The School Busing Controversy: 1970-75

The School Busing Controversy: 1970-75

Editor: Judith F. Buncher

Contributing Editors: Charles Monaghan and Henry H. Schulte, Jr.

Contributing Writers: Joseph Fickes and Stephen Orlofsky

**FACTS ON FILE 119 West 57th Street
New York, New York**

The School Busing Controversy: 1970-75

Copyright, 1975 by Facts on File, Inc.

(Cover photo by United Press International)

Library of Congress Catalog Card No. 75-1737
ISBN 0-87196-359-0 (cloth), 0-87196-360-4 (paper)
9 8 7 6 5 4 3 2 1

PRINTED IN THE UNITED STATES OF AMERICA

Preface

"Busing's just got to be, man. Got to be. We got it coming to us. We got to open up ourselves, spread out. Get into this city, man. Move into all those places we can't go at night, you know. Go to good schools, live in good places like white folks got. You got all that stuff. My folks don't, so they want it for me and my brothers. That's why they're busing us."

—11-year old black student,
being bused to South Boston[1]

"I'm not against any individual child. I am not a racist, no matter what those high-and-mighty suburban liberals with their picket signs say. I just won't have my children bused to some god-awful slum school, and I don't want children from God knows where coming over here. We put our last cent into this home. We both work to keep up with the mortgage and all the expenses.... We just want to live peacefully out here. We want our children to grow up in a quiet, decent neighborhood.... We want to see them off to school, and not sit for the rest of the day wondering, are they safe, and will there be a fight, and are they afraid even to walk home if they miss the bus?"

—white mother,
living in South Boston[2]

The school bus became a symbol of public school integration in the 1970s. As a symbol, it tended to represent simultaneously the emotions of integrationists (who saw it as a vehicle of escape from the ghetto and towards equality) as well as supporters of "neighborhood schools" (to whom the practical concepts of safety and property were more meaningful than the more abstract "equal opportunity.") The resort to busing as a means to achieve integrated education was caused by an array of devices designed to maintain segregated schools: the closing of public schools, the creation of private schools, a southern governor's "standing in the classroom door" to prevent physically the enrollment of two black students in a university of thousands, the linking of integrationists with communists. Underlying all these methods, the chief defense against public school integration since 1954 has been procrastination. Busing presented an immediate, direct threat to the varied manifestations of procrastination.

Forgotten in the anger generated by the sight of the school bus bringing "them" in and taking "ours" out of the neighborhood has been the public acceptance of school transportation in the United States. Beginning with Massachusett's 1869 authorization of public funds to transport children between school and home, public school transportation was provided in every state by 1919.[3] Mr. Chief Justice Burger, writing the Supreme Court decision in *Swann v. Charlotte-Mecklenburg Board of Education*, refers to this contrast between busing's acceptance in the case of the consolidated and segregated schools and the opposition it provoked when used for purposes of integration: "The [court-ordered] trips for elementary school pupils average about seven miles and the District Court found that they would take 'not over 35 minutes at the most.' This system compares favorably with the transportation plan previously operated in Charlotte under which every day 23,600 students on all grade levels were transported an average of 15 miles one way for an average trip requiring over an hour."

The courts' struggle with the differing decision-making groups in American society clearly illustrates the democratic process. In few other countries of the world today could the courts consistently lead where the Congress hesitated to follow and the Chief Executive reiterated his aversion to following. Public reactions to the controversy between the judiciary and the other bodies of the federal government were expressed through polls, elections, resolutions, and demonstrations.

June 1975   Judith F. Buncher

[1] Quoted by Thomas J. Cottle, "Bus Start," *The New York Times Magazine*, March 9, 1975, p. 20.
[2] Quoted by Robert Coles, *The Buses Roll* (New York: W. W. Norton and Co., 1974), p. 27.
[3] Nicolaus Mills, *The Great School Bus Controversy* (New York: Teachers College, Columbia University, 1973), p. 4.

Contents

School Desegregation 1954-75

May 14, 1954: The Supreme Court rules in *Brown v. Board of Education of Topeka, Kansas* that "separate educational facilities are inherently unequal."

July 6, 1954: The Louisiana legislature passes a plan to use the state's police power to maintain segregated schools.

Dec. 21, 1954: Mississippi voters approve by a 2–1 majority a state constitutional amendment to permit abolition of public schools to avoid racial integration of school children.

May 31, 1955: The Supreme Court rules that racial segregation in public schools must be ended "with all deliberate speed," but it sets no deadline. The courts are to "require that the defendants make a prompt and reasonable start toward full compliance," and "may find that additional time is necessary to carry out the ruling in an effective manner."

Sept. 3, 1955: The National Association for the Advancement of Colored People (NAACP) report reveals that 11 of the 17 states where segregation was required by law have taken some steps to comply with the desegregation ruling. Six states have refused to comply: Alabama, Florida, Georgia, Louisiana, Mississippi, and South Carolina.

Nov. 7, 1955: The Virginia Supreme Court of Appeals rules unanimously that, under the state constitution, state funds can not be used to support private schools.

March 11, 1956: Nineteen United States senators and 77 congressmen from 11 southern states issue a manifesto denouncing the Supreme Court's public school desegregation on legal grounds. They pledge by "all lawful means" to have it reversed.

March 13, 1956: *The New York Times* survey reports that Alabama, Georgia, Mississippi, South Carolina, and Virginia are "resisting" the Supreme Court decision; Florida, Louisiana, North Carolina, Tennessee, and Texas are "divided or delaying"; and Delaware, the District of Columbia, Kentucky, Missouri, Oklahoma, and West Virginia are "integrating."

July 5, 1956: The House defeats the Powell Amendment (introduced by Rep. Adam Clayton Powell Jr. [D, N.Y.]) along with the school bill. The anti-bias rider would have barred school aid funds from segregated public school in states "which fail to comply with the decision of the Supreme Court."

Aug. 29, 1956: A mob of 1,000 whites demonstrates against the enrollment on Aug. 26 of 11 black students in the 800-student Clinton, Tennessee high school. A 600-man Tennessee National Guard unit is called out to enforce the admission of the 11 students.

Sept. 9-10, 1957: Nashville's new $500,000 Hattie Cotton Elementary School, with a registration of one black and 388 white children, is virtually destroyed by a dynamite blast. The 13 black 6-year olds who integrate the three elementary schools Sept. 9 are jeered at, spat upon, and made targets of sticks, stones, and bottles.

Sept. 24, 1957: President Dwight Eisenhower orders 1,000 members of the 101st Airborne Division to Little Rock to take up posts outside of the Central High School. The nine black children who were forced to leave the school by a crowd of 800–1,000 white supremacists the day before re-enter the school, protected by the paratroopers.

Sept. 12, 1958: The Supreme Court unanimously orders the resumption of racial integration at Central High School in Little Rock. Gov. Orval Faubus retaliates with a directive to close the four high schools on Sept. 15, the opening day of school.

Sept. 29, 1958: The Supreme Court unanimously rejects the claim of Gov. Faubus and the Arkansas legislature that they are not bound by the Supreme Court's 1954 decision. The ruling cites Chief Justice John Marshall's 1803 decision that the Constitution is "the fundamental and paramount law of the nation." The Court declares that "state support of segregated schools, through any arrangement, management, funds or property can not be squared with the [14th] Amendment's command that no state shall deny to any person within its jurisdiction the equal protection of the laws."

Nov. 4, 1958: Louisiana voters approve a referendum to use state funds to create a private school system.

Feb. 18, 1959: The Dade County School Board yields to a federal court order and votes to admit four blacks to a Miami elementary school in September. They would be the first blacks in an all-white Florida public school.

May 17, 1959: NAACP Executive Secretary Roy Wilkins claims that Alabama, Florida, Georgia, Louisiana, Mississippi, and South Carolina have not made even token compliance with the Supreme Court's order.

April 9, 1960: *Southern School News* reveals 94% of southern black students still attend segregated schools.

Nov. 23, 1960: The Louisiana legislature unanimously passes a resolution accusing President Eisenhower and the federal courts of "making common cause with the Communist conspiracy."

Nov. 28-30, 1960: White pupils almost completely boycott two integrated New Orleans schools. The two white children and their accompanying parents who attend the Frantz School on Nov. 28 and Nov. 30 are shoved and taunted by mobs of white women. The three black first-graders are the only pupils in the other integrated school.

Jan. 10, 1961: Charlayne Hunter and Hamilton Holmes enroll at the University of Georgia in Athens, the first desegregation of Georgia's public education.

Sept. 6, 1961: Of the southern states, only Mississippi, Alabama, and South Carolina still maintain completely segregated public school systems.

April 16, 1962: Three Louisiana segregationists are excommunicated by Roman Catholic Archbishop Joseph Francis Rummel for continuing to "provoke . . . disobedience" to his March 27 order that New Orleans Archdiocese schools be desegregated.

May 10, 1962: *Southern School News* reports that 92.4% of southern black students still attend segregated schools.

Sept. 30-Oct. 1, 1962: Thousands of white segregationists clash with federal marshals and troops in a futile effort to prevent James Meredith from enrolling at the University of Mississippi at Oxford. Meredith's enrolling as the first black as the university marks the desegregation of public schools in Mississippi.

May 27, 1963: The Supreme Court declares that it "never contemplated that the concept of 'deliberate speed' would countenance indefinite delay in elimination of racial barriers in schools."

June 11, 1963: Gov. George Wallace at first physically blocks the registration of two black students, Vivian Malone and James Hood, at the University of Alabama. Wallace leaves the building after President Kennedy places the Alabama National Guard under federal orders.

Aug. 18, 1963: James Meredith graduates from the University of Mississippi with a BA in political science.

Aug. 28, 1963: More than 200,000 black and white integrationists march on Washington from throughout the United States. The massive demonstration calls attention to demands for immediate equality of blacks with whites.

Sept. 3, 1963: Eleven black students attend previously all-white elementary and high schools in Charleston for the first public school desegregation in South Carolina.

Sept. 10, 1963: Gov. Wallace concedes that he "can't fight bayonets with [his] bare hands" after President Kennedy federalizes the Alabama National Guard. Wallace ordered the Birmingham schools closed Sept. 5 and used state troopers Sept. 6 to block the already delayed opening of the Huntsville schools set to accept one black student each. Wallace allowed Tuskegee, Mobile and Birmingham schools to open Sept. 9, but blocked the entry of black students by using state troopers and deputized National Guardsmen.

Sept. 12, 1963: President Kennedy is asked at his news conference if he considers it right to "wrench children away from their neighborhood—family area—and cart them off to strange, faraway schools to force racial balance." The president replies, "I would not approve of the procedure you described."

Feb. 3-26, 1964: Boycotts of northern schools are held to protest *de facto* segregation. On Feb. 3, 464,362 (44.8% of all students) boycott in New York City; Feb. 11, 19,000 in Cincinnati; Feb. 25, 172,350 in Chicago; Feb. 26, 20,500 in Boston.

July 2, 1964: President Lyndon Johnson signs the Civil Rights Act. Title VI bars discrimination in any federally-assisted activity and provides for aid cut-off, subject to judicial review.

Oct. 26, 1964: Presidential candidate Barry Goldwater says he favors "our system of neighborhood schools" and does not "want to see them destroyed or be sacrificed by a futile exercise in sociology" as "forcibly busing your children ... just to meet an arbitrary racial quota."

Jan. 4, 1965: The Justice Department files suits against Bossier County, La. and Campbell County, Tenn. They are the first federal school desegregation suits to be filed under the 1964 Civil Rights Act.

Feb. 15-24, 1965: The South Carolina, Georgia, and Mississippi Boards of Education agree to sign pledges to comply with federal school desegregation policies. The states would then become eligible to receive respectively $11.8 million, $55 million, and $23 million.

March 1, 1965: The Supreme Court refuses to review a 1964 ruling of the Denver appeals court that holds that *de facto* school segregation does not violate the constitution. The Supreme Court ruled (in a case involving the Kansas City, Kans. Board of Education) that although the Constitution barred the segregation of public school pupils by race, it did not require integration.

April 29, 1965: Education Commissioner Francis Keppel announces that the nation's 27,000 school districts will be required to desegregate all public schools completely by September 1967, or steps will be taken to eliminate federal school funds.

Nov. 8, 1965: The Supreme Court declines to hear an appeal of a New York court's upholding of "school pairing" plans for New York City. The parents of the students involved in the pairing of Jackson Heights and Corona students contend that the plan violates the Supreme Court's 1954 decision by requiring children to travel out of their former districts for racial reasons.

Jan. 3, 1966: The Southern Education Reporting Service reveals that 89% of the school districts in southern and border states are technically desegregated, but that only 16% of the black students are enrolled in integrated schools.

April 11, 1966: Over 500 people attend the Sacramento, Calif. hearings on desegregation plans. The Sacramento Mothers Association distributes pamphlets warning that busing would separate parents from children in case of an atomic bomb attack.

May 2, 1966: The Sacramento school board adopts the boundaries for 1966–67. Of 1,075 children reassigned, 875 are expected to be bused. More than this number have been bused in special education programs and in outlying suburban areas.

March 22, 1967: A three-judge federal court in Montgomery orders the desegregation of all Alabama public schools at the start of the fall term. This is the first time since 1954 that an entire state is placed under a single injunction. The order is upheld by the Supreme Court on May 22.

June 19, 1967: U.S. District Judge J. Skelly Wright declares Washington, D.C.'s *de facto* segregation unconstitutional. The Wright decision extends the 1954 Supreme Court ban on school segregation to separation caused by population patterns.

Sept. 6, 1967: The Providence Plan is implemented in Rhode Island. Any student assigned to a school more than a mile away will be bused. Black students represent 70% of the 2,655 students in grades 1–6 to be transferred. More than 40% of the students will be able to walk to their new elementary schools.

May 27, 1968: Department of Health, Education and Welfare (HEW) figures show 14% of black pupils attended desegregated schools in 11 southern states during the 1967–68 school year.

June 14, 1968: Mount Vernon, N.Y. begins a busing plan grouping elementary school pupils by age rather than neighborhoods.

Sept. 16-17, 1969: Vice President Spiro Agnew says he opposes busing school children simply as a means to achieve racial balance. The White House announces that Agnew expresses Administration policy.

Sept. 17, 1969: The 16 southern and border state governors vote down efforts to condemn student busing. They pass instead a resolution urging the Administration to employ "restraint and good judgment" in using busing.

Sept. 21, 1969: HEW Secretary Robert H. Finch says that his department will continue to use busing as long as segregated school systems exist.

Jan. 14, 1970: The Supreme Court sets September 1970 as desegregation deadline in public schools in Alabama, Florida, Georgia, Louisiana, Mississippi, and Texas.

Feb. 6, 1970: Nearly one-third of Denver's school buses dynamited.

Feb. 11, 1970: Judge Alfred Gitelson orders a desegregation plan involving the busing of 240,000 students in Los Angeles.

Feb. 18, 1970: The Senate passes the Stennis Amendment barring *de facto* school segregation.

March 3, 1970: White crowd in Lamar, S.C. storms buses carrying black students.

March 24, 1970: President Richard Nixon states, "Transportation of pupils beyond normal geographic school zones for the purpose of achieving racial balance will not be required."

April 4, 1970: Gallup poll finds 86% oppose busing.

July 16–28, 1970: Congress passes education bill barring the use of the appropriated funds for busing to promote desegregation.

Oct. 1, 1970: New York State's antibusing law is declared unconstitutional.

April 5, 1971: Judge Robert Merhige approves cross-district busing plan for 20,000 students in Richmond.

April 20, 1971: The Supreme Court upholds busing as constitutional in *Swann v. Charlotte-Mecklenburg Board of Education.*

May 14, 1971: HEW recommends cross-town busing to integrate Austin, Tex. public schools.

Aug. 3, 1971: President Nixon disavows HEW's Austin busing plan, commenting, "I am against busing as that term is commonly used in school desegregation cases." He instructs HEW Secretary Elliot Richardson and Attorney General John Mitchell to "hold busing to the minimum required by law."

Aug. 31, 1971: Chief Justice Warren Burger claims that the Supreme Court's *Swann* ruling does not require "a fixed racial balance or quota" to desegregate schools.

Sept. 1971: Schools open with resistance to desegregation in North and West, minimum of disruption in South.

Sept. 8, 1971: Nine students injured in Pontiac, Mich. antibusing riots.

Sept. 11, 1971: Gallup reports 76% oppose busing.

Nov. 5, 1971: House passes three antibusing amendments.

March 8, 1972: House "insists" antibusing amendments adopted in November be kept intact, barring compromise with Senate.

March 14, 1972: Florida voters oppose busing (74%) and choose Gov. Wallace as Democratic primary winner (41%).

March 17, 1972: President Nixon asks for a moratorium on all new court-ordered busing.

May 30, 1972: Appeals Court upholds busing of 49,000 Nashville children.

June 14, 1972: Judge Stephen Roth orders 310,000 Detroit students bused between the city and the suburbs.

Aug. 18, 1972: House bars court-ordered cross-district busing.

Oct. 12, 1972: Senate filibuster kills antibusing legislation.

Feb. 16, 1973: U.S. District Court Judge John Pratt orders HEW to begin proceedings to cut off federal funds from public school systems not desegregating.

April 30, 1973: Chattanooga ordered to implement busing plan by the Circuit Court of Appeals, upheld Nov. 5 by the Supreme Court.

May 21, 1973: The Supreme Court fails to establish a precedent in judging Richmond cross-district busing.

June 21, 1973: The Supreme Court rules in Denver case that *de facto* segregation in North must be treated as southern *de jure* segregation.

Dec. 19, 1973: Judge Frank Gray Jr. orders HEW to review its refusal to grant Nashville funds for purchasing buses.

Jan. 28, 1974: New York City housing patterns ordered changed in area supporting a school with "racial imbalance."

April 23, 1974: The Supreme Court upholds Memphis desegregation plan that would retain 25 all-black schools.

July 25, 1974: The Supreme Court rejects cross-district busing in Detroit case.

Aug. 30, 1974: Busing of 23,000 Denver students begins.

Sept. 12, 1974: Boston schools open with court-ordered busing plan; violence erupts.

Dec. 14, 1974: Senate adopts Scott-Mansfield proposal to add "...except as it may be required to enforce non-discrimination provisions of federal law" to Rep. Marjorie S. Holt's bill prohibiting use of the education bill's funds to assign students to schools on the basis of race.

March 10, 1975: The District Court of Appeals in California overturns Judge Gitelson's 1970 order for busing Los Angeles students.

March 11, 1975: U.S. Commission on Civil Rights warns that segregation is likely to increase in northern and southern urban areas.

March 14, 1975: Judge Pratt orders HEW to enforce desegregation in 125 school districts in southern and border states.

March 31, 1975: *The Boston Globe* reports 23 antibusing proposals pending in Congress.

April 21, 1975: The Supreme Court declines to review cross-district busing plans in Indianapolis and Louisville.

May 10, 1975: Judge W. Arthur Garrity Jr. orders the final busing plan for Boston, involving the busing of 21,000 students.

May 17, 1975: The NAACP sponsors march in Boston to commemorate the 21st anniversary of the *Brown* decision. Restore Our Alienated Rights (ROAR) simultaneously holds convention to begin a nationwide antibusing movement.

Court Decisions: 1970-71

The Supreme Court: The South

Feb. 1 integration deadline set. In a brief unsigned order Jan. 14, the Supreme Court overturned a Dec. 1, 1969 U.S. Fifth Circuit Court of Appeals ruling that set September 1970 as a pupil desegregation deadline for public schools in Alabama, Florida, Georgia, Louisiana, Mississippi and Texas. The court set a Feb. 1, 1970 desegregation deadline, rejecting a Justice Department request that the September deadline be approved.

Acting on appeals backed by the NAACP Legal Defense and Educational Fund Inc. involving 14 school districts in five of the states, the court said: "Insofar as the Court of Appeals authorized deferral of student desegregation beyond Feb. 1, 1970, that court misconstrued our holding in *Alexander v. Holmes County Board of Education*"—the court's Oct. 29, 1969 decision ordering desegregation "at once." The justices had issued orders to the districts Dec. 13, 1969 instructing them to be prepared to meet a Feb. 1 deadline if the appeals court decision were overturned.

Although there were no dissents to the order Chief Justice Warren E. Burger and Justice Potter Stewart signed a "memorandum" stating that they did not join the action because they felt the court should have considered arguments pertaining to the decision of the appeals court, which, they said, "is far more familiar than we with the various situations of the several school districts." Justices John M. Harlan and Bryon R. White stated that they concurred with the ruling but suggested that the court set eight weeks as the maximum allowable time between a court integration order and actual desegregation of a school district. Justices Hugo L. Black, William J. Brennan Jr., William O. Douglas and Thurgood Marshall termed the eight-week period a "retreat" from the court's Oct. 29 position.

California

L.A. school integration ordered. A Superior Court judge in Los Angeles Feb. 11 ordered officials of the Los Angeles school system, the second largest in the U.S., to present a formula by June 1 for the integration of the district's 555 schools and to implement the plan no later than September 1971. Judge Alfred E. Gitelson issued the order in a suit instituted by the American Civil Liberties Union (ACLU) on behalf of Mexican-American and Negro schoolchildren.

According to Judge Gitelson, the Los Angeles district set boundaries "preventing or prohibiting or impeding minorities from attending white or substantially white schools."

Los Angeles school superintendent Robert F. Kelly said he would recommend an appeal "at the earliest possible time." Kelly said the order would require the busing of 240,000 of the district's 674,000 students. He warned that the costs of reshaping the district "would mean the virtual destruction of the school district."

Judge Gitelson said in his ruling that the district was guilty of "expending millions in tax funds for the protection, maintainance and perpetuating of its segregated schools . . . " The judge also accused the district of building new facilities "knowing that the schools, would be, upon opening, segregated or racially imbalanced."

Pasadena integration plan approved. A federal district court judge in Los Angeles March 4 approved a plan submitted by school administrators in Pasadena, Calif. to integrate the city's elementary and secondary public schools. Judge Manuel L. Real had ordered the district to formulate a plan Jan. 20.

Real rejected a petition by the attorneys general of three Southern states —Alabama, Mississippi and Louisiana— to enter the case as a "friend of the court."

The Southern officials had sought to enter the Pasadena case because in their view the time allowed Pasadena educators to design a desegregation arrangement was excessive. The Southerners contended that the California district should be ordered to "integrate now," which, according to the attorneys general, was the order handed down to their states.

The plan approved by Judge Real called for busing students up to 10 miles within zones set up inside the Pasadena district. Under the plan, the 30,622-pupil district was to be fully integrated by September. Pasadena administrators estimated that the busing would cost $700,-000 to $1 million annually.

Pasadena backs board on busing. The residents of Pasadena, Calif. narrowly voted down Oct. 14 three referendums to recall three members of the local school board who had supported a school integration plan that called for extensive cross-town busing.

The plan was implemented when the Pasadena schools reopened for the fall term. Under its terms, 30,000 students were to be bused at a cost of $1 million to Pasadena and three neighboring communities which were involved in the busing arrangement.

Final but unofficial returns showed that Albert C. Lowe, the board president, was retained by a vote of 23,522 to 21,610. Mrs. LuVerne Lamotte retained her seat by a vote of 23,009 to 22,410 and Dr. Joseph Engholm kept his seat by a vote of 23,281 to 22,258.

The recall campaign was started during the spring after the three board members voted not to appeal to a higher court the March 4 decision of the U.S. federal district judge who approved the integration plan.

Michigan

Pontiac school integration ordered. A federal judge in Detroit Feb. 17 ordered the industrial community of Pontiac, Mich. to completely integrate its schools at the student, faculty and administrative levels by the fall of 1970. Judge Damon J. Keith ordered that "such integration shall be accomplished by the revising of boundary lines for attendance purposes, as well as by busing so as to achieve maximum racial integration."

Keith called on the Pontiac school board to submit for his approval by March 16 an arrangement for the integration of the entire Pontiac school system. Pontiac's two high schools, six

A junior high schools and 29 elementary schools included 24,000 students.

Pontiac school plan submitted. Public school officials in Pontiac, Mich. submitted a plan March 21 for total desegregation of the city's school system in compliance with a court order, but at the same time they said they would appeal the U.S. Court order for integration.

B Federal District Judge Damon J. Keith had handed down the desegregation orders Feb. 17, telling school officials to implement desegregation plans by the fall of 1970.

The Pontiac school board, in filing the plans, argued that if Keith accepted its formula it would be so costly to the school district that it would impair the quality of education for all of Pontiac's 24,000 students.

C Under the plan submitted by the school board, each pupil in grades one through six would attend his neighborhood school for two years and transfer to other area schools for the other four grades. This would mean that every child in the Pontiac system would be bused for four of his first six school years.

The Supreme Court: North Carolina

D **Busing plan delayed.** The Supreme Court declined March 16 to overturn a decision by the U.S. Court of Appeals for the Fourth Circuit which had granted officials in Charlotte, N.C., a delay in implementing a school desegregation plan. There was no dissent.

The desegregation order was scheduled to be implemented April 1 for Charlotte's elementary schools and May 4 for secondary schools. But with the Supreme Court's action sustaining the lower court's ruling, the plans could not be implemented before the end of the 1970 school year. The plan, which would have required the most massive busing program in the South, had been singled out by Southern leaders as a symbol of disruptive integration and had been criticized by Secretary of Health, Education and Welfare Robert H. Finch as "totally unrealistic."

F The purpose of the delay granted by the Fourth Circuit court was to permit Federal District Judge James P. McMillan to hear evidence on opposing contentions regarding the impact of the busing orders. The desegregation order handed down by the circuit court had called for a racial balance in Charlotte's schools of about 71% white students and 29% Negroes in 100 of the district's 103 schools.

G ***School integration date reset.*** U.S. District Judge James B. McMillan March 25 granted public school administrators in Charlotte, N.C. a six-month delay in implementing court-ordered school desegregation plans. McMillan rescinded an earlier order by his court that had set

an April 1 desegregation target date and extended the deadline to Sept. 1.

The judge indicated that recent decisions by other federal circuit courts had removed pressures to desegregate "at once," and instead allowed school boards a longer period to implement plans. His postponement came after Charlotte school officials pleaded that they did not have the time, the financial resources nor the buses to comply with McMillan's earlier order that called for the busing of 13,000 Charlotte students. The district had for some time been busing 24,000 other pupils under the orders of McMillan's court.

U.S. enters N.C. school case. The Nixon Administration joined the controversial Charlotte, N.C., school desegregation case April 8, suggesting that the U.S. district judge who had ordered a busing plan to be implemented had committed "an abuse of discretion." The action was in the form of a brief filed by the Justice Department in the U.S. Court of Appeals for the Fourth Circuit in Richmond, Va.

The National Education Association (NEA) entered the case the same day with a brief representing the Negro schoolchildren of Charlotte. The NEA argued that the busing order, handed down by Judge James B. McMillan, was the proper means of achieving desegregation and would not place a burden on the Charlotte school district.

According to the terms of McMillan's order, a maximum of 13,300 pupils would be added to the 24,000 now being bused. The order also would require the pairing of schools so that no school in the district would be more than one-third black. He had ordered the plan to be put into operation by April 1, but March 25 he amended it to take effect Sept. 1. The Fourth Circuit and the Supreme Court upheld the change.

The Fourth Circuit Court opened its hearings on the appeal April 9 in Richmond and heard a government attorney say that it was time that the Supreme Court ruled on the legality of all-black schools. The attorney, David L. Norman, deputy assistant attorney general for civil rights, told the court that Nixon Administration policy permitted the existence of predominantly Negro schools in urban centers and said the Supreme Court should decide whether judicial policy would be the same.

Norman indicated that he was speaking for President Nixon, who March 24 had laid down his Administration's guidelines for public school desegregation.

Norman concentrated his case on the question of whether Judge McMillan's order for busing was too "extreme." Norman said that the Justice Department and the Department of Health, Education and Welfare (HEW) "have drawn hundreds of desegregation plans at the instruction of the courts and

we do not have one that resembles" the arrangement ordered by McMillan.

One of the attorneys representing the NEA and the Negro schoolchildren of Charlotte was Stephen J. Pollak, a former deputy attorney general for civil rights in the Johnson Administration. Pollak argued that the existence of segregated neighborhoods could not be used in the Charlotte case as a basis for maintaining all-black schools since, he said, the school segregation was not de facto, or segregation resulting from housing patterns.

Busing limited in Charlotte case. The U.S. Court of Appeals for the Fourth Circuit ruled May 27 that not every school within a district must be integrated in order to fulfill the Supreme Court's demand that de jure school segregation be eliminated at once.

The order, by a 4-2 vote, was handed down in a case brought to the appeals court sitting in Richmond, Va. by officials of the Charlotte-Mecklenburg County school district in North Carolina, who argued that a desegregation plan ordered for their district was too extreme. The Justice Department entered the suit April 8, contending that the judge who had ordered the desegregation plan which called for massive student busing had "committed an abuse of discretion." The government asked that the case be remanded for a drafting of a milder desegregation plan.

The decision set aside the order for implementation of the desegregation plan that would have made it necessary for the district to bus 13,300 more students than the 24,000 already participating in the busing arrangement. The ruling left standing the original order for integration of the district's junior and senior high schools but ordered that a new plan for the district's elementary schools be drawn up.

The majority decision, written by Judge John D. Butzner Jr., said busing of students was a "permissible tool" for achieving integration but no "panacea" for solving all problems that arise out of school desegregation.

"Not every school in a unitary school system need be integrated," the court said. The Supreme Court had not yet fully defined what it considered to constitute a unitary school system.

The majority view said if a school board had made "every reasonable effort to integrate the pupils under its control," an "intractable remnant of segregation" should not void an otherwise sound plan for the establishment of a unitary school system.

U.S. judge orders Charlotte busing. Federal Judge James B. McMillan Aug. 3 ordered administrators of the Charlotte-Mecklenburg County, N. C. school system to begin using a student busing plan when the schools reopened for the fall term Aug. 31. The busing plan, which Mc-

Millan had approved Feb. 5, was designed to increase the incidence of desegregation in the county's public schools.

The plan called for busing 13,300 students. The plan had been returned to McMillan's district court after Charlotte officials had sought relief from the U.S. Court of Appeals for the Fourth Circuit on grounds that the busing plan was too harsh. The appeals court upheld parts of McMillan's Feb. 5 decision but ordered one part re-examined for a "rule of reasonableness." McMillan Aug. 3 upheld his earlier ruling.

McMillan gave Charlotte officials the option of adopting portions of a plan drawn by its liberal minority. That plan would require busing of more students but generally over shorter distances than the ones incorporated in McMillan's ruling.

In sustaining his Feb. 5 decision, McMillan said that constitutional rights take precedence over reasonableness. He wrote in his decision: "Reasonable remedies should always be sought. Practical rather than burdensome methods are properly required. . . . However, if a constitutional right has been denied, this court believes that it is the constitutional right that should prevail against the cry of unreasonableness. If, as this court and the circuit court have held, the rights of children are being denied, the cost and inconvenience of restoring those rights is no reason under the Constitution for continuing to deny them."

Georgia

Atlanta busing barred. U.S. District Judge Frank A. Hooper ruled March 20 that 56 Atlanta public schools that were either all-black or all-white did "not exist because of discrimination" but rather evolved from the city's residential patterns and could not be further desegregated by any other plan acceptable to the court. He said there was no legal precedent that would require him to order massive student busing.

Hooper's ruling was part of an order requiring that students in Atlanta be assigned to schools on the basis of geographic zoning. His order eliminated an earlier order under which two high schools and two elementary schools were paired for integration purposes. Judge Hooper said under his plan, desegregation in Atlanta's public schools would be increased from 57.5% to 64.5%.

The Supreme Court: Florida

Kirk school appeal denied. Florida Gov. Claude R. Kirk Jr.'s continuing efforts to have a court-ordered school desegregation plan for Manatee County discarded, suffered a serious setback April 20 when the U.S. Supreme Court denied his petition for an immediate hearing on the legality of the order.

In a brief unsigned order, the court dismissed without comment Kirk's request that the justices transfer the Manatee County school case from the Fifth Circuit Court of Appeals in New Orleans to the Supreme Court. Kirk had gone to New Orleans April 13 to deliver a friend of court brief asking the federal district court to overturn a lower court's ruling that ordered a desegregation plan which included the cross-county busing of 2,600 Manatee County students.

While the legal bickering over the technicalities of the plan continued, the busing, which got under way April 14, continued through April 21 without incident. Manatee County officials reported that a few parents refused to permit their children to be bused, but said the arrangement was working without disruption. Newsweek magazine reported that attendance in the Manatee schools was no more than 2 or 3 percentage points off normal.

Kirk yields school control. Florida Gov. Claude R. Kirk Jr. capitulated to the federal district court in Bradenton April 12 and pledged to end his weeklong acts of defiance against a Supreme Court-approved school desegregation plan for the Manatee County public schools. Kirk, who had suspended the Manatee district school officials on the day before the plan was to be implemented April 5, had been repeatedly warned by the federal court that he faced contempt citations and fines of $10,000 a day until he relinquished control of the county's public schools.

Kirk made the announcement that he was reinstating the district's officials in a taped TV broadcast. He said he would officially put the school board members and the local school superintendent back in control and direct them to put the desegregation plan into operation April 14. The desegregation plan ordered by U.S. District Judge Ben Krentzman began operation April 14 with 2,600 students bused cross-county to new schools.

He said he had agreed to relinquish his control over the Manatee schools because "the solutions to our problems must lie in the duly constituted courts." The "problem" Kirk referred to involved the implementation of the school desegregation plan that Kirk termed "illegal" because it required the forced cross-county busing of students to achieve a racial balance in the Manatee schools. He said he would go to New Orleans to seek a reversal of the order from the U.S. Fifth Circuit Court of Appeals, currently sitting in that city. He also said he had received assurances from the Justice Department that it would join him in the appeal to the Circuit Court. The governor declined to identify who had given him the assurances.

The drama unfolded April 3 when the Supreme Court rejected a request by Manatee County officials for a delay in implementing the desegregation ar-

rangement. Soon after the court's decision was announced, Manatee's school board announced it would implement the plan immediately.

Kirk flew to Bradenton April 5 and ordered the district's 17,000 public school pupils to ignore the court order and continue to attend the neighborhood schools in which they were presently enrolled. He suspended the school board and the local superintendent, he said, by the power of "executive order" and said he was assuming personal control of the district's school system.

The Nixon Administration said April 6 that it was prepared to cooperate with the federal court in enforcing the school desegregation order that Kirk had defied. White House Press Secretary Ronald L. Ziegler said that the "Justice Department will cooperate with the court in carrying out the court order." The Justice Department announced that Judge Krentzman, in ordering Kirk to show cause why he should not be held in contempt, had also brought in the department as a friend of the court.

Judge Krentzman April 7 ordered Kirk to relinquish control of the Manatee schools and return control immediately to the local officials. He also ordered that the controversial busing plan be put into operation by April 9. He said that any orders issued by Kirk to the contrary were to be ignored. Kirk ignored Krentzman's order to appear in his Bradenton court despite the governor's claim that he was anxious "to have my day in court."

Kirk, however, ignored Krentzman's order to have the busing arrangement set in motion and returned to Bradenton April 8 to insure that the integration plan was not implemented. Two of the governor's aides took physical possession of the school board offices while Kirk himself warned that any Manatee school official who agreed to implement the plan would be suspended.

U.S. Attorney John Briggs announced April 9 that the federal government would assume control of the Manatee county public schools despite a phalanx of heavily armed Florida state troopers and a reported warning that federal marshals would be fired upon if they moved against the school offices. An aide to Kirk quickly denied the report that Florida troopers would use force to keep the marshals from entering the district's school offices. Briggs, who was assigned by the Justice Department to see that the court-ordered desegregation plan was carried out, said the integrity of the federal court system was at stake. Kirk moved into the offices late April 9 and said he would resist any effort of the federal marshals to take control of the schools. He said he would order Florida troopers to arrest the first marshal who tried to serve him with subpoena papers or take over school property.

Kirk vacated the Manatee County school board offices April 10.

A

B

C

D

E

F

G

A Colorado

Denver school integration ordered. A U.S. District Court judge May 23 ordered the Denver public school system to desegregate 15 of its minority-group schools by 1972 and enact sweeping changes at two others. Judge William E. Doyle, ruling in a segregation suit filed against the Denver Board of Education by eight Denver families, said de-

B segregation was essential to improving the quality of education at the 17 schools.

Each of the schools had an enrollment of at least 70% black or Spanish-American, with the exception of one, which was 60% black. The drawing up of desegregation plans was left to the school district and the plaintiff's lawyers, but Doyle set down several guidelines. He ordered the 14 elementary schools covered by his ruling to be desegregated

C by the fall of 1972. At least seven of them had to be desegregated by the fall of 1971. When integrated, each school had to have a white, non-Spanish enrollment of more than 50%. Doyle also ordered one predominantly Spanish-American junior high school fully desegregated by the fall of 1972.

Doyle also touched on the sensitive issue of student busing. (In February nearly one-third of Denver's school

D buses were dynamited in a parking lot. Authorities believed the blasts were linked to opponents of a plan to use busing to integrate Denver's schools.)

Doyle said mandatory busing should be avoided "to the extent possible" but that it "may well be necessary to effectuate much of the court's plan."

New York

E **New York antibusing law voided.** New York State's 17-month antibusing law was struck down as unconstitutional Oct. 1 by a three-judge federal court in Buffalo which held that it violated the 14th Amendment. The statute had made it illegal for appointed school boards to reshuffle pupil assignment plans to achieve racial balance without the consent of their parents.

F The law had been copied by school administrators in the Deep South seeking to forestall desegregation in their district's classrooms.

The judges held in their 24-page decision that the law violated the U.S. Constitution because it "constitutes an explicit and invidious racial classification and denies equal protection of the law." They granted a permanent injunction against all future enforcement of the law.

The order was signed by Circuit

G Judge Paul R. Hays, Chief Judge John O. Henderson of the Western District of New York and District Judge Harold P. Burke.

The law, which was enacted in May 1969, applied to appointed school boards, but not to elected school boards. The litigation challenging the law was

brought by a group of black and white Buffalo parents.

The judges said that an examination of the objectives and effect of the law "supports the proposition that the statute serves to continue segregation in the school and thus significantly encourages and involves the state in racial discrimination."

The Supreme Court: The South

Court hears school arguments. The Supreme Court Oct. 12–14 heard arguments on student busing and racial balance in the schools in the Deep South. The arguments were heard by the court as part of appeals filed by attorneys representing school districts in Charlotte, N.C. and Mobile, Ala.

During the three days of hearings, lawyers for Negro schoolchildren, the U.S. solicitor general representing the federal government and attorneys for Southern school officials called on the Court to adopt different proposals to solve the busing problem. The court itself was reportedly divided in its reactions to the proposals advanced by the petitioners.

Attorneys for the N.A.A.C.P. Legal Defense and Educational Fund, Inc., representing the Negro children, argued Oct. 12 that each Negro child had a constitutional right to be enrolled in a school that was not recognizably "black." The lawyers said that based on this premise, any school plan that did not eliminate every all-black school should be adjudged inadequate. The Fund attorneys told the court that it would be undermining its own 1954 decision in *Brown v. Board of Education* if it now permitted some Southern school districts to maintain some recognizably "black" schools.

Solicitor General Erwin N. Griswold, arguing for the Justice Department, rebutted the Fund's arguments Oct. 12 and 14. He said Oct. 12 that the Fund's petition amounted to a demand for racial balance in the schools and "I cannot find that in the Constitution." He told the court that if a school board had done everything feasible to eliminate all traces of state-imposed segregation, then it had satisfied the Constitution even if some all-black schools remained. In response to a question by Justice Thurgood Marshall, who argued the *Brown v. Board of Education* case before the court in 1954, Griswold said it was "surely an objective" of a school board to see that each Negro child received a desegregated education, but that the court could not require it because "it's not in the 14th Amendment."

In his second appearance before the bench, Griswold warned Oct. 14 that white students might flee the South's public schoolrooms if school desegregation were pressed too vigorously. He insisted that the plan advocated by the Fund— abolition of all recognizably black

schools—would in the long run produce less integration. Griswold said that "if you require too much, you aggravate the problems of withdrawals. There suddenly comes a place where the whites' fleeing is accelerated or becomes complete."

At the same time Griswold rejected arguments by lawyers for the Mobile and Charlotte districts that the Constitution prohibited assigning children to schools on the basis of race in order to break up segregated schools. He also accepted the idea that limited busing of children to schools outside their immediate neighborhood might be necessary to achieve integration.

Lawyers for the school districts told the court Oct. 13 that the 1954 *Brown v. Board of Education* decision was being violated by court-ordered integration plans that assigned children to schools by race. A group of the Southern lawyers argued that the 1954 ruling required "color-blind" assignment of students and that the busing of schoolchildren to increase the incidence of integration was unconstitutional.

Lawyers for the Southern appellants repeatedly used the 1954 *Brown* decision to bolster their arguments against the integration plans ordered for the Mobile and Charlotte districts. An attorney for a group of white and black parents whose children were bused away from their local schools when the Charlotte schools reopened Sept. 9 with desegregated facilities, said that "we plead the same constitutional rights here that the plaintiffs pleaded in *Brown*."

1971
North Carolina

Court approves school busing. North Carolina's Supreme Court Jan. 20 sustained the state's policy of providing school buses for city-dwelling children involved in desegregation programs as long as the state used funds to transport children from rural areas to their schools.

The decision struck down a lower court injunction that would have prohibited the state from using funds for busing. The injunction was not in effect pending the decision of the state Supreme Court.

In effect, the court's action gave the state legislature the choice of continuing busing for all children who needed it, or dropping it altogether. In either case the state would have to apply its decision uniformly to rural and city children.

An assistant state attorney general said the court's decision could not be appealed because it did not involve any constitutional issue.

Virginia

Richmond school plan ordered. A federal judge in Richmond, Va., who for two years had heard arguments over various desegregation plans for the city's public schools, April 5 ordered city officials to go ahead with a plan that would increase busing of schoolchildren by about 50%.

The plan approved by U.S. District Court Judge Robert R. Merhige affected all the city's 50 public schools. Of about 50,000 pupils, 20,000 would be bused to increase the incidence of desegregation.

Earlier plans submitted to Merhige by the Department of Health, Education and Welfare (HEW) and backed by the Richmond School Board had no provisions for busing students for desegregation purposes.

Under the plan ordered by Merhige, the city was required to buy 56 more school buses at a cost estimated at $500,000 for the first year. Each high school and elementary school would have a student population of at least 17% white or 33% black under the new plan.

Richmond school plan proposed. The Richmond, Va. school board May 4 unveiled a unique desegregation plan that would use a lottery system to determine which schoolchildren would be bused from their neighborhood schools to other schools.

The plan was submitted to U.S. District Court Judge Robert R. Merhige, who had ordered the board April 5 to set up a plan that would integrate Richmond's predominantly black inner city schools with the white suburban schools.

George Little, an attorney for the school board, said he could find no precedent for a desegregation plan based on a random lottery system. He said the lottery was patterned after the one used by the Selective Service System to call up men for the armed forces.

The lottery would determine which white students would be bused in from two white suburban communities and which black students would be bused to the suburban schools. The plan, which would involve the daily busing of 35,-000 schoolchildren, would use a child's birth date to set up the lottery system.

The Supreme Court: North Carolina

Supreme Court upholds busing. The Supreme Court, in a series of unanimous decisions, told the Charlotte-Mecklenburg County, N.C. joint school system and all the other school districts of the South April 20 that busing children as a means of dismantling dual school systems was constitutional.

The rulings brought to a close final legal efforts by Southern school boards to stave off busing students to achieve racially-balanced schools.

Chief Justice Warren E. Burger wrote the opinions for the entire court in the four cases on which it ruled.

In addition to upholding a far-reaching school busing plan in the *Swann v.*

Charlotte-Mecklenburg case, the Court struck down as unconstitutional an anti-busing statute enacted by the North Carolina legislature, ordered Mobile, Ala. school officials to use "all available techniques" to correct segregation in their schools and overturned a Georgia Supreme Court ruling that had said certain desegregation efforts in Athens were unconstitutional.

"Desegregation plans cannot be limited to the walk-in school," Burger wrote for the court. The justices held that busing schoolchildren was proper unless "the time or distance is so great as to risk either the health of the children or significantly impinge on the educational process." The court added that at times busing was an indispensible method of eliminating "the last vestiges" of racial segregation.

The court made it clear, however, that the rulings in the Charlotte and its companion cases did not apply to de facto segregation, caused by neighborhood housing patterns and found most often in the North.

In upholding the constitutionality of busing, the court brushed aside the arguments of the Nixon Administration and the Justice Department which had backed **Southern school officials seeking relief from the court. Justice Department lawyers had contended that Southern school districts should be permitted to assign students to schools in their own neighborhoods even if it slowed down the pace of desegregation.**

Lawyers for the Southern districts argued that in the North, communities were allowed to have neighborhood schools and that it would be discriminatory if the South were not allowed the same "privilege."

(Several hours after the decision was announced, White House Press Secretary Ronald L. Ziegler, speaking for President Nixon, said "the Supreme Court has acted and their decision is now the law of the land. It is up to the people to obey that law." He declined to answer questions of whether the President was pleased or dissatisfied with the ruling.)

The court imposed some limits on its decisions. It stopped short of ordering the elimination of all-black schools or of requiring racial balance in the schools. In addition, the court said that young children may be improper subjects for busing if it was over long distances.

The major portion of what Burger described as "guidelines" for the "assistance of school authorities and courts" came in a 28-page decision involving the Charlotte school district. The court upheld the action of U.S. Judge James B. McMillan who approved a school desegregation plan that required massive crosstown busing of schoolchildren to increase the incidence of integration. His ruling was overturned by a U.S. appeals court on the grounds that it was unreasonable and burdensome. In upholding McMillan's decision, the court said the Charlotte

school board had failed to propose an acceptable alternative plan and that McMillan was forced to draw up his own.

In the other North Carolina case, the justices ruled that the legislature violated the Constitution when it enacted an anti-busing law and that the statute, "apparently neutral" and "color-blind" in form, "would render illusionary" the concept of a unitary school system. Burger wrote that bus transportation had been an "integral part of all public educational systems" and that it was unlikely that an effective remedy could be devised "without continued reliance upon it."

In the Mobile case, the justices overturned a desegregation plan that city officials had devised and ordered further desegregation.

The Supreme Court: Housing

Housing project veto sustained. The Supreme Court April 26 upheld the constitutionality of state referendum laws that allowed a majority of voters in any city, state or county to block low-rent public housing in their community.

By a 5–3 vote the court sustained California's referendum law, on the books since 1950, which required public approval of the low-rent projects before they could be built.

California voters had used the law to block construction of almost half the low-rent housing proposed for the state since its passage.

In the opinion written by Justice Hugo L. Black, the court described the law as consistent with "devotion to democracy, not to bias, discrimination or prejudice."

Chief Justice Warren E. Burger and Justices John M. Harlan, Potter Stewart and Byron White joined Black in the majority decision. Justices Harry A. Blackmun, William J. Brennan Jr. and Thurgood Marshall dissented. Justice William O. Douglas did not take part in the case.

The court had been asked in a host of friend-of-court briefs to strike down the California law on the ground that it frustrated efforts to erect low-rent public housing for the poor. Among those filing briefs were the National Urban Coalition, the National Association of Home Builders, the American Institute of Architects and the Justice Department.

The Urban Coalition said the ruling "may have rendered meaningless" its unanimous April 20 decision approving **busing to dismantle dual school systems. The organization's statement said development of "black and poor central cities and white and affluent suburbs" will frustrate such "piece-meal approaches" as busing.**

The South

Court asked to order integration. The 5th Circuit Court of Appeals was asked

May 11 to order total integration in more than 200 school districts across the South that had been overlooked in earlier court desegregation orders. In all, 25 cases involving school suits were filed with the appeals court in New Orleans.

Lawyers for plaintiffs in the 25 cases asked the court to order total integration by the beginning of the 1971–72 school year. They asked the appeals court to instruct lower district courts to order busing if necessary to achieve "complete dismantling of the remaining vestiges of segregation in the school systems."

The more than 200 districts were in Texas, Louisiana, Mississippi, Florida, Alabama and Georgia. More than 100 of those were in Alabama and 81 in Georgia. Among the school systems affected were those in Atlanta, Columbus, Augusta and Albany, Ga., Bessemer, Ala., Jackson and Biloxi, Miss., and Fort Lauderdale, Fla.

Michigan

Court backs Pontiac busing order. The U.S. Court of Appeals for the 6th Circuit let stand May 28 a federal judge's order requiring extensive busing of students as part of a school desegregation plan for Pontiac, Mich.

The appeals court, sitting in Cincinnati, sustained the original decision handed down in February 1970 by Judge Damon Keith of the U.S. district court. Under Keith's order, the busing was to have begun in the fall of 1970 but an appeal lodged by the school board delayed its implementation.

The busing plan ordered by Keith and sustained by the appeals court called for all elementary schoolchildren to be bused at some time. Elementary schools would have two grades and each child would attend his neighborhood school for two grades and be bused for four of the six years.

Tennessee

Nashville busing plan ordered. A federal district judge in Nashville, Tenn. approved June 28 a crosstown busing plan submitted by the Nixon Administration to desegregate the Nashville-Davidson County public school system.

Judge L. Clure Morton adopted the integration plan drawn up by the Department of Health, Education and Welfare (HEW) with some modifications. He ordered the plan implemented when the schools reopened in September.

The HEW plan would require the daily busing of about 47,000 students, an increase of some 13,500 over the number bused during the 1970–71 school year. The Nashville-Davidson school system, the second largest in Tennessee, had an enrollment of about 95,000 students. Under the plan, the system's all-black schools would be completely eliminated, although 36 of the system's 141 schools would remain mostly white.

The number of black schoolchildren required to ride buses would almost double while the number of whites to be bused would increase by only one-third.

Texas

Austin school plan rejected. A U.S. district court judge in Austin, Tex. June 28 rejected a federal desegregation plan for the city's schools that called for extensive crosstown busing of pupils. Judge Jack Roberts ordered the federal government and Austin school officials to try to draw up a school plan that would keep the busing to a minimum.

Roberts held that the federal government had failed to prove its main point— that the Austin district discriminated against Mexican-Americans. Roberts added that the government had failed to prove its charge that the district had perpetuated the segregation of black students since 1955.

The U.S. plan rejected by Roberts would have involved the busing of more than 13,000 students daily over a distance of 15 miles.

U.S. busing plan for Austin rejected. A U.S. district court judge in Austin, Tex. refused to accept July 18 a federal school desegregation proposal for Austin's schools that would have required extensive crosstown busing.

District Court Judge Jack Roberts accepted instead the school desegregation plan filed by the Austin school district.

Under the district's plan for elementary schools, new centers would be established for fine arts, avocations, social sciences and sciences. Pupils of all races would be bused to the new centers for a portion of the school day.

The district's plan for junior high schools called for the reassignment of all black pupils to schools "that are not identifiable as Negro schools."

The district and the Department of Health, Education & Welfare had previously agreed to a plan for the desegregation of Austin's senior high schools which provided for the closing of a predominantly black high school with reassignment of all black students to schools not identifiable as black schools.

Corpus Christi busing plan delayed. Supreme Court Justice Hugo L. Black granted school officials in Corpus Christi, Tex. Aug. 19 a temporary delay in implementing a desegregation plan that called for extensive busing.

Black said he agreed with Corpus Christi officials and the Justice Department, which had supported the school board's request for the stay, that the 15,-000 elementary schoolchildren should not be bused immediately. Black called the situation "very anomalous, new and confusing."

He said he was ordering the stay without comment on the "wisdom or propriety" until the 5th Circuit Court of Appeals or the full Supreme Court acted on the issue.

The busing plan had been drawn up by the Department of Health, Education and Welfare at the request of U.S. District Court Judge Woodrow Seals. In a suit filed by private plaintiffs, Seals had ruled that the Corpus Christi district discriminated against both blacks and Mexican-Americans.

School officials said they could not afford the busing costs, which were estimated at $1.7 million. The Justice Department had told the Supreme Court that there was "serious question" as to whether the board had discriminated against Mexican-American children.

The key issue in the case was whether the Corpus Christi school board had segregated Mexican-American schoolchildren purposely. Most of them were in predominantly Mexican-American schools, and Seals had ruled that the board had put them there and kept them there illegally.

Chief Justice Burger

Burger cautions on busing. Chief Justice Warren E. Burger said Aug. 31 that he feared federal judges were "misreading" the Supreme Court's April 20 ruling on busing to achieve racial desegregation by interpreting it to require racial balance in every school. Burger delivered a clarification of the landmark busing decision, which he had written for the court, in refusing to stay the enforcement of a court-ordered busing plan for the Winston-Salem, Forsyth County, N.C. school system.

Burger rejected the plea for a stay because of the lateness of the appeal and the lack of sufficient information to overturn the plan ordered by Judge Eugene A. Gordon. Schools there had opened Aug. 30 under a plan involving busing of 34,000 of the district's 50,000 students.

In his 10-page opinion, unusual in a denial of a stay, Burger said the unanimous April ruling did not require "a fixed racial balance or quota" in order to constitutionally desegregate schools. He said a school district's racial balance should be used as "a starting point" to determine "whether in fact any violation existed." But he quoted language from the April ruling on the Charlotte, N.C. school system saying that judges need not require "that every school in every community must always reflect the racial composition of the school system as a whole."

Michigan

Detroit segregation called deliberate. A U.S. judge in Detroit, who has been at the center of a two-year legal battle over integration of the city's schools, said Sept. 27 that Detroit's public school system had been deliberately segregated.

Judge Stephen J. Roth said he would delay ordering specific plans to integrate

Detroit's schools pending further hearings.

Roth's decision came in a 13-month civil suit still being contested. The suit was filed by the National Association for the Advancement of Colored People (NAACP) as a class action suit on behalf of all the city's schoolchildren and their parents. In December 1970, Roth had ordered a school integration plan based on an entirely new concept in school desegregation, but hearings and appeals delayed the plan's implementation.

According to Roth, the Detroit system promoted segregation by constructing small primary schools, redrawing attendance zones to circumvent integration and using busing to move some black students to other black schools rather than white ones. He said "state and local government actions have played a substantial role in promoting segregation" of the schools.

But he added that "there is enough blame for everyone to share." "Government actions and inactions at all levels—federal, state and local—have combined with those of private organizations such as loaning institutions, real estate associations and brokerage firms" to cause a pattern of housing segregation, Roth said. He said segregated housing fostered segregated schools.

Roth also put some of the blame on blacks, who to some degree he said, "like other ethnic groups in the past, have tended to separate from the larger group and associate together."

Detroit school plan ordered. Federal Judge Stephen J. Roth directed the Michigan Board of Education Oct. 4 to propose within four months a school integration plan that would encompass Detroit's inner city schools and schools in outlying suburban areas.

Roth had ruled Sept. 27 that Detroit's public school system had been deliberately segregated.

In his instructions, Roth said the plan should result in the creation of a metropolitan school district integrating inner city and suburban schools. He said that only some type of metropolitan plan appeared to have "a chance to succeed."

Roth insisted that he had not decided on any integration plan, but his comments on an inner city-suburban district stirred fears in the suburbs that the plans would require crosstown busing of schoolchildren.

In a related development, Michigan's top Democratic party leadership went on record Oct. 2 endorsing busing "as an imperfect and temporary mechanism to help erase the imbalances in our educational system." Among those who signed the busing statement were Sen. Philip A. Hart, State Attorney General Frank Kelley, Secretary of State Rich-

ard Austin, Democratic State Chairman James M. McNeely and Jerome Cavanagh, former mayor of Detroit.

The South

Judge limits Florida busing. Federal Judge George Young said Sept. 17 that a crosstown busing plan set for Orange County, Fla. could not involve transfer of more than 5,000 of the district's 90,000 students.

School board members in Orange County had vowed to resist more sweeping busing at the risk of being jailed. The school board had requested a delay in implementing the busing plan until after the Christmas recess, but Young ordered the busing plan to be implemented by Oct. 4.

Alabama law invoked. An Alabama judge invoked a new state law for the first time Oct. 18 as he ordered Birmingham school officials to admit five white students to the school of their choice rather than the ones to which they had been assigned as part of a desegregation plan ordered by a U.S. court.

Judge William C. Barbour ordered Birmingham school authorities to enroll the students after they had been turned down in their bids for transfers.

The law which Barbour invoked required school boards to honor transfer requests if parents determined that their child's health or education was endangered by busing. The law was passed at the urging of Gov. George C. Wallace, who had stirred a debate over busing in Alabama when he ordered a number of districts to disregard federal desegregation plans.

Atlanta school case kept open. The 5th U.S. Circuit Court of Appeals overruled two federal judges Oct. 21 and in so doing kept open an Atlanta school desegregation case that began in 1958.

The appeals court, sitting in New Orleans, overruled a district court which had said there was no point in ordering busing or any further desegregation of Atlanta's public schools. The district court judges, Sidney O. Smith and Albert J. Henderson Jr., had dismissed a busing plan for Atlanta as neither "reasonable, feasible nor workable."

The appeals court returned the case to the district court with an order to grant the National Association for the Advancement of Colored People (NAACP) a hearing to propose a busing plan for the court's consideration.

Jackson, Miss. ruling. U.S. District Court Judge Dan Russell issued a permanent injunction Oct. 20 enjoining the State of Mississippi from interfering with a desegregation plan for public schools in

Jackson or withholding funds from the Jackson district because of busing.

Russell ordered the state tax commission, state auditor and attorney general not to interfere with implementation of a court-approved desegregation plan.

Jackson officials had sought relief from the federal court after Gov. John Bell Williams directed state agencies Sept. 11 to withhold education funds until the system showed that it was not using the money for busing purposes.

The Supreme Court: Michigan

Court declines to review Pontiac busing. The Supreme Court declined Oct. 26 to hear an appeal by the Pontiac, Mich. school board of a court-ordered busing plan that had evoked widespread community opposition and violence by the Michigan Ku Klux Klan.

By refusing to hear the case, the court avoided ruling on the controversial issue of busing in the North to achieve racially-balanced schools.

For the most part, school segregation in the North was fostered by neighborhood housing patterns, or de facto segregation. In the South, school segregation was generally the result of officially constituted acts or de jure segregation. The court had yet to rule on de facto segregation.

The court's action in the Pontiac case meant that lower court judges would remain free to order school busing plans in other Northern school cases.

The court did not give reasons for refusing to hear the appeal by the Pontiac school board, which maintained that school segregation in Pontiac was a result of neighborhood patterns and not of discriminatory actions by either school or public officials.

Pontiac's appeal was the first Northern case to reach the Supreme Court since it upheld the constitutionality of school busing in three cases in April 1971.

Alabama

Alabama law voided. Alabama's law against mandatory school busing was ruled unconstitutional Dec. 3 by U.S. District Court Judge Sam C. Pointer.

Judge Pointer cited a U.S. Supreme Court decision overturning a similar North Carolina law, and said freedom of choice plans would be ruled out in Birmingham "at least until a unitary system has been in operation for a sufficient length of time to escape the tendency such option would have towards reestablishing a dual system."

SUPREME COURT SETS FEB. 1 DEADLINE FOR DEEP SOUTH SCHOOL INTEGRATION

The U.S. Supreme Court Jan. 14 overturned a lower court decision that had granted Mississippi and five other Deep South states a temporary reprieve in implementing federal school desegregation guidelines. The new ruling, which set a Feb. 1 desegregation date, represented a setback for the Nixon Administration, since the Justice Department had requested the high court to sustain the original September 1970 deadline.

Richmond Times-Dispatch

Richmond, Va., January 20, 1970

The U.S. Supreme Court has set a near-impossible task for many school divisions in the Deep South states by ordering desegregation by Feb. 1 of public schools attended by some 300,000 pupils.

Wednesday's decision reversed a ruling by the U.S. Court of Appeals for the Fifth Circuit which on Dec. 1 had set next September as the deadline for desegregation of school districts in Alabama, Florida, Mississippi, Louisiana and Georgia. The ruling will also apply to some school districts in Texas, the sixth state within the Fifth Circuit's jurisdiction.

As a result of Wednesday's decision it seems likely that other school districts in the South, under court order to desegregate by Sept. 1, will be forced to accept the accelerated deadline.

The decision is also certain to step up the exodus of white pupils from public schools, particularly in Mississippi, and leave many of its school districts almost all-black.

Many educators view the midyear deadline as educationally unwise and say that mere physical effort involved will prove impossible. It is probable that some school districts will simply close, thus forcing other court actions.

Yesterday, Florida Gov. Claude Kirk told the Supreme Court that his state is "financially and physically unable" to meet the midyear deadline and Louisiana has submitted a motion to the court for emergency consideration of a petition for a rehearing of the case.

The Supreme Court's decision was a setback for the Nixon administration, since the Justice Department had requested the Sept. 1 desegregation date and had told the Fifth Circuit that if that deadline were approved the department would use "all available resources" to see that it was enforced.

Chief Justice Warren E. Burger and Justice Potter Stewart did not join the court's action, announcing in a "memorandum" (but not labeled as a "dissent") that they believed it to be unsound to overrule the Fifth Circuit Court's decision without considering arguments in briefs and oral hearings. They said that the Fifth Circuit, which sits in New Orleans, "is far more familiar than we with the various situations of those several school districts ... and has exhibited responsibility and fidelity to the objectives of our holdings in school desegregation cases."

Although the Burger-Stewart memorandum seems a more logical approach to the problem, it cannot be considered a significant departure from the court's usual unanimity in school desegregation cases for the past 16 years.

In another separate opinion — again, not a dissent — Justices John M. Harlan and Byron R. White, suggested an eight-week deadline.

Regardless of whether the Feb. 1 deadline should or should not have been set, the fact remains that the damage being done to public schools is deeply distressing. Admittedly, however, the results might have been substantially the same in the fall, as far as long-range effects on the schools are concerned, if integration had been delayed until then.

The Dallas Morning News

Dallas, Tex., January 22, 1970

THE FEB. 1 deadline for massive mixing of a number of Southern schools is building toward a showdown between the Supreme Court and several Southern governors on the question of whether the court can order bussing in defiance of an act of Congress.

John McKeithen of Louisiana has drawn approving echoes from several other governors by pointing to the 1964 Civil Rights Act's ban on bussing as a means of achieving racial balance in schools.

Since the high court's mixing formula calls for racial balance, bussing is essential to overcome built-in residential racial patterns.

McKeithen says it is illegal. He has drawn "a line in the dust" against bussing. George Wallace of Alabama echoes him. So do the governors of Florida, Mississippi and Georgia. McKeithen says he is not violating the law—he's upholding it.

Who's right? Up till now, the law and the court haven't collided over the integration issue—but only because first the Department of Health, Education and Welfare and later the courts simply defied the 1964 act.

CONGRESS hasn't complained, but now the Southern governors are complaining. If they persist, then the massive transfer of black and white students across neighborhood school district lines won't take place. That would put the next move up to the high court.

The looming confrontation differs from those in the past when U.S. marshals or even the National Guard were called to integrate schools trying to retain segregation. But, as official policy, segregation is dead in the South. The open-door or freedom-of-choice policy has been substituted for it.

That wasn't enough for HEW. HEW has wanted racial balance from the first. And HEW invented "zoning" and "pairing" of distant attendance districts to overcome residential patterns. HEW has had the power of the purse, but the courts—in adopting HEW's policies—are expected to make some show of constitutionality.

THEY HAVEN'T done so; there simply has been a gradual shift in judicial policy from outlawing official segregation to demanding positive integration by the means already laid down by HEW.

So HEW and the court have been equally guilty of breaking federal law. That's what McKeithen and the others are talking about. Since the Supreme Court has never asserted the supremacy of its policies by outlawing the 1964 act, the governors have firm ground to stand on.

Are we a nation of laws or not? That is the question. It's bigger than bussing, but the governors have chosen bussing as a test of the question.

Much of the country's discontent with the ambiguous hypocrisy of a judicial policy that seeks a social goal in disregard of federal statute comes to a focus in the challenge the governors are flinging down.

THE RICHMOND NEWS LEADER

Richmond, Va., January 26, 1970

The Supreme Court could not have acted more capriciously nor more irresponsibly than by ruling, as it did on January 14, that all school districts in Alabama, Florida, Georgia, Louisiana, and Mississippi must integrate by February 1. The results of this order have brought widespread disruption, bordering on total chaos, to the schools in these States, interrupting the education of 300,000 youngsters before semester's end.

Quite understandably, the parents of these children are bitter. In Mississippi, where the compulsory school attendance law was repealed in 1965, many white parents have decided to keep their children at home. Thousands of others have entered their children in private schools. The court's ruling ultimately could bring a deterioration of quality in education; white taxpayers are not likely to support tax increases or new bond issues for public schools to which they do not send their children.

The high court's hell-bent quest for instant integration thus has reached the level of high folly. From the *Brown* decision of 1954, outlawing segregation enforced by law, the court has steadily moved in the direction of integration enforced by law. In its latest decision, the court also flirted dangerously with the question of *de facto* segregation, or segregation that results from living patterns rather than by law.

In effect, the high court has destroyed the neighborhood school system in much of the South and has assumed the authority for telling school officials which children must attend which school. From a position of color-blindness, the court has moved to a position of color-consciousness. The lunacy of the Federal judiciary's obsession can be seen in the predicament of a 14-year-old boy in Little Rock, Arkansas. He wants to continue to attend his neighborhood school; in fact, he refuses to attend the school several miles away to which he has been assigned. So the Federal court in Little Rock has sentenced his parents to 30-day jail terms and fined them $1,000 for refusing to make their son attend a school he doesn't like.

Of course, the Supreme Court's decrees, however unreasonable, are the law of the land and must be obeyed. The fruits of civil disobedience, come to harvest in a breakdown in law and order, have proved the necessity for obeying all laws, however unpalatable those laws may be. The parents and children affected by the January 14 Supreme Court order may circumvent the order legally, but school officials in the five Southern States have no choice but to comply.

Civil rights activists scarcely can contain their glee at this punitive ruling. In their view, the five Southern States have dragged their heels for almost 16 years now, and they have no justification for further delays. They also are highly critical of Southern States for using every legal means open to them to delay compulsory integration. But the right to appeal, and to continue appealing until all legal remedies have been exhausted, is also part of the law of the land, available to litigants in any legal action.

Yet, within the democratic process, there should be some redress, short of outright defiance and civil disobedience, open to hundreds of thousands of parents who want to retain control over their children's education. Of course, the U.S. Constitution provides that Congress can limit the appellate authority of the Supreme Court, and thus limit its high-handed interference in public education.

That is not likely, unless the Department of Health, Education, and Welfare and the Department of Justice were to extend their crackdown on *de facto* segregation to the North. Certainly if *de facto* segregation is illegal in the South, it must be illegal in the North as well. If the chaos imposed on public education in the South were to be inflicted on Northern districts, public pressure could force enough congressmen to say that the Federal government's obsession with instant integration had gone too far.

Congress then might clamp some restrictions on the Supreme Court, and approve legislation forbidding HEW to demand busing and racial quotas. These are the only remedies that might be hoped for by thousands of parents who are fed up with the arrogance of HEW and with the dictates of a high court intent not on justice or mercy, but on integration at any price.

The Birmingham News

Birmingham, Ala., January 15, 1970

Without belaboring the merits of the specific case, the Supreme Court's order yesterday that 14 Southern school districts, including the Bessemer and Jefferson systems, have less than two weeks to desegregate amounts to what well may be an administrative impossibility.

While they in no way questioned the point that segregated schools are illegal, Chief Justice Warren E. Burger and Justice Potter Stewart offered the entirely logical comment that the school districts concerned with the education of 300,000 children should have been given the opportunity of a hearing, certainly not an unreasonable courtesy, if nothing else.

Additionally, the dissenting justices suggested that the U.S. Circuit Court in New Orleans, which had given the defendants until next fall to implement desegregation plans, *had* heard arguments in the case and was in a much better position to weigh "the varying problems" confronting the areas concerned.

This was an entirely reasonable position and the court majority's insistence that those responsible for the education of hundreds of thousands of youngsters move headlong into changes will create, for the time being, more problems than corrections.

It is no longer arguable that segregated schools will be tolerated by the courts. And it is true that some school systems have been delinquent in implementing court orders, as distressing as those edicts have proved to be in many cases.

Despite the high court's irritation over prolonged resistance on the desegregation issue, the course of wisdom in this most recent case would have been to listen to the counsel of the district court, which is aware of the "varying problems" which exist and won't disappear by February 1 simply because the Supreme Court insists they must.

St. Petersburg Times

St. Petersburg, Fla., January 16, 1970

Of course it will be difficult to desegregate Florida's schools.

It will be inconvenient, disruptive and expensive to both students and teachers.

But 200 years of segregation since the Civil War have been difficult, inconvenient, disruptive and expensive for many black Americans.

And 16 years of segregation since the United States Supreme Court declared it unconstitutional also have been inconvenient, disruptive and expensive.

Since 1954 the Supreme Court has been telling every Florida school board to desegregate with "all deliberate speed." A thousand excuses and legal tricks followed.

Since Oct. 29 the Supreme Court has been telling every Florida school board to "integrate at once."

THE COURT ran out of patience this week. It said integrate by Feb. 1.

There has been a surprised, emotional reaction. Gov. Kirk asked for delay. Education Commissioner Floyd Christian talked about the difficulties. Pinellas Supt. Thomas Southard said, "This will not apply to us." State Rep. Jerome Pratt, D-Palmetto, who seems to fear integration more than ignorance, has called for repeal of the compulsory school attendance law.

It is time for reason. It is time to lose patience with those who preach law and order for others but violate the law themselves. It is time to desegregate our schools coolly and voluntarily. It is past time.

The Greenville News
Greenville, S.C., January 24, 1970

Only six people in the whole wide world can do anything to avert the disruptive public school crisis faced by the people of Greenville County in February—and they probably won't. They are the following associate justices of the United States Supreme Court:

Hugo F. Black
William J. Brennan Jr.
William O. Douglas
John M. Harlan
Thurgood Marshall
Byron R. White

They are the six justices who on January 14 decreed that Southern schools under court orders must integrate totally and immediately. Only they — nobody else — can change that decision.

It is, of course, theoretically possible that plaintiffs in the Greenville and Darlington integration suits could avert the crisis simply by withdrawing their complaints. But that is a practical impossibility. The plaintiffs are figureheads only. The lawyers pushing the suits are the agents, not of individuals, but of an organization, the National Association for the Advancement of Colored People. It is hardly likely that organization would agree to withdrawal.

And so the only source of relief is the half-dozen majority on the Supreme Court. If three of them could be persuaded to change their votes and join Chief Justice Warren Burger and Associate Justice Potter Stewart, who dissented, the mid-year school disruption could be averted.

But the only way to get to the Supreme Court is through judicial channels.

Therefore the demands of thousands of anguished, angry Greenvillians upon public officials, from the President of the United States on down, are misdirected and futile.

President Nixon has no power to set aside or ignore Supreme Court rulings. Neither does the attorney general of the United States. Both are sworn to uphold the Constitution and the processes of law.

South Carolina's United States senators and representatives can do nothing.

Governor Robert McNair is powerless in the matter. He can do no more than Governor Faubis did in Arkansas or George Wallace in Alabama some time ago. Neither could do a thing to stop integration and each finally bowed before the orders of the court, despite a lot of meaningless talk and bluster before, during and since.

Chief Judge Clement F. Haynsworth Jr. of the Fourth Circuit Court of Appeals and District Judge Robert Martin cannot change the situation. Both are bound, completely and irrevocably, by the Supreme Court's instant integration ruling, unless and until the Supreme Court modifies it.

And certainly the Greenville County school board and administration cannot defy the rulings of the court.

In a sense Governors Kirk of Florida and Maddox of Georgia are following the only practical course, although each has been guilty of inflaming the public unduly by rash statements. They are following due process of law, Governor Maddox by ordering an "equal protection" suit filed in an effort to halt integration in Georgia until all states are integrated, Governor Kirk by becoming a party to the Florida case and personally going before the Supreme Court.

Governor McNair of South Carolina is both right and wrong in his approach to the Greenville and Darlington County school crises. Our governor was correct to insist that South Carolinians follow due process of law and to observe the law, as interpreted, no matter how distasteful it might be.

Promising to do everything possible to alleviate the situation, Governor McNair warned that "when we run the course, we're not going to defy the courts, defy the law of the land, regardless of our personal feelings. Open defiance is not the nature of South Carolina."

That is the type of leadership which best serves South Carolina and Greenville County, no matter if it is somewhat unpopular hereabouts in the heat of this moment. Governor McNair, who called attention to the course being followed in Florida, is to be commended highly for that portion of his stand on the current situation.

However, Governor McNair "slipped" a little by asking the President of the United States to set aside or delay a binding court order. The President simply has no more right or authority to defy the courts than Governor McNair. By asking the President, in effect, to "stand in the schoolhouse door" in his place, the governor has weakened to a degree his own position regarding respect for the law.

Although the governor's request is understandable in view of the heavy pressure upon him to "do something," it is nevertheless unfortunate, and should be corrected if possible. Certainly Governor McNair should not repeat the error.

The same can be said for similar action by the Greenville County Legislative Delegation's majority. Such action may be politically popular, but it ill serves the people to raise false hopes and it undermines respect for law to ask the President to ignore the law as interpreted by the courts.

In the present unfortunate situation, the only realistic course of action is to pursue the matter further in the courts, as Florida and Georgia are doing. The schools can ask for a rehearing, which undoubtedly will have to be denied by the Fourth Circuit. The way then will be open for appeal to the Supreme Court, asking the six associate justices to grant relief.

Let us follow that course if we must "do something" about the situation. But let there be no false hopes about the outcome.

As Senator Ernest F. Hollings said a few years ago when he was saying farewell to the General Assembly before leaving the governorship, it appears "we have run out of courts."

TWIN CITY SENTINEL
Winston-Salem, N.C., January 21, 1970

THE school board's December decision to completely desegregate the faculty in every school has now been vindicated. A federal court has decreed precisely what was expected of it, and the only question left open is how deeply our people are committed to the concept of "law and order."

There are, of course, a number of people saying these days that the desegregation orders of the Supreme Court are not in the Constitution and therefore are not "law" at all. That would be true if it weren't for 150 years of American history and legal precedent. For it was in 1819 that the Supreme Court, under Chief Justice John Marshall, took upon itself the authority to interpret the Constitution, and that authority has never been seriously challenged to this day.

This is not to say that it cannot be challenged. Any time Congress chooses, it can pass an amendment to the Constitution and 38 of the 50 states can ratify it into law. In this manner —or by Constitutional Convention — The Supreme Court's power of "judicial review" can be removed, or Supreme Court decisions on desegregation, legislative reapportionment or anything else can be changed or nullified.

But in 16 years of court decisions on school segregation, no serious legal challenge to the court has ever been mounted for the simple reason that the majority of the American people have not been behind such a challenge. (Moreover, not one member of the 435-member House of Representatives has proposed impeachment proceedings against a member of the Supreme Court in these 16 years, and one member is all it takes to introduce a bill of impeachment.)

Therefore the Supreme Court's decisions on school segregation, based on the court's interpretation of the 14th Amendment, are indeed *the* law, and no amount of argument can change that fact.

Therefore it is the duty of us all, teachers, students, parents and officials, as American citizens to obey the law scrupulously until or unless it is legally changed.

There can be little doubt that the vast majority of people in this county accept this responsibility. But we also have a responsibility to obey the law, however unpopular it is, in the best spirit possible. For to do otherwise will inflict more harm on our children than any hardships that might be caused by court orders.

NEW ORLEANS STATES-ITEM
New Orleans, La., January 17, 1970

The temptations of demagoguery traditionally have been difficult for politicians in the Deep South to resist.

Playing upon public fears, race-baiting and flailing away at Yankee demons have only served to distract white and black Southerners from their real problems in the past.

We had hoped Gov. John J. McKeithen and Gov. John Bell Williams had recognized the need to have done with the glib and dangerous language of the past.

Louisiana and Mississippi are in difficult times which call for forthright, courageous leadership. The abrupt desegregation of public schools in the two states has caused disturbing and complex problems for whites and blacks. But the rulings of the Supreme Court are the law of the land, and regardless of what they feel and think, the citizens of both states must accommodate themselves and their children to the new school situation as best they can or work to change the laws.

In the final analysis the public school systems must be saved, although it will not be easy. Patient and courageous leadership by ordinary citizens and elected officials will be required.

Attacking Northern "hypocrites" —even though there may be some justification in the term—as Gov.

McKeithen did recently in New Orleans will not alter the Supreme Court ruling or help salvage the public school system in Louisiana. The same goes for Gov. Williams' ridiculous claim that the court ruling represents some diabolical Yankee scheme to sabotage Mississippi's industrial prospects.

Both governors have demonstrated that they are capable of better.

Neither is Gov. McKeithen leading when he declares in grandstand fashion at the Louisiana Assessors' Conference. "I want to see the candidate for governor who will have in his platform a plank to support equalization on a statewide basis. You talk about a slow death. When the farmers, the store owners and small home owners get through with him, there'll be only a grease spot left."

That's fairly clever stump talk, but it hardly is leadership. It's championing the status quo. It's admitting you're licked before the bell sounds.

And we're not so sure the governor is right. Times *are* changing. We believe the public increasingly is recognizing the need for a forthright approach by public officials to the mounting problems of states and municipalities.

Evasive politics and erratic excursions into demagoguery will not help Louisiana or Mississippi in 1970.

THE MIAMI NEWS
Miami, Fla., January 16, 1970

HARD TIMES are upon the Dade County schools. In almost every way, the system and the students will suffer because of the instant desegregation demanded by the U.S. Supreme Court.

It is a pity matched only by the now dawning realization that the problem should have been faced more directly years ago.

Because ways have been found in the past to dodge the moral and legal responsibilities of desegregating, the students today must pay a heavier price in disruption than is their proper share.

The financial costs could have been spread out over the years. The shifts of teachers and students that cause disruption could have been paced. But those things were not done, and now we must do it all at once.

There is no way now to reach back into the years and make those old sinners pay. Their children will have to pay double. And unless the community bends every effort to meet its school obligations here and now, the cost to the children may balloon even higher.

Let us spare ourselves and our children the screaming and hollering that we are being put upon unfairly. That has no purpose and no relevance now.

Dade County's moral and legal obligations are clear, and a way must be found to meet them. The costs are high, and rising.

The Washington Post
Washington, D.C., January 20, 1970

The essential point to bear in mind in reading the Supreme Court's Wednesday order telling public school authorities in five Southern states to desegregate now—at once, instanter, immediately, forthwith and without delay of any kind—is that it was handed down 16 years after the court's initial order to desegregate the public schools "with all deliberate speed." The court can hardly be called heedlessly impatient. It has simply had all the delay and all the deliberation it could stomach without sacrifice of its authority. And the government of the United States has looked on at the South's flouting of the Supreme Court with a complacency that invited Negroes to lose all faith in the judicial process—and in the whole idea of orderly social change.

The inaction and indifference of the Eisenhower administration in the 1950s, so far as implementation of the original desegregation ruling was concerned, had much to do with the rise of "massive resistance." The President, in the 1950s, withheld the support of his own leadership and moral authority from the court decree and maintained a neutral aloofness from the great national struggle for equal rights. Noncompliance became a general pattern throughout the old Confederacy in consequence.

The Nixon administration has been lending much

the same sort of encouragement to entrenched patterns of segregation in the South. The Department of Justice seems always able to find sympathy for the travail of white citizens who must make a painful adjustment to the ideal of racial equality, yet is rarely able to muster up much feeling for blacks who have had to adjust to inequality for the whole of their lives and seek something better for their children.

There was a positive effrontery in the assertion of the Department of Justice that it would undertake an all-out program of lawsuits to desegregate the entire South this fall if the court would only postpone the deadline for compliance to next September. Will the Department now sulk idly in Washington because it has not had its dilatory way?

Further delay in desegregation is a misfortune for everyone in the South—for whites no less than for blacks. It simply perpetuates turmoil and compounds confusion. The change to unified schools has simply got to be made. The sooner it is made, the sooner the South will be able to deal with the manifold problems of improving its educational system for the children of both races. Acceptance of the idea of change, of equality, is the key to progress, alike in education and in the economy of the Deep South.

THE MILWAUKEE JOURNAL
Milwaukee, Wis., January 23, 1970

The purported shock and dismay of southern politicians over the Supreme Court's latest decision that five southern states must desegregate *now* has to be a sham. They complain that the court is being hasty, that it is trying to get progress too fast, that the South is being given no time to act.

It was 16 years ago that the Supreme Court ordered desegregation of schools "with all deliberate speed." Time and again since then it has batted down efforts to stall and reiterated that it meant what it said in 1954.

To claim that the latest ruling is precipitate is like saying that a prediction that the sun will rise tomorrow lacks scientific basis. The court is merely saying what it has been saying for more than a decade and a half. States that pretend to be horrified by the latest reiteration either haven't been listening or are intent on continuing the illegal stall.

GOV. KIRK DEFIES FEDERAL COURTS OVER SCHOOL INTEGRATION ORDER

To forestall compliance with a Supreme Court-ordered school desegregation plan, Florida Gov. Claude Kirk, Jr., suspended Manatee County school officials April 5 and declared he was assuming personal control of the school system. Kirk ordered the district's 17,000 public school pupils to ignore the court order and continue to attend neighborhood schools rather than take part in busing to achieve racial balance.

Two days later U.S. District Judge Ben Krentzman, in turn, ordered Kirk to relinquish control of the schools, and he ordered the busing plan to become effective April 9. Kirk ignored the court order and moved into the district's school board offices April 9, vowing to resist any effort by federal marshals to take control of the schools. The Justice Department then dispatched its federal marshals, despite a phalanx of heavily armed Florida state troopers. There were several confrontations. Ultimately, faced with contempt citations and $10,000-a-day fines, the governor capitulated. He vacated the offices, reinstated the district's school officials and directed them to put Judge Krentzman's desegregation plan into effect April 14.

The Miami Herald
Miami, Fla., April 14, 1970

By seeking to place himself above the law of the land, Governor Kirk has moved into the league with George Wallace and Orville Faubus, to say nothing of little ol' Lester Maddox.

The governor took control of the Manatee public school system and in doing so, he probably won a lot of votes from emotional and prejudiced residents on the west coast of Florida opposed to busing of students.

But the governor, through his politically-inspired devices, will lose more for the state than he will gain.

He will lose prestige in the eyes of the nation, he will lose whatever status the state may still have left with the White House, and he erodes hopes for equality of educational opportunity.

We hope, however, Mr. Kirk will learn in a short time that courts interpret the laws, rather than governors.

As an advocate of law and order, Mr. Kirk sets a poor example when he defies legal orders of the judiciary.

THE MIAMI NEWS
Miami, Fla., April 14, 1970

CLAUDE KIRK JR. is no longer only a simple embarrassment to the State of Florida but a danger to its peaceful, legal existence.

He may also be a danger to himself.

The governor has taken over, literally and physically, the school system of Manatee County, installing himself as "Superintendent Gov. Claude Kirk Jr." in the office of the ousted superintendent.

Ninety state officers, presumably but not visibly armed, stood guard yesterday at the school headquarters.

U.S. District Atty. John Briggs reports he was "told by the governor's office that if the U.S. marshals try to enter the area and arrest anyone, they will be fired on."

Yesterday Kirk snubbed a federal court's show-cause contempt order and further defied the courts. He had called the U.S. attorney a "liar" and had denounced a newsman as a "fool."

"They ain't gonna lay a hand on Claude Jr.," said the governor, "and they better keep their hands off Erik," a son born in Tallahassee a few hours before.

Whatever the legal case that Kirk is trying to prove in a strutting demonstrating of ego, this is most erratic behavior. It goes far beyond the posturing of other demagogues who have appeared to resist law and order, only to back down on sober second thought.

If Kirk persists in this manner in pretending to represent the interests of Florida he should be impeached and removed from office as unfit to serve.

Megalomania has no place in a state house, in command of men who may bear arms, or in the conduct of a school system serving 17,000 children held as pawns to a grandiose ambition.

In sum, Claude Kirk Jr. is no longer a joke. He is a dangerous and intolerable public nuisance.

New York Post
New York, N.Y., April 7, 1970

After barging into a Florida school district preparing to proceed with integration, Republican Gov. Kirk intoned magisterially yesterday: "We have come this way reluctantly. We have not been given our day in court." Evidently he had forgotten last Jan. 23.

That was the day when the Governor made another personal appearance at Supreme Court in Washington—to attempt further stalling of its desegregation edicts. Not long after his departure, the high court rejected Kirk's publicity plea and his case as well.

The Governor assumed what he called "custodial supervision" of the Manatee County public schools yesterday. In other words, he demonstrated his contempt of the courts by obstructing their integration program. Queried about the developments, the White House explained that the federal government will help see to enforcement of appropriate court orders. How? By pressing forward with the nomination of Florida's own G. Harrold Carswell, whose restrictive opinions in racial cases have been regularly rejected and reversed?

Can there any longer be serious doubt that it is the Administration's "Southern strategy" that emboldens the Kirks and leaves men of good will in the South—school officials and others—exposed to new fire for striving to comply with the law?

THE PLAIN DEALER
Cleveland, Ohio
April 10, 1970

Florida Gov. Claude Kirk who some feel is a superficial phony, is not merely setting himself above the law, he acts as though he IS the law.

For the second time the governor has defied a U.S. district judge and for the second time has ousted the Manatee County school board and taken over operation of the schools to thwart federal court orders to integrate by busing.

By provoking these confrontations, Kirk is doing a disservice to education, good race relationships and proper administrative and judicial procedures.

OKLAHOMA CITY TIMES
Oklahoma City, Okla., April 15, 1970

IT is good that Gov. Claude Kirk of Florida has decided to go the legal route and quit trying to flout the federal courts on an integration order.

Doubtless he has accomplished his purpose of wooing voters on his anti-busing stand. But in a nation where there has been so much defiance of the courts, whether by air controllers, mailmen, self-styled revolutionaries, or Back Panthers, Gov. Kirk only added new mockery to our legal institutions by the way he confronted them.

Incidentally, it may be that Kirk crossed up the Nixon administration and justice Department strategy on busing, which apparently is to delay a showdown as long as possible. An article elsewhere on this page speculates that's why the Justice Department brief in the case was so curt with him.

THE ARIZONA REPUBLIC
Phoenix, Ariz., April 14, 1970

Florida Gov. Claude Kirk stopped just short of forcing a bitter state-federal showdown when he bowed to federal court orders and reinstated school officials of Manatee County with instructions to implement a district court's integration order. Even at that, however, Kirk's initial defiance of a federal district court's school integration order can only contribute to additional undermining of the law.

Heaven knows, Kirk can always point to postal workers, school teachers, sanitation workers and many others who have defied federal law and federal courts in pursuit of what they consider to be a higher good. And those who preach the gospel of civil disobedience, and always and everywhere find excuses for draft resisters, campus militants, mad bombers, and everyone else who puts his personal conviction above the law, are obviously in no position to criticize Governor Kirk . . . although it goes without saying that this has not deterred them from tsk-tsking at Kirk's defiance.

But those who have consistently pleaded for respect for law and order can and must criticize Kirk.

It may well be, as he claimed, that his dramatic defiance was intended to force a Supreme Court decision on the legality of forced busing of public school pupils to achieve racial balance (an objective this newspaper has consistently opposed). But there are ways to force such a decision that do not undermine the federal court system, and Kirk had a duty to seek them out.

We condemn unequivocally Governor Kirk's defiance of the courts . . . and we shall continue to condemn every individual or organization that sets itself above the law.

Newsday
Long Island, N.Y., April 7, 1970

President Eisenhower had trouble accepting the original Supreme Court school desegregation decision in 1954. He equivocated in his public discussion of the ruling, and—more or less in consequence—was handed a first-class constitutional crisis at Little Rock in 1957. Now President Nixon is having his own doubts and reservations about the value of integration, and is about to harvest his own dragon's teeth. Governor Kirk of Florida—one of the noisiest of the "law and order" advocates—has personally seized control of a county school system and is out to emulate Orval Faubus and Ross Barnett. There is no question that Kirk is in defiance of the Supreme Court and of the law of the land. If another wave of Southern defiance is to be avoided, the President and the courts are going to have to deal forthrightly with this challenge to federal authority. Governor Kirk belongs in jail and Richard Nixon must choose between his Southern strategy and his role as the nation's chief executive.

San Francisco Examiner
San Francisco, Calif., April 15, 1970

FLORIDA'S flamboyant Governor, Claude R. Kirk Jr., may have reaped a certain amount of cheap southern political hay from his week-long defiance of federal authority in a school desegregation ruling. Whatever new redneck votes he may have won, however, are no match for the damage he has caused.

What was i n e x c u s a b l e about Gov. Kirk's week-long show of dramatic defiance was his cynical knowledge that it was a phony act from start to finish. He knew he couldn't win; he had no intention of suffering for the cause he professed. Faced with the imminent reality of a $10,000-a-day fine for contempt of court, he quickly rang down the curtain on his bombastic charade.

If all this seems a little rough, consider the inexcusable damage the Governor has done to the cause of law and order. The damage can never be measured, and may even be minimal. But the spectacle of a state's chief executive defying — however briefly — the supreme law of the land is hardly conducive to orderly process elsewhere in our troubled society.

Florida deserves a better leader than Claude Kirk.

THE SUN
Baltimore, Md., April 14, 1970

One way to say it would be that the Governor of Florida has an identity problem, complicated by selective astigmatism. In his quarrel with the federal district court at Tampa, his sense of self had impaired his vision of the political ambiance in which he operates. That ambiance is determined by the United States Constitution.

It is quite true that the Constitution acknowledges a certain sovereignty in the several states of the union. There is thus no doubt that Mr. Kirk is Governor of a sovereign state. But to conclude, as he did, that "no federal judge can order a sovereign governor of a sovereign state around" was to go astigmatic at Article VI of the Constitution where it says, "This Constitution and the laws of the United States . . . shall be the supreme law of the land. . . ."

It was this mandate which Judge Ben Krentzman of the Tampa court had in mind when he held Governor Kirk to be in civil contempt for the flouting of school-desegregation orders issued by the same court. Fines of $10,000 a day were to toll against the Governor—unless he agreed by noon Monday to do what the court said. The Governor agreed Sunday. It was one of the quickest vision corrections in recent political history.

St. Petersburg Times
St. Petersburg, Fla., April 14, 1970

"What I have said speaks for itself — neither I nor my staff will have any further comment. Thank you."

That is how Gov. Claude Kirk ended his week-long recess on sanity, public responsibility and respect for law in Manatee County, Florida.

He closed a crisis-that-should-not-have-been with a victory statement-that-really-wasn't . . . and he deftly headed off any questions which might expose his antics for what they were.

SUCH IS THE nature of the politics of confusion. Its practitioner feed upon bewilderment and ignorance, on impressions rather than facts.

The facts are these:

✔ He failed to get the busing issue before the Supreme Court, which was his announced intention.

✔ He did not, as he claimed in his statement Sunday, win Justice Department support for an effort to "modify" U.S. District Judge Ben Krentzman's desegregation order.

✔ He delayed implementation of a court - ordered desegregation plan for one week . . . a delay that really began in 1954, and continued in 1965, when the suit was filed.

✔ He disrupted an entire school system for one week and robbed Manatee school children of what little harmony and instruction might have been accomplished under the circumstances.

✔ He needlessly and recklessly stirred emotions to a point from which only the greatest of good fortune allowed us to retreat without bloodshed.

✔ He used his office to erode respect for law and order in Florida as no Black Panther, Ku Klux Klansman, American Nazi or SDS Weatherman ever could.

✔ He converted the dignity of former governor and justice Millard Caldwell into a mere stage prop.

✔ He exposed the danger which the Nixon Administration's "southern strategy" poses for the law of the land The President's silence before such open defiance by a governor hardly discourages rebellion by others.

KIRK ALSO diverted public attention from the mismanagement, reckless spending and scandal which have colored his Administration since it took office more than three years ago.

He hopes he has won re-election.

Claude Kirk already was establishing himself as Florida's costliest politician financially.

Now he is assaulting the state's dignity and insulting its intelligence.

He has misjudged the capacity of its people to recognize selfish opportunism — and to strike it down.

The forces for equal justice and opportunity in America will not be stopped by such antics.

THE COMMERCIAL APPEAL
Memphis, Tenn., April 7, 1970

IT IS DIFFICULT to figure out the motivation of Gov. Claude Kirk of Florida in his determination to challenge the federal courts by personally taking over the school administration of one of his counties.

As governor, Kirk must realize that the court's word must be observed by all officials and citizens so long as that word stands. This is the essence of law and order which the governor is sworn to uphold.

There is no doubt about the court's position on the Manatee County situation. The federal district court at Tampa had ordered into effect a desegregation plan last Jan. 28. Manatee County school officials had appealed that order all the way to the United States Supreme Court which just last Friday turned down the school officials' request that the plan be delayed until next September.

The plan undoubtedly would work considerable hardship on the Florida county involved. It called for shifting 2,617 of the county's 2,700 students and 187 of the teachers to different schools in mid-term. Yet, the county officials and even the state education commissioner were resigned to making the required adjustments this week. Only the governor is standing in the way of compliance with the orders of the federal court.

There remains, however, the fundamental question of just how far the United States Supreme Court really expects schools to go in this matter of school integration. Despite some actions in cases such as this one involving the Manatee County schools, usually actions referring back to lower courts or declining to hear the cases, the Supreme Court still has not spelled out its position.

The result has been that in some communities busing and other devices are being required to achieve desegregation by numbers in each school while in other communities there remains unchallenged the segregation that results from housing patterns in the school districts.

It is this lack of clear policy on the part of the highest court that gives the appearance of validity to such challenges as the one being made by Governor Kirk. Until the Supreme Court defines its position in terms much more clear than any it has used thus far, opportunist politicians can continue attempting to use the issue for their personal ends.

The Charlotte Observer
Charlotte, N.C., April 12, 1970

The issue posed by the tactics of Florida's Gov. Claude Kirk is spelled out in a Wall Street Journal editorial, "Law-And-Order Albatross."

"Just when we were beginning to think the need for law and order was once again being recognized more widely, albeit sometimes grudgingly," says The Journal, "now we find Governor Claude Kirk of Florida defying the Federal courts over integration.

"The important thing in this dispute is not the merits of the court's plan . . . . The important thing is respect for and loyalty to the process by which that decision was reached. If the governor of a state does not treat court decisions as legitimate, how can other citizens be asked to do so?"

But it is not only the institution of the federal courts that is endangered by Kirk's action. Federal law enforcement has suffered, too, in its sputtering performance against Kirk's defiance of a court order.

Whether Kirk was engaging in a display of demagoguery, as The Miami Herald suggested, or is acting out of deepest conviction, federal authorities have allowed him to play out too long a string.

Kirk kept demanding his "day in court" while refusing to show up when summoned. He surrounded himself with sheriff's deputies and state troopers to outnumber federal marshals seeking to carry out the court order, relenting to allow aides to be served with subpoenas. And the United States attorney in the district said threats had been made to fire on federal officers if they tried to oust Kirk from the educational office he had seized.

The Florida government has either run the biggest bluff in the history of school desegregation or has engaged in the most wanton defiance of the federal government by any Southern chief executive.

In either case, he has all but begged the federal court to cite him for contempt and even put him in jail. And both the federal court and the Justice Department have dallied too long.

This display by a Republican governor must be especially embarrassing to a Republican president, whose vacation White House is also located in this particular governor's state. The question still remains: Will the executive branch move against Kirk as President Eisenhower once moved against Faubus of Arkansas and President Kennedy moved against Wallace of Alabama and Barnett of Mississippi?

As The Wall Street Journal sums the matter up:

"Some of us try to take the phrase law-and-order as a high ideal, meaning decorous debate about any grievances and peaceful acceptance of decisions reached through the processes society provides to resolve the grievances.

"That ideal is a pressing necessity today, whatever name you give it. It is an ideal hard enough to uphold under the best of circumstances, let alone when it is encumbered by the kind of albatross Governor Kirk is fashioning for its neck."

THE BILLINGS GAZETTE

Billings, Mont., April 13, 1970

Gov. Claude Kirk of Florida, a member of that branch of the Republican Party most concerned with Law'n Order, has decided not to obey a federal court order to integrate the Manatee County, Fla., school system.

Kirk said he would defy, with force if necessary, the U.S. Marshals sent to enforce the court order. He has threatened to jail the marshals if any of his aides are arrested.

A U.S. attorney says a Kirk intermediary told him that marshals attempting to enter school board headquarters would be shot at.

Kirk denies that, but that's about all. He has called out county sheriff's deputies and state troopers to protect him from the feds, presumably in defense of state rights.

Is Kirk planning to "stand in the school house door," as did another southern politician a few years ago? Is he planning to take out after the "anarchists" and run for president as a third or fourth-party candidate?

We don't know. But we trust Spiro Agnew will denounce Kirk as he does all those who defy government authority.

And we wouldn't be surprised at an announcement of secession very soon by the Florida Legislature.

THE CINCINNATI ENQUIRER

Cincinnati, Ohio, April 11, 1970

FLORIDA'S GOV. Claude Kirk has reminded the nation that the challenge to law and order is not the exclusive preserve of the New Left and its lieutenants.

To roughly the same extent as the flag desecrators, the draft-card burners and all of the others who have defied the law to demonstrate their discontents, Governor Kirk has injected himself as a barrier to the implementation of a Federal court order.

If anything, Governor Kirk's defiance is more reprehensible than that of the militant radicals. He, after all, is a public official sworn to uphold—rather than to challenge and defy—the law.

The issue that afforded Florida's chief executive his platform for defiance was the desegregation of the schools in Florida's Manatee County. A U. S. District Court, after examining the facts, found in Manatee County a willful policy of resisting the establishment and maintenance of an integrated school system. The court ordered, accordingly, that school officials proceed with the busing of students as a means of achieving a reasonable racial balance in each of the county's 27 schools.

Governor Kirk's response was to seize the school system to forestall execution of the court order.

There may be a case to be made against enforced busing to achieve racial balance or against instituting such a plan so close to the end of a school year.

But Governor Kirk manifestly chose the wrong way to make his case. He has made it all the easier for others to defy laws about whose justice they have doubts.

There can be no defending his decision.

The Courier-Journal

Louisville, Ky., April 14, 1970

FLORIDA'S flamboyant Governor Kirk has been one of the nation's louder advocates of law and order. So it came with particularly ill grace that in the Manatee County school case he chose to defy the law and the courts rather than seek the peaceful and orderly redress of his grievance.

As all but the blind could foresee, the governor's capitulation Sunday night was complete. The best he could get from the government was a promise to review the court-imposed busing plan, but not to delay it.

It would be a mistake, though, to jump to the easy conclusion that the whole messy affair was some kind of momentary aberration that can now be forgotten. Governor Kirk, for all his reckless attempt to gain re-election votes by challenging the federal government, has a legitimate grievance.

As he has said all along, he wants to bypass all lower courts and take directly to the Supreme Court an issue that cries for judicial interpretation; forced busing of school children. And the issue, as he saw it, was pressing. Manatee County had been ordered by federal court, effective eight days ago, to bus 2,700 of its 17,000 pupils to achieve in each of its schools a racial balance roughly equal to the balance in the school population as a whole. It's 22 per cent Negro.

But Governor Kirk is not alone, nor is the Manatee County ruling as stringent as some others. Los Angeles has been ordered by a state court to adopt a busing plan whose cost is estimated at $40 million for the first year alone. Charlotte, N.C., is under federal court order to add another 13,000 pupils to the 24,000 already being bused.

These cases, and others, add urgency to the appeals—including one from the Justice Department itself — that, in light of President Nixon's March 24 statement on school desegregation, the Supreme Court quickly give some national guidance.

The gravity of the issue should not be underestimated. Over the weekend the U.S. Commission on Civil Rights came down hard on the President's policy statement. And whether one agrees or not with the commission's observation that the Administration seems to be backing away sharply from enforcement of school desegregation, it is indisputable that the scattered federal courts have lacked any kind of central judicial direction.

As the President observed in his message, the Supreme Court itself has recently cited a number of "basic practical problems" that it has not resolved. Among them, in Chief Justice Burger's words: ". . . to what extent transportation may or must be provided to achieve the ends sought by prior holdings of this court."

Mr. Nixon took the view that "it is preferable, when we have to make the choice, to use limited financial resources for the improvement of education . . . and for the upgrading of the disadvantaged areas in the community, rather than buying buses, tires and gasoline to transport young children miles away from their neighborhood schools." Consequently, he instructed officials of his administration that, in enforcement of desegregation, "Transportation of pupils beyond normal geographic school zones for the purpose of achieving racial balance will not be required."

Such an administrative ruling is not binding on the courts, of course; but it echoes the congressional intent, expressed in the 1964 Civil Rights Act, that federal officials and courts not be empowered to order racial balance through busing. So the gulf is widening, and only the Supreme Court can resolve the disparities between action and intent.

Manatee County is no Los Angeles or Charlotte, either in size or in the complexity of its urban problems. So it could very well be that a Supreme Court ruling on busing—or on the broader issue of whether, and to what extent, "desegregation" means "integration"—would bring relief to one locality and not another. But that's not what's at stake.

Governor Kirk has dramatized the issue. But in doing so he resorted to illegality himself, and thereby encouraged public disrespect for the very system which is all that stands between anarchy and "law and order." By such a reckless course in such uneasy times he did a severe disservice to both his state and the nation.

HIGH COURT RULES UNANIMOUSLY: BUSING IS CONSTITUTIONAL

The Supreme Court, in a unanimous decision April 20, told the Charlotte-Mecklenburg County, N.C. joint school system and all other school districts of the South that busing children as a means of dismantling dual school systems was constitutional. In addition, the court struck down as unconstitutional an anti-busing statute enacted by the North Carolina legislature, ordered Mobile, Ala. school officials to use "all available techniques" to correct segregation in their schools and overturned a Georgia Supreme Court ruling that had said desegregation actions in Athens were unconstitutional. All the decisions were unanimous.

Although they were landmark decrees, the rulings were by no means definitive. Chief Justice Warren Burger, writing the opinions for the entire court, declared emphatically: "Desegregation plans cannot be limited to the walk-in school." And the justices held that busing was at times an indispensable method of eliminating "the last vestiges" of racial segregation. They stopped short, however, of ordering the elimination of all-black schools or requiring racial balance in the schools. The court also made it clear that the rulings in the four cases did not apply to de facto segregation caused by neighborhood housing patterns and found most often in the North.

In upholding the constitutionality of busing, the court brushed aside the arguments of the Nixon Administration and the Justice Department which had backed Southern school officials seeking relief from the court. Justice Department lawyers had contended that Southern school districts should be permitted to assign students to schools in their own neighborhoods even if it slowed down the pace of desegregation.

—Systems that continue to have a school or schools all-black or all-white are not necessarily violating the law, but school authorities must make every effort to desegregate across the board.

—School authorities can consider the health of children and any "significant" impingement on the educational process in determining the degree of busing to achieve a unitary system, but district courts have broad, strong review powers on these decisions.

The thrust of the Supreme Court's decision held true not only in the Charlotte-Mecklenburg case but in important cases from Clarke County, Ga. (Athens) and Mobile, Ala. The Court overruled the Georgia Supreme Court's prohibition of a busing plan that achieved a better racial balance in the schools of Clarke County. It reversed the 5th Circuit Court in the Mobile case, where a limited desegregation plan had been approved.

All citizens who have based their opposition to Judge McMillan's orders on the grounds that they couldn't "take the word of one man," now have the highest authority in the land saying the same thing. This unanimous Court includes President Nixon's "strict constructionist" appointees, led by a new Chief Justice who had called on the Court to lay down fresh guidelines.

There can be no excuse now in Charlotte-Mecklenburg for failing to see clearly the "law and order" path where the public schools are concerned.

That path leads to completion of the current school year with adequate transportation and financing. Then it leads to a summer that provides ample time to arrange better transportation, better scheduling and better financing to make our newly acquired unitary system work. There also needs to be better arrangements for pupil assignments so that schools on the Westside are not so badly out of balance or overcrowded.

Judge McMillan must feel that a great burden has been lifted from his shoulders. That burden is now borne principally by the Supreme Court whose earlier decisions necessitated Judge McMillan's ruling in the Charlotte-Mecklenburg case.

The local record shows that McMillan several times made reasonable overtures to the Board of Education and the community. He asked repeatedly for voluntary compliance plans less severe than the board majority finally "acquiesced" to.

All along, the judge showed a willingness — to the degree permitted by law — to make the painful transition as easy as possible for us. But in emotional and often angry tones, people in positions of leadership made him the villain of the piece. This included shameful expediency by elected officials at local, state and national levels.

There should now be a recognition of new responsibility by all public leaders. It should begin here with elected bodies and extend to the Chamber of Commerce, the Community Relations Committee, the Parent-Teacher Association and all civic organizations.

That responsibility is to create a new climate of compliance with the law that will overcome the negativism of the past two years. It is to organize the energies and talents of citizens to make the school desegregation plan work. It is to shape the public schools so that the educational benefits will extend to all our children.

The Charlotte Observer

Charlotte, N.C., April 21, 1971

The unanimous Supreme Court decision upholding Federal Judge James B. McMillan's orders in the Charlotte-Mecklenburg school case should end the long months of doubt, dissension and indecision surrounding the operation of our school system.

Chief Justice Warren Burger's written opinion for the Court speaks with legal finality on 1) the busing issue, 2) the pairing and grouping of schools to achieve a unitary school system and 3) assignments of pupils by race when needed to end unlawful segregation.

Unanimously, the nine members of the Supreme Court said Judge McMillan was acting within his District Court's powers in ordering drastic redistricting and pairing, even if that required extensive busing.

The Court added that it was well within the capacity of local school authorities to carry out the orders of Judge McMillan's court.

That had already been demonstrated this school year in the reluctant but relatively successful use of makeshift transportation to get thousands of students to their new schools.

Busing has entailed many difficulties for the system and individuals. Pupils and teachers have found the adjustments hard in many instances, and there have been racial flare-ups at the junior and senior high school levels.

But, by and large, the education job has been carried out as well as could be expected while the community hedged its support against the possibility of reversal by the Supreme Court.

Past community divisions on the question become less significant now. The Supreme Court has ruled on what must be done to operate our public school system lawfully. The basic framework is that already approved by the District Court, which retains the power to review and revise operation of the plan.

The Supreme Court has provided up-to-date guidelines that are largely those already adhered to by Judge McMillan:

—Transfers are essential (especially majority-to-minority transfers) in making one constitutional school system of what had been two segregated systems.

—Transportation undoubtedly will be needed to effect the kinds of transfers needed.

—Fixed racial ratios are not required in each school to reflect the overall ratio in the system, but a certain amount of "racial balance" may be needed to end unlawful segregation. Guidelines used in the local case were ruled acceptable.

TWIN CITY SENTINEL

Winston-Salem, N.C., April 22, 1971

THE Supreme Court's ruling in the Charlotte-Mecklenburg case went a long way toward laying down ground rules for future pupil assignments in the South.

In effect, the decision affirmed the use of court-approved busing, school-pairing and racial "balancing" as means of desegregating the state's largest school system. It overturned a North Carolina law that prohibited the busing of students to achieve racial balance; and it enlarged the scope of the federal courts' remedial power to end school discrimination — thus vindicating, after the fact, Judge James B. McMillan's initial ruling in the Charlotte-Mecklenburg case.

This is what the decision affirmed as law, and it effectively ends whatever hope many parents had of seeing Judge McMillan left out on a judicial limb.

The decision will be a difficult one to live with, for it imposes on the Charlotte-Mecklenburg school system a responsibility that will tax the patience and ingenuity of everyone involved.

And for those who see in this decision a reason for gloating, they might ponder the thought that no judicial ruling under the sun can ever take the place of a community's collective will.

If this decision prompts a flight of middle-class Charlotteans to private academies or (as happened in Washington and Philadelphia) across the nearby state line, it could do irreparable damage to the school system. The federal judiciary is not a shepherd and the people of Charlotte are not sheep. They and they alone must decide the future of their schools; and in this collective decision rests the fate of thousands of urban black children, for whom the integrated classroom is nothing less than a training ground for life in a plural society.

We hope these parents — for it rests with the parents — make the right choice, just as we hope parents in the Winston-Salem and Forsyth system make the right choice when it is presented to them. For if those now living do not, in Justice Burger's words, "eliminate the discrimination inherent in dual school systems," then those who follow us will have the job to do—and against much greater odds than any we might face in the next decade.

WINSTON-SALEM JOURNAL

Winston-Salem, N.C., April 22, 1971

ALTHOUGH the Supreme Court did not answer the old question of what is a "'unitary" school system in its momentous decisions Tuesday, the court made the question largely academic.

The court said, in effect, that the district and circuit courts in the South will answer the question differently for each school district—but it also gave the lower courts far more definite guidelines about the tools they can use, and about the results to be sought, than these courts have had in the past.

Most people were surprised, if not actually astonished, that this more "conservative" court, led by a Republican Chief Justice appointed by President Nixon, did not retreat from the advanced positions taken by the Warren court; that this court in fact moved them forward, and did it unanimously.

Perhaps the biggest surprise was that the court upheld the desegregation plan put into effect in Charlotte and Mecklenburg County, which desegregated every school in the district in rough accordance with a "racial quota" system and used widespread busing of children to accomplish this.

In opinions written by Chief Justice Warren Burger on the Charlotte-Mecklenburg case and several others, the court held that:

—Transportation of children to schools outside their neighborhood was a constitutional means of breaking down the effects of dual school systems that had been set up by old segregation laws. But it also held that busing is objectionable if "the time or distance of travel is so great as to risk the health of children" (particularly younger ones) or "significantly impinge on the educational process."

—The existence of one-race or virtually one-race schools is not necessarily proof that segregation is being carried on through official action, but the *presumption* is in this direction; and school boards must prove to the contrary if such schools are to continue to exist.

—The use of "racial quotas" in an assignment plan is not necessary in every school in a system but can be "a starting point in shaping a remedy . . ."

—"Pairing" and "clustering" of schools for assignment purposes "is a permissible tool" for breaking down segregation."

—North Carolina's antibusing law, which forbids the use of buses to achieve racial balance, is unconstitutional because it attempts to prevent court-ordered desegregation plans.

It is now clear that school boards have far less room for maneuver than they had before these decisions came down. Many southern school boards (and that probably includes our own) will be required to make the choice of desegregating more schools or letting the court do it for them.

Perhaps the language that most clearly expresses the philosophy reflected in these decisions, particularly regarding busing, is this:

"All things being equal, with no history of discrimination, it might well be desirable to assign pupils to schools nearest their homes. But all things are not equal in a system that has been deliberately constructed and maintained to enforce racial segregation. The remedy for such segregation may be administratively bizarre in some situations and may impose burdens on some; but all awkwardness and inconvenience cannot be avoided in the interim period when remedial adjustments are being made to eliminate the dual school systems."

So now it is up to the lower federal courts "to grapple with the flinty, intractable realities of day-to-day implementation of (the Supreme Court's) constitutional commands," and the path before them — though allowing for local variations—is far more clearly blazed than before.

Undoubtedly these decisions will be unpopular in many places in the South, and in some areas they may speed up the movement of pupils into private schools. It also appears that these decisions do little or nothing to impose a requirement on the North and West to eliminate de facto segregation in the schools.

But they do remove many uncertainties for parents, pupils and school officials in the South, and they hasten the day when this 17-year-old struggle will be behind us.

And the fact that this "conservative" Burger court, like the Warren court before it, spoke with a single voice makes it compellingly clear that the last vestiges of the old dual school system will soon be eliminated.

St. Petersburg Times

St. Petersburg, Fla., April 21, 1971

There will be no return to segregated schools.

That's what the United ·States Supreme Court said again yesterday. It added, with considerable force, that school boards and lower court judges might as well begin work immediately to desegregate schools.

How the court spoke, and the climate into which it delivered its opinion, were almost as significant as its reaffirmation of the original school decision on May 17, 1954.

THE DECISION was unanimous, a remarkable event itself. Since President Nixon's campaign criticizing the court, since the retirement of former Chief Justice Earl Warren, and the appointment of Justices Burger and Blackmun, the court has been torn with bitter divisions.

The justices standing together as one demonstrated the great importance all these men of the law place upon purging the schools of racial discrimination.

Then they underscored it by announcing these related decisions only, and no others.

Since the last presidential election, a feeling has been encouraged in this country that perhaps integrated schools could be avoided after all. The court stepped down firmly upon that falsehood. It specifically rejected the argument that busing was fine for maintaining segregation but somehow illegal and immoral for obtaining integration.

It unanimously overruled the U.S. Circuit Court in Richmond, Solicitor General Erwin N. Griswold, the Justice Department and President Nixon's wishes.

Behind the decision was the still larger principle that ours is a nation ruled by laws rather than by men.

Changing presidents, with the consent of the Senate, can alter the balance of the court. They can change its direction and its style. But even a president cannot change the independent court's respect for the integrity of the law — a respect that far overrides personality, judicial patterns and legal philosophy.

✔ ✔ ✔

Yesterday's decision flashed a green light for the Pinellas School Board to complete its desegregation in a way that will be best for all the county's children.

The present court-ordered desegregation plan has created unstable schools and increasing flight. It must be changed.

At the urging of some parents, the School Board already has begun plans for "clustering." In this respect, Pinellas is ahead of most other areas.

THE MEANING of yesterday's decision was that the School Board should complete its work as quickly as practical, adopting the sectional clustering plan now under discussion to desegregate all schools in the county next September.

It should be done because it would be best for the children, best for all communities and because the Supreme Court of the United States correctly has ruled that it must be done.

The Virginian-Pilot

Norfolk, Va., April 22, 1971

Now all of us know Chief Justice Warren E. Burger much better. He is Chief Justice of the United States Supreme Court, not of the Nixon Administration. Like all proper judges, he is committed to precedent. His thinking is orderly, and with pen he is capable of vigor and clarity. He is aware of the limitations of man and his institutions, yet demanding of both. And he is patient.

This is evident from Mr. Burger's decision, shared by the full Court, in the important *Charlotte-Mecklenburg Board of Education* and three related Southern school cases. In contrast to President Nixon's professed devotion to neighborhood schools and other polite devices of segregation, he held that busing, school groupings and pairings, gerrymandered districts, and mathematical race-ratio goals are Constitutional remedies to dual systems, to be prescribed by Federal District Court judges in proportion to the default by local school authorities.

The Supreme Court in *Brown*, delivered 17 years ago next month, charged District judges with dismantling segregation "at all deliberate speed." Acceleration long since has been urged; Mr. Burger called for more. Yet throughout his decision he reached back to *Brown*. "At no time has this Court deviated in the slightest degree from that holding or its Constitutional underpinnings," he wrote at an early point· in Tuesday's ruling.

Significantly, he employed *Green v. New Kent County School Board* (1968), one of several Virginia suits to reach the Court during Chief Justice Earl Warren's time, as a launching pad for his extended judgment. There Justice Brennan ruled that while the "freedom-of-choice" concept, then much favored by Southern school boards, could be a valid remedial measure in some circumstances, its failure to promote integration in New Kent required that "the burden of a school board today is to come forward with a plan that promises realistically to work . . . now . . . until it is clear that the state-imposed segregation has been completely removed."

Green was much criticized for saying what was wrong without indicating what would be right. ". . . The Court missed an important opportunity to provide guidance by rearticulating the reasons for and the very meaning of 'desegregation,'" complained the *Harvard Law Review*. ". . . In more difficult cases, where not all the factors point the same way, the Court will have to refine its analysis of the concepts 'dual system,' 'unitary system,' 'segregated,' 'integrated,' and 'racially unidentifiable.'" Attorneys for the Norfolk School Board meanwhile urged the Court to clear up the issue of *de facto* and *de jure* segregation—of spontaneous segregation, which supposedly explains the Northern and Western phenomenon, as distinguished from Southern segregation rooted in now-discredited laws.

But Mr. Burger would not enter the semantics thicket. Mere words "are poor instruments to convey the basic sense of fairness inherent in equity," he wrote. Nevertheless, he fixed "unitary" as the objective of school systems, and emphasized that at some point — mark that phrase, *at some point* — they must reach it. Time until then will be interim: an action period, overseen by insistent District Court judges amply stocked with law.

And what will identify that point? How will judges and school boards recognize the Promised Land? Mr. Burger did not undertake to provide an answer, just as he pleaded, on the certainly that "one vehicle can carry only a limited amount of baggage," that the occasion was inappropriate for delving into "myriad factors of human existence which can cause discrimination in a multitude of ways on racial, religious, or ethnic grounds" — a rather impressive euphemism for Yankee segregation.

Similarly, Mr. Burger declined to say whether racially identifiable schools are permissible, although he noted that unbalanced units and unitary systems need not be in conflict; or at what point "transportation of students" (he shied away from the term "busing," doubtless for its emotionalism) might prove to be a health and educational menace to children, while recognizing the potential risk; or how residential patterns and new-school construction are to be reconciled, a segregation problem of which he indicated awareness. "No fixed or even substantially fixed guidelines can be established as to how far a [lower] court may go, but it must be recognized that there are limits," he wrote. "The object is to dismantle the dual school system."

That is at once an acknowledgement of incapacity at the top of the judicial system and an order for performance below. We do not find it contradictory. For 17 years the Supreme Court has been relying on the District and Appeals Courts to carry out its broad dictums, and Mr. Burger clearly is satisfied with the precedent; *Charlotte-Mecklenburg*, after all, is an endorsement of a District Court judge's far-reaching order to a school board. The suggestion here — indeed, the inevitability — of a continuation of litigation in the various districts, including Norfolk, is patent. But Chief Justice Burger, as we commented at the outset, is patient.

And, as we also said, he is demanding. The mystical "some point" at which full compliance with *Brown* must be achieved is for the entire South to reach; until a school board arrives there, it must occupy itself with race as well as all the other complexities of education.

The hope of that, we may only pray, will prove to be greater than the despair.

Leadership

Governor Linwood Holton responded to the Supreme Court's Charlotte decision with the reassurance that "Virginia will continue to maintain and support high quality schools as the Constitution requires.

"As everyone knows," continued the Governor, "I'm extremely pleased at the way young Virginians have handled this adjustment and I expect they will continue to furnish leadership."

Who can say what agony and turmoil would have been averted if Senator Harry F. Byrd Sr. had reacted to the *Brown* decision as moderately, and as wisely?

The Cincinnati Post
TIMES ✦ STAR

Cincinnati, Ohio, April 21, 1971

Any notion that the Supreme Court might modify its rulings on school desegregation was snuffed out this week in a series of unanimous decisions which should erase any vestige of "Separate-but-equal" education in the South.

It was the most definitive action since the old Warren court struck down dual school systems as unconstitutional in 1954 and ordered a racially "unitary" school system instead.

Now, in two North Carolina cases, a Georgia case and an Alabama case, the high court has ruled that:

• Busing for reasonable distances is a legitimate tool of desegregation and cannot be prohibited by state law.

• Simply assigning children to the nearest neighborhood school may not be enough to comply with desegregation standards.

• Local school boards and federal judges should be given a great deal of latitude in using busing, gerrymandering of attendance areas or any other means to eliminate classroom segregation.

Chief Justice Warren E. Burger, who wrote the opinions in all four of the cases, said the rulings apply only to situations (in the South) where school segregation was sanctioned by law.

This means the court has yet to speak on school segregation in the North—much of it caused by all-black or all-white housing patterns.

The new decisions are bound to be a bitter disappointment to busing foes in all parts of the country, and particularly in southern cities like Charlotte, Richmond, Mobile and Memphis.

They also are a rebuff to the Nixon adminstration, which argued with merit last fall it is "constitutionally acceptable" to assign students to the nearest school regardless of the color mix.

"Desegregation plans cannot be limited to the walk-in school," Justice Burger commented.

IN PRACTICAL TERMS, this means the court-imposed desegregation plan in Charlotte has been upheld even though it involves the daily cross-busing of thousands of students.

And it means that Mobile will have to draw a new desegregation plan that breaks up a black enclave not touched by the current plan.

Perhaps the most promising aspect of the new court rulings is that they lay down needed guidelines for dealing with desegregation.

The court points out, for example, that "every school in every community" need not have the same racial balance. In fact, in some rare cases, it may be permissible to operate a one-race school.

In the final analysis, however, the court has decreed that desegregation—at least in the South—is more important than whether a child can walk from home to school.

This is not an easy or a popular principle to apply. It may have to be tempered in cases where prolonged busing could have an adverse effect on young children.

But the mandate of the court is clear. And the message is to desegregate—by whatever means are necessary.

Oakland Tribune

Oakland, Calif., April 25, 1971

Nearly 17 years have elapsed since the landmark U.S. Supreme Court decision outlawing state-imposed segregation in public schools, but the explicit mandate of the Court has yet to be fully obeyed.

Despite violations of their constitutional rights as spelled out in the unanimous opinion, many black children in the South reportedly still do not have access to an education equal to that afforded white youngsters.

In the interim years, Warren Burger has replaced Earl Warren as chief justice, six of the eight concurring justices have been replaced and many additional decisons have come down to reaffirm in all particulars that original opinion.

The latest came last week on the issue of busing, and the chief justice spoke for the entire Court.

While attention was centered on the failure of some southern school districts to desegregate "with all deliberate speed" as ordered in 1954, an important part of the opinion carried a clear warning to n o r t h e r n schools which to date have been outside the purview of the court.

Calling for school boards to devise plans to use busing, zoning, pairings of schools or pupil transfers to end segregation, Burger used plain language that realistically dealt with the specific situation at hand.

In emphasizing that the issue was not de facto or accidental segregation resulting from social conditions or population patterns, he made clear his opinion principally concerned the constitutional question of discrimination as it continues to be practiced in the South.

He did not reject the premise of neighborhood schools, often validly defended by anti-busing forces in all parts of the country, but he simply warned that "desegregation plans cannot be limited to walk-in schools."

Thus the practical rationale of the Burger opinion strikes at the heart of the issue as brought before the high court: "All things being equal, with no history of discrimination, it might well be desirable to assign pupils to schools nearest their homes.

"But, he added all things are not equal in a system that has been deliberately constructed and maintained through enforced racial segregation."

Busing, Burger said, is a valid and legal tool to insure the quality of education is the same for all pupils in a system, particularly if that system has previously been guilty of evasive segregation schemes or deliberate defiance of the U.S. Supreme Court.

The Court was not asked, and thus did not answer, any question about eliminating accidental segregation that might occur from other than discriminatory action.

But school boards everywhere were alerted to avoid magnifying accidental segregation patterns by their manner of locating new schools or closing old ones.

Within the next few weeks, the Supreme Court will decide if it will hear several cases where segregation in the North is charged, and one in particular would seem subject to the Burger warning last week.

In an Illinois case, U.S. Federal District Court Judge Julius Hoffman ruled school officials had inherited a segregated and discriminatory system which they "subsequently fortified by affirmative policies and practices."

There is sound reason to expect the Court to rule against examples anywhere in the nation of segregation borne of discrimination, regardless of whether it was begun purposely or accidentally.

Thus in California as in much of the rest of the nation, the challenge to insure equal educational opportunities for all is a local one that can best be met by local school boards, without any help from the courts.

It is perhaps of some benefit to know that busing is in fact constitutional, but far more important is the need for all school officials to maintain their dedication to the principles of equal education opportunities and to use all resources available to achieve that end.

DESERET NEWS

Salt Lake City, Utah, April 22, 1971

There can be no reasonable quarrel with the principle that black children should get an education just as good as that of white children.

Indeed, social conditions being what they are, it may be that massive busing is not only a constitutional way of achieving this objective — as the U.S. Supreme Court ruled this week — but perhaps in some situations the most feasible way.

But busing is one thing as a stop-gap measure. As a long term proposition, it just won't do.

The Supreme Court put its collective finger on the crux of the matter when, in this week's ruling, it observed:

"All things being equal, with no history of discrimination, it might well be desirable to assign pupils to schools nearest their homes. But all things are not equal in a system that has been deliberately constructed and maintained to enforce racial segregation."

So be it. Supreme Court rulings are the law of the land, and — while this week's ruling on busing no doubt will add impetus to the growing popularity of private schools — Americans are law-abiding people.

Even so, busing has some serious drawbacks that no court ruling can banish. To begin with, busing forces children to spend many hours aboard buses — hours that could be better spent in extra-curricular activities, in the classroom, or studying at home.

When children must leave school when the bus leaves, it's hard for them to get involved in athletics, plays, debating or any number of other extra-curricular activities that involve staying after normal school hours.

When a bused child becomes sick at school, his parents may face great difficulty in getting him home. But that's the least of the parents' problems.

Parents seem bound to be more knowledgeable and interested regarding a school in their own neighborhood than one located miles away. With busing, parents wishing to talk personally with teachers about their children's education can be seriously inconvenienced. In fact, how many mothers will venture alone at night into an inner-city ghetto to attend a PTA meeting?

Moreover, busing means a school district must lay out more money for transportation — money that could be better spent on teachers, books, and classrooms. And increased school costs can mean increased taxes.

The challenge now is to make sure the schools in the ghettoes become as good as those in the suburbs so that in years to come no child need board a bus to get a good education.

Chicago Daily Defender

Chicago, Ill., April 26, 1971

In what is second only to the 1954 benchmark ruling in the Brown versus the Board of Education case, the U.S. Supreme Court order on busing has knocked the remaining props from under the swaying structure of school segregation. The effect of the new order is to insure perpetuity of racial balance not only as a conformity with a constitutional requirement, but as a safeguard against clandestine erosion of the democratic process in the intellectual conditioning of American youth for enlightened and responsible citizenship.

The Court wisely observed: "All things being equal, with no history of discrimination, it might well be desirable to assign pupils to schools nearest their homes. But all things are not equal in a system that has been deliberately constructed and maintained to enforce racial segregation."

The constitutional and social implications of the court's judgment are immense. This closes all avenues of intentional misconstructions of the meaning and inference of the law and of the use of the relevant mechanism to insure proper exercise of the principle of equal educational opportunity.

It further burrows into the consciousness of the people, both North and South, the kernel of social justice as a moral imperative or our democratic avowals.

The fact that Chief Justice Warren Burger made the major statement in a decision in which there was unfragmented concurrence, testifies to the importance that the Court itself attaches to the case from Charlotte, N. C., where the state had challenged a District Court order for increased busing in the elementary schools.

The suggestion that the Burger Court would veer away from the Warren Court, particularly on civil rights questions, proved thus far to be both premature and incorrect. This Court not only reaffirms the judicial concept of its predecessor, at least in school matters, it serves notice that the philosophical norm which guided the action of the previous tribunal on school racial balance, will not be swept aside for the constructionist legalism on which President Nixon had placed repeated emphasis.

This historic action of the comparatively new Court brings the black man deeper into the stream of American society.

THE ANN ARBOR NEWS

Ann Arbor, Mich., April 30, 1971

IT IS coming up on 20 years since the segregated school concept was dealt its first telling blow in the Supreme Court's historic 1954 ruling.

The integration of the nation's public schools did not take place at a pace fast enough to please many Americans, including the Supreme Court. Finally, the court ordered integration — by any means—NOW.

The court has killed the last hopes of the segregationists and foot-draggers by ruling that mass busing of children is a legitimate means to desegregate public schools.

School integration is the law of the land. We have concluded in this country that mixing white children and black children at more than a token level is beneficial in that it puts all children on an equal footing educationally.

Is busing a contrived means of bringing into being the desired product? Of course it is. Chief Justice Burger alluded to remedies which were administratively awkward, inconvenient and even bizarre. These remedies are called for because, all things being equal, the system was not equal to start with.

* * *

BUSING has many and eloquent foes, some of whom have participated in Ann Arbor's busing disputes. But if busing is a contrived device, so is the segregated school. And so is the housing development which zones out black people.

Equal educational opportunity isn't going to come about until racial integration is established in the schools. Beyond that, it is a matter of Americans accepting the idea that integration is learning, living and building together —whether in the neighborhoods or in social circles or on the job.

The court did not require playing the numbers game, i. e., busing children from one school to another to achieve perfect proportional representation. But merely going through the motions of upsetting racial imbalance won't be accepted, either.

Record American

Boston, Mass., April 23, 1971

It is significant, particularly from a local point of view, that the U. S. Supreme Court excluded consideration of "de facto" segregation from its milestone decision legitimizing the use of busing to eliminate racial imbalance from the natian's public schools.

Left unanswered for the time being, therefore, is the direct question of how the ruling will be applied to Boston and other northern cities, where neighborhood residential patterns are often the major influence determining which schools are black and which are white.

How long it will remain unanswered, however, is uncertain.

The court practically ruled out the neighborhood school as a viable educational concept in multi-racial communities, however traditional it may have been in Boston and other Massachusetts cities and towns. Most would not have been affected, in any case, by the busing ruling, because their populations are racially homogeneous. Besides, they have been busing children for years.

But for Boston and a few others with large non-white groups, it may eventually present school administrators with baffling logistics problems — and the taxpayers with another expensive program.

It is also worth noting that while federal district courts were directed to do more to break down racial imbalance, the supreme court specified that desegregation does not require that every school in every community at all times must reflect the racial composition of the system.

This, of course, could leave broad discretion to a local federal district court.

Boston has no "history" of state-imposed segregation such as the court held up to suspicion, even though it has 63 imbalanced schools. In this regard, the court noted, the existence of "some small numbers of schools of one race, or virtually of one race, is not alone proof" of racial discrimination.

And, fortunately, the city has embarked on a costly program of school construction, which should serve to improve its image while asking for state aid in adjusting district lines and planning the interchange of pupils from contiguous school districts to achieve greater racial balance.

By its action, the Supreme Court has now rendered null and void, it appears, any plan by anti-bus forces in the city to repeal Massachusetts' imbalance law.

Defiance of the court is an idle gesture. Boston schools can still control their destiny by perfecting to the satisfaction of the state Dept. of Education plans to balance certain school districts for 1971-72. Otherwise they run the risk of mass busing designed by a federal court as it was in Charlotte, N. C.

The San Diego Union

San Diego, Calif., April 22, 1971

The decision of the United States Supreme Court this week which empowered federal district courts to apply stricter guidelines in school integration brings with it many problems. At the same time it gives renewed hope for attainment of genuine racial equality.

The unanimous decision written by Chief Justice Warren Burger gives lower courts the power to establish racial ratios in schools after they determine that a historic pattern of legal segregation has existed.

It further permits the lower jurists to order busing of school children to attain ethnic balance in proportions that the court establishes for the schools involved.

The Supreme Court also suggests that many schools could more accurately reflect desirable ethnic compositions by realignment of attendance districts.

To the extent that the historic Supreme Court decisions move America toward the goal of equal educational opportunities for all, they must be applauded. At the same time it must be recognized that the road ahead is likely to be rocky.

The decision, for example, deals only with "de jure" segregation — that imposed by state or local laws. It does not address "de facto" segregation — that which results from economic circumstances, housing patterns or the legitimate choices of the people involved.

As a result many Southerners already are convinced that the Supreme Court is seeking only to punish them since it is mainly in the South that "legal" segregation is found. The decision thus will result in divisivness, more pressure for private schools and more effort to find loopholes. A further source of difficulty will be that the court was not specific in its ruling on ethnic ratios. The decision held that ratios are not a constitutional mandate, but rather a discretion of the federal district judge. Under these terms, latitude could be immense.

Finally, not even the busing portion of the Supreme Court decision is totally unequivocal. Justice Burger said legitimate complaints against transporting of students could be raised if the travel impaired health or the education of children because of time or distance. This, also, promises to be grist for continuing litigation.

Taken in its totality, the real value of the Supreme Court school integration decision last Tuesday is that it exhibits that the United States of America is a self moderating society.

There were many who predicted that the efforts to achieve genuine racial equality would be set back by the conservative Burger court. Now we have seen that responsibility generates sobriety; that although haltingly, perhaps inefficiently, the United States will nevertheless continue to move toward a society which offers all persons equal opportunity— and that all of this can be accomplished through the existing structures of government.

The Greenville News

Greenville, S.C., April 21, 1971

A unanimous U. S. Supreme Court formally recognized and at least for the time being tacitly accepted a dual system of school racial law in these United States — one rule requiring rigid integration policies in the South, the other permitting widespread racial segregation elsewhere in the nation.

The Supreme Court spelled it out in unmistakable words by saying specifically that integration rulings for states which formally required racial segregation by law do not apply to other states.

In addition the court armed federal district judges in the South with broad discretionary powers to enforce integration standards upon Southern school districts, if they do not implement acceptable plans of their own.

Furthermore the court undercut the neighborhood school concept for Southern schools and said widespread busing of school pupils is permissible in the South in order to achieve and maintain racially integrated schools. This amounts to judicial reversal of President Nixon's anti-busing, neighborhood school policy, insofar as it affects Southern schools, but in effect allows it to stand for the rest of the country.

In some respects the latest series of decisions, written by Chief Justice Warren Burger, reverses or twists the rulings of former Chief Justice Earle Warren in the 1954 school desegregation cases. The old "color blind" theory of law has been replaced by a new theory commanding that color be recognized in such a way as to achieve school integration.

Specifically the Supreme Court laid down these broad guidelines in four separate cases:

—Substantial pupil busing can be required in order to root out the "evil" and the "last vestige" of segregation in formerly legally segregated school districts. A modified, flexible ratio of white and black student bodies may be employed.

—All Southern school plans must be "effective" in bringing about desegregation. If the neighborhood system does not achieve integration in the South, it is invalid. Furthermore, Southern districts cannot return to segregation by building new schools in white suburbs far removed from Negro population centers.

—Georgraphic attendance zones in the South may be changed in order to bring about integration.

—State anti-busing laws are invalid if they prevent integration.

Barring unexpected approval of pending legislation in Congress to require one nationwide set of school racial standards, the immediate effect of yesterday's decision will be to bring about and keep racially integrated schools in Dixie, and segregated schools in the North, where racial living patterns are increasingly segregated.

Yesterday's decisions will have little or no effect upon Southern school districts like Greenville and Charlotte. The Charlotte plan was approved specifically by the Supreme Court and it is almost identical to the Greenville plan if not more drastic.

In one respect the decisions are useful. They do tell Southern school officials and Southern school patrons exactly where they stand under the dual law of the land. They may result in less litigation and fewer long-drawn-out appeals from decisions of district judges handling Southern school cases. To that extent the decisions do give a little more stability to the Southern school situation.

On the national level a renewal of the controversy concerning segregated Northern schools is certain to occur, in Congress and elsewhere. Over the long haul, a dual system of racial law cannot stand in a nation united by one Constitution which applies to all sections as well as all people. Sooner or later whatever standards required for Southern schools must be applied to the rest of the nation.

The Birmingham News

Birmingham, Ala., April 21, 1971

The U.S. Supreme Court's package of decisions yesterday on the series of school desegregation cases which were before it—including one from Mobile—will be a disappointment to those who had hoped that the court would act effectively to rein in some of the more far-ranging interpretations of the court's requirement that school districts eliminate all vestiges of state-imposed segregation.

No one expected the court to reverse that requirement—nor should the court have been expected to do so. The principle of nondiscrimination in the operation of schools is by now generally accepted.

But while there is little dispute any longer of the correctness of the constitutional principle, there has persisted a great deal of disagreement over the practical implementation of the principle and a great deal of confusion over what, exactly, the court did require.

What was hoped for was a Supreme Court statement to the effect that the Constitution does not require the use of such measures as massive busing of students to achieve integration or establishment of ratios to determine acceptable racial balance in each school in a given district.

That the justices declined to say. They held that the courts may properly order busing to achieve desegregation, observing that "desegregation plans cannot be limited to the walk-in school"—in effect holding against the neighborhood school concept; and, while declaring that fixed racial ratios are not required in every school in a district, "very limited use" of mathematical ratios (as in Charlotte, N.C.) is permissible.

The court said, in effect, that the federal district courts' power to order local school districts to take action to eliminate segregation is virtually unlimited. This offers small comfort to those who believe that in some cases the courts have gone far beyond reasonable criteria in determining whether a district is in fact in compliance with the law or in ordering additional steps to satisfy the courts' view of compliance.

On the other hand, the jurists said that the presence of a few all-white or all-black schools within a single district does not in itself constitute discrimination, and they declined to rule on the question of school segregation resulting from housing patterns.

If the court ultimately rules that the latter kind of situation—with large concentrations of black and white students in separate schools as a result of housing patterns (de facto segregation)—is not unconstitutional, it could mean that the court would approve a "neighborhood school" attendance system in districts where it was convinced the system was not deliberately designed to *promote* segregation (de jure).

On the other hand, the Supreme Court conceivably could hold, as some lower courts have implied, that *no* segregation in the South can be considered "de facto" since separate schools were built in white and Negro neighborhoods to perpetuate segregation. This would have the effect of applying any "de facto" exemption only to school districts in other parts of the country—many of which are more segregated than any in the South.

Be that as it may, Southern school districts would do well to heed this paragraph in Tuesday's opinions by the nation's highest court: "If school authorities fail in their affirmative obligations (to eliminate racial discrimination) . . . judicial authority may be invoked."

In other words, there should be no cause for judicial intervention if the school authorities are making honest and conscientious efforts to do what the law requires of them. If they try to evade their obligations, then they must expect the courts to act—and the Supreme Court has now indicated that their power to act is considerable and far-reaching.

This newspaper continues in the belief that educational factors should be the predominant consideration in making decisions and operating programs in the public schools, rather than any arbitrary numbers game based on the pupils' race—always with the reservation that there must be no discrimination *based* on race.

Failure of all concerned—including school authorities, parents and children of both races, and, yes, federal judges—to meet this challenge with reason, restraint and responsibility can only do damage to the goal we all presumably seek: Quality education for every child.

If the public schools are destroyed (or collapse because of a withdrawal of public support, including willingness to pay for them through taxes), what will we have gained?

THE ATLANTA CONSTITUTION

Atlanta, Ga., April 21, 1971

There's likely to be a good deal of sound and fury about the Supreme Court's decision this week which held, in part, that the busing of school pupils is a proper means of ending school segregation.

This is such an emotional issue, however, that is is important to try to understand exactly what the court decision means.

It does not mean, for example, that "every school in every community must always reflect the ratio of composition of the school system as a whole," to quote the exact words of the decision. In fact, the decision states, there is no constitutional requirement to achieve a specific ratio of racial balance within any school system.

It is a carefully worded detailed decision involving four different cases, one affecting the Athens, Georgia, school system.

The basic decision upheld a desegregation plan for Charlotte, North Carolina, previously ordered by a federal judge. That plan involves the busing of students in Charlotte and surrounding Mecklenburg County to eliminate previously segregated schools. The decision also struck down a North Carolina anti-busing law passed by the state legislature in direct reaction to the Charlotte desegregation order.

In Athens, the decision had the effect of upholding a school desegregation plan which involved busing some students to eliminate segregation. And, it ordered a new desegregation plan for Mobile, Alabama, one which would produce greater desegregation and which would involve more crosstown busing of students.

The unanimous Supreme Court decision amounted really to four separate opinions. All four were written by Chief Justice Warren Burger.

Burger said that the objective of the present decision is identical with the aim of the 1954 Supreme Coure decision on school segregation: "To eliminate from the public schools all vestiges of state-imposed segregation."

He noted that both federal judges and local school officials have had great practical problems in seeking this objective. "Nothing in our national experience prior to 1955 prepared anyone for dealing with change of the magnitude and complexity encountered since then," said Burger.

At a number of points in the decision, he indicated his awareness that this area is too complex for hard-and-fast rules. "Conditions in different localities will vary so widely that no rigid rules can be laid down to govern all situations," he said.

We believe that Southern school officials and parents, white and black, have struggled courageously to deal with the difficult social change involved in ending dual racially segregated school systems. We are certain that the school officials in districts directly affected will comply with this court decision. We would hope, however, that this is discussed and debated—as it will be—in a reasonable manner. Some politicians will be unable to resist the obvious temptation for cheap emotional political demagoguery. But then we've survived that kind of shoddy rhetoric before.

The Miami Herald

Miami, Fla., April 22, 1971

SOUTHERN school officials who have been clamoring for guidelines on desegregation have them at last. In a 9-0 ruling the U.S. Supreme Court has held among other things that "the importance of bus transportation as a normal and accepted tool of educational policy is readily discernible in this and the companion case."

The case is the U.S. District Court order in Charlotte, N.C., affecting the Charlotte-Mecklenburg County school system. The judge had directed extensive busing and got, in the main, an uproar. An appellate court subsequently overruled him. And now he is sustained by the highest court in the land which, a spokesman for President Nixon tersely reminds the nation, must be obeyed.

In strictly legal terms which define local responsibilities, the guidelines roughly are these:

1—Schools do not need to reflect the racial composition of systems as a whole but a judge may specify mathematical ratios of whites and blacks, as Judge James McMillan did in Charlotte.

2—"Some small numbers" of schools of one race or the other may exist but where there is "a history of segregation" the schools must explain why this is not discriminatory.

3—School officials are expected to foster integration by measures such as gerrymandering boundaries to include both races, "pairing" schools (as has been done in Dade County) and fixing school zones combining noncontiguous areas in racially diverse neighborhoods.

4—The anti-busing language of the Civil Rights Act of 1964, a war cry in the 1970 elections, is out. The courts must enforce the 14th Amendment and its guarantee of equal protection of the laws.

So, there it is, after 17 years, natural anxieties, political demagoguery, tumult in the educational process and restatement if not achievement of what many regard as the American dream.

IN THESE years there has been painless desegregation as well as confrontation, violence and defiance of court orders.

Typical mid-Southern Black Belt cities such as Greenville, S.C., have integrated peacefully within the last year. Over 90 per cent of Florida's pupils are now in integrated schools. There has been perhaps three to four times the amount of desegregation during the Nixon administration as under any previous one.

Oddly, though, the decision of the Warren Burger court, while moderate and reflecting some of President Nixon's views, is independent of and perhaps is a repudiation of administration policies.

The so-called "Southern strategy" in 1970 which is the subject of a forthcoming book under that name by Editors Reg Murphy and Hal Gulliver of The Atlanta Constitution, stands in disarray as a consequence.

The administration has mounted an overt effort to slow down school desegregation. Mr. Nixon made speeches last year denouncing busing. Integration-minded officials of HEW in the Southern region were fired rather brazenly.

Now that Strom Thurmond has had his half a pound of flesh (half being better than none) perhaps the scene can shift from the politics of race to the politics of national interests and needs in a spirit of American unity.

For the rest, the court has overcome its constitutional timidity by charting the course, "however imperfect," which the law not only allows but demands.

There need be little more confusion in the thousands of school boards within the region once governed by de jure segregation and covered by the decision of April 20 one month before the historic 17th birthday of Brown v. Topeka.

It has been long enough.

THE DENVER POST

Denver, Colo., April 21, 1971

THE FOUR UNANIMOUS decisions handed down Tuesday by the U.S. Supreme Court may have answered fairly definitely most questions Southern school districts and courts have had about what is required of those who seek to remedy the injustices caused by state-imposed school segregation.

But those Denverites — including us — who had been hoping the high court would provide guidelines applicable to Denver's school desegregation dispute will have to wait a while longer. The answer to Denver's problem may well be found somewhere in Tuesday's decisions, but only a court — quite possibly only the Supreme Court — can say where.

What the high court did Tuesday was to put together four opinions dealing with specific situations in North Carolina, Georgia and Alabama.

The rulings are interesting and instructive: a federal district judge in North Carolina was found within his rights in ordering more busing than the local school district wanted, in order to improve "racial balance" in the schools; another judge in Georgia was right to approve cross-busing of black and white kids; a "neighborhood school" plan in a Mobile, Ala., ghetto was rejected as too segregative.

But even more interesting — and more thought-provoking for Denverites — are long sections of "dicta" in these rulings: passages of philosophic advice, legal precepts and guidelines to help school officials and lower courts interpret the court's thinking on school integration.

In theory, none of this applies to Denver. Chief Justice Burger, who wrote all the opinions, says several times that they apply only to school districts engaged in eradicating the last vestiges of "dual" (segregated black and white) school systems. Denver, of course, has never had such a system.

And, although part of the Denver case involves "de jure" (by force of law) segregation, the federal district court proposal which concerns Denverites most is the one to cross-bus minority children out of and Anglo children into 14 now-segregated elementary schools. And that requirement is proposed as a remedy for "de facto" (caused by racial change in neighborhoods) segregation.

Still, what are we to make — as an indication of the court's thinking — of a phrase like this in the "dicta": "Absent a constitutional violation there would be no basis for judicially ordering assignment of students on a racial basis."

This phrase is taken from a partial text of the court's opinion. How much it means is impossible to determine without the full context. But this is what makes us say the "dicta" in this case are highly interesting.

THE FIRST HINT of what these opinions all add up to, as far as Denver is concerned, could come when the Supreme Court, or one of its justices, rules on the Denver plaintiffs' plea to overturn a stay of execution issued by the 10th Circuit Court of Appeals.

A more explicit reading should come, a week or so later, from the 10th Circuit Court itself. That will at least tell us what the appellate court thinks the Supreme Court means.

But Denver's case is so different from the Southern ones decided Tuesday that we may well have to wait for the high court itself to spell out its thinking on the Denver issues.

THE CINCINNATI ENQUIRER

Cincinnati, Ohio, April 22, 1971

IN WHAT IS ALREADY being hailed as its most significant pronouncement on school integration since 1954, the Supreme Court has moved to answer many of the questions that have arisen during the past 17 years. But its decision leaves a number of others unresolved.

In essence, the court reaffirmed the 1954 decision holding segregated public education to be illegal. And it reinforced that view by affirming the power of the federal courts to employ a wide range of tools to make certain that designed segregation is, in fact, abolished.

If, for example, it is shown that a school system has acted to frustrate the purpose of the 1954 ruling, the federal courts may require the busing of students to achieve integration.

Significantly, however, the court stipulated that not every school in every school district must be racially balanced. And it held further that imbalance in itself is not evidence of a calculated effort on the part of school officials to perpetuate segregation. Similarly, it held that there are valid grounds for objecting to busing — in circumstances where the well-being of the students involved may be jeopardized.

What the court did not do in its decisions this week was to speak out on the issue of de facto school segregation. Its decisions, in short, were related solely to Southern schools, which, prior to 1954, required dual schools for Negro and white children. They did not relate to Northern schools in which segregation has tended to continue not as the identifiable result of calculated official policy, but as the consequence of housing patterns over which school officials obviously have no control.

The Sixth Circuit Court of Appeals in Cincinnati has already taken the position that school officials have no positive responsibility under the law to end that kind of segregation.

Elsewhere, however, courts have held otherwise and required the imposition of busing or other plans aimed at achieving racially balanced schools throughout the system.

The court's far-ranging decision came less than a week after Sen. John C. Stennis (D-Miss.) took the Senate floor once more to articulate his favorite theme — that the federal government employs one yardstick to measure school integration in the North and an altogether different yardstick in the South.

Last year, the Mississippi lawmaker proposed an amendment (approved by the full Senate but eliminated later by a Senate-House conference committee) that would have enforced desegregation equally in the North and the South.

Yesterday, the Senate rejected a similar measure.

In the course of defending his position, Senator Stennis cited a series of statistics for the 1968 school year revealing continued segregation in most Northern schools — at a time when Southern schools were being beset by federal court orders to overcome similar imbalances.

In Cincinnati, for example, Senator Stennis contended that, as of the fall of 1968, 16.9% of the Negro youngsters in the district's public elementary and secondary schools were attending all-Negro schools. The same survey, he said, showed 33.9% of the district's Negroes were in schools that were between 50% and 100% Negro. Only 21.9% were in schools that were 49.9% or less Negro.

Negroes constitute 42.9% of Cincinnati's public school population, according to Senator Stennis' statistics, and thoroughgoing school integration would find all of the district's schools with roughly the same proportion of Negro students.

In other parts of the country, according to Senator Stennis, the imbalance was even more pronounced. In Chicago, for example, 47.4% of all Negro public school students were in all-Negro schools, and 96.8% were in predominantly Negro schools. In New York, 80.3% were in predominantly Negro schools, in Los Angeles 95.3%, in Detroit 91%, in Philadelphia 90.4%, in Washington 99.1%, in Louisville 86.5%.

Those who had hoped that the court, in re-examining the whole, broad issue of school integration, would move to remedy such imbalances where possible across the country were destined, for the moment at least, for disappointment.

In the weeks ahead, the lower federal courts — and the nation generally — will have an opportunity to determine how specifically this week's decisions will be applied to a wide variety of local problems and situations.

The nation's first impression must be that the court is standing its ground in its resolve to destroy the vestiges of statutory segregation that once gripped the South, but that it is not yet willing to move decisively against the kind of segregation that continues its growth in the North.

ARGUS-LEADER
Sioux Falls, S. D., April 22, 1971

To say that a certain act is constitutional is one thing. To say that it is wise or unwise is another.

The U.S. Supreme Court decreed this week that busing is a legitimate way of compelling desegregation of the public schools. It said, in consequence, that laws against such busing are contrary to the U.S. Constitution.

In its decision, the court in effect took a position that does not conform with the views expressed recently by President Nixon. He said about a year ago that he was opposed to massive involuntary busing and said the government could not require local school districts "to transport children beyond normal geographic school zones" in order to achieve a racial balance.

But the court has held otherwise. And the White House now says that the court's edict is the law of the land and that's that.

The current White House position is understandable and there can be no quarrel with the contention that the verdict of the Supreme Court is final.

But does it reflect common sense? There is a sharp difference between a type of school segregation that is established by special effort. It is different when the school attendance fits into a perfectly normal pattern. Many parents have objected with vigor and good reason against the busing of their school children outside of their normal school areas. And their objection has nothing to do with prejudice or color. They simply want to have the children as close to home as possible. There are families that acquire homes close to schools to avoid difficulties in transportation and other problems. Is it illegal for them to do so?

THE DALLAS TIMES HERALD
Dallas, Tex., April 22, 1971

IT WAS MR. Chief Justice Hughes who many years ago remarked that "We are under a Constitution, but the Constitution is what the judges say it is."

Today, we know e x a c t l y what Hughes was talking about. For the Supreme Court, in its school busing decision of last Tuesday, performed a truly dazzling rewrite job on the Fourteenth Amendment to the Constitution.

As the high court sees it, federal judges are perfectly within their rights in contriving any desegregation plan which "promises realistically to work, and promises realistically to work now." Busing of pupils, therefore, is okay; so is "the very limited use of mathematical ratios" of black students to white students.

But—and this is no inconsequential "but"—the decision applies only where school segregation was once by law established. That, as you've doubtless guessed, means the South.

Thus we behold a doubly impressive instance of "judges saying what the Constitution is." No matter that the Warren court, in the historic Brown case of 1954, went only so far as to hold that the state may no longer sponsor school segregation. The Burger court has discovered it isn't enough that all schools should, in theory alone, be open to children of both races. It's now up to school districts to see to it that children of both races take advantage of this—

whether the children want to or not. Thus a negative prohibition of segregation is translated into a positive duty to achieve desegregation.

The really shameless aspect of the decision, however, is that it applies only to one section of the country. We'd ap-p r e c i a t e Mr. Chief Justice Burger's showing us where the Constitution says the Fourteenth Amendment has no effect north of Mason-Dixon. But wait—we forgot. The Constitution is what the judges say it is.

The implications of this judicial rewrite job are staggering. We can't begin to guess at all of them. But certain it seems that a hard blow has been struck at individual and local liberties.

There's just one positive aspect to the decision. The nine justices refrained from setting a South-wide standard for desegregation. Not only did they rule that individual student bodies need not reflect a school district's racial composition—they told lower federal judges to continue using their discretion in writing desegregation formulas.

The f o r m u l a s these judges have written in the past have ranged from the onerous to the merciful. Some have taken local conditions into account; others haven't. But at least there's room for flexibility here. That's about the only hope with which the S u p r e m e Court has left the school districts of the South. For the moment, it will have to suffice.

Richmond Times-Dispatch
Richmond, Va., April 25, 1971

As appalling as it was for its approval of busing as a desegregation tool and for its exclusion of most Northern communities from its effect, the United States Supreme Court's latest school decision may not be as harsh and unyielding as a first reading indicated. Here and there, one can find a phrase that lifts the spirits, that kindles hope for a restoration of sanity and stability to the pupil assignment systems of the South's public schools.

Public officials and private citizens sincerely interested in preserving public schools as institutions of superior quality should study these encouraging phrases with the utmost care. Lawyers may quibble about what they mean, but some of them deserve to be tested. Public education is too important to Richmond, too important to Virginia and too important to this nation to wither simply because no one had the zeal or the courage to defend it against the blighting effects of massive busing.

One hopeful phrase in the court's opinion is this:

"An objection to transportation of students may have validity when the time or distance of travel is so great as to risk either the health of the children or significantly impinge on the educational process."

Some who have studied the opinion, including some distinguished attorneys, are convinced this statement limits the busing powers of federal district judges. To what extent any busing plan constitutes a "risk" to the health of the children or "impinges on the educational process" is arguable. Public officials and citizens have a clear right to challenge any plan they believe to be in conflict with the Supreme Court's conclusion.

A second encouraging phrase seems to suggest the ultimate restoration of the neighborhood school concept. Noting that communities do not "remain demographically stable," the court stated:

"Neither school authorities nor district courts are constitutionally required to make year-by-year adjustments of the

racial composition of student bodies once the affirmative duty to desegregate has been accomplished and racial discrimination through official action is eliminated from the system. This does not mean that federal courts are without power to deal with future problems; but in the absence of a showing that either the school authorities or some other agency of the State has deliberately attempted to fix or alter demographic patterns to affect the racial composition of the schools, further intervention by a district court should not be necessary."

Now place this statement beside the court's observations that not "every school in every community must always reflect the racial composition of the school system as a whole," and that one-race schools may be permitted in a unitary system clearly, the decision does not make each district judge a permanent educational czar, empowered to redraw boundaries and reassigning pupils year after year simply to satisfy his own arbitrary notions of

desegregation. Once a community has moved to a Constitutionally acceptable unitary system, a federal judge would not be justified in ordering additional busing to alter student body racial compositions compositions that resulted solely from changing neighborhood racial patterns.

Possibly this point could be cited against the proposed consolidation of the Richmond, Henrico and Chesterfield school districts. If Richmond does all that it is required to do to desegregate its schools, on what authority would the Richmond Federal District Court order a consolidation? After all, neither Henrico nor Chesterfield was created deliberately to "alter demographic patterns to affect the racial composition" of the city's schools.

These, then, are some of the more hopeful notes in the opinion. They are but weak beacons of hope, to be sure, but any light is welcome to those who are searching for a way out of the darkness of despair.

Chicago Tribune

Chicago, Ill., April 21, 1971

The Supreme Court yesterday handed down the most important rulings on school desegregation since the Brown vs. Board of Education case in 1954. Its major findings were that school authorities in states that once officially maintained segregation may—but are not required to in all circumstances—assign pupils to schools outside their neighborhoods and bus them to their destination, but that segregation arising from residential patterns rather than state or local restrictive action was not necessarily unconstitutional.

The court submitted four decisions, all unanimous, from five different school systems, the most important of which upheld a federal District judge who ruled that the schools of the city of Charlotte and surrounding Mecklenburg County in North Carolina should reflect the racial composition of the community. The lower court fixed a pupil ratio of 71 per cent white to 29 per cent black, to be achieved by busing. The Supreme Court held North Carolina's anti-busing law unconstitutional.

The court also ordered more busing to achieve a racial mix in the schools of Mobile, Ala., and also upheld the authority of federal judges to assign teachers in order to achieve a degree of faculty desegregation. The teacher ruling could have an effect on implementation of the Justice Department's order to the Chicago Board of Education to have the federal Department of Health, Education and Welfare draft a plan to reassign teachers to achieve faculty integration.

The court, in handing down guidelines which it admitted were incomplete and imperfect, made these general rulings:

—There is no constitutional right to have "any particular degree of racial balance or mixing," but mathematically ratios of one race to another in a school system may be used as a "starting point."

—There is no binding requirement that every school have some mix of races among students, and "the existence of some small numbers of students of one race or virtually one race in a school is not in itself illegal."

—There is no requirement that students be assigned to the schools nearest their homes, but objections to busing may be valid when the time or distance of travel is so great as to risk the health of the children or significantly impinge upon the educational process.

—School officials may be required to use busing as "one tool of school desegregation."

The underlying theme of the court was that remedial action may be ordered by federal courts only in those areas where state and local officials in the past clearly acted to keep the races apart. But the court cited the Civil Rights Act of 1964 in saying that Congress intended that de facto segregation arising from housing patterns was not unlawful in the absence of a showing that this was brought about by discriminatory action of state authorities.

In addition to cases arising in Charlotte-Mecklenburg and Mobile, the court also disposed of two allied Virginia cases and one from Clarke County, Ga.

The decisions were qualified in so many directions that no universally applicable rule emerges, and the South may argue that the decisions discriminate against it because most school segregation resulting from residential patterns occurs in Northern cities.

The Washington Post
Times Herald

Washington, D.C., April 22, 1971

In common usage—but not in the eyes of the law—there are three types of racial "segregation" in our schools. One is that which exists in schools mostly—but not exclusively—in the South, where it can be demonstrated that there has been deliberate intent on the part of the government officials at some level to segregate school children solely on the basis of their race. The dual school systems of the South and a number of school systems in the North where such (covert) intent has been established, fall into this category of segregation which was outlawed by the Supreme Court in 1954. A second type of school "segregation" is that which can be demonstrated to proceed, at least in part, from the racially discriminatory actions of government officials in areas *other* than education—in housing, for example. This category would include much of the so-called "de facto school segregation" on the constitutionality of which the court has yet to speak. The third type is simple racial concentration in our schools for which no specific government intent or activity in any field is held accountable. This too has not been before the high court.

The wise and well-written decision which Chief Justice Burger handed down for a unanimous court on Tuesday, in fact dealt exclusively with the first of these categories. This point was one the Chief Justice stressed repeatedly throughout the decision, and it is worth remembering. For in the central case at hand—*Swann versus the Charlotte-Mecklenburg (N.C.) Board of Education*—the court made abundantly clear that *only in the context of remedying a state-inflicted wrong,* of *overcoming the effects of past segregation on an official, deliberate basis,* was it upholding the authority of federal courts to impose school desegregation plans that might involve busing, non-contiguous zoning, racial proportioning and the rest. Thus:

"All things being equal, with no history of discrimination, it might well be desirable to assign pupils to schools nearest their homes. But all things are not equal in a system that has been deliberately constructed and maintained to enforce racial segregation. The remedy for such segregation may be administratively awkward, inconvenient and even bizarre in some situations and may impose burdens on some; but all awkwardness and inconvenience cannot be avoided in the interim period when remedial adjustments are being made to eliminate the dual school systems."

And again, in one of the companion rulings:

"The Constitution does not compel any particular degree of racial balance or mixing, but when past and continuing constitutional violations are found, some ratios are likely to be useful starting points in shaping a remedy."

There are not just "starting points," but also terminal points suggested in these decisions: Chief Justice Burger made evident that the Supreme Court does not view these remedies and compensations as carrying on in perpetuity for past wrongs, but rather as steps leading to a conclusion, to some point where the offending districts will have fulfilled their responsibility to dismantle their dual school systems and overcome the vestigial effects traceable to them.

Although the court confined its ruling to school districts that have been (or yet may be) found guilty of deliberate, officially inspired segregation, the language of the decision did have some implication for the kinds of cases on which it has yet to rule. Chief Justice Burger was very tidy and specific in limiting the scope of the decision and in distinguishing between the two principal types of case the court has not heard. Of what we have called the second category of segregation, he observed:

"We do not reach in this case the question whether a showing that school segregation is a consequence of other types of state action, without any discriminatory action by the school authorities, is a constitutional violation requiring remedial action by a school desegregation decree."

He thus left open the possibility that the court might find a constitutional violation, say, in a case where school segregation was found to be a direct consequence of officially abetted housing discrimination. But he did not leave a lot of room for such a finding in an outright racial balance case where no official intent could be found to have produced racial concentrations of students. Thus:

"If we were to read the holding of the District Court to require, as *a matter of substantive constitutional right,* any particular degree of racial balance or mixing, that approach would be disapproved and we would be obliged to reverse." (Italics added)

All this, of course, has yet to be spelled out in actual high court rulings, but the line of thought behind the distinctions made by the Chief Justice is one that we find important and persuasive. The notion that government should be empowered, even directed, to deal with citizens solely on the basis of their race for a purpose no matter how well-intended is one that we find particularly perilous and repugnant. That, however, is the notion behind much of the current movement to establish racial proportions on a fixed formula basis in the public schools, particularly Senator Ribicoff's plan. We have discussed before—and we will shortly come back to—our reasons for finding Senator Ribicoff's proposed legislation in this field a bad bill and a prospective hindrance rather than help to the achievement of racial justice in the schools.

Desegregation of the schools in the North conceivably will be expedited by some future court decision on housing-related racial concentrations in the schools. But we are convinced that it could be expedited now by a concerted, forceful effort to demonstrate that many Northern school districts are in fact guilty of discrimination within the meaning of the Supreme Court's rulings from Brown down to the present case.

TULSA DAILY WORLD

Tulsa, Okla., April 21, 1971

THE U.S. SUPREME COURT has knocked another prop from under segregation in American public schools. Busing of pupils to achieve racial mixing is now clearly legal.

Without reading the actual opinions filed by the Court yesterday it would be presumptuous to try to interpret them fully. But some main points seem to be clear, and one of them is that local laws cannot block busing of pupils when their effect is essentially to protect segregated schools.

There is some question as to what result the opinions will have on the "neighborhood schools" concept. The Court did not specifically rule on the question of school segregation caused by neighborhood housing patterns— a common basis of enrolment lines now in use. Chief Justice WARREN BURGER said this issue was not specifically presented in the cases being decided.

"We are concerned in these cases," he said, "with the elimination inherent in the dual school system, not with myriad factors of human existence which can cause discrimination in a multitude of ways on racial, religious or ethnic grounds."

At the same time, the rulings seem to give lower Courts a great deal of leeway in providing the means to bring about desegregated schools. The neighborhood concept can hardly be considered a safe refuge for segregation any longer, even though it is the traditional basis of school enrolment.

It makes no sense to many Americans—both black and white—to bus children great distances to satisfy some arbitrary standard of racial mixing. But until the High Court rules on that specific point, local Judges seem to have it in their power to order busing or whatever other methods they deem essential to bring about racial balancing.

It goes without saying that yesterday's SUPREME COURT rulings put new pressure on the Tulsa Board of Education, which was already straining to satisfy JUSTICE DEPARTMENT requirements for greater racial distribution throughout the school system. The options open to local Boards are becoming narrower and narrower.

THE ROANOKE TIMES

Roanoke, Va., April 22, 1971

Reasserting its historic role of independent-mindedness and forcefully reaffirming a 17-year commitment to nondiscriminatory public schooling, the U.S. Supreme Court now has laid down tough desegregation guidelines in the most unmistakable terms to date. Every urban community in the South, consequently, is now to be compelled to undertake sweeping steps to accomplish integration.

Tuesday's decision—significantly, a unanimous ruling from a court otherwise deeply split and increasingly conservative—will have an inestimable, immediate, regionwide impact. The whole educational process—and virtually every other aspect of community life, from race relations to tax rates—will be affected.

The court has given an explicit greenlight for massive busing, large-scale alteration of attendance lines, limited use of racial-balance assignments and thus a de-emphasis of the cities' traditional neighborhood-school concept. No one of these methods of accelerating classroom integration is new, or a legal surprise; taken together, however, they constitute a stern, no-compromise policy that will mean: (1) inconvenience for thousands of bus-riding students; (2) serious classroom disruption in Deep South communities still unprepared for social change; (3) panicky flight to the suburbs by whites living in a few mostly-black cities; (4) a costly new school-budget burden for core cities that can least afford the huge expense of buying and maintaining huge fleets of buses.

This having been said, it seems to us that there is much in the decision written by Chief Justice Burger that is constitutionally indisputable; that there is, at various points, a sensible mixture of idealism and pragmatism; that there is, to the extent humanly possible, a most-welcome pattern of flexible yet specific rules and regulations. And it is on these matters that public attention ought to be focused.

To be sure, the court has not yet answered all of the profoundly troubling questions that relate to school desegregation. "One vehicle can carry only a limited amount of baggage," Chief Justice Burger observed Tuesday; so for now at least, the nation is still left with an unacceptable double standard—one that requires affirmative desegregation actions in all of the cities in the South, yet is still not applied by the high court in those cities of the North where subtle governmental actions have caused one-race neighborhood schools.

Unfortunately, when other "vehicles" were available in the past— when, for example, the court was being asked to rule on totally contradictory lower-court rulings involving segregation of schools in the North— it did nothing. Now, though, the court must recognize that the South's rules have to be made fully applicable to any Northern city where discrimination has occurred.

All that the court did on Tuesday —and all, as a practical matter, that it could do at this time—was to state what the rules are to be in the South. If the new guidelines are still somewhat "incomplete and imperfect," as the chief justice in effect acknowledged, nonetheless they represent a far more precise set of yardsticks than heretofore were available. That being so, we share the view of the Athens, Ga., school superintendent who expressed gratification that the court "has finally made a decision . . . so that all of us in education will know what is expected of us."

What is expected? As we interpret it, the high court is saying that district federal judges have almost limitless powers—especially in communities where school boards do not take the initiative—to eliminate holdover effects of the old, state-compelled dual school system. A statistically perfect system of racial balance in every school must not be compelled; yet, for one year only, judges can use mathematical ratios as a suggested starting point—if not applied in every school.

Similarly, busing can be required —as writers of anti-busing legislation always secretly knew—if transportation proves necessary to end discrimination. Yet, the court added, busing need not be forced "when the time or distance of travel is so great as to risk either the health of the children or significantly impinge on the educational process." Charlotte's district judge saw no such risk in his city, yet the Fourth U.S. Circuit Court thought otherwise; now, the high court has reaffirmed the district ruling—hinting that reasonableness, as measured by a district judge, will prevail if it is "fair."

Because the court has left at least some room for considering local conditions and has sanctioned the existence of predominantly one-race schools if their segregation is "minor and unintentional," neither local school boards nor district judges have been locked into mistaken and possibly fatal policy rigidities that some integrationists desired. Some fuzziness remains, however much Mr. Burger might have wished otherwise; for our part, we think that kind of fuzziness is essential, notwithstanding the burdens it puts on judges and school officials. Obviously, what is feasible for Roanoke is not practical in some other city with a different racial mix or geography.

We wish, frankly, that the court's needed guidelines could have been even more vague on one or two points—so that, for example, public education would not have been threatened in those few communities where "white flight" will lead inescapably to resegregation, poorer education for blacks and chaotic financial and social problems for city halls. The court has given irrefutable evidence, however, that it will not cut back in the slightest on the nation's belated commitment to equal justice, and equal educational opportunities. Coming from a court that has been largely reshaped to a conservative mold, that affirmation is gratifying. Incalculable problems remain, nonetheless.

The Detroit News

Detroit, Mich., April 22, 1971

The U.S. Supreme Court's ruling that bussing may be used to dismantle dual school systems is a reasonable forward step in the long campaign against discrimination in U.S. education.

While giving lower courts a tool for correcting flagrant cases where states circumvent federal law, the ruling recognizes sane limits to the use which the courts may or should make of that tool.

Far-reaching though the ruling may be, it certainly does not signal a mandatory, widespread and massive program of bussing of American school children in the name of desegregation. The clear intent of the Supreme Court is to remedy hard-core instances of arbitrary segregation where no sincere or effective effort has been made by local school systems to improve themselves.

Some Southern school districts will be profoundly affected. But we judge from the court's language that the effect upon de facto segregation in Northern states will be considerably less. The ruling says:

"We are concerned in these cases with the elimination of the discrimination inherent in the dual school systems, not with the myriad factors of human existence which can cause discrimination in a multitude of ways on racial, religious, or ethnic grounds."

Observing that the bussing order which it upheld does not set a mandatory ratio of white and black students, the Supreme Court asserted that the command to desegregate

"does not mean that every school in every community must always reflect the racial composition of the school system as a whole."

The important thing, in the court's view, is that school assignments not be made as a part of state-enforced segregation. The existence of one-race schools within a district "is not in and of itself the mark of a system which still practices segregation by law."

While upholding the use of buses in the case in question, the Supreme Court justices added that no fixed guidelines for a lower court can be established.

Bussing was deemed sensible in the case in question because the use of buses is within the capacity of the school system, because the time and distance involved are short, and because the system had offered no satisfactory alternative plan.

This week's decision, like the 1954 decision outlawing the concept of "separate but equal" schools, must be regarded as a landmark ruling in civil rights. But, like the decision of 1954, it is by no means definitive.

The 1954 decision stated a broad doctrine, opening the door for endless litigation to determine the means by which that doctrine might be legally applied. This week's ruling resulted from a piece of that litigation but in turn leaves questions to be answered.

A series of rulings by lower courts and reviews by the Supreme Court will obviously take place to establish with more precision the circumstances under which bussing may or may not be required.

The Philadelphia Inquirer

Philadelphia, Pa., April 23, 1971

Four unanimous decisions by the U. S. Supreme Court Tuesday, principally the one dealing with the Charlotte-Mecklenburg school system in North Carolina, are likely to be a landmark in our country's continuing and often agonizing efforts to eliminate racial discrimination in public schools. What the court says about the use of busing to foster the integration of schools may have far-ranging impact extending, in the long run, to many communities not directly involved in these cases.

But, to put the decisions in perspective, they need to be evaluated in terms of what the court does not say or require as well as what it does.

Just as the landmark Supreme Court decision of 1954—which declared unconstitutional the dual system of public schools segregated by state law on the basis of race—had only limited application geographically and did not produce instant integration of all public schools in the South, so is the court's latest landmark limited in application and scope.

★ ★ ★

First of all, the court is dealing with de jure racial segregation exclusively, not the de facto kind that exists in varying degree in many northern cities, including Philadelphia. The issues before the court concerned ways and means of integrating public schools where dual systems, one black and one white, had been mandated by state law prior to the 1954 decision.

Chief Justice Burger, who wrote the opinions in all four cases, made this clear when he said in the Charlotte decision:

"We do not reach in this case the question whether a showing that school segregation is a consequence of other types of state action, without any discriminatory action by the school authorities, is a violation requiring remedial action by a school desegregation decree. This case does not present that question and we therefore do not decide it. Our object in dealing with the issues presented by these cases is to see that school authorities exclude no pupil of a racial minority from any school, directly or indirectly, on account of race; it does not and cannot embrace all the problems of racial prejudice, even when those problems contribute to disproportionate racial concentrations in some schools."

In the Charlotte case the Supreme Court has upheld the public school integration plan of U. S. District Court Judge James B. McMillan which requires busing of both black and white students to schools outside their immediate neighborhoods. Although the court authorizes other Federal judges in similar circumstances to order busing of pupils away from neighborhood schools as a device to further racial integration, it provides no guidelines.

Chief Justice Burger put it this way:

"The scope of permissible transportation of students as an implement of remedial decree has never been defined by this court and by the very nature of the problem it cannot be defined with precision. No rigid guidelines as to student transportation can be given for application to the infinite variety of problems presented in thousands of situations."

And the chief justice also said, in elaborating on this point:

"An objection to transportation of students may have validity when the time or distance of travel is so great as to risk either the health of the children or significantly impinge on the educational process."

The Supreme Court specified that the presence of one-race schools does not necessarily mean unconstitutional racial discrimination exists in the school system. Mr. Burger said:

"It should be clear that the existence of some small number of one-race, or virtually one-race, schools within a district is not in and of itself the mark of a system which still practices segregation by law."

On a related point the chief justice noted that public schools do not necessarily need to have the same racial balance as the community:

"The constitutional command to desegregate schools does not mean that every school in every community must always reflect the racial composition of the school system as a whole."

And, quoting again from the Supreme Court's unanimous opinion in the Charlotte case, Mr. Burger declared:

"Neither school authorities nor district courts are constitutionally required to make year-by-year adjustments of the racial composition of student bodies once the affirmative duty to desegregate has been accomplished and racial discrimination through official action is eliminated from the system."

Thus, while the Supreme Court may have given a qualified indorsement to busing as a tool to fight racial segregation in public schools, and while it may have dealt a blow to the neighborhood school concept, it seems to have raised as many questions as it has answered.

Like the 1954 decision, the latest landmark will not end the controversy or the litigation. One predictable result will be a massive surge of new court cases focusing on questions still unanswered.

THE DAILY OKLAHOMAN

Oklahoma City, Okla., April 22, 1971

HISTORICAL antecedents aside, the racial segregation that still persists in public schools throughout the nation is attributable overwhelmingly to segregated housing.

It's a lawyer's quibble and always has been a quibble to argue that the only kind of school segregation the courts need to be concerned with is the kind that occurs in the 20 or so states which had laws requiring it before the United States Supreme Court acted in 1954.

Oklahoma was one of those states, but the existence of legally-imposed segregation wasn't the only or even the basic reason why whites and blacks attended separate schools in this state. For the most part, they attended segregated schools because they lived in segregated neighborhoods.

Segregated housing still is the rule everywhere in the nation and there's not much the courts can do about it, since the usual effect of legal efforts to mix the races is white flight and the gradual "resegregation" of formerly all-white neighborhoods into all-black neighborhoods.

The problem acquires such massive dimensions in sprawling metropolitan areas such as New York City and Los Angeles that any attempt to apply busing requirements evenly would be socially explosive and financially ruinous.

The Supreme Court recognized this in the Charlotte-Mecklenburg County case when it upheld the authority of federal judges to order busing as a means of desegregating schools, but said that racial ratios weren't required in all schools of a community. Still undefined are most of the key expressions that crop up repeatedly in the literature of desegregation, including language the court itself used in handing down its Charlotte-Mecklenburg ruling.

It differentiated between a "unitary" system and a "dual" system without defining what it meant in either instance. Exactly where is the line between "token" desegregation and "full implementation" of the law? The reason why answers aren't forthcoming is that guidelines which would accommodate every conceivable combination of circumstances couldn't be formulated.

For that reason the courts predictably will go right on considering each case on an ad hoc basis, with the result that the precedents governing in one instance won't govern necessarily in other instances. But in the process, gross disparities are developing in the way the law is being applied. As the courts have interpreted it up to now, the Constitution requires federal intervention only in the states of the old Confederacy and a few states outside the South which formerly practiced "de jure" segregation. The "de facto" segregation which reflects segregated housing patterns is ignored, although Chief Justice Warren Burger indicated it might not be in the future if the location of new schools was intended deliberately to attract white families into segregated suburbs.

The former Warren Court's 1954 ruling banning legally-imposed segregation held it to be a denial of the 14th Amendment's equal protection guaranty. But the multitude of separate and often conflicting findings of the lower federal courts will continue to represent a denial of equal protection in themselves unless the Supreme Court at some point endeavors to reconcile them.

Even in the North it's being acknowledged that a double standard prevails. Connecticut Sen. Abraham Ribicoff is not without justification in accusing New York Sen. Jacob Javits of "hypocrisy." But a northern lawmaker couldn't possibly hit upon a surer way of alienating his constituents than by voting for Ribicoff's bill to desegregate schools in northern metropolitan areas.

HOUSTON CHRONICLE

Houston, Tex., April 22, 1971

The Burger Supreme Court, at least in matters of school integration, has proved to be virtually indistinguishable from the old Warren court.

The new chief justice, Warren Burger, and his fellow Minnesotan, Justice Harry A. Blackmun, have given the court a new and more conservative orientation in some regards. But in its latest and enormously important school desegregation ruling the court's philosophy is unchanged.

This will be disappointing to the millions of Americans — President Nixon and Congress included — who have serious doubts about the wisdom of compulsory busing for the purpose of achieving racial balance.

The decision, written by Chief Justice Burger for a unanimous court, goes right down the line in upholding cross-town busing and the "pairing," "clustering" or "grouping" of schools for the purpose of eliminating remaining vestiges of dual educational facilities for whites and blacks.

The court's decision ignores Mr. Nixon's expressed disapproval of busing for racial purposes and also the reluctance of Congress to use federal funds for this purpose. It also ignores hundreds of resolutions from local school boards and legislatures, statements by governors and petitions by individuals who oppose cross-town busing as an encroachment on the concept of the neighborhood school.

These decisions undoubtedly are going to set off a new shock wave of protest across much of the nation, especially in the South where the courts and the federal government have most vigorously applied their enforcement of integration laws and court decrees.

One regrettable aspect of the ruling is the fact that it is directed at de facto segregation in the South rather than at de facto segregation in the nation as a whole.

Burger wrote that schools all or predominantly of one race in a mixed-population district "is not in and of itself the mark of a system which still practices segregation by law." Such schools will require close scrutiny. But in a system with a history of segregation, the need for remedial change warrants a presumption against the system. In such instances, school authorities have the burden of proving their school assignments are genuinely nondiscriminatory.

This suggests there will be one standard for the South, where racial segregation was supported by law, and another standard for the rest of the nation, where segregation was not sanctioned by law.

The decisions have, at least, cleared the air. There no longer can be any doubt, as there previously was, about where the Supreme Court stands on the issues of busing, pairing, freedom-of-choice, and the maintenance of the neighborhood school.

"If a state-imposed limitation on a school authority's discretion operates to inhibit or obstruct the operation of a unitary school system or impede the disestablishment of a dual school system, it must fall; state policy must give way when it operates to hinder vindication of federal constitutional guarantees," the court said.

Fixed racial ratios are not required, but the court said it's not enough for school attendance lines to be neutral. Rather, school officials must foster integration by affirmative, remedial action if that's necessary to achieve truly nondiscriminatory assignments.

The court has spoken. This is the law — until some future court or a constitutional amendment changes it. We fear it is going to hasten the white exodus from our central cities to the suburbs, a process already well under way.

The Sun Reporter

San Francisco, Calif., April 24, 1971

The unanimous Supreme Court decision which upheld crosstown bussing and other controversial steps as instruments to be used in the destruction of school segregation represents another milestone in the 17-year struggle of Black folks to force whites, previously in the South but now throughout the nation, to accept the 1954 unanimous Supreme Court Decision declaring segregation in public education an unconstitutional denial of equal protection of all citizens before the law.

Think of the tremendous public and private funds wasted on the treadmill of opposition to the Supreme Court's constitutional mandate! The sickness even invaded San Francisco, where His Honor the Mayor's opposition to bussing was a covert effort to deny racial minority youngsters their constitutional rights.

The evils of the Wakefield Act are glaringly condemned. We would hope that those who struggled for equal quality integrated education in America could now give a great sigh of relief with this victory, and redirect their energies from a defense of the constitutional protection against segregation in public education toward creative initiatives to enrich the quality and the meaning of public education in America. Who will gainsay that America's most precious asset, its children, deserve and demand no less?

Yet, our long experience with that old debble, racism, tells us that our opponents who support racial segregation will not accept this latest unanimous Supreme Court mandate, but will continue to divide the nation with new techniques and procedures to deny to non-white children their constitutional rights of equal quality, integrated public education.

What great evils men do in the name of State's Rights and individual rights, which are predicated upon the paranoia of racial superiority!

THE PLAIN DEALER

Cleveland, Ohio, April 22, 1971

The U.S. Supreme Court ruling approving the busing of pupils as a means to achieve racial integration of southern schools are decisions of far-reaching consequence which we find warranted and appropriate.

Most notably, they set guidelines for the original 1954 desegregation order of the court and give broad power to local courts to enforce compliance with that law.

The 28-page unanimous opinion, written by Chief Justice Warren E. Burger, virtually spells an end to a dual education system in the South.

The four decisions compel school officials to foster integration by even resorting to "administratively awkward, inconvenient and even bizzarre" measures such as busing and gerrymandered school districts.

The court rejected the position of the Nixon administration that the neighborhood school concept should be retained. Racial integration can no longer be limited to "walk-in schools, the court ruled. Busing, it held, is proper except where the distance is so great as to be injurious to the health of the pupil, or significantly affect the educational process.

The decisions could be politically injurious to President Nixon in the South. Nixon, who had advocated a go easy policy on school integration, last year deplored the disruption and expense of busing, criticized the "automatic assignment" of children by a "mathematical formula," and supported the concept of neighborhood schools. The decisions are likely to force the Nixon administration into taking a stronger stance on desegregation.

In this regard, it is noteworthy that the unanimous opinion was written by Chief Justice Burger, one of two conservative justices appointed to the court by President Nixon.

While the court made it clear that the opinion did not apply to northern "de facto" segregation based upon neighborhood patterns because "one vehicle can carry only a limited amount of baggage," there appeared principles that could affect northern cases now pending. These concern construction of new schools to block integration of existing schools and discriminatory action by school officials in drawing school boundaries.

Los Angeles Times

Los Angeles, Calif., April 22, 1971

The Supreme Court has tried mightily to sweep away quibbles, and doubts, and delays.

The Supreme Court has said that "the constant theme and thrust of every holding from (1954) to date is that state-enforced separation of races violates the equal protection clause" of the Constitution. The Supreme Court has said that school authorities must exclude no pupil of a racial minority from any school, "directly or indirectly," on account of race. The Supreme Court has said that to this end cross-town bussing is permissible; school assignment by race is permissible; gerrymandering of districts is permissible. The neighborhood school concept falls before the command of the Constitution: official racial discrimination is not allowed.

The decisions were unanimous. The justices who made them were appointed by Presidents Roosevelt, Eisenhower, Kennedy, Johnson and Nixon. The four opinions were written by Mr. Nixon's appointee, Chief Justice Warren E. Burger. The decisions are the law of the land, and they have behind them the force of a constitutional, philosophical and indeed political consensus.

The Court has gone far toward settling the arguments about what the South must do to undo the results of the separate school systems it once supported. The Court has been as precise as it could be. It cannot be absolutely precise; and the working out of school desegregation plans in the South, or anywhere else for that matter, is extraordinarily complicated. Much depends on the willingness of the Administration, which sought a less rigorous resolution than the Court reached, to support the Court's commands with the affirmative action of the federal government.

And the Court hasn't yet tackled, as Burger pointed out, the whole tangled question of what must be done by school systems outside the South. (Neither, of course, has Congress; note that the Senate Wednesday voted down Sen. Abraham Ribicoff's proposal to require the integration of inner-city black children into white suburban schools throughout the nation.)

But you cannot conclude that Los Angeles and other California and Northern cities are wholly unaffected by the Court's chain of reasoning.

"We do not reach in this case the question whether a showing that school segregation (as) a consequence of other types of state action, without any discriminatory action by the school authorities, is a constitutional violation requiring remedial action by a school desegregation decree," Burger wrote.

That statement and others by Burger leave well open the possibility that even in non-Southern school districts, which never operated overtly separate school systems, discriminatory action by school authorities would require remedial action by the courts. Which, in fact, relates to what former Superior Judge Alfred Gitelson found in Los Angeles: that by selecting sites, building schools, drawing district lines and denying transportation to minority students, the Los Angeles Board of Education was unconstitutionally discriminating.

Judge Gitelson may well be upheld; this, for Los Angeles, is the principal message in the Court's decisions.

For the country, the larger message, it seems to us, is that we are definitely going to proceed toward becoming an integrated society.

The process is going to be difficult; the problems, multitudinous.

Burger confessed that the Court cannot make every wrong right; and he was careful not to insist upon precise and rigid balancing of the races in the schools. "In an area as sensitive as we deal with here," he said, "words are poor instruments to convey the sense of basic fairness inherent in equity." Yet it was to that sense of basic fairness, inherent in the Constitution and in the traditions of the nation, that the Court addressed itself; and its four decisions show the country what it truly is, and what it must become.

ARKANSAS DEMOCRAT
Little Rock, Ark., April 21, 1971

The Supreme Court said yesterday that when it comes to desegregating schools in the South, anything goes.

Busing, pairing, gerrymandering, abandoning schools, building new ones, assigning faculty . . . Nothing can stand in the way — state laws, acts of Congress, lower court decisions, lack of funds, neighborhood living patterns, or inconvenience.

The Supreme Court said lower courts may order anything for the purpose of eliminating all forms of segregation caused by the dual school system, which, of course, means the South. As always, the court announced it was dealing only with segregation that had come about because of laws. It was not dealing with the big-city ghetto school that was created by neighborhood living patterns because no such case was before it. Another reason is that the court probably thinks, as do even some members of the NAACP Legal Defense Fund, that the schools of Harlem, South Bronx and Chicago can never be desegregated. This very practical matter always makes an impression on judges, it seems, but other practicalities, such as where dirt-poor Southern school districts are going to get the money for transportation systems, don't get much consideration.

This time the Supreme Court went further than we dreamed it would go. Although this is the very fuzzy part of the decision, it comes very close to decreeing racial quotas for schools. However, it denies it has done this, saying in fact, that the Constitution does not demand that "every school in every community must always reflect the racial composition of the school system as a whole."

Yet, the court makes it plain that neighborhood schools (Chief Justice Warren Burger calls them "walk-in" schools) will have to go and that district judges will be "concerned with the elimination of the one-race school." Especially significant is that this decision upholds the Charlotte-Mecklenburg integration plan, which called for the purchase of $1 million worth of school buses to move 13,300 school children (9,000 of them in grade school) so that every school would have an enrollment that was 71 per cent white and 29 per cent black. In language that must win a prize for ambiguity, the court says that we must not conclude that its approval of this plan means it approves of racial quotas. The 71-29 ratio was not a quota but a "starting point for shaping a remedy." Racial quotas are not called for by the Constitution, the court declares.

We also don't think "starting points" are mentioned in the Constitution. Either all of us are equal before the law, or we aren't. Our color shouldn't make any difference, and certainly it does when a child is going to be forced to go to a different school — one that he wouldn't normally attend — because some judge has prescribed the number of whites and blacks that have to be in each school. This makes school kids the creatures of the state and pretty well wipes out the theory of individual freedom we prize so highly in our country.

We think that now we will see "starting points" laid down by all judges, who are assured from this point on that the Supreme Court will uphold just about anything they require. The Charlotte-Mecklenburg decision will be the guide, especially for courts like the Eighth Circuit Court of Appeals, which has already demonstrated its impatience with a moderate approach to desegregation.

Before it right now are appeals from the reasonable desegregation plans now in effect in the Little Rock, North Little Rock and Pulaski County School districts. We can judge how quick this court will seize the precedent of the Charlotte-Mecklenburg decision by the fact that it already has taken the unprecedented step of stopping school construction on demand of some Negro lawyers who said the new buildings would increase segregation. Our reading of the decision makes us believe that all school administrators in Pulaski County had better get ready for wholesale busing in the fall and the breakup of many neighborhood elementary schools.

LEDGER-STAR
Norfolk, Va., April 21, 1971

For those who had hoped the new Supreme Court rulings on school desegregation would establish hard-and-fast policies that might hasten an end to the seemingly endless litigation, the decisions yesterday fell short.

Chairman Vincent Thomas of the Norfolk School Board, for example, observed: "I can't see anything on the surface to lead the way to a final determination of what we should do or what we have to do. That's what we are looking for."

The frustration in Norfolk is understandable. The Norfolk suit has been in the courts for 14 years.

What the Supreme Court did say yesterday was that busing is a permissible device for achieving greater mixing of the races in the schools. Chief Justice Burger described segregation as an evil and reiterated a 1968 decision that school authorities have an affirmative duty to eliminate racial discrimination "root and branch."

But the uncertainty remains—just as Mr. Thomas noted—over how best to carry out such a mandate, and uncertainty surrounds, too, the definitions of what constitutes compliance.

Even as these questions go unanswered, though, there is guidance to be found in this latest Supreme Court opinion. And it could be helpful to the lower federal courts and to the local school authorities in attempting to square two considerations that are not always compatible: total desegregation and an efficient, quality educational program.

For the Court has said that precise racial balance throughout a system is not required. It has said also that the existence of schools of a single race in a district "does not, by itself, demonstrate that the school board is violating the Constitution." The opinion seemed also to encourage from lower federal courts discretion in deciding school mixing suits. "Once a right and a violation have been shown," the Burger opinion read, "the scope of a district court's equitable powers to remedy past wrongs is broad, for breadth and flexibility are inherent in equitable remedies."

The Court's decision not to spell out too specifically the criteria for establishing a unitary school system no doubt will mean further uncertainty for local school districts. Lower courts will still be searching for the answers. But the breadth and flexibility that the Supreme Court has emphasized can in themselves be guides to acceptable answers for communities and both their black and white citizens—providing that when they are applied in order to eliminate segregation they do not ignore the requirements of education.

CHICAGO DAILY NEWS

Chicago, Ill., April 22, 1971

The Supreme Court's unanimous decision in the Southern school desegregation cases made one thing quite plain: There will be no backtracking in the fight against state-imposed separation of the races. The long and consistent line of decisions beginning with the historic Brown case of 1954 is extended and broadened by the new rulings.

Chief Justice Warren E. Burger wrote the opinion, and the full concurrence of the other justices destroyed any lingering hopes or fears that Nixon administration politics would alter the direction of the high court as it affects the South. In some respects, particularly in approving busing as one means of achieving racial balance, Burger parted company with the public statements of President Nixon, who appointed him. The court also rejected the arguments of the Justice Department, which had intervened in behalf of the neighborhood school concept in a way that could have slowed the pace of desegregation in the South.

This ruling establishes guidelines that should overcome the last legalistic barriers to desegregation. North Carolina's antibusing statute was knocked aside; a Georgia Supreme Court ruling against pupil assignment by race was overturned. The court held firmly that any means necessary might be ordered toward the end of wiping out the old pattern of dual school systems.

It stands to reason that a sweeping opinion of this kind will have some fallout in the North, where more subtle ways of tinkering with racial balance have been devised. Yet it would be premature to apply the stern prohibition laid down here against state-sponsored segregation to the situation that exists in Northern cities.

The Burger opinion in fact specifically excluded the question of "de facto" segregation resulting from factors other than "discriminatory action by the school authorities." By giving federal district courts broad discretion to determine whether school authorities have acted in good faith, the ruling may open avenues toward future cases where the "de facto" issue becomes paramount. At the same time, the high court seemed to be warning against trying to right all wrongs by using the schools as a lever. "It would not serve the high purpose" of the Brown decision, the court said, "to seek to use school desegregation cases for purposes beyond their scope, although desegregation of schools ultimately will have impact on other forms of discrimination."

Even with the new and somewhat clearer guidelines, puzzling questions remain. And as the court recognized, conditions differ so widely from one state, city or hamlet to another that each case will have to be judged on its own. Busing may be the answer in one place, but not in another. Integration by a percentage formula may apply in one district, but be impractical in the one next door. We are left with a problem of infinite complexity and many of the answers are still obscure.

The one certainty, however, is that the goal has not changed or been lost to sight. And for those who feared that might be the case with the changed makeup of the court, that in itself is reassurance in large measure.

Pittsburgh Post-Gazette

Pittsburgh, Pa., April 22, 1971

IN WHAT may be the most significant decision on school desegregation since the original Brown ruling in 1954, the U.S. Supreme Court Tuesday backed busing and other tools for combating segregation in Southern education.

The significance was two-fold.

► The rulings in four cases were unanimous and were written by Chief Justice Warren E. Burger himself. This  **Mr. Burger** removed the last vestige of hope for anti-integrationists expressed in many quarters in the 1968 campaign that if a more conservative candidate such as Richard M. Nixon were elected President and got his men on the U.S. Supreme Court that somehow the line of rulings on integration could be turned in a different direction. (The placing of Mr. Burger and of Justice Harry Blackmun on the court indeed has made a difference in criminal justice rulings, but, it now is apparent, not in school integration.)

► The court approved a whole range of "tools" for integration, such as busing, racial quotas, pairing and gerrymandering of attendance zones, if needed to attain the goal of removing "all vestiges of state-imposed segregation." In a real sense, therefore, the high court moved beyond desegregation as the requirement to integration.

Now it should be clearly understood that the court outlined certain limitations to its own sweeping doctrine. It did not order the elimination of all-black schools. It did not require racial balance in every school.

But it did say that the existence of all-black schools creates an assumption of discrimination and held that Federal district judges may use racial quotas as a guide in fashioning desegregation decrees.

Finally, the court rulings clearly applied to Southern states where there once was legal "de jure" segregation and not elsewhere in places where segregation is "de facto," by happenstance of neighborhood housing patterns.

But Northerners would be ostrich-like if they did not realize the import of the rulings and of the two elements of significance outlined above. For the continuing attitude of the court on integration and the tools it now has approved for integration purposes ultimately can apply North as well as South.

What now appears is that we will continue for years to have the uneasy but seemingly unavoidable relationship of courts as well as school boards fashioning the schools. Even within these guidelines there will be latitude for motivation, interpretation, and implementation, all subject to litigation.

* * *

But the trend now is clear. When a chief justice courageously rules at cross-purposes with the pronouncements of the President who appointed him with the expectation of change, there can be no lingering question.

Now persons of good will of all races can work together to make integrated schools good schools, secure in the knowledge that whatever the changes of administration there will be judicial support from the U.S. Supreme Court on down.

THE MILWAUKEE JOURNAL

Milwaukee, Wis., April 22, 1971

The Supreme Court's unanimous decisions of Tuesday renewed the thrust of its historic 1954 directive that school segregation by law must be wiped out. The court gave broad latitude to achieve that goal. The rulings also have important implications for de facto segregation that could shake Northerners out of the belief that their more subtly evolved racial separation is out of judicial reach.

Noting that "the measure of any desegregation plan is its effectiveness," the court said that so-called color blind attendance policies and other circumventing devices in the South are not good enough. It upheld a variety of desegregation tools for use and said that "administratively awkward, inconvenient and even bizarre" measures might be needed. A wave of new Southern desegregation orders from the courts can now be expected.

Some interpretations hold that the court, despite rhetoric seemingly to the contrary, set groundwork for legal attack on segregation Northern style. The court argued that a school board's location of new buildings in expanding white residential areas could constitute creation of segregated schools. This may strengthen such Northern cases as Atty.

Lloyd Barbee's against the Milwaukee School Board, in which a conscious board policy of perpetuating racial separation is alleged.

The implications for the North in Tuesday's rulings are inescapable. There is, for one thing, the encouragement given to integration. Chief Justice Burger went aside from constitutional questions to say: "School authorities have wide discretion in formulating school policy and, as a matter of educational policy, school authorities may well conclude that some kind of racial balance in the schools is desirable quite apart from any constitutional requirements."

More important, the court practically said that the neighborhood school has no constitutional protection, thus seeming to deprive integration foes of their most emotionally powerful argument. The court validated such controversial integration methods as bussing, pairing and grouping even of noncontiguous districts, gerrymandering attendance boundaries, locating new schools with racial mix as a criterion and using a flexible white-black ratio as a starting point.

In elaborating on bussing, the court noted that such transporting of schoolchildren historically had been an integral factor in education and that nearly 40% of

American pupils today are bussed.

Not only did the court sweep aside Justice Department arguments on behalf of the Southern districts in these cases, but it contradicted President Nixon's personal views, expressed last year, against bussing and arbitrary racial mixing.

The court still has not provided a badly needed national norm for school integration, although the pattern being set in the South eventually may spread to all districts if just the right de facto segregation case gets before it. It is conceivable that congressional action may reach that point first. Sen. Ribicoff (D-Conn.) is again jabbing with true aim at the consciences of Northern liberals, shaming them toward support of his bill to require substantial integration in all metropolitan areas within 12 years as a provision of continued state and federal support.

A new voice heard increasingly across the land claims that integration is no longer fashionable, that blacks demand their own first rate schools. It is a voice eagerly joined by traditional segregationists. Such feeling sorely lacks sufficient vision. A racially integrated society must be a foremost national goal, just as first rate schooling for all must be, whether white bigots and militant blacks like it or not.

The Oregonian

Portland, Ore., April 22, 1971

The U. S. Supreme Court—the Burger court—has unanimously and emphatically affirmed the Warren court's major decisions outlawing state-imposed racial segregation in the public schools and endorsed busing as a means of achieving a reasonable degree of integration.

The series of decisions written by Chief Justice Warren E. Burger directly concerned southern cases, and the court's repeated emphasis against state-enforced segregation focused its rulings on the South. The chief justice wrote that "in a system with a history of segregation, the need for remedial criteria of sufficient specificity to assure a school authority's compliance with its constitutional duty warrants a presumption against schools that are substantially disproportionate in their racial composition."

"All things being equal," he added, "with no history of discrimination, it might well be desirable to assign pupils to schools nearest their homes. But all things are not equal in a system that has been deliberately constructed and maintained to enforce racial segregation."

This might be read as exempting from the ruling the bulk of northern districts without a record of a dual school system supported by law. But such an interpretation may well be in error. The decisions mentioned a number of devices by which school authorities have sought to

maintain segregation, such as the location of new schools in white neighborhoods distant from black residential areas. If such policies were to be found anywhere in the nation, presumably they would be subject to correction by federal court action, including the ordering of busing programs.

It does not appear, however, that school districts which, like Portland's, have made sincere efforts to diminish classroom segregation growing out of housing patterns will be under legal compulsions through these decisions, even though some of a city's school buildings continue to have a much-too-high proportion of black pupils and some are all white, as in Portland.

The decisions have the effect of enlarging the powers of the federal courts to deal in detail with desegregation in those areas in which state or local authorities still resist the basic principles enunciated by the court in the Brown case 17 years ago.

"Breadth and flexibility are inherent in equitable remedies," the court said. But it added: "In seeking to define even in broad and general terms how far this remedial power extends it is important to remember that judicial powers may be exercised only on the basis of a constitutional violation (i.e., official state or local action encouraging segregation.) Remedial judicial authority does not put judges automatically in the shoes of school authorities whose powers are plenary."

The rekindling of federal judiciary pressure on the South to eliminate racial discrimination in education, "root and branch," will unquestionably have the effect of increasing the moral responsibilities of school authorities in other regions to press for higher degrees of integration.

The Supreme Court, in giving its blessing to busing as a means of integration, has noted that buses have come into common use as school districts have consolidated. It pointed out that 39 per cent of the nation's pupils ride buses to and from school. The percentage is even higher in Oregon—53 per cent. A symptom of the trend is the Ribicoff amendment, rejected by the Senate Wednesday, proposing that metropolitan area schools—inner-city and suburbs—be required to integrate classrooms in racial proportions based on the population pattern of the entire area.

Even in the South, the court agreed, busing would have its limits. "An objection to transportation of students," it said, "may have validity when the time or distance of travel is so great as to risk either the health of the children or significantly impinge on the educational process."

But if the objections to busing are merely reflections of prejudice against mixing of the races, they have no validity legally—or morally. That is a principle worth honoring everywhere in the nation.

The Des Moines Register

Des Moines, Iowa, April 28, 1971

The U.S. Supreme Court decisions upholding school busing are a temporary reprieve for the North, and they should be read with due regard for the consequences of half-way measures on racial matters.

The Court ruled specifically on five cases originating in the South, and Chief Justice Burger advised a crowded courtroom that the justices did not deal with issues arising from Northern-style segregation caused by neighborhood housing patterns.

It would be a grave mistake, however, to conclude that the court has narrowed its view of segregation only to the vestiges of the South's dual, black-and-white public school systems. On the contrary, the busing decisions point in the other direction.

The rulings are a strong reaffirmation of the original court decision against school segregation in the Brown case of 1954. As if to underscore that point, all the decisions were written by Burger, just as the Brown ruling was given by Chief Justice Earl Warren, who was Burger's predecessor.

Not content with this reaffirmation, the justices gave broad powers to the federal courts to write prescriptions for school integration. These can include orders for busing of school children far from their homes, drawing new school district boundaries and, if necessary, other inconveniences, costs and burdens.

Having gone that far, it seems reasonable to expect that the court will not impede the efforts of lower courts to deal with other forms of racial discrimination. Housing authorities and zoning boards which can influence racial living patterns probably will not be immune from judicial scrutiny.

The busing decisions amount to a rebuke to the Nixon Administration. In the matter of housing as well as schools, Nixon has indicated that he would not push integration beyond the narrowest reading of the law. Justice Department lawyers sided with the Southern schools in the busing cases, arguing that pupils should be assigned to schools in their own neighborhoods even if that slowed the pace of desegregation.

"All things being equal, with no history of discrimination, it might well be desirable to assign pupils to schools nearest their homes," Burger wrote. "But all things are not equal in a system that has been deliberately constructed and maintained to enforce racial segregation."

In his summation, the chief justice said that "substance, not semantics, must govern" in determining equity. That judgment will surely produce increasing demands from civil rights groups for action in the North as well as the South. It is a judgment all Americans would do well to heed.

St. Louis Globe-Democrat

St. Louis, Mo., April 22, 1971

The Supreme Court took a long bus ride Tuesday, but unfortunately the contraption got somewhat out of control.

The damage done, however, is not nearly as much as some people might think.

Before trying to analyze the ruling, it is best to outline what it actually did and did not do.

The ruling affirms the federal district courts' broad powers to desegregate school systems where discrimination has been created by law or other artificial means, as is the case in dual school systems in the South.

It does not apply to school systems where housing patterns or other causes beyond the control of school boards have caused racial imbalance, as is the case in many northern cities.

In authorizing district courts to order busing or racial quotas in instances where the Constitution has been violated, the high court put limits on how far district judges might go. Thus, this is in no sense an edict authorizing massive busing, as some observers are claiming.

*   *   *

It is a blow against the neighborhood school system, but certainly not a crippling one. The neighborhood school system is just as valid today as it was before the court's ruling. Those who would try to use the Burger court ruling against the neighborhood school idea won't find the ammunition they seek.

In simple terms, the Supreme Court said that if a federal district judge found that busing could be useful "as a tool of school desegregation" in a dual school system, he has the power to order its use, along with other remedial measures.

But at the same time the court pointed out "an objection to transportation of students may have validity when the time or distance of travel is so great as to risk either the health of the children or significantly impinge on the educational process . . ."

*   *   *

The principal objection to the decision is that it opens the door to possible abuse by judges who might feel inclined to become reformers, as well as jurists.

We can see how a district judge might well have to consider the validity of a busing plan as part of a solution to desegregation.

But if this same judge takes it upon himself to start drawing up busing plans of his own, fixing arbitrary racial quotas and spelling out other means for accomplishing integration rather than desegregation, he could go off the deep end rather easily.

The much-heralded decision seems largely superfluous. District judges already had the power to rule on the constitutionality of state antibusing laws and school desegregation plans. It shouldn't be necessary for the Supreme Court to spell out in detail how they should or should not exercise this authority.

The matter of school busing generally should remain in the hands of local school boards and parents of school children in the district. Any intervention by a federal district judge should be rare and only when a federal statute or the Constitution has been violated.

The Hartford Courant

Hartford, Conn., April 22, 1971

There would appear to be both virtues and shortcomings in the decision of the United States Supreme Court ruling that federal courts may order busing of public school children as a means of segregating schools.

The paramount virtue is that the decision unswervingly reiterates the landmark ruling by the high bench in 1954 when it said, both in the name of the Constitution and of human justice, that black children are entitled to education equal to that received by white children.

This was the beginning of desegration as it is now generally understood. But in the decade and a half since then, it has been fought and dodged in states bent on enforced segregated education, or it has been legally misunderstood or befogged through a multitude of circumstances. Prominent among the issues has been busing, of course, debated in many states and towns.

As Chief Justice Burger says, since 1954 federal judges have struggled in hundreds of cases with a host and variety of problems to implement the original directive. And now, he points out, "the court is offering up-to-date guidelines for judges and school officials as well."

Again, as far as this goes, it is a virtue of the latest ruling. Up-to-date guidelines patently are needed, as the experience since 1954 shows.

But whether they are now actually provided, except in the specific edict on busing, is more difficult to say. The court may be correctly standing on principle, but the application and the working out lie ahead. Justice Burger himself says, "We are concerned with the elimination of the discrimination inherent in the dual school systems, not with the myriad factors of human existence which can cause indiscrimination in a multitude of ways on racial, religious or ethnic grounds." Further, he says that "The remedy for segregation may be administratively awkward, inconvenient and even bizarre in some cases . . ."

If this estimate of the situation proves correct — and it is hard to see how it will not — the ruling just handed down is likely to be fought over as often and in as many ways at the original one in 1954. Constitutional principles have been rightly reasserted, but attempts at specific application or objection will probably lead right back to the welter of the courts again. Just for an example, even while handing down its decision the high court held that fixed racial ratios are not required in all schools of a community, thus leaving open a question sure to be brandished pro or con. Nor did the decision close in on the question of de facto school segregation, the common source of racial separation in many Northern communities as opposed to de jure segregation in the South.

Again, coming to the specific issue of busing, the Supreme Court's decision may be correct constitutionally, but from the point of education it is bound to meet the same objections that obtained before. From the Administration down, there are sincere educators who believe in the neighborhood-school concept as the best way to give good education, and who oppose busing for the sake of all youngsters alike. They may be right, they may be wrong, but for all the Supreme Court's ruling the argument will continue. This is hardly to say the court has not striven its very best to insure equal education. It is only to point out that the problem is an intensely complicated one, and that while guidelines have been laid down once again, the working out is decidedly yet to come.

The New York Times

New York, N. Y., April 22, 1971

Although the Supreme Court has ruled unanimously that busing of pupils to achieve school desegregation is constitutional, the issue at the heart of Chief Justice Burger's opinion is not busing at all. It is rather the Court's belief that the school authorities of Charlotte, N. C., and other Southern districts, have openly defied the 1954 Supreme Court ruling that outlawed the maintenance of dual school systems.

Chief Justice Burger does not minimize the legitimate objections to extensive busing, particularly to that of young children over long distances. He also acknowledges the undesirability of fixed mathematical norms—and explicitly recognizes that some schools, because of their location, will in fact remain segregated.

But the ruling—with all nine Justices in agreement—emphasizes that the district under review had deliberately maintained a segregated system at least until 1969 and that the school board had "totally defaulted in its acknowledged duty to come forward with an acceptable plan of its own, notwithstanding the patient efforts of the district judge. . . ."

Because busing has become so intensely political an issue—made more so since President Nixon has deliberately exploited it—the real significance of the Burger ruling is in danger of being obscured. The opinion underscores the fact that bus transportation has been an integral part of public education for years, making possible the transition from the one-room schoolhouse to the regional school. A giant transportation system is used by well over one-third of the total public school population, largely unrelated to integration.

But busing has also long been the tool of many Southern districts for the specific purpose of maintaining segregation. The Charlotte district, for example, had been transporting 23,600 pupils of all ages for an average one-way trip of over an hour. Under the district court's ruling, now upheld by the Supreme Court, one-way transportation would not have required "over 35 minutes at most."

The Chief Justice concedes that in the absence of a history of discrimination, "it might well be desirable to assign pupils to schools nearest their homes." It is precisely because, in the case under review and many others like it, discrimination has been deliberately perpetuated in direct violation of the 1954 ruling that some uncomfortable remedies are now held legitimate. Even so, the opinion emphasizes the need to make such remedies realistic and workable.

At the same time, Chief Justice Burger has served notice to those inside and outside the Administration who would ignore or obstruct earlier rulings identified with his predecessor that he does not intend to allow the Supreme Court to be undercut or influenced by political pressures in the area of civil rights.

THE SUN

Baltimore, Md., April 22, 1971

A unanimous Supreme Court has taken the next logical step in the series of rulings that began in 1954, when forced school segregation by race was held to be unconstitutional. Since then the federal judiciary has said time and again that not only must old separate school systems be discarded, but also that officials have a duty to take affirmative actions to see that actual desegregation follows legal desegregation.

Though the court was once again unanimous in its finding, this most recent decision is going to be controversial. There are two aspects of the ruling to which many Southerners strongly object, and there is no shortage of political leaders willing to make political capital out of this resentment. True political leadership would be to urge acceptance of the inevitable ruling, and to search for ways to improve both the educational systems in the region and the relations between the races. We single out the South because the ruling singles out the South and the Border states which once had dual school systems.

The aspect of the ruling Southerners will object to most is of course that having to do with busing. The court says that the neighborhood school concept is not acceptable in a formerly dual system if the results are segregation. Since that is the usual result, the affirmative action school systems may be ordered to take, the court ruled, is busing students past their "neighborhood school" to a distant one. For years that practice has been accepted in the white South if the schools at the end of the trip were all-white. Those who oppose it now do so for reasons that are race-related. The court has said very clearly now for 17 years that such opposition to school desegregation may not prevail.

The second aspect of the court's ruling that Southerners are going to object to is that having to do with racial ratios. The court said these may be used by school officials to decide how students will be assigned, and by courts to test the equity of assignment plans. Southerners have insisted that since assigning pupils to meet a ratio meant using race as a basis for official action, this was forbidden by the 1954 decision. The court now has unequivocally rejected that argument.

Many Southern spokesmen are saying that the court is discriminating again, and that de facto school segregation in the North is allowed to stand even though that is no different from what now exists in the South. That is true. The court said pointedly that the constitutionality of the sort of school segregation that exists where there was never a dual school system is not an issue in "this case":

"We do not reach in this case the question whether a showing that school segregation is a consequence of other types of state action, without any discriminatory action by the school authorities, is a constitutional violation requiring remedial action by a school desegregation decree." Many people believe de facto segregation does result from state actions and is unconstitutional.

What this decision does is force the South to be equal to the North in doing away with every vestige—and legacy—of a dual school system. School systems that meet that requirement and then resegregate along Northern lines will presumably be as constitutional in North Carolina as in North Dakota. Or as unconstitutional. The Chief Justice said, "It does not follow that the communities . . . will remain demographically stable. . . .

Neither school authorities nor district courts are required to make year-by-year adjustments of the racial composition of student bodies once the affirmative duty to desegregate has been accomplished."

"This case" then has brought the South to equity with the North. That is the meaning of the decision. Some future case will deal with the national problem of segregated schools in our society. Perhaps busing and racial ratios will be required everywhere. What seems clear now is that they will eventually be required everywhere or nowhere.

That is exactly as it should be. Rights of Americans should no more be based on geography than on race. Furthermore, as many Negro children attend schools in the North and West as in the South now. So both the Census and the Supreme Court have set the stage for a national resolution of our dilemma. Yesterday the Senate refused to face up to the issue, when presented with a plan for national desegregation. But the issue is here to stay, and senators will, we hope, think some more about such plans.

Minneapolis Tribune

Minneapolis, Minn., April 25, 1971

The beginning of the so-called Southern Strategy was seen in the presidential campaign of 1968. Candidate Richard M. Nixon told a television audience in Charlotte, N.C., that while he agreed with the 1954 Supreme Court decision against school segregation, he did not agree that the federal government and courts should act as local school districts in determining how to carry out the decision.

The end of that strategy came last week when the Supreme Court upheld massive school busing, as ordered by a federal court, to eliminate the dual school system in that same city of Charlotte. The importance of the ruling, in our view, cannot be overemphasized. The court directly rejected President Nixon's oft-stated case against compulsory busing to achieve racial balance, implicitly exposing the hypocrisy of northerners and southerners who have used busing to achieve racial separation. The court, in effect, said that a federal judge was "reasonable" in ordering the cross-town busing of an additional 13,000 students in Charlotte and Mecklenburg County to reach, as closely as possible, a 71-29 white-black ratio in each school. The court ruling was unanimous, it had the support of two Nixon appointees, it was written by Chief Justice Warren E. Burger.

The Supreme Court, it is true, did not rule on the issue of de-facto school segregation in northern schools. That issue was not before the justices, and the court traditionally is not prone to go beyond the immediate questions in a case up for decision. But the court did give powerful support to the cause of school integration in the North. The court did so first by its sanction of busing as an integration vehicle. The court did so most of all by exerting a leadership on the integration issue that has been so lacking at both the local and the national levels.

This leadership, this assertion that there are certain principles that must be followed, can have a powerful influence on public attitudes. The Harris Survey has shown that the effect of last fall's Supreme Court decree against school segregation was to increase public support for desegregation. Now, as a result of court rulings, the South actually is leading the North on school integration. The ratio of black pupils attending integrated schools went from 18 percent to 38 percent in the South in the past two years, while the ratio remained at 27 percent in the North. So, as Minneapolis agonizes over a two-school pairing plan, whites in Sumter, S.C., are attending a junior high school where they are outnumbered by blacks 4 to 1.

And in a fascinating reversal of roles, a white student says, "It's all right. Quite a few Negroes are friendly with us in class now. They weren't at first, but they are now. They cut up with us just like we are all the same race."

Detroit Free Press

Detroit, Mich., April 22, 1971

THOUGH the Supreme Court disclaims any intent to apply its findings in southern school cases to northern situations, those who read Chief Burger's opinion carefully will find it freighted with implications for schools everywhere, including the Detroit metropolitan area.

The nub of the court's finding is this: "All things being equal, with no history of discrimination, it might well be desirable to assign pupils to schools nearest their homes. But all things are not equal in a system that has been deliberately constructed and maintained to enforce racial segregation."

Thus, the court concludes, there is very little, if anything, that can be construed at this point as de facto segregation in a school system where a history of discrimination exists. Discrimination in southern cities is no accident, the court concludes, and the district courts have broad, albeit not completely unlimited, powers to decide on appropriate corrective actions.

The court has decided the case on the simplest ground it could find—that southern cities such as Charlotte have a history of affinity for a dual, and therefore, illegal, school system and that the vestigial segregation because of neighborhood patterns is in fact a result of public policy.

It is a short leap, although the court chose not to make it now, from there to the argument that there is virtually no such thing as accidental or de facto segregation in the country. The Detroit case, now before the federal district court, is exploring this very issue. Already there has been elaborate testimony that the segregation that exists in Detroit schools is also no accident and that it results from official policies, if not from the policies of the school board itself.

Detroiters ought not to feel too secure, we daresay, behind the argument that the Detroit schools are not characterized by the same history of discrimination that has brought southern schools under the Supreme Court's watchful eye. It is our conviction that the courts will ultimately tell us that public policies—past use of contracts, school site location, political subdivision lines—have tended to perpetuate discrimination and that new policies must be drawn to change the pattern.

The court is closing in on all the accumulated record of discrimination that exists in the country. It has thus far limited itself to the South, but the clear implication is that a great deal of the segregation in America is vulnerable to the finding that it is intentional.

That tendency may not work to its logical conclusion before the people of Charlotte chafe some more against what will seem to them to be, and doubtless is, a double standard. Our past hypocricies are catching up with us, though, and we may soon learn that the due bill for those years of "accidental" segregation is greater than we imagined.

Ironically, Chief Justice Burger's opinion in effect tells the lower courts dealing with urban southern school districts to get on with the job and be done with it. The promise for southerners is that the end of the agony over desegregation is at hand.

For others whose records on patterns of discrimination are less than spotless, the promise is that the court will deal with our misdeeds too.

THE KANSAS CITY STAR

Kansas City, Mo., April 23, 1971

What the Supreme court is saying on racial integration or desegregation in the schools is unclear at this point. The court seems to have said that federal judges can order bussing to achieve a racial mix. But under what circumstances and where? The court says this *may* be done. Does this then mean that when a suit is filed in a given locality that the federal district judge decides the issue on the basis of his own background and inclination? What is enough integration and what is too much desegration and how far can people be either accommodated or inconvenienced to achieve a racial balance?

Anguished outcries are coming from the South where it is believed that the court has once again singled out the old Confederacy as a target of persecution. Yet the decision does not appear to be the final downfall of school segregation that exists because of real estate selling practices that have set population distribution in a metropolitan area. In fact Chief Justice Warren E. Burger says that the series of decisions marks the end of official or state sanctioned *de jure* segregation. That would seem to leave alone the *de facto* segregation in the schools

that exists not because of any overt attempt by school officials but through real estate patterns which in many metropolitan areas separate the central city and the suburbs. The chief justice does mention discriminatory action by school authorities leading to a *de jure* condition out of one that had been merely *de facto* in the past. It appears that the federal district courts have been given wide latitude to step in and decide what is right or wrong, and which children can be bussed and under what circumstances.

Yet the rulings are far from plain. Do they apply only within a district—such as the Kansas City district with a mixed racial population—or would they fall with equal force in the Shawnee Mission school district or the Center, Raytown or North Kansas City districts with the judges able to cross district boundaries and other political subdivisions including county and state lines? It would be meaningless to say that Shawnee Mission or North Kansas City should integrate further because there are so few minority students in those districts. Such an order could have an entirely different meaning in the South, or in Kansas City or Kansas City,

Kansas, where there are substantial minority populations within the district.

If judges can't order bussing across boundaries, then the result of the decisions from Washington might only speed the flight to the suburbs across state, county or district lines. The intent of the court is not clear and there is wide disagreement on what the justices really mean. There does seem to be a constant, common failing in Washington in all branches of government to recognize that some of the biggest urban concentrations in the country are spread over many school districts and counties and sometimes over two or more states.

As of now various partisans are interpreting the court decisions according to their diverse hopes and fond wishes. Some are saying that the South is finally doomed. Others say that the decisions apply everywhere, in the North and across boundaries. But nobody knows. Surely the high court cannot have intended that these matters be left to judicial whim on a regional basis. The word from Washington is obscure.

ALBUQUERQUE JOURNAL

Albuquerque, N. M., April 21, 1971

Seventeen years after the Warren Supreme Court's historic decision calling for a halt to school segregation, the end may be finally in sight.

This week the nation's highest tribunal under Chief Justice Warren E. Burger unanimously ruled that federal courts may order busing of public school children as a means of desegregating schools.

The landmark o p i n i o n established guidelines — which school officials across the South

long had claimed were lacking — on busing, revamping of school district boundaries, plus a certain amount of deliberately imposed "racial balance" if needed to eliminate "all vestiges of state-imposed" segregation.

Dismissing arguments against busing, the court said transportation has been an integral and normal part of the public education system for years, with 18 million (39 per cent) of the nation's public school children

trnsported by bus in 1969-70.

"Desegregation plans cannot be limited to the walk-in school," the court declared.

B u r g e r ' s opinion said neighborhood school zoning also is unconstitutional if it does not accomplish desegregation. "All things being equal, with no history of discrimination, it might well be desirable to assign pupils to schools nearest their homes. But all things are not equal in the system that has

been deliberately constructed and maintained to enforce racial segregation.

The court's stand runs counter to announced Nixon administration positions in opposition to massive busing and in support of the neighborhood-school concept.

But as Burger said: "Our objective remains what it was May 17, 1954 — to eliminate state-imposed segregation. At no time has the court deviated from this objective."

The Boston Globe

Boston, Mass., April 22, 1971

The once popular Federal District Judge James B. McMillan, whose school desegregation decision has been unanimously upheld by the United States Supreme Court, can no longer get up a golf foursome at his Charlotte, N.C., club even though he is an excellent golfer and a witty companion at the 19th hole.

This is how deep racial bigotry runs in his community. And yet, all that he had ruled and all that the Supreme Court now has upheld is the truth that all men are created equal (though they certainly do not remain that way) and that the violation of one group's constitutional rights can be permitted only at the intolerable risk of the constitutional rights of all.

Judge McMillan for 54 years had shared in what he now describes as "ingrained centuries of Southern white prejudice against the Negro without thinking through the prob-

lem." He would very much have liked to arrive at a decision that would have pleased his neighbors:

"But if the people of the community knew the facts as the court has been required to learn and understand them, they would reach about the same conclusion this court"— and now the Supreme Court—"has reached."

These conclusions are far from earth-shaking as either new or revolutionary doctrine. The surprise, if it is one, is that the Burger Court has the same strong convictions as did the Warren Court 17 years ago. This alone should convince segregationists that their's is, as it ought to be, a losing battle against common decency and good sense—not to mention good law. The decision merely suggests that there is nothing sacred about the neighborhood school, and that busing children to other schools

is a constitutional way of dismantling legally enforced but illegal separation of races.

The decision does not even touch de facto segregation in the North, which could be one reason for Southern charges of discrimination—odd word in this context. For that matter, it does not ban "some small number of one-race or virtually one-race schools within a district" except where "a school system has been deliberately constructed and maintained to enforce racial segregation." The dismay of some Southerners is inexplicable, for they are denied nothing which is theirs either legally or by any other right.

The decision is interpreted by some as indicating that Chief Justice Warren E. Burger "is charting his own course without regard to the disposition of President Nixon, who appointed him." Cited are the

facts that Mr. Nixon esteems the neighborhood school as almost sacrosanct and Mr. Burger so regards it only when all else is equal. Only the justices can settle this one, and they are hardly likely to make the effort.

The decision is a good one. But, busing or no busing, it is the quality of education at the end of the line which is the important thing, as state Superintendent of Schools Neil V. Sullivan has said. And again, busing or no busing, de facto segregation, as in Boston, is as evil in fact if not intent as is de jure segregation in the South.

Busing is a necessary step at this time. But the final answer to integration in the schools lies in the long overdue integration of the whole society and of the opportunities enjoyed by its members. The decision in this is a moral one, not in the court's jurisdiction.

WINSTON-SALEM JOURNAL

Winston-Salem, N. C., September 2, 1971

ONCE again, statements by a high government official have thrown parents, school officials and lawyers into complete confusion about a school desegregation case. First it was the President. Then it was Gov. Wallace. And now it is the Chief Justice of the United States himself, Mr. Warren Burger.

The chief justice's comments on the Winston-Salem/Forsyth County school case have, of course, produced maximum confusion here, but people all over the South are trying to figure out what the chief justice was getting at, and what possible effect his remarks will have in their own school systems.

Let us try to sort things out.

First of all, it is clear that the school plan and all the buses will continue to roll into the fall, perhaps into the winter — and possibly from now on. The chief justice refused to allow the school board any delay in carrying out the new assignment plan.

Secondly, the chief justice obviously thinks that in the controversial matter of "racial balance," both the school board and the Middle District Court misinterpreted the Supreme Court's April decision in the Charlotte-Mecklenburg case.

But apparently the misinterpretation is mainly a matter of *language*, not of substance. In April, the Supreme Court made it clear that it was not requiring "racial balance" — that is, a situation in which "every school in every community must always reflect the racial composition of the school system as a whole." The court went on to say that if the Charlotte plan had required exact mathematical ratios in every school, or something very close to it, the court would have rejected the plan. But, the court said, this "racial balance" was used only as a starting point, and significant differences in racial composition were allowed by the lower court — therefore the Charlotte plan was acceptable.

It is true that the *language* used by our own school board's attorneys seemed to show that the board had misinterpreted the ruling. The school board stated in its brief that it was "required . . . to achieve a racial balance throughout the system which will be acceptable to the Court." And that, of course, was not true. But what the board said and what it *did* in devising a plan are two different things. If enrollments which vary from 18 per cent black children in some schools to 36 per cent in others amounts to "racial balance," then the term is utterly meaningless.

Further, we can find nothing whatever in the District Court's order of June 22 which suggests that this court demanded "racial balance" from our own school board.

Thirdly, the chief justice criticized the school board for not supplying enough details on our busing for him to determine whether a delay should be granted or not, and in this rebuke he seems to be at least partly justified. School board members say that it was impossible to supply exact times and distances before the plan was actually put into effect, but some effort should have been made to supply the chief justice with educated guesses, at any rate.

Fourth, there is no positive assurance in the chief justices's statements about busing that the Supreme Court (if it agrees to review our case) will order a reduction of busing in the current school plan. He did restate the court's opinion that busing was not necessary in cases where the health of the children or the education process would be harmed and that ages, distances and other factors could be considered. But in a footnote to his comments Tuesday, the chief justice said that he would consider as "extreme" a situation in which children rode the bus for three hours daily. And except where foul-ups occur, no Forsyth child is bused that long. The chief justice may well have picked three hours at random, and he is also speaking for himself, not the full court. So no one can predict whether the court will consider *some* of the busing in this county as "extreme."

Finally, the chief justice was obviously irritated not only by what he considered insufficient information, but by the fact that he was pressed for time because the school board's appeal reached him less than a week before school opened here. The chief justice's opinion in the Pentagon Papers case showed great irritation at the fact that the court was pressed into acting quickly on the case, and apparently his irritation is no less in the Forsyth County case.

Although granting a delay would have caused a break in the school term and unlimited difficulties for school authorities here, perhaps we would have been better off if the chief justice had done just that. It would have been better still if he had made no comment at all. Instead, he said in effect, "Keep the buses rolling, but from the little information I have, somebody is mixed up down there."

And now, thousands of parents and children have gotten the totally mistaken idea that no further desegregation than last year's plan was really required, while others are justifiably wondering: Will this confusion ever end?

TWIN CITY SENTINEL

Winston-Salem, N. C.

September 2, 1971

SINCE his appointment to the Supreme Court, Chief Justice Warren Burger has shown himself to be a testy man with a short fuse on his patience.

On at least one public occasion he exploded at the sight of a microphone and demanded that it be removed before he would speak.

In the recent case involving the New York Times and the Pentagon papers, he recorded his resentment at being hurried into an opinion and demonstrated his irritation during the questioning of the Times' attorneys.

Now, in the Forsyth County school case, the chief justice was again asked to act in a hurry—that is, in four days or less. Again he showed his irritation. And in letting this irritation sway him he inexcusably added further confusion to an already bad situation.

This irritation led him into an apparently unjustified criticism of Judge Eugene Gordon. It was Judge Gordon's opinion of June 22 requiring the Forsyth schools to do as much in the way of desegregation as the Charlotte schools that gave impetus to the school board's present busing plan.

Throughout the chief justice's opinion of Tuesday runs the assumption that Judge Gordon required the board to achieve "racial balance" in the schools. We have carefully searched Judge Gordon's opinions in the Forsyth case and we find no evidence whatsoever to support this assumption by Chief Justice Burger.

Almost certainly the chief justice was drawn into this mistake by the Forsyth school board's brief. This brief says that the board was "required" by the federal courts to "achieve a racial balance throughout the system."

Despite this language, however, it is perfectly clear that the school board's plan does not achieve "racial balance," or anything very close to it. Different schools have enrollments of black children that range all the way from 18 per cent to 36 per cent, and Judge Gordon specifically gave the school board the authority to make limited changes even in *that* widely varying range.

It is entirely possible — though by no means certain — that the Supreme Court will review the Forsyth case later this year and will hold that *some* of the busing here works too great a hardship on the children and on the education process. At best, one might guess, 1,000 or so children out of 18,000 added to the busing lists might be affected.

But this is by no means made clear in the chief justice's language of Tuesday or in the April decision of the Supreme Court.

Meanwhile, the chief justice has vastly increased the bitterness and confusion here by sounding off — but not doing anything tangible — about a school plan which, he confesses, he knows very little about.

He could hardly have done a greater disservice to the people of this county.

The Charlotte Observer

Charlotte, N. C., September 3, 1971

Chief Justice Warren Burger's statement about the Winston-Salem schools ought to make clearer what already should have been clear: that the Supreme Court's Charlotte-Mecklenburg school decision does not compel schools everywhere to have a racial balance.

In that decision last April the court said if Judge James McMillan had held that "any particular degree of racial balance was a matter of constitutional right" it would have reversed him. "The constitutional command to desegregate schools does not mean that every school in every community must always reflect the racial composition of the school system as a whole," the court said. But, it noted, Judge McMillan was within bounds in requiring his "very limited use of the racial ratio" as "a starting point."

The court stressed that the judge's decision was within his discretionary powers and fitted Charlotte-Mecklenburg's circumstances. And repeatedly it emphasized that circumstances elsewhere might require different solutions. The objective is to dissolve dual school systems, not to put children on buses or keep them off buses.

In Winston-Salem, U.S. District Judge Eugene Gordon has ordered a desegregation plan that has some parallels with Charlotte's. The Fourth Circuit Court of Appeals has approved it. It is important to note that Chief Justice Burger, although he suggested that Judge Gordon may have misread the Charlotte decision as a mandate to do the same everywhere, did not stay the Winston-Salem order. It remains to be seen whether the full court will reverse Judge Gordon.

In any event, the court's order in the Charlotte case stands.

We cannot judge the propriety of Judge Gordon's ruling in Winston-Salem. We cannot say whether Judge Gordon misread the Charlotte decision, or whether he acceptably fashioned his Winston-Salem solution from the specific circumstances at hand there. It does appear that Judge Gordon was not quite doing what the chief justice suggests: in the Winston-Salem plan, the percentage of black students ranges from 18 to 36 — hardly a flat racial-balance requirement throughout. We will simply have to wait to see what the full court says.

In any case, Chief Justice Burger's comments on Winston-Salem were certainly no retreat from Chief Justice Burger's decision on Charlotte. In the chief justice's view, some Southern federal judges apparently think they **must** require racial ratios under virtually any circumstances. He simply wanted to further emphasize that no one is entitled to racially-balanced schools by constitutional right, but that racial-balance orders sometimes may be found to be the best way of undoing past segregation.

Charlotte can move on according to plan. Chairman William E. Poe of the Charlotte-Mecklenburg Board of Education, although he still seems to have unfounded hopes that the Supreme Court will back away from the Charlotte decision, has sounded a good note in saying there has been a turn in attitude in Charlotte. "Most people are right impatient now to get on with the job of education," he said Wednesday night. We thing, so, too, and we see the new school opening as the beginning of a new and better era.

The Birmingham News

Birmingham, Ala., September 4, 1971

Many people have waited a long time for the U. S. Supreme Court to define clearly the terms it uses in its school integration decisions.

For instance. the "unitary" school system: At what point does a "dual system" become a "unitary" system?

It seemed from the court's decision on Charlotte, N. C., in which it upheld busing as an instrument to implement desegregation plans, that racial balancing was the criterion; that each school had to reflect the racial ratios of the system as a whole to be properly 'unitary."

Now Chief Justice Warren E. Burger has dispelled this notion. In refusing to stay a busing plan for Winston-Salem and Forsyth, N.C., he said that federal judges misunderstood the high court if they thought racial balance in every school was required.

In one sense, this clarification— if it can truly be called that—is welcome. Precise racial balancing as a requirement would be arbitrary and troublesome to implement if it were to be applied in every case. For one thing, it requires the assignment of students to schools on the basis of race—something which the court rejected in 1954. For another, it would work hardships on school officials— as indeed it already has in areas where it is in force — in providing transportation and school facilities out of existing funds.

In another sense, the Burger statement unglues whatever certainties might have formed since Charlotte. Now the judges, lawyers and school officials up and down the line must be puzzling once again over just what is required.

So there will be even more confusion.

But while racial balancing has the precision inherent in numbers, it is nevertheless unreasonable as a requirement in every school system.

The confusion, then, will be worth it if it is temporary: That is, if the court will move soon to formulate some criteria which are reasonable and at the same time clear.

But we cannot continue forever to wallow in this sea of uncertainty. The court must become as articulate in stating what is required and acceptable as it has been in rejecting that which is not acceptable and observing what is not required.

Meanwhile, those who wait for certainty on the issue are left once again treading water.

St. Petersburg Times

St. Petersburg, Fla., September 2, 1971

President Nixon, whose previous words have given encouragement to the disrupters and boycotters, now has relayed word that he is proud of the quiet acceptance of desegregation in many southern school districts. That is like a child who played with matches admiring the work of the fire department in putting out the fire.

We have difficulty in believing the President's sincerity — both times.

AS ALWAYS, racial issues this year have brought out some of the best in many people and the worst in some politicians. Two examples:

✔ Chief Justice Warren E. Burger seemed to be playing Mr. Nixon's politics with his strange restatement of the court's April 20 decision on Charlotte, N.C. Burger felt the Winston-Salem school board misunderstood. A chief justice hardly was needed to tell the board to re-read the original decision. Of course there is no constitutional command of uniform racial ratios. There IS a command to end discrimination. And many school boards wisely have decided that there are sound educational reasons to achieve a stable racial makeup in all schools. Burger's expression changes nothing. His timing certainly does not increase confidence in the non-political performance of the chief justice.

✔ Elliot L. Richardson, secretary of Health, Education and Welfare, apparently lacks the backbone to stand up for his own convictions. He now is in "total agreement" with Mr. Nixon on busing. Well, why did Richardson prescribe busing in Austin, Tex., which Mr. Nixon disavowed? When thousands of southern schools were built in locations to maintain segregation, how else does Richardson intend to achieve integration?

THE LOUISVILLE TIMES

Louisville, Ky., September 3, 1971

Chief Justice Burger's unusual pronouncement this week confuses rather than clarifies the murky and emotional school busing debate. By choosing to follow the White House line rather than reiterating what the Supreme Court said in its unanimous ruling last spring, he presumes to speak for his fellow justices while undermining their independence of the political process.

Both actions are dangerous.

The Chief Justice suggested, in refusing to delay a plan to use busing to achieve racial balance in schools in Winston-Salem, N.C., that some federal judges are misreading the court's April busing decision involving schools in Charlotte - Mecklenburg County, N.C. He found it "disturbing" that the Winston-Salem board believed "it was required to achieve a fixed 'racial balance' that reflected the total composition of the school district" because that "suggests the possibility that there may be a misreading" of the Charlotte opinion.

There was nothing unclear about that opinion. The syllabus in the court's own official reports sums it up quite well:

1. "The constitutional command to desegregate schools does not mean that every school in the community must always reflect the racial composition of the system as a whole; . . . limited use of the racial ratio . . . as a starting point in shaping a rem-

edy . . ." is within a court's discretion.

2. "While the existence of a small number of one-race, or virtually one-race, schools does not in itself denote a system that still practices segregation by law, the court should scrutinize such schools and require the school authorities to satisfy the court that the racial composition does not result from . . . discriminatory action. . . ."

3. ". . . A student assignment plan is not acceptable merely because it appears to be neutral, for such a plan may fail to counteract the continuing effects of past school segregation . . . No rigid rules can be laid down to govern conditions in different localities."

4. ". . . . The remedial technique of requiring bus transportation as a tool of school desegregation" is within the power of the courts. "An objection to transportation of students may have validity when the time or distance of travel is so great as to risk either the health of the children or significantly impinge on the educational process. . . ."

"No fixed or even substantially fixed guideline can be established as to how far a court can go, but it must be recognized that there are limits," the chief justice went on to write in that opinion. "The objective is to dismantle the dual school system." To

do so, he continued, the Supreme Court "must of necessity rely to a large extent . . . on the informed judgments of the district courts . . . and on courts of appeals."

There is a danger in this even greater than the one posed by the chief justice's apparent willingness to subordinate the law to White House politics. It is that this nation will be diverted by the red-herring of busing from the pressing demand, as the Supreme Court put it in 1968, that we push forward ". . . now . . . until it is clear that state-imposed segregation has been completely removed."

What the chief justice said this week—and what Mr. Nixon has been saying all along — has no weight alongside those words. The President is playing politics with all his talk about busing to the "minimum necessary extent" and his praise for the virtues of the neighborhood school while ignoring the continued presence of racial segregation. Now the chief justice appears to join him, without waiting for judicial questions raised by the April decision to come— as they eventually will—before the high court. All his words will do is make more timid, less certain of what is demanded of them, district and appeals judges and school officials all over the nation.

Honolulu Star-Bulletin

Honolulu, Hawaii, September 2, 1971

With a specific statement on the subject by Chief Justice Warren E. Burger, it appears that the concept of busing to achieve racial balance in public schools, already under widespread attack, faces its severest test to date.

Last spring the Supreme Court issued a decision which has since been widely interpreted by lower courts as requiring racial balance in each separate school. Busing to achieve this effect was thereupon ordered.

Among the schools where such an order is being carried out are those in the judicial circuit including North Carolina. The Chief Justice is the member of the high court who supervises this district. He said in a statement Tuesday— the Supreme Court is in summer recess—that it would be inappropriate for him as supervising judge to interfere at this stage in the Winston-Salem desegregation program. But in an unusual 10-page opinion he wrote:

"If the court of appeals or the district court read this court's (the Supreme Court's) opinion as requiring a fixed racial balance or quota, they would appear to have overlooked specific language of the opinion in the case to the contrary."

He then quoted language from the relevant decision that said "the constitutional command to desegregate schools does not mean that every school in every community must always reflect the racial composition of the school system as a whole."

He said the judges must calculate a school district's racial balance as a starting point to decide "whether in fact

any violation existed," but that the judges were not required to use busing in an attempt to achieve this balance in each school.

What the Chief Justice appears to be saying is that there must be a racial balance in the district but not necessarily in each school. Why he didn't say precisely this, if this is what he meant, is what often baffles the layman who attempts to read judicial language. He admits by implication that the wording of the original decision was sufficiently obtuse to have confused lower court judges attempting to apply it.

President Nixon is, of course, on record as opposing busing to achieve racial balance in individual schools. He has said the neighborhood school should be preserved. Chinese families in San Francisco are up in arms over the prospect of having their children bused to mixed schools where they will lack instruction in Chinese culture. Gov. George C. Wallace of Alabama is militantly refusing to obey the court order which Chief Justice Burger has now appeared to water down. And children as well as parents, both white and black, are reluctant to be transported across town just to sit in schoolrooms with children of another race.

Busing, it appears, is in for its severest test. The Chief Justice has opened the biggest loophole for those who oppose it. He has now said that the Supreme Court didn't say what the lower courts have generally agreed it did say in the case of Swann v. Charlotte-Mecklenburg Board of Education.

THE DAILY OKLAHOMAN

Oklahoma City, Okla., September 1, 1971

ONCE the courts had read into the Constitution a mandate against discrimination in the schools, it followed that factors other than race would emerge eventually to complicate a situation already becoming chaotic.

Not race but social and economic status is the governing consideration in a far-reaching decision by the California Supreme Court which threatens public-school financing not only in that state but in most of the other 49 states.

The court says California's public-school financing system — based largely on property taxes — is unconstitutional because it discriminates against the poor. Because of its wide application if allowed to stand, the ruling predictably will be appealed to the United States Supreme Court.

The California ruling falls back on the 14th Amendment's commodious equal protection clause which provides the constitutional writ for just about the entire body of new law the courts have been generating in this field ever since the Supreme Court entered the thicket back in 1954.

The concept that the public schools are under an obligation to strive for socio-economic as well as racial balance isn't new. U. S. Circuit Court of Appeals Judge J. Skelly Wright propounded it in a ruling on June 19, 1967, ordering drastic measures to modify de facto segregation in the public schools of the District of Columbia.

In the abstract, there's much to be said for the principle of equalizing educational opportunities through a more even-handed distribution of available school funds. Wide acceptance of this principle underlies the various equalization formulas used by most states as a means of supplementing the revenues of their poorer districts.

The California court correctly notes that the amount a school district can spend depends largely on its tax base. "Although the amount of money raised locally is also a function of the rate at which residents of a district are willing to tax themselves," says the court, "as a practical matter, districts with small tax bases simply cannot levy taxes at a rate sufficient to produce the revenue that more affluent districts reap with minimal tax efforts."

But in their efforts to run the schools, the courts too often confine themselves to the philosophical aspects without paying sufficient heed to the practical consequences of what they are ordering. To junk the present financing system and replace it with statewide taxes to be applied evenly on a per-pupil basis would have profound repercussions on school districts already staggering under far-reaching and often unrealistic busing requirements.

Public resistance to court-ordered busing is hardening as enforcement efforts spread from the South to other sections of the country where classroom segregation long has reflected segregated housing patterns. Resistance ranges all the way from a new spate of anti-busing litigation to bus bombings and outright defiance of court orders by local school boards.

President Nixon says he is instructing the attorney general and the Department of Health, Education and Welfare to "work with individual school districts to hold busing to the minimum required by law." But what is the law? Chief Justice Warren Burger indicates that some of the lower courts mistakenly are reading into the Supreme Court's Charlotte-Mecklenburg ruling a constitutional requirement for "racial balance" in every district.

Once the Constitution is accepted to mean whatever the judges choose to read into it, there is only confusion. In the words of Macaulay, the Constitution then is "all sail and no anchor."

The Chattanooga Times

Chattanooga, Tenn., September 3, 1971

We wouldn't have believed it possible, but Chief Justice Warren Burger has managed to confuse the public to an even greater extent on judicial authority to end racial segregation in public schools.

In refusing to permit a delay in a court order involving a North Carolina county school system—a matter ordinarily disposed of in a very few words — the Chief Justice wrote a 10-page opinion setting out what the Supreme Court meant, or didn't mean, in its now famous *Swann* busing decision of last April.

Two points need to be made right here. One is that the Chief Justice refused to hold up a program ordering the extensive busing of children in order to achieve a given racial ratio in the schools of the affected county. The second is that the order is not an opinion of the Supreme Court and carries no such weight or authority. It may have been intended as clarification; if so, we fear it missed its mark.

Mr. Chief Justice Burger then warned lower courts they were not to interpret the decision as requiring "a fixed balance or quota" in all the schools of a system. Certainly, it has not been so considered here. The city school board, in drawing up its plan for pairing schools and busing students to achieve a generally greater degree of integration than now exists, fixed white to black racial ratios ranging from 20-80 to almost 50-50. U.S. District Judge Frank Wilson approved the program with the exception of the high schools, a situation on which he asked for greater information.

In this week's order, the Chief Justice said judges were not required to use busing in order to achieve a higher degree of integration. He did not say they could not or should not, merely that they were not required to.

What did the *Swann* opinion say? It noted that bus transportation had been an integral part of U.S. schooling for generations and is a permissible remedial technque when ordered to implement desegregation. "Desegregation plans cannot be limited to the walk-in school," it held.

Locally, the school board submitted a program of pairing schools and zoned attendance which, for the convenience and safety of the children, it felt, involved the busing of approximately one-third the students in the system. It was the board's program Judge Wilson approved. The board made busing a part of it.

Actually, someone has figured, the longest bus route planned for public school students is of less distance than the shortest bus trip provided for students of the two major boys preparatory schools here. And, right now, a private school located in the far reaches of suburbia is advertising it can arrange for the transportation of students from any portion of the city—a busing experience of greater duration and without approved vehicles or drivers than conceived for the vast majority of public school students.

As simply as we can put it, the situation is this: The city school board of dedicated citizen-members, under a directive to lower the racial imbalances over the system as a whole, devised a plan it considered best for the students and for the cause of quality education. Judge Wilson, a resident of the community, approved it as falling within the requirements of the higher courts.

No one suggests it pleases everyone; no plan would. But it was locally drawn and locally affirmed. Its acceptance calls upon the highest sense of responsibility of a citizen—obedience to lawful orders from constituted authorities. And that will require the best that lies within us all, thinking now, acting later.

The New York Times

New York, N. Y., September 3, 1971

Secretary of Health, Education and Welfare Richardson, in bowing to President Nixon's antibusing rhetoric and proclaiming it the department's avowed policy, appears to have chosen a familiar political trail. Still visible on that trail are the footsteps of Robert H. Finch, Mr. Richardson's predecessor. He, too, had walked away from his subordinates who felt it their duty to enforce the desegregation law, despite White House orders to put oft-stated principles in cold storage.

Mr. Richardson, after his meeting with the President, insisted that the policies of his department on school busing are "perfectly clear." That clarity obviously eluded those conscientious members of his staff whose desegregation plans were scuttled on orders from the White House and who now face transfer or dismissal if they go beyond the President's mandate for a holddown on busing.

Precisely what the President's policy is, other than a political message to appease George Wallace, remains foggy. H.E.W. staff members are left to tremble under a warning that they will be penalized if they seek to impose busing beyond the minimum required by law. Without a more concrete definition of "the minimum" by Mr. Richardson, his aides are likely to choose between two courses—sit it out in safe passivity or get out.

Secretary Richardson's only hint of how he now interprets the department's mission was in his suggestion that busing should be invoked only where it is required by the courts. This threatens once again to put on Federal judges the major burden of what by now ought to have become largely an administrative responsibility.

No sensible plan of school zoning, whether for educational or integration purposes, should call for unnecessary busing, particularly over long distances. On top of that, Chief Justice Burger has again explained what should have been evident from a reading of earlier rulings—that desegregation does not call for the artificial creation of a "fixed racial balance."

Yet the unmistakable message of this latest, as well as all previous, court rulings is relatively simple: just as busing is indispensable in daily getting millions of children to their schools, it is part and parcel of a wide variety of ways to remove racial barriers which have been deliberately erected and carefully maintained for many decades.

The President's antibusing statements have made doubly difficult the task of those Southern school boards and educators who have sought conscientiously to obey the law. Mr. Richardson's surrender has now put them on notice to expect no moral support from education's spokesman in Washington.

The Washington Post
Times Herald

Washington, D. C., September 3, 1971

"Clear as a bell"—that is the way we characterized Chief Justice Burger's opinion for a unanimous Supreme Court in the Swann case in April—the ruling which held that lower federal courts may authorize a considerable measure of busing, non-contiguous zoning and related procedures for the purpose of overcoming the effects of past official school segregation. What was utterly clear, in our view, was that the court was *not* requiring the use of these techniques for the purpose of creating racial balance; it was upholding their use as an instrument of desegregating school systems that had formerly been segregated by law. This perception did not require an enormous amount of interpretative skill on our part—the Chief Justice made it very plain in the rulings that came down that day:

"If we were to read the holding of the District Court to require, as a matter of substantive constitutional right, any particular degree of racial balance or mixing, that approach would be disapproved and we would be obliged to reverse."

And again:

"The Constitution does not compel any particular degree of racial balance or mixing, but when past and continuing constitutional violations are found, some ratios are likely to be useful starting points in shaping a remedy."

In our estimation, the Chief Justice did no more than restate these principles in his comment the other day on a school case in Forsyth County, North Carolina. While refusing Forsyth County school officials a stay they were seeking (in his capacity as Circuit Justice), Mr. Burger was careful to point out that his turning down of their plea on circumstantial and procedural grounds in no way amounted to an endorsement of certain views taken by the district judge in their case— views that may or may not misread Swann but which suggested to the Forsyth County Board of Education that in consequence of the Swann decision, it was obliged to bus its way to "racial balance." The Chief Justice did not comment on any of the other Southern (or Northern) busing cases now working their way through courts.

There may have been valid reasons for the Chief Justice to restate these fairly obvious facts, to enunciate once again exactly what the court had and had not said in its so-called busing decision last spring, although we are not exactly sure what they were. It is unusual for a justice to write several pages dealing with the merits of a lower court's judgment when he is refusing to stay its execution and the impact of the Chief Justice's words is to question the correctness of that judgment even though he took pains to say the record was too skimpy to permit a definitive conclusion. But be that as it may, the most troubling aspect of the Chief Justice's opinion is the interpretation that may be placed on it by those who oppose busing for any purpose. Because he emphasized only the limits of the Swann decision his words are likely to be used in an effort to persuade lower court judges to do less than that decision actually requires.

This latter point is also applicable, unfortunately, to the White House's repeated forays into the subject. Mr. Nixon and his spokesmen have unceasingly restated their opposition to mandatory busing for the purpose of "achieving racial balance" as if they were opposing something that has been authorized by statute or Supreme Court rulings. The President and his advisers must know as well as anyone else that the overwhelming preponderance of busing schemes now being tested in the courts as well as those which have been put into effect are not the result of court orders to bus for the purpose of achieving "racial balance." Rather they are schemes that come within the meaning of the Swann ruling that certain such measures are permissible and may even be necessary as a means of erasing the vestiges of the old, mainly Southern *de jure* segregated school systems.

After his meeting with the President the other day, HEW Secretary Elliot Richardson indicated that he and Mr. Nixon were in accord on busing—and then went on to restate their position. It is, again, essentially no more and no less than federal statutes and the Swann ruling prescribe. By implying that it somehow *is* different, however, the White House has managed, over time, to undermine public confidence in those busing schemes which have been ordered, to suggest that they are being undertaken in the name of furthering racial balance for its own sake, not in the name of completing the process of desegregation. It is a clever ploy, but has not done much for public understanding. And it has done real harm to those school officials and community leaders in the South who are trying—at some social and political risk to themselves—to gain public acceptance and support of what the courts have authorized, of what is bound to come about.

Arkansas Gazette.

Little Rock, Ark., September 3, 1971

CHIEF JUSTICE Warren Burger has a natural talent both for complicating issues and for saying whatever he has to say at the very worst time or place. So it is that Mr. Chief Justice Burger has chosen the opening week of school, in the climactic stages of desegregation, to unload 10 pages of dicta in a one-judge interim decision that will confuse well-meaning school boards and encourage the enemies of integration to make more mischief.

The Chief Justice's latest performance, in the Winston-Salem integration appeal case, is almost as undiscerning as was his speech delivered in London last month attacking the American system of jurisprudence at the convention of the American Bar Association. Whatever he had to say about the weaknesses of American justice, in contrast to what he clearly regards as the superior British system, would better have been reserved for delivery at home.

Mr. Burger's 10-page dissertation on desegregation lamented what the Chief Justice regarded as a misunderstanding in interpretation of the recent (unanimous) decision in the Charlotte (N.C.) "busing" case. Burger said he was disturbed that the Charlotte decision had been interpreted by the Winston-Salem School Board to mean that fixed racial ratios were required in each school.

What we suspect is that the Chief Jus-

tice has been snookered by the Winston-Salem School Board in its innocent-appearing claim to believing that fixed ratios were required. As the Chief Justice pointed out (and as Governor Bumpers of Arkansas suggested in comment Wednesday), a reading of the Charlotte case opinions makes it explicitly clear that fixed ratios are *not* demanded. We find it difficult to believe that the school board in Winston-Salem did not actually know better than to put words in the Supreme Court's mouth, as it did in the appeal to Mr. Burger.

It has *never* occurred to us that the Supreme Court in the Charlotte case meant that every last school had to have the same racial ratio, equal to the ratio of the school district as a whole. The court's opinions in the Charlotte case made it quite clear that practicalities would be taken into account in each school district. It would be entirely reasonable for a school board, for good reason, to have (let us say) a 20 per cent integration of one school and a 35 per cent integration of another. Yet it does not seem to have occurred to the Chief Justice that the most practical arrangement of all, everything considered, will often be in a plan where all schools are t r e a t e d equally and approximately equal ratios are planned, at least at the beginning, as they have been planned here in the Little Rock School District

In Little Rock, for example, the school

administration can argue rather persuasively that all junior high schools and senior high schools have been treated about the same, with approximately two whites to every black and "busing" provided as necessary. Such an arrangement gives the school system heavy protective armor against charges of favoritism. Once the goal of eliminating racially identifiable schools has been undertaken, there is much to be said for doing a thorough, systematic job of it, as many district courts and school systems have set out to do.

In tight specifics, the Chief Justice's opinion in the Winston-Salem case does not mean very much, because (1.) he did not even stay the extensive integration plan for Winston-Salem (and Forsyth County) that had been ordered, and (2.) he could not speak for the entire court, or indeed for anyone but himself, in delivering himself of this random commentary in a case limited to the stay-order jurisdiction of a single justice.

In its effect on public opinion in the South, however, the Chief Justice's dicta in the Winston-Salem appeal will clutter the business of getting on with school integration, and of employing buses, as it is necessary, to transport students from point X to point Y in the immemorial school bus tradition. Burger's opinion will be used for purposes that he may find unrecognizable.

The Courier-Journal

Louisville, Ky., September 2, 1971

SEVENTEEN YEARS after the Supreme Court declared racially segregated schools inherently unequal, and therefore unconstitutional, the nation is still floundering in a morass of conflicting opinions on the undoing of the sins of the past.

Almost unheard now are the voices, so loud and strident in other years, that called upon the seamier side of the popular mind to defend such ineffable causes as the "Southern way of life" and the "virtue of white womanhood." The sheer monotony of their theme and tone and the evil cloaked in the pious words did them in—first before the bar of justice, later in the minds of the American people. The George Wallaces of the land have had to learn a new vocabulary.

Yet the old fears and prejudices persist, and fearful citizens have gone to extraordinary lengths to avoid embracing the spirit of the law as well as the letter. Western Louisville, for instance, was once an integrated neighborhood with segregated schools. Now it's largely segregated neighborhood with segregated schools. *De jure* merely changed into *de facto* as many of the area's white residents moved farther into the suburban countryside—some in search of an all-white community that could guarantee them an all-white school. The same thing has happened in other parts of the city, other parts of the South, other parts of the nation.

'I'm for . . . whatever it is'

But separate still means unequal, the courts have persisted, and white and Negro children

will go to the same schools even if some have to ride buses across town to find the equality that segregation has made impossible.

So the "neighborhood school" becomes the new rallying point. A bigot like Louise Day Hicks becomes a popular heroine in Boston—that one-time "Athens of the New World"—and rides into Congress on the school busing issue. The same issue throws school boards—many of them well-intentioned—into turmoil, clogs federal court dockets, and resurrects the moribund political life of George Wallace.

Efforts of the Department of Housing, Education and Welfare (HEW) to enforce decisions of the courts are stymied by a President who tells his own appointees to stop what they're doing, but won't tell them what to do instead —not until after the next Election Day, anyway. A once conscientious HEW Secretary backs down and says that he supports whatever it is the President has in mind, if anything.

School boards, sensing from the obfuscation and inaction that the pressure is off, renege on previous agreements. In Michigan, nightriders take the matter into their own hands and burn the buses which would carry their children to school.

The Chief Justice of the United States, after reading what was thought to be a landmark decision authorizing busing in Charlotte and Mecklenburg County, North Carolina, then complains that some federal judges who order busing in their districts are misreading the intent of the Supreme Court's decision.

Confusion. All is confusion, resulting in almost universal unhappiness, very little progress, very little justice.

Because of the refusal of our elected leaders to lead, the citizens are forced once again to start the slow trip up the judicial ladder. The Kentucky Civil Liberties Union and the Legal Aid Society must take to the law to gain a hearing for a plan they say would desegregate Jefferson County's Newburg Elementary School without extensive busing, by redrawing some of the county's school district lines. Similar suits must be filed elsewhere.

Communities divided

Meanwhile, many whites still flee, in search of some all-white, all-affluent Valhalla where they can forget that their country is inhabited by many who are unlike themselves, and the President hints in his "open-housing" policy that it's still possible to build such dreamlands if the suburbanites just play their cards right and watch the language they put into their zoning ordinances.

The fact is, a large number of our people aren't committed to such revolutionary ideas as equality, justice, or any meaning of American patriotism that can't be interpreted in full on a bumper sticker.

This is what's tearing apart many of our schools and our communities. The raucous fights over busing—as distasteful and inadequate as that measure appears to be—are only a symptom of the far more serious disease that troubles us. And the timidity of our leaders suggests that—to them, at least—the disease is preferable to the cure.

Court Decisions: 1972-73

The Supreme Court:
Colorado

C

Court to hear Denver school case. The Supreme Court agreed Jan. 17 to hear the appeal of a group of Negro and Mexican-American parents who were seeking a busing order for desegregation of Denver's public school system.

It would be the court's first school busing case involving a city outside the South.

D

The court would determine what actions, if any, a community had to take to eliminate de facto segregation, which was fostered by segregated housing patterns. In virtually all earlier school integration cases, the court had found de jure segregation, or discriminatory acts by public officials, to be at the root of the segregation and had ordered it eliminated.

The Denver case also presented the court with the problem of deciding whether a large city with many all-black schools resulting from de facto segregation must desegregate at all if it was shown that segregation in some of the schools was encouraged by acts of public officials.

E

The plaintiffs had been seeking in the lower courts an order requiring busing and other integration steps to break up what they said was a concentration of minority group students in 15 of Denver's inner-city schools.

Michigan

F

Detroit school plans barred. U.S. District Court Judge Stephen J. Roth ruled March 28 that "relief of segregation in the public schools of the city of Detroit cannot be accomplished within the corporate geographical limits of the city." He rejected three proposed integration plans limited to Detroit city students, despite a March 23 plea by the Justice Department for a delay of further action pending possible passage by Congress of President Nixon's proposed moratorium on court busing orders.

G

The ruling came under an integration suit originally brought by the National Association for the Advancement of Colored People. Roth had ruled in

1971 that Detroit segregation had been fostered by official actions in the past, although he acknowledged that the city had made attempts to eliminate segregation. He had ordered the Michigan State Board of Education to devise a Detroit metropolitan area school integration plan. His finding of de jure segregation was being appealed by the Detroit Board of Education and the state attorney general.

The state Board of Education submitted six different plans to the court Feb. 3, without expressing preference, ranging from a merger of 36 metropolitan school districts into six regions with equal black-white ratios, to a simple increase of funds and community control for black schools in Detroit.

The Justice Department entered the case after Nixon pledged March 16 that his Administration would seek to overturn court busing orders. Judge Roth had not yet acted on the department's plea when he rejected the three desegregation plans.

In rejecting the plans, Roth said school district lines were arbitrary, and could not be used to deny constitutional rights. He called it his "duty" under the 1954 *Brown* decision to "look beyond the limits of the Detroit school district for a solution."

Detroit developments. U.S. District Court Judge Stephen J. Roth refused May 9 to allow the Justice Department to intervene in the Detroit school integration case, saying that federal law permitted the department to intervene in civil rights cases only on the side of the plaintiff—in the Detroit case the National Association for the Advancement of Colored People. U.S. Attorney Ralph Guy Jr. had argued that suburban communities were not adequately represented in the case, and asked for a delay in any busing order "because of a strong public feeling in the area."

Michigan Attorney General Frank J. Kelley asked the U.S. Supreme Court May 8 to assume immediate jurisdiction over the Detroit case. The 6th U.S. Circuit Court of Appeals in Cincinnati had earlier refused as premature Kelley's request to appeal Roth's finding that Detroit segregation had been caused by

official state and city action and inaction. But in his new plea Kelley argued that the issues in the case should be heard at a higher level before "hundreds of thousands" of students were bused and school programs were disrupted.

Detroit area busing ordered. U.S. District Court Stephen J. Roth June 14 ordered a massive busing effort to integrate Detroit city and suburban schools. It was the most extensive desegregation order issued by a federal court.

Under the plan, which was based largely on a proposal of the National Association for the Advancement of Colored People, 310,000 of 780,000 pupils in Detroit and 53 suburban school districts would be bused across Detroit city lines. City high school districts would be paired or clustered with suburban districts, and teachers would be reassigned so that each school had at least 10% black faculty and staff.

Roth wrote that under his order, "the greatest change would be in the direction of the buses," and set a general maximum of 40 minutes for a one-way ride. But he added that "transportation of kindergarten children for upwards of 45 minutes one way, does not appear unreasonable, harmful or unsafe in any way."

Roth set up a nine-member panel to fill in the details and establish a schedule within 45 days, with full implementation set for the fall 1973 term. Problems of adjusting administration, personnel contracts and financing with the plan were expected to be complicated by a Detroit fiscal crisis. The Detroit School Board had adopted an emergency budget plan June 6 reducing the 1972-73 school year from 180 to 117 days, in a plea for more state aid.

The Detroit schools had 290,000 students, about 65% black, while 29 of the 53 suburban districts were all white and the rest overwhelmingly white.

A stay of the judge's ruling, or of the final desegregation order to be issued after hearings on the nine-member panel's recommendations, could be sought under the education act cleared by Congress June 8 and awaiting presidential signature. The bill provided that school busing orders be stayed pending appeals or until Jan. 1, 1974. The 4th U.S. Circuit Court of Appeals had overturned a city-suburb school consolidation plan for Richmond June 6, but the ruling was not binding in Michigan, which was in the 6th Judicial Circuit.

Detroit panel sees fall busing. An 11-member panel named by U.S. District Court Judge Stephen J. Roth to work out details of his busing order recommended that Michigan be ordered to pay $3 million for 295 available school buses to begin busing 50,000–80,000 children in the fall, it was reported July 5.

Court stays busing. A panel of the Sixth U.S. Circuit Court of Appeals issued a stay July 21 of orders by U.S. District Court Judge Stephen J. Roth for plans to desegregate Detroit metropolitan area schools through massive use of busing.

Judge Roth had ordered the state of Michigan July 10 to buy 295 buses to begin implementing the first stage of his plan, though state officials argued that they had no constitutional or legislative authority to purchase the buses.

The Justice Department had joined Michigan's appeal of the order July 17, relying in part on the recently passed antibusing amendments to the higher education bill.

The appeals court said the 11-man panel named by Roth to draw up details of the plan should continue its work, and scheduled an Aug. 24 hearing on the merits of the case.

Detroit busing stayed. A three-judge panel of the Sixth U.S. Circuit Court of Appeals issued an indefinite stay in Cincinnati Aug. 24 of a lower court order that would have begun a massive busing program to integrate Detroit metropolitan area schools. At the same time, the court began to hear arguments on the constitutionality and applicability of a busing moratorium law passed by Congress in June.

Chief Judge Harry Phillips said the "size of this record and the complexity of this question" made impossible any ruling before the school year began. The court promised to issue a ruling as soon as possible. Written arguments were submitted Sept. 5.

Michigan Attorney General Frank J. Kelley, Democratic candidate for the U.S Senate, and David L. Norman, head of the U.S. Department of Justice's Civil Rights Division argued for a reversal of U.S. District Court Judge Stephen J. Roth's busing order.

Detroit busing upheld. A three-judge panel of the 6th U.S. Circuit Court of Appeals in Cincinnati ruled Dec. 8 that a city-suburb school integration plan was necessary to assure equal rights for black schoolchildren in Detroit.

But the judges ordered another hearing in Detroit U.S. District Court, to give 18 suburban districts a chance to comment on the plan before final lines were drawn.

The Supreme Court: Virginia

Court orders free Norfolk buses. The Supreme Court refused by an 8–0 vote May 15 to review a ruling by the 4th U.S. Circuit Court of Appeals in Richmond that Norfolk, Va. must provide free transportation of 24,000 children assigned to schools beyond walking distance under an integration plan. The court also voided a stay issued by the appeals court that plaintiffs said would have prevented implementation of the integration plan in the coming school year. Justice Lewis Powell Jr. excluded himself from the case.

Norfolk had argued that it had never provided free school transportation, and that the court had intervened in budget decisions and imposed its views "as to what constitutes wise economic and social policy." The appeals court ruled that it would be "a futile gesture" and a "cruel hoax" to "compel the student to attend a distant school and then fail to provide him with the means to reach that school."

Virginia

Richmond plan overturned. The 4th U.S. Circuit Court of Appeals in Richmond overturned a lower court order June 6 that would have merged the school districts of Richmond and two suburban counties and bused thousands of schoolchildren to achieve racial integration. The Richmond School Board immediately ordered its lawyers to appeal the case, regarded as a crucial turning point in desegregation law, to the Supreme Court, which had already agreed to review a school busing case in Denver.

The court ruled by a 5–1 vote that U.S. District Court Judge Robert R. Merhige Jr. had interpreted the 14th Amendment in an "excessive" manner when he ruled that governmental actions had helped lead to an increasingly black central city and a ring of white suburbs, and that the resulting school segregation was unconstitutional whatever the cause. In "exceeding his power of intervention," the court said, Merhige had slighted the "principle of federalism incorporated in the 10th Amendment," which reserved powers to the states.

Judge James Braxton Craven Jr. wrote for the majority:

"Neither the record nor the opinion of the district court even suggests that there was ever a joint interaction between any two of the units involved (or by higher state officers) for the purpose of keeping one unit relatively white by confining blacks to another. We think that the root causes of the concentration of blacks in the inner cities of America are simply not known, and that the district court could not realistically place

on the counties the responsibility for the effect that inner city decay has had on the public schools of Richmond."

The court said the mere fact that the city school population was 70% black while the suburban school population was 90% white did not constitute a constitutional violation. Any county actions to enforce segregation had been "slight" compared to other "economic, political and social" factors. Furthermore, "school assignments cannot reverse the trend" of racial concentration.

In a dissent, Judge Harrison L. Winter cited "the sordid history of Virginia's and Richmond's attempts to circumvent, defeat and nullify" Supreme Court integration rulings, which he said would be further "frustrated" by the appeals court decision.

Suburban Henrico and Chesterfield counties had been joined in their appeal of Merhige's ruling by the Justice Department after President Nixon set down new antibusing guidelines March 16. The NAACP Legal Defense and Educational Fund, which had brought the original suit, had been joined by the Richmond School Board in the lower court, and by the National Education Association, the American Civil Liberties Union on appeal.

Among those who commented on the decision, Virginia Sen. William B. Spong, Jr. (D) said the ruling did not vitiate "a compelling need for legislation that will spell out a national school policy not requiring massive enforced busing."

Joining Judge Craven in the majority were Chief Judge Clement F. Haynsworth Jr. and Judges Albert V. Bryan Sr., Donald S. Russell and John A. Field Jr.

Tennessee

Nashville order approved; Memphis plan stayed. The 6th U.S. Circuit Court of Appeals in Cincinnati, in two separate rulings, May 30 upheld a lower court plan that required 49,000 Nashville area schoolchildren to be bused for integration, but granted a stay June 5 to the Memphis Board of Education, which had been under a lower court order to begin a busing program in the fall.

In the Nashville case, the court upheld U.S. District Court Judge Clure Morton, who had ordered the Metropolitan County Board of Education of Nasvhille and Davidson County to implement the busing plan during the current school year. The board claimed it lacked funds for full implementation, and lacked taxing power to acquire the funds. The Justice Department had intervened in favor of the board's appeal, although the plan had originally been proposed by the Department of Health, Education and Welfare.

In the Memphis case, the court overruled U.S. District Court Judge Robert M. McRae Jr., who had denied a stay of a plan to begin busing 14,000 pupils in the fall. The Memphis Board of Education had argued that without a stay it would have had to commit itself to buy or lease buses before it knew the final disposition of the case.

Memphis to start busing. The Memphis Board of Education voted a $252,000 budget item Oct. 17 to begin busing some 12,000 students in January 1973, after the Supreme Court refused to stay lower court integration orders.

The 6th U.S. Circuit Court of Appeals, in a split decision, had ordered the plan into effect Aug. 29. In the majority opinion, Judge Anthony Celebreeze wrote that the school board had failed to prove that the 128 of 162 schools that were segregated were not "in any way the product of its past or present discriminatory conduct," which would be the only way the board could refute charges that it had "failed to eliminate its dual system," according to Celebreeze's interpretation of Supreme Court decisions.

Dissenting Judge Paul C. Weick said the court had "given scant consideration to the "constitutional rights" of "black and white children who do not want to be bused away from their neighborhood schools." The district had 145,000 pupils, 53.6% black. NAACP leaders in Memphis said Aug. 29 that the busing plan did not go far enough.

Texas

Texas busing decisions reversed. The 5th U.S. Circuit Court of Appeals in New Orleans reversed lower court school integration rulings for Austin and Corpus Christi, Tex. Aug. 2, and rejected the use of large-scale busing until all neighborhood-oriented remedies had been tried.

In the Austin case, a U.S. district court judge had rejected plans for crosstown busing, and ordered instead that special learning centers be set up for visits from neighborhood schools. The appeals court, although agreeing that the district judge "knows the situation better than we do," said he could not "totally reject the use of busing as a permissible tool," and ordered him to request new plans for further desegregation from all parties. The court ordered a final plan in time for the start of the 1972–73 school year.

In Corpus Christi, the appeals court reversed a U.S. district court ruling that called for extensive crosstown busing, and ordered instead that the judge adopt a new pupil reassignment plan. The court also ordered the use of pairing and clustering of schools, and relocation of portable classrooms. But pairing of non-contiguous school districts would be barred "until the court had exhausted every other possible remedy which would not involve increased student transportation."

The court ruled that Mexican-American pupils had suffered unconstitutional discrimination in both cities, although they had never been officially segregated by state law, because school boards had failed to act against neighborhood ethnic concentrations, and had used pupil assignment and building location to reinforce segregation.

A minority of the 14-judge panel (the circuit court sat en banc rather than the usual three-judge panel) dissented in both cases, claiming that all remedies short of large scale busing had already been unsuccessfully tried. Judge John M. Wisdom, in a dissent, said the rulings were "the first backward step" for the appeals bench, which had been noted for leading the way in implementing Supreme Court desegregation rulings.

Broomfield Amendment

Moratorium stays denied. In the first court tests of the Broomfield Amendment, the only antibusing measure to win Congressional approval, stays of desegregation orders were denied for Oxnard, Calif., Augusta, Ga., Las Vegas, Nev., but granted for Chattanooga, Tenn. The Amendment was passed Nov. 1971 and provided for postponement of court-ordered "transportation of any student or students" until all appeals of the court order are exhausted or the appeal time expired.

The Ninth U.S. Circuit Court of Appeals in San Francisco rejected a plea Aug. 22 by the Oxnard school board and the Justice Department to suspend a busing plan begun in the 1971–72 school year. The court ruled that the Broomfield measure could not be applied retroactively, despite Justice Department arguments that the moratorium was intended to apply in all cases in which appeals had not been exhausted.

Supreme Court Justice Lewis F. Powell refused Sept. 1 to stay a busing plan for Augusta, on the grounds that the bill applied only to orders issued for the purpose of achieving racial balance. The Augusta plan, he wrote, had been ordered to correct unlawful segregation. A Justice Department appeal Sept. 5 that the entire court provide an "immediate interpretation" of the law was rejected Sept. 8 by Chief Justice Warren E. Burger.

Justice William O. Douglas rejected a plea Sept. 12 by Las Vegas school officials, supported by Justice Department lawyers, to stay a busing plan in that city, "it not being shown that the conditions of the Broomfield Amendment of the Education Act have been met." The schools involved in the plan, which clustered predominantly black and predominantly white schools, had remained closed during the appeal.

In Chattanooga, U.S. District Court Judge Frank Wilson Jr. ordered a delay

Aug. 11 of a busing order he had issued earlier for the lower grades, although leaving in effect a high school integration plan. Wilson said he did not think his order required "a racial balance," as specified in the bill, but approved the delay requested by the school board since he could not "ignore the popular use of the English language," which equated busing for desegregation with racial balance. The stay would remain in effect only during the 18-month lifetime of the bill.

Georgia

Atlanta integration ordered. The Atlanta school board voted 4–2 Oct. 9 to appeal to the Supreme Court an order by the 5th U.S. Circuit Court of Appeals to implement an integration plan within seven weeks. The two black members of the board constituted the minority.

A three-judge panel of the appeals court had overruled two lower court rulings Oct. 7, calling the Atlanta system "virtually totally segregated." The panel ordered the school board to devise a plan that would "at a minimum" use "pairing or grouping of contiguous segregated schools," paying "special attention" to 20 schools "which have never been desegregated" and remained "all or virtually all white." Superintendent of Schools Ed Cook said the number of such schools had declined to 17.

Since the filing of a National Association for the Advancement of Colored People (NAACP) suit in 1958 that led to the ruling, Atlanta's schools had become over 75% black. The court said that 106 of 153 schools were at least 90% of one race, and most of them had always been so.

The U.S. district court in Atlanta had rejected an NAACP plan in June which the appeals court had ordered it to consider, which would have bused 33,000 of Atlanta's 95,000 pupils. The appeals court, in its latest ruling, said "the fear of white students' flight shall not be utilized as a factor in composing this plan," but cited as guidelines for Atlanta two recent decisions in Austin and Corpus Christi, Texas, that condoned some busing but barred cross-town busing until all other remedies were tried.

Atlanta plan delayed. A Nov. 27 deadline for a desegregation plan for Atlanta schools was delayed Nov. 24 by a three-judge panel of the 5th U.S. Circuit Court of Appeals in New Orleans, which remanded the case to a lower court. A compromise plan worked out by officials of the Atlanta branch of the National Association for the Advancement of Colored People and the school board had aroused the opposition of the NAACP Legal Defense and Educational Fund as being inadequate. Only eight of 29 black plaintiffs in the case had approved the compromise.

1973
Michigan

New Detroit appeal granted. The 6th Circuit Court of Appeals agreed in Cincinnati Jan. 16 to a new hearing, before all nine judges, of an appeal of a district court school busing plan for Detroit and its suburbs. The ruling vacated a December 1972 ruling by three of the appeals judges, who upheld the busing plan with some reservations. The action halted all further district court hearings on implementation of the plan.

Detroit busing ordered. The 6th Circuit Court of Appeals in Cincinnati June 12 upheld the principle of merging city and suburban school districts to achieve racial balance while ordering a lower court to work out a new busing plan for Detroit and its suburbs.

The issue of metropolitan area busing had remained open after the U.S. Supreme Court refused May 21 to uphold a similar plan for Richmond, Va. Because Justice Lewis F. Powell Jr. had been a member of the Richmond and Virginia state boards of education, he did not participate. The voting resulted in a 4–4 tie vote, and no precedent was set.

Writing for the 6–3 majority in the Detroit case, Chief Judge Harry Phillips said the constitutional right to equality before the law could not be "hemmed in by the boundaries of a school district."

The court set aside the original busing plan on the ground that the suburban districts had not been given proper opportunity to object in court. Also set aside was an order that Detroit immediately buy 295 school buses to implement the plan. While returning the case to the federal district court, the appeals court suggested that the best solution might come from the state legislature. But if the legislature failed to correct segregation, the court said, "a federal court has both the power and the duty to effect a feasible desegregation plan."

In a dissenting opinion, Judge Paul C. Weick urged a new trial to consider a Detroit-only plan. A merger, he said, would deny individual children "their right not to be substantially burdened solely on account of their race."

Attorneys for the suburban districts announced June 15 that the case would be appealed to the U.S. Supreme Court.

Detroit school merger to get review. The Supreme Court said Nov. 19 it would review a federal district court plan ordering the merger of the predominantly black Detroit public school system with 52 contiguous, white suburban school districts.

A federal district court judge had ruled that the merger was the only feasible means of eliminating racial segregation in the 65% black Detroit system. An appellate court upheld the lower court

finding but remanded the case to the trial court to give dissenting suburban districts an opportunity to be heard.

HEW

Bias fund cuts ordered. A federal judge in Washington ordered the Department of Health, Education and Welfare (HEW) Feb. 16 to begin proceedings to cut off federal funds from school districts and state college systems that had not complied with desegregation requirements.

U.S. District Court Judge John H. Pratt had ruled in November 1972 that HEW had violated the law in refraining from any fund cutoffs since early 1970. In his latest order, Pratt set timetables for HEW action in several categories of cases, and ordered the department to submit detailed progress reports every six months to the NAACP Legal Defense and Educational Fund, which had filed the suit. HEW was ordered within 120 days to begin cutoff procedures, which included notification of districts, hearings, and notification of Congress, against 10 states which operated racially segregated systems of higher education, and had either failed to submit desegregation plans or submitted plans rejected by HEW. Proceedings within 60 days were ordered for 74 school districts that had been found by HEW by 1970–71 to be out of compliance with submitted desegregation plans.

Sixty-day limits were set for 42 districts found by HEW in violation of a 1971 Supreme Court ruling by maintaining schools with "substantially disproportionate" racial ratios without justification, and for 85 other districts, which had not yet been required by HEW to justify disproportionate enrollments.

Desegregation aid cut. The Administration reported March 1 that it would defer spending some $223.6 million of $270.6 million appropriated in fiscal 1973 to aid school districts undergoing desegregation.

An official of the Office of Education said most of the 336 districts applying for funds had filed unsatisfactory applications. The Office of Management and Budget had imposed a $50 million limit for the program in fiscal 1973, as an economy measure and because of the limited time available since the Emergency School Aid Act went into effect Feb. 1.

The withheld funds would be budgeted for programs in fiscal 1974, and $271 million budgeted for that year would be used for fiscal 1975.

HEW warns of bias cutoffs. HEW's Office for Civil Rights ordered 25 school districts in 12 states March 24 to submit new plans by April 10 that would "eliminate the vestiges of" their "former dual school systems" by the fall of 1973, and warned that failure to comply might lead to legal action and a cutoff of federal aid.

The action had been ordered by a federal district court judge in February, and

acting civil rights director Peter E. Holmes told the districts that the government would "pursue its legal efforts to appeal the case." The Justice Department had asked the judge March 8 to stay the order pending appeal.

The civil rights office also requested 10 states to submit higher education desegregation plans by April 23, in accordance with the court order.

Aid cuts upheld. A court order directing the Department of Health, Education and Welfare (HEW) to cut off funds from school districts and state college systems not complying with desegregation requirements was upheld June 12 by the Circuit Court of Appeals for the District of Columbia.

In upholding District Court Judge John H. Pratt's order as "unassailable," the court said HEW was "actively supplying segregated educational institutions with federal funds, contrary to the expressed purpose of Congress."

The South

Atlanta plan ordered. A U.S. district court in Atlanta ordered into effect April 4 a compromise school integration plan that some civil rights attorneys had first accepted, then rejected.

The plan had been devised by the school board and the local chapter of the National Association for the Advancement of Colored People (NAACP), but then rejected by the NAACP national office and the NAACP Legal Defense and Educational Fund, an independent group whose attorneys had participated as counsel for the black plaintiffs in the long-standing desegregation suit.

The court said "federal courts have held a settlement agreement once entered into cannot be repudiated by either party."

Chattanooga integration ordered. The 6th U.S. Circuit Court of Appeals in Cincinnati April 30 ordered implementation of a lower court plan for the integration of the public schools in Chattanooga, Tenn.

The plan established a ratio of not less than 30% but not more than 70% of any race in all but five of the city's elementary schools and in junior high schools. A plan for high schools remained under study.

Jonathon Mapp, whose suit had resulted in the original ordering of the plan in 1971, contended before the court that the plan placed a disproportionate burden on black students by ordering the closing of some black schools but not white schools. The Chattanooga Board of Education said the plan went too far in requiring pairing and clustering of schools and large expenditures for the purchase of buses to transport students.

Supreme Court upholds Chattanooga busing. The court Nov. 5 refused to overturn a federal district court order that Chattanooga, Tenn. officials bus students to achieve racial balance in the schools and that city authorities provide funds for the busing.

The Supreme Court

Alabama decision upheld. The Supreme Court April 18 allowed to stand a lower court order integrating outlying districts into the school system of Pleasant Grove, Ala. The city had said it could not afford the cost of buses.

Denver ruling bars de facto bias. The court ruled June 21 that Northern school systems with substantial pockets of segregation would be treated the same way as had Southern school systems with de jure patterns of segregation.

In a case involving Denver, the court said school board policies that fostered segregation even in limited parts of a metropolitan area might affect the whole system, and the whole system required desegregation, "root and branch."

Black and Mexican-American parents had sued the Denver school board, charging it with the creation of segregated schools through manipulation of attendance zones, school site selection, and a neighborhood school policy.

Justice Rehnquist dissented, and White, a native Coloradan, did not participate.

The Denver ruling was the high court's first decision dealing with the question of de facto segregation. While the court stopped short of eliminating the distinction between de jure and de facto segregation, it said "proof of state-imposed segregation in a substantial portion of the district will suffice to support a finding by the trial court of the existence of a dual system. . . . Where the finding is made, as in cases involving statutory [de jure; Southern] dual systems, the school authorities have an affirmative duty to effectuate a transition to a racially nondiscriminatory school system."

The court ordered the case returned to the federal district court in Denver to allow Denver school authorities to prove they did not intend to provide racial separation.

Indiana

Indianapolis busing ordered. U.S. District Court Judge S. Hugh Dillin July 20 found the State of Indiana guilty of maintaining segregated school systems and ordered the state legislature to devise a permanent integration plan for the Indianapolis metropolitan area. For the 1973–74 school year, Judge Dillin ordered an interim plan under which almost 6,000 black students from Indianapolis would be bused to 18 suburban districts.

Judge Dillin said if the legislature did not act within a reasonable time, the court would devise its own plan. Legislative leaders said they might let the case reach the U.S. Supreme Court before taking any action.

Under the interim order, suburban districts were required to accept black students from the city in numbers equal to 5% of total enrollment. City schools were ordered to reassign pupils so that no school had less than 15% black enrollment. Dillin said schools in the metropolitan area should eventually reflect the 19.5% black enrollment in the area, but added that "perfect racial balance . . . is not required by law, and will not be ordered."

Tennessee

Knoxville plan upheld. The U.S. Court of Appeals for the 6th Circuit July 18 upheld a desegregation plan for the Knoxville, Tenn. schools calling for pairing of schools, adjustment of school zones and the closing of two schools—one all black and the other all white. The plan did not provide for busing.

The ruling affirmed a 1971 order by District Court Judge Robert L. Taylor, who had said busing of a large number of pupils "to obtain a certain percentage of black students in each school" was not required.

Memphis busing upheld. The U.S. Court of Appeals for the 6th Circuit Dec. 4 upheld a court-ordered plan for busing of public school students in Memphis, rejecting contentions by the National Association for the Advancement of Colored People that the plan left too many all-black schools.

Citing Supreme Court precedents, the court said there was a "necessity of tolerating some one-race schools because minority groups concentrate in urban areas."

The court also upheld a lower court's finding that the city of Memphis had acted improperly by cutting its transportation budget in an attempt to avoid implementation of the busing order.

HEW busing aid refusal voided. U.S. District Court Judge Frank Gray Jr. ruled Dec. 19 that the Department of Health, Education and Welfare's (HEW) refusal to consider applications for transportation aid funds had "impeded" a court-ordered busing plan for Nashville, Tenn. public schools and was "illegal and unconstitutional."

Gray ordered HEW to review within 30 days its earlier refusal to grant the city funds to purchase buses to transport about half of Nashville's 95,000 students.

Massachusetts

Boston school plan upheld. The Massachusetts Supreme Court Oct. 29 upheld a state plan to redraw Boston's school district lines to achieve racial balance by September 1974.

The plan, which would involve large-scale busing, had been drawn to conform with a state law limiting the number of black students in any school to 50%.

RICHMOND SCHOOL MERGER DECISION OVERTURNED BY U.S. APPEALS COURT

The 4th U.S. Circuit Court of Appeals in Richmond, Va. overturned June 6 the ruling of District Court Judge Robert R. Merhige Jr. ordering the merger of Richmond's predominantly black public schools with those of two white suburban counties. Merhige's Jan. 10 ruling had, in effect, held that the right to equal educational opportunity in racially integrated schools took precedence over the right of local governments to set the geographic boundaries of school districts. At the time, the ruling was viewed as a precedent which could have a momentous and nationwide impact on school desegregation. The Appeals Court Feb. 8 had granted the State Board of Education a stay in implementation of Merhige's order while hearing the appeal.

In its 5–1 decision, the Court of Appeals ruled that Merhige had interpreted the 14th Amendment in an "excessive" manner, "exceeding his power of intervention" and slighting the "principle of federalism incorporated in the 10th Amendment." In the lone dissent, Judge Harrison L. Winter cited "the sordid history of Virginia's and Richmond's attempts to circumvent, defeat and nullify" Supreme Court desegregation rulings, which he said would be further "frustrated" by the appeals court decision. The Richmond School Board announced it would appeal the decision.

The overturning of the Richmond school desegregation order came as Congress gave final approval to the 1972 Higher Education Act June 8. The bill contained provisions forestalling further court-ordered busing for 18 months or until all appeals were exhausted. It was signed into law by President Nixon June 23.

Chicago Tribune
Chicago, Ill., June 7, 1972

The United States Court of Appeals in Richmond yesterday overturned an inflammatory federal court ruling which would have compelled the busing of thousands of children between the predominantly black school districts of Richmond and the white districts of its suburbs, even in adjacent counties.

In the original ruling, issued last January, Federal Judge Robert R. Merhige [rhymes with courage but not with wisdom] held that because political boundaries are set by the state, then any racial segregation that may result in the schools is state-imposed and therefore unconstitutional by definition of the Supreme Court. Judge Merhige's order for busing across boundaries hit the country like a red flag in a bull ring. It has aroused a storm of fear and opposition, and has led to similar orders elsewhere, notably in Detroit and its suburbs.

Had Judge Merhige's ruling become the law of the land, it could have imposed staggering problems on school districts and cities all over the country.

The appellate court has come to the sensible conclusion that municipal and county boundaries established many years ago can hardly be blamed for today's segregation; that any segregation is therefore de facto rather than de jure, and that Judge Merhige therefore "exceeded his power of intervention."

We have said all along that the busing squabble should be straightened out in the courts, where it began, rather than by resorting to a constitutional amendment or by trying to deprive the courts of jurisdiction.

The issue has already become far more entangled in politics and emotion than it deserved, and has threatened to embroil the country in a dispute with racial overtones in an election year. What is at stake is really rather limited: it simply involves the right of courts to order busing between established communities against the will of those communities.

The court is not denying the right of a school district to bus pupils within its borders, if it wants, or even to agree with an adjacent school district on busing between them. The court is not ruling on the social merits of busing, which are unproved but may be positive, at least in the lower grades, or on its educational merits, which are dubious at best.

Very likely this case or another like it will go to the Supreme Court for a definitive ruling on the matter. That is where it should come from. A good deal of the shouting in Congress and elsewhere will then prove to have been emotional, politically-motivated, and unnecessary.

Los Angeles Times
Los Angeles, Calif., June 7, 1972

The U.S. Court of Appeals has reversed, by a vote of 5 to 1, a federal district court order calling for consolidation of the Richmond, Va., city school district, which is 70% black, with two neighboring suburban school districts, which are 91% white, to form a new and enlarged district that would be 66% white. In the absence of "invidious discrimination," the federal appeals court ruled, there is no Constitutional basis for a court to restructure local government in this way.

It is now for the Supreme Court to decide whether Dist. Judge Robert R. Merhige Jr., in his original consolidation order, or the appeals court was right in interpreting the Constitution.

Judge Merhige had relied heavily on last year's unanimous decision of the Supreme Court in the Swann vs. Charlotte-Mecklenburg Board of Education case. In that decision, the Supreme Court supported court intervention to require busing in an extensive metropolitan area to overcome segregation. But there is a technical difference in the cases, for Charlotte city and Mecklenburg County are part of the same school district, while Richmond City and Henrico and Chesterfield Counties have separate school districts.

The appeals court found that the Richmond racial situation is similar to other American urban situations, including Los Angeles. The central cities are getting blacker, the suburbs whiter. But the judges concluded that this white flight to the suburbs was not the fault of the schools in this case.

"Whatever the basic causes, it has not been school assignments, and school assignments cannot reverse the trend," the judges said.

The parallel to Los Angeles is evident. Los Angeles schools cover an area about the size proposed for the consolidated Richmond system, but Los Angeles has more than six times as many students. The Los Angeles schools are divided by the Santa Monica mountains; south of the mountains, 64% of the students are black or brown; north of the mountains, 85% are white. Los Angeles itself is awaiting outcome of an appeal to court-ordered desegregation.

The Supreme Court that will hear the Richmond case is different from the Supreme Court that decided the Charlotte-Mecklenburg case and the Supreme Court that made the first great school segregation decision in 1954. Some concern already has been expressed because of the addition of conservatives to the court. But this is to ignore a singular fact: The school segregation question has not divided conservatives and liberals on the Supreme Court. As the Warren court was unanimous, so has been the Burger court.

In affirming this fundamental justice, the Supreme Court has also sought to define limitations for the courts. This is essential.

In the preoccupation with the courts, it is easy to forget that the primary responsibility for erasing segregation rests not with the courts but with grass roots government. To argue that the courts may not have authority to order consolidation of the Richmond area schools is not to deny that the consolidation would contribute to social justice and thereby to an element of educational quality. To appeal a court order for massive busing, whether in Richmond or Los Angeles, is not to argue that America is better and stronger when divided and segregated.

Congress, encouraged by President Nixon, has now ordered a moratorium on desegregation while appeals are exhausted. The target of the action is busing. The only predictable result is to push the matter deeper into the courts while those politically responsible, from the White House to the local school boards, perpetuate a dangerous illusion, an illusion that segregated schools somehow are not a problem that every American should be working to eliminate.

CHICAGO
Daily Defender

Chicago, Ill., June 12, 1972

The action of the 4th U. S. Circuit Court of Appeals in Richmond in overturning a District Court order on school desegregation, is disquieting in its eventual impact on a number of school cases now pending before the courts in various districts.

The Appeals Court swept aside a District Court order that would have merged Richmond's predominantly black schools with those of two suburban counties with mostly white school populations.

Without a single dissenting voice, the Richmond Board of Education paraded before the District Court a preponderence of evidence in pleading for the establishment of racial balance in its school system.

It showed the administrative difficulties it must surmount to operate a dual school system, to say nothing of the heavy budget that such an operation requires. Moreover, the board feels that it has both a moral and legal responsibility to carry out the directives of the provisions of Section 6 of the 1966 Civil Rights Act.

It was the logic and practicality of this argument that led U. S. District Court judge Robert R. Merhige Jr., to intervene on the side of the Richmond school board. The racists in that old confederate Virginia city want neither integration nor busing. And the board went to court to stay undue interference with its normal functions.

Merhige's decision touched off a storm of disapproval among the white suburban county residents, resulting in angry rallies and a massive motorcade to Washington to protest busing. It would seem the Appeals Court, which ruled that Merhige had exceeded his power of intervention, was merely acting in response to the agitation against his mandate.

If Merhige's ruling had been upheld it would have established a healthy precedent for the other school cases that are pending. The climate of public opposition to busing, ushered by President Nixon, is having its malevolent effect on federal courts which seem eager to comply with Mr. Nixon's negative, reactionary views.

The Washington Post
Times Herald

Washington, D.C., June 9, 1972

The decision by the Fourth Circuit Court of Appeals in the Richmond school case undoubtedly will be described by many as a victory for those who oppose any further desegregation of the public schools or any additional busing of students. In a sense, it is, because the decision, unless overturned by the Supreme Court, declares that all has already been done that will be done by the courts to desegregate the schools in and around this particular southern city. But in a larger sense, the decision is a stand-off. Given the terms in which the Court framed its work, this decision seems to us to have changed very little the general understanding of what the Constitution requires and to be unlikely to provide much, if any, of a precedent to guide judges confronted with similar situations elsewhere.

As we read the opinion of Judge Craven, and the blistering dissent of Judge Winter, the Richmond case turned solely on its facts. The majority of the Court held, contrary to Judge Merhige, that the evidence did not establish any conduct by the state which had led to the situation in which Richmond's schools are predominately black and those in the two suburban counties, Henrico and Chesterfield, are almost totally white. One can quarrel with that conclusion and we, at least, find Judge Winter's dissent on the point far more persuasive than the majority's opinion. But even if the Court's conclusion on the facts in this particular case is correct, the thrust of the majority opinion is that if the facts had been different Judge Merhige's consolidation might well have been upheld.

Thus, the Court's opinion seems to stand not so much for the proposition that urban and suburban districts will never be consolidated in a desegregation case but that they can be consolidated given a proper set of facts. It is true, of course, that the Court said busing and other transfers of students are not to be required by lower courts solely for the purpose of establishing racial balance in the schools. But that is not new. The Supreme Court has said it in a case involving school districts where students were never deliberately segregated by race. And it is also true that the Court weighed in with some strong words about the power of the states under the Tenth Amendment to regulate their own affairs. But even the latter was qualified by a recognition that if a state uses the lines of its political subdivisions to circumvent "the Fourteenth Amendment equal protection right of blacks to attend a unitary school system" those lines must fall. In the same view, it is worth noting that the Court specifically said, "This is not a busing case. That remedy . . . has been utilized in Richmond and is not challenged on appeal."

The basic question, then, remains unanswered in all the cases—from Richmond, Detroit, Denver—involving efforts to ameliorate the ghetto conditions of urban schools by joining them with suburban schools. That is how much or what kind of action, or inaction, by public officials is required to persuade the courts that the resulting segregation is the product of unconstitutional state action. It is to this issue that the Supreme Court will have to address itself someday and it could choose the Richmond case as an appropriate vehicle.

In the meantime, however, the Richmond decision ought to serve to take some of the emotion out of the busing issue in this year's presidential campaign. There will be no busing across school district lines in Richmond this fall and, we suspect, little of it elsewhere. That, alone, should make discussion of the question somewhat less emotional. But it should not foreclose such discussion for the problem of segregated schools still remains in both urban and suburban areas. At most, all this decision says is that in some situations that problem cannot and will not be solved by the courts as a matter of constitutional right, but that the problem ought to be solver in all situations, as a matter of social policy, by legislation or other means if not by the courts.

Chicago
today
American

Chicago, Ill., June 11, 1972

SCHOOL BUSING has become such an emotional issue that even people who should know better are led into intellectual traps by it. It has such a strong hold on Congress and the administration that they are trying hard to tell the courts how to rule on the subject. And it has led at least one judge, Robert R. Merhige Jr. of the Federal District Court in Richmond, Va., to try to legislate school boundaries.

In this he has been properly overruled by a U. S. Appeals Court in a case that may, and should, go to the Supreme Court. Judge Merhige ordered the merger of city and suburban school districts of Richmond—including districts in other counties—to facilitate busing from black areas in the city to white schools in the suburbs.

No doubt Judge Merhige acted on what he considered good and humanitarian grounds to correct a sharp racial imbalance. But it was an arbitrary decision apparently based on the judge's personal feelings; it had nothing to do with the only justifiable goal of busing, which is to provide quality education for pupils who otherwise wouldn't get it; and it would serve only to further the negative function of busing, which is to impose an artificial kind of integration in areas that are in fact segregated.

The appellate court's decision won't resolve the busing issue. But it at least rejects the emotional approach to it and helps to establish a reasonable atmosphere in which other courts can operate. And the responsibility is clearly up to the courts; they alone should decide when and to what extent busing benefits the communities and citizens it affects.

Before the courts can go ahead with their job, tho, a couple of things need to be straightened out. The Supreme Court should define, once and for all, the limits within which the lower courts can work. It should also make clear that these limits are not to be tampered with by either the legislative or executive branches. The best way to keep emotion out of busing is to keep politics out of it.

The New York Times

New York, N.Y., June 12, 1972

The United States Court of Appeals for the Fourth Circuit, in striking down a Federal District Court order to merge the predominantly black school district of Richmond with its two largely white suburbs, has done little to clarify a complex issue. The consolidation order was based primarily on the contention that the state had consistently used its power to preserve segregation and to keep the suburban districts white by locking the blacks into the city. Federal District Judge Robert R. Merhige Jr. said that both in the pattern of housing and of school construction the state had directly facilitated the maintenance of a segregationist wall which had the effect of perpetuating dual school systems.

The appeals court has challenged those findings. But, as the strongly worded dissent by Judge Harrison L. Winter makes clear, the record of that court not only shows little sensitivity to civil rights but actually contains rulings which helped to create smaller districts as deliberate white enclaves.

The basic question which is sure to be brought before the Supreme Court is whether Judge Merhige was right in finding that the state's political authority had been abused to uphold segregation. Judge Winter insists that it has. He states in his dissent: "The sordid history of Virginia's, and Richmond's, attempts to circumvent, defeat and nullify the holding of *Brown I* has been recorded in the opinions of this and other courts."

Neither *Brown* nor subsequent Supreme Court rulings require a racial balancing of school enrollment. This newspaper disagreed from the outset with those who hailed the Merhige rulings as a blanket judicial demand for a merger of urban and suburban districts everywhere, with its risk of undermining community involvement and local commitment to public education.

The importance of Judge Merhige's ruling seemed to us that it put suburban districts on notice that discrimination in housing and the deliberate use of school zoning powers to exclude black children amounts to *de jure* segregation. If these were the conditions in Richmond—as Judges Merhige and Winter maintain—then the effect of the appeals court's ruling is to protect an illegal barrier.

The Supreme Court, beginning with *Brown* in 1954 and most recently with *Swann v. Charlotte-Mecklenburg* in 1971, has ordered that such barriers be dismantled. The Richmond reversal presents the Supreme Court with an opportunity to eliminate those existing ambiguities which have encouraged evasion of the 1954 desegregation ruling.

The San Diego Union

San Diego, Calif., June 9, 1972

The federal courts appear to be moving toward a belated recognition of the right of citizens at the local level to make basic decisions about the structure of their school systems. We can thus hope for some cooling of judicial fervor to launch fleets of busses for the sole purpose of achieving racial balance in our schools.

The 4th U.S. Circuit Court of Appeals now has overruled the federal district judge who ordered the consolidation of the Richmond, Va., school district with the districts of two suburban counties. The message to the judge is that the right of these school districts to exist as separate entities is protected by the Constitution unless it can be shown they are maintained deliberately to discriminate against children in the Richmond area.

There is no evidence of such discrimination in the Richmond case, even if there is a predominance of Negro pupils in the city schools and a predominance of white pupils in the suburban schools. As undesirable as this racial imbalance might be from the standpoint of social theory, the Circuit Court of Appeals recognizes that for school district boundaries to be abolished by court order is not only undesirable but unconstitutional.

The simple fact is that the same Constitution which contains a 14th Amendment protecting citizens against racial discrimination also contains a 10th Amendment protecting the right of citizens to set up and operate local school districts. This is the "states' rights" amendment which all too often recently has been given a back seat in the eagerness to achieve a more precise racial balance in public schools.

The Supreme Court in 1954 decreed that "states' rights" offered no justification for maintaining separate schools for whites and Negroes, as was then the custom in many states. It is quite another matter, however, to declare that the states have no right to maintain local school systems in which the racial composition of student bodies simply reflects the racial composition of the neighborhoods in which schools are located.

Just as the 1954 decision spelled out clearly that deliberate segregation of the races in public schools cannot be condoned, an equally clear-cut decision is needed to settle the still-cloudy issue of how far local school officials are obliged to go in achieving racial balance in classrooms when there was no deliberate segregation to begin with.

President Nixon, sensing the potential for bitterness and strife in our society as a result of unfair and unworkable integration plans, has recommended that Congress impose a moratorium on court-ordered school bussing. It would be far more desirable if such a moratorium were to arise from the wisdom of the courts themselves, and there are signs that this finally may be coming to pass.

FORT WORTH STAR-TELEGRAM

Fort Worth, Tex., June 9, 1972

The 4th U.S. Circuit Court of Appeals ruling in the Richmond, Va., school case is certain to spark a furor among integration-at-any-price advocates.

It overturned U.S. District Judge Robert R. Merhige Jr.'s order for the merger of city and suburban school districts in the Richmond area. In so doing it knocked down, by a potent 5-1 count, the first federal court decision ordering busing of pupils across political boundaries — a decision that had been regarded as an omen that politically separated white suburbs would be forced to help correct school racial imbalances resulting from the increased percentage of blacks in inner-city populations.

Across the nation, the district court order was viewed with alarm or rejoicing, depending on one's stand on the issue of racial balance in the schools. But of the ruling's effect, if allowed to stand, there was little question. It would have opened the door to the imposition of the racial-balance doctrine on schools across the nation — regardless of personal hardships and inconveniences it might force on members of all races, regardless of social and economic disruptions it might cause, regardless of the violence it might inflict upon proven principles of government.

In reversing the district judge, the appellate jurists rendered an opinion that was both judicially sound and sociologically practical.

The decision held that, in his concern for implementation of the 14th Amendment's equal-protection provisions, the lower court judge had ignored "a fundamental principle of federalism incorporated in the 10th A m e n d m e n t." That principle, of course, is that powers not delegated to the federal government by the Constitution are reserved to the states, or the people.

So much for a federal judge's right to "compel one of the states . . . to restructure its internal government for the purpose of achieving racial balance in the assignment of pupils to its public schools." This definitely is not power the Constitution delegates to the federal government.

The reversal decision also pointed up the superficiality of the sociological premises of the lower court ruling. The racial patterns around Richmond, the opinion stated, are similar to those of other cities across the nation, and the causes of these patterns are "simply not known." Then came the clinching line: "Whatever the basic causes, it has not been school assignments and school assignments cannot reverse the trend."

The case will be appealed to the Supreme Court, and there the circuit court may be overturned. But its decision has already served two good purposes. It has provided a timely reminder that there are other things in the Constitution worth preserving besides the 14th Amendment. And it has underscored one of the most rampant follies of the age — the idea that basic trends, stemming from deep-flowing socio-economic currents, can be harnessed and controlled by judicial decree.

THE ATLANTA CONSTITUTION
Atlanta, Ga., June 8, 1972

The U.S. Fourth Circuit Court of Appeals Tuesday overturned the lower court decision requiring the merger of the Richmond, Virginia, school system with two suburban school systems, the aim of the initial decision being to achieve racial balance in schools.

We believe the decision a sound one, not because we oppose court rulings to end separated, segregated schools but because there comes at some point a limit to what court decisions alone can do. We think that limit was reached at Richmond, in the lower court decision. If the effort to achieve desegregated schools, on some sort of percentage basis, is reason enough for abolishing school systems entirely, well . . . our feeling is that at this point there seems no end to it. If we merge three school systems on this basis, why not five? Or ten? We think the Fourth Circuit court made a wise decision.

The Evening News
Newark, N.J., June 8, 1972

Reversal of a federal judge's order to merge the schools of Richmond, Va., with those of two adjoining counties has implications as significant as the United States Supreme Court's desegregation ruling of 1954. It could signal the end of wholesale busing as a viable means of achieving desegregation. At least it is likely to hasten a long-awaited ruling on the busing question by the highest court.

The original ruling would have merged three vast educational systems serving 101,000 students into one disparate system, with massive problems of administration and adjustment, requiring 78,000 youngsters to be shifted back and forth daily.

In terms of educational costs, turmoil, lost time and exacerbation of bitterness, the risks of chaotic failure are high.

Justification may be found in some cases for metropolitan-wide busing. Indeed, most inner cities sustain a certain amount of busing for practical reasons that achieve a measure of integration as well, and there are scattered experiments around the country where busing has been adopted specifically for desegregation purposes. Their success has been uneven, taken as a whole.

There seems little justification in inter-city busing. At best, the result could be a deepening frustration on the part of minority families that, while their children are permitted to attend predominantly white schools, they are barred by restrictive zoning laws and prejudices from living in white neighborhoods and attending neighborhood schools.

Mass busing and gerrymandering of school districts are not compelling answers to the question of how best to achieve racial desegregation in America. The Supreme Court, to which the Richmond plaintiffs will appeal, may finally be unable to sidestep the thorny issue in view of widespread resistance to busing and strong evidence that state and local laws have deliberately contributed to exclusive housing patterns in the North as well as the South.

Achievement of significant and enduring integration lies primarily in the removal of the prejudices that lock minorities into ghetto housing and low-pay job status in all parts of the nation. How that achievement is to be reached with maximum fairness to all concerned is turning out to be the most vexing social problem of our age.

THE POST-TRIBUNE
Gary, Ind., June 9. 1972

To a layman, some of the language used by the 4th U.S. Circuit Court of Appeals in the controversial Richmond, Va., school case could carry it considerably beyond its immediate importance as a potent new argument in the school busing controversy.

What the appeals court decided in litigation still likely to reach the Supreme Court was that the district court order linking the school districts of Richmond and its suburbs in an effort at racial balance was wrong.

The key to the ruling was the appeals court view that a district judge could not "compel one of the states of the Union to restructure its internal government for the purpose of achieving racial balance" in schools unless there is "invidious discrimination in the establishment of local governmental units."

But if it is wrong to "compel" a state to "restructure" for racial reasons, then what of some other restructurings?

It would appear to us to involve "restructure" when a state is required to ignore long-established county lines in setting up new legislative districts (and, perhaps, congressional districts, though there is a federal question there) in order to carry out earlier top court "one man-one vote" concepts.

It would appear to us to involve "restructure" when several counties within a state are required to unite in forming regional planning establishments for the approval and handling of a variety of federal grants.

Our argument here is not that such requirements forced on the states by Congress and the judiciary are wrong. We think in the main, both in the legislative and planning instances, they have been healthy.

However, if it is wrong to require "restructure" to effect racial equality which the 15th Amendment to the Constitution and the Supreme Court in its recent decisions have viewed as just, then is it not also wrong to require restructure to give everyone a more equal voice in representative government or to assure more useful social planning?

The busing issue will continue controversial throughout the current election campaigns and for a considerable time in the courts. But if it is solved on what seems a pure states' rights concept, then it is going to open a lot of other debates as well. The states should have rights, but it has been the view of the court that they should not exercise them in a way to deny individual and general welfare rights guaranteed by the Constitution. That could be the ultimate issue.

DETROIT-SUBURBAN SCHOOL BUSING ORDERED BY U.S. DISTRICT JUDGE

Only eight days after the 4th U.S. Court of Appeals reversed Judge Robert Merhige's ruling ordering the consolidation of Richmond's city and suburban schools, a federal judge in the 6th U.S. District in Detroit delivered the most extensive busing order to date. Judge Stephen J. Roth June 14 ordered 310,000 of the 780,000 pupils in Detroit and its 53 suburban school districts to be integrated through busing. Setting a general maximum of 40 minutes for a one-way ride for school children, Roth ordered a nine-member panel to work out details and establish a schedule within 45 days with the goal of implementation for the fall 1973 school term.

Chicago today American
Chicago, Ill., June 17, 1972

WHATEVER else might happen as a result of Federal Judge Stephen J. Roth's massive school busing order in Detroit, it is certain to start a battle that will end up in the Supreme Court, possibly involving more than busing. Roth's order calls for integration of 780,000 school children and 53 suburban school districts—with busing of 310,000 children, both black and white.

His order came within a few days after Congress passed an anti-busing measure that in effect tells federal judges not to direct school busing unless school districts request it [a silly provision on its face, because judicial orders are needed only when districts don't want busing]. It also tries to undermine the judiciary in other ways, such as providing that busing should not be carried out until all appeals have been exhausted—a stinging slap at district courts.

Roth's ruling was the first major one to collide with the anti-busing law, and so is destined for a test. That law clearly needs a test, too. To what extent can Congress interdict the courts and stay within the Constitution? Legislative and judiciary are separate branches of government, but the judiciary has suddenly come under attack—and not only from Congress. The anti-busing legislation was instigated by President Nixon, so the executive and legislative are in effect ganging up on the judiciary.

So Judge Roth's order may have as much to do with a basic constitutional question as with busing, and maybe more. Its aftermath will be worth watching. The question is not solely on the merits of a desegregation ruling for Detroit, but more fundamentally on Congress' right to put a leash on federal judges.

The Dallas Morning News
Dallas, Tex., June 22, 1972

The movement for an antibusing constitutional amendment has been pushed nearer a showdown by a federal court ruling that Detroit and 53 suburban districts must achieve racial balance by merging 800,000 pupils into a single school district.

Judge Stephen Roth's order makes all previous busing programs look like class excursions. More than 300,000 students would have to be bused up to 40 miles a day to achieve the 80-20 white-black ratio he demands.

President Nixon has on his desk a bill just passed by Congress forbidding busing until all appeals are exhausted, but Judge Roth has made it plain that neither the electorate, President Nixon nor Congress is going to stop him.

He may be right. Only a Supreme Court decision or an antibusing amendment could stop him for certain—and the high court will have the opportunity of deciding just how wide a circle courts can draw in pursuing the will-o'-the-wisp of racial balance.

It will surely get Roth's order on appeal just as it will get an appeal from a Fourth Circuit Court ruling, which countermanded a substantially similar order that would have mixed Richmond, Va., and its suburbs.

The Fourth Circuit said in that recent decision that restructuring of internal government to achieve racial balance isn't constitutionally justifiable. Either Roth or the Fourth Circuit is wrong.

In any case, Michiganders, who voted 51 per cent strong for anti-buser George Wallace, can testify that busing isn't the "phony issue" liberals say it is. A lot of other Americans will agree.

They can hope that the Supreme Court will halt the social experimenters at school district lines—but the only real guarantee of escape from the experimenters is an anti-busing constitutional amendment.

The Oregonian
Portland, Ore., June 16, 1972

The federal court ruling ordering integration of Detroit's schools with those of 53 suburban school districts is the most sweeping decision of its kind in the nation's history. It would provide for the daily busing of more than 300,000 of the 780,000 pupils in an area of about 300 square miles, with one-way trips of as much as 20 miles lasting 45 minutes.

In terms related to the Portland area, it would mean the busing of four times the Portland school enrollment over an area more than three times the city's size.

All this is to be done to bring down to an average of about 25 per cent the black enrollment in schools throughout the area; in Detroit schools, it is now about 65 per cent.

The largest integration busing program now in effect is that in Tampa, Fla., where 52,000 pupils, about half the total enrollment, are being bused.

The Detroit order could be overruled on appeal, as was a similar city-suburbs integration decision in Richmond, Va. Or it could be delayed by the terms of a bill now on President Nixon's desk for signature and providing that no court-ordered transfer of pupils for racial balance can be put into effect until all appeals are exhausted. The U. S. Supreme Court, which has the last word on such matters, has a Denver busing case before it, but it is not expected to rule on the issue until early next year. The Detroit court's order directs a beginning on the plan this fall.

This goes far beyond the U. S. Supreme Court's original school desegregation order of 1954 striking down the laws enforcing dual school systems. The Detroit judge would impose upon the schools the entire burden of integrating the races and, in the process, take one and a half hours out of the day of each of thousands of school children, black and white, and render them strangers to their neighborhoods. Moreover, Detroit schools, like Portland's are strapped for funds. The next school year there may be shortened, as was Portland's, to stay within an inadequate budget. The millions for additional busing would mean that much less for education.

Unquestionably, pupils of any race or cultural background benefit from association with others. Black children deserve special consideration in the schools because of the handicaps imposed by centuries of discrimination against blacks. But black children, too, would suffer under the Detroit plan; and polls indicate that black adults in the Detroit area are split on the question of busing.

This is one of those issues that is extremely personal. If it's your child, yes, put him on a bus. But if it's mine, no. The court, unfortunately, is very impersonal in determining how much of the school day will be spent — on a bus.

Some busing plans have worked fairly well to reduce concentrations of black pupils. But none comes near the magnitude of that ordered in Detroit. Its proportions are awesome, its implications of judicial fiat frightening. Michigan's Gov. William Milliken had it right in his response to the Detroit order: "Massive busing will not only be disruptive but counterproductive." And if it sticks in Detroit, it will be a precedent for similar damage to metropolitan area schools throughout the nation. The judge has added fuel to a hot election-year issue.

The Detroit News

Detroit, Mich., June 16, 1972

You have to hand it to Judge Stephen J. Roth. When he dives into the water, he makes a splash. His tricounty school bussing order is a sprawling belly flopper, executed in the face of a congressional moratorium, a higher court opinion, a presidential plea and an outraged public.

Since Roth is a federal judge and therefore an intelligent man, we assume he realizes the enormity of his action and the absurdity of his demands upon those who must develop and comply with his defiant and sweeping order.

If he acted with that realization, he must have been prompted by some overriding consideration. It has been suggested, for example, that he c o n s i d e r e d precipitate action necessary in order to get his picture on the cover of Time before the bussing issue is settled by the Supreme Court.

Even as he acted to integrate Detroit schools with those of 52 suburban districts, Roth seemed to be saying: "Will some one put a stop to all this?" For on the first page of his findings he noted that he has never taken proofs on whether the suburban districts are guilty of de jure segregation. This is exactly the point on which the state and the suburbs have based an appeal to the Supreme Court.

Roth's order is vulnerable in so many ways that we have difficulty deciding where to start.

Consider his selection of seven members for the nine-man panel which will develop the details of the integration plan. The panel includes some of the people who held key positions in the Detroit school system during the years when the alleged de jure segregation was taking place. Roth seems willing to put the foxes to work guarding the chicken roost.

Four of the seven members come from the Detroit system, although the majority of children affected by the order live in the 52 suburban districts. Those 52 suburban districts will be allowed to name a total of one member to the panel to represent their interests.

Roth gives the panel 45 days to develop a plan. Actually, the time allowed is more like 38 days, since the panel won't get its full nine members and start its deliberations until next week. In those 38 days it must figure out how to shuffle, assign and reassign 780,000 school children; how to bus the students to and from the schools they will attend; how to reassign faculties and staffs within the desegregated areas. Roth is asking nothing short of a miracle.

The state is strapped, Detroit is strapped and many of the suburban districts are strapped. Where do they get the money to pay the panel's costs? And going beyond the planning costs, where do they get the money for the massive and staggeringly expensive bussing program that will follow?

It is clear in the minds of ordinary citizens, if not in the mind of Judge Roth, that the Roth order must never be allowed to go that far.

First, every legal appeal and device will be employed to delay the implementation of the o r d e r; second, a definitive statement on cross-district bussing will be sought from the Supreme Court; finally, but only if necessary as last resort, the Constitution will be amended to restore rationality in a situation where the irrational for the moment has gained the upper hand.

June 19, 1972

If there is any rationale for supporting a bussing order that would transport some 300,000 schoolchildren away from their neighborhoods, it is that racial integration should lead to quality education for all. But the link is tenuous. The scientific proof is lacking. And, in Judge Stephen Roth's decision, the goal is almost foreclosed by wording which protects the status quo.

In his order, Judge Roth requires that each school district make provision "to insure that the curriculum, activities and conduct standards respect the diversity of students from differing ethnic backgrounds."

In the findings of fact and conclusions, the judge expands his c o m m e n t s to include "student codes" and the "entire grading, reporting, counseling and testing program."

This is more than a recognition that inner city children do not now perform as well as suburban students. If it were only that, we could have no quarrel with an attempt to ease the transition in a hypothetical integration plan. But Judge Roth seems to be requiring "special" treatment or "preferential" allowances that solidify existing quality differences.

Moreover, in his own mind, he is not dealing with a hypothetical case. He is talking about something he perceives to be as real as next fall. And if a superior but newly integrated school system were to follow this approach, we would immediately have two separate but unequal educational systems: one for inner city transferees, one for remaining neighborhood children.

But Judge Roth goes on to say that no test or "track" system will be allowed to separate children into ability or aspirational groupings.

So, if standards, testing and grading are to recognize existing lower performances by inner city children and if the children cannot be separated according to ability, we are left with only one likely result: Standards, testing and grading for all students will be reduced to some lowest common denominator and the concept of quality education will be diluted for all students, black and white, inner city or suburban.

Under Judge Roth's bussing plan, the highest "quality" education we could expect would be mediocre. With that, any vestige of justification for cross-district bussing disappears.

Detroit Free Press

Detroit, Mich., June 16, 1972

WHETHER ONE accepts Judge Stephen Roth's solution to the inequity of education in metro Detroit or not, one point is stripped naked by this case: The present system of organizing and financing schools is tragically unfair and must be changed.

For what appear to be legal and tactical reasons, Judge Roth in his order this week brushed past the complicated questions of finance, governance and administration that will be involved in integrating the metro area's schools. The state, he says, must return with recommendations on how to deal with those problems as it carries out integration.

Yet we wonder whether the question of racial integration can be separated from, and dealt with in advance of, the issue of long-term equalization of program, staff, finances, safety and facilities. Indeed, to carry out Judge Roth's ruling without first coping with these problems would not end inequality but compound it.

Beyond that, we must wonder whether the state could not reduce drastically the inequities that exist even if the busing of school children is ultimately rejected by the courts.

Take the matter of class size, for one major illustration. Judge Roth notes: "The rated capacity of classrooms in the Detroit public schools is 32; in some of the suburban districts the average rated capacity is as low as 24 or 25." That kind of difference, he says, has to be rectified.

Left unanswered, though, is the question of how that equalization is to take place. Does the state provide a special supplement in districts where class size must be reduced? Does it reassign the personnel of one district to another to bring low class size districts up and high districts down? What, then, of local millages?

Though Judge Roth has chosen not to deal directly with the question of finance, the issue is implicit in everything about his order. The state cannot ignore finance.

If Judge Roth's order stands, the inequalities will be dramatized and, quite probably, corrected. His decision would force the issue. A parent, knowing that his child might have to go to school in some other district, would be less tolerant of that district's lack of adequate facilities or teachers, or its over-sized classes.

But why only if the Roth order stands? If, as seems likely to us, the Roth order does not stand up, the consciences of Michigan people ought to be shamed by the inequities that have been exposed. They are unconscionable under any system of pupil assignment.

The local millage system is not the only villain making for inequality in Michigan, but it is one of the more pernicious. And the state cannot evade that question, whether or not it is required to bus school children, whether or not there is to be integration of city and suburbs.

The presence of such inequalities makes a mockery of any pretense that we believe in equal educational opportunity in this state. Such injustices must end whatever happens to the Roth decision.

THE CINCINNATI ENQUIRER

Cincinnati, Ohio, June 22, 1972

QUITE APART FROM the fact that it would entail the most ambitious school-busing operation in the nation, U.S. District Judge Stephen J. Roth's order for the desegregation of public schools in Detroit and its environs was a bombshell for several notable reasons:

• It came on the heels of a congressional mandate, voted after many weeks of debate, that the federal judiciary refrain from issuing any additional busing orders for the attainment of school integration through 1974.

• It came also on the heels of a decision in the U.S. Court of Appeals for the Fourth Circuit overturning a similar integration plan in Richmond, Virginia.

• It came in the face of a decision handed down by the Sixth Circuit Court of Appeals three years ago that there exists no constitutional right to attend a racially integrated or racially balanced school.

The issues in Detroit are akin to those that prevail in many of the nation's other urban centers. The public schools inside the Detroit school district are roughly two-thirds Negro. That circumstance made it impossible for Detroit schools even to approach what some regard as an optimum racial balance. Hence, Judge Roth chose the same course that had been chosen earlier by U.S. District Judge Robert R. Merhige Jr. in Richmond — consolidation with the suburbs. But whereas Judge Merhige had ordered Richmond's schools merged with those in two adjacent suburban counties, Judge Roth ordered Detroit's schools merged with those in 53 suburban communities. And whereas Judge Merhige's decision, if it had stood, would have entailed the busing of an estimated 78,000 students, Judge Roth's would mean the busing of an estimated 310,000 of the 780,000 students in the school districts involved. Some inner-city students would have to be bused to the suburbs; some suburban students would have to be bused to inner-city schools.

Not surprisingly, the State of Michigan is expected to appeal Judge Roth's decision to the Sixth Circuit Court of Appeals, which sits in Cincinnati.

Three years ago, the Sixth Circuit Court of Appeals, considering a suit brought by the National Association for the Advancement of Colored People (NAACP) against the Cincinnati School District, ruled, in effect, that there exists no constitutional right to attend a racially balanced school.

"Boards of education," wrote Judge Paul C. Weick, one of three jurists who heard arguments in the case, "can hardly be blamed or held responsible for neighborhood residential patterns."

The court also took the position that "federal courts are ill-fitted to instruct boards of e d u c a t i o n where to select school sites, draw zone lines or how to operate the public schools. We should intervene only where there has been a clear invasion of constitutional rights, and in our judgment that has not occurred here."

The Fourth Circuit Court of Appeals, in the same fashion, found no willful effort on the part of school officials in Richmond or its environs to perpetuate a dual school system. Precisely the opposite finding emerged from a somewhat similar case in Charlotte, N.C., where, in a landmark ruling, the U.S. Supreme Court held busing on a countywide basis the only feasible method of building a unitary school system.

If, as expected, the Detroit decision is appealed, the crucial issue could well be whether the dilemma Judge Roth has sought to resolve has resulted from willful action on the part of school officials to maintain racially unbalanced schools or whether the cause of integrated education has simply suffered from the continuing movement of white families from the inner city to the suburbs.

The Detroit case could also produce a first test of Congress' ability to restrict the federal courts in the area of school integration. Congress took its stand in the face of allegations that the legislative arm of the federal government could not constitutionally interfere with the judicial arm, notwithstanding a provision of the Constitution that gives the Supreme Court such "appellate jurisdictions, both as to law and fact, with such exceptions, and under such regulations as the Congress shall make."

Clearly, Judge Roth has fired the first salvo in what could prove one of the most significant legal struggles of the decade.

The Charlotte Observer

Charlotte, N.C., June 20, 1972

Reaction to Federal Judge Stephen Roth's order for school desegregation in Detroit was predictable. It was the same kind of complaint we heard in Charlotte, throughout North Carolina, and more recently in Richmond. Governors, congressmen, senators and others complained of the "massive" busing that would result.

Yet a look at the figures raises the question: When is busing busing and when is it "massive" busing?

In Detroit today there are 750,000 school children. Of these, 225,000 already are riding a school bus every day. Judge Roth's order would mean the busing of 85,000 more. If 85,000 is "massive," what is 225,000?

In Richmond there are 104,000 students. Of these, 68,000 already are bused. Judge Robert Merhige's desegregation order would have meant the busing of 10,000 more. If 10,000 is "massive," what is 68,000?

In North Carolina there are more than 1 million children. Of these, 410,000 were riding school buses prior to court-ordered desegregation. The orders required that an additional 86,000 be bused. If 86,000 is "massive," what is 410,000?

In Charlotte-Mecklenburg there were 79,569 public school students at the end of last term. Of them, 41,028 were riding buses. Prior to desegregation, 28,300 were being bused; thus, federal court orders here increased busing by 12,628 students. If 12,628 is "massive," what was 28,300?

We do not mean to dismiss the difficulties involved in some of these orders. But this has been a year of loose talk about "massive busing," and the facts often do not bear out the strident words used in the discussions.

THE SAGINAW NEWS

Saginaw, Mich., June 19, 1972

The spotlight on busing—the issue that has divided the people, the parties and even families like no other issue since Vietnam—now focuses squarely on Detroit. It also focuses squarely on the urgency of the U.S. Supreme Court to decide once and for all what limits, if any, are contained in all rulings to end school segregation by busing since the high court struck down the separate but equal doctrine in 1954.

In the wake of U.S. District Judge Stephen J. Roth's order that the city of Detroit and 52 suburban school districts brgin implementing cross-district school desegregation by September, we can only repeat what we said on June 9.

First, we are not surprised by Judge Roth's official order. The man has been of a single, idealistic and highly independent mind onthis ever since he issued his first finding — that Detroit schools were segregated due to "actions and inactions" of state and local governing bodies. From that point he has moved to the final conclusion that they are so hopelessly integrated that only cross district busing on a mammoth scale can achieve equal distribution by race ratio in the schoolroom. In getting there he was not deterred by a Justice Department request that he hold up his ruling until Congress could act on the President's request for legislatinon staying further court busing orders until all present case appeals had been heard.

Second, in spite of its impact—which has been virtually total across this state—Roth's order and the entire cross-district busing issue remains in legal limbo.

The difference between now and a couple of weeks ago, however, is that a sense of urgency has been injected into it as far as the Detroit order goes. It has been further complexed by various factions opposed striking out in all directions seeking legal review and the infusion of politics.

The Roth order is so sweeping in context that like Richmond, it is deserving of higher judicial review. And this is where the matter should be properly determined. The question is will it get it in time to clear the air before September? Right now that appears doubtful. The Sixth Circuit Court of Appeals would be the logical place to start. But that court earlier refused review on grounds that a review was premature until Roth had ruled.

Now the governor and the state attorney general have bypassed the 6th Circuit and carried their request direct to the U.S. Supreme Court. But the high court is soon to go into recess which could preclude any decision there before fall.

And now the President himself has entered the picture using the Roth ruling to get at Congress for failing to write into the Education Aid Bill the tougher anti-busing amendments he asked for.

In effect Mr. Nixon's comments can be read as an "I-told-you-so." The President says the present aid bill would have no effect on the Roth order—and that the only way to get a stay is to follow his proposal which would legislate a halt to implementation of all court-ordered busing for at least 18 months, perhaps longer, until all appeals were exhausted.

This Congress has been reluctant to do knowing full well it would put the legislative and the judiciary on a collision course—and raise the possibility of a Constitutional crisis. It would.

Thus we return to our original thesis. It is incumbent that the courts decide these busing questions, not Congress—and they should not be forced by Congress to act decisively. Until that happens busing will remain the confused issue that it is—and it will stay in legal limbo.

Our final observation also remains unchanged. Busing is now destined to become one of the stormiest issues of the election campaign. Perhaps in the long run Judge Roth's ruling has forced it to a head. For certain Detroit dwarfs Richmond.

THE RICHMOND NEWS LEADER

Richmond, Va., June 15, 1972

Today the people of the Richmond area have a particular kinship with the people of the Detroit area, because yesterday a Federal District judge in Detroit did to the people there what Federal District Judge Robert R. Merhige, Jr., did to the people here five months ago. Federal District Judge Stephen Roth ordered 53 suburban school systems in the Detroit area to dump the 780,000 students within their combined jurisdictions—one-third of the public school children in Michigan—into one giant mixmaster. His reason, of course, is race.

As in the Richmond case, Judge Roth has required the assignment of school children to achieve a precise racial ratio in each school. Of the 780,000 students, 25 per cent are black. So under the plan that Judge Roth has ordered for implementation in part this fall, each school would have to have an enrollment closely approaching a 75-25 white-black ratio. Clearly Judge Roth has been afflicted by the same germ that somehow escaped from the Petri dish in the pseudo-scientific laboratory of the nation's sociologists and bit Judge Merhige. The people of the Detroit area will not be comforted by the knowledge, which the people of the Richmond area can give them, that egalitarian orders of racist judges cannot be licked by taking two aspirin every four hours and getting plenty of rest.

The people of the Richmond area will be forgiven a moment of private rejoicing. If the residents of another region had to be skunked—if the racial blending of public school children had to be ordered anywhere else besides here—it is fortunate for us that it has been ordered in an unequivocally Northern city such as Detroit. There cannot be even the most roundabout insinuation that the racial condition in the Detroit area schools was created by any form of State—or de jure—action. Heretofore it has been the particular fate of the South to have had the most vindictive sorts of judicial orders forced upon it because, said the Federal courts, segregation in the South used to be State policy whereas in the North it was not. Under such a malicious distinction, segregated school situations in the North have remained largely untouched.

The Detroit case may at last compel the Supreme Court to toss that distinction onto the pile that history reserves for its most pernicious follies. To suggest that man can be remade by other men is the highest form of intellectual pretention. Yet here we have two Federal judges—one in Richmond, and now one in Detroit—who, despairing over the failure of man to fashion a more just society, have undertaken to recast our offspring from integrationist molds. Any social policy based solely on race is the most desperate form of clutching at suicidal scientific straws, and it will not work. When given the opportunity, the Supreme Court should rule such policies illegal as well.

SUPREME COURT VOTES 4–4 AGAINST RICHMOND CROSS-DISTRICT BUSING

The Supreme Court May 21 in an unannounced 4-4 vote upheld an appellate court ruling that the merger of the predominantly black Richmond, Va. school district with the heavily white, adjacent school districts of Henrico and Chesterfield was unconstitutional. Justice Lewis F. Powell Jr., a former member of the Richmond and Virginia state boards of education, did not participate.

Federal District Court Judge Robert R. Merhige Jr. had ruled Jan. 10, 1972 that the merger of the districts was the "only remedy promising immediate success" in ending an increasing pattern of unequal and segregated education. The 4th U.S. Circuit Court of Appeals overturned Merhige's order June 6, 1972 by a 5–1 vote. It charged Merhige with interpreting the 14th Amendment in an "excessive" manner and with exceeding his power of intervention by slighting the "principle of federalism incorporated in the 10th Amendment," which reserved power for the states. The appellate court said Merhige was in error in blaming the outlying counties for excessive concentrations of blacks within Richmond.

The Virginian-Pilot

Norfolk, Va., May 22, 1973

While the Supreme Court's 4-4 vote of yesterday set no precedent on interdistrict school busing for the nation, it is operative in the Richmond-suburbia c a s e. T h e Fourth U.S. Circuit Court of Appeals was upheld in its June 1972 rejection of Judge Robert R. Merhige Jr.'s order for the consolidation of Richmond's mostly black schools with Chesterfield and Henrico Counties' mostly white ones. And the Virginia Gubernatorial campaign was incidentally denied its potentially most explosive—and least worthy—issue.

Considering the vast amounts of litigation and emotion invested in the Richmond School Board's suit for consolidation, the Supreme Court's unsigned, one-sentence judgment was less than satisfactory. A decisive vote was lacking because the ninth Justice, Lewis F. Powell Jr., is a former member of the Richmond School Board. As that experience, along with Mr. Powell's further service on the Virginia State Board of Education, would suggest, he is the Court's leading expert in public-school affairs; just recently he demonstrated that in writing a complex Texas school-financing opinion. With his necessary abstention, the Richmond split decision followed ideological—and maybe political—lines.

The split is significant. For 17 years, on through the important *Swann* ruling of April 1971, requiring extensive busing in Charlotte, the Court maintained unanimity in school desegregation cases. When finally it cracked last June, the issue was whether Emporia, a Virginia town, could secede from the Greensville County school district and thus lower its black-to-white pupil ratio. The four Nixon-appointed Justices, who include Mr. Powell, were willing, but overruled. If Emporia did not set the Court's course for Richmond, it at least removed the obstacle of Court solidarity.

Meanwhile, massive school busing became increasingly unpopular all over the country. The Nixon Administration opposed it. Congress came close to passing antibusing legislation. When the Circuit Court slapped down Judge Merhige's consolidation order by a 5-1 vote, this newspaper noted that it "took the popular view." Judge Merhige's name had been mud in Virginia—even in Richmond, whose schools he would rescue from black re-segregation—ever since he signed his findings in January 1972.

Maybe the Supreme Court now is being influenced in some degree by the national climate. For many months, in any event, Chief Justice Warren E. Berger has been backing away from the decision he wrote in the Charlotte case. Lower court judges misread in his words a requirement for racial balances in schools, he has complained.

His complaint may be spied in yesterday's stalemate, as it clearly could be in the Emporia dissent. Whether it will prevail finally on the district consolidation question may be answered in the Detroit case.

That is the only case similar to Richmond's now under appeal in the Federal courts. In spite of certain peculiarities, the fundamental question, as in Richmond, is whether inner-city and outlying school districts should be merged in the interest of metropolitan desegregation. Because of Detroit's size and location outside the South, in some ways it offers a better Constitutional test than Richmond did.

As for Richmond, it is subject to the Circuit Court's declaration that it cannot try to solve its school problems by r e a c h i n g across boundaries into neighboring school districts. How Richmond schools will fare as a result is a dismal prospect. But it is just as well that Virginia suddenly is without a live busing hassle for exploitation in the budding political season.

THE RICHMOND NEWS LEADER

Richmond, Va., May 21, 1973

Early today, the Supreme Court upheld the ruling of the Fourth Circuit Court with these nine words: "The judgment is affirmed by an equally divided Court." So by the narrowest of all possible votes, the Supreme Court has forestalled all the social demolition that consolidation here — and throughout the nation — would have brought about. Consolidation remains only a bad dream bred of crackpot suggestion. Reason has prevailed.

In the *Swann* decision two years ago, the Court said: "No fixed or even substantially fixed guidelines can be established as to how far a court can go, but it must be recognized that there are limits." The Court ruled today that Federal District Judge Robert R. Merhige, Jr., went beyond those limits when he ordered consolidation. His was an order grounded in the anachronistic premise that no black child can acquire a quality education unless blacks in the school he attends constitute a numerical minority. It was an order based on the simplistic proposition that all the problems in Richmond's public schools derive from jurisdictional boundaries. It was an order dedicated to the theory that if blacks and whites cannot be persuaded to establish their own racial ratios, then they must be compelled to do so.

This was a balance case. Racial balance is one of today's more fashionable addictions which — thankfully — has not been legitimized by the Supreme Court. Nor, with today's decision, can anyone argue rationally that opposition to consolidation is the peculiar intellectual deviation of bigots and the idiot right. Today's decision may have been the closest of the close, yet in it there is nourishment for those parents and students in the metropolitan area who fed so long on anguish and fear.

And now. . . now let us be done with litigation involving the races in Richmond area public schools. All of our school systems are "unitary" in the sense that they exclude no one on the basis of race, and that is good. If the public schools of Richmond face particular difficulties, let the administrators of those schools meet the most profound obligation of any educator: *I.e.*, to help every student realize his true potential. But with today's decision from the Supreme Court, let us have no more attempts to impose abstraction on reality. We all have endured enough.

Richmond Times-Dispatch

Richmond, Va., May 22, 1973

The Decision ...

At last, the brakes. Until yesterday, the juggernaut of coercive school busing seemed uncontrollable and threatened to roll on and on, smashing whatever barricades of reason and constitutional principle might arise in its path. But yesterday, the United States Supreme Court began to apply the brakes. By affirming the U. S. Fourth Circuit Court of Appeals' decision against the consolidation of the Richmond metropolitan area's school systems, the high court ruled that there is a limit to how far the juggernaut can go.

It cannot roll across the legitimately established boundaries of political subdivisions merely for the sake of achieving racial balance in public schools. The circuit court so ruled, and by affirming that decision, the Supreme Court has so ruled. Thus, the school systems of the city of Richmond and of the counties of Henrico and Chesterfield will continue to operate as they have traditionally operated: separately. There will be no busing of children from deep in the heart of Richmond to the outer regions of the counties, or vice versa, to make certain that all schools in the area have a predominantly white enrollment.

The consolidation proposal was an offense to both the U. S. Constitution and to reason. Nothing in the Constitution requires racial quotas for public schools, the circuit court ruled and the Supreme Court has affirmed, but the adoption of the consolidation plan approved by U. S. District Judge Robert R. Merhige Jr. would have been the equivalent, the circuit court declared, "of the imposition of a fixed racial quota." The boundaries of Richmond, Henrico and Chesterfield were drawn, basically, years before school integration and busing became legal issues; and race had nothing whatever to do with their establishment. Moreover, if Richmond could reach out for white children in Henrico and Chesterfield to dilute its predominantly black school population, what would prevent it from acquiring white students from still other counties in the future if it so desired? Indeed,

Judge Merhige himself suggested that other counties in the region easily could be added to a consolidated system.

Obviously, approval of the principle of consolidation, as outlined in the Richmond case, would have constituted an invitation to chaos in the area's public schools. Transportation problems and racial statistics would have supplanted education as the primary concerns of school administrators. Public resistance to massive, long distance busing would have accelerated the exodus of white pupils from public schools and the proliferation of private schools, all to the detriment of public education. Finally, approval of the principle of consolidation for racial purposes could have foretold the abolition of the right of states to determine the structure of their local governments, for if political boundaries could be ignored to achieve racial balance in schools they could be ignored to achieve other racial goals.

Yesterday's victory against consolidation came, it must be noted,

by the narrowest possible margin. The court split 4-4, with Justice Lewis F. Powell Jr. of Richmond, once chairman of the Richmond School Board, not participating. Such a split automatically confirms an appeals court decision.

To be sure, consolidation questions remain alive in other cases the court probably will consider in the future. Conceivably, the court could subsequently order the consolidation of public schools in, say, the Detroit area. But such a ruling would not necessarily affect Richmond. Two cases are seldom identical, and the court could conclude that different circumstances prevail in Detroit; that, for example, school district boundaries in that area are racially tainted, and that, as a result, consolidation is legally justifiable. We hope that such will not be the case. On the contrary, we hope the Richmond decision will become the controlling decision in all similar disputes and that court-ordered consolidation for racial purposes will soon cease to be a threat anywhere.

... And Richmond's Future

Any jubilation over the outcome of the metropolitan school consolidation decision ought to be tempered by concern for the future of the Richmond public schools and the city itself.

Now community leaders must unite in support of a strong system of public schools for Richmond. The courts have grappled with the legalisms, but metropolitan leaders must come to grips with the human problems, which remain.

Taking a commendably positive approach yesterday was the Rev. Miles J. Jones, chairman of the Richmond School Board, who was disappointed by the decision but who refused to be embittered by it. The legal verdict, said Mr. Jones, "does not spell disaster for Richmond," and with the exercise of genuine, good-faith black-white leadership, the community can find solutions to its problems.

Educationally, the school system has begun in recent months under the leadership of Mr. Jones, who is black, and Superintendent Thomas C. Little, who is white, to take strides toward rebuilding

public confidence. In the reading improvement program, the clarified disciplinary procedures, and the expansion of "model" or alternative schools, the system has set some of the building blocks for future progress.

But as a part of this effort, biracial leadership needs to be exercised to resolve a lingering legal problem. The Court's decision prevents busing across political boundaries, but left in effect as of the moment is a District Court-approved plan under which thousands of children are being bused across the city, in some cases to be put into a minuscule racial minority. The city schools have lost close to 10,000 white pupils since cross-city busing began in 1970. Continuation of this kind of pupil assignment in the wake of the consolidation ruling can only be self-defeating, leading eventually to an all-black school system.

Is there a more moderate alternative? Possibly the biracial school board and its legal counsel

will be able to discern one from past court decisions. Yesterday's Supreme Court rendering leaves the 4th U. S. Circuit Court of Appeals' decision of June last year as the controlling word on area desegregation. In that opinion, Judge J. Braxton Craven held that Richmond had "done all it can do to disestablish to the maximum extent possible the formerly state-imposed dual school system within its municipal boundary." All three metropolitan systems were "unitary" racially, the court said. In that context, let it be remembered that the Supreme Court, in the 1971 Charlotte case, said that once a school system has reached a "unitary" status, it is not required to make year by year adjustments of racial compositions of student bodies.

Thus, the city might be on solid ground in seeking relief from strict cross-city busing in U. S. District Court, under a contention that it has fulfilled its Constitutional duty to dismantle a state-imposed dual school system. Judge Robert R. Merhige Jr., who approved of consolidation, has himself been skep-

tical of the merits of "sprinkling," or assigning children across town to be part of a very small minority in a particular school.

As an incentive for remaining in the Richmond system (and to draw "lost" and new patrons), students might be given the option of transferring to the school or special program of their choice, even if it happened to be a "neighborhood" school. Certainly, any new system would have to be carefully thought out so that it would in no way be a return to compulsory segregation. Elements to safeguard individual educational rights might include the provision of free transportation and widespread advertising of educational options throughout the city.

We don't suggest that we have the answers, only that this community is capable of finding answers. It is time, as Mr. Jones suggests, "to see what real black and white leadership can do in the city of Richmond." We believe it can work wonders.

The New York Times

New York, N.Y., May 27, 1973

A deadlocked four-to-four vote by the Supreme Court has vacated an original order that would have forced a merger of Richmond's predominantly black school system with its surrounding, predominantly white suburban counties. The judicial tie has the effect of upholding last year's opinion by the United States Court of Appeals for the Fourth Circuit, which overturned the original merger order issued by Federal District Judge Robert R. Merhige Jr. Specifically, the Appeals Court rejected Judge Merhige's claim that the state of Virginia, by means of discriminatory housing and school construction policies, had directly facilitated the maintenance of a segregationist wall and a dual school system.

The Supreme Court's action is a setback for the cause of school integration, particularly since such a division is, in accordance with tradition, not accompanied by any opinions or explanations. This newspaper disagreed from the outset with those who viewed Judge Merhige's ruling as a first step toward mergers of urban and suburban districts everywhere. But we had hoped that a reasoned Supreme Court opinion would point the way and serve as a warning to suburban districts that abuse of the zoning power to exclude black residents or black schoolchildren would henceforth be treated as unconstitutional *de jure* segregation

The case, moreover, seemed to offer long-overdue opportunity for the Court to sort out a variety of conflicting claims and to eliminate those ambiguities which threaten to erode the integration gains achieved since the 1954 desegregation ruling. An ideal opening for a searching examination of the issues was provided not only by Judge Merhige's detailed account of segregationist gerrymandering but by Judge Harrison L. Winter's strongly worded dissent from the Appeals Court ruling. "The sordid history of Virginia's, and Richmond's, attempts to circumvent, defeat and nullify the holding of *Brown I* has been recorded in the opinions of this and other courts," wrote Judge Winter.

The charges of such deliberate evasion constituted the basic issue to which we had hoped the Supreme Court would address itself. It could have done so without resorting to a merger order, thereby upholding that measure of local control over public education which seems to us desirable for the maintenance of community commitment to school support. But at the same time, the Court could have moved against policies which turn local control into a camouflage for segregationist zoning and planning.

It would be an act of defeatism to accept the Court's disappointing deadlock as a signal that the end had come to an era during which the courts and the country moved toward attainment of equal rights in the nation's schools. Quite to the contrary, it remains for the proponents of civil rights to carry to the Supreme Court any violations of *Brown* with renewed determination. The Court's evasion of the hard questions in Richmond must be deplored as a temporizing delay; it should not be accepted as a call for retreat.

LEDGER-STAR

Norfolk, Va., May 22, 1973

The Supreme Court has now upheld the judgment of the U.S. 4th Circuit Court of Appeals in rejecting court-enforced consolidation of the Richmond and two adjoining school systems as a means of achieving broader racial balance.

In the large context of general directions in school desegregation rulings, the high court's action was not conclusive. The affirmation of the lower appellate court, which had overturned District Judge Merhige's order for the three systems to consolidate, came by way of a 4-4 division. Justice Powell, formerly associated with both the Richmond school system and the State Board of Education, did not take part.

But for the parties to the specific case, the result is conclusive. And its effect is to bring to an end a long period of uncertainty not only for Richmond itself, with a school system that is 70 per cent black, but for the counties of Chesterfield and Henrico, whose enrollment is about 90 per cent white.

Many, of course, saw a great deal of merit in the school merger idea. It not only would more evenly balance the races in the Richmond schools; it also would provide strong guarantees against resegregation, a continuing problem for many central-city school districts.

★ ★ ★ ★

But the issue here really is neither education nor integration. And in promoting these as the issues, Judge Merhige extended the role of the court beyond any reasonable limit. Because the basic flaw in the approach remains the fact that the consolidation would have been court-ordered. And the issue is whether the court has the right to impose on two separate school districts the responsibility for solving the problems of a third district. Within what should be the restricted framework of law, those two districts do not own any such responsibility.

★ ★ ★ ★

The case is, to be sure, complex in the sense that many provocative and troubling questions are raised, including the cross-busing issue. And at the risk of over-simplification, we quote from the government brief. The government, which entered the case in opposition to the consolidation order, accused Judge Merhige of acting as a "problem solver implementing programs and policies contrary to state law that some might find enlightened or desirable."

It is this penchant for problem solving that has led the courts astray in so many instances, and most especially with respect to specific, court-ordered plans that have emerged to overcome racial imbalances in the schools.

The Supreme Court will face other cases presenting issues quite similar to those contained in the Richmond plan even though some circumstances doubtless will be different and some new legal questions may be posed. But in a subsequent case, with nine justices voting, a decision would be conclusive insofar as establishing legal precedent.

The court will be serving not only the interests of law but ultimately the cause of problem solving itself if it can refrain from perverting the law in order to provide short-cuts to those solutions that ought to be pursued in other ways. And now, presumably, will be so pursued in Richmond.

THE ARIZONA REPUBLIC

Phoenix, Ariz., May 23, 1973

The Orwellian obsession to engineer racial mixing in America, no matter what the violence to human choice, is an unrelenting social scheme.

It has flourished most vividly in schools, where the device of busing-for-integration has been the manipulative machinery. Think tanks are alive with new notions of the Orwellian theorists, the newest being how to regulate the racial mixture of residential housing.

Something of a slap in the face has been dealt the social engineers in this week's U.S. Supreme Court ruling to strike the infamous Virginia integration decision of Federal Judge Robert Merhige.

The ruling was not thunderous. It was a split 4-4, with Justice Powell abstaining because of his own preappointment involvement in the Virginia case.

Nonethless, the ruling has derailed the Virginia plan outright, and probably stalled for the time being the madness of other schemes to juggle Americans by skin color to meet numerical quotas.

It was 16 months ago that Judge Merhige decided that the only salvation for Richmond's 70 per cent black schools was to merge them with those of 92 per cent white Henrico County nearby, and 91 per cent white Chesterfield County.

By shaking all 101,000 students well within the 752-square-mile consolidated district, Judge Merhige hoped to achieve a 66-to-34 per cent racial mix.

Blacks as well as whites posed volumes of logical legal arguments against the proposal.

One which Judge Merhige shrugged off was that thousands of students would spend hours daily on buses. Richmonders were outraged at the judicial indifference — since Judge Merhige sends his own son to a predominantly white private school within walking distance of his home.

Nowhere did the judge produce any eloquent or persuasive evidence that education would be served. It was a numbers game of color quotas through and through.

If Judge Merhige's decision had been left to stand, the consequences are too dreadful to contemplate. No political subdivision nor political boundary would be immune from judicial fiat to move citizens at the will of the court to meet racial quotas — perhaps even across state lines.

DE FACTO SEGREGATION OUTLAWED IN 7-1 DENVER SCHOOL RULING

The Supreme Court ruled 7-1 June 21 that Northern school systems with substantial pockets of segregation would be treated the same way as had Southern school systems with de jure patterns of segregation. In a case involving Denver, the court said school board policies that fostered segregation even in limited parts of a metropolitan area might affect the whole system, and the whole system required desegregation, "root and branch." Black and Mexican-American parents had sued the Denver school board, charging it with the creation of segregated schools through manipulation of attendance zones, school site selection, and a neighborhood school policy.

The Denver ruling was the high court's first decision dealing with the question of de facto segregation. While the court stopped short of eliminating the distinction between de jure and de facto segregation, it said, "Proof of state-imposed segregation in a substantial portion of the district will suffice to support a finding by the trial court of the existence of a dual system.... Where the finding is made, as in cases involving statutory [de jure; Southern] dual systems, the school authorities have an affirmative duty to effectuate a transition to a racially nondiscriminatory school system."

The court ordered the case returned to the federal district court in Denver to allow Denver school authorities to prove they did not intend to provide racial separation.

Justice William H. Rehnquist dissented, while Justice Byron White, a native Coloradan, did not participate in the court's decision.

The New York Times

New York, N.Y., June 26, 1973

The Supreme Court has taken an important step in assuring the nation's racial minorities that the protection of their children from the evils of school desegregation applies throughout the United States, and not just in the South. The 7-to-1 ruling in a case involving the Denver schools holds that when a district has been guilty of a deliberate policy of racial discrimination, the burden is on the public education authorities to show why they should not repair the resulting harm by desegregating all the schools.

The ruling flows naturally from the 1954 Brown decision, even though that historic case dealt specifically with the Southern legal tradition which had authorized the maintenance of "separate but equal" schools. In terms of practical consequences, the more surreptitious policy of racial gerrymandering of school zones in Northern cities is hardly distinguishable from the *de jure* maintenance of dual school systems. Once administrative fiat had separated a city's children by race, it followed almost inevitably that they would be dealt with "separately" and usually unequally in matters of financing and pedagogy. Thus, equality of opportunity—and therefore equal protection under the law—became a myth.

The point driven home by the Court is that deliberate school board policies have all the earmarks and impact of state law. It is not enough to show that past evasions are no longer engaged in today; it is the responsibility of the school authorities to correct the present effects of past injustices.

The Court's action should dispel doubts and misconceptions about the future of desegregation which have been fostered by segregationists and exploited by politicians. The Court has made it clear that the 1954 desegregation order was not an aberration, imposed by a temporarily liberal Court. There is a vital message in the agreement between Justices William O. Douglas and Lewis F. Powell Jr., respectively the symbols of liberalism and conservatism, that desegregation is required of *all* schools—and is fixed policy under the Constitution.

THE DENVER POST

Denver, Colo., June 24, 1973

FOR THE NATION, especially its northern and western cities, the U.S. Supreme Court enunciated a sweeping but sensible new doctrine Thursday in the Denver school desegregation case.

This doctrine is that where the schools in any substantial area of a city have been segregated by school board policies or actions, the legal presumption is that schools in the whole system have been affected and will require desegregation.

This was one of the most basic contentions of the plaintiffs in Denver and the high court's ruling is a significant victory for them.

However, for Denver as a whole, the decision could mean in practice another delay of a year or more in settling the case. This we regret. We had been hoping the Supreme Court would settle the whole matter, one way or another, and end the uncertainty about a host of integration-related issues.

Since the high court hasn't done that, we wish the new school board could find some way to do it.

What the court did do was affirm the findings of both district and circuit courts that the actions and policies of school boards in the 1950s and 1960s contributed to the segregation of a set of elementary schools in or near Park Hill.

IN VIEW OF THIS proven fact, the court said, ". . . Common sense dictates a conclusion that racially inspired school board actions have an impact beyond the particular schools that are the subjects of those actions." That is, there must be other schools in Denver that are nearly all-Anglo because black students were confined to schools in the Park Hill area.

To be fair, the high court is giving the Denver school board a chance to rebut the newly-established legal presumption. In district court, the board will have a chance to try to prove that segregation in Park Hill area schools didn't affect schools elsewhere in the city. Otherwise it must desegregate the schools citywide.

But we wonder whether there is any point in the board trying to prove this point. The majority of the board may feel obligated to try, but it would be a long, uphill fight. It would certainly simplify life for the board, and for all the citizens of Denver, if the board could manage now to work out some settlement of this case acceptable to all elements of the community.

One significant sidelight of the Supreme Court decision is the fact that the court found that District Judge William E. Doyle erred in separating Negroes and Hispanos for purposes of defining a "segregated" school.

The court noted "much evidence that in the Southwest Hispanos and Negroes have a great many things in common" and that Hispanos suffer from the same educational inequities as Negroes and Indians. Therefore the high court felt that Doyle should have included schools "with a combined predominance of Negroes and Hispanos. . .in the category of segregated' schools".

Now although it is true that Hispano children often suffer the same educational inequities as blacks, it is also true that most Hispanos in Denver—the articulate ones at least—apparently do not want their children to have the same degree of school integration sought by most blacks.

If this be so, the Denver school board might save everyone a lot of legal hassling by trying to work out differing settlement terms with the black and Hispano communities.

WE HOPE, at any rate, that the new board will consider this possibility. The Supreme Court ruling has set new ground rules within which everyone will have to work.

Now that we know what they are, it would help if the schools could settle this case somehow, within those rules, and concentrate their full energies and resources on improving the quality of education in Denver.

The Detroit News
Detroit, Mich., June 24, 1973

As the courts laboriously grind out opinions in school segregation cases, pro-bussers and anti-bussers alike find grist for their causes. Last week it was the anti-bussers' turn to take heart.

They got their first substantial evidence that Justice Lewis F. Powell Jr., who may be the man who will cast the "swing" vote in future bussing cases that come before the U.S. Supreme Court, strongly opposes bussing as a means of achieving racial integration.

Not that Powell is a segregationist. On the contrary, he voted with the majority of the court last week to send the Denver case back to a lower court, where the school board must answer the charge that it deliberately shaped school policy to maintain segregated ghetto schools. Justice Powell argued at length for the desegregation of all schools. Whether in North or South, he said, segregation must be removed "root and branch."

However, Justice Powell regards the school bus as a very poor tool for such work. In his view, "Any child, white or black, who is compelled to leave his neighborhood and spend significant time each day being transported to a distant school suffers an impairment of his liberty and his privacy."

We see no inconsistency in Justice Powell's position. Bussing is not the only means of getting rid of the segregation which he and all other fair-minded persons deplore. He suggests other steps: redrawing neighborhood attendance zones, building new schools, integrating faculties.

Justice Powell's approach follows closely that of President Nixon, who last year proposed a plan under which courts would avoid issuing bussing orders until a variety of other remedies had been exhausted. The idea is so practical and logical that no court has yet grasped it.

In the bussing controversy, however, you lose some and you win some.

Earlier this month, the U.S. Court of Appeals (6th Circuit) handed down a ruling which upheld the essential parts of Judge Stephen J. Roth's order contemplating massive cross-district bussing for Detroit and 52 suburban school districts.

That setback for the anti-bussers must be weighed against two recent decisions by the U.S. Supreme Court. In one, the Supreme Court upheld a ruling by a lower court that Federal Judge Robert Merhige had exceeded his authority in merging the Richmond, Va., school district with two surrounding counties. The high court's decision came on a 4-4 tie vote, Justice Powell, once a member of the Richmond school board, abstaining.

The second decision, the one last week, suggested the possibility that Justice Powell may be the man who will break that 4-4 deadlock, thus producing a 5-4 decision against cross-district bussing, when and if the Detroit case comes before the Supreme Court for final judgment.

The Evening Star and The Washington Daily News
Washington, D.C., June 30, 1973

In its Denver school decision, the Supreme Court finally began dealing with segregation outside the South, and the effect promises to be momentous. No longer may officials in the North or West, or anywhere else, place much confidence in the argument that their school desegregation is a de facto situation, deriving from residential patterns, rather than the de jure kind which, in the South, bears the stigma of origin in old racial laws.

Indeed those distinctions may begin to fade away, for the court extended the de jure scope to every city in the nation where any conscious official action—such as zoning or construction of facilities—has resulted in a pocket of school segregation. If this condition exists, a city can be required to desegregate its whole system, not just the affected area, and the court's strong implication is that this is the road Denver must follow.

Furthermore, civil rights lawyers think that the same factors can be found in most other cities, and probably they are right. So this decree raises the prospect of citywide busing all across the country to attain thorough racial distribution. The court did not spell out methods that would be acceptable, but it did seem to indicate some appreciation of the practical dilemmas involved. In allowing further district court consideration, it gave Denver a bit more time to get started on difficult adjustments.

No one will win very much, we suspect, if massive busing finally emerges as the primary court-approved remedy for racial imbalance in urban schools. A great deal of damaging discord and waste of resources may be avoided if the court's requirements stop short of that, and can be fulfilled through other measures, including rezoning, and even relocation of schools in some areas. The justices are right in not dealing lightly with segregation caused by calculated official actions, past or present. But they have yet to grapple with the reality of new urban residential concentrations that, sadly enough, have created too many separate racial communities of vast expanse. The main hope of overcoming this division lies in improved economic mobility for minorities, and housing reforms. Attempting to deal with it at the educational level through enormous expenditures for transportation may be much more than the American public is willing to bear, and of dubious value to minority students.

In any case, much remains to be clarified by the court, but this surprisingly lopsided 7-1 ruling made plain that desegregation is going to be expanded, one way or another. Soon the justices will take up the question of whether to require school desegregation between cities and suburbs, and there's good reason to hope they will not go to such lengths. The court's tie vote that cancelled such a plan in the Richmond area indicated that whatever busing is required at least may be restricted to existing school districts.

Chicago Daily Defender
Chicago, Ill., June 26, 1973

A new federalism that translates itself into local option underlines the Supreme Court decision on obscenity. There are enough multiple variables to be read into action that various states will have varying constitutional interpretations as to what constitutes, in the language of the court, "redeeming social value" where and when pornography is at issue.

Of the four other cases on which the Justices ruled, the Denver School case was the most significant in that it touched upon a fundamental social question affecting the whole spectrum of democracy in practice. The question had been dragging far too long without a substantive judicial guideline to remove it from the whims of injudicious partisan courts.

Though the Justices did not go all the way in their definition of de facto segregation as an unconstitutional warrant, they did establish, to the astonishment of many of their critics, that any Northern school system with a substantial pocket of demonstrable segregation will be construed as an entirely dual system with an unconstitutional level of discrimination.

Some students of the law believe that the Supreme Court missed a precious opportunity to end any legal distinction between de facto discrimination and de jure segregation. Except for the rare case in which geography divides a school district into separate units, the court declared:,

"Proof of state imposed segregation in a substantial portion of the district will suffice to support a finding by the trial court of the evidence of a dual system."

A clear and unobstructive distinction between de jure and de facto segregation was glossed over, the Justices strongly indicated that they would apply rigorous desegregation standards to areas where racial separation is a product of social pattern rather than former law.

Viewed in its broad context, it is a great decision. It takes, at long last, school desegregation out of the fog which had enveloped it and removes the Burger court from the shoal of doubts of its position on the issue of racial imbalance in the nation's public school system.

It was feared that with the Nixon doctrine of "strict constructionism" and the presence of his appointees on the court that there was no longer an alignment of the Justices of sufficient numerical strength to carry on the legal precedent inherent in the court's 1954 desegregation mandate.

Could it be the flood waters of Watergate have flushed out of the constitutional holes to which the Nixon appointees had been consigned? This is not a rhetorical question, but an inquisitive supposition.

The Birmingham News

Birmingham, Ala., June 29, 1973

School desegregation, which took the South by storm during the Sixties, may stir analogous controversies in the North in the Seventies as the courts move toward a uniform national policy on the issue.

The U. S. Supreme Court recently established a precedent in the Denver, Colo., ruling which, in effect, declared unlawful the particular form of segregation widely practiced in Northern metropolitan school districts.

In the Denver case, the court held that if even a part of a metropolitan school system is segregated, the rest of the system necessarily will be affected; therefore, the entire system must be desegregated "root and branch."

For many years the terms "de facto" and "de jure" had been used to construct an untenable distinction between Northern and Southern segregation. Not unreasonably, the forces of the federal government first attacked segregation where it had been maintained for generations by law — meaning the South.

Now, however, the percentage of black students in the South attending mostly white schools, 44 per cent, is much higher than the corresponding percentage in the North, 29 per cent.

Schools in the South have been ordered paired, closed, consolidated and any other form of change which would facilitate racial balancing. School children have been zoned, bused and balanced to achieve the numerical ratios by race which would satisfy the courts' demands for an end to Southern dualism.

Now it is time to end dualism, Northern style.

If a policy is fair, equitable and constitutionally required of one section of the nation then it must also be applied to other regions.

Separate and unequal policies, North and South, clearly are hypocritical and unjust.

The methods employed in Northern desegregation may not be any more palatable there than they have been here to many people. Many parents, black and white, resent having their children transported long distances each day to achieve a certain ratio of blacks to whites in schools. Reassigned faculty members also may be inconvenienced by the hundreds. And many middle-class families, black and white, may be fearful of having their children subjected to the social problems commonly associated with children of the slums

But the Denver ruling is evidence that the Supreme Court intends to continue in, rather than turn back from, the direction in which the nation has been going for the past two decades.

Unquestionably, a national policy against deliberate segregation by race is sound in principle. It is axiomatic that where low-income minorities are segregated, their children's educational opportunities are vastly lower than those of the children of the affluent.

But the practical problems which have arisen from desegregation are many, making it evident that school desegregation in itself is no panacea to the nation's racial and social problems. The nation must approach the deep underlying problems in unity, however — not in a piecemeal fashion which decrees a standard for one region but exempts the rest.

Richmond Times-Dispatch

Richmond, Va., June 24, 1973

The Denver school case indicates a majority of the U. S. Supreme Court is ready to move against Northern-style segregation, but only when a school board can be assumed to have "intended" to foster separation of the races by some of its actions.

Justice Lewis F. Powell Jr. of Richmond concurred in the 7-to-1 decision to the extent that he felt a Constitutional standard which had been laid down for Charlotte, N. C., a "Southern" city, should be fair enough for Denver, Colo., a "Northern" city.

However, in a separate opinion possibly of major importance, Mr. Justice Powell proposes that the court, first, eliminate all distinctions between Northern and Southern school cases including historical differences and questionable presumptions of "intent" by the judiciary, and, second, adopt a uniform rule of reason for the nation that would recognize the value of the neighborhood concept in urban education.

The Powell plea is eloquent. In his usual manner, he carefully balances the competing interests and attempts to find the path of moderation where lies the most equitable solution. This man who contributed so hugely to the betterment of public education for all the children of Richmond and Virginia is offering here a common-sense approach for the schools of the nation. May his plea be heard!

What is Justice Powell proposing? Certainly not that school boards can renege on the responsibility of maintaining a desegregated school system. Neighborhood school boundaries can be adjusted to promote the most integration practicable. New schools can be constructed at sites most likely to attract a racially-diverse student body. Faculty integration is attainable. Students can be given the freedom to transfer to schools where they are in the racial minority and be given a free ride there. Powell is absolutely right that in this new era no person of a racial minority should be demeaned by being made to feel that, solely because of his race, he is barred from attending particular public facilities in his locality.

But what of the practice of barring students from their neighborhood schools solely because of their race and transporting them great distances, ostensibly to promote integration? Clearly, Powell believes the massive busing remedy suffers from an excess of zeal and a shortage of wisdom. In a single-minded concern over racial percentages, the court has strayed from the original 1954 *Brown* decision, which was supposed to forbid assignment of pupils by race. It is well to remember, he reminds his colleagues, what the goal is, or should be: "the best possible educational opportunity for all children."

Bizarre busing schemes that focus entirely on racial distribution are not constructive of that goal. Citizen support of public education may correlate with a sense of closeness to school: "distance may encourage disinterest." (The woeful decline in P-TA attendance at Richmond schools since the start of busing in 1970 bears out that conclusion.) Courts ordering widespread busing risk hastening an exodus from public to private school and from city to suburb. Busing has divided communities, not brought them together.

"Communities deserve the freedom and the incentive," Powell concluded, "to turn their attention and energies to this goal of quality education, free from protracted and debilitating battles over court-ordered student transportation."

These are tremendously encouraging words coming from an associate justice of the Supreme Court, and all the more so because they come from a member whose position may be pivotal in coming tests of the limits of metropolitan busing. Mr. Justice Powell's first extensive opinion on the busing issue may prove to be a landmark in restoring reason to the difficult desegregation process.

The Dallas Morning News

Dallas, Tex., June 25, 1973

THE SUPREME COURT has avoided treating the North and the South the same in segregation suits, but it has decided — for the first time — that the North, too, can be guilty of segregation.

So far as high court pronouncements have gone, the North has been secure until now behind the automatic defense that if there are no state segregation laws there can be no wrongful segregation.

But lower courts have found a deliberate case of segregation within the Denver school system—and on this the high court has founded a new policy of ordering mixing, based not on wrongful laws but on deliberate policy decisions made by school boards outside the South.

In ordering the Denver board to prove that the rest of its system isn't tainted by a deliberate antimixing policy decision, the high court is saying that deliberate intent to segregate is just as bad as the old Southern laws that spelled out separate schooling.

NOTHING like this has been said to the North before. The court, moreover, piled the burden of proof not on the people suing the Denver system but on the system itself. Instead of the plaintiffs having to show discrimination, the Denver board (and all others to be sued outside the South) must prove conclusively that deliberate policy had no part in creating racial imbalance.

Plausible explanations won't do, said the court—the board must show that the whole thing was accidental, free from the effect of any deliberate human agency. If the board fails, then its whole system will be ordered mixed, just as in the South.

THE SPECTER of busing in the North will grow larger, because once guilt is established all the remedies, including busing, will apply.

The immediate result should be to strengthen the drive for an anti-busing constitutional amendment. Northern lawmakers should feel strong pressure from home to join the South in halting the bus. If mixing itself can't be halted, Americans are pretty much of a mind that its offspring—busing—should be kept within firm bounds.

The obvious next step is for the court to set a uniform national mixing policy.

In the latest pornography decision, the high court acknowledged that the states, in their own individual constitutional exercises of power, each has the right to enforce some laws according to the standards of the community. But where federal enforcement of laws is involved, that enforcement must be under a single national standard. The federal government cannot justly enforce its own law by one standard for one region and a different standard for the others.

Court Decisions: 1974-75

New York

Integration of NYC school ordered. In what was said to be the first decision of its kind, a federal district court judge in New York City Jan. 28 ordered federal, state and city housing authorities, along with city departments of education, police, parks and transportation, to cooperate in formulating plans to integrate a junior high school in the borough of Brooklyn. As of 1973, 43% of the school's pupils were black, 39% hispanic and 18% white.

Ruling in a suit filed by the National Association for the Advancement of Colored People, Judge Jack B. Weinstein ordered housing officials to provide a joint plan "to undo the racial imbalance" in publicly-supported housing in the area served by the school. Weinstein said all levels of government had failed to take "available steps" to reverse trends toward segregation in both housing and education, and concluded that "federal complicity in encouraging segregated schooling through its housing programs" was unconstitutional.

Noting that entrenched segregation at the school had discouraged white families from moving into the area's public housing, Weinstein said the plans should include "advertisements and inducements" directed at the white middle class to "stabilize" the district's population.

Weinstein ordered the city's transportation department to provide busing plans for short-term balancing of the school's enrollment; the police department was to submit plans for adequate protection of children in the area; and the parks department—whose facilities were heavily used by the school—was ordered to provide a separate plan.

Weinstein said the plans should be submitted by March 1 and put into effect in September.

Court retreats on NYC school order. U.S. District Court Judge Jack B. Weinstein issued a final ruling July 26 which considerably softened his earlier landmark decision that city, state and federal agencies must cooperate to alter housing and social patterns in order to integrate a junior high school in the Borough of Brooklyn.

Weinstein gave the city's central school board and the district board until the beginning of the 1977 school year to raise the number of white students in the school to 70%, the overall percentage of white junior high pupils in the district. Currently, 18% of the one school's students were white.

To attain this proportion, Weinstein ordered that feeder patterns within the district be redrawn to reflect the racial make-up of the district as a whole. The junior high school would also be made a special "school for gifted children" to attract students from throughout the district. Weinstein noted that such plans would conform with the recent Supreme Court decision against cross-district busing.

Weinstein retained the right to order an extensive intra-district busing program if it appeared within the first year that the softer plans were failing to attract sufficient numbers of white students.

The South

Montgomery busing rejected. U.S. District Court Judge Frank M. Johnson Jr. May 22 accepted an integration plan offered by the Montgomery County, Ala. school board that would, in general, allow elementary school pupils to attend neighborhood schools. Johnson rejected plans involving cross-city busing submitted by black groups and the federal government, ruling that while some schools would have high percentages of black students under the school board plan, all students would attend a "substantially desegregated school for a majority of their school careers."

Supreme Court

Memphis desegregation plan upheld. The court unanimously refused to disturb a lower court order upholding a Memphis school desegregation plan that retained 25 all-black schools in the interest of saving money and limiting busing, it was announced Apr. 23. Justice Marshall did not participate in the ruling, which was made without comment.

Court rejects cross-district busing. The Supreme Court July 25 struck down a plan to desegregate the predominately black Detroit school system by merging it with mostly white, neighboring districts. The 5–4 decision all but banned desegregation through the busing of children across school district lines.

Chief Justice Warren E. Burger, author of the court's majority opinion, was joined by Justices Harry A. Blackmun, Lewis F. Powell Jr. and William H. Rehnquist, all appointees of President Nixon, and Potter Stewart, named to the court by President Eisenhower.

In his opinion, Burger noted reasoning by lower courts that Detroit's schools, which were 70% black, would not be truly desegregated unless their racial composition reflected the racial composition of the whole metropolitan area. However, Burger challenged what he called the lower court's "analytical starting point" —that school boundary lines might be casually ignored and treated as mere administrative conveniences.

Such notions were contrary to the history of public education in the U.S., Burger wrote. "No single tradition in public education is more deeply rooted than local control over the operation of schools; local autonomy has long been thought essential both to the maintenance of community concern and support for public schools and to quality of the educational process. . . . local control over the educational process affords citizens an opportunity to participate in the decision-making, permits the structuring of school programs to fit local needs and encourages experimentation, innovation and a healthy competition for educational excellence."

Moreover, Burger continued, consolidation of 54 historically independent school districts into one super district would give rise to an array of new problems concerning the financing and operation of the new district. In the absence of a complete restructuring of the laws of Michigan relating to school districts, the proposed interdistrict remedy would cause the federal district court to become "first, a de facto 'legislative authority' to resolve these complex questions, and then the 'school superintendent' for the entire area," Burger said.

"Disparate treatment of white and Negro students occurred within the Detroit school system and not elsewhere, and on the record the remedy must be limited to that system. The constitutional right of the Negro respondents residing in Detroit is to attend a unitary school system in that district. Unless petitioners drew the district lines in a discriminatory fashion, or arranged for white students residing in the Detroit district to attend schools in Oakland and Macomb counties, they were under no constitutional duty to make provisions for Negro students to do so. . . . We conclude that the relief ordered by the district court and affirmed by the court of appeals was based upon an erroneous standard and was unsupported by record evidence that acts of the outlying districts affected the discrimination found to exist in the schools of Detroit."

In a dissent, Justice Thurgood Marshall charged that the court's answer to this problem was to "provide no remedy at all. . . , thereby guaranteeing that Negro children in Detroit will receive the same separate and inherently unequal education in the future as they have been unconstitutionally afforded in the past."

Failing to perceive any basis for the state's erection of school boundary lines as "absolute barriers" to the implementation of effective desegregation remedies, Marshall castigated the court majority for seeming to have "forgotten the district court's explicit finding that a Detroit-only decree . . . 'would not accomplish desegregation.' "

The state, not simply the Detroit board of education, bore the responsibility for curing the condition of segregation in the Detroit schools, he asserted. Marshall pointed out that the state, under the 14th Amendment, bore responsibility for the actions of its local agencies. Given that Michigan operated a "single, statewide system of education, Detroit's segregation could not be viewed "as the problem of an independent and separate entity," Marshall said.

Denver busing begins. Supreme Court Justice Thurgood Marshall refused Aug. 29 to block implementation of an integration plan for the Denver public schools involving busing of about 23,000 pupils. The plan had been ordered into effect by a lower court.

School officials said as classes opened the next day that some pupils were apparently being enrolled in private Roman Catholic schools, which reported their first enrollment increase in five years. The Denver archdiocese had said the parochial schools would try to avoid becoming a "haven" for those attempting to avoid busing.

Massachusetts

Boston busing ballot barred. The Massachusetts Supreme Court ruled April 16 that a proposed binding referendum on a plan to use large-scale busing to integrate Boston schools would be unconstitutional. However, the court said a nonbinding "opinion poll" could be allowed on the ballot.

The ruling noted that the bill setting the referendum would prohibit assignment of students without parental consent, thus blocking enforcement of the state's earlier racial balance law. Gov. Francis W. Sargent, who had requested the court's opinion, vetoed the bill April 17.

In a related development, the court May 1 ordered the Springfield School Committee to implement a busing plan by September to racially balance the city's schools. The ruling rejected the city's appeal of a plan ordered earlier by the state board of education.

Boston school bias found. U.S. District Court Judge W. Arthur Garrity Jr. ruled June 21 that Boston had deliberately maintained a segregated public school system, and ordered that a state-devised racial balance plan be implemented in September.

Ruling in a suit filed by black parents and the National Association for the Advancement of Colored People, Garrity said school officials had knowingly carried out a system segregating both teachers and students through special attendance and grading patterns. Garrity ruled that the plaintiffs were entitled to every legal means of relief, including busing, no matter how "distasteful."

Under the state plan, the number of black-majority schools would be reduced from 68 to 40. At least 6,000 pupils, black and white (out of 94,000) would be bused.

Garrity orders School Committee to develop integration plan. U.S. District Court Judge W. Arthur Garrity signed a final order Oct. 30 requiring the Boston School Committee to develop by Dec. 16 a city-wide school integration plan to replace the interim court-ordered program of busing for desegregation. The new plan, which would go into effect in the fall of 1975, would free several million dollars in emergency desegregation aid from the Department of Health, Education and Welfare (HEW). In his order, Garrity urged the Committee to draft plans that would achieve desegregation with a minimum of busing and reassignment of students.

In another action, Garrity Nov. 8 approved a special School Committee plan for a crash tutorial program for chronically absent students. Aimed at the approximately 8,500 pupils boycotting the schools during implementation of Garrity's interim desegregation program, the plan required these students to attend classes for at least half the school day. In conjunction with the tutoring plan, city officials launched a drive Nov. 11 to crack down on truants, especially those in three South Boston high schools most directly affected by the desegregation program.

The Justice Department announced a federal grand jury's indictment Oct. 24 of two men on charges stemming from the beating of a black man Oct. 7. Joseph E. Griffin Jr., 33, and Ronald B. King, 32, were accused of beating and injuring Andre Yvon Jean Louis, 32, in order "to intimidate black students from attending Boston public schools without discrimi-

nation" and with interferring with the federal court order to desegregate the schools. If convicted, each man faced total maximum penalties of 11 years in prison and fines of $11,000.

Boston school panel defies judge's order. U.S. District Court Judge W. Arthur Garrity Dec. 18 ordered three members of the Boston School Committee to show cause by Dec. 27 why they should not be held in civil contempt of court.

In defiance of an Oct. 31 order by Garrity to adopt a busing plan for citywide school desegregation for the fall of 1975, the School Committee, by a 3–2 vote Dec. 16, rejected a plan drawn up by the school system's attorneys and staff. Despite the committee's vote, two copies of a 530-page busing plan were delivered to Garrity by the School Committee's attorney, John O. Mirick, who said that his duty to "the system as a whole" outweighed his obligation to comply with his client's wishes. (Mirick filed a motion with Garrity Dec. 16, asking that his law firm, Hale and Dorr, be allowed to drop the committee as a client.)

In disavowing the busing plan, John J. Kerrigan, chairman of the School Committee, said, "I can't in good conscience be an architect of a plan that would increase the bloodshed and hatred in the city of Boston." The other four members of the committee indicated full agreement with Kerrigan, but two voted to approve the citywide plan. Failure to endorse a plan, the two dissenters argued, might cause Judge Garrity to strip the committee of its authority.

The program submitted to Garrity called for busing 35,000 pupils in all sections of the city. The city would be divided into six zones, each extending into the predominantly black neighborhood of Roxbury. (The interim desegregation plan currently in effect mandated busing of 18,000 of the city's 82,000 students.)

3 Boston school officials in contempt. U.S. District Court Judge W. Arthur Garrity Jr. Dec. 27 held three members of the Boston School Committee in civil contempt of court for their refusal to approve a citywide busing plan for school integration. Garrity Dec. 30 ordered the committee members fined and barred from participating in school desegregation matters unless they endorsed a new integration plan by Jan. 7, 1975. The judge also ordered proceedings to see if two of the members, who were lawyers, should be suspended from practicing in federal court while they were in contempt. The three committee members were Chairman John J. Kerrigan, John J. McDonough, both attorneys, and Paul J. Ellison.

In a related development, the 1st U.S. Circuit Court of Appeals Dec. 19 unanimously upheld Garrity's finding June 21 that Boston had deliberately operated a segregated school system. The three-judge appellate panel ordered desegregation of the schools to continue.

1975
Massachusetts

Voluntary Boston school plan submitted. The Boston School Committee Jan. 27 submitted to a federal court judge a plan for desegregating the city's public school system in the fall of 1975. Unlike the interim, court-ordered busing plan currently in effect, the new proposal provided for voluntary student enrollment in biracial classes.

Three of the committee's five members had been cited for civil contempt by U.S. District Court Judge W. Arthur Garrity Jr. Dec. 27, 1974 when they refused to approve a desegregation plan. However, Garrity ruled that the school committee dissidents would purge themselves of contempt if they "authorized" an integration plan by Jan. 7. Garrity subsequently extended the deadline after he was informed that a voluntary plan was being readied for submission. On receiving the 600-page proposal, the judge ordered further hearings. He said he would appoint "masters" to study the committee's plan and the blueprints for integration filed by 15 other government agencies and community organizations.

The school committee's plan relied heavily on so-called "magnet schools" located in six different zones in the city. Children already attending integrated classes would be given the first chance to enroll in the varied learning programs at the magnet schools, and "an attempt then will be made to accommodate every student who applies for a citywide magnet school," a summary of the plan said.

Based on the make-up of surrounding neighborhoods, the remaining schools would be designated either "predominately white" or "predominately minority." Pupils of the opposite category then would be allocated to these schools. Children attending schools that still failed to meet federal court guidelines for racial mixture would participate in compulsory scholastic activities at a "neutral" site one day a week.

Violence persists. Meanwhile, violence continued to plague high schools of the South Boston area. More than 100 policemen patrolled the corridors of Hyde Park High School Jan. 14, after racial clashes the day before had resulted in three injuries and 13 arrests. Racial fighting had also resulted in arrests of 15 Hyde Park students Jan. 9 on charges of disorderly conduct.

South Boston High School, closed since a Dec. 11, 1974 stabbing incident, reopened Jan. 8. The approximately 400 students—31 of them black—who returned to classes were guarded by an estimated 500 state, metropolitan and city policemen. Judge Garrity Jan. 2 had denied a motion by Boston city attorneys to permanently close the school, which had been the focal point of opposition to the court-ordered, forced busing plan.

Boston's Phase Two plan submitted. A second plan to desegregate the Boston schools was submitted to Judge W. Arthur Garrity March 21. Phase Two, or the masters' plan, was drawn up by Dean Robert Dentler and Associate Dean Marvin Scott, both of the Boston University School of Education, upon recommendations from four court-appointed masters.

Among the plan's proposals:

■ Ten multiracial school districts would be formed (nine community and one citywide), replacing six larger districts established under Phase One in September 1974. Each school would then reflect the ethnic composition of the district, rather than the city.

■ The number of students involved in mandatory busing would be reduced from the 17,000 under Phase One to a maximum of 14,900.

■ Students would be assigned schools within their districts on a nearest available seat basis, as long as the assignment contributed to racial balance.

■ Racial percentages would vary according to district, from 85% to 25% white.

■ Seventeen colleges and universities in the Boston area would be paired with Boston schools for consultation on "the provision of program and instructional support, assistance and development."

The masters wrote in the proposal, "We believe that our plan distinguishes sharply between voluntary and compulsory student transportation. Voluntary transportation by school buses leased by the School Committee and by mass transit has been going on for six decades in Boston. The School Department estimated in 1972, for example, before Phase 1 desegregation had been devised, that more than 30,000 public school students used school buses and mass transit to and from school daily in Boston. In that year, the School Committee leased 129 buses for student transportation purposes.... At the minimum estimate, not more than 15 percent of the students enrolling in the Boston public schools would undergo compulsory busing. At the maximum estimate, not more than 22 percent would be so bused. This contrasts, even for a very large city, with proportions that range from 32 to 45 percent in desegregated cities and counties throughout the southern states, where compulsory busing for desegregation has been mandated for as long as 20 years."

The masters are Francis Keppel, former Commissioner of Education and dean of the Harvard Graduate School of Education; Dr. Charles V. Willie, a black professor of education at the Harvard Graduate School of Education; Edward J. McCormack Jr., former Massachusetts Attorney General, born in South Boston; and Jacob J. Spiegel, retired justice of the State Supreme Judicial Court.

Reaction to the Phase Two plan. Martin Walsh, regional director of the Justice Department's community relations service, March 21 called the masters' plan "a very positive, innovative approach to desegre-

gation, although there will be difficulties. It certainly is an attempt to minimize the hardships while carrying out the court order." State Rep. Michael F. Flaherty from South Boston commented, "I see nothing that will help the situation in Boston at all. We're still being told where to send our children. I don't think the people of South Boston will buy it."

Garrity issues final busing plan. Judge W. Arthur Garrity Jr. issued his final desegregation order for Boston May 10. He adopted most of the masters' plan: community district councils, city-wide schools, and collaboration with universities in the area. The city would be divided into eight neighborhood school districts, and 21,000 students would be bused (of the 72,000 in the Boston school system.)

Since East Boston is separated by Boston harbor from the rest of the city, it was not included in the nearest integrated school district, and will remain 95% white. Dean Robert Dentler, one of the authors of the masters' plan, said that East Boston's desegregation would require 40-minute bus rides and an additional 5,000 busing assignments.

According to the order, within any of the eight school districts the average distance between home and school will be under 2.5 miles. The longest trip is estimated at five miles. Travel time is expected to average 10–15 minutes, with a maximum of 25 minutes.

Mayor Kevin White commented May 11 that Garrity's final plan "has virtually guaranteed a continuation of the present level of tension and hostility throughout the city." City Councillor Louise Day Hicks, an antibusing leader, called the order "outrageous" and "the death knell of the city."

Supreme Court declines hearing. The Supreme Court May 12 declined to review Judge Garrity's 1972 ruling that the Boston schools were unrepresentative of the school population. Mayor White had attempted to argue that school segregation had never been official policy in Boston.

California

Los Angeles school bias ruling reversed. The 2nd District Court of Appeals of California March 10 overturned a controversial 1970 lower court decision that would have required large-scale busing of Los Angeles' 600,000 public school children. Reversing the finding of former Superior Court Judge Alfred Gitelson that the city's board of education was guilty of de facto segregation policies, the three-member appellate panel ruled that the board had not "intentionally discriminated against minority students by practicing a deliberate policy of racial segregation." The panel, returning the case to a lower court, said that "segregation was ignored rather than intentionally fostered."

A

B

C

D

E

F

G

A   The court based its ruling on the 1973 Supreme Court decision on the Denver schools, where it was held that segregation must be "deliberate" or intentional to violate students' constitutional rights. In Los Angeles, the court said, "the specified acts or omissions of the [school] board could have had a reasonable basis untainted by any purpose or intent to deprive any student or group of students of a constitutional right."

B   The American Civil Liberties Union (ACLU) announced that it would appeal the decision to the California Supreme Court. The ACLU had originally brought the desegregation suit against the district in 1962. Ramona Ripston, executive director of the ACLU's southern California branch, called the court's decision "not only a setback for black and brown kids but a setback for civil rights in general.

C   She added that "Continued racism in the United States is the biggest problem facing us today." She defined the problem as one of "intent." "We're talking about the selection of sites, feeder patterns, transportation. The fact that they [the board] did nothing indicates to me an intent."

Superintendent of Schools William Johnson said he was extremely gratified by the ruling. The board president, Donald Newman, commented that the board was vindicated, and that the court decision "reaffirms that the district has not undertaken any action to segregate its students."

Former Judge Gitelson was defeated for reelection after he ruled on the case in 1970. He commented March 10 that he was "truly perturbed" by the court's decision. "I think we have gone back to the equal opportunity conception of 30 years ago," he said. The Gitelson decision was never implemented because it was immediately stayed by the appeal court, pending the outcome of the school board's appeal.

Kentucky, Indiana

Supreme Court declines hearing. The Supreme Court April 21 declined to review two lower court decisions on merging school districts in Indianapolis, Ind. and Louisville, Ky. The two cases were each somewhat different from the Detroit proposal, which was rejected by the Supreme Court in 1974. In Detroit, the two separate school systems would be combined only for purposes of integration. The Indianapolis and Marion County governmental functions had been united into a "Uni-Gov" metropolitan area in 1969, and only the school systems remained to be merged. The appeals court found that the separate school systems in Louisville and adjoining Jefferson County had been discriminatory, which had not been proven in Detroit and its suburbs.

SUPREME COURT REJECTS
CROSS-DISTRICT BUSING

The Supreme Court July 25 struck down a plan to desegregate the predominately black Detroit school system by merging it with mostly white, neighboring districts. The 5–4 decision all but banned desegregation through the busing of children across school district lines. Chief Justice Warren E. Burger, author of the court's majority opinion, was joined by Justices Harry A. Blackmun, Lewis F. Powell Jr. and William H. Rehnquist, all appointees of President Nixon, and Potter Stewart, named to the court by President Eisenhower.

In his opinion, Burger noted reasoning by lower courts that Detroit's schools, which were 70% black, would not be truly desegregated unless their racial composition reflected the racial composition of the whole metropolitan area. However, Burger challenged what he called the lower court's "analytical starting point"—that school boundary lines might be casually ignored and treated as mere administrative conveniences. Such notions were contrary to the history of public education in the U.S., Burger wrote. "No single tradition in public education is more deeply rooted than local control over the operation of schools; local autonomy has long been thought essential both to the maintenance of community concern and support for public schools and to quality of the educational process.

In a dissent, Justice Thurgood Marshall charged that the court's answer to this problem was to "provide no remedy at all…, thereby guaranteeing that Negro children in Detroit will receive the same separate and inherently unequal education in the future as they have been unconstitutionally afforded in the past." Failing to perceive any basis for the state's erection of school boundary lines as "absolute barriers" to the implementation of effective desegregation remedies, Marshall castigated the court majority for seeming to have "forgotten the district court's explicit finding that a Detroit-only decree … 'would not accomplish desegregation.'" The state, not simply the Detroit board of education, bore the responsibility for curing the condition of segregation in the Detroit schools, he asserted. Marshall pointed out that the state, under the 14th Amendment, bore responsibility for the actions of its local agencies. Given that Michigan operated a single, statewide system of education, Detroit's segregation could not be viewed "as the problem of an independent and separate entity," Marshall said.

Washington Star-News
Washington, D.C.,
July 27, 1974

The Supreme Court ruling barring the busing of students across jurisdictional lines to achieve racial balance means that school boards can concentrate now on providing quality schools instead of wasting time trying to figure out how to haul children somewhere else to obtain some mathematical proportion of blacks and whites in every school.

By a 5 to 4 decision in a case involving Detroit and its suburbs, the Supreme Court Thursday held that for the courts to require busing between or among separate governmental jurisdictions would do violence to the tradition of local control of schools and would be disruptive of the educational process. "The notion that school district lines may be casually ignored or treated as a mere administrative convenience is contrary to the history of public education in our country," Chief Justice Burger wrote in the majority opinion.

The court left the door open for cross-jurisdiction busing if a showing can be made that deliberate actions among the governing units or by one unit was the reason for racial imbalance. But the stringent test would appear to rule out most such busing.

The court majority obviously did not agree with the opinion of one of the dissenters, Justice Marshall, that the ban would be a "giant step backwards" — and neither do we. Massive, long-distance busing is not the remedy for racial imbalance. The disruption to school systems and to the pupils themselves simply is not worth whatever advantage, if any, there is in obtaining a pre-conceived ratio of white and black students.

If the concept of neighborhood schools has any validity — and we believe it does — there are going to be predominantly black or white schools so long as there are concentrations of blacks and whites in separate places. The hope for overcoming racial imbalance in schools in such situations lies not in spending vast amounts on pupil transportation systems but rather in economic mobility for minorities and in governmental action, through zoning laws, housing subsidies and the like, that would help change housing patterns.

Where racial imbalance exists in schools because of discriminatory governmental actions, it must be corrected. But it is neither right nor publicly acceptable to force one governmental unit to correct the mistakes of another.

TULSA DAILY WORLD
Tulsa, Okla., July 26, 1974

ANYONE who truly believes that the law should be color blind must applaud the U.S. SUPREME COURT'S rejection of the Detroit busing plan.

If approved, the Detroit scheme would have required transportation of pupils from one school district to another for the sole purpose of achieving a certain racial proportion.

The Court's ruling was by no means a complete solution to the problems of integration and busing. In the first place, it was reached by a 5-4 vote which means that at some future time, cross country racial busing could be revived. Furthermore, the Court did not reject the inter-district hauling concept outright. It merely held that there was no evidence that the districts involved had failed to operate integrated school systems. It goes back to a lower Court where it could be resurrected by new evidence.

Nevertheless, the decision tends to put some limit on the notion that race must be the first consideration in determining where a child attends school. Without saying so directly, the Court seemed to imply that there are other values and considerations in the education of children that are at least as important as the number of black and white skins that may be counted in a particular classroom.

St. Louis Globe-Democrat
St. Louis, Mo., July 26, 1974

In its most important school decision since striking down legally imposed school segregation in 1954, the U.S. Supreme Court Thursday struck down the self-anointed authority of courts to bus pupils across school district lines or merge districts to achieve wider integration. The opinion should demolish two current local suits, one pressing for a merger of the Kinloch, Berkeley and Ferguson-Florissant school districts, and the other seeking to merge St. Louis schools with 21 of the 25 St. Louis County districts. And the opinion should result in the abolition of existing multi-district plans throughout the country.

Chief Justice Warren E. Burger, who wrote the majority decision, was joined by Justices Stewart, Blackmun, Powell and Rehnquist. Dissenting were Justices Douglas, Marshall, Brennan and White.

The 5-4 decision is of monumental importance —the first definitive ruling on multi-district plans, which judges in recent years have imposed without benefit of law. These judges have engaged in social scheming of dubious educational merit in order to establish quotas or percentages of ethnic groups in wide areas beyond governmental lines. They abolished school boards, reset boundary lines, imposed tax levies, restructured curricula and, in general, acted as benevolent despots.

For example, in the landmark case decided by the court Thursday, a federal judge was exercised that the Detroit school system, although integrated itself, was 64 per cent black. Some 50 suburban districts, although integrated, were predominantly white. His solution was to bus pupils in Detroit and throughout a three-county area to achieve neat quotas of blacks and whites. In doing so, all 50 school districts would have been essentially destroyed. Local government, and democracy, would have been a farce.

If citizens have no control over their children, what do they have control over? If courts can merge governmental units for school busing, what is to prevent courts from merging cities and towns for other noble-sounding purposes, such as equalizing tax loads or achieving better housing mixes? Such tyrannical edicts by authoritarian judges have suffered a setback by the Supreme Court's ruling.

The decision does not affect desegregation plans within a single district, which were permitted in some instances by the Supreme Court in the Denver case in June 1973. But even here, courts must determine that alleged segregationist policies of a school board are so pervasive that the entire district must be desegregated. This means segregation must be de jure (legally imposed or deliberately fostered by a board) rather than de facto (segregation that happens to occur because of voluntary housing patterns or other happenstance).

THE ATLANTA CONSTITUTION
Atlanta, Ga., July 26, 1974

It was just four years ago this summer that Detroit's metro school busing desegregation case started moving its way through the courts to the U.S. Supreme Court.

This week in a far reaching decision — one that will affect Atlanta among other cities — the high court ruled 5-4 against requiring widespread busing in greater Detroit to achieve racial desegregation . The decision sets precedent. It means that the pending lawsuits to force Atlanta and surrounding schools to combine through a metro busing desegregation plan are doomed to failure.

The question at issue in Detroit involves a situation found now in Atlanta and in a number of other American cities. The school system of Detroit proper, as is also true in Atlanta, has now a majority of black pupils. The nearby suburban school systems have mostly white pupils. The thrust of the lawsuit was to ask the federal courts to order a busing plan that would bus white pupils into the city and black pupils into the suburbs to achieve a racial balance in schools.

The court ruled, in our view, with considerable wisdom in deciding against such a proposal.

Racial discrimination is wrong and unfair in the public schools or anywhere else. And there is no doubt that some politicians and people who speak against "busing" are in fact voicing racist sentiments, even if they use codewords to do so. But, having said that, there is considerable doubt about the value of busing pupils great distances and literally from one school system to another to create a certain black-white racial percentage. Black and white parents alike have expressed reservations about such plans, in Atlanta and in other cities.

The Supreme Court decision in the Detroit case was a long awaited one. It at last helps clear up an area of confusion involving Atlanta and surrounding school systems.

LEDGER-STAR
Norfolk, Va., July 26, 1974

The federal judiciary's embrace of busing as a school desegregation tool is drastically loosened by the latest Supreme Court decision. And that's one of the healthiest national developments in a long time.

The court did not cast aside the device altogether or rule in a way that would sweepingly reverse earlier actions. For one thing, if all the school systems in an area were judged guilty of operating on a segregated basis, their merger and cross-busing could be commanded, under the court's logic.

But with the crossing of political boundaries already barred in the Richmond case through the effect of an even split on the high tribunal, and now the five-to-four ruling against combining various districts in the Detroit area, surely a major shift in judicial direction has taken place.

This is a direction change which Congress is currently in the process of trying to force by legislation, though its particular prescriptions have all along looked to be futile. Since the court has assumed the power to specify the instruments for righting what it deems to be a wrong, under the Constitution, the court seemed likely to have its way, despite any statutory instructions.

But one thing which strong action by Congress against busing has had the capacity to do is to serve notice on the courts of the dangerous ground the advance of busing was intruding upon, both in terms of logic and the public sense of outrage.

Perhaps some of that message is getting through already. And perhaps, too, the courts from here on in will be using ever more restraint when it comes to extreme devices for achieving racial balance. And maybe the judiciary will even move away from the balance idea itself, which seems to have been regarded by judges in earlier decisions as some kind of anti-discrimination touchstone.

That has been one of the most pernicious notions of all and the most in need of scrapping.

𝕿𝖍𝖊 🌳 𝕾𝖙𝖆𝖙𝖊

Columbia, S.C., July 29, 1974

MANY Southerners, reacting to the Supreme Court's long-awaited decision in the Detroit school case might be inclined to think that the federal court, which imposed school desegregation on the South with heavy hand, is now letting the North off lightly.

This argument might have some validity if we were dealing with the same Supreme Court. The idealistic Warren court that cracked down so hard on the South's *de jure* (legal) segregation had a vastly different make up than today's Burger court, which has four reasonable and realistic justices appointed by President Nixon.

In the Detroit case, the Supreme Court dealt definitively for the first time with *de facto* segregation, or segregation caused not by official actions but by housing patterns, economic conditions, etc. Basically the racial mixture in the Detroit area schools were the result of non-governmental acts, although the lower court there held that some of the more subtle segregation devices were employed officially.

The Detroit area had developed essentially as other large metropolitan areas throughout the nation have. The core city school district has become increasingly black as more whites move to suburbs.

U.S. District Judge Stephen Roth ruled in 1971 and in subsequent hearings that district lines should be ignored and that school children should be bused in and out of Detroit.

This ruling and those like it in other large cities with *de facto* segregation spread fear and anger among whites, proving that Northerners were not much different from Southerners on racial issues.

The Detroit decision was called a major retreat from previous desegregation decisions by the four holdovers from the Warren Court who voted in the minority.

It was not that at all. It was just not a forward leap. In the first place, the majority opinion by Chief Justice Warren Burger would permit urban-suburban mixing if it can be shown certain official acts such as gerrymandering districts, contributed to segregation. But, of course, the decision will make it difficult or impossible to impose a racial balance plan on an entire metropolitan area.

The impact of this decision will fall not only on Northern cities but on Southern as well. Now that most vestiges of *de jure* segregation have been eliminated in the South, such segregation as remains here arguably is *de facto*.

The decision will produce a mixed bag of benefits and liabilities. The authority of individual school districts is sustained, and thus the neighborhood school concept is enhanced. To use a local example, suburban Richland County School District Two cannot, in the absence of official skullduggery, be required to exchange students with Columbia's District One in order to even out the racial balance.

In addition, the school systems will not be required to spend large sums for noneducational items such as buses. (Judge Roth ordered the Detroit area districts to buy 295 extra buses to shuffle the kids in and out of the city.)

But the decision could increase the problems of the core-city districts and contribute, unless imaginative planning and action are employed, to the deterioration of center cities.

Perhaps we will see a new emphasis on open housing, because this remains a viable way to spread out black students.

The Detroit decision decreases the likelihood of more disruptive court interference with education in metropolitan areas. But it increases the need for good will, understanding, and cooperation between the races in center cities to assure an improved quality of education for all children, particularly the blacks.

𝕽𝖎𝖈𝖍𝖒𝖔𝖓𝖉 𝕿𝖎𝖒𝖊𝖘-𝕯𝖎𝖘𝖕𝖆𝖙𝖈𝖍

Richmond, Va., July 26, 1974

Schoolchildren in a generation not yet born will read in their history texts that on July 24, 1974, the United States Supreme Court handed down one of its most significant decisions in the 200-year history of the republic—holding that a President's claim of executive privilege must yield to the need for evidence in a criminal trial.

It may well be that many of those same schoolchildren will be enrolled in good, stable public schools because of a decision rendered by the court the very next morning, yesterday, July 25, 1974. Another landmark was posted, even though this time it was a divided, not a unanimous, court that spoke. As it did in *The United States v. Richard M. Nixon* the day before, the court, in ruling against multidistrict, racial-balance busing in Detroit, sharply circumscribed the power of one of the three branches of the national government. But like the Nixon-Watergate case, which confined *presidential* authority, the Detroit decision curbed the power of the *judicial branch* itself in one important area of American life. Thus, if an "imperial presidency" is a less foreboding possibility today, so, too, is a tyrannical judiciary — at least insofar as education is concerned.

━━

No longer may lower courts consider that they have a free hand to reach across local political boundaries to rearrange school populations solely to satisfy some arbitrary, dreamy conception of what constitutes a perfect racial mixture. As Chief Justice Warren E. Burger observed in writing for the majority, the district court in Detroit and the appellate court in Cincinnati "shifted the primary focus from a Detroit remedy to the metropolitan area only because of their conclusion that total desegregation of Detroit would not produce the racial balance which they perceived as desirable."

The courts had directed 52 suburban districts to exchange pupils with Detroit on a racial basis despite the absence of evidence that any of the districts had denied admission to children because of race, or that the lines of the districts had been drawn purposely to exclude blacks. Chief Justice Burger said that desegregation plans must be confined to the boundaries of a single school district unless it can be proven that all districts in a particular region were guilty of unconstitutional discrimination. Had not the high court thus drawn the line, it is difficult to imagine to what lengths some judges might have gone in dispatching school buses to chase after the fleeting Utopia of universal racial balance. Schools would have faced intolerable uncertainty and chronic instability, as students could never be quite sure in what school or even what county they might be needed to fill out a racial quota. And as individuals rebelled against this infringement of their personal liberties, by moving or enrolling in private schools, support for public education would have been further drained.

━━

Yesterday's decision has the gratifying impact locally of removing the last shred of uncertainty surrounding the Richmond School Board's efforts to consolidate city schools with those of Henrico and Chesterfield counties for the purpose of seeking a white majority in every school. Consolidation is dead. All the area school systems are independently operating on a racially-unitary basis. Some schools will continue to be heavily black but that does not mean that such schools ought to be regarded as inferior. Local officials and citizens ought now to shift from their preoccupation with race to a whole-hearted concentration on teaching children, wherever they are, the skills they need to survive and preferably to excel in a complex age.

Some of the concerns of the Supreme Court minority, articulated by Justice Thurgood Marshall, ought to be shared by many persons who favor the legal and practical wisdom of the majority opinion. The thought that city schools might lose all of their white and middle-class black patrons because of continued cross-city busing is not a pleasant one. But with inter-district busing now clearly barred, the judiciary may be more receptive to pleas from cities for relief from unrealistic, self-defeating *intra-district* busing plans.

THE WALL STREET JOURNAL.

New York, N.Y., July 31, 1974

If the impeachment hearings hadn't occupied everyone's mind, last week's Supreme Court decision in the Detroit school desegregation case would probably have been the most widely discussed ruling of the year. Chief Justice Burger's opinion signals a major, and to our mind, much needed shift in social policy. Although headlines focused on busing, the true question was whether the business of producing an abstract numerical ratio of black and white overrode every other consideration. Justice Burger answered no, that some other things must also be weighed in the balance—in this case the integrity of local school districts if they haven't been shown to be violating law or the Constitution.

The case involved several lower court orders that would have abolished 54 local school districts in the Detroit metropolitan area for the sake of obtaining a certain proportion of the races in the Detroit city school system. The suburban districts had not been implicated in segregation, but to correct racial imbalance in Detroit, busing of some 300,000 school children would have been required. This plan was the logical outcome of absolutist reasoning on integration, which would define segregation as any situation where a public school was more than 50% black. But large-city school systems are overwhelmingly black: more than 95% in Washington, D.C., and over 67% in Detroit itself. So you have to pull in white faces from the suburbs, dismantling school district lines.

The court, by a 5 to 4 vote, has rejected this course. As Justice Burger emphasized, local control of the schools is an important American tradition, not to be overturned lightly when there has been no proof of wrong-doing by some of the districts involved. We suspect that the emotional force of the busing issue came not from racism, but from the notion that a federal judge or bureaucrat could reach into a community, almost at random, and overturn its local school system, for no clearly stated reason except for a vague appeal to dubious social science. After all, it's hard to blame racism for George Wallace's most significant 1972 triumph, the Michigan primary by 51% of the vote.

The court's decision should defuse this issue, to the relief of every politician this side of Mr. Wallace. But, Thurgood Marshall to the contrary, it won't undercut enforcement of the kind of desegregation called for by Brown v. Board of Education. Lost in the emotional exhaust was Chief Justice Burger's explicit statement that busing was a legitimate tool to integrate a single district. Furthermore, he continued, it could be used for several districts if all of them had taken part in producing the original pattern of segregation, for instance if the districts have been deliberately gerrymandered to exclude blacks.

The judicial attack on segregation has been a noble and very worthy enterprise. Segregation, a social policy based on racial distinctions, was vicious and offensive, as well as infinitely stupid. But the attack on segregation, partly because of its judicial character, has been fixated on the source of this stupidity, concern with the racial makeup of a classroom. Instead of insuring that race is irrelevant, the goal has been to obtain a class with a fixed proportion of black and white. But of all the elements that go into learning, skin color is probably about the least important.

Detroit Mayor Coleman Young, the first black man to hold that post, was on the right track when he commented that he "shed no tears for cross-district busing." This controversy has diverted too much attention and energy from the real albeit excruciatingly difficult issue, successful teaching of impoverished minority students so that they have a real chance at breaking their "cycle of poverty." Mayor Young would concentrate on increased school financing. Others might urge curriculum reform and efficiently planned teaching programs. These measures are by no means easy or certain, but at least they are directly related to the heart of the problem, as busing is not.

We hope, finally, that the Detroit decision will be the first step in easing away from quotas, goals and the counting up of racial proportions. Such devices make sense only as a temporary and very extraordinary corrective, and this theme seems to underlie Justice Burger's decision. In the end, we have to find our way back to the principle that the Constitution is color-blind.

The Boston Globe

Boston, Mass.,
July 26, 1974

The US Supreme Court ruling in the Detroit school case will have no effect on what happens in Boston next fall since Judge W. Arthur Garrity Jr.'s school desegregation order is limited to the core city. But, in Boston as in Detroit, any obstacle to a metropolitan approach is bound to restrict the options for poor and increasingly black urban school systems in the future.

And such an obstacle clearly exists in yesterday's five-to-four ruling that courts may not order busing across municipal boundaries unless there is evidence that the suburbs involved have deliberately practiced racial segregation in their schools. That is something that is extremely hard to prove. And in Detroit, where 53 suburbs are involved, the burden may be insuperable.

It is important to note that the door to a metropolitan plan for school desegregation is not entirely closed.

The majority ruling did not declare such a solution unconstitutional. And the finding was narrowly based on the fact that the late Judge Stephen J. Roth did not gather evidence of illegal segregation in Detroit's suburban schools or hear arguments from the local school boards. In returning the case, the lower court is now directed to take such evidence.

And waiting in the wings is a recent three-judge metropolitan ruling in Wilmington, Delaware, based in part on a finding that during the mid-1960s the state failed to redraw school district lines for the city even though racial segregation would clearly result unless the boundaries were changed.

Ultimately the suburbs must get involved. The cities cannot be condemned to make it on their own while the surrounding communities remain largely white and largely untouched by the problems afflicting the core city school system. Urban whites as well as urban blacks are the victims of this treatment. And as the core decays the suburbs themselves will suffer.

Twenty years after Brown v. the Board of Education the courts are still being asked to take the lead in bringing to all Americans, justice not just in education but in housing and jobs. This untimely and significant pause is the first faltering they have shown. We hope that it is only a stumble on a long and difficult road.

The New York Times

New York, N.Y., July 28, 1974

In its 1954 decision in *Brown v. Board of Education,* the Supreme Court ruled that "separate but equal" in education was unconstitutional. It has reaffirmed that view in decision after decision during the ensuing twenty years; but last week, in *Bradley v. Milliken,* a Detroit case, despite reaffirming the essence of the Brown decision, the Court clamped tight limits on the remedies it is disposed to grant in order to rectify unconstitutional deprivations suffered by minority school children.

Lower Federal courts had found unconstitutional discrimination against black school children in Detroit. Because of the complicity of the State of Michigan in that discrimination and the racial makeup of the school population of the area—blacks comprise 67 per cent of the Detroit school population but only a little more than .23 per cent of the school population of the entire metropolitan area—the lower courts envisioned a metropolitan-wide solution because a "Detroit only" solution would have been virtually meaningless. The remedy would have involved busing school children across presently existing school district lines.

The Detroit case was the first test of whether the full Court would require interdistrict solutions in order to achieve the constitutional results it had decreed in the Brown case. The decision was critical because most of the remaining school segregation in the United States occurs in big cities. In 1972, one half of all black school children were enrolled in the 100 largest school systems and two thirds of them were enrolled in schools which were more than 80 per cent black.

The essence of the decision rendered by the 5-to-4 majority was that "disparate treatment of white and Negro students occurred within the Detroit school system and not elsewhere, and on the record the remedy must be limited to that system." The Court also relied heavily on the importance of local control of the schools. It sent the case back to the District Court to fashion a remedy within the confines of the city of Detroit.

* * *

The decision seems as wrong as a matter of law as it is unfortunate as a matter of social policy. It is clear on the record that the State of Michigan retains plenary control over the schools throughout the state. It retains, for example, authority to consolidate and to merge school districts without the consent of those districts. It provides about a third of the public school budgets throughout the state and its credit is pledged for the construction of all school buildings in the state.

The Fourteenth Amendment imposes the requirement on the state to provide equal treatment to all of its citizens. The state has that power but did not choose to exercise it, so the lower courts decreed a solution that the state might have effected on its own. The aim was equality of educational opportunity for all school children. One tool was the use of school buses to the extent necessary to achieve that aim—not as an ideological exercise but as one of various devices to be used within reasonable bounds.

The Court's majority has now in 1974 shrunk from imposing the same constitutional stringency on large metropolitan areas that it imposed on the South twenty years ago. In so doing, it has cast a long cloud over the future. Judge J. Skelly Wright of the United States Court of Appeals for the District of Columbia said recently, "If the Supreme Court should ever hold that the mandate of Brown applies only within the boundaries of discrete school districts, the national trend toward residential, political and educational apartheid will not only be greatly accelerated, it will also be rendered legitimate and virtually irreversible by force of law."

More to the point, Justice Thurgood Marshall, writing in dissent said, "Unless our children begin to learn together, there is little hope that our people will ever learn to live together." Thus, in refusing to fashion a remedy sufficiently broad to correct the constitutional wrong which it found, the Court's majority has made us all, not just the black children of Detroit, the losers in the long run.

THE MILWAUKEE JOURNAL

Milwaukee, Wis., July 27, 1974

The US Supreme Court's ruling in the Detroit desegregation case is a serious setback to the cause of racial justice in America. Although the court found that the constitutional rights of black children in the city schools were violated, it provided no adequate remedy.

The case began as a typical desegregation suit within Detroit, but the late Federal District Judge Stephen Roth found that the only meaningful way to break down unconstitutional segregation, when nearly two-thirds of Detroit's enrollment was black, was to include many white suburban districts in the desegregation plan.

Roth persuasively argued that "government actions and inaction at all levels, federal, state and local, have combined with those of private organizations, such as loaning institutions and real estate associations . . . to establish and to maintain the pattern of residential segregation throughout the Detroit metropolitan area." And since "school district lines are simply matters of political convenience and may not be used to deny constitutional rights," Roth had said, interdistrict desegregation is necessary. The Sixth Circuit Court of Appeals upheld Roth.

The Supreme Court disagreed, and in a narrow legal sense, its conclusion was not illogical. It noted that the case originally had dealt just with Detroit, and that there simply had been no offering of evidence that anyone but Detroit was responsible for the school segregation there. Before setting aside school district boundaries, the high court said, "it must first be shown that there has been a constitutional violation within one district that produces a significant segregative effect in another district." The court did not hold that there had been no such discrimination, but only that it had not been shown in court.

The decision is especially devastating in combination with the court's March, 1973, ruling in the Rodriguez case, in which it had refused to recognize that wealth based inequities in school spending unconstitutionally deprive children in poorer districts of equal access to education. In that case, as in Thursday's Detroit decision, the court majority showed deplorable timidity in expressing fear of the wide ramifications for school financing, governance and similar matters had it reached the opposite conclusion.

Perhaps it is not naive to see some reason for hope in the court's explanation of its Detroit decision, as well as in the fact that, as with the Rodriguez case, it was on a 5 to 4 vote. A few different circumstances might swing the majority the other way in a future case.

Chief Justice Burger, in the majority opinion, declared that "boundary lines may be bridged where there has been a constitutional violation calling for interdistrict relief . . ." He added: "Of course, no state law is above the Constitution. School district lines and the present laws with respect to local control are not sacrosanct. . . ."

Certainly the Detroit decision must not kill efforts toward achieving the integrated society that has been the promise of America historically, and that the future viability of the country demands. New effort, perhaps a new tack in litigation, is needed. The whole array of "government actions and inaction" and private practices, which Judge Roth recognized as the basic problem, must be confronted.

Perhaps states, rather than just school districts, must become the chief targets of desegregation suits. After all, despite traditions of local control, school districts and municipalities are merely creatures of the state, with their legal roots in state law. The State of Michigan, as such, was not even a party to the Detroit case.

The court's Detroit ruling surely must not be welcome to big central cities — the heavily black Detroits as well as the still predominately white Milwaukees — for it perpetuates the lure of white suburban sanctuaries, beyond reach of constitutional equity. The origins of these sanctuaries may be complex, but a society that cannot find ways to break them down, so as to fulfill the historic promise of its great Constitution, will continue to live in shame.

Detroit Free Press

Detroit, Mich., July 26, 1974

FOR THE short run in metropolitan Detroit, the U.S. Supreme Court's rejection of a multidistrict solution to racial segregation will mean far less hassle and less tension.

The original decision to impose a metropolitan solution, rendered by the late Stephen Roth, as federal district judge, had excited passions and frightened many people. It was so sweeping that even people who supported its objectives found it hard to contemplate.

All this is gone now. The court ordered hearings on a Detroit-only integration plan and rejected by a 5-to-4 vote the idea that the suburbs should be involved in the solution. The court has spoken, the fears of many will be calmed and there will be no massive attempt at solving the problem of racial isolation in the metropolitan area.

Although the court did not completely close the door on a metropolitan solution under certain circumstances, the standards it set are so tough that no such plan is likely to be approved in the near future.

The issue that the court did not confront is what will happen in the absence of some such comprehensive effort to eliminate racial isolation. Perhaps the courts were not equipped to confront this question, though a minority felt the Supreme Court erred in not trying. As Justice Thurgood Marshall put it, "In the short run, it may seem to be the easier course to allow our great metropolitan areas to be divided up each into two cities — one white, the other black — but it is a course, I predict, our people will ultimately regret."

That argument is, of course, now academic. If a Detroit-only integration plan automatically means an all-black city then there is no remedy for that to be found in the courts. If the rejection of metro solutions means that the city will remain black and the suburbs white for a generation or more, the remedy will have to be nonjudicial.

Is it possible to avoid that result? Is the state interested in avoiding it? We question whether it can be done, and we doubt even more strongly whether there is a will to avoid and reverse the trend toward the ghettoization of the central city. That is a problem too difficult, too massive, too requiring of courage to get the kind of action needed.

In this election year, it is unlikely that the state's political leaders will do more than heave a sigh of relief that they don't have to deal with busing as an issue on the stump. Now that the specter of court-ordered busing has been removed, however, the state's leaders ought surely to weigh carefully what can be done to prevent even more severe segregation than we now have.

Their options may not be all that great. But we think it imperative that they do what they can: By promoting the equalization of education through the use of money, through the technical skills that the city schools sometimes lack and through a consistently manifested concern.

This state has burned up a lot of energy over the past few years saying "no" to busing and other such solutions. What we will have to see now is whether there is any interest at all in saying "yes" to other less onerous, less draconian attempts to solve the problems of racial isolation in Southeast Michigan.

The problems, we can be sure, have not been waved away by the magic wand of the Supreme Court decision.

Los Angeles Times

Los Angeles, Calif., July 28, 1974

Justice Thurgood Marshall is right when he asserts that the Supreme Court decision in the Detroit school busing case will make certain that the black children of Detroit will continue to receive "separate and inherently unequal education."

The court has denied those children the one remedy that could have ended the segregation of their schools. That remedy is integration with the surrounding suburban schools, as had been ordered by the federal district court and upheld by the federal circuit court of appeals.

This decision cannot be separated from another regressive decision of the high court in the Rodriguez case last year. In that decision, the Supreme Court reversed the finding of the lower courts that the present basis for financing public education is unconstitutional.

In the Rodriguez case, the Supreme Court acknowledged the inequality of education because of its financial base, but insisted that this was not in violation of the Constitution. In the Detroit case, the Supreme Court acknowledged the problem of segregation in Detroit schools but found the only available remedy exceeding the authority of the Constitution.

Fortunately for Californians, the Serrano decision of the state Supreme Court will provide a basis for continuing efforts to provide more equitable financing of schools regardless of the U.S. Supreme Court decision in the Rodriguez case.

But the Detroit decision almost certainly will slow the search for solutions to the problem of segregation through revised school district lines.

Both the Rodriguez and the Detroit decisions seem to leave without remedy those trapped in segregated and under-financed schools. They are essentially the poor of the big cities.

This is not a good thing for those children and it is not a good thing for the nation. Justice Marshall pointed to the real problem when in his dissent in the Detroit case, he said: "In the short run, it may seem to be the easier course to allow our great metropolitan areas to be divided up each into two cities, one white, the other black. But it is a course, I predict, our people will ultimately regret."

To reverse this process of segregation between city and suburb, however, is easier said than done.

And to try to find a remedy is to threaten those thousands whose move to the suburbs has been, in part, a move to escape a multiracial circumstance.

The Detroit situation underscores the problems. The concept of forcing the integration of the separate school districts of three counties, which would have required busing as many as 310,000 students, raised the possibility that the disruption caused by the reorganization would counterbalance any social gain resulting from the integration. Furthermore, the order imperiled the tradition of local control of education without offering any solution for the political, financial and social problems raised by the court order.

If the court used the narrowest constitutional interpretation in this decision, it nevertheless kept alive the important constitutional authority for federal intervention. That is good.

"No state law is above the Constitution," Chief Justice Warren E. Burger reminded the nation in the opinion. "School district lines and the present laws with respect to local control are not sacrosanct and if they conflict with the 14th Amendment, federal courts have a duty to prescribe appropriate remedies."

In other words, nothing in the Detroit decision was intended to interfere in the intervention of federal courts to order busing as a remedy to segregation within school districts. The Supreme Court itself intervened effectively just a year ago to enforce integration in the Denver schools. The strong position being maintained by Judge Manuel Real to enforce the school busing plan in Pasadena is another example of the appropriate exercise of authority by the federal courts to provide the equal protection guarantees of the 14th Amendment. And this has most recently had new sanction from the House and Senate, in the conference committee compromise on the busing amendment to the federal school legislation; the committee acknowledged the authority of the courts to order busing when necessary to protect the constitutional rights of minority children.

The massive busing of the Detroit plan may not have been the right solution. But the segregation of children into black city schools and white suburban schools is clearly wrong. The Supreme Court decision must stand as a challenge to find new solutions.

CHICAGO
Daily Defender

Chicago, Ill., July 30, 1974

The Supreme Court dealt a solar plexus blow to desegregation when it rejected the Detroit busing plan that had been approved by a District court and sustained by the U.S. 6th Circuit Court of Appeals in Cincinnati in 1972.

The decision is a smashing victory for the Nixon Administration which had urged the Supreme Court to reverse the lower court actions. The 5 to 4 opinion in which all the Nixon appointees to the court including Chief Justice Burger concurred should serve as a warning that the nation's commitment to civil rights for which so much black blood has been spilled is in danger of erosion by an unfriendly court.

Two decades of a protracted, bitter struggle to equalize educational opportunity for black children and give substance to the dream of better days, may be swept away by the harsh ruling of unconscionable, politically-minded, anti-social justices.

Justice Burger's opinion that the lower courts had authorized "a wholly impermissible remedy" by including 53 Detroit suburban school districts in the integration plan, is a reasoning whose rational is consonant with racist thinking.

We are being pushed back to the 1896 era of separate-but-equal accommodation as a reminder of our unaltered status as second-class citizens. The decision, which dooms countless generations of black children out of the main stream of American society, is a challenge we must meet with all the vigor we can muster. Black leaders with a moral sense of their responsibility to the masses, must now gird themselves for the new struggle that looms ahead and prepare to fight for every inch of the ground lost on the civil rights front.

This is a Nixon victory by a Nixon court. We would be forfeiting our constitutional claim to equal protection as ordained by the Fourteenth Amendment, should we allow this court decision to stand unchallenged.

THE DAILY HERALD

Biloxi, Miss., July 30, 1974

The Supreme Court has decided that busing pupils across school district lines from a black inner city to white suburbs would be improper and contrary to the tradition of local school control.

The ruling spurred predictable reactions. Anti-busing forces in the North were "delighted." Busing advocates everywhere were "disgusted." and here in Mississippi, Attorney General A. F. Summer said the decision only reinforced the dual-standard which applies to the integration issue in the North as compared ato the South.

Said Summer: "The court said a lot of pretty words that would have been beautiful had they said the same words in the decisions affecting Mississippi and the South. Its general effect is that we remain where we are without further recourse and the big northern cities can relax."

In a sense, Summer was correct. As a matter of fact, the "tradition of local school control" has been treated as little more than reactionary nonsense as the courts moved to desegregate the South. Neither has any regard been given the concept of "neighborhood schools" in the hot pursuit of integrating the South.

And no efforts have been made in the South to distinguish between "de facto" and "de jure" segregation. The federal centers of influence, instead, have judged all shades of segregation in the South as inherent evil created by white society.

For years the courts were able to evade the problem of racial injustice in other regions of the nation by clinging to the theory that "de facto" segregation was a condition, however unfortunate, which didn't justify the harsh mandates applied to the South, where segregation had been enforced by law.

But, in essence, there was scarcely a "dime's worth of difference," to borrow George Wallace's phrase, between racial injustices in the schools of the South and those of other regions. Civil rights advocates were eventually able to make that clear and break the barrier of "de facto" desegregation.

The Supreme Court has now turned again to declare "de facto" segregation, in some instances, justified. It is yet too early to determine how broad or narrow the implications of this ruling might be in the long run.

In dissenting, Justice Thurgood Marshall called the decision a "giant step backwards" toward separate and unequal schools. While it might be something of an impediment to the advance of equal civil rights in education, it is difficult to view the ruling as such a "giant" leap in any direction.

It is at least encouraging, however, to see the nation's highest court again recognize the value of neighborhood schools and local control, even if in a specific case.

The neighborhood school concept is good for the entire country, certainly including the South. The concept of integrated and equal public education has no less value for American society.

The idea is for the two concepts to be merged without destroying one or the other.

The Kansas City Times

Kansas City, Mo., July 27, 1974

In its narrow 5-4 decision on bussing, the Supreme Court has at least temporarily made things a little simpler for suburban schools. It has done nothing to improve—and may have made more difficult—the lot of the urban school districts whose populations reflect the reality of real estate patterns in racial distribution.

The court said, in effect, that an order in the Detroit area to bus students across district lines to achieve integration was not valid because there was no finding that the suburban districts involved had sought to avoid integration. The lower court was directed to devise a desegregation plan without regard to nearby suburban districts.

This is all very well, and perhaps it could have been no other way without completely turning upside down half the school districts in the country. But the dilemma of the big-city districts remains. The central school system in the average metropolitan area is likely to become predominantly black, if it is not already that, and the court action could have the effect of accelerating that process.

If city school districts must integrate as if they exist in a vacuum, the result will be to speed polarization. People move to the suburbs for many reasons, and the hope to enter their children in virtually all-white schools probably is not high on the list among them. But it is a factor. As long as they want to move farther over the horizon and tax themselves to build and establish schools, there is nothing to stop them. The hard reality of de facto segregation in housing is the key. Fair housing laws at federal, state and local levels have not made great impressions on the pattern of residential development. The economic limitations are what count. Proportionately few blacks can buy the kind of housing that is being built.

Yet would it really be fair or acceptable to subject either suburban or inner city children to massive bussing either across great cities or metropolitan counties? If it is generally agreed that integrated schools are better schools and that integration is in the long-range interests of the American society, it cannot be demonstrated that the wholesale bussing of millions of children would be worth the cost and the stress of great dislocations. Nobody really likes the idea of bussing very much. It is merely one of various possible tools—none of which seems very practical—to promote integration in education.

So the dilemma is with us still. The immediate hope is for proportionate racial stabilization in the cities. The long-range hope is for really integrated housing on the basis of area population. But that will wait on a much greater degree of economic equality than now exists.

The Providence Journal

Providence, R.I., July 26, 1974

Metropolitanization of urban school districts, the last real hope of America's large predominantly black cities of mixing black and white students in the classroom, remains an issue to be dealt with despite yesterday's Supreme Court ruling in the long-awaited Detroit case.

The court, on a 5-to-4 vote, held that the federal courts may not impose cross-district desegregation plans when it has not been established that all districts involved had failed to integrate their systems. Said Chief Justice Warren Burger, "To approve the remedy ordered by the court (the late Judge Stephen J. Roth, U.S. District Court in Cincinnati, 1971) would impose on the outlying districts, not shown to have committed any constitutional violation, a wholly impermissible remedy."

While the court thus upset the Detroit plan to reassign black students to schools in 53 heavily white outlying districts, it did not reject the concept or the possibility that future litigation may prove suburban districts culpable and therefore subject to a metropolitan plan.

The sharp division in the court suggests that under different circumstances conforming to provisions laid down yesterday, approval of cross-district busing might be forthcoming. In the Richmond, Va. case last year, the court blocked a plan that involved not only student reassignment but also the total consolidation of the city system with systems in neighboring Enrico and Chesterfield counties. It did so, however, on an evenly split 4-to-4 vote with Justice Lewis F. Powell Jr. abstaining. It was his vote yesterday that broke the tie.

The idea of crossing jurisdictional boundaries generates vigorous opposition for a number of reasons but an important one, certainly, is its defiance of tradition. The fact remains that in cities like Detroit, Richmond, Atlanta, Louisville and Indianapolis, white flight to the suburbs has meant larger and larger ratios of blacks to whites in the inner city and virtually resegregated the races into separate residential groupings.

State responsibility for public education is well established. This fact in part formed the basis of Judge Roth's decision in which he found that after the Detroit School Board initiated a school desegregation program, the state legislature drew new district lines in effect nullifying the plan. He held that means must be taken to correct such practices and that the only feasible way in Detroit was by cross-district busing.

The high court has by no means closed the door on a concept that under certain circumstances may offer the only hope of remedying the refusal or inability of city and suburbs to comply with the Supreme Court's historic desegregation ruling of 20 years ago.

William L. Taylor, director of the Center for National Policy Review, spoke to this question at a conference of journalists in Washington last January. Political subdivisions, including school districts, are the creation of the state, he said, and they may be altered.

That is what metropolitanization is really all about.

Pittsburgh Post-Gazette

Pittsburgh, Pa., July 26, 1974

THE U.S. Supreme Court decision in the Detroit school integration case could be an unhappy landmark in the history of major American cities as well as in the annals of the long school desegregation struggle.

By a 5 to 4 vote the high court struck down a plan for mixing students from the predominantly black Detroit school district with pupils in suburban white schools to achieve racial balance for integration purposes. In so doing the court:

► Barred busing of students between cities and suburbs to achieve school desegregation, except in the rarest of cases.

► Said racial balance no longer is the overriding criteria.

* * *

Unquestionably, the decision will ease one set of tensions, that of white suburban parents who feared long-distance busing of their children into the central cities. Certainly the high court "followed the election returns" in responding to anti-busing fervor across the country. One of President Nixon's campaign promises in 1968, to change the court's stand on the subject, now has been fulfilled with his four appointees plus Justice Potter Stewart forming a new majority.

But the Detroit decision may increase tensions in the central cities as both white and black parents find themselves locked into desegregation plans which may include busing, but without hope of relief by the inclusion of suburban school districts.

In turn this may increase the flight to the suburbs by white parents and thus exacerbate the problems of the big cities, and not just with schools. Undoubtedly, the Detroit decision will increase pressure by anti-busing central city residents, on the theory that what's sauce for the goose should be for the gander.

Will citizens of the central cities, white as well as black, be left to work out their problems by themselves?

Chief Justice Warren Burger in the majority opinion held that the suburban districts shouldn't be involved because they had not committed any constitutional violation. This, of course, overlooks the fact that suburbs are part of the problem.

As Justice Thurgood Marshall in dissent wrote: "The rippling effects on residential patterns caused by purposeful acts of segregation do not automatically subside at the school district border."

Pittsburgh is in a better situation than many cities because it has retained a large white population within its boundaries. But yesterday's decision likely dooms hopes of creating a better school racial balance in the eastern part of the city, for instance, by combining with adjacent largely-white districts.

It would be a mistake, however, to cry woe too much. The long line of desegregation decisions has accomplished much for America, particularly in ending the dual and unequal system of education in the South, and will continue to do so.

But psychologically, if not actually, yesterday's decision will have its effect.

As dissenter Marshall noted: "We deal here with the right of all of our children, whatever their race, to an equal start in life and to an equal opportunity to reach their full potential as citizens. These children who have been denied that right in the past deserve better than to see fences thrown up to deny them that right in the future."

* * *

If the suburbs cannot be included in the solutions to the central cities' desegregation problems, how do we forestall a slide into a "two societies" situation of largely black central cities and white suburbs?

One answer is a greater effort at enforcing civil rights legislation to overcome for blacks discrimination in jobs and housing so that they may climb the economic ladder. But also Americans must be willing to provide extra funds at the federal and state levels for big-city schools.

Money obviously isn't everything, but without heavy financial infusions the central city schools with antiquated facilities and an overloaded tax base will not be able to compete in quality with suburban schools. Such assets as a better ratio of teachers to pupils, counseling, special reading courses, and the variety of subject offerings needed in a city school system all cost money, more money than for a college preparatory type of suburban school.

* * *

Dissenter Marshall gloomily noted: "In the short run it may seem to be the easier course to allow our great metropolitan areas to be divided up each into two cities — one white, the other black — but it is a course, I predict, our people will ultimately regret."

White Americans in general have made clear they don't want busing as a way to provide for the blacks the "equal opportunity" described by Justice Marshall. Now for suburban parents, at least, that threat is removed.

Can Americans now realize that in lieu of that tool, that other, often costly remedies must be tried?

Chicago Daily Defender

Chicago, Ill., December 5, 1974

The rally at the Boston Common which drew a crowd of some 5,000 persons, most of them white, was a heartening manifestation of democracy in action. The people gathered at that historic place to show support for the court order which made busing an integral mechanism of the Boston school system. The order enraged some racist Bostonians who are violently opposed to racial integration in any form or shape.

Dr. Martin Luther King's widow, Coretta Scott King, told the crowd that racism, not busing, was at the bottom of the riotous demonstrations that led to beating of blacks and stoning of buses carrying black children to their designated schools.

Mrs. King correctly pointed to those disgraceful incidents as undemocratic assaults on equality. The court busing order simply provided the occasion for a display of racist emotions that has been heretofore suppressed.

The rally at the Boston Common was not only a symbol of massive support for integration but also an attempt at redeeming the soiled image of a historic city long known as the cradle of liberty.

It should be recorded for students of social history that most of the active participants at the street disturbances that followed the court's decision were immigrants who came from the Old world in search of freedom and opportunity to partake of the culture and the wealth of this American society.

But they soon forgot their past and want now to deny to black Americans the very same opportunity they once sought—integration into the American society. History and time will catch up with them.

THE COMMERCIAL APPEAL

Memphis, Tenn., December 20, 1974

SOUTH BOSTON and the Boston School Committee have blinded themselves to what saves this diverse, interdependent society from self-destructive conflict — the law. Laws that offend the people can be changed. But until they are they must be obeyed. Otherwise the people will be much more offended by anarchy.

The situation in South Boston is admittedly complex. Self-righteous advice from afar will not do any good. White ethnic groups bitterly resent black students bused to their schools while their own children are sent to formerly all-black schools outside the area. There is a deeply imbedded "turf" psychology at work. There are also racial prejudice and fear. Everything possible must be done to ease the violent tensions that have built up, but they can't be allowed to flout the law. It is tragic that South Boston has to learn for itself the lessons of desegregation in the South and such Northern cities as Pontiac, Mich.

The school committee should be taken to task for failing to comply with a federal court order to file a new busing plan by last Monday. Committee Chairman John Kerrigan said he voted to defy the court because "I can't in good conscience be an architect of a plan that would increase the bloodshed and hatred in the City of Boston." How much more bloodshed and hatred will there be because the protesters have seen their elected officials siding with them against the court?

Kerrigan presumably would have the court back down in the face of public protest. Then the scene would be set for renewed demonstrations all over the country in places where desegregation is finally being achieved peacefully and with greater biracial understanding and cooperation. What way do men like Kerrigan want this country to go? Ethnic and racial bigotry will not be eliminated quickly or easily, but before the law they must be rejected.

IN TIME laws may be passed to do away with or restrict busing for desegregation purposes. Until then, bused students must be given a chance to get their education in orderly schools. The violence and intransigence in South Boston shame the nation and do untold harm to the lives of both the students and adults who are affected.

The Providence Journal

Providence, R.I., December 17, 1974

Recent events have underscored the need to isolate the most dangerous single source of contagion in the City of Boston before racial polarization reaches epidemic proportions. South Boston High School ought to be closed, at least for the remainder of the academic year.

The incident of last week in which a student was stabbed precipitated the worst outbreak of violence seen in New England in recent memory. It was as though a reservoir of hatred, building since early fall, had suddenly been released. No longer was there any semblance of restraint in the South Boston neighborhood. Anti-black feelings accompanied by racial epithets burst from those who previously had couched their sentiments in the pseudo-respectable language of the anti-busing crusade. The boil, so to speak, had burst.

On Saturday, thousands of angry demonstrators led by the Rev. Ralph Abernathy marched to Boston Common in support of the city's desegregation program. Not unlike the civil rights marches of the 1960s, the rally was infused with the kind of spirit that implies confrontation. Indeed, a brief clash with the police did occur. From around the nation people had come to protest what is happening to a city now paying a high price for 10 years of self-deception — a period in which the city's education officials supported the pretense that racism and de jure segregation were outrages unique to the Southern states.

Within 24 hours the Common became the scene of a counter demonstration.

Easily lost sight of amid the din of rhetoric and the horrors of flying rocks and fists, is the fact that turmoil has not spread throughout the city. It is limited almost entirely to the South Boston district.

The fact is that trouble has erupted infrequently in other parts of the school system. Until the incident late last week, attendance had been rising steadily. And even now the most vocal anti-busing spokesmen seem to have grasped the constitutional imperatives of Judge W. Arthur Garrity Jr.'s orders. That awareness is implicit in the call — a call, incidentally, which we cannot endorse — for a constitutional amendment as the only alternative.

Closing South Boston High, in effect, would remove the principal target of fury. Without daily opportunities for trouble, without racial symbolism in the neighborhood as a daily reminder of court-ordered educational change, tensions would have an opportunity to abate.

Not unexpectedly, the Boston School Committee has chosen to defy the court's deadline for submitting a permanent plan. In doing so, it has given further encouragement to those Bostonians whose determined opposition to a constitutional mandate has brought shame to a city once known affectionately around the world as the "Cradle of Liberty." For this latest act of defiance and all that preceded it, the committee bears a heavy burden of responsibility.

On the facing commentary page today is a column by Jonathan Kozol, the author and teacher, who has observed the workings and non-workings of the Boston school system for many years. In a few words he has reduced the city's present tragic situation to its core. "South Boston is no fortress in this city; nor can this city be a fortress in the state or nation," he writes. "We are one people, one population; we will survive as one, or we will not survive at all."

THE CHRISTIAN SCIENCE MONITOR

Boston, Mass., December 18, 1974

Constructive plans for desegregation of Boston schools struggle for attention against scenes of hate and disruption televised to the nation. Though such scenes are largely confined to a single part of the city, South Boston, they should not be minimized as a representation of diehard resistance to the law, complete with ugly evidence of racism. Nor should the positive feelings involved — neighborhood pride, concern for educational standards — be ignored.

Yet the law will eventually have to be carried out, unless the Constitution is amended or its interpretation of the past 20 years reversed. And Congress currently has been showing how reluctant it is to rule out even such a controversial means of implementing the law as the busing of students.

So Boston and other cities facing desegregation need to proceed promptly with plans that both comply with the law and display as much regard as possible for the strains placed on the first generations of parents and children to be caught in the transition. This week a majority on the Boston School Committee risked contempt of court citations to vote against the new plan for the next phase of desegregation as ordered by U.S. District Judge Garrity.

Their action unfortunately represents the lack of official leadership in Boston which has compounded the problem of compliance. If the leadership had moved ahead in the past, there seems little doubt that legal desegregation could have been accomplished without the court-ordered busing that now fuels resistance.

The new plan for the next phase of desegregation also includes busing — indeed, more of it in the whole city — but it offers parents and students several options as to the kind and location of schools.

Now is the time for critics and well-wishers to come forward with improvements or alternatives before Judge Garrity's Jan.

20 deadline for such inputs. There are many sources for innovative thinking on the subject. For example, Cleveland lawyer and former school board member Hugh Calkins has joined with a law student to propose a detailed "partial remedy" involving voluntary regional integrated schools and a financial incentive system. If a student chose to leave his neighborhood school for a regional school, his former school would pay only two-thirds of the cost of his education at the regional school, which would receive the additional third from the state.

Flaws may be found in such plans. But the time for wide-open thinking rather than obstruction is now. In Boston, communication would be aided by the wholehearted cooperation of parents in the biracial councils called for by Judge Garrity.

Is there hope? Yes, in the sense that these problems have come as the result of previous successes. Mississippi journalist Hodding Carter 3d puts them in perspective as "second-generation" problems. He recently told a Boston group how far the South, where

almost all black students are now in desegregated schools, has come after those agonizing scenes which Boston is reliving. As he noted:

"There have been obvious failures, yet what has to be remembered is that in a society which said 'never' in a way that you have not even begun to approximate in South Boston, we have today, now, a society which says, grudgingly, 'We'll live with it,' and in some aspect feels free to go beyond that and say, 'We are going to make the best of it' and even beyond that to say, 'Thank God, I'm part of it.' "

The Boston Globe

Boston, Mass., December 17, 1974

A three to two majority of the Boston School Committee has chosen once again to defy the law, embodied in the US Constitution and in Judge W. Arthur Garrity Jr.'s order, by refusing to endorse a plan to desegregate the Boston schools. The consequences of this action could be more bitterness for the city as a whole.

In fairness to Boston and its citizens, the background of the present situation needs to be spelled out clearly. Political opportunists for too long have been encouraging people to believe that, if there is enough public opposition, the law will somehow disappear. In fact it is because this city ignored the law for so long that we are now under a court order to comply.

Legally speaking, the situation stems from a US Supreme Court ruling made 20 years ago and upheld or strengthened in dozens of subsequent high court decisions. Based on the 14th Amendment, the Supreme Court justices unanimously concluded in the 1954 Brown decision that "in the field of public education the doctrine of 'separate but equal' has no place." And, in spelling out the remedy a year later, the court insisted, "It should go without saying that the vitality of these constitutional principles cannot be allowed to yield simply because of disagreement with them."

Massachusetts did not wait for a case to be brought. Instead, the Legislature passed a law in 1965 requiring the state's cities and towns to take action when any school became more than 50 percent non-white or face a cut-off in state aid to the public school system.

At the time the state law was passed, Boston had 46 imbalanced schools and a minority population of 23 percent. Last year the city had 64 predominantly black schools and a non-white enrollment of 38.5 percent. This year the minority enrollment is 43.5 percent of the school population.

Ten years ago this city could have been desegregated without

busing, by redrawing attendance lines and by building new schools where they would attract a mixed enrollment.

But in the wake of the Brown decision and subsequent rulings affecting school systems across the country, the Boston School Committee continued to perpetuate largely separate schools. Despite the state law, the committee, in 1966 and 1971, let millions of dollars in state aid be withheld rather than balance the school system. Even when Federal funds were cut off by the US Department of Health, Education and Welfare in 1973, the Boston School Committee failed to act.

A 14th Amendment suit in Boston was inevitable in view of the spreading separatism. When it came, US District Court Judge Garrity delayed his ruling, apparently hoping the Supreme Court would ease the burden on cities by approving suburban involvement in the Detroit case. But that did not happen and Judge Garrity had no choice but to move. His findings, last June 21, were damning:

"... the court concludes that the defendants took many actions in their official capacities with the purpose and intent to segregate the Boston public schools and that such actions caused current conditions of segregation ... It is ordered and adjudged that the defendants ... be permanently enjoined from ... maintaining segregation in any school ... in the Boston school system ..."

Lawyers agree that Judge Garrity's rulings have been conservative. He has broken no ground for Boston that has not already been broken throughout the South and in other northern cities where desegregation through busing has been accomplished more smoothly.

If there is a difference between Boston and cities like Detroit, Denver and San Francisco, it stems from the fact that lack of cooperation by the School Committee left Judge Garrity no alternative but to start with a plan drawn up by the state Board of Education. If there was a reason that President

Ford singled Boston out for public comment it was because a request for Federal troops to deal with disruption was being discussed here.

In its 1958 ruling on Little Rock, the Supreme Court emphatically stated that "the constitutional rights of respondents are not to be sacrificed or yielded to the violence and disorder which have followed the actions of the governor and Legislature." And the same can now be said of the actions of the Boston School Committee.

The antibusing rider proposed in Congress, or similar measures in past statutes, will in no way wipe out Judge Garrity's order. The only possible way to circumvent the Judge Garrity ruling would be to amend the Constitution, which requires a lengthy procedure involving a two-thirds vote of each house of Congress or a constitutional convention initiated by two-thirds of the state legislatures.

The point is that, while it is Judge Garrity's duty to see that white and minority students share space and thus share an interest in every school building, at all grade levels in the city, it is only by default of the School Committee and the people who back up that committee that it becomes his duty to determine how that desegregation shall be accomplished.

The plan rejected by a majority of the School Committee is a hopeful plan. It moves to deescalate tensions by going beyond neighborhoods to mix students on neutral sites. It goes beyond the simple mathematics of desegregation to deal with a better education for Boston schoolchildren. And it leaves room for more community give and take input into school policy and programs.

For all these reasons, we are glad the plan will reach Judge Garrity even without endorsement. Now, if the common interests of the whole community can be mobilized to respect the law and build from it for next fall, Boston could still emerge with benefit to everyone.

The Standard-Times
New Bedford, Mass., December 19, 1974

Once again, the Boston School Committee has managed to add another irresponsible absurdity to its record in the area of racial desegregation. This time, a majority of the committee (3 to 2) decided to defy a court order to endorse and submit a plan to desegregate the city's schools.

The School Department's lawyer, to his great credit, submitted the plan, prepared by the department's staff, to U.S. Judge W. Arthur Garrity despite the committee's action.

What has a majority of the committee accomplished? Well, they have effectively removed themselves from having any real voice in dealing with a tension-laden situation that just will not go away.

Two of the committee's lawyer-members, Chairman John J. Kerrigan and John J. McDonough, admitted privately their outright defiance of the court order could result in their being cited for contempt — even being suspended or disbarred.

The School Committee's action may also jeopardize millions of dollars in state and federal aid. Also in danger of being lost are additional millions in federal funds impounded until Boston begins implementing effective desegregation action.

Furthermore, the 3 to 2 vote is more of the same sort of expressed or implied attitude that has encouraged Boston parents to believe for nearly a decade that if they stall long enough, the school racial imbalance problem somehow will go away. It won't.

The committee can't say this is a situation that sneaked up on them unaware, leaving them without enough time to take corrective action. When the state racial imbalance law was passed in 1965, Boston had 46 imbalanced schools. Last year the number of schools with more than 50 per cent non-white populations had grown to 64.

Certainly, the city's non-white population had increased in the intervening years, but this is what Judge Garrity had to say about the committee's conduct during that era:

"... The court concludes the defendants (committee) took many actions in their official capacities with the purpose and intent to segregate the Boston public schools and that such actions caused current conditions of segregation."

Lawyers (except for a few running for public office on an anti-busing plank) agree Judge Garrity's ruling broke no new ground, that similar decisions have been handed down — and implemented — both in the South and in other Northern cities.

The three-member majority's action Monday is totally indefensible. As Boston Mayor Kevin H. White said of the Garrity ruling months ago, "It is time for us as a city to live up to and face reality."

THE SPRINGFIELD UNION
Springfield, Mass., December 23, 1974

Busing as a means of school integration probably will be around for as long as it takes school systems to replace it with an alternative — such as centralized school complexes— and even then busing will play some part in the system.

Busing foes who gathered on Boston Common recently reflected the bitterness of Bostonians over violence that accompanied that city's school busing program. Federal Judge W. Arthur Garrity, who issued the final busing order, was the target of some speakers.

But as State Rep. Raymond L. Flynn, D-South Boston, one of the rally organizers, pointed out, a federal constitutional amendment is the only way court -ordered busing could be overturned. That process, even if successful, could take several years.

The amendment, which would prohibit the assignment of students to schools on the basis of race, creed or sex, would require a two-thirds supporting vote by both houses of Congress and then ratification by three-quarters of the states.

Only the day after the Boston rally, Congress nullified an anti-busing amendment as part of an education money bill. Opponents regarded the amendment as a means of getting around the Civil Rights Act of 1964, under which the Health, Education and Welfare Department is authorized to enforce school desegregation.

While the amendment did not refer specifically to busing, it would have barred HEW from requiring that schools receiving federal school funds classify students and teachers on the basis of race. This, in effect, would take away the government's power to enforce integration.

The prevailing sentiment in Congress might have been the same had an anti-busing constitutional amendment been under consideration. Conflict with the 14th (equal protection of the laws) amendment might have been claimed.

In any case, U.S. communities with bi-racial school systems are likely to find school building programs a quicker remedy for massive busing than action through the courts or through legislative bodies.

Boston Herald American
Combining the best features of the Herald Traveler and Record American
Boston, Mass., December 31, 1974

Mayor Kevin White's decision to join the Boston School Committee in appealing federal Judge W. Arthur Garrity's desegregation order all the way to the U.S. Supreme Court — and his pledge that the city will pay the full cost of that appeal — were wise and appropriate, in our opinion.

Though the Mayor's move came as a surprise to most people and has been criticized by some, it deserves and has received the support of many on both sides of the school busing controversy.

Several members of the school committee and other anti-busing leaders described the Mayor's action as too little or too late. But they'd already gone on record as favoring the appeal and for the most part they were delighted with the news that the city would pick up the legal tab.

That tab could be expensive and is regarded as a waste of money by some of those who support Judge Garrity's decree or think it is futile to appeal it. But it represents only a small fraction of what already has been spent to enforce and implement that order — or to resist it, legally and otherwise.

Meanwhile, the Mayor's decision was hailed as "logical and sensible" by Rep. Royal Bolling Sr., a leading spokesman for the black community. Though he agrees with Judge Garrity's ruling, he says it is only fair for those who do not agree with it to have their day in court.

That was one of the points stressed by the Mayor in his announcement. And it is a point that is very valid, in our opinion. For the crisis that has erupted in our schools and divided the city's people isn't likely to end until the issue is resolved once and for all by the Supreme Court.

The high court has, of course, handed down a number of school desegregation decisions in the past 20 years. But the precedents and principles involved in those cases may not apply exactly to the situation here.

The chances that the Supreme Court will reverse Judge Garrity's decree are perhaps "remote," as the Mayor has conceded. But whether it sustains or overrules the decree, its decision will be final.

Then and only then, as the Mayor remarked, will the tension, the doubt and the uncertainty hovering over Boston's schools begin to subside. Only when every legal avenue of appeal has been exhausted and the debate has ended, as he put it, can we hope to restore order and resume the vital task of educating our children.

St. Petersburg Times

St. Petersburg, Fla., December 31, 1974

Historic events may not be recognized at first as historic. They may come too fast or be seen as only a local matter or be blurred by other issues requiring the public's attention, such as pocketbook concerns. That seems to be the way it is in Boston.

THE EVENT is the mostly emotional one of school busing for desegregation. The Constitution is being tested. Actions are being taken, and not taken, that will influence race relations, ideas about law and violence, and the 14th Amendment for years. A turning point — forward or backward — appears certain.

What happens should be up to the people of Boston, as it was up to the people of St. Petersburg when busing began some four years ago. But the public in Boston has not rallied to support equal opportunity in education; three of five members of the Boston School Committee have defied the law; civic and official city leadership has been weak. Now it rests with President Ford whether violence will continue when Boston's schools reopen after the first of the year.

Needed from the President is an expression of sympathetic concern for the children of Boston and a firm pledge that court rulings will be supported, that law will be enforced, that pupils will not be endangered going to school in a nation based on concepts of justice and an equal opportunity to become whatever one's abilities permit.

GIVEN THE hot feelings in Boston, fanned by extremists, Mr. Ford's pledge would need to be backed up with a promise — or warning — to deploy U.S. troops to Boston if necessary. The Kent State University tragedy reduces confidence in federalized National Guard forces. Well-trained Army regulars would be necessary to calm the fears of parents and pupils and to ensure order.

Mr. Ford is, we think, a decent man, who considers the ethical as well as political consequences of his decisions. He has not indicated that he is a racist. Yet, his anti-busing statements and his lack of unequivocal support for the law encourage racists. If the public cannot look to decent men for leadership, to whom can they look?

BUSING IS as imperfect for school desegregation as it always has been for getting children to school. But it can be used as long as it is necessary. It always has been. St. Petersburg and Charlotte, among other places, show it is a useful desegregation tool when used carefully with the welfare of pupils and parents in mind and when made fair to all, as with rotation here.

To refuse to desegregate the North, to set in motion a reversal of desegregation gains already made elsewhere because of successful defiance in Boston would make shameful history and signal that mob power is an acceptable alternative to law. It could proclaim the 14th Amendment an empty ideal, worthless in fact. For the well-being of the nation, President Ford dare not allow that.

Amsterdam News

New York, N.Y., December 28, 1974

The time clock of racial violence is ticking away in Boston while President Gerald Ford, like Nero of old, fiddles as the racial fires burn.

The NAACP and others standing for decency in this country have appealed to President Ford, to take urgently needed action in enforcing law and order in Boston.

But in spite of the fact that a Black man was beaten and almost lynched on October 7th by white mobs, and despite the fact that Boston's racist violence has become a regular weekend occurrence nevertheless, there is no new word from the White House on Boston.

The last word we had from the White House on Boston was that the President did not agree with the judge who told the Boston bigots to desegrate their schools.

What do we have to do in order to get the President to take responsible action in Boston? Must we wait until someone is killed in the violence?

There was a time when this nation deplored Dwight Eisenhower's reluctance to act. That was the time when Orvil Faubus thumbed his nose at federal laws and used the National Guard to take away the rights of Black children in Little Rock.

But even Dwight Eisenhower had his breaking point, and he finally did what he should have done earlier. He sent federal troops into Little Rock to restore law and order and uphold the Constitution.

What does it take to get Gerald Ford to act?

THE ARIZONA REPUBLIC

Phoenix, Ariz., December 29, 1974

Responding to outbreaks of racial violence following his orders to compel the busing of school-children in Boston, Federal District Judge W. Arthur Garrity has imposed limits on the speech and assembly rights of the citizens in that city.

The judge has banned any gathering of persons within 100 yards of South Boston High School. He has also banned the utterance of "racial epithets" on school grounds.

The United States Constitution forbids any abridgment of "free speech and of the press or the right of the people peaceably to assemble to petition the government for a redress of grievances."

Because busing is among the most widespread and obnoxious grievances the American people have with their present government, it would seem that speech and assembly to protest busing are constitutionally protected.

But, it must be conceded, the men who wrote our Bill of Rights probably never imagined that such an infringement of rights as forced busing would ever occur under the document they had written.

Chicago Tribune

Chicago, Ill., December 31, 1974

Busing for racial integration of schools continues much in the news from Boston—and not only from there. Racial segregation by school authorities was with good reason outlawed by the Supreme Court in Brown v. Board of Education [1954]. But identifying de facto segregation with de jure segregation has caused unending troubles. In Topeka, Kas., where the test case of Brown v. Board arose, some schools were segregated de jure in a substantially integrated society. But in Boston, is it right to thrust upon school authorities and school pupils the task of integrating schools in a de facto segregated society?

By now, hardly anyone wants busing except federal judges. This fact is eloquently illustrated by a special supplement to the current issue of Ramparts, the radical magazine. There Andrew Kopkind, a contributing editor of Ramparts, says, "In Boston, at least, nobody wanted busing, altho various spokespeople for the black community were compelled to support it for historical and poltical reasons—or because the original opposition had come from their enemies." But now blacks in Boston and elsewhere are far more interested in community control of schools in black neighborhoods than in crosstown busing. Mr. Kopkind's judgment is that busing proposals in Boston are "unworkable and unwise at best, and damaging at worst." He is even more emphatic: "It was always a crazy idea to bus Roxbury kids into Southie, or vice versa."

Eight other writers contributed to a Ramparts symposium on busing. None of them favors it. Some quotable remarks: "Busing doesn't integrate the community. It just moves the kids around during the school day."—Herb Kohl. Unwanted busing "is the height of callousness, injustice, and political stupidity."—John Holt. "Instead of pushing for better schools, black people and white people are fighting over who will sit next to whom in some of the worst schools in the nation."—Noel Day.

"Busing is a racist, lazy, selfish, decision made by people who don't want to take the time to do the work required to improve the quality of education in all of our schools."—Ericka Huggins. "I see no reason why children of either race or any social class should be conscripted into a 20th century crusade of social justice."—Edgar Z. Friedenburg. "What you have in Boston is the spectacle of working-class people fighting among themselves to get into or to retain schools that everybody knows victimize all students, black and white."—Malecai Andrews.

These are not judgments of reactionary white bigots. None of the persons quoted above is a rightwinger, and half of them are black.

Busing raises two vast, unsolved issues—crippling, dangerous race prejudice; and the miserable state of many public schools. In situations where nobody wants it, busing helps neither problem. It is high time the courts ceased making extreme, doctrinaire demands for "racial balance" in public schools. It would be no betrayal of Brown v. Board of Education for the courts to content themselves with striking down official actions to segregate.

If the Boston School Committee has gerrymandered districts, let it be required to draw better maps.

But busing? Who in Boston, besides Judge W. Arthur Garrity, wants it?

THE CINCINNATI ENQUIRER

Cincinnati, Ohio, December 30, 1974

THE SCHOOL-INTEGRATION crisis in Boston proceeds unabated. Demonstrations, counterdemonstrations, the willful violation of court directives by the Boston School Committee—such developments as these have brought Boston close to the halfway mark of the school year with no clear answer in view. Indeed, passions are far more furious today than they were when the current school-integration crisis come to the fore in September. Even if a technical solution could be found next week, the animosities these few months have engendered would not disappear in a lifetime.

Therein, perhaps, is the ultimate tragedy. For when the Supreme Court declared in 1954 that schools segregated by law were unconstitutional, the hopeful expectation was that there lay ahead a fresh era of racial amity and understanding—an era in which a new generation of Americans would grow up essentially blind to racial differences.

As matters have developed, however, such communities as Boston are seeing more racial acrimony than ever before, and it is an acrimony that will be shaping attitudes and insights for perhaps generations to come.

What has made most acts of defiance of court orders in the area of school integration particularly deplorable is that they are potentially explosive short-cuts. They set precedents for those who are looking for an excuse to ignore one law or another. They contribute, accordingly, to a gradual erosion of respect for law, for the orderly processes of government.

There have been eras in history in which there was no practical alternative to such acts of defiance—eras in which there were no "safety valves" for the use of the aggrieved. In nearly all cases today, however, there *are* safety valves: there are opportunities for judicial or legislative appeals to right wrongs.

The distressing aspect of the Boston integration crisis is that there is a growing *feeling* that no such safety valves exist. The opponents of mandatory busing appear to be feeling more and more that there is no alternative available to them but the alternative of dogged resistance.

This growing and potentially dangerous attitude has been examined by Jack Nusan Porter, a sociologist specializing in race relations, who teaches at Pine Manor College in Brookline, Mass.

The whites in Boston, Mr. Porter has written for the Los Angeles Times, "do not want extremism, mob violence or anarchy—what they do want is *attention*. If a phrase could describe the white ethnics of South Boston—and indeed the white ethnics of today's America—it would be that they feel 'a sense of impotent isolation.'

"By and large, white ethnics are insecure—economically, politically and psychologically. They are frightened of crime in the streets, frightened of economic recession, frightened of losing their community—their schools, churches, stores, sense of belonging.

"Middle Americans," Mr. Porter goes on, "are heartsick to see their children bused into what they consider high-crime areas. They want their little ones to come home for lunch, home to mommy, instead of being transported to the other side of town—or even into the next neighborhood.

"With the advent of busing in the big cities of the North, what made working-class white ethnics so angry was that the liberals in the wealthier suburbs could be in favor of busing and integration—as long as it didn't involve *their* children."

These, if Mr. Porter's analysis is correct, are the factors that have generated the hatred—the furious, ineradicable hatred—that Americans are seeing on their television screens every evening. It is a hatred born of frustration by a segment of the Boston community that feels it has no voice. Whenever, in any community, there are such feelings of alienation and abandonment, there are grave and ugly dangers.

THE MILWAUKEE JOURNAL

Milwaukee, Wisc., December 21, 1974

A thoughtful analysis of the Boston school desegregation controversy by a Massachusetts sociologist makes the point that the issue is not racism but what the white ethnics of South Boston consider the basic human freedom of choice in schooling their children. It is an understandable view, but it misses the mark.

Freedom of choice in schooling is a myth. The laws of every state require parents to send their children to school. These laws make no guarantee of schoolhouse proximity. Nearly half the schoolchildren in America live so far from school that they must ride buses daily to class. School districts short of classrooms at times of burgeoning enrollments have often shuffled different grade levels among buildings from year to year to fit everyone in. The neighborhood school may be a tradition in much of urban America, but it is not a right, by law or Constitution, and never has been.

Even if it were a right, history records many examples of legitimate rights in conflict, with resolution of such conflicts by assignment of higher precedence to one right over another. Usually it has fallen to the US Supreme Court to make those decisions. The history of school desegregation throughout the South amply demonstrates that the right of black children to an equal educational opportunity must take precedence over white parents' feelings about freedom of choice in schooling.

The Boston Globe

Boston, Mass., December 24, 1974

The appeal of the Boston school desegregation case to the US Supreme Court could conceivably bring a final answer on this troublesome issue by next June, and that could be a helpful thing for Boston as it moves toward citywide implementation of a court order next fall.

A still more positive effect of an appeal, brought by the Boston School Committee, is that in acting to bring their case before the highest court in the land, the committee implies a willingness to abide by that court's decision.

Earlier the state courts twice found the School Committee in violation of the now defunct Massachusetts law regarding racial balancing in the city's schools. The US Department of Health, Education and Welfare also found the committee guilty of operating a dual school system in violation of Federal law. Now both a US District Court and the US Circuit Court of Appeals have found the Boston School Committee guilty of constitutional violations under the 14th Amendment.

But the last legal door will not be closed until the case has been brought before the US Supreme Court in Washington.

Under ordinary procedures, it could take five months for an appeal to reach the Supreme Court. And there could be a risk of a stay on the lower court rulings if four justices agree that the case merits being held over until next fall for a hearing.

But if the court refuses to hear the case, thus leaving lower court rulings intact, the School Committee would have no further options and would have to comply with Judge Garrity's orders. So long as any legal remedy exists, the committee has a right to try it even though its own attorney has declared the attempt would be "frivolous." But a Supreme Court ruling would resolve the legal question not only for the Boston School Committee, but for all those in this city who now believe their rights are being violated.

The San Diego Union

San Diego, Calif., January 3, 1975

Federal Judge Arthur W. Garrity is inviting a test of his constitutional powers in his threat to fine three members of the Boston School Committee. The committee members are resisting the judge's order to draw up a school integration plan even more sweeping than the one which already is causing disorders.

Whether the judge's integration orders are justified or not, this impasse finds an appointed federal officer ordering three local elected officials to do something that they believe to be wrong for their community. Under our system of government to whom do elected representatives answer? To a judge, or to the people who elected them?

THE CHRISTIAN SCIENCE MONITOR

Boston, Mass., January 2, 1975

As Boston's public schools reopen today, including those closed since a stabbing incident Dec. 11, nine unsung Americans are giving their country the kind of example it needs on the thorny path to school desegregation.

In the midst of South Boston's obdurate resistance to the law as interpreted by U.S. District Judge Garrity and upheld by the circuit court of appeals, nine South Boston parents have come forward in support of the law. They have volunteered to serve on one of the biracial neighborhood councils ordered by Judge Garrity.

These councils are part of the effort to ameliorate the acknowledged strains requiring compassion for the transitional generation of parents and students called upon to make the first difficult steps away from unlawful segregation. Whatever the outcome of new legal moves to resolve the Boston crisis, the future of harmonious community relations clearly lies in a multiplication of constructive individual decisions to comply with the law and cooperate with one's fellow man.

But this reponsibility of individual citizens does not absolve their leaders from likewise setting an example of regard for law and man. Thus there is no excuse for the leadership's failing to carry out the law while the latest legal efforts to test it are in the making. The present interim desegregation plan, including its court-ordered busing, should be implemented with all the police assistance necessary to protect students and public. The Phase 2 plan for next fall, with its new educational options, should be pursued in the light of revisions and alternatives which can be submitted until Jan. 20.

The three-man majority of the school committee were given the opportunity to purge themselves of Judge Garrity's recent contempt rulings against them by voting to "authorize" submission of an appropriate plan even if they do not personally "approve" it. The difference illustrates the way many individuals are being asked to consider obeying the law even if they disagree.

For the school committee and city leadership to go along with further hampering and delay not only undermines respect for the rule of law but undercuts the already interrupted education of students at a time when the dwindling job market demands as many educational advantages as possible.

Meanwhile, the school committee's appeal to the Supreme Court to overrule Judge Garrity ought to be expedited both by the committee and the Supreme Court. Mayor White's guarantee of city financing for the appeal may be a debatable use of taxpayers' money, since the constitutional issue appears to have been long settled and he himself regards a successful appeal as "remote." But the guarantee removes any financial excuse for delay, and it can be supported as going that extra mile to assure all concerned that every legal step has been taken.

The school committee has every right to this process. And, if the decision is against it, there is every right for the predicted next step of seeking a constitutional amendment that could have the effect of overthrowing Judge Garrity's decision.

But insofar as these are merely delaying tactics, they are to be deplored. The test of their motives will be in the dispatch with which the appeal is pursued — and the degree to which the outcome is adhered to, whatever it may be.

Here is where not only local but national leadership can play a role in meeting the future constructively rather than destructively. Here is an opportunity for President Ford to undo the damage of his previous statement that played into the hands of those defying the law. By wholly supporting compliance with a Supreme Court decision, not to mention the law that stands in the meantime, he could help to provide the climate for more Americans in Boston and elsewhere to follow the example of those nine unsung volunteers.

THE INDIANAPOLIS STAR

Indianapolis, Ind., January 4, 1975

The awesome power of a Federal judge has lately shown itself in Boston.

In that city, scene of the Boston Tea Party, an early American blow for freedom and the concept of self-government, United States District Court Judge W. Arthur Garrity this week ordered three members of the five-member Boston School Committee fined and stripped of their authority to act on matters concerning desegregation of the Boston school system unless they vote with the other two members to file by Jan. 7 a new citywide desegregation plan.

Garrity issued in writing his intention to act in this manner after holding the three committeemen in civil contempt of court for their refusal to vote for submission of the new plan by a Dec. 16 deadline he had previously specified.

In the background of these events lies an earlier integration plan ordered into effect by Garrity last September which has been the cause of serious outbreaks of violence in some areas of Boston.

Though primarily involving South Boston High School and considerably less wide in scope than the new plan, scheduled to replace it next fall, the current plan has already produced such violent reactions — including the stabbing of one student by another — that school officials and Boston police now consider it unsafe for South Boston High School to be kept open.

There seems little room for doubt that the refusal thus far of the three-member majority of the school committeemen to agree to submit a new citywide plan is based on fear that a new and wider plan could do harm far surpassing that already brought about under the existing plan.

On one side of this issue is a single individual, a Federal judge, an appointed official, who presumably reads the Constitution and rulings of the U.S. Supreme Court as requiring him to command creation in Boston of a situation which, if current conditions point accurately, could play havoc with the Boston public school system and possibly lead to widespread disorder and violence. We deplore the disorder and violence, but they are facts of the situation.

On the other side is a majority of the Boston School Committee, the members of which are duly elected by the people of Boston and thus empowered by them, in accordance with the principles of self-government, to serve as the policy-making and controlling authority in respect to the Boston public school system.

The current situation in Boston would suggest a usurpation of powers vested in the people in their duly elected representatives by a single appointed official who holds the awesome power of the law to command obedience to his dictates.

That such a situation apparently has arisen in a city the very name of which is a symbol of freedom and self-government to Americans is ironic — and tragic.

THE RICHMOND NEWS LEADER

Richmond, Va., January 13, 1975

Two weeks ago Federal District Judge Arthur Garrity found three members of the Boston School Committee — the equivalent of our School Board — in civil contempt of court for refusing to approve a plan that would bring still more compulsory busing to Boston. Judge Garrity fined the three and barred them from participating in any desegregation matters that might come before the Committee.

In that ruling and in the position of the three Committee-members lie fundamental questions. The judge's position, like the position of those who tend to endorse compulsory busing, is that the basic issue is the rule of law. The position of the three Committee-members is that imposition of the "law" — *i.e.*, compulsory busing — in Boston has polarized the races and endangered public school children; they regard it as an assault on the neighborhood way of life. To see that the Committee-members are essentially correct, one need only open one's eyes.

In contemplating the situation in Boston, it is worth keeping in mind that the five-member School Committee there is popularly elected. Moreover, in an advisory referendum last June, the populace voted 13-1 *against* the imposition of any compulsory busing plan. Yet here we have a situation in which a federal judge seeks to compel three members of the School Committee to approve a plan in which they — as elected representatives of the public — do not believe; a plan, indeed, that the public manifestly does not want.

So some questions to answer are these: (1) Would the three members of the School Committee be carrying out their popular mandate if they approved a compulsory busing plan that they believed the public does not want? (2) Would the Committee-members be carrying out their mandate if — when ordered by a federal judge — they approved a plan they sincerely believed would threaten the safety of school children? (3) Is the safety of children secondary to balancing them racially in the public schools? (4) Ought Judge Garrity to intercede between the public and the Committee the public has elected?

It is all very well to charge the School-Committee members with segregationist subterfuge. It is all very well to point out that without adherence to the law in his matter, we risk anarchy. It is all very well to maintain that the "Christian response" to rulings of federal judges is to submit to those rulings. But whatever their national image now, Bostonians are the inheritors of a long tradition — a tradition that goes back 200 years — of not subordinating their own interests to legalist demands.

We recall a time not so long ago — from the mid-1950s to the mid-1960s — when many of those who are subscribing to Judge Garrity's position now, were subscribing to the Rev. Dr. Martin Luther King's position then. And his position, like the position of Henry David Thoreau before him, was that if it was necessary to break "laws" to emphasize their immorality, then breaking them was altogether defensible and honorable, even noble. And so, as an enunciator of the public conscience, he broke the law. Are the members of the Boston School Committee any less noble for refusing to endorse a plan they believe to be equally as wrong as the lunch-counter laws in Montgomery two decades ago?

The three members of the School Committee have their principles, too. Should they sacrifice their principles for expedients? Is the morality of the Committee-members inferior to the morality of law? Are they any less the representatives of majority opinion than the Rev. Dr. King was? Is it proper to redefine passive resistance as massive resistance when we object to it?

We are told to love our neighbor, but nowhere are we told to love our neighbor to the neglect of our own children. To make such a recommendation is to leave undischarged certain intellectual obligations. Sanctioning the busing of one's own child — to his detriment and for the sole alleged benefit of another child — is not noble; it is derelict. And surely that is what the three members of the Boston School Committee feel they would be if they went along with the good judge: derelict. For they seem to know, as he evidently does not, that the heart of the covenant that he proposes for the public school children of Boston is...self-immolation.

St. Louis Globe-Democrat

St. Louis, Mo., January 6, 1975

Boston, the Citadel of the liberal Eastern Establishment, will appeal to the U.S. Supreme Court an order by a federal judge which has brought forced busing to the city. Bostonians have found, in the four bloody and venomous months since their children were first marched into strange neighborhoods, that they are little different from citizens in other areas—generally the South—who were confronted with judicial fiat.

They have the same bigotry and the same animosity. But they also have the same legitimate concern for neighborhood schools (race considerations aside), and the same justifiable outrage at judicial decrees that supplant legislation arising out of the will of the citizenry. They don't like the rights of the majority being totally taken away to give dictated specious "civil rights" to a minority—imposed "rights" that must be exercised even if the minority wishes to refrain from them.

In short, black children simply must leave their local schools and be bused to schools in other areas, whether they want to go or not. The same is true of whites. A state court ruling that the Boston schools must realign their racial make-ups was protested by a huge 13 to 1 margin in a non-binding Boston referendum in June. But shortly thereafter, U.S District Judge W. Arthur Garrity ordered immediate realignment among some schools, with all 200 schools in the city to face racial quotas next September.

☆ ☆ ☆

CLEARLY THE JUCIAL FIAT imposing crosstown swapping of children in every school in Boston is an indication that racial quotas are an end unto themselves. If schools were deliberately segregated through gerrymandering, as alleged by the court, the solution would be to redraw school attendance boundaries where violations occur, not establish arbitrary quotas at every school in the city. The demographics of Boston are such that it is ludicrous to contend that there is deliberate segregation at all schools. Rather, the segregation results from voluntary housing patterns.

What thoughtful Bostonians object to is the forced movement of children being conducted not to correct deliberate segregation, but to satisfy what one judge thinks is a proper racial balance among all school children, wherever they may be. This is social scheming, not civil rights, and it has had a dreadful effect on the social fabric of all of Boston.

The same sort of judicial do-goodery appears evident in a recent local case. As in Boston, the key question was whether any segregation results from economic factors or from racial considerations, but the case involved housing rather than schooling. The U.S. Court of Appeals for the Eighth Circuit overruled a district judge's finding that a Black Jack zoning ordinance prohibiting multi-family housing was not racial discrimination.

The Court of Appeals reasoned that "the ultimate effect of the ordinance was to foreclose 85 per cent of the blacks living in the metropolitan area from obtaining housing in Black Jack" because they could not afford the single-family homes in Black Jack.

☆ ☆ ☆

OBVIOUSLY THE ORDINANCE was an economic "discrimination," in the sense that only blacks and whites who could afford single-family homes could live in Black Jack. But twisting the cost of something into a matter of racial discrimination is specious logic as long as there is no racial impediment to those who can afford the item.

The ruling represents a new intrusion into the right of citizens to set minimum standards for everyone—black and white—in that community or group.

The role of the judiciary and of government agencies such as the Department of Justice is to insure that all citizens have no roadblock to such things as employment, housing and schooling that results because of their race (or religion, creed, etc.). In Boston and Black Jack, anyone was free legally to move to any house and to attend the school in that locale. The fact that blacks and whites generally live by choice in communities that are predominantly of their own race, or that black incomes as a whole may be lower than those of whites, has no legal bearing on discrimination charges.

By judicial legislation on racial happenstance, as in Boston and Black Jack, courts are taking away the right of citizens to voluntary association and to exercise free will within the bounds of civil rights laws and the Constitution.

The Afro American

Baltimore, Md., January 7, 1975

Having convinced himself that cooperation and appeasement of the anti-busing element in Boston was falling flat, federal judge W. Arthur Garrity has decided to brook the defiance of law. That Boston School Committee.

Judge Garrity has found three members of the committee — John J. Kerrigan, chairman; Paul Ellison and John J. McDonough — guilty of contempt of court for not approving a desegregation plan by Dec. 16 and ordered them to purge themselves or face fines.

The Defiant Three have threatened to go to jail rather than obey the law but it is doubtful they will do that, or if they do, that they will stay for very long. Even the jails are desegregated.

Violence, threats of violence and disruptions of the kind that once prevailed in Dixie, have plagued Boston since busing was ordered in the school system.

There has been too much toleration of the lawbreakers in Boston.

The Defiant Three and their vocal and violent white supporters are the ones who are threatening education in Boston.

It is not busing to bring about school desegregation that has Boston in turmoil but the defiance of law. That fact must not be twisted into an ugly lie behind which those who are promoting racism and division can hide.

In this country approximately 19 million children are bused to schools daily. Busing has not destroyed any school systems. It has not prevented children from getting educations. Busing, in fact, has made it possible for millions of children to be able to get public school educations.

Only when desegregation is involved does busing become "forced busing" and, according to opponents, a threat to the education system.

It still remains a fact that less than 6 per cent of all the children in the nation are bused for reasons that have to do with desegregation. So it is not busing that threatens to destroy educational systems.

The culprit is racism and classism. Both are targets of the Supreme Court rulings demanding public schools be desegregated and permitting busing to be employed as a tool to that end.

Getting rid of dual school education and inequalities is more important than the added costs or inconveniences of busing.

Desegregation and teaching young people to live together is so much more important than holding on to area or city all-white culture patterns that these pale into relative insignificance.

South Boston, or any other section of any other city that prides itself on a pattern of conduct that attempts to restrict other racial groups' participation in tax-supported activities, indulges in illegal, immoral and unAmerican schemes.

It is unfortunate in Boston that the leadership there, including its communications media, could not get that message through.

That minority of Boston citizens who have carried on a war against law, has been asking for tougher treatment from the courts.

While it is regrettable it had to come to this, it is encouraging to see that at long last Judge Garrity has decided to respond properly to the defiance. Time will prove desegregation, even by busing, a necessary development that will be beneficial to the education of our children and the betterment of the society at large.

The Providence Journal

Providence, R.I., January 11, 1975

Judge W. Arthur Garrity Jr., the beleaguered federal district judge whose superb handling of the Boston school crisis has earned widespread admiration, in effect has postponed for at least two more weeks a final decision on the kind of desegregation program the city will be required to adopt next fall.

In declaring three school committee members purged of civil contempt for having authorized creation of a plan based on voluntarism, Judge Garrity was opting for a cooling-off period. The court had ruled them in civil contempt for failing to submit a new plan last month. On Wednesday he said, "The court will not today deprive them of that opportunity."

It was clear from his remarks, however, that the crisis is by no means at an end. Rather, it has been postponed until sometime after Jan. 20, the committee's new deadline for filing its voluntary program. "After the defendants have filed the amended plan, which they have in mind," Judge Garrity said, "the question whether citywide desegregation may be achieved without (assignment of students to schools outside their neighborhoods) can then be settled once and for all."

Certainly, the desirability of voluntary integration is not an issue. The concept comes as close as any could to universal acceptance. The hitch is the record of voluntary plans. It is extremely poor.

In the South, during the 1960s, so-called freedom-of-choice plans became a popular means of circumventing school desegregation. The Supreme Court, in *Green v. County School Board of New Kent County, Va.* (May, 1968) ruled that while not themselves unconstitutional, such plans were inadequate unless they sought explicitly to dismantle a dual system and transform it into a unitary system.

Judge Garrity's pessimism, therefore, is easily understood. He cited the Dec. 27 testimony of John J. Kerrigan, the former school committee chairman, who had said, "The only way you are going to desegregate city schools is through forced busing." And the judge added that the chances of a voluntary plan meeting the requirements of the court order "are remote in the extreme."

Thus, resolution of Boston's school problem is hardly imminent. The next two weeks are likely to be critical to the final outcome. If the period is used by defiant school committee members and others to build false hopes and further inflame anti-busing sentiments, the chances of a tranquil opening of schools next fall could be dangerously undermined.

If, however, the time is used in fact as a cooling-off period in which the people of South Boston heed the pleas and example of a neighborhood parent, Mrs. Margaret Coughlin, there can be new hope. A mother of nine and grandmother of four, Mrs. Coughlin has organized volunteers to monitor the schools. She has preached the importance of avoiding confrontations. And she has urged parents to end the boycott and prove that those who believe the safety of students cannot be ensured are wrong.

Judge Garrity has performed his duties with exemplary restraint and understanding. He has provided another fortnight's margin for conciliation and resignation; it must not be wasted.

The Boston Globe

Boston, Mass., March 24, 1975

Judge W. Arthur Garrity Jr. will open oral arguments tomorrow on a citywide school desegregation plan that goes far beyond the basic arithmetic of racial mixing to involve the whole community in an educational program that could make the Boston school system one of the best and most exciting in the country.

Certainly there will be problems with a plan that cuts back on desegregation in favor of ethnic stability, that calls for a broad realignment in the administration of the city's school system, and that requires an unprecedented involvement in the schools by business and the universities. They are now on the spot and they cannot fail.

But those who say it cannot be done, those who say the plan still goes far in terms of social intervention, should consider the alternatives available under the existing jurisdiction of a Federal court order.

In striking out for relevant, high-quality education, the plan submitted by the four court-appointed masters Friday seeks to meet the Constitution's broad requirements for desegregation, at the same time preserving the integrity of the city's neighborhoods.

There is something in this plan for everyone, designed as it is to achieve school desegregation "by means that are responsible, fair and efficacious."

Minority students will no longer be isolated in substandard schools. But the racial mix will range from 85 percent white in East Boston to 25 percent in Jamaica Plain, a degree of variation that was not permitted under the state's now defunct racial imbalance law.

The character of Boston's neighborhoods is preserved in the drawing of nine compact community school districts. And that's a good thing. But, for the first time in the city's history, Boston parents and especially minority parents will have a voice in policy-making through participation in local school district councils. And in every case there should be strong new support from the larger community in terms of educational programs and job training.

The local high schools will stand as the focus of an educational program based on "the needs and interests of residents and students" within those districts. This is a specially poignant gain for areas such as South Boston, Roxbury, Hyde Park and Charlestown. There will also be a citywide complex of magnet schools for which students may apply as one of several options built into the plan.

Compulsory transportation will be cut back from 17,000 students now to a maximum of 14,000 students next year and two out of three students may be able to walk to their nearest school. Seniors may apply to remain in their 1974 high school until graduation and students may elect to remain in their Phase One school or apply to another district, a magnet school or the Metco program.

There will be mandatory assignment of pupils, based on address rather than geo-codes. But it will be within districts closely related to 1973 ward and precinct lines and designed "to enable parents and students to plan a coherent sequence of learning experiences within an identifiable series of schools that culminate in a community district high school." And the program is designed to maximize freedom of choice within Constitutional limits.

The greatest challenge and the greatest opportunity for gain will come in the proposal to contract directly with businesses and universities for massive support services to specific programs and schools.

The tax-exempt universities and colleges, which comprise the largest industry in the Boston area, have so far been free with advice but have stood on the sidelines when it came to taking real action. Businesses, too, have been half-hearted in their commitment to the city's school system. All of this could change and bring additional Federal funding if Judge Garrity supports the masters in ordering visible, paired sharing of expertise from these two sources.

It may not be easy to work out the details in an area of administrative heirarchy that includes the universities, the community school district councils, a citywide supervisory agency and the existing superintendencies and school committee.

But the plan's emphasis on educational quality, its perception of the schools as a functioning part of the whole community, the new flexibility in ratios of black and white students and the very significant reduction in desegregation-related busing cannot help bringing a thrill of hope that Boston can once again break new ground in an area where we have seemed to be deadlocked in bitterness.

Every change in society involves compromise and good will on all sides. And the masters' plan represents an extraordinary and imaginative example of such compromise. If it can be made to work, everyone who has suffered anguish over the past year in Boston will have given a little and gains a little. It was King Solomon's understanding of this principle that made him wise.

THE SACRAMENTO BEE

Sacramento, Calif., January 4, 1975

The spectacle of massive resistance, violence and parent-instigated boycotts in the Boston public school system is profoundly disturbing.

True, it is not the first such instance of defiance of court-ordered busing to achieve racial balance in our schools — more than half of Boston's schools are nonwhite in enrollment — but the lamentable situation has special significance in this city which cradled the nation's liberties.

The crux of the matter is whether or not this is a nation of law.

What has been happening in Boston is a flagrant defiance of the law, mandated by the U.S. Supreme Court 20 years ago, which ordered racial integration of the schools.

A large and vocal segment of Bostonians, clinging to the "neighborhood school" tradition, has vehemently resisted a court-ordered desegregation. The opposition includes three recalcitrant school board members presently under contempt of court citation.

They have refused adamantly to "approve" the desegregation plan and busing ordered by Federal Judge W. Arthur Garrity Jr. The judge has given them until Jan. 7 to reconsider, after which he will impose daily contempt fines.

Garrity did offer the three a prudential compromise way out. He agreed to let them "authorize" rather than "approve" the desegregation program. This way they could abide by the law without compromising their conscience.

These school board members, and the parent organization fighting to block integration, would be wise to weigh seriously the consequences of the course they have taken.

It amounts to nothing less than defiance of the law. If ours is to be a society of laws, not of individual whim or bias, such defiance simply cannot be countenanced.

The emotion-laden reasons for this resistance and the attachment to the neighborhood school tradition are not hard to understand.

Sooner or later, however, Boston's citizens and parents will have to accept the constitutional mandate for integration of the city's schools. The longer this is delayed, the longer unreasoning resistance goes on, the harder it will be to achieve a harmonious, workable resolution of the present impasse.

Boston Herald American

Combining the best features of the Herald Traveler and Record American

Boston, Mass., March 25, 1975

Late last summer we suggested that if there were a sufficient display of goodwill, Boston's troubled schools could reopen with a minimum of disruption under the federal court's desegregation order.

It is not possible at this point, unfortunately, to say that is the way it worked out. Still it is important to recognize that the anti-busing violence, as might have been expected—tended to overshadow the fact that for the great majority of the city's 90,000 public school children, life went on very much as it always had.

Now there is greater need than ever before for cooperation and compromise, as oral arguments begin today before Judge W. Arthur Garrity, Jr., on a revolutionary city-wide plan by four court-appointed masters, which surprisingly suggests a greater concern for quality education than a slavish commitment to racial integration.

In the end, the odds are that this plan, too, will not satisfy everyone. What plan possibly could? But it certainly deserves the chance to be judged on its own merits. It ought to be weighed honestly, without bias or prejudice, and then compared with the alternatives.

The masters plan is unique in many respects. Its proposal to involve universities and business directly in the educational process marks an historic departure from the norm. If it were successfully implemented, it could change the course of public school education in the country.

How the masters could estimate less busing than under the initial phase which went into effect last fall is puzzling to many. In fact, there is much about the plan which is not easy to grasp at first reading—and consequently has created hangups about several of its concepts.

The expansion of the narrow neighborhood into a broader community within prescribed ward and precinct lines, and the creation of semi-independent administrative districts with their own advisory councils are among them.

For example, it is difficult to foresee the court stripping constitutional authority from an elected school committee and transferring it to regional advisory councils, after the idea had been rejected so recently by the electorate.

On the other hand the new degree of flexibility in pupil ratios to reflect the de facto racial composition of the various communities rather than the arbitrary requirements of the old state imbalance law could relax the discontent many feel toward adjustment of the racial population of the schools.

There is the seed for change in the masters' plan and that is precisely why it must not now be regarded from frozen positions. Public opinion on this emotional issue has been polarized too long. With so much at stake—the education of thousands of children and the peace of the community—an open mind and a new willingness to compromise are in order.

Springfield Republican

Springfield, Mass., March 23, 1975

The city of Boston and its school board have appealed to the U.S. Supreme Court for review of a ruling that the board has deliberately operated a segregated school system.

That was the basis of a finding by U.S. District Judge W. Arthur Garrity, Jr., which resulted in the order for school busing to desegregate Boston's schools.

But Boston — like Springfield, which has already appealed its own racial imbalance case to the high court — probably won't realize its hopes for reversal of the busing order.

Both cities are busing because, basically, they failed to take significant action for desegregation over a period of years. The busing programs, as a means of integration, are not likely to be terminated by the high court.

The Detroit News

Detroit, Mich., May 23, 1975

Detroit parents may find it interesting that the voluntary "magnet" concept of school desegregation is a key part of the new plan for Boston, where massive forced bussing heretofore has produced nothing but turmoil.

A "magnet" plan has been offered as one solution in the Detroit school desegregation case but thus far has aroused small enthusiasm on the part of the judge or the various participants in the litigation.

One year ago, Judge W. Arthur Garrity ordered the bussing of Boston schoolchildren for the purpose of racial integration. When school officials began carrying out the order in September, the school system disintegrated amid demonstrations, violence and absenteeism.

Profiting from this experience, Judge Garrity has ordered a revised plan for next September. The new plan, shaped with the help of court-appointed experts, provides for a network of magnet schools—schools which depend on quality education to attract a mixture of blacks and whites.

These magnet schools, Judge Garrity asserts, form the "crux and the magic" of the new integration plan and will give the schools "an enormous safety valve" which the previous program of massive bussing did not offer.

Detroit is in a fortunate position. It does not have to try an unmitigated plan of massive bussing in order to find out what does not work. Boston has already demonstrated the answer to that and has advanced to another stage of experimentation.

Will Detroit profit from Boston's experience? Or must Detroit find out the hard way? The court's disposition of the proposed Detroit "magnet" plan will help answer that question.

Chicago Daily Defender

Chicago, Ill., March 31, 1975

After conducting public hearings and reviewing 18 evaluations and proposals, four experts in law and education, submitted a draft proposal for city-wide desegregation of the Boston Public Schools next fall. Under the plan the number of pupils under compulsory busing would be reduced from 18,000 to 14,000.

The plan's basic objective is to radically revamp educational boundaries by dividing the city of Boston into nine self-contained community school districts in which classroom would reflect the racial composition of that district. U.S. District Court Judge W. Arthur Garrity, Jr., ruled last June that the Boston School Committee, which serves as a board of education, had intentionally practiced segregation.

Under the new plan, schools in South Boston, the working class Irish-Italian neighborhood where most violent dissent against desegregation has occurred, would be grouped with Roxbury, a predominantly black inner-city community.

There may be substantive merits to the plan. However, unless it is properly supervised and policed, racial clashes will erupt again in September when schools reopen.

The Evening Gazette

Worcester, Mass., May 14, 1975

Twenty years ago, 15 years ago, even 10 years ago, few people would have believed that Boston would become the symbol of diehard school segregation in the nation's bicentennial year.

Trouble was somehow expected in places like Charlotte, N.C., and Louisville, Ky., when the courts began ordering school integration. But Charlotte and Louisville and many other Southern cities have integrated their schools smoothly while Boston remains recalcitrant. Many people are puzzled by this.

The paradox is not really that puzzling. School segregation in the South 20 years ago was built on the proposition that the Negro was not the equal of the white, must not be allowed to associate freely with whites, and would be consigned to grossly inferior schools than whites. That concept was manifestly contrary to the Constitution and had to be changed. Despite the overt resistance of some Southern whites, the majority of whites accepted the court decision.

Segregation in Boston was and is different. It is based on neighborhood living patterns, often ethnic in nature. Desegregation in Boston means the end of the neighborhood school, in the old sense. Desegregation in many Southern cities, on the other hand, often meant the reinforcement of the neighborhood school. No longer would black children be bused 10 miles away from home and their neighborhood schools to preserve the principle of segregation.

There are other differences. Twenty years ago, the schools were relatively peaceful places. Today, the junior highs and senior highs are plagued with vandalism and violence, even when no racial tensions are involved. When the racial factor is added, tension is increased further.

These comments are not meant as excuses for Boston, but as partial explanations. When it comes to assessing blame for the Boston situation there is plenty to go around. There has been a shameful lack of community leadership. The politicians have seemed to compete with each other to poison the atmosphere.

Given the general climate of opinion in Boston, it seems unlikely that Judge W. Arthur Garrity's Phase 2 desegregation order, issued last weekend, will be any more successful than his Phase 1 order in achieving calm and orderly integration in the schools. Despite the fact that it was painstakingly worked out by court-appointed specialists, despite the fact that it will reduce the length of many bus rides, despite the plain truth that Judge Garrity is required by the Constitution and higher court rulings to order an end to segregation, the outlook is not bright. Judge Garrity and school officials in Boston are up against an explosive feeling of hatred, fear and frustration that makes discussion meaningless.

When the Supreme Court decided, more than 20 years ago, that school segregation was unconstitutional, millions of Americans hoped that this would signal the eventual end of bigotry in this country. After Little Rock, Louisville, Charlotte, and other cities were successfully integrated, not always easily, it seemed as if the hope would be fulfilled.

But somehow, something happened by the time the issue was forced on Boston. It is very hard, judging as an outsider, to see what positive good has been accomplished by forced busing there. It is very easy to see what harm has resulted — thousands of children who have abandoned school for good, the growth of hate and prejudice among the young, the disruption of the learning process, and the continued exodus of whites from Boston.

Perhaps, in the long run, a better, more tolerant society will result. We certainly hope so. But, at best, the price will be exceedingly high.

The Des Moines Register

Des Moines, Iowa, May 20, 1975

The U. S. Supreme Court has declined to review lower court decisions that found examples of deliberate segregation in the Boston school system. The Boston School Committee and Mayor Kevin White had asked the high court for a review, but the justices let the decisions stand without comment.

The effect of the court's refusal is to give backing to a school busing plan ordered last June by Federal District Judge W. Arthur Garrity. The judge has been blamed for the violent outbreaks over the busing of blacks to predominantly white schools, especially South Boston High School, the scene of ugly disturbances last fall and this spring.

Garrity and the Circuit Court of Appeals which reviewed his order agreed that the Boston School Committee had directed blacks into three-year high schools and whites into four-year schools, had refused to transfer whites from overcrowded white schools to empty places in predominantly black schools and had granted "hardship" transfers to whites wishing to leave schools that were becoming largely black.

The School Committee contended that the judicial criticism found fault "not for doing something bad, but for not doing enough good." School officials argued that the busing order put an almost impossible burden on them.

The Circuit Court insisted that the School Committee was obligated to make a "positive showing" that its policies were not the result of "intentionally segregative acts."

Over the weekend Judge Garrity issued his final plan to integrate Boston's public schools next September. It would require busing of 12,000 grade school youngsters for the first time, bringing to more than 20,000 the number of pupils riding buses to schools.

Boston officials predicted that Garrity's new order, coupled with the Supreme Court refusal to review his previous one, would further inflame racial tensions among the city's residents.

The clashes in South Boston and television coverage of them have obscured the subtle policies by which the School Committee tried to sidestep its responsibility to integrate schools. The courts had little choice but to call attention to the official shortcomings and to try correcting them.

Angry whites are misdirecting their outrage at the courts instead of voicing displeasure with the School Committee, whose evasions needlessly prolonged the integration trauma for Boston's school-children and their parents.

THE CHRISTIAN SCIENCE MONITOR

Boston, Mass., May 14, 1975

The painful but necessary process of desegregating Boston's public schools received further legal underpinning in this week's United States Supreme Court action. By refusing to accept appeals to review lower court decisions, the Supreme Court in effect upheld their findings of unconstitutional segregation in the Boston school system.

It is this unlawful legacy, allowed to grow by a series of city and school administrations, that has led to a situation requiring the utmost compassion for a generation of parents and students. On them falls the brunt of dislocation and adjustment that could have been tempered through leadership toward constitutionally demanded desegregation over the years.

As it is, the federal district court has decided that the controversial resort of compulsory busing is among the means necessary to achieve the long-deferred compliance with the law. And though the eventually desegregated schools hold out the best long-term hope for the best education for the greatest number, there is no minimizing the strain on the "pioneers" in this forward movement. Families of all races face poignant decisions about whether to plunge into the latest desegregation plan with hope, to resist it in the vain expectation that somehow the law can still be changed, or to give up living in a city belatedly and sometimes turbulently coming to grips with the problem.

Judge Garrity's recently announced Phase 2 plan for implementing the law may be challenged in the courts — as his segregation decision, now affirmed, was. It presents difficulties of operation, fairness, and expense. But it has been worked on with experts and with public input. It is the court's plan, and it ought to be complied with forthrightly and without obstruction.

Mayor White does not help the situation by talking against the plan. But his position of having to take on this inherited burden virtually alone is understandable. Governor Dukakis has spoken favorably of the plan. And, with Boston the seat of state government, the state might well use more of its own hard-pressed budget to help the city in its time of travail. Washington, too, ought to see what can concretely be done to assist Boston in observing federal law (rather than hampering it as Mr. Ford's anti-busing words last fall did).

Meanwhile, the people of Boston certainly must continue to have their rights of free expression on the subject, as confirmed by Judge Garrity. But, as he warns, free expression cannot be allowed to become obstruction of the law. He is seeking means to prevent such obstruction, and the kind of violence that broke out previously.

All Americans have a stake in the peaceful, legal resolution of this problem in a city so close to the nation's roots of freedom and equality.

THE SACRAMENTO BEE

Sacramento, Calif., March 13, 1975

It is a regrettable setback for efforts to end de facto segregation in the schools that a three-judge appeals court in Los Angeles has reversed a 1970 Superior Court order that the huge Los Angeles city school district must desegregate its schools.

Superior Judge Alfred Gitelson, now in private law practice, had ruled nearly five years ago that Los Angeles' de facto school segregation — segregation resulting from housing patterns — is implicitly embraced by the U.S. Supreme Court's decision of more than 20 years ago that public schools cannot be segregated deliberately by law, or de jure.

What makes the appeals court's decision unfortunate, with potential nationwide repercussions, is that de facto segregation is the principal barrier still to be surmounted in achieving racial balance in the schools.

De jure segregation — the kind deliberately set by school district policy — has pretty much been eliminated, particularly in the South, where it was all but universal.

In most of the rest of the country, however, studies show de facto segregation is widespread, especially in major Northern and other regional urban centers. A recent report by the U.S. Commission on Civil Rights said more than 71 per cent of blacks in these regions still attend mostly minority schools, as a result of de facto segregation.

The commission warned this intolerable situation is getting worse instead of better, portending ominous racial divisions and strife.

Gitelson's 1970 ruling sparked wide community furor because its implementation would require extensive busing. Busing for racial balance has been the catalyst for most of the fight against efforts to end de facto segregation.

It should be emphasized, however, that busing is but one option available in such situations. There are alternatives. They can and must be used, along with busing when necessary and feasible. The segregation problem, with its deprivation of equal educational opportunity, will not simply vanish.

The sad import of the appeals court decision is that it fosters an atmosphere in which school districts are tacitly encouraged to ignore de facto segregation. Hopefully, further appeals will take the issue back to the U.S. Supreme Court for a decisive order ending de facto segregation.

SAN JOSE NEWS

San Jose, Calif., March 12, 1975

The courts may not be moving with all deliberate speed in clarifying the school segregation issue. They are moving, however, and that is a blessing.

A three-judge Court of Appeals in Los Angeles has reaffirmed intent as the key in de facto segregation cases. These are situations in which racial imbalance results not from state laws or local ordinances but primarily from housing patterns.

In 1970 a Superior Court judge ordered Los Angeles schools to end de facto segregation. This week's ruling overturns that order.

The Appeals judges said that the earlier findings "do not show that the (school) Board intentionally discriminated against minority students by practicing a deliberate policy of racial segregation." It is "purpose or intent" that is the controlling factor in such cases, the Court ruled.

This ruling is based on a U.S. Supreme Court finding in a Denver school case two years ago.

This principle could affect efforts to force busing on a number of California districts, including several in Santa Clara County.

A school board, of course, could foster segregation through location of schools, manipulation of attendance boundaries or establishment of transfer or transportation policies. In such cases the courts can and should move in.

In the absence of evidence of such connivance, however, the schools should be allowed to concentrate on their primary job, educating youngsters.

A better racial balance in the schools, desirable as that is, will have to await a more gradual change in housing patterns.

Los Angeles Times

Los Angeles, Calif., March 12, 1975

The California Court of Appeal, in reversing the Los Angeles city schools integration order, has unwisely narrowed the constitutional protections afforded public school students. It is appropriate that the decision is to be appealed and that the California Supreme Court will have an opportunity to clarify the issues.

The legal and constitutional considerations are but part of the problem. Regardless of the outcome of the appeal, there will remain the problem of what to do.

Superior Judge Alfred Gitelson, in his original integration order five years ago, proposed percentage formulas for each school to break down the widespread segregation. His order responded to a history of failure by the Board of Education to take significant action to reverse the increasing isolation of the district's black and Mexican-American students. But his order ignored the unique geography of the district, which in effect is two districts divided by mountains. The geography makes the solutions that have been used effectively in other segregation cases impractical.

We had hoped that the Court of Appeal, in reviewing Gitelson's decision, might have concentrated on the reasonable limits of judicial power to enforce a remedy. Instead, the Court of Appeal has remanded the case to the lower court for further fact-finding on the ground that no constitutional violation was proved.

We disagree with the conclusion that there is insufficient evidence that the Board of Education took actions intended to segregate students.

We also disagree with the Court of Appeal that the protections of the 14th Amendment can be applied only when it can be proved that the segregation resulted from overt acts of the state intended to create segregation.

The appeal judges relied on an interpretation of decisions by both the U.S. Supreme Court, in the Denver case, and the State Supreme Court, in the Santa Barbara case.

The relevance of the Denver case is somewhat obscure because the Supreme Court chose to treat it as it had treated the Southern school segregation cases—that is, as de jure segregation, imposed overtly by the state. In so doing, the Supreme Court neatly avoided a definitive decision regarding the constitutionality of de facto segregation—that is, segregation resulting from housing patterns or other factors not imposed by law.

Nevertheless, the U.S. Supreme Court in the Denver case affirmed that the protections of the 14th Amendment apply not only to segregation intentionally brought about but also to segregation "maintained by state action." How can it be argued that segregation has not been maintained by the Los Angeles Board of Education?

In the Denver case, the Supreme Court revived a definition it had used in an earlier Southern school segregation case, stating that the difference between de jure and de facto segregation is intent. It is a reasonable definition. But the Court of Appeal has seized on that definition to argue that intent to impose segregation must be proved if constitutional protections are to be provided by the courts. That does not appear to us a reasonable interpretation of what the Supreme Court was saying.

Furthermore, the Court of Appeal has, it seems to us, misunderstood the State Supreme Court. It cites one decision to underscore the power vested in local school boards. But it seems to dismiss the more fundamental finding of the State Supreme Court that the existence of segregation, regardless of its causes and origin, can represent a deprivation of constitutional rights.

Five years have now gone by since Gitelson handed down his integration order. Fortunately, school officials have attached sufficient respect to that order to start some modest integration programs. It would be everyone's loss if the school board should now interpret this reversal as justification to avoid further steps.

Segregation exists. It serves no good purpose. The community can only be strengthened by working for its end.

Des Moines Tribune

Des Moines, Iowa, April 29, 1975

The U.S. Supreme Court has let stand two appeals court decisions that require desegregation only when it has been proved that government officials sanctioned segregation. The lower-court rulings left room, however, for desegregation moves across metropolitan district lines in unusual circumstances.

The high court let stand a ruling of the U.S. Sixth Court of Appeals requiring the Louisville and Jefferson County, Kentucky, school districts to root out "vestiges of state-imposed segregation [that] had not been eliminated."

In Kentucky, the appeals court said, the county is the basic educational unit. School district lines in the state, it added, "have been ignored in the past for the purpose of aiding and implementing continued segregation."

The lower court had made a point of contrasting its Louisville-Jefferson County case with the 1974 Detroit desegregation case. In that ruling, the Supreme Court said the Detroit school desegregation plan could not involve suburban districts that had not committed specific acts of segregation or operated dual black and white school systems.

The appeals court said the "vital distinction" in the Detroit case is "that there was no evidence that the outlying school districts had committed acts of de jure segregation or that they were operating dual systems." In Louisville and Jefferson County, "exactly the opposite is true," the court ruled. Both systems were "guilty of maintaining dual school systems."

State-created school district lines, the court said, must impose no barrier to accomplishing desegregation. It ordered a lower court to offer a desegregation plan and cross district lines within the county and even across county lines if necessary.

The Louisville system is about evenly divided between black and white. The county system is 96 per cent white.

In the other case, involving Indianapolis, the Seventh Court of Appeals had ordered further study of a proposal to merge the Indianapolis city school system with the systems of several towns in adjacent Marion County and two small neighboring cities.

The districts outside the Indianapolis system were not found to be deliberately segregated, but a pattern of segregation was found in the city system.

The court sanctioned the hearing on the proposal that the outlying districts — even though not guilty of de jure segregation — be included in desegregation plans because of a 1969 "Uni-Gov" merger of Indianapolis and Marion County governmental bodies.

The hearing would determine whether the government merger requires merger of the educational systems as well.

Springfield Republican

Springfield, Mass., April 27, 1975

In declining to review two desegregation rulings by appeals courts, the U.S. Supreme Court has confirmed a shifting stance on the question of inter-district busing.

By upholding the lower court ruling, the high court left the way open for desegregation plans to reach across the boundaries of certain districts in Kentucky and Indiana. This decision was in keeping with an earlier one by the Supreme Court.

That decision, handed down in 1974, allowed cross-district busing in cases where unconstitutional segregation in one district had brought about segregation in another.

The court did not expand on that position in the Kentucky and Indiana cases. But the cases emphasized the vulnerability of suburbs which undertake deliberate steps to maintain segregation as a community.

By enforcing discriminatory zoning ordinances, for instance, a suburb could keep black families out, and in the process maintain all-white schools.

Such a policy would force minority youngsters to remain in imbalanced schools and be deprived of equal education. This apparently is the unconstitutional segregation that would justify cross-district busing, in the court's view.

In that light, it is reasonable to expect also that lower federal courts will be supported by the Supreme Court in regarding consistent failure to remedy imbalanced schools within a district as discriminatory— or in effect deliberate segregation.

An example of such lower court action in Massachusetts was federal Judge Arthur Garrity's order for busing in the Boston schools, on the grounds the school board had "knowingly" kept the schools segregated, by delays and "pervasive practices."

ARKANSAS DEMOCRAT

Little Rock, Ark., April 28, 1975

The federal courts are going to continue chasing Americans who flee from school busing into the suburbs. That much is made plain by the U.S. Supreme Court's refusal to review the cases of Louisville and Indianapolis.

Both cities are under appeals court orders to bus across school district lines so as to achieve racial balance in their metropolitan areas.

In Louisville's case, the order is to root out "all vestiges of state-enforced discrimination." Under the high court's current approach to busing, there needn't be or have been a law on a state's books providing for segregation. "State enforced" can mean that districts have simply adopted segregationist policies. Whereas Southern states were made to bus because of segregationist laws, more northerly states have been judged by their deeds.

In both cases, however, the remedy is the same, busing. The cross-district busing issue has only been a temporary complication that slowed but did not stop the buses. Last year the Supreme Court ruled that cross-district busing is permissible when official policies in one district produce segregation in another district.

Whether that applies to Louisville and Indianapolis or not isn't clear because the high court dismissed their appeals from cross-district busing without comment. In short, the court, as has been its custom from the first, in laying down mixing doctrine, seldom clarifies its own comment.

But its silence in this case will probably stimulate more district court rulings ordering cross-district busing — and, of course, more of the white flight that such rulings are vainly aimed at stopping.

How far will the judicial chase of white flight reach? How far will the buses roll in pursuit of people who opt out of the senseless policy of destroying the neighborhood school?

The answer doesn't lie with the Supreme Court. Its course is set, though the scope of the pursuit is not yet determined. The answer lies, as it has lain for years, with Congress. Only Congress can authorize the antibusing amendment to the Constitution that will allow Americans to vote, state by state, on the question of whether they want busing.

Their answer, South and North, is already plain: From three-fourths to four-fifths of Americans oppose busing. The Supreme Court knows it and the Congress knows it. But even the spread of the bus to the North hasn't yet produced the legislative consensus among the people's representatives needed to stop the bus.

Maybe the Supreme Court, by its latest decision, is simply telling the lawmakers that if they want the buses to stop rolling — across district lines, across county lines and perhaps even state lines — that they've got to give the people a constitutional referendum on the question.

Certainly, the court can't do it. It's up to Congress.

The Detroit News

Detroit, Mich., April 23, 1975

Further notice that cross-district bussing remains a live issue came from the U.S. Supreme Court this week in rulings on school desegregation cases involving Indianapolis and Louisville and their suburbs.

These new rulings are consistent with the Supreme Court's 1974 decision in the Detroit case. That decision sent the case back to the lower court for the making of a Detroit-only plan but left the door open for interdistrict plans where segregation in adjacent suburbs can be proven.

Federal Judge Robert E. DeMascio is working on the Detroit-only solution but has ruled that the NAACP may file an amended complaint against suburban districts. Thus, Detroit again has entered the cross-district bussing controversy.

Against this background, it's clear the Supreme Court in the Indianapolis case added nothing new when it upheld a lower-court decision which merely requires further study of an interdistrict merger of school systems.

Likewise, the Supreme Court followed the logic of its Detroit decision when it upheld a cross-district plan for the Louisville metropolitan area after finding discrimination within the school systems involved.

In short, these steps toward cross-district integration—and, inevitably, cross-district bussing—conform to the law as interpreted by the Supreme Court.

Whether the law is a good law remains very much open to question. What is good about the massive disruption of school districts in broad areas merely in order to seat children according to a certain racial pattern?

The Dallas Morning News

Dallas, Tex., April 23, 1975

BY REFUSING to get involved in a couple of busing decisions by lower courts, the Supreme Court may have opened the door for another wave of grand designs for cross-district busing.

If the lower federal courts choose to embark on a renewed campaign to move schoolchildren about, there are apparently no serious legal barriers to their doing so.

The practice of moving children from school district to school district has not been ruled out, per-se, by the high court. Though the American people oppose busing by one of the largest and most consistent majorities seen in modern times, they have not been successful in translating this opposition into political action. Congress sits on its hands.

And so the five per cent of the population that—according to Gallup—favors busing may get its way over the objections of the 70 to 80 per cent that does not. The five per cent controls the decision-making process that counts in this matter.

But before the federal courts launch another round of busing plans to redesign society, we hope that someone on the bench will consider what is happening to society and the schools now.

Not just the riots in Boston. Not just the rising toll of classroom violence, a subject that several senators have recently discovered to be a headline-grabber for the ambitious orator. These are dramatic symptoms of the schools' troubles, but we believe that more significant evidence can be found in recently published statistics that bear on the schools' primary reason for being.

The schools' main purpose is the education of the young. Not so long ago, that would have been considered so obvious that it hardly needed to be stated. But in recent years, the main purpose has tended to be overlooked in the zeal of federal courts and agencies to use the schools as a vehicle for modifying society to meet their specifications.

This disregard of the main purpose, education, has been paralleled by a steady decline in the schools' ability to carry out that purpose.

In the Scholastic Aptitude Tests, a battery of examinations for prospective college students, American high school students have demonstrated this decline with steadily falling scores. Since 1962, the average scores on verbal tests have dropped from 478 to 440. On mathematics tests, averages have dropped from 502 to 478, out of a possible 800.

The federally funded National Assessment of Educational Progress tested 90,000 schoolchildren on science and found a downward trend in that subject, also.

A third study, by HEW, compared public school students' reading skill. Reading levels, it concluded, have been falling since the mid-1960s.

No reasonable observer would claim that busing and other federal social designs are the sole reason for this alarming downtrend. But neither can there be much argument with the case for putting the highest priority on reversing the trend as quickly as possible. The school system that fails to teach is not likely to succeed at any secondary purposes that the courts have in mind.

For that reason, if for no other, let us hope that the federal courts give some thought to this simple question: In the schools' attempt to reverse this decline in effectiveness, are new busing decrees likely to help or to hurt?

The Courier-Journal

Louisville, Ky., April 30, 1975

SUPREME COURT rulings last week in the Louisville and Indianapolis school desegregation cases appear to offer civil rights supporters a bit of fresh hope that the justices haven't yet closed the door on metropolitan solutions to segregated inner-city schools.

Granted, the question of court-ordered merger or of cross-district busing in Louisville and Jefferson County was made moot by the Kentucky Board of Education's imposition of merger April 1. But widely overlooked in reaction to the Supreme Court's denial of appeals on whether city and county schools are in fact segregated was the decision's impact on the tiny, all-white 350-student Anchorage system in eastern Jefferson County.

Denial of appeals for the city and county systems meant that the Supreme Court had upheld the decision of the U.S. 6th Circuit Court of Appeals in Cincinnati. That court ordered a desegregation plan to be fashioned without regard to school district boundaries, and said the Anchorage system was to be included in the plan if necessary.

This preserves at least some hope for the principle of including more than one school system in the same desegregation plan in order to guard against resegregation of the inner-city. The Indianapolis case is somewhat broader in scope, but it too indicates that the Supreme Court's rejection last year of a multidistrict plan in Detroit may not have been the retrenchment that some first feared.

Not insurmountable

In both Louisville and Indianapolis, the Supreme Court stuck to the principle enunciated in Detroit. This is that there must be proof that the policies of one district had a segregative effect on another, or that school lines were crossed in the past for segregation.

In the Indianapolis case, the Supreme Court denied appeals from 10 suburban districts in Marion County. The districts objected to an order from the U.S. 7th Circuit Court of Appeals in Chicago, directing District Judge S. Hugh Dillin to hold further hearings on whether they should be included in a desegregation plan for Indianapolis. Originally, 23 districts in and around Marion County had been included in an order by Judge Dillin, but the districts outside Marion County were dropped from the case after the Supreme Court struck down a similar plan in Detroit.

The specific issue now in Indianapolis is whether creation in 1969 of metropolitan city-county government (known as UniGov), which excluded schools from the reorganization, had the effect of perpetuating segregation in Indianapolis city schools and the 10 suburban schools in Marion County.

The Supreme Court is expected to receive appeals soon from a three-judge panel's decision to order cross-district busing in Wilmington, Delaware. Metropolitan school desegregation plans also seem certain to be raised in Hartford, Cincinnati and Cleveland cases.

While it's regrettable that the Supreme Court chose to ignore the obvious realities of white flight in its Detroit decision, it's clear that civil rights groups are determined to make the most of the legal door that was left ajar. Tough new rules of evidence will apply in school desegregation cases. But those rules aren't insurmountable, as the recent Supreme Court actions in Louisville and Indianapolis indicate.

Federal Government Policies: 1970-71

The Senate

Busing ban sought. Sens. John C. Stennis (D, Miss.) and Strom Thurmond (R, S.C.) led a parade of a dozen Southern senators who took the Senate floor for more than three hours Feb. 5 demanding that the new federal school desegregation guidelines be applied to Northern school districts or be abandoned altogether.

Stennis's action opened his campaign to amend the $35 billion, four-year, House-passed education bill now before the Senate to bar compulsory busing of schoolchildren to achieve racially integrated schools in the South, and to restore "freedom of choice" school arrangements where they had been struck down by federal courts. Stennis had announced his intention to seek a rider to the education bill Nov. 30, 1969.

Stennis said "parents are not going to permit their children to be boxed up and crated and hauled around the city and the country like common animals." He called on the senators who believed that there was wide support for busing to "get your ear a little closer to the ground."

The amendment that Stennis and the other Southern senators sought to attach to the bill was almost an exact copy of a law passed by the New York State Legislature in 1969 prohibiting the assignment of students "on account of race, creed, color, or national origin or for the purpose of achieving equality in attendance or increase attendance or reduced attendance at any school of persons of one or more particular races, creeds, colors or national origins."

Thurmond maintained that approval of an antibusing measure "would prevent our schools from becoming the laboratories of fanatical social reformers and race-obsessed judges."

Sen. Sam J. Ervin Jr. (D, N.C.) noted during the debate that the amendment sought by the Southern senators had been approved and signed into law by "that great liberal in the field of civil rights, Gov. Nelson Rockefeller."

The bill pending before the Senate would extend for another four years the 1965 Elementary and Secondary Education Act and the impacted aid program to districts educating children of federal employes. The bill would also increase the ceiling for the elementary and secondary programs.

Measure gains Northern support. Sen Abraham A. Ribicoff (D, Conn.) Feb. 9 became the first Northern liberal to announce his intention to vote for the amendment sponsored by Stennis that called for a uniform policy for enforcement of school desegregation guidelines. Ribicoff called on other Northern state senators to drop their "monumental hypocrisy" and admit that Northern school systems were just as racially segregated as those in the South.

Ribicoff said: "if Sen. Stennis wants to make honest men of us Northern liberals, I think we should help him." "Northern communities have been just as systematic and consistent as Southern communities in denying to the black man and his children the opportunity that exists for white people."

Ribicoff's speech was immediately hailed by both Senate conservatives and liberals. Sen. George D. Aiken (R, Vt.), a liberal, praised Ribicoff for "your courage and if I may use the term, nobility, in standing up before the Senate and telling the truth."

Another Senate liberal, Claiborne Pell (D, R.I.), agreed that many Northerners "go home and talk liberalism to each other, but we don't practice it."

Ribicoff emphasized that he would not support the amendment also sponsored by Stennis that would prohibit busing to achieve racial balance. Ribicoff warned that such an amendment would "bring to a halt federal efforts to enforce school desegregation."

Senate passes segregation curbs. The Senate, by a 56–36 vote Feb. 18, curbed de facto school segregation by cutting off federal funds to those school districts whose racial imbalance was a product of residential patterns. If the amendment passed the House, it would extend to many predominately white and predominately black school districts in the North the same penalties currently enforced in the South for noncompliance with court-ordered desegregation arrangements. The amendment was part of the $35 billion education bill (HR514).

Sen. John C. Stennis (D, Miss.) the sponsor and floor manager of the amendment, called the passage "a landmark . . . a new gateway . . . a turning point." Stennis, along with other Senate conservatives, had indicated his belief that increased pressure to desegregate many schools in Northern school districts would result in a different attitude toward the Deep South's defiance of federal efforts to integrate the South's schools.

"If you have to do that [integrate] in your area," Stennis told Northern senators, "you will see what it means to us."

Stennis and his forces successfully guided the amendment through passage by winning the support of senators from outside the South. Only 26 of the votes for the Stennis proposal came from Southern and Border state senators.

Stennis credited Sen. Abraham A. Ribicoff (D, Conn.) a liberal who backed the Stennis move Feb. 9 after denouncing "hypocrisy" by Northern states, with a major role in rallying enough Northern votes to insure passage of the amendment.

The proposal had to be cleared by a House-Senate conference committee, and then by the House itself.

Stennis and his supporters secured passage of the proposal after they had first beaten down two moves designed to dilute the language of their amendment. First they defeated a motion by Sen. Hugh Scott (R, Pa.) to pass an amendment that would only restate the existing laws concerning desegregation. They then turned back a proposal offered by Sen. Jacob K. Javits (R, N.Y.) that was a similar copy of the Stennis proposal except that a significant phrase had been deleted from the Southern-backed amendment. Sen. Javits' amendment had stricken the words "without regard to the origin or cause of such segregation."

The Stennis amendment:

"It is the policy of the U.S. that guidelines and criteria pursuant to Title VI of the Civil Rights Act of 1964 and Section 182 of the Elementary and Secondary Education Amendments of 1966 shall be applied uniformly in all regions of the U.S. in dealing with conditions of segregation by race, whether de jure or

A de facto, in the schools of the local educational agencies of any state without regard to the origin or cause of such segregation."

Other successful amendments. Southerners in the House and Senate waged their second successful assault on federal desegregation guidelines Feb. 19 by incorporating into two appropriations bills four riders designed to restore "freedom-of-choice" school arrangements and prohibit the federal government from busing schoolchildren to achieve racial balance.

B In the House, Southern congressmen succeeded in securing the incorporation in a new $19.4 billion health and education appropriations bill three freedom-of-choice amendments and antibusing provisos designed to curb the Government's power to enforce school desegregation.

The House amendments to restore the freedom-of-choice plans were sponsored by Reps. Jamie L. Whitten (D, Miss.) and Charles R. Jonas (R, N.C.). Whitten's two amendments specified that none of the education funds "may be used to force any school district to take any actions involving the busing of students, the abolishment of any school or the assignment of any student attending any elementary or secondary school to a particular school against the choice of his or her parents."

D The effect of the Whitten amendments would be to sanction the freedom-of-choice plans for school desegregation that in many cases the courts had struck down.

Jonas' amendment carried Whitten's proposal one step further. He supported a move that would let parents, not educators, determine how to implement the freedom-of-choice plans. His amendment provided that none of the bill's funds "shall be used to provide, formulate, carry out or implement any plan which would deny to any student the right or privilege of attending any public school of his or her choice, as selected by his or her parent or guardian."

E Southerners in the Senate waged a successful campaign to include in the $35 billion educational authorization bill a provision to bar busing of schoolchildren as part of federally-sponsored desegregation arrangements.

F Sen. Sam J. Ervin Jr. (D, N.C.) led the fight to incorporate into the bill the antibusing provisions. He succeeded in tacking on to the bill a ban to prohibit busing to "alter racial composition."

Education funds bill approved. The Senate approved, 68–0, a second version of the controversial education appropriations bill after more than nine hours of Saturday debate Feb. 28. The measure was trimmed to $19 billion after President Nixon vetoed the original version of the fiscal 1970 bill as inflationary Jan. 26.

G The second version also contained a spending limitation that would empower the President to withhold funds appropriated by the bill if he felt it necessary to hold down inflation.

(The House voted, 228–152, March 3 to accept the Senate's version of the bill. House Republican leaders, who had been summoned to the White House, said President Nixon would sign it soon after it reached him. In approving the Senate version, the House avoided a battle over school desegregation, since the Senate had modified two amendments that had been incorporated into the House version, and had struck out a third antibusing rider.

The House also agreed to accept the Senate's clause that provided that only 98% of the appropriations could be spent.)

The Senate passed the bill after it had first voted down a group of Southern-inspired amendments designed to erase or curb the government's power to enforce federal school desegregation laws. The Senate rejected outright three riders sponsored by Southern senators aimed at prohibiting pupil assignments or busing as means of achieving school desegregation, while a coalition of Republicans and liberal Democrats voted 42–32, and 41–34, to insert into the bill a six-word amendment that diluted the antibusing amendment that was incorporated into the House version of the bill which passed Feb. 19.

(The House had passed its revised version of the $19.4 billion bill, 315–81, after a Republican effort to cut it by $433 million was turned back. The House also deleted a House Appropriations Committee's amendment that would permit the President to withhold the bill's funds if he deemed it necessary to curb inflation. The same provision had been incorporated and passed in the Senate's version of the bill.)

The Senate coalition of liberals also voted 43–32 to knock out altogether a passage from the House bill designed to reinstate "freedom-of-choice" school plans. The amendment, sponsored by Rep. Jamie L. Whitten (D, Miss.), would have prohibited the use of federal funds for any plan that would deny a student "the right or privilege of attending any public school of his or her choice as selected by his or her parent or guardian."

The Senate liberals succeeded in diluting the language of the House's antibusing amendment by inserting a six-word amendment sponsored by Sen. Charles McC. Mathias (R, Md.), who said that President Nixon opposed the restrictive language in the House's version. Under the rider incorporated in the House bill, none of the bill's funds could be used "to force any school district to take any action involving the busing of students, the abolishment of any school or the assignment of any student to a particular school against the choice of his or her parents."

The Mathias amendment inserted the words "except as required by the Con-

stitution" before the House's provision, virtually nullifying the antibusing clause since the courts had interpreted the Constitution to require integration of all Southern school systems. The same qualifying language had been inserted in the original bill, but after the President vetoed it, the House removed the Senate's clause. Thus it was reinstated for the second time by the Senate Feb. 28. Southern senators, led by John C. Stennis (D, Miss.), James O. Eastland (D, Miss.) John L. McClellan (D, Ark.) and John J. Sparkman (D, Ala.), argued unsuccessfully the Senate's move to delete the antibusing amendments from the House version.

The Administration

School issue discussed. In a series of released statements, the Nixon Administration moved Feb. 6–17 to stake out a position regarding a proposal sponsored by Sen. John C. Stennis (D, Miss.) and backed by other Southern senators to press new federal school desegregation guidelines in the North or be abandoned altogether. Stennis was seeking to attach his proposal as a rider to a $35 billion education bill now pending before the Senate.

The first statement outlining the Nixon Administration's position was released Feb. 6 in a letter from Commissioner of Education James E. Allen Jr. to Sen. Clairborne Pell (D, R.I.), the floor manager of the education bill. Allen said the Administration was opposed to any Southern-sponsored legislation that would preserve racially segregated schools in the South.

Allen said that he was "convinced that segregation by races in our nation for any reason is unsound educationally, regardless of geography." He added, however, that there were "serious questions as to the legal effect and implications" of the Southern-backed proposal to press school desegregation in the North.

White House Press Secretary Ronald L. Ziegler indicated Feb. 12 that President Nixon believed the North and the South should be subject to federal school desegregation orders. Ziegler indicated that the President was not opposed to Stennis' efforts to extend to school districts in the North the same desegregation guidelines being enforced in the South.

Ziegler told newsmen that to "the extent the uniform application amendment offered by Sen. Stennis would advance equal application of the law, the Administration would be in full support of this concept." The press secretary would not, however, interpret the President's remarks as an outright endorsement of the Stennis proposal.

Ziegler re-emphasized that Nixon had "consistently opposed and still opposes compulsory busing of school children to achieve racial balance." Ziegler restated the President's desire to "preserve rather than destroy the neighborhood school."

Despite Ziegler's Feb. 12 statement, a White House source reported Feb. 13 said the Nixon Administration would neither endorse nor oppose Stennis' plan to attach a rider to the education bill. According to the statement, "The Administration has no formal position on this specific amendment," and although the positions may vary slightly, "if we had to go on record we would say no position one way or the other."

President Nixon said Feb. 17 that although he understood the confusion and disruption caused by massive school desegregation, the courts had ordered an immediate end to school segregation. He said the law must be obeyed. In a formal statement, Nixon promised federal assistance to school districts "in complying with the courts' requirements."

The President made the statement during his announcement of a cabinet-level committee to aid schools as they implemented court-ordered desegregation arrangements.

Advisory panel formed. President Nixon established a Cabinet-level task force Feb. 16 to provide assistance and counsel to school districts under court orders to desegregate their schools immediately. The President said the group, which he termed "an informal Cabinet-level working group," would work with school administrators to execute the desegregation orders and still preserve the public education system.

Chairman of the group was Vice President Agnew. Vice chairman was George P. Shultz, secretary of labor. Other members were Attorney General John N. Mitchell, Postmaster General Winton M. Blount, Secretary of Health, Education and Welfare Robert H. Finch, Donald Rumsfeld, director of the Office of Economic Opportunity, and Presidential counselors Bryce Harlow and Daniel P. Moynihan.

Nixon, Agnew score mob violence. President Nixon and Vice President Agnew March 4 denounced as "senseless" the attack March 3 by a mob of angry whites who stormed school buses carrying Negro schoolchildren to a formerly all-white high school in Lamar, S.C. Ronald L. Ziegler, White House press secretary, said Nixon's reaction was that "any right-thinking American would deplore" the mob's action.

Agnew summoned newsmen to his White House office to criticize the attack by Lamar whites. Agnew told reporters that "there is no excuse for this reprehensible and entirely senseless mob action." He said he wanted "to make it clear that this Administration does not condone and will not tolerate violence resulting from the lawful desegregation of schools anywhere."

Nixon's school policy outlined. President Nixon pledged March 24 that his Administration would not abandon or undermine the school desegregation gains since the Supreme Court's 1954 ruling outlawing "separate but equal" educational facilities. The President said it was his "personal belief" that the 1954 decision "was right in both constitutional and human terms."

The President's commitment was included in an 8,000-word document on the problems of elementary and secondary school desegregation. White House officials said it was the most comprehensive statement by any president on the issue of school integration. The policy statement, judged to be too long for a televised broadcast, was given to news correspondents at the White House.

In his report, Nixon vowed to apply all of the government's available resources towards elimination of officially imposed, or de jure, segregation in the South's public schools. He said, however, that until the courts provided further guidance he could not require elimination of de facto segregation, in the North or South, resulting from residential housing patterns.

At the same time, President Nixon revealed that the government planned to allocate $1.5 billion over the next two years to help school districts in the North and the South alleviate the effects of racial segregation stemming from de facto segregation.

Much of the President's statement dealt with the two forms of racial segregation, de facto and de jure. Nixon said the Supreme Court had already ruled on de jure segregation when it handed down the landmark decision in *Brown v. Board of Education* in 1954. The President pledged to carry out the court's mandate by relying on the "good faith" efforts of local Southern officials to comply with the court's orders.

The President said, however, that the courts had not spoken out on what, if anything, to do to overcome de facto segregation. He said that while segregation as a by-product of housing patterns was undesirable in practice, it remained fully constitutional in theory. Nixon said he was offering a set of possible remedies at an administrative level.

Nixon's suggestions encompassed two positions that he had often stated before. He repeated his opposition to student busing simply as a means of achieving racially balanced schools without improving the quality of education, and he said that he was in favor of the neighborhood-school concept.

His main proposal was to offer funds for technical assistance to public school districts in the North and South that wanted to eliminate de facto segregation on their own initiative or to mitigate the government" to be guided by the basic principles and policies laid down in his statement.

The President offered these principles:

Deliberate racial segregation of pupils by official action is unlawful, wherever it exists. In the words of the Supreme Court, it must be eliminated "root and branch"—and it must be eliminated at once.

Segregation of teachers must be eliminated. To this end, each school system in this nation, North and South, East and West, must move immediately, as the Supreme Court has ruled, toward a goal under which "in each school the ratio of white to Negro faculty members is substantially the same as it is throughout the system."

With respect to school facilities, school administrators throughout the nation, North and South, East and West, must move immediately, also in conformance with the Court's ruling, to assure that schools within individual school districts do not discriminate with respect to the quality of facilities or the quality of education delivered to the children within the district.

In devising local compliance plans primary weight should be given to the considered judgment of local school boards—provided they act in good faith and within constitutional limits.

The neighborhood school will be deemed the most appropriate base for such a system.

Transportation of pupils beyond normal geographic school zones for the purpose of achieving racial balance will not be required.

Federal advice and assistance will be made available on request, but Federal officials should not go beyond the requirements of law in attempting to impose their own judgment on the local school district.

School boards will be encouraged to be flexible and creative in formulating plans that are educationally sound and that result in effective desegregation.

Racial imbalance in a school system may be partly de jure in origin, and partly de facto. In such a case, it is appropriate to insist on remedy for the de jure portion, which is unlawful, without insisting on a remedy for the lawful de facto portion.

De facto racial separation, resulting genuinely from housing patterns, exists in the South as well as the North; in neither area should this condition by itself be cause for Federal enforcement actions. De jure segregation brought about by deliberate school-board gerrymandering exists in the North, as the South; in both areas this must be remedied. In all respects, the law should be applied equally, North and South, East and West.

School integration rise seen. Secretary of Health, Education and Welfare (HEW) Robert H. Finch indicated April 7 that President Nixon's March 24 policy statement on school desegregation would cause little or no change in his department's enforcement of school desegregation guidelines. Finch said there would be no "backward motion" and he predicted that the number of Negro children in schools with whites in the South would double by fall.

Finch told newsmen that he and his HEW aides foresaw no change in the department's practice of busing as one means of enforcing either court-ordered or HEW-ordered school desegregation in the South. (President Nixon had said in his March 24 statement that he was opposed to student busing simply as a means of achieving racially balanced schools without improving the quality of education.)

Finch said that since nearly 90% of the South's public schools used student busing "it's not as though we're calling for a whole new lot of buses."

One of Finch's key aides, Jerry H. Rader, HEW's equal educational opportunity director, said that where busing already was used to maintain segregation, there would be little problem in rearranging it to accommodate school desegregation.

A second HEW assistant to elucidate the department's policy was J. Stanley Pottinger, the new director of HEW's

A Office of Civil Rights. Pottinger said his office would continue to work to eliminate school segregation whether it be de jure (through law) or by de facto (through housing patterns) means. "We have striven mightily," he said, "to eliminate all-black schools and we will continue to do so. Our policy on that has not changed a bit." He acknowledged later, however, that the policy now applied only to de jure segregation.

B Finch said the task of determining whether discrimination was de jure or de facto would be "very, very difficult" and that it would have to be done on a school-by-school basis.

The Manatee County, Florida case. The Nixon Administration, which had entered the case when the Justice Department dispatched federal marshals to oversee implementation of the desegregation plan, continued to play a major role. A spokesman for the Justice Department said April 11 that the government planned to file a brief with the Fifth Circuit Court suggesting that the judge who ordered the desegregation plan (Ben Krentzman of the district court in Tampa, Fla.) might have "abused" his discretion with the order. A second spokesman for the department said later that the department "will not ask for any modification of the initial plan," but would ask the appeals court to refer the controversial plan to the Department of Health, Education and Welfare (HEW), which was instrumental in drawing up most government-ordered desegregation plans.

Two other Nixon Administration actions were taken April 13:

E Solicitor General Erwin N. Griswold, in a memorandum filed with the Supreme Court, said that "any confrontation between the governor [Kirk] and the United States would be entirely of his own making." Griswold reported in the memorandum that he opposed Kirk's effort to have the high court take on direct appeal his request for a decision on the Manatee County school order.

The second move came when the Justice Department followed through with its April 11 plan and filed a brief with the Fifth Circuit Court in New Orleans, suggesting that Judge Krentzman had erred in rejecting an alternate school desegregation plan for the Manatee County schools that used more "modest" techniques. The department conceded in the brief that the alternative plan would not have produced as much desegregation as the arrangement approved by Krentzman.

G ## The House

Education funds. The House passed and sent to the Senate April 14 a $4.1 billion fiscal 1971 education appropriations bill (HR16916) with amendments to curb the use of federal funds to force school integration. The amount of funds was $745 million more than requested by the Administration but far less than the authorization recently enacted. The bill's $1.5 billion for aid to schools with large numbers of poor children was only 41% of the amount authorized.

The House rejected attempts to add $191 million to the bill for additional funds for construction of college facilities, impacted area schools and library programs. The additional funds for the first two programs would have raised them to the current funding level.

The integration curbs were added to the measure by the House Appropriations Committee and upheld by House votes. One, sponsored by Rep. Jamie L. Whitten (D, Miss.) and upheld by a 106-63 vote, would bar use of the funds to force a school into further desegregation by busing or transferring students to achieve racial balance over objections of the students or their parents. Another, sponsored by Rep. Charles R. Jonas (R, N.C.) and upheld by a 101-87 vote, would bar use of the funds to implement a desegregation plan denying any student the right to attend the public school of his choice.

The Administration

'Unreasonable' busing scored. Attorney General John N. Mitchell said April 16 that every citizen had "the right to reject unreasonable requirements of busing and to send their children to neighborhood schools." Mitchell said this right was "just as important as the right of all of our citizens to be assigned [to the schools] without regard to their race." Mitchell's antibusing remarks drew cheers and applause from many of the 1,200 Republicans who were attending the party's 1970 leadership conference in Washington, D.C.

The attorney general told the GOP leaders that despite the balancing of constitutional rights and antibusing rights, the Nixon Administration "has brought about more school desegregation than any previous administration." He said he hoped that by the beginning of the next school year in September "this burning issue of school desegregation will be behind us and be laid to rest."

Agnew claims Administration successes. In two speeches in South Carolina April 24 and 25, Vice President Spiro T. Agnew claimed the Nixon Administration had met with success in reducing the crime rate and in its policies in Vietnam. Agnew also denounced liberal critics of the Administration and said that what had been criticized as a "Southern strategy" was simply an attempt to treat the South the same as the rest of the nation.

Agnew pledged the President would continue to try to reshape the Supreme Court by nominating "strict constructionists." He said: "Under this Administration, there will be no forced busing to achieve racial balance, and the neighborhood school concept will prevail unless, of course, the Supreme Court should nullify the President's policies."

The Congress

Education funds. A $4.4 billion education appropriation bill was passed by a 357-30 House vote July 16 and 88-0 Senate vote July 28. The total was $453 million more than the Administration requested.

The bill was sent to the President for signature, and senators from both parties appealed to Nixon July 28 not to veto it. At a news conference July 20, Nixon had called the appropriation in excess of his budget "an unacceptable amount" that would have to be made up elsewhere if a veto were to be avoided.

The funds were for public school programs and for grants and loans to college students. Among the items were $75 million to help school districts desegregate, $551 million for districts where enrollments were impacted because federal facilities were housed in the area, $167.7 million for educational grants to college students and $243 million for direct loans to college students.

As enacted, the bill retained a House amendment barring use of the funds to force school closings or busing or transfer of pupils without parental consent to promote school desegregation. In the Senate debate July 28, Sen. Charles McC. Mathias (R, Md.) read a letter from Elliot L. Richardson, secretary of health, education and welfare, stating that the provision would not interfere with the Administration's desegregation program in the South.

The Administration

Mitchell vows integration enforcement. Attorney General John N. Mitchell vowed Aug. 13 that school desegregation laws would be "decisively" enforced in the fall. However, in testimony before the Senate Select Committee on Equal Educational Opportunity, he said that the Justice Department did not intend to send a special task force to the South to enforce desegregation. Instead, he said, the federal officials already in the South would handle any problems and would be supplemented by "whatever additional personnel are necessary."

Stressing that he did not foresee "any great noncompliance" with the laws in the South, Mitchell said: "We do not plan to use federal officials as substitutes for local police officers whose responsibility it is to maintain good order." He added, however, that "we will not permit federal laws and court orders to be violated."

In response to questions, Mitchell said citizens who submitted complaints on the violation of desegregation laws to U.S. attorneys need not fear retaliation. He pledged "the swiftest, most drastic action available" against any retaliation.

Referring to Supreme Court consideration of the issue of "racial balance" in schools, Mitchell said: "My study of the cases leads me to believe that the Fourteenth Amendment does not incorporate the concept of racial balance. Until the higher courts decide differently, we will continue to apply the standard of reasonableness." He admitted that such policies might result in the toleration of all-white or all-black schools in urban areas where extensive busing would be required.

In a news conference Aug. 19, Mitchell charged that too many court decisions on school desegregation had made "yo-yo's" out of many Southern students and expressed hope that the Supreme Court would not issue a ruling requiring "racial balance" during the school year.

"I would hope that the Court would look at the time factors involved and would not tear up the pea patch in the middle of the term," he said. If the Court did adopt a "racial balance" plan, Mitchell added, "we would have to go through the whole process [of desegregation] all over again," since Administration desegregation plans emphasized neighborhood schools, rather than the elimination of all-white or all-black schools.

Agnew scores busing. Vice President Spiro T. Agnew spoke in Grand Rapids, Mich. Sept. 16. Attacking "the general permissiveness that has brought rioting in the streets and on the campuses," Agnew said the working man was "fed up with watching college buildings destroyed in the name of academic freedom."

Agnew identified the working man, whose vote he was soliciting, as those earning between $5,000 and $15,000 a year and "supporting his family with no handouts from Uncle Sam," as the "forgotten American" who had "strong family ties and keeps faith with his religion" and as a person who "does not enjoy being called a bigot for wanting his children to go to a public school in their own neighborhood."

500 complaints cited on school bias. Assistant Attorney General Jerris Leonard Nov. 17 told newsmen at an incident-marred press conference that the Justice Department had investigated about 500 complaints of racial discrimination in Southern school districts that had desegregated their classes during 1970.

Shortly before the press conference began, representatives of six news organizations walked out of the conference after they were told by the Justice Department's public information director that Leonard's statements were not for attribution to him. Leonard was chief of the department's civil rights division.

Six newsmen remained to take part in the session. Leonard reportedly told them that the department had filed somewhat fewer than 100 motions in courts to end the alleged in-school discrimination. He termed the discrimination within the 500 districts a "significant problem."

According to one of the reporters who remained, most of the complaints were of separate classes and buses for white and black students, the dismissal of black teachers and the transformation of attendance zones to fit racial living patterns.

1971

The Administration

Integration in North to be pushed. The Nixon Administration said Jan. 14 that it would soon turn the machinery of government to the task of increasing the rate of school integration in the North. More attention would be focused on Northern schools, the Administration reported, because there were now more integrated school systems in the South than in the North.

Announcement of the government's intended drive was made by Elliot L. Richardson, secretary of health, education and welfare (HEW). Richardson said HEW's Office of Civil Rights had found after a survey that only a slight change had occurred in the rate of school integration in the North and West since 1968.

According to the survey, the percentage of blacks attending integrated schools in the North and West rose from 27.6% to 27.7%.

This compared with a two-year rise of 19.7% in the percentage of Negro schoolchildren attending integrated schools in the South. According to HEW data, the rate increased from 18.4% to 38.1%.

Richardson made public the statistics during a news conference at which several reporters openly challenged the validity of the figures. Several newsmen also used strong language in questioning the secretary about the Administration's plans to deal with school districts in which black principals and teachers had been dismissed.

(Richardson was reportedly upset at the tone of some of the questions. He said he would not let the newsmen "put me on the defensive about these figures.")

HEW's figures marked a change in Administration procedure. Earlier data had used figures relating to school districts rather than pupils. In the earlier reports, the Administration had asserted that 97% of all school districts in the South were desegregated. However, civil rights groups challenged the statistics, claiming that students, rather than districts, should be counted.

Richardson said the new figures "show clearly and dramatically that unprecedented progress has been made in school

desegregation since 1968." He singled out the gains in the South, attributing them to "the way in which people, black and white alike, have carried out the requirements of the law."

Richardson said the Administration would now turn its attention to the schools in the North because of what he described as satisfactory strides taken by school systems in the South to desegregate facilities.

"The pupil desegregation battle in the South has been brought to the point where the only remaining steps are to follow up the job," Richardson said. "But the back of [segregation] has been broken."

South's integration praised. Seven top officials of the Nixon's Administration met March 6 with representatives of Southern school systems in Atlanta and praised their efforts to end school segregation as "a record of remarkable progress."

Following the closed door session, Elliot L. Richardson, secretary of health, education and welfare (HEW), lauded the educators' desegregation achievements. He told newsmen that "as far as the actual achievement of desegregated school systems . . . the South now had proportionately more black people attending desegregated schools than the North has."

Richardson and the six other Administration officials, all members of the White House Committee on Education, conferred with leaders of seven state education advisory committees set up by the White House to help ease problems arising from the desegregation of the South's public schools.

Other officials at the Atlanta meeting were George Shultz, director of the Office of Management and Budget; Attorney General John N. Mitchell; Postmaster General Winton M. Blount; George Romney, secretary of housing and urban development; Donald Rumsfeld, director of the Office of Economic Opportunity; and Robert H. Finch, a White House adviser.

The Senate

Senate passes school aid bill. After a week of rejecting some amendments sponsored by Southerners and accepting others, the Senate April 26 approved a compromise bill authorizing $1.4 billion in federal aid to help school districts integrate their schools. The vote was 74–8.

The vote followed acrimonious debate that focused primarily on the distinctions between school integration in the North and in the South.

The legislation was sent to the House, which passed a slightly different desegregation bill in 1970. It died when the Senate failed to act on it.

The bill passed by the Senate would give communities broad discretion over use of most of the funds allotted. In applying for grants, however, school districts would be required to have a broad plan for eliminating segregation and use a portion of their grant to create at least one "stable, quality, integrated school."

According to the measure, the model schools would have a "substantial portion of children from educationally advantaged backgrounds" but would be substantially representative of the racial makeup of the community.

School districts that were under U.S. court orders to desegregate could be exempted from the requirement to set up a model school.

The bill was a compromise measure worked out by Secretary of Health, Education and Welfare (HEW) Elliot L. Richardson and a group of civil rights advocates, among them Sens. Jacob K. Javits (R, N.Y.), Walter F. Mondale (D, Minn.) and Claiborne Pell (D, R.I.). The primary area of disagreement between the Nixon Administration and the civil rights proponents was over how the money should be allocated.

During the week the bill was debated, Southern senators proposed a number of amendments, all but one of which were turned down.

The only one to get the Senate's backing was authored by Sen. John C. Stennis (D, Miss.) and approved April 22 by a 44–34 vote. The amendment put the Senate on record as declaring that it was "the policy of the United States" to enforce federal school desegregation laws in communities where the segregation resulted from housing patterns as well as in areas where the segregation had been sanctioned by law.

Stennis said his amendment would eliminate the "dual standard" of enforcement under which he said Southern schools were threatened with forfeiture of federal funds if they failed to desegregate while schools in Northern cities and suburban areas remained segregated.

Other efforts to attach Southern-sponsored amendments to the bill were rejected. The Senate turned down April 26 a series of amendments put forward by Sen. Sam J. Ervin Jr. (D, N.C.) designed to relax some of the U.S. desegregation guidelines. One amendment would have permitted communities with "freedom-of-choice" school plans, under which a student could enroll in any school in the district, to be exempt from further desegregation efforts.

Another Ervin amendment would have prohibited a U.S. judge or official from ordering a desegregation plan that called for the busing of schoolchildren for racially balanced schools. A third would have prohibited the federal government from stopping a child from attending the public school nearest his home.

The Administration

Nixon will heed Court. President Nixon April 29 stated his views on busing at a news conference. Now that the Supreme Court had "spoken" on the issue, whatever he had said that was inconsistent with the court's decision was "now moot and irrelevant because . . . nobody, including the president. . . , is above the law as it is finally determined by the Supreme Court."

The law was "that where we have segregation schools as a result of governmental action . . . that then busing can be used under certain circumstances to deal with that problem. And so we will comply with that situation and we will work with the Southern school districts, not in a spirit of coercion but one of cooperation, as we have during the past year. . . . "

Until the court offered a decision on segregated school patterns arising not from governmental action but housing patterns, he said he would hold to his original position "that I do not believe that busing to achieve racial balance is in the interest of better education."

U.S. backs Austin school busing. The Nixon Administration, complying with the Supreme Court's mandate upholding school busing, May 14 recommended "extensive" crosstown busing as part of a plan to desegregate the public schools in Austin, Tex.

The desegregation proposal was the first made by the government since the Supreme Court April 20 brushed aside the Administration's objections to busing and declared it constitutional as a means of dismantling dual school systems.

Officials in the Department of Health, Education and Welfare (HEW) submitted the plan to Judge Jack Roberts of the U.S. district court in Austin. It called for the crosstown busing of an undetermined number of students to achieve a mix among the black and Mexican-American minorities and the white majority. The plan would leave all but one school in the city with a white or "Anglo" majority.

Austin, the sixth largest city in Texas, had about 56,000 students in 56 elementary schools, 19 junior high schools and eight high schools. About 15% of the students were black and about 20% Mexican-American. Austin had two secondary schools and seven elementary schools that had virtually all-black enrollments, all in all-black neighborhoods.

J. Stanley Pottinger, director of HEW's Office of Civil Rights, said the Austin plan was "the first indication" of the government's interpretation of the Supreme Court's busing decision.

Attorney General John N. Mitchell said May 13 that HEW's proposal for Austin "will be broad enough to satisfy the [Supreme Court] mandate and, hopefully, to meet the educational needs of the community."

Will Davis, president of the Austin school board, expressed dissatisfaction May 14 with the way the government presented its desegregation plan. Davis said, "I think this is the shabbiest kind of treatment, especially filing the plan before we have even seen it."

Nixon disavows Austin school busing. President Nixon dissociated himself Aug. 3 from his Administration's proposal for a school desegregation plan for Austin, Tex. that would require extensive crosstown busing.

In disavowing the plan drawn up by the Department of Health, Education and Welfare (HEW), Nixon reasserted his strong opposition to busing as a means of racial balance:

"I am against busing as that term is commonly used in school desegregation cases. I have consistently opposed the busing of our nation's schoolchildren to achieve a racial balance, and I am opposed to the busing of children simply for the sake of busing."

Nixon also directed HEW Secretary Elliot L. Richardson and Attorney General John N. Mitchell to "work with individual school districts to hold busing to the minimum required by law" as Southern school districts altered desegregation plans to comply with the Supreme Court's April 20 ruling upholding busing.

The President left no doubt, however, that his Administration would continue to enforce the order of the court, including court-ordered busing.

Nixon said the Justice Department would appeal on "limited constitutional grounds" the ruling by a federal district court judge in Austin that the Austin school board bus elementary students as part of a desegregation plan.

(The judge, Jack Roberts, July 19 had accepted the board's plan for the creation of centers for fine arts, social sciences, avocations and science and to bus elementary schoolchildren to the centers for periodic "cultural" experiences.)

The President said Mitchell had advised him that he "must appeal" the board's plan for periodic interracial sessions "because that decision is inconsistent" with the Supreme Court's ruling.

The federal government was believed to be planning to base its appeal on the ground that part-time desegregation did not meet the test of the court's mandate to put an end to dual school systems.

Nixon also instructed Richardson to submit to Congress an amendment to the proposed Emergency School Assistance Act that would "expressly prohibit" using any of the act's $1.5 billion for busing. The bill, already cleared by the Senate, was before the House. The bill would authorize $1.5 billion in federal aid to help school districts desegregate their schools.

U.S. warns 39 school districts. The Nixon Administration notified 39 school districts in 11 Southern and Border states June 22 that they would probably be required to complete additional integration under the Supreme Court's new desegregation guidelines.

In letters from the Department of Health, Education and Welfare's (HEW) Office for Civil Rights, the districts were told they would have to comply with the court's new orders or face the loss of federal aid to their schools. The civil rights office said that 80–100 districts in the Southern and Border states would get warning letters.

The first 39 letters were sent to districts in Delaware, Florida, Kentucky, Maryland, Mississippi, North Carolina, Oklahoma, South Carolina, Tennessee, Texas and Virginia.

The letters represented the first step taken by the Nixon Administration toward enforcing compliance with the court's new desegregation guidelines, which were handed down April 20. The 39 districts which were to get the letters had been desegregating under executive enforcement of the Civil Rights Act of 1964, which prohibited discrimination in any federally-assisted program. Most other school districts across the U.S. were integrating under federal court order.

J. Stanley Pottinger, director of the Office for Civil Rights, indicated that although the court said that a precise racial balance in every school would not be required, the existence of schools easily identified as a "white school" or a "black school" by the makeup of student enrollment, faculty or faculties was sufficient evidence of a violation of the Constitution.

Pottinger also noted in the letters that the court had called for additional busing, merging of attendance zones and other steps for desegregation, which HEW did not require as part of President Nixon's policy on integration.

Pottinger wrote that "to the extent that policy issued by this office in the past may conflict with or are different from rulings by the Supreme Court, the court holdings of course must prevail."

Nixon warns aides on busing. The White House said Aug. 11 that President Nixon had warned government officials, orally and in writing, that they risked losing their jobs if they sought to impose extensive busing as a means of desegregating schools throughout the South.

Nixon's directive was made public by White House Press Secretary Ronald L. Ziegler eight days after the President had dissociated himself from his Administration's proposal for a school desegregation plan for Austin, Tex. that would require extensive crosstown busing.

Ziegler said Nixon had warned officials in the Justice Department and the Department of Health, Education and Welfare that he wanted the busing of schoolchildren for integration purposes kept to the minimum required by law. Ziegler told newsmen that while the federal bureaucracy had not always been responsive to Presidential directives, "they are going to be responsive" to the busing order.

"And those who are not responsive," Ziegler warned, "will find themselves involved in other assignments or quite possibly in assignments other than the federal government."

According to Ziegler, the Administration did not object to busing plans drawn up by local school officials and would enforce any direct court orders requiring widespread busing.

But he said the President had instructed government personnel to carry out school desegregation without using the busing of schoolchildren as a "major technique."

According to the New York Times Aug. 11, HEW Secretary Elliot L. Richardson had considered resigning after the President disavowed HEW's plan for busing in Austin. Richardson was said to have decided against stepping down after discussions with his staff.

Richardson, who was on vacation in Alaska, was unavailable for comment.

Executive Agencies

Richardson backs Nixon on busing. Health, Education and Welfare Secretary Elliot L. Richardson said Aug. 31 that he was in complete agreement with President Nixon's policy limiting school busing. Richardson denied that he had considered resigning after the President repudiated a school desegregation plan drawn up by HEW that required extensive crosstown busing in Austin, Tex.

Speaking to newsmen after an hour-long conference with the President in San Clemente, Calif., Richardson said: "My understanding of the President's policy on school busing was perfectly clear before all this occurred and is perfectly clear now. He believes that busing should not be used except to the minimum necessary extent. He believes it is a good thing in principle for children to attend school in their neighborhoods. I knew this was his view, I supported that view before Aug. 3, and it was understood by my colleagues before Aug. 3" (the date Nixon commented on the Austin plan).

It was Richardson's first extensive comment on the busing issue since the President's statement. Richardson said, "I did not consider resignation." He said the President's statement was not a repudiation of HEW but a necessary clarification to combat "misunderstanding and even distortion" of his policies.

Asked why the HEW plan requiring considerable busing was submitted in the Austin case, Richardson said "the specific application of policy in any given case is always a matter of judgment." In response to a question of whether it was fair to say he was "in total and complete agreement with the President's policy and the President's statements in support of that policy and with the spirit of that policy," Richardson answered, "That is correct." Richardson refused to answer a question relating to Alabama Gov. George Wallace's antibusing actions.

Richardson said he and the President had only "touched on" the busing issue in a discussion of the progress of school openings in the South.

Civil Rights Commission

Texas busing challenged. The U.S. Commission on Civil Rights charged Aug. 3 that an Air Force base in southwest Texas was seeking to continue the illegal busing of schoolchildren on the base to a nearby predominantly white district.

The panel charged that the busing transferred 850 children from Laughlin Air Force Base to a district other than the one in which it was located.

George Bradley, assistant general counsel of the commission, said the children were bused to a predominantly white school district in Del Rio, bypassing an adjacent district in San Felipe that was overwhelmingly Mexican-American. Bradley said the Air Force had petitioned the Justice Department to intervene in a federal suit in Texas and seek permission for the Laughlin base to continue the cross-district busing.

In July, the Texas Education Agency had advised the Del Rio district that it could no longer accept the base's students because of a federal district court ruling that transfers perpetuating segregation were illegal.

The Air Force had denied that it was seeking to perpetuate segregation in its busing arrangement. According to the Air Force, the San Felipe district did not have sufficient educational facilities to handle the 850 children bused daily.

The Air Force was seeking a one-year extension of the busing plan.

U.S. panel criticizes bus policy. The U.S. Commission on Civil Rights said Aug. 12 that President Nixon's directive to keep busing for racial integration to a minimum would undermine efforts to desegregate schools.

The panel sharply criticized Nixon's policy in a statement adopted unanimously by its six members.

The commission said the "transportation of students is essential to eliminating segregation." The panel added that for purposes other than integration, "busing has been a common feature of American education."

The commission said that "what is at issue in this matter is not—to use the President's phrases—busing for the sake of busing or even busing solely for racial balance. The major issue is the kind of education available at the end of the trip."

The panel pointed out that a school desegregation plan drawn up by the Department of Health, Education and Welfare and based on extensive crosstown busing for Austin, Tex. had been "courageously accepted" by Austin officials as the standard.

"What the nation needed was a call to duty and responsibility, for the immediate elimination of the dual school system, and for support of all those officials who are forthrightly carrying out their legal obligations," the commission said.

"Unfortunately, the President's statement almost certainly will have the opposite effect, the effect of undermining the desegregation effort."

Rights panel assails Administration.

The U.S. Commission on Civil Rights again used stern language Nov. 16 to accuse the Nixon Administration of failing to adequately enforce the nation's civil rights laws.

It was the third time in 13 months that the panel had sharply rebuked the Administration over its civil rights policy.

Nixon's disavowal of school busing for purposes of racial integration was singled out by the commission. "For example, as this commission has pointed out, the President's comments opposing busing to facilitate school desegregation, by failing to offer a realistic alternative, may well be interpreted as a sign of a slowdown in the federal desegregation effort," the report charged.

Senator Muskie

Muskie assails Nixon on busing. Sen. Edmund S. Muskie (D, Me.) Sept. 7 sharply criticized President Nixon's attempt to block the use of any of $1.5 billion in federal education funds by school systems to acquire buses for **integration purposes. At the same time, Muskie expressed his distaste for the busing of students to desegregate public schools.**

Muskie's remarks, his first on the controversial issue of school busing, were made at a news conference in San Francisco, one of his first stops on a tour of California.

In voicing his distaste for busing, Muskie agreed with at least part of the President's view on busing.

"Like everyone else, I don't like busing," Muskie told newsmen. "It's inconvenient to parents, consumes time that students could better use for studying, and it uses up resources for the purchase of buses and so on that might be better used."

However, Muskie said, until U.S. cities were successfully integrated, "we're going to have to rely on busing to some extent to deal with the problem."

President Nixon had instructed the Department of Health, Education and Welfare Aug. 3 to submit to Congress an amendment to the proposed Emergency School Assistance Act that would "expressly prohibit" using any of the act's $1.5 billion for busing.

Muskie said the President's position "has had the effect of disrupting movements that have been under way, plans, that have received the support, however reluctant, [of parents] as they accepted the necessity for moving toward the integration of their schools."

Muskie called Nixon's proposed amendment "a disservice to those communities." He said the proposal "has a disruptive effect on public opinion in those communities."

When asked for his own solution to the busing issue, Muskie said there was "no perfect answer" to a problem rooted in "a distortion of our values over a long period of time, which has produced communities that are segregated and separates peoples from each other for reasons that are wrong in terms of the American ideal."

The House

House panel rejects busing ban. The House Education and Labor Committee set the stage for a floor fight on school busing when it approved Oct. 5 the Nixon Administration's proposal to give federal aid to school districts desegregating their schools. The committee passed the legislation by a 24–3 vote.

Before the final vote, the committee rejected President Nixon's request that districts receiving federal financial assistance be forbidden to use the funds for busing to achieve racial integration.

But antibusing forces in the House were expected to offer the restriction as an amendment when the bill reached the floor.

(There were reports that the House would not vote on the bill in 1971. The Rules Committee, which passed on legislation before it reached the House floor, had announced it would not consider legislation that had not cleared committees by Oct. 1.)

The Administration bill, known as the Emergency School Assistance Act, would provide $500 million in fiscal 1972 and $1 billion in fiscal 1973 for districts that were desegregating, either voluntarily or as the result of a court or administrative order.

The measure was passed by the House in 1970 but was not acted on in the Senate. The Senate passed a bill in April similar to the one adopted by the House committee Oct. 5.

House sets curbs on busing. Republican and Democratic congressmen with widely divergent political philosophies voted overwhelmingly Nov. 5 against busing schoolchildren for purposes of racial integration.

The House opposition to busing came in the form of three amendments to President Nixon's proposal to spend $1.5 billion over the next two years to help communities that were desegregating their schools.

After the three amendments were passed, the House approved Nixon's school aid bill as part of the final version of a multi-billion higher education bill. The final vote on the patchwork measure was 332–38.

But the significance of the final outcome lay in the three antibusing amendments which made it clear that the House agreed with the President in its opposition to busing.

The key antibusing amendment would prohibit the use of the $1.5 billion to pay for buses, drivers or any other cost of transporting children out of their neighborhood schools for the purpose of racial integration. Dozens of liberal Democrats voted with nearly all Republicans and Southerners to pass that amendment by a 233–124 vote.

Another amendment would not allow federal court orders requiring busing to go into effect until all appeals had been exhausted or until the time for appeal had passed. That amendment (the "Broomfield Amendment") passed 235–125.

A third amendment, adopted by a vote of 231–126, would forbid U.S. education officials from requiring, or even encouraging, communities to institute busing plans.

The final vote on the final bill was completed shortly before 2:30 a.m. after several hours of emotional debate.

(White House Press Secretary Ronald L. Ziegler said Nov. 6 that the President was pleased with the passage of the antibusing amendments. Ziegler said the vote "supports the posture that the President has taken regarding busing.")

The antibusing bandwagon hit full stride near midnight when Rep. Edith Green (D, Ore.), a foremost House education expert and mother of two sons, took the floor.

Rep. Green said "we cannot go back 100 years to make up for the errors of our ancestors. The evidence is very strong that busing is not the answer to our school problems. I never bought a home without looking first to find out about the schools my boys would attend. If the federal government then is going to reach its long arm into my house and say, 'Well, we are sorry you bought your home here, but your children are going to have to be bused 30 miles,' I say the government has gone too far."

Passage of the House bill set the stage for a protracted Congressional battle over busing, with the opening rounds to be fought in a House-Senate conference.

The Senate had passed versions of the higher education bill and $1.5 billion desegregation aid bill that were quite different from the ones passed by the House. The Senate version of the $1.5 billion school aid bill was passed April 26 after attempts to handcuff it with antibusing amendments failed. The final Senate measure did not contain any restrictions on busing and would require a good deal of school integration before communities could seek federal financial assistance.

Before the bill came to the House floor for a final vote, it was sent on a circuitous parliamentary route to free it from committee. The bill had been bottled up in the Rules Committee, which had refused to pass it on under normal procedural rules for amendment.

STENNIS PROPOSES ANTI-BUSING RIDER; RIBICOFF SCORES NORTHERN HYPOCRISY

In the Senate Sen. John Stennis (D. Miss.) attempted to amend the four-year $35 billion education bill by adding a rider forbidding compulsory busing to achieve racially integrated schools in the South and restoring "freedom of choice" school arrangements where they had been struck down by federal courts. Stennis gained some unexpected support from a Northern liberal—Sen. Abraham Ribicoff (D, Conn.). Announcing his intention (Feb. 9) to vote for the section of the Stennis amendment that called for uniform enforcement of school desegregation, Ribicoff urged other Northern senators to drop their "monumental hypocrisy" and admit that Northern school systems were just as racially segregated as those in the South.

The Hartford Courant
Hartford, Conn.
February 11, 1970

Few thinking persons would attempt to deny United States Senator Ribicoff's contention that racial segregation is widespread in the North. Whether it is as serious as in the South is a rather needless comparison. Racism is despicable in any quantity or locality. Measuring it may have some advantage in Senate tit-for-tat, but the real problem is what to do about it.

When the Senator says, however, that Northerners are guilty of "monumental hypocrisy," there is more room for discussion.

"Do not our people realize," he asked, "that on the high school and junior high levels children go to school in an armed camp, where there are knives and guns, blacks versus whites, police in schools to regulate, principals and teachers who are afraid . . .? Yet we turn away from problems that are six blocks away from where we live."

We realize these things all right, Senator. But hypocrisy is not the beam in our eye entirely, when and if we remark the mote in the eye of the South. There is also a monumental frustration in many cases. The whole problem of how whites and blacks may share equally in this land is so vast, so long-standing, so snarled, that people sometimes turn away from it—whites and blacks alike—in despair of ever being able to solve it. At the risk of being called double-dyed hypocritical, one may point out that in the South there has been a red-necked, axe-handle way of settling many issues between whites and blacks. W-h-a-c-k, and that was it.

Racism and hypocrisy are not to be excused because they are universal and timeless sins of mankind. And Northerners will not try to deny their share in such vices. Still, many of us also try to tackle all kinds of segregation problems in all fields—schools, jobs, housing, community-wise—grabbing the tasks where we can and hanging on for dear life though the solutions to the problems still elude us over and over. There may be monumental ignorance, monmental frustration. But perhaps the amount of pure hypocrisy is not deserving of the same adjactive.

For example, Senator Ribicoff says that two lines could be followed to meet the situation in the North. One must involve strenuous efforts to open up good jobs and housing to Negroes in the suburbs. The second must bring all-out support for improvement in the ghettos where many black families are going to have to live for years. But these suggestions are the merest generalities. And there's the rub. Putting them into effect is what must be worked out—and in this, hypocrisy is but one obstacle to success. Right, we have to make the attempt to start with. In some cases we have. In all cases we have a long way to go, many mistakes to survive, much to learn, years to put in. We'd be very happy to have the advice of all the company of Senators, as well as the castigations and suggestions of Senator Ribicoff.

The Providence Journal
Providence, R. I., February 13, 1970

No one ever has seriously leveled the charge of conformity at Sen. Abraham A. Ribicoff of Connecticut. As governor of that state, as Secretary of Health, Education and Welfare in the Kennedy administration, and as a leader of Senate Democratic liberals he has followed a career filled with surprises. No step he has taken, however, has contained the shock value of his recent declaration of support for Sen. John Stennis of Mississippi on the issue of school desegregation.

Every armchair analyst from New York to Sacramento can be expected to probe the senator's psyche unmercifully for the next few weeks in an effort to find a rational explanation.

Did the senator take his stand out of sincere conviction that it is time to declare *de facto* segregation in the schools illegal? Does he believe such a law could be enforced? In comforting the South in its hour of "need," does he hope to gain a greater measure of progress in ending dual systems in a region where racial separation is enforced by state and local governments? These and countless other questions have been raised by the senator. There seems reason to predict his answers will be less than electrifying.

Senator Ribicoff has been eloquent in defending his stand. He has discussed the problem of racism in this country with vision and sensitivity. His analysis is as knowledgeable and as nearly faultless as any on the subject issued by a government official.

The North is guilty of racism. It has ghettoized the Negro into urban pockets of misery and segregated its schools in fact by the *de facto* actions of prejudiced whites as surely as the South has done it by official and popular design.

When all the senator says is conceded, however, there remains all he has failed to say. He has preached a valid principle, but where is his plan? He has called for an end to the distinction between *de jure* and *de facto* segregation but it is the Supreme Court's ruling of 15 years ago that enforces that distinction by holding the former illegal while remaining silent on the latter. He affirms his opposition to the busing of school children with remarkable obscurity as to what will replace it. The wish may father the deed, but the deed of integrating residential neighborhoods in the North or the South is at best generations in the future.

Mr. Ribicoff's show-stopper was indeed a felicitous way of gaining national attention for pronouncements that have been made time after time and warrant constant repetition. To be charitable, that may have been his motive. Conversely, it is difficult to see how labeling all Northerners hypocrites and easing the mounting pressure on Southern segregationists will weaken in the least the steadfast, 15-year defiance of a high court ruling.

To describe the Ribicoff move as an effort to undercut the South is to indulge in wishful thinking. The Nixon administration has demonstrated repeatedly its willingness to grasp any excuse for easing the screws, for delaying federal insistence on Southern compliance. Wouldn't it be tragic if the senator from Connecticut unwittingly served up just what Southern intransigents and their political allies considered made to order?

Richmond Times-Dispatch

Richmond, Va., February 11, 1970

Sen. Abraham A. Ribicoff's speech on school desegregation was as welcome as a sparkling sunrise after a stormy, troubled night. Dawn comes at last. And in its early light, Northern liberals can see that they truly have been guilty of "monumental hypocrisy", to quote the Connecticut Democrat, on the agonizing issue of school integration.

In its original desegregation decision, the United State Supreme Court sought to nullify the double standard that had governed public school admissions policies throughout most of the years that have followed that decision, the federal government has adopted a double standard of its own, a policy as unfair and as obnoxious as the South's old practice.

Federal authorities have attempted to bludgeon Southern states into adopting integration policies that often defy common sense and ignore the wishes and welfare of whites and blacks alike. At the same time, they have virtually ignored segregation in Northern schools, moving against it there only sporadically.

Now, Sen. John Stennis of Mississippi has urged Congress to put the whole nation on one standard. If segregated schools are evil and illegal in Mississippi, Georgia, South Carolina and other Southern states, they're evil and illegal in New York, Rhode Island, Pennsylvania, New Jersey, New York and Connecticut. Accordingly, Stennis has introduced two amendments to the education bill, one calling upon the federal government to apply its school desegregation standards "uniformly in all regions of the United States" and another giving local school boards exclusive authority to determine whether to bus children to achieve racial balance.

Similar proposals have been advanced before, but to no avail. This time, however, Ribicoff greeted the Stennis plan with a generally approving speech, a people-who-live-in-glass-houses-shouldn't-throw-stones kind of speech.

The North is "guilty of monumental hypocrisy in its treatment of the black man," said Ribicoff. It is "just as racist" as the South, he said, and "perhaps we of the North needed the mirror held up to us by the Senator from Mississippi in order to see the truth."

Ribicoff promised to support the Stennis proposal calling for the uniform application of desegergation standards. Regrettably, the Connecticut liberal vowed to vote against the Mississippi Senator's plan to make busing a purely local matter, even though New York has a similar law. Yet, Ribicoff recognized the absurdity of busing except on a severely restricted scale.

Most of the segregation that exists in public schools today is the result not of law but of segregated living patterns, he noted. To seek to circumvent this reality by busing children from a school in their own neighborhood to a school in another far away is to flirt with disaster, the Senator warned.

"You couldn't do anything worse to a black child than to bus him into middle-class suburb. The psychological shock and the philosophical shock are as cruel as anything that can be done."

A more cogent argument for freedom-of-choice probably never came from the lips of a Southern senator.

The best way to brighten the Negro's future, as Ribicoff stressed, is not to bus his children to distant schools but to improve schools in his own neighborhood, increase his economic opportunities, and give him the mobility and the freedom to flee the ghetto.

Ribicoff's impressive speech could be a turning point in the school integration battle that has kept education in turmoil for 16 years. It might persuade Congressional liberals to halt their senseless search for a racial golden mean in school enrollment and to concentrate instead on the most urgent educational task facing this country, which is to rescue its public schools from the quagmire of crime, vice and violence into which they are steadily sinking.

THE BILLINGS GAZETTE

Billings, Mont., February 11, 1970

Monday was the day that was in the U. S. Congress. It marked the beginning of an end of an era.

It took a liberal to do it and one of the most liberal of them all did it.

Sen. Abe Ribicoff, the Connecticut Democrat, asked his fellow northern liberals to drop their "monumental hypocrisy" on the school segregation issue.

Ribicoff's support of a southern amendment brought amazed cheers. The amendment provides that federal school desegregation standards shall be applied uniformly in all regions of the U.S. . . . without regard to the origin of cause of such segregation.

Ribicoff's argument was there is no real difference between actual segregation in the north due to residential separation than that by state law in the south.

He also hit at the busing efforts in saying "You couldn't do anything worse to a black child than to bus him into a middleclass suburb. The psychological shock and the philosophical shock are as cruel as anything that can be done."

Honest Abe is right. It is time the north quit using the south as-a scapegoat and the south quit using the blacks likewise.

Education requires favorable environment to be properly absorbed.

True, there have been those who rose to educational heights on an undernourished belly. But, oh, so few. None if there was protein deficiency in the first two years.

We need equal education, north and south. We didn't say separate and equal — just equal.

It is the business of our governments, local, state and national, to bring it about.

Ribicoff's startling speech of February 9, 1970, may speed the action.

St. Louis Globe-Democrat

St. Louis, Mo., February 12, 1970

Sen. Abraham Ribicoff of Connecticut must have been playing to the grandstand when he accused the North of "monumental hypocrisy" as he called for support of a proposal by Sen. John Stennis of Mississippi under which schools segregated because of residential patterns would be considered in violation of civil-rights laws.

To approve the Stennis measure could bring chaos to many northern cities. In numerous instances it would be impossible to comply by any means. There just aren't that many buses to do the job, even if this were justified—which it isn't.

Schools were never meant to be used as a means of solving racial imbalance brought on by housing patterns.

What the Constitution and its amendments guarantee is the right of every child to attend a school without being segregated by such means as the dual-school system used in some sections of the South.

It is possible that a school board could be guilty of causing segregation by gerrymandering school districts. This would be in violation of the Constitution.

But in areas where the population is predominantly white or black, there is no justification for seeking racial balance by artificial means, such as busing.

This attempt to avoid de-segregation in Mississippi by trying to put an impossible burden on northern schools will fall of its own weight. Any logical person can see that it is neither feasible nor desirable.

St. Petersburg Times
St. Petersburg, Fla., February 15, 1970

President Nixon's Lincoln Birthday statement on the desegregation controversy was a masterpiece of political duplicity.

It opposed "compulsory busing," encouraging white opposition in the South to federal court orders attempting to eliminate racial discrimination.

It took a hedged, indirect position for nationwide school desegregation, too weak to give any encouragement to black Americans.

But it dealt only with the top of the iceberg, not with the huge problem that touches the farthest corners of the American character and divides it into separate and unequal societies.

OUR COUNTRY really has two race problems:

✔ The more apparent one, and it may prove to be the easier to resolve, is the southern remnant of 90 years of state-enforced segregation.

✔ The second problem is the racism that has seeped into some of the American character. It is hard to face. A presidential commission has warned against it. A new federal school survey documents it with evidence that racial isolation exists in every section of the country and is growing fastest in Northern cities.

American politicians — ranging all the way from George Wallace to Adam Clayton Powell — are skilled in exploiting both of these problems. In recent weeks, there has been a particularly virulent outbreak of exploitation in Florida.

This will pass. But the challenge will remain of melting this iceberg both above and below the surface.

It is easy to be against "compulsory busing."

But where was the leadership to oppose compulsory busing that maintained segregation? Where are those who want to be part of the solution instead of part of the problem?

Where was the leadership against enforced residential segregation? Until two years ago the St. Petersburg Charter granted the city the power "to designate, establish and set apart the territorial limits or districts of said city within which white persons may reside, and separate territorial limits or districts of said city within which Negroes may reside."

ON THE PROBLEM of national racism, two senators are showing America the alternatives.

Sen. John C. Stennis, D-Miss., has offered legislation to apply to schools across the country the same desegregation regulations pressed upon the South.

Sen. Stennis' objective is not to integrate North and South. He hopes to arouse in the North racial antagonisms that will stop integration in the South.

As the Tampa Tribune put it, "The South needs Northern allies."

In truth, it is Americans with vision to see the urgency of bringing our country together into a single society who need allies in all sections of the country.

One of those with such vision is Sen. Abraham A. Ribicoff, D-Conn. He took Sen. Stennis at his word, and courageously supported this as a way "to open up our suburbs."

Needed now is leadership as clear as that of Abraham Lincoln.

The America that could not exist in 1860 as a house divided against itself cannot exist in 1970 as a black house and a white house.

CHICAGO Daily Defender
Chicago, Ill., February 14, 1970

The revolt of five Southern states — Alabama, Georgia, Louisiana, Mississippi and Florida — against the Supreme Court's immediate school desegregation mandate, should not surprise anyone. The Justice Department's request for postponement of that order was all that was needed to show the folk in Dixie that President Nixon was truly against the court's orientation on the whole question of school integration.

Mr. Nixon had made it abundantly clear e v e n before his assumption of the Presidential powers that he was opposed to enforced integration. The ground was, thus, well laid for the Southern uprising. The Governors of the revolting states received aid and comfort from Mr. Nixon's open criticism of the racial philosophy of the nation's highest tribunal.

The Nixon stance is a shocking departure from the moral commitment of three previous Administrations. Presidents Eisenhower, Kennedy and Johnson felt they had a moral and executive obligation to sustain the judgment of the court on the issue of desegregation of America's public schools. They saw that any other stand would have impaired the authority of the court and viciated the promise of democracy.

Mr. Nixon is, in fact, challenging the authority of the Supreme Court. The consequence of the challenge may plunge the whole nation into an unprecedented constitutional crisis.

This is indeed a strange anomaly. By and large, Mr. Nixon got into office on the strength of his strident support for "law and order." We were constantly being reminded during the days of the urban riots, and during the 1968 Presidential campaign that "ours is a government of laws, not of men." Mr. Nixon repeated this with the fervor of a liturgical prayer.

Public school desegregation is the law of the land. This law, perhaps more than any other, cannot be circumvented without inviting corresponding disorder. To allow the revolting Southern Governors the right to challenge the authority of the court is tantamount to saying that the Supreme Court is not supreme in the exercise of its judicial functions. Such a view runs afoul of the constitutional foundation of the court, and is, of course, untenable. Were this view allowed to prevail, the country would be thrown into the worst form of anarchy and violence ever witnessed in modern times.

Not only is a crisis impending, the very political future of the Republican Administration is at stake. Nixon may well be an unwilling one-term President. The Southern Strategy which he is pursuing with vigor and passion may sound his death knell.

Arkansas Gazette.
Little Rock, Ark., February 14, 1970

Given the "Southern strategy" of the Nixon administration, it was no surprise to find President Nixon issuing a statement that appeared to support the Stennis amendment on school segregation and appeared to oppose the use of bus transportation in school desegregation.

We do not doubt that Mr. Nixon made some cheap points in the South but we are not sure that what the President said meant very much, if anything.

Mr. Nixon said he favored having the same desegregation rules apply for North and South, but his press secretary, on questioning, said the President was not necessarily endorsing the Stennis amendment to an HEW appropriation bill. The amendment, virtuous on its face, states that desegregation standards shall be applied uniformly throughout the country. What it is principally designed to do is to give Southern school boards an argument in court that they should not have to break up their de jure segregation until all the cities in the non-South have broken up de facto segregation. The argument, at the least, would work to delay further the breakdown of de jure segregation in the South.

The statement issued at the White House came out foursquare against "compulsory busing" to achieve racial balance, but here again there is semantic confusion. The 1964 Civil Rights act forbids busing to attain such balance in the schools but does not forbid busing to break down racial discrimination. There is a fine line between the two purposes. What's more, the use of the word "compulsory" complicates Mr. Nixon's meaning, because, so far as we know, nobody has advocated that anyone be *compelled* to ride a school bus anywhere for any purpose.

What he Nixon statement, like the Stennis amendment, actually does is to encourage popular resistance to the courts in the current, climactic assault on the Southern systems of racial segregation by law.

Detroit Free Press
Detroit, Mich., February 11, 1970

SEN. ABRAHAM Ribicoff has done a rare and useful thing: He has told his colleagues the truth, which is that many of them would rather flay the dying carcass of southern segregation than face the racism in their own bailiwicks.

For too long we have deluded ourselves that racism, which indeed has a more rigid pattern in the South, was something that only southern sheriffs practiced. Even after the rude awakening of the big city riots of the mid-1960s, it was easier to mount a public campaign against a lynching that took place 15 years ago in the South than to face the wrongs done in Detroit every day in 1970.

This is not to say that Detroiters are worse racists than Mississippians, or even in the same league necessarily. In spite of the backlash, a large number of Detroiters, black and white, remain committed to the ideal of an integrated and open society. Certain practices and prejudices that are commonplace in the South are unthinkable here.

But the cleavage between the Inner City —it is put in capital letters and it always sounds ominous—and the suburbs is as impenetrable for many as any wall of segregation ever erected in the South. Even a white southerner may find himself shocked by the stereotyped thinking and self-righteous prejudices that he finds in the white fringe of Detroit.

As Sen. Ribicoff says, "The North is guilty of monumental hypocrisy in its treatment of the black man."

What, we are forced to ask ourselves, can we do about this? The sheer size of Detroit defies even the kind of integration that is now being created in many southern communities. Housing patterns are breaking down, but mostly they are breaking down within the city of Detroit itself. There can be no integration of truly effective scope unless there is effective integration of suburbs. As Sen. Ribicoff says, that is where the new housing and the new jobs are being created. One survey he cited showed that 40,000 blacks in Detroit would seek housing in the suburbs near their jobs if they could get it.

Are you listening, Dearborn?

Sen. Ribicoff also had a pungent comment on the doctrine of separatism, which blacks in their search for cultural identity have endorsed and which many parlor liberal whites have rushed to endorse:

"Many will argue that blacks no longer want integration. And whenever a black man says this, you can almost hear the sigh of relief in the suburbs. Many may not want integration. But many will. And our responsibility is to provide access to that opportunity."

Our responsibility is also to provide a decent place in the central city for those whites who choose to live here. Lafayette Park as a renewal project has had its weaknesses, but it has at least served the purpose of easing the apartheid of the metropolitan area. The mere rebuilding of ghettos should not be our goal.

There is no simple formula for ending the separatism and the white and black racism that fosters it. We can at least face the problem honestly though, as Sen. Ribicoff has done.

That won't solve the problem, but it will at least get us to the point of looking for flaws in our own performance rather than looking south, past our own transgressions.

CHICAGO DAILY NEWS
Chicago, Ill., February 11, 1970

When the Supreme Court finally ordered the Deep South states to dismantle "now" their dual school systems — one for white and one for black — Sen. John Stennis of Mississippi offered a legislative remedy. It was deceptively simple. His proposed amendment to a school bill provided that federal school desegregation standards "shall be applied uniformly in all regions of the United States without regard to the origin or cause of such segregation."

Southern senators eagerly jumped on the Stennis bandwagon, but Northerners stayed clear. Except for Sen. Abraham Ribicoff (D-Conn.), who rose this week to blast his fellow liberals for "monumental hypocrisy" and announce he would vote for the Stennis amendment.

On its face, the Stennis proposal makes a certain amount of sense. All right-thinking people surely agree that desegregation standards should be "applied uniformly in all regions of the United States." Most would also agree with Ribicoff that hypocrisy has run strongly through the North's efforts to purify the South while its own city school systems maintained large proportions of all-white or all-black schools.

But the hooker in the Stennis formula lies in the final clause: "without regard to the origin or cause of such segregation." No senator could be unaware that its intention was to wipe out the distinction between "de jure" and "de facto" segregation.

This is a large distinction indeed, and one that cannot be so easily erased. Southern schools have been segregated by law (de jure), and for nearly 16 years the Southern states have worked every angle they could find to avoid compliance with the Supreme Court's ruling that such legal separation is unconstitutional.

In contrast, the force of law in the North has been on the other side, to build school systems in which no color bars existed. Especially in the large cities, segregation by race undeniably does exist in fact (de facto). But this outgrowth of housing patterns and migration is hardly the same as a planned system of separation enforced by law.

The aim of Stennis and his colleagues is to build a backfire against the heat now being applied to the remaining areas of enforced segregation. As a moral challenge to the North to do a better job of integration than it has done, his proposal has some merit. But its total effect would be to blur the clear line between the two varieties of segregation, and hinder progress against both.

Ribicoff fell into the trap. We trust the majority of senators will not.

ST. LOUIS POST-DISPATCH
St. Louis, Mo., February 13, 1970

Senator Abraham Ribicoff of Connecticut has made a speech about public school integration in which he properly condemns Northern hypocrisy and makes astute observations about the racial issue. He also comes up with the wrong answer.

The Senator says "we're just as racist in the North as they are in the South" and perhaps he is right. He asserts that the fundamental problem is a dual society "in every metropolitan area" and that we must "include the suburbs in our solution" and undoubtedly he is right. He holds that the black man must have the freedom to choose where he wants to live and work, and certainly that has to be the basis of the ultimate social solution of the race issue.

But because Senator Ribicoff opposes the North's "monumental hypocrisy," he says he will vote for a school segregation amendment sponsored by Senator John Stennis of Mississippi. This amendment would apply federal school desegregation standards uniformly throughout the nation "without regard to the origin of such segregation."

The origin of most Northern segregation is de facto or neighborhood living patterns. It is wrong and it wrongly affects education and community life in general, but segregated housing cannot be cured by moving against segregated schools. Nor can de facto school segregation be cured by ignoring de jure segregation, meaning segregation by law, which is characteristic of the South.

There is of course nothing wrong with applying the same desegregation standards to North and South alike. They should be so applied. But when the problem is segregated neighborhoods, that is the problem to be attacked uniformly, and when the problem is de jure segregation of schools, that is what ought to be attacked uniformly. The Stennis amendment, now backed by the Nixon Administration, would spread thin the Federal Government's efforts to enforce desegregation in the South by applying it to other states where it is least applicable.

We fear that Senator Ribicoff, an able and sincere man, is wearing a hair shirt over Northern hypocrisy, forgetting segregationists know what they want. They want segregation. That is the purpose of the Stennis amendment.

BOTH HOUSES OF CONGRESS PASS SCHOOL SEGREGATION AMENDMENTS

The Senate voted 56–36 Feb. 18 to curb de facto school segregation by cutting off federal funds to those school districts whose racial imbalance was a product of residential patterns. If passed by the House, the amendment would extend to many predominantly white or black school districts in the North the same penalties currently enforced in the South for non-compliance with court-ordered desegregation. The amendment was part of the $35 billion education bill. Sen. John Stennis of Mississippi, sponsor of the measure, credited Connecticut Sen. Abraham Ribicoff with a major role in rallying enough Northern votes (30) to insure passage of the amendment. The Senate also passed another amendment which would forbid the busing of school children to "alter racial composition."

In the House, Rep. Jamie Whitten (D, Miss.) successfully sponsored two amendments specifying that no educational funds "may be used to force any school district to take any actions involving the busing of students, the abolishment of any school or the assignment of any student attending any elementary or secondary school to a particular school against the choice of his or her parents." An amendment sponsored by Rep. Charles Jonas (R, N.C.) would let parents, not educators, determine how to implement the freedom-of-choice plans.

JACKSON DAILY NEWS
Jackson, Miss., February 19, 1970

The healthiest manifestation of the 56 to 36 victory of the Stennis amendment in the Senate will be the impact this will have on honest, well-meaning white voters in the North.

So long as the South was the whipping boy, non-South politicians could make all manner of speeches advocating race-mixing, civil rights and get legislation approved to ship bundles of your tax dollars into the hands of minority groups. This could change.

If final congressional approval is given this amendment hypocritical politicians can no longer get by with slapping the South on civil rights to garner minority votes without disturbing the peace of mind of Northern whites, for the latter considered civil rights legislation as something special for those strange drawling people who eat grits for breakfast.

But various opinion polls and information gathered independently indicate the white people elsewhere in the nation are deeply even gravely concerned about the fate of their children and their educational systems.

If non-South members of Congress recognize the hypocrisy of the double standard of race-mixing and the Stennis amendment is made national policy, then in the future office-seekers across the nation can ill afford the wrath of the concerned white majority by yelping civil rights to capture minority votes.

The national political complexion may well be changed by this one victory. It's about time!

Meanwhile, let no thought be spawned that the fight for sanity has ended. The chaotic school situation demands that the fullest efforts of all right-thinking persons be channeled in a sustained campaign to correct many evils brought on by the appeasement of agitators whose appetite for demands is insatiable.

Their radical, extremist movement has gone too far. Their paid agitators are not going to cease demanding.

The Congress must say "whoa."

The Senate has made the first move in a sensible direction.

The Providence Journal
Providence, R.I., February 21, 1970

All the hoorah about a major Southern victory on the issue of school desegregation is somewhat premature. Certainly, the strategy devised by Sen. John C. Stennis of Mississippi, endorsed by President Nixon and force-fed to the Senate with the help of Connecticut's Sen. Abraham A. Ribicoff, has achieved the monumental purposes of confusing the issue and of deflecting federal pressures against historic traditions of white supremacy in the Southern schools.

An exchange of views by any three Northerners now is likely to demonstrate the result of what has transpired in Congress over the last few weeks. Where once there was solid agreement that the Supreme Court ruling of 1954, reaffirmed in the strongest possible terms a few months ago, must be enforced, now there is almost total disarray. Now the view expressed by many is almost a playback of the Stennis view—let the North look to its own sins before hurling missiles at its brethren in the South.

There is an air of unreality sufficient to shake the confidence of the most resolute civil rights advocate. That is true. But it is still too early to despair of reason's winning out.

The Stennis amendment to withhold federal school aid funds from any school district failing to desegregate regardless of the circumstances passed the Senate by the remarkable margin of 56 to 36 but still faces some formidable obstacles. It must be approved by a conference committee dominated by unfriendly forces. It then will go to the floor of the House. Should it survive those tests it would become, not law in the enforceable sense, but "the policy of the United States."

"Mercifully, this is a mere policy and therefore not binding," said Sen. Hugh Scott of Pennsylvania, Republican floor leader. "It's a good thing it's policy, because any genuine attempt in good faith to enforce this language would require all the police forces in America and a good many of our troops overseas."

Exactly. That is the precise rationale for the long-range Stennis drive. Link Northern housing patterns with every hamlet, town, city and state in the South where racial separation in the schools is enforced by government rule and Dixie's battle first to emasculate, then to reverse the integration edict is won.

Unfurl the banners of all-or-nothing — and nothing will be done. Preach universal application of the law and it is widely assumed that this has not been the case heretofore. The high court did not proscribe *de jure* segregation in the South alone, but *wherever* it exists and that remains the law of the land. Dump felonies and misdemeanors in the same hopper and confusion reigns and that is just what Mr. Stennis and his colleagues want.

Some black leaders in the past have tried to talk up separatism and rightly have been criticized for myopia. Let Congress fail to countermand the action of the Senate, and we will hear those voices once again.

A victory for Mr. Stennis and the South? Perhaps it is temporary obstruction and rhetorical device. It is impossible to believe, however, that such blindness will be permanent. Union forces suffered setbacks — Chickamauga, Chancellorsville, Fredericksburg — but federal forces persevered and the Union still lives on.

THE PLAIN DEALER
Cleveland, Ohio, February 26, 1970

Desegregation of schools is not an end in itself.

The aim of the Supreme Court's 1954 decision in the Brown case was to put an end to separate-and-unequal schooling, so that black children would get equal, not inferior, education.

Desegregation can be a means — not the only means — of improving the education of black, low income or other discriminated-against groups' children. It must be used only with caution.

To start busing massively thousands of public school children in order to achieve desegregation at some mathematical optimum mixture would be folly. It would also be painful and damaging to many children, especially black children.

Sen. Abraham Ribicoff, on the Senate floor on Feb. 9, said it was hypocrisy to compel southerners to desegregate their de jure separate schools while northern schools continued segregated de facto.

Ribicoff blamed the separation in schools upon the separation of races, geographically and socially. He pleaded for an end to that separation.

But he also warned: "It is indefensible to bus a child 20 miles away to comply" with some integration order. "We could do nothing worse to a black child from a poor ghetto than to take him and bus him into a middle-class school."

"The psychological and philosophical shock to that child is crueler than anything that could be done," the liberal senator said.

Many a southern metropolis has, under pressure from the federal courts, ended de jure segregation of its schools, but now has the same de facto segregation which is prevalent in northern big-city school districts. In that regard, Atlanta is now similar to Cleveland.

In Cleveland's public school district, the black pupils are concentrated in East Side areas. Around the outer edge of the East Side there are some integrated school districts. But the majority of white pupils are thickly bunched on the West Side, with a wide downtown and industrial valley interposed.

Where it is not done artificially, integration in schools is an advantage. It has educational values, as the Coleman report and other studies show, particularly for black or other minority children.

But high quality education, not integration, is the number one goal. Many black thinkers, including columnist William Raspberry, consider integration itself a blind alley. One black writer says: "Integration as a reality was as great a hoax on black people as the melting pot myth."

Busing to reach a black-white balance in Cleveland public schools, assuming it would work and the public accepted it, would cost $15 million a year, says Supt. Paul W. Briggs.

It takes hard-scrabble advocacy in Columbus and here to get Cleveland schools the tax money they need to get by. They still lag at about two-thirds the per pupil expenditure of well-off suburbs.

Those $15 millions should go to buy high quality instruction, not to pay a corps of bus drivers. Nor should children be used as pawns in some futile attempt to cure adult segregation by manipulations of student bodies in classrooms.

THE DALLAS TIMES HERALD
Dallas, Tex., February 22, 1970

IT WILL BE a few days more before Senate and House agree on the precise character of the school desegregation provisions to be written into the education appropriation bill.

It will be even longer—much longer, in all likelihood—before anyone can judge the effect of the provisions.

But one thing, in any event, is certain: On this tortured and long-vexed question, Congress' heart is at last in a location that approximates the right place.

The overall effect of the congeries of antibusing and national desegregation policy amendments (a congeries that must be reconciled by conference committee) is to recognize the profound human problems inherent in forced desegregation.

Such a recognition is unprecedented. And yet so also are our contemporary desegregation problems unprecedented.

To comply with recent court decrees ordering full integration, Southern school districts find they must resort to busing children out of their own neighborhoods. Meanwhile, even as the South faces its worst desegregation problems yet, the North rests secure and untroubled in its practice of segregated schools.

It is to these grievances that the Senate and House addressed themselves, if in differing fashions.

Last Wednesday, the Senate amended the education appropriations bill by declaring that desegregation in the North, as well as in the South, should henceforth be national policy. Later, the upper chamber adopted another amendment forbidding federally ordered busing.

The House, for its own part, has approved amendments okaying freedom-of-choice desegregation plans and banning busing.

There is thus a considerable degree of divergence between the approaches of the two chambers. Still, it seems fairly certain that the inevitable conference committee will undo little of what has been done.

Likely it will write some sort of antibusing language into the final bill. We hope in addition it will retain the House's freedom-of-choice provision (defeated by the Senate) and the uniform national desegregation policy amendment. If one of the two has to fall, however, we hope the freedom-of-choice amendment survives. It is, in its essence, a simple and just answer to the problem of who shall attend school where. The amendment would leave it up to the students themselves.

There is one complicating factor in all of this. If the appropriations bill in question is more costly than the President wants, he may veto it—busing amendment and all.

That would be unfortunate. The Senate's and the House's actions stand to benefit the nation by introducing a note of realism and understanding into a heretofore discordant chorus of anger and exasperation. Even if the bill exceeds the President's recommendations by a couple of hundred millions, he should sign it. This chance is too precious to be lost.

The Hartford Courant
Hartford, Conn., February 20, 1970

Luckily, there are still hurdles remaining that may prevent the Stennis proposal on school desegregation from becoming law.

As of the moment, the Senate has succeeded in voting to cut off Federal aid to school districts that fail to desegregate even though their racial imbalance is a product of residential patterns and not illegal. But the language, which brackets de-jure and de facto segregation, still must be cleared by a House-Senate conference committee and by the House itself, and ultimately the over-all educational bill of which it is part must be signed by President Nixon.

Surely somewhere along the line the Stennis proposal must be seen for what it is. It is a vengeful plan to hamper desegregation rather than advance it. The South, where de-jure segregation has prevailed bitterly and stubbornly, merely wants the shoe to be on some other foot for a while, and "see how you like it."

Senator Stennis has said as much himself. During debate on his proposal, he told Northerners, "If you have to integrate in your area, you will see what it means to us." What the South wants, he said, is a live-and-let-live policy. What the South obviously hopes is that when the North faces the problems of school desegregation, it will be tempted to treat the South less stringently, more charitably, more "understandingly." In short, with the shoe on its own foot, it will be inclined to let the South off the hook in a misery-loves-company, undercover agreement on — as the Senator said — live and let live. "Don't press us and we won't press you" is the eventual attitude the South wants from the North. Obviously this means short shrift for desegregation the country over.

The point is, however, that racism has traditionally hampered desegregation of Southern schools, while in the North, as has been said, the imbalance is largely the result of residential patterns. In theory, imbalance may be imbalance, period. And certainly it should be corrected across the nation equally. No one denies this. But where federal penalties are to be assessed in districts that fail to desegregate, there indubitably must be a distinction between districts that won't abide by statute or moral law, and those that can't. This is where the distinction between de-jure and de-facto segregation obtains, however the courts may handle such a difference.

No wonder Senator Stennis hails the action on his proposal as a "new gateway, a turning point." It could be a gateway indeed for those Southern districts that still want out from desegregation. It could be a turning point indeed in the sense that some de-facto northern districts, frustrated by a problem they would like to cope with but can't, finally decide to turn their eyes from what goes on in the de-jure South.

Senator Stennis gives major credit to Senator Ribicoff of Connecticut, who joined the Mississippian's forces last week, for passage of the de-jure-de-facto proposal. Even granting that Senator Ribicoff is right in principle that desegregation should be equally promoted all across the country, it is hard not to believe he has unwittingly been had by Southern strategists whose aims are something different altogether.

ARKANSAS DEMOCRAT
Little Rock, Ark., February 22, 1970

If they become law, no one can be certain of the effect of the anti-busing bills that passed the Senate last week. Surely they will slow down the experimenting guideline writers in Health, Education and Welfare. But the effect on the federal courts, which really control desegregation, probably will be only intuitive. Federal Judges base their decisions on the constitution, not statutes.

But this is okay. In fact, it's a real victory for the moderates in this country, who have accepted desegregation as a fact of life but who do not want their children to be bused or their schools to spend their meager resources on experiments. With these bills, Sen. John Stennis, D-Miss., and Sen. Sam Ervin, D-N.C., have begun the first serious discussion of integration and education in this country since the Supreme Court decision in 1954.

They pointed out that there were all-black schools outside of the South. And they asked that the same remedy be applied to them as was being applied to the South — busing. But upon examination this appears impossible. As a practical matter, how could you bus suburban whites 20, 30 miles into core-city ghettos and the blacks out? And how could you force Charlotte to bus but not Chicago? Is this fair? All answers were negative. Slowly a few converts stepped forward, chief among them Sen. Abe Ribicoff, D-Conn. Listen to what this liberal said on the Senate floor:

> Let us not kid ourselves. Wherever we go across the nation, when blacks move in, the whites move out, and if they have children, they move as far away as they can. What shall we do? Shall we chase them with buses, with helicopters, or with airplanes to try to get an equitable distribution?

Finally, the roll was called and three bills were passed that ordered application of the same desegregation rules nationwide and the end to busing. The landmark vote was the one on equal application of the laws, and the inherent fairness of this brought other liberals besides Ribicoff to the side of the Southerners — Montoya of New Mexico, Mansfield of Montana, McIntyre of New Hampshire, Burdick of North Dakota and Aiken of Vermont. (It also caused wet-noodle liberals like Kennedy of Massachusetts, Nelson of Wisconsin, Hartke of Indiana, Hatfield of Oregon to duck and not vote at all)

Only a fool would expect these bills to stop desegregation, or to allow any city to perpetuate or revert to a dual school system. Also, no one pretends that these bills contain the answer for effective and painless integration. Rather all they show is that one answer wasn't working. As Ribicoff says, we must continue to look for the solution.

It might even be busing in some situations. At least we hope that these bills, if they become laws, wouldn't be interpreted so as to prevent a local school district from using buses to strike a racial balance IF it wants to. In fact, more flexibility is the best result we could hope for from the Senate's actions last week—flexibility and the abandonment of what seemed to be a national effort to destroy neighborhood schools in the South but nowhere else.

HERALD-EXAMINER
Los Angeles, Calif., February 23, 1970

Sen. John C. Stennis, (D-Miss.) pushed through an amendment directing the federal government to enforce desegregation of schools equally in the North and the South — whether it was the result of laws or neighborhood residential patterns.

The senator argued that school desegregation efforts should be "applied uniformly in all regions of the United States without regard to the origin or cause of such segregation."

However, segregation problems in the South and in the North can hardly be equated. There is a vast difference between Southern laws which create segregated dual school systems and geographic, population factors which cause racial imbalance in many western and northern cities.

The first duty of Congress is to enforce those integration laws already on the books. Legally constituted school segregation in the South is wrong.

De facto segregation is another matter. Residents of Los Angeles, for example, do not object to their children attending racially mixed schools. The nearly unanimous objection in all parts of the community is uprooting 240,000 children from their neighborhood schools and transporting them many miles away each day to a distant school to satisfy a a local judge's order that a specific racial balance must be maintained.

WINSTON-SALEM JOURNAL
Winston-Salem, N.C., February 21, 1970

THE TWO TOP Republicans in the Senate, Hugh Scott, the minority leader, and Robert Griffin, the party Whip, are said to be greatly confused about President Nixon's actual position on school desegregation. And well they might be. In recent days the administration's course has zigged and zagged like a destroyer under bombing attacks.

Last week the President's press secretary announced that Mr. Nixon believes the same standards for school desegregation should apply in the North and in the South; that he is opposed to involuntary busing to achieve desegregation; and that he favors the concept of neighborhood schools. (Zig).

In the same announcement, however, the press secretary indicated that the President stopped short of endorsing proposed amendments by Sen. John Stennis that would seek to write these sentiments into law. (Zag).

Four days later Leon Panetta, the man in the Department of Health, Education and Welfare who has been the most vigorous enforcer of southern school desegregation, resigned under pressure from Congress — pressure which he said was reflected in the White House. (Zig).

Within minutes after Panetta's resignation, however, the President's press secretary had more word from Mr. Nixon. The President, said his aide, "feels the best education is integrated education. The President does not feel segregated education is good." (Zag).

On the very same day, Congressman Gerald Ford, the President's leader in the House, said he favored two amendments to an appropriations bill that would prevent the use of federal funds to deny children "freedom of choice" or to enable school districts to bus children involuntarily. (Zig).

But the President's own Secretary of Health, Education and Welfare told the House Rules Committee that he was opposed to the same amendments. (Zag).

While all this was going on, the Senate was debating the Stennis amendment that would require the North to desegregate just as fully as the South. Sen. Scott, who breakfasts with the President nearly every morning, promptly introduced a bill which he said was backed by the President—and southerners pointed out that the Scott (or the President's) bill would destroy the intent of the Stennis amendment. It would require very little desegregation in the North. (Zag).

Sen. John Tower, Republican from Texas, denied that the Scott amendment was supported by the President. Sen. Tower said that Bryce Harlow, the President's own counselor, had said that "This substitute does not have the imprimatur of the White House." (Zig).

Sen. Scott, outraged, consulted the White House. He was soon able to produce a letter from Mr. Harlow which said, "Your amendment is administration language, preferred in existing circumstances over the original or amended Stennis amendment." (Zag).

But the letter also said that "other approaches would also accord with the President's basic object — equal treatment under the law—to the degree that they would give validation to *de facto* segregation in the South in the same degree that it is constitutionally permissible in the rest of the country." (Zig).

For a President who has an apparently unbreakable habit of saying, "Now let me make one thing perfectly clear," Mr. Nixon has managed to render the administration's policy on school desegregation perfectly indecipherable.

Small wonder that Senators Scott and Griffin are confused. They must now agree with James Reston of *The New York Times* who once wrote that Mr. Nixon "could steer between Scylla and Charibdis and carry both precincts."

Arkansas Gazette.

Little Rock, Ark., February 21, 1970

SOME DETAILS — important details, to be sure — remain to be settled in the differing versions of segregationist amendments that were added this week, in House and Senate, to the appropriations bills for the federal Department of Health, Education and Welfare.

It is perfectly clear, however, that the gravest injury has been done to national policy on racial integration and equal rights. Indeed, what has happened finally is that both the legislative and executive branches of the government have largely abandoned the cause of civil rights and racial equality.

What happened this time around was that the Senate joined the House in the game of hooking segregationist riders to the HEW money bill. The Senate adopted two key amendments, one purporting to require equal application of desegregation laws everywhere *"without regard to the cause or origin"* of segregation at issue, the other forbidding HEW to require bus transportation of students in order to "alter racial composition" of a school.

The first, or "Stennis," amendment purports to equate de facto school segregation — which is the circumstantial segregation of housing patterns — with de jure segregation, which is the artificial, systematic imposition of segregation by law. The one amendment gives HEW a perfect excuse to abandon all inforcement, because it could not possibly break up de facto school segregation nationwide. The other apparently forbids HEW to require any kind of bus transportation in desegregation planning.

All the Nixon administration has wanted is an excuse to abandon its diminishing effort in Southern school integration. The effort, in fact, has grown so weak — with Secretary Finch himself being undermined by Nixon's agents in the Department — that Leon Panetta, the civil rights division's director, finally resigned this week in a climactic confrontation with the White House.

The emasculation of HEW is now complete. Its leading enforcer of desegregation requirements has been forced out. Congress has sharply restricted HEW's authority to act in any case. In Congress, the critical defections this time were among Northern Democrats in the Senate — and the most dreadful responsibility lies upon Senator Abraham Ribicoff of Connecticut, who was taken in by the Stennis amendment and joined cause with the Senate's segregationist gang. The administration, for its part, played its usual clever game of pitting both sides against the middle, but seeing to it that the "Southern strategy" prevailed in the end.

* * *

SO IT IS that the nation has come full circle back to 1954, when the Supreme Court took its stand — alone among the three branches — in declaring that all Americans, regardless of color, are equal under the Constitution. How far we have regressed from the crest of 1964, the year of the floodtide in civil rights, when the national conscience had at last been awakened after generations!

Now the conscience of the nation sleeps again, and the courts stand alone again, abandoned by a craven Congress and a cynical president.

It is up to the courts now, as it was in 1954, to preserve and defend the rights of the minority. Indeed, the burden on the courts is all the more formidable, for, from every indication, it is the courts that will determine now whether the Second Reconstruction, like the first, comes to the same dead end. Their strength, as ever, is in the Constitution.

Daily Defender

Chicago, Ill., February 28, 1970

Public school desegregation as ordered by the U. S. Supreme Court in its 1954 decision is today threatened with counter measures that aim at reducing it to nothing more than a thin paper requirement. The Stennis Amendment, which passes under the guise of uniformity of application of the desegregation order, is a veiled attempt to undermine by legislative fiat the very structure of the court's directives in the assignment of races in school districts throughout the nation.

The Stennis Plan would make school desegregation applicable with equal force North and South. De facto segregation which prevails in the North rests upon perpetuity of residential bias which follows the gerrymandering of school districts by racist-minded school boards.

De jure segregation below the Mason and Dixon Line, which is vouchsafed by 200 years of anti-social mores is the measure by which the South wants to preserve its ethnic superiority by keeping the Negro at armlength.

The distinction between the two categories of racial bias is one of georgraphy, not of substance. Segregation under whatever name or rationable it may be described. The ultimate objective of the Stennis Plan is not equalization of the procedural p r o c e s s, but a means to get the North to converge its forces along with those of the South on a single target: School Desegregation.

The double-barreled convergence is intended to wipe out the 1954 desegregation order in all its ramifications and implications. Without the support of the Executive branch of the government, t h e present Court, already weakened by the absence of outstanding liberals, will not dare resist the challenge of its authority.

That's the meaning of the Stennis Amendment which the Senate has approved and which President Nixon has endorsed. It is crystal clear that the President is part of the conspiracy to cancel out the purpose and intent of public school racial balance, heighten white supremacy and by the same token keep the Negro down as a second class citizen. In so doing, the Nixon Administration is repudiating the Supreme Court and the moral commitments of three previous Administrations.

Thus a nation that boasts of being indivisible is dashing itself upon the rock of racism which is bound to s p l i t asunder. Mr. Nixon is building a legacy of ill-will which will haunt the Republican Party for years to come and which will damage the N e g r o cause beyond redemption.

Amsterdam News

New York, N.Y., February 28, 1970

The news from Washington grows grimmer and grimmer as far as blacks are concerned.

President Nixon's vow to bring the country closer together seems to have been directed towards the South and the South alone.

The bid for the lowering of our voices seems to have been meant for everyone but Vice President Agnew, whose strident pronouncements clang out every week against just about everything blacks, the poor and other minorities have held out hope for in the new decade.

The Stennis-backed move for uniform enforcement of school integration across the nation is nothing more than a slick trick sponsored by Southern legislators to insure the slowing down of school desegregation in the South. It will do, passed however, with the compliance of the White House. It will do nothing on the other hand to insure desegregation in the North.

The smokescreen of busing to insure desegregation has obscured the whole issue, since it has long been an established fact that the South bussed white and black children long, long distances in order to maintain segregated schools.

Nevertheless, the White House has now named a conservative on the school desegregation issue to head the staff designated to aid Southern school districts "struggling" with court-ordered desegregation.

The man, Robert C. Mardian, has already criticized such tactics as "school desegregation plans requiring inordinate busing of children".

The NAACP last week pointed out this "new and strange combination of enemies: the Southern segregationist die-hards, the President of the United States, and advocates of racial separatism", calling them an "unholy combination" joined to slow the advancement of the black American.

It certainly seems to be just that. And the news from Washington grows grimmer and grimmer.

THE MINNEAPOLIS STAR

Minneapolis, Minn., February 21, 1970

THE STENNIS amendment designed to apply federal school desegregation guidelines uniformly throughout the country—irrespective of whether segregation is caused by law, custom or happenstance—promises to put the country and some of its loftier concepts to a stringent test.

The amendment, passed by the Senate, still has to go to the House and the President. How it would be applied, if it is adopted, is still being debated. But it is clear that many of its supporters feel it will soften federal desegregation efforts in the South because desegregation in the big cities of the North, which could be accomplished only by massive busing, would be too costly and, more important, politically impossible.

Meanwhile, the House has passed a measure prohibiting forced busing. If that move is successful, then uniform application of desegregation guidelines, as called for by the Stennis rider, would seem likely to amount to very little application at all.

What happens then to the melting pot theory of America—the concept that this singularly favored nation could take people of varied ethnic backgrounds and transform them by some beautiful red, white and blue alchemy into unhyphenated Americans? Has the fire gone out?

Integration is not just going to happen in this generation or maybe in the next or next. If it occurs, it will be as the result of conscious public and governmental design and effort—including busing, vastly improved education, innovative and courageous housing programs, employment opportunities and presidential and congressional leadership.

The Des Moines Register

Des Moines, Iowa, February 21, 1970

The U.S. Senate has adopted the amendment offered by Senator John Stennis (Dem., Miss.) for equal enforcement of racial desegregation of schools, North and South. The amendment (to the school aid authorization bill) would require federal officials to apply the same guidelines "uniformly in all regions" for eliminating de facto segregation (caused by housing patterns) as for eliminating de jure segregation (created by law).

Stennis, expects his amendment to have little direct impact on school segregation in the North. He hopes to generate Northern resistance which will slow school desegregation in the South. Action against de facto segregation is likely to be slow. Neither Congress nor the federal courts have declared it illegal or unconstitutional.

Southern charges of "Northern hypocrisy" on school desegregation hit home. The school segregation caused by racial discrimination in housing is as real as that caused by official action in school assignments.

However, the federal courts have acted against presumed de facto segregation where they found that school boards perpetuated segregation by drawing attendance lines or by locating new buildings on sites which perpetuated segregation by racial neighborhoods. A state court judge in California last week ruled that such actions by the Los Angeles School Board contributed to school segregation which "was not, is not de facto. It is de jure."

The U.S. Supreme Court declared school segregation by law unconstitutional in 1954. It ordered its elimination with "all deliberate speed" in 1955. Congress finally created federal machinery for enforcement (the most effective: denial of federal aid) in 1964. And the court closed the last escape hatch for avoiding integration in 1968 when it said that phony "freedom of choice" plans under which black children were still "choosing" all-black schools were unacceptable.

The federal courts were directed to eliminate "root and branch" the vestiges of the South's old dual schools. In some Southern cities they have ordered busing to overcome segregation which, though it originated in law, is now as much related to housing patterns as that in Northern cities. But the courts are forbidden by the 1964 Civil Rights Act from requiring busing to correct de facto segregation.

The Administration acknowledged this anomaly by endorsing, as a substitute for the Stennis amendment, a measure proposed by Senator Hugh Scott (Rep., Pa.) which would accept de facto segregation in the South as well as the North until such time as the courts might declare it unconstitutional.

Stennis rejected this. In many Southern districts school segregation is unrelated to residential patterns. (The desegregation court order for Natchez, Miss., simply assigns children to the nearest school.) So the Scott proposal would not help them avoid desegregation.

Some Northern liberals also objected. They said the measure would be a further barrier to efforts to overcome existing Northern school segregation. The measure lost.

We disagree with the purpose of Senator Stennis's amendment, but he raises a valid issue. The federal government should become more vigorous against Northern racial discrimination. Congress needs to provide clear statutes directing this and should establish civil rights enforcement staffs of a size equal to this task.

But it need not declare a recess in the 15-year-old battle against the evils of segregation by law to do this.

The Courier-Journal

Louisville, Ky., February 24, 1970

WATCH WHAT WE DO, not what we say, Attorney General Mitchell admonished a questioner of the administration's civil rights policy a few months ago. Those of us who have attempted to reconcile deeds with words in the year just past are deeply disheartened about both.

The deeds of last week wrecked a ten-year effort to bring some measure of equality to the nation's schools. Patterns of housing in the North made this a difficult and frustrating exercise but the effort in most cases was at least an honest one. Throughout most of the South obstruction and defiance kept dual school systems largely unchanged. There were a few shining exceptions.

Last week with the passage of the Whitten amendment in the House and the Stennis amendment in the Senate, stubborn white Southerners were told that the heat was off. In spite of the Supreme Court, including the panel headed by Mr. Nixon's choice; in spite of the patient efforts of federal education officials, the South now has the right to keep its double and unequal school system at least until the North manages to solve the far more difficult questions of housing and social segregation which are the real keys to equal schooling.

During this long tussle the role of the President has been demeaning and hypocritical. There was much talk of hypocrisy stirred up by the odd speech of Senator Abraham Ribicoff who would have it that the hypocrites were congregated up North. The President's record on the issue of school desegregation can set a model for hypocrites on both sides of the Mason-Dixon line.

In the autumn of 1968 when Mr. Nixon was a candidate, points out The Washington Post, the Whitten amendment was presenting its annual appearance. On its surface it is merely a plea that the Department of Education be forbidden to use its funds in such a way as to force children to attend schools not of their parents' choice, for the provision of forced busing or for the closing of certain schools. What it actually does is to prevent HEW from carrying out the provisions of the Civil Rights Act or the several directives of the Supreme Court.

So, in 1968 Candidate Nixon sent his friend Melvin Laird to the House Republicans to say that he—Mr. Nixon—was against the Whitten amendment and that he hoped they would vote against it. In 1969 when Mr.

Whitten returned with his amendment, Attorney General Mitchell informed House members that Mr. Nixon was, in fact, not opposed and so it passed the House.

Mr. Finch, Secretary of HEW, returned to the battle in the Senate, saying that yes, the administration did oppose the amendment. He and Minority Leader Hugh Scott worked diligently to get the Senate to drop the amendment and substitute one less damaging. But this year, Education Commissioner James E. Allen Jr. was publicly contradicted by the President's press secretary after he assured a Senate subcommittee that the administration opposed the amendment.

Mr. Nixon, you will notice, has not said a word. His press secretary Ronald Ziegler allowed it to be known in Key Biscayne that Mr. Nixon also was partial to Senator Stennis's companion amendments to the Senate bill. To make it unmistakable, the White House ordered the harsh and insulting firing, at a moment's notice, of HEW's enforcement officer, Leon Panetta, who had lobbied against the Stennis amendment under the mistaken impression that his President opposed it.

"Watch what we do, not what we say." It is hard to decide which is the more disillusioning.

The Washington Post

Washington, D.C., February 22, 1970

It was not just the public that found itself completely baffled by the end of the week as to what was going on in the Senate on the subject of school desegregation. Rarely has there been more confusion—*de jure* and *de facto*, as it were, or deliberate and inadvertent—than that which marked the Senate debate over John Stennis's amendment calling for equal application of desegregation law in the North and South. What, after all, could be wrong with that? Was not the North, in Senator Ribicoff's phrase, guilty of "monumental hypocrisy" in its attitude toward the racial concentration in its own schools?

The answer to the second question is, Yes—but not in a way that has much, if anything, to do with what was going on in the Senate. For in relation to the pitch the Southerners were making, and as the term "monumental" goes, it was to compare Grant's Tomb with the Mausoleum at Halicarnassus. Consider only Senator Talmadge's observation that there has been no officially-imposed racial segregation in the South since the Supreme Court outlawed the practice sixteen years ago. It could get you to wondering on what grounds, then, Attorney General Mitchell, who is not exactly in the vanguard of the civil rights movement, had brought suit against the state of Georgia to desegregate its schools in the fall of 1969.

To untangle some of the mysteries attending this question of equal application of the law, it might be well to consider, first, what Federal law currently is; second, the way in which it already applies to the North; and, third, what the Stennis amendment (passed in the Senate) could or could not do to affect the situation. Elsewhere on this page, an excerpt from the debate, goes to the same points.

First, for the law. It is embodied in several Supreme Court decisions, the Civil Rights Act of 1964, and various measures related to Federal aid to education. The court has held that it is unconstitutional for governmental authorities at any level in the public school system to segregate children "solely on the basis of race." To do so, of course, was the publicly stated, official practice of Southern (and some Northern) school systems prior to the Brown decision in 1954. Ten years later, the Civil Rights Act of 1964 incorporated the court's views on the illegality of discrimination of this kind and made compliance with those views a condition of receiving Federally-dispensed money:

"No person in the United States shall, on the ground of race, color, or national origin, be excluded from participation in, be denied the benefits of, or be subjected to discrimination under any program or activity receiving Federal financial assistance."

The passage of this law preceded by only a short time the passage of the Federal aid to education act and similar Great Society legislation which, for the first time, made significant sums of money theoretically available to (and withdrawable from) state operated schools and other institutions that had continued to defy the court's ruling against racial discrimination. That was when the fuss over the "guidelines" hotted up. Defiant Southern school districts, wanting their money, attempted to meet the Civil Rights Act standard merely by saying they were desegregated in the sense that they no longer publicly espoused discrimination ("freedom of choice"); HEW, which had the funds to dispense, countered that in numerous districts only the rhetoric had changed; the Supreme Court, in 1968, then took another step in the law: it ruled that so-called "freedom of choice" or desegregation by proclamation, was not in itself sufficient evidence of compliance with the law. It thus gave HEW authority to apply its own measures of good faith or lack of it in the districts under consideration.

How does all or any of this affect the North? It is important to note, first, that where official intent to segregate children in schools "solely on the basis of race" has been established in the North—usually a covert intent, but an intent, nonetheless—those school districts have come under the same pressures and orders as those in operation in the South. Most of the more famous "de facto" cases in the North and the West, in fact, have been prosecuted and resolved on "de jure" grounds. So in that sense the law already is equally applicable; it's just that people have assumed that any ruling against a Northern or Western district must, of its nature, be a "de facto" ruling.

"De facto" itself is a term that is losely applied to cover any situation in which official intent to discriminate has not been perceived, but where large racial concentrations exist in the schools. Some lower courts have ruled that such concentration in itself is a form of illegal "segregation." Most have ruled otherwise. And more important, the Supreme Court has declined to take any view on the question. The Civil Rights Act, however, does take a view, specifically distinguishing between racial concentration caused by discriminatory state action and racial concentration that is not the apparent result of such official action. It has forbidden the federal government to use its funds merely to establish racial balance where no state discrimination can be found. The Stennis amendment, being merely a kind of policy statement, will thus have little practical effect in bringing about "desegregation" in the North, since the court's silence and the Civil Rights Act's directive render it almost without legal meaning.

What it can provide, however, is yet another weapon for resisting districts in the South. They will be able to attempt a new stalling maneuver on the grounds that they do not have to move any faster than, say, Cleveland. So with adroit legal manipulation (at which they have never been slouches) they may gain a little more time. We should be clear whom we are talking about here. Of some 4,470 school districts in seventeen states where the dual, black and white system had some official standing, only a few hundred (mostly rural) districts are still going through the agonies with the Federal government over their refusal to dismantle their dual school systems. Those are Senator Stennis's clients; they are what the fuss has been all about.

Still, we may all owe the Senator a debt of gratitude. Only this skirmish could have focused national attention on the *real* problems in the North (and in some cities of the South, which have complied with law but found their schools "resegregated" on a "de facto" or neighborhood basis). So now we can get down to considering the authentic questions—which plans work and which plans don't; how, without proving discriminatory intent, you can move children around on the basis of their skin color and not establish precedents or practices that are as dangerous as they might be well-intended; whether racial concentration, in itself, can be officially stigmatized without creating state doctrine that a given number of black children in a school automatically defines that school as one that is defective; what the real sources and dimensions of the problem are—and what its practical solution. On account of Senator Stennis's effort this week (though despite his opposition to the idea), there will now for the first time be a select Senate committee charged with making a serious and responsible inquiry into these questions, questions the Congress has done its best to ignore over the years. That was the one really useful thing to come out of the Senate debate.

Pittsburgh Post-Gazette

Pittsburgh, Pa., February 20, 1970

WHATEVER its ultimate fate — and legislative hurdles remain — the Stennis amendment to a federal education aid law which the Senate approved this week serves the useful purpose of focusing attention upon racial integration in the schools as a national rather than a regional problem.

The amendment states that "it is the policy of the United States that guidelines and criteria" governing the distribution of elementary and secondary educational funds "shall be applied uniformly in all regions of the United States in dealing with conditions of segregation by race whether de jure or de facto in the schools of the local educational agencies of any state without regard to the origin or cause of such segregation."

Since this is put as a statement of policy rather than an outright law, there is doubt that it could be enforced even if it should find clear sailing through the remainder of the legislative waters. But the intent of Senator Stennis, a Mississippi Democrat, is clear enough. He hopes that his amendment would, by shifting an enforcement burden to the North, slow down or end federal enforcement of laws against de jure (by law) segregation in the South.

De jure segregation has been ruled out by Supreme Court decisions and by statutes reaching as far back as 1954. The problem has been and will continue to be enforcement. We think the Nixon administration should not back away from enforcement whatever the fate of the Stennis amendment.

If de facto segregation resulting from housing patterns, should become illegal, it would, as Senator Scott has said, impose a tremendous new problem of enforcement. And yet to argue that it couldn't be done is to concede the truth of Senator Ribicoff's recent charge that this country has a double standard on racial integration of the schools.

Congress is dealing with an enormously complicated and highly emotional issue. The issue does not lend itself to easy solutions, as educators and public officials all over this country are painfully aware. In fact there may be no solution to the racial problem short of a moral and spiritual revolution which has not yet been evidenced.

This is not to throw up our hands in despair. Much progress has been made in integrating the schools of the South and we expect to see more. We would hope, too, to see more movement toward an end to de facto segregation in the North. There is no room for self-righteousness wherever this problem exists. It would be much easier of solution if all of us were more willing to practice what we preach.

The Birmingham News

Birmingham, Ala., February 20, 1970

With the House of Representatives voting to ban busing to achieve racial balance and to give sanction to freedom-of-choice as a method to effect school desegregation, only one day after the Senate voted to require equal desegregation standards nationwide, the country has passed a milestone in the years-long attempt to resolve the "how" and "how much" school integration questions.

The Senate's passage of the Stennis amendment to the educational appropriations bill won't automatically end all the confusion or solve all the problems attendant to school integration.

For one thing, the amendment still has a way to go before it becomes law. It will have to survive a Senate-House conference and then be approved by both houses as part of a final bill. (As the House-passed amendments to the HEW bill must yet pass the Senate.)

For another, Sen. Stennis's proposal to have school desegregation standards apply nationwide, with no distinction made between de jure and de facto segregation, would not directly relieve pressure on the South to take steps—such as closing of some schools and long-distance transfers of teachers and students to achieve racial balance—which a majority of Southerners (including many who do not object at all to the principle of desegregation) consider unreasonable and impractical. The House measures, if they survive, would attack this point more directly.

What it *would* do—and the Mississippi senator made it plain that this was his motivation—is subject the other parts of the country to the same kind of pressure. Sen. Stennis and other Southern governors and congressmen believe that if that is done, there will be a great deal more understanding of and sympathy for the South's position than there has seemed to be in the past.

Carrying that a step farther, they believe that if Northern and Western districts are faced with to the same requirements Southern districts have been ordered to accept, the nationwide reaction will be in the direction of relaxation of some of the requirements—not a move to go back to segregated schools, but in support of neighborhood schools and freedom of choice.

That the Southerners' campaign to bring the other parts of the country under the same gun whose barrel the South has been staring down is having some effect can be seen in the fact that the Senate would pass the Stennis amendment at all. Until now, it wouldn't have touched it with a ten-foot pole.

Just as clearly the House of Representatives wouldn't have passed the anti-busing a n d freedom-of-choice amendments it tacked onto the HEW appropriations bill yesterday if there had not been a significant change in Congress' appreciation of the South's point of view.

One of the more curious comments on the Stennis amendment came from Sen. Hugh Scott, the Senate Republican leader, whose compromise proposal, which Southerners said would have been meaningless, was rejected before Stennis's was approved.

If the amendment becomes law in its present form and if efforts are made to enforce it, Scott said, it would take all the troops in the country and we'd have to bring the ones home from Vietnam.

The Pennsylvanian seemed to be saying that the North and the West would resist vigorously any attempt to require of them the same thing that Southerners have had to live with. If those requirements are so unacceptable to the rest of the country, then why should there be any surprise that they have been resisted in the South as well?

We all will be better off, it seems to us, when the emphasis shifts back from precise racial balance to provision of the best quality education for all children, black and white, on an equal basis, with each student or his parents free to choose the school he wishes to attend and the state using its resources to make that school the very best possible.

Newsday

Long Island, N.Y., February 20, 1970

With the adoption of the Stennis amendment, this country's backward march to the fifties—the pre-1954 fifties—quickens its pace. The South now has, in addition to its own transparently obstructionist devices, the sense of the U.S. Senate that it need not take integration orders too seriously so long as segregation continues in the North. Moreover, it has the increasingly overt backing of the President. Not only did Mr. Nixon's hedged but unmistakable endorsement provide the final impetus for Senate approval of the Stennis proposal, but he added to that an anti-busing statement couched in the sort of code-words ("neighborhood schools," "quality education") that backlash candidates usually employ to signal their devotion to the cause of lily-white schools.

Except as a question of convenience, it has never been demonstrated that there was any particular educational advantage in sending children to schools in their own neighborhoods. That is a myth dear to confirmed segregationists and faint-hearted integrationists. Southern states have not hesitated to bus white children by the thousands, or to bus black children over 20 miles. in the interests of keeping the schools segregated. In any number of Northern cities and suburbs children regularly ride buses or subways to schools, public or private. Busing presents formidable problems in some places, by the nature of the local demography. In other places it works. It is scarcely in and of itself the evil that segregationists and their comforters would have us believe, and for all its drawbacks it remains one of the few realistic tools for redistributing a school population along racially balanced lines.

Even more disturbing than this latest token of the President's infatuation with the South was the stampede of non-Southern Senators that helped pass the Stennis amendment by a vote of 56 to 36. No less than 30 of the approving votes came from well above and beyond the Mason-Dixon line. In approving a measure that would trigger endless wrangling and delay by insisting on uniform application of desegregation laws, the Senate majority was acknowledging the sway of a potent new constituency. They have been variously characterized as "the forgotten man," "middle America," "the silent majority." More accurately, they are the great frightened majority, conservatives, moderates and liberals from all corners of the country, who first began to coalesce in the sixties, when the reality of the black man's quest for equal rights started hitting too close to home.

In the seventies, the new constituency grows bolder as it senses its power. In an election year, any major political figure defies them at his peril. So the backward march goes forward, to the inglorious past. Small wonder that Sen. Stennis of Mississippi could hail the passage of his regressive bill as "a landmark . . . a new gateway . . . a turning point."

NIXON DEFINES SCHOOL SEGREGATION: DE JURE ILLEGAL; DE FACTO UPHELD

In a 10,000-word text issued to newsmen at the White House March 24, President Nixon, for the first time since his election, set forth Administration policy on school desegregation.

Differentiating between *de jure* segregation—that which is officially imposed—and *de facto*—that which exists as a result of residential housing patterns, Nixon said it was his "personal belief" that the landmark Supreme Court decision (*Brown vs. Board of Education, 1954*) outlawing "separate but equal" educational facilities "was right in both constitutional and human terms." He pledged that the Administration would "carry out the law fully and fairly" with regard to de jure segregation of pupils and teachers, relying on the "good faith" of Southern officials to comply.

However, he asserted that until the courts provided further guidance, *de facto* segregation, though undesirable in practice, remained constitutional in theory. He said that student busing would "not be required . . . for the purpose of achieving racial balance." Instead, he proposed administrative remedies, and announced that the Administration would allocate $1.5 billion over the next two years to assist school districts throughout the country that wished to eliminate *de facto* segregation on their own initiative, or to remedy the effects of racial imbalance by providing supplementary educational facilities for students in segregated schools.

THE BLADE

Toledo, Ohio, March 29, 1970

THE FIRST question raised by President Nixon's statement on school desegregation is why he thought it necessary to make it. "We are not backing away," he said. "The constitutional mandate will be enforced." Why should a president need to say that he intends to support the Constitution?

The answer, of course, is that the so-called southern strategy of the Nixon administration, with its transparent attempts to attract and hold the support of the South, have resulted in a widespread suspicion that the Administration might, indeed, be backsliding on the enforcement of the 1954 Supreme Court decision. In defense, Mr. Nixon now says flatly that he is not, and this is good. But he can hardly complain if his statement itself is received with skepticism among civil rights forces.

Insofar as the substance of the statement is concerned, there is much in it that is reasonable and straightforward, given the vast complexity of the subject. He rightly distinguishes between the de jure segregation of the South, where children were racially separated by law, and the de facto segregation of the North, where the neighborhood school reflects the housing patterns of the area it serves. The President further stated that the Government will not try to establish an arbitrary racial balance for the schools, nor order bussing on a large scale to achieve this goal.

Mr. Nixon pledged his Administration to eradicate deliberate school segregation throughout the country, including northern districts where gerrymandering and other techniques are used solely to keep white and Negro children apart. As far as the South is concerned, it would not be inconsistent with this policy to require some bussing. A recent story in The Blade pointed out that some southern districts have bussed Negro children up to 93 miles a day (past white schools) in order to get them to Negro schools. It certainly would not be unfair to require such districts to bus for the purpose of achieving desegregation as they have been doing to segregate their school children.

School districts doubtless will welcome the $1.5 billion which the President proposed for a two-year period to help them achieve desegregation, and to improve the quality of education in "racially impacted" schools where de facto segregation exists. Money also is to be provided to support innovations designed to supply "educationally sound interracial experiences" for children in such schools. The specifics are far from clear, but presumably the President means that avoiding the demonstrated disadvantages and complications of massive bussing or arbitrary racial-balance quotas as answers to de facto segregation does not necessarily mean permanently accepting the status quo.

Mr. Nixon's declared goal of a free and open society is a matter of established national policy. What remains to be seen is how well the rhetoric which the President used to outline the objectives will be matched by actions toward achieving them.

The Philadelphia Inquirer

Philadelphia, Pa., March 25, 1970

President Nixon's statement detailing his views on problems relating to racial integration and segregation in public schools is carefully worded in a manner that, perhaps intentionally, allows a variety of interpretations.

He is realistic, scrupulously so, in documenting all the obstacles, both legal and practical, that stand in the way of ending quickly and totally the widespread separation of America's schoolchildren on the basis of race.

But he seems to be rather matter of fact, almost eager, in his readiness to concede that all such obstacles are insurmountable.

The Inquirer agrees, up to a point, with much that the President says in regard to the utter impracticalities of attempting drastic measures to abolish completely de facto segregation in the public schools.

We believe he is correct in drawing a distinction between de jure segregation and de facto segregation.

De jure segregation, declared unconstitutional by the Supreme Court, involves the operation of a dual system of public schools with mandatory separation of pupils on the basis of race.

De facto segregation, which has never been declared unconstitutional by the Supreme Court, is the result of housing patterns which cause neighborhood schools to be entirely or predominantly of one race.

We support the President in his view that massive busing of pupils, of whatever race, from one neighborhood to another, for purposes of attaining some arbitrary standard of racial balance, ought not to be required.

We welcome his proposals for federal aid to improve the quality of education in substandard schools, although the one and a half billion dollars that he proposes to spend over a two-year period will achieve no miracles.

We indorse wholeheartedly his declaration that civil rights laws, as all laws, should be applied equally in all parts of the country—provided this sound principle is not distorted and subverted so that it provides an excuse for non-enforcement.

Despite its grim logic and its undeniable truths there seems to be something lacking in the President's statement.

The substance of his arguments, when all is said and digested, seems to be that a racially divided America is acceptable. He seems to embrace the separate - but - equal doctrine.

We believe the President might well have given more attention to the need for trying to overcome obstacles instead of yielding to them.

The New York Times

New York, N. Y., March 25, 1970

President Nixon raised new hopes in the preamble of his statement on desegregation when he pledged that the painstaking work of a decade and a half will not be undermined and reaffirmed his "personal belief" that the 1954 Supreme Court ruling was right "in both constitutional and human terms."

But the promise of his initial appeal was not sustained, and by the time the 8,000 words had run their course, it was difficult to see how the document could succeed in reducing "the present confusion."

That confusion is the result of the Administration's own inconsistencies. It is not likely to be diminished by the President's warning to local communities not to provoke the lower courts into conflicting or "extreme" rulings, when it was the deliberate policy of the Justice Department itself to shift the burden of enforcement from administrative guidelines to litigation in the courts.

The President pointed with pride to progress in the South; but he ignored the fact that these gains are largely attributable to the guidelines. Yet, the guidelines are dead, killed by the Administration and now buried by the President.

The most tangible contribution of the President's message is in its effort to clarify the differences between de jure and de facto segregation, the former largely confined to the South, the latter characteristic of the North. Mr. Nixon made it clear that the South cannot be allowed to delay and obstruct until such time as Northern cities are fully integrated.

"Words ring empty without deeds," the President said. "In government, words ring even emptier without dollars." This is precisely why it is difficult to assess Mr. Nixon's promise of special funds to be used in what he calls "racially impacted" schools. Since the money is to be diverted from other domestic allocations, who can tell whether this will merely be a reshuffling of dollars for the already shaky school subsidy?

Mr. Nixon's philosophy of education is divided against itself. He complains that past policy has demanded too much of the schools by asking them to accomplish "a social transformation." But despite his limited view of the schools' mission, the President admits that school desegregation is most important to national "unity and progress."

Even within the limited and occasionally contradictory mandate of the President's statement, progress is possible. The question is ultimately whether he allows his lieutenants to exploit its doubts or expects them to advance its commitment. Mr. Nixon said: "This matter of good faith is critical." It remains up to the Administration to earn that faith.

THE KNICKERBOCKER NEWS
••• UNION-STAR •••

Albany, N. Y., March 26, 1970

President Nixon has made a valiant effort to sort out, as it were, court opinions, expressions of national will and actual practices of his own administration in the matter of school integration. That done, he sought to give direction to the course his administration will follow on schools in the year ahead.

He did all this in a message of more than 8,000 words. It is a complex message. As is common in many presidential statements, it proclaims the administration's desire to be, "perfectly clear" without quite accomplishing that laudable aim. It is a message that will be studied deeply in many quarters and interpreted diversely. No one yet really knows whether it is a message of obfuscation or a great message. It could prove to be the latter.

It reveals President Nixon as a man who puts limits of practicality on the horizons of the idealist. That is not always a bad thing to do.

Thus he appears to revert to the "deliberate speed" concept of the Supreme Court in school desegregation, although the court has since indicted that deliberate speed should have brought the nation more rapidly to school integration than is the case.

Likewise he appears to revert—in part at least—to the Supreme Court ruling of "separate but equal" schools, a ruling that gave way to later rulings ordering integration.

Civil rights leaders are distressed, contending the President thereby is acquiescing in the continuation of segregation. His supporters would argue that the President is recognizing that the de facto segregation of the north — and in some instances in the south — is going to continue, even though under court order the segregation by law in the South is being eliminated. And from that premise they observe since there will continue to be black schools and white schools, the practical President is seeking to make the black schools as good as the white schools. He would do that with money and with a ban on the segregation of teachers everywhere.

One of the most controversial elements in the President's statement rests in his continuing opposition to busing as a means of achieving integration. The President opts for the neighborhood school concept. Here he can expect the support of all those suburban whites who would object to the busing of their children to a ghetto area or even to an in between area and, quite possibly, the support of slum dwellers who prefer that their younger children, at least, receive their schooling close to home. He will be opposed by those who view integration as a part of education, and school integration as an essential first step to the national goal of a truly integrated America.

Yet even in this matter of neighborhood schools, the President takes care to warn against the gerrymandering of schools to achieve segregation.

What will follow these not entirely clear guidelines of the President? No one knows today. But we do know that their interpretation provides a test of the administration's good faith and good will. We remain hopeful.

St. Louis Globe-Democrat
St. Louis, Mo., March 25, 1970

President Nixon's critics can no longer say they do not know where he stands on desegregation.

Mr. Nixon's 10,000-word statement outlining his position is said to be the most detailed ever given by an American President.

In our estimation, it revealed the President has been doing an excellent job in desegregating United States schools within the framework of the Constitution.

He has rejected the extremist, desegrate-all-schools-now approach for a more balanced program that takes into account such limiting factors as housing patterns, the effect on the educational program and the welfare of the children involved.

In general, the Nixon Administration's accomplishments to date in desegregation, when weighed against those of previous Administrations, must be rated excellent.

For example, in the last year the number of black children attending southern schools that are complying with desegregation orders has doubled—from less than 600,000 to nearly 1,200,000, which represents 40 per cent of the Negro student population in that region.

Mr. Nixon's critics have avoided all mention of such progress, usually resorting to smear attacks and innuendo rather than the facts.

They resent the fact that the President rejects the completely unsound and impractical idea of trying to eliminate de facto segregation that results from housing patterns.

In his statement Tuesday the President said "deliberate racial segregation of pupils by official policy is unlawful, wherever it exists" and must be eliminated.

But he asserted that de facto segregation "resulting genuinely from housing patterns" is not by itself cause for federal enforcement actions.

He also pointed out that "transportation of pupils beyond normal geographic school zones for the purpose of achieving racial balance will not be required."

President Nixon's major surprise was a proposal to spend $1.5 billion to improve the quality of education in all schools, but to concentrate on what he termed "racially impacted" schools and on "equalizing those schools that are furthest behind."

This was an impressive and encouraging statement. It should answer most questions of reasonable Americans who had wanted clarification of the President's views on desegregation.

We believe a great majority of the people will applaud this conscientious, fair-minded approach to a most difficult problem.

THE ROANOKE TIMES

Roanoke, Va., March 27, 1970

President Nixon has said, emphatically, that the Supreme Court's school desegregation mandate—which he recognizes was right in both legal and human terms—will be enforced.

"We are not backing away. . . from the painstaking work of a decade and a half," he has declared.

That a President should have to make such a public affirmation of his duties is, 15 long years after the court first spoke, somewhat incredible. For that, however, Mr. Nixon has himself to blame—himself, his ambiguous past statements on race, his attempts to woo the Deep South's Wallace vote, his whole ill-defined "southern strategy."

In his lengthy, long overdue policy statement on school desegregation, Mr. Nixon manages once again to place himself on nearly all sides of a multi-sided issue. On the face of it, his statement seems unequivocal as it deals with each of the major aspects of the matter. Yet, taken together, it produces new questions and contradictions, and indicates to the country that this administration will do only what is demanded by the Supreme Court — nothing more — in pushing ahead with integration.

Philosophically, it is difficult to quarrel with the President's view that society perhaps asks too much of its educational system when it insists that schools be used not only to educate, but also to accomplish a social transformation. And, pragmatically, it is impossible not to concur in Mr. Nixon's view that "there are limits to the amount of government coercion that can reasonably be used . . (that) with housing patterns what they are in many places in the nation, the sheer numbers of pupils and the distances between schools make full and prompt school integration in every such community impractical."

But, those truths notwithstanding, one wonders if the President is not, once again, following instead of leading, throwing out a few sops to each segment of our society, shaping policy on the basis of what the silent majority thinks it wants rather than on a basis of national interests.

Mr. Nixon insists that the schools must not be used as the lever with which to break down historical patterns of racial separation. Yet, since nothing else seems to work, the schools may in fact offer the only possible way of accelerating a breakdown of separatist attitudes, forcing blacks from the outset to compete with whites, and thus fulfilling what Jack Greenberg, the director-counsel of the NAACP, sees as the very purpose of schools: "to raise a generation according to our national ideals."

Mr. Nixon acknowledges that "we must give the minority child that equal place at the starting line that his parents were denied—and the pride, the dignity, the self-respect, that are the birthright of a free American." Yet, having said that, he slams the door on the whole concept of racial balance in the schools, even though—if we are to believe the education studies—nothing else offers hope of quickly guaranteeing the black child that "equal place."

Like the President, we find nothing in the Constitution, or in the Supreme Court's school opinions, to support the Stennis-Ribicoff view that segregated schools in Chicago ghettos are, like those in a rural Mississippi county, automatically illegal. Several lower courts see it differently, however, and the Supreme Court must resolve the issue quickly.

Moreover, we think the President is exactly right in saying that "where the existing racial separation has not been caused by official action . . . increased integration is and should remain a matter for local determination." Where

Mr. Nixon errs, however, is in refusing to design discretionary grant-in-aid incentives or to use the power of his office in other ways to actively encourage localities to achieve more integration if they can.

Instead of doing this, the President proposes a two-year, $1.5 billion program to try to raise the quality of education in the inner-city schools, North and South. And he does this, seemingly, without blinking an eye, even though a month ago he was telling the country that federal school aid ought not to be further increased without proof that it will achieve results.

In our opinion, enrichment programs can, with proper follow-through, help overcome some of the disadvantages of race, poverty and cultural lag. For large metropolitan communities where racial balance is not feasible, remedial-education programs are in fact essential, however mixed the results to date. Mr. Nixon's support for this concept is therefore praiseworthy, if belated.

What we fail to understand, however, is why the President doesn't desire, additionally, to help s m a l l e r urban communities where total integration is in fact feasible. For if he believes, as he states, that "racial integration in the classroom can be a significant factor in improving the quality of education for the disadvantaged," he ought to be taking positive steps to encourage it, instead of adhering so steadfastly to his neutral, politically safe posture.

Deep South segregationists will find little comfort in the President's statement, thankfully; n e i t h e r, however, will those who feel that the nation's racial crisis now requires a non-judicial recognition that separate schooling for blacks and whites may always be unequal, whether or not it results from official policy, and whether or not compensatory-aid programs are operative.

The Courier-Journal

Louisville, Ky., March 26, 1970

PRESIDENT NIXON'S lengthy statement on school desegregation no doubt achieved the political effect he wanted. Both Southern segregationists and civil-rights leaders are displeased with it. This makes it appear that the President is taking a moderate, "middle-of-the-road" stance.

The trouble is the presidential pronouncement doesn't clarify very much. As a policy it is hard to see what practical effect it will have, how it will affect the present Nixon course.

The President said that *de jure* segregation —that is, segregation that results from a deliberate official policy—must go. The Supreme Court said that some time ago, and so did Congress in 1964. The court has not yet set any guidelines for eliminating *de facto* segregation, which in most instances is caused by housing patterns, and President Nixon therefore concluded that he could do nothing about it administratively. He did propose spending $1.5 billion during the next two

years to improve the quality of education in schools racially segregated because of neighborhood patterns. The money can be helpful, if used in the right way. It is not clear, however, just how it will be spent. Moreover, this is not an attack on the problem of *de facto* segregation. Rather, it is an acceptance of it as an insoluble problem. It may very well be insoluble until housing patterns change, and so far the administration has shown no willingness to spend the money and effort necessary to break up the ghettos.

The President made the ritual condemnation of busing as a remedy for *de facto* segregation—he didn't say how we felt about the use of busing to preserve segregation—and endorsed the concept of the "neighborhood school," whatever that means.

When it comes to the problem of *de jure* segregation, which is peculiarly a Southern problem, the President's statement is long on promises but short on how they are to be delivered, and what he did say on the subject is disquieting.

He said his administration plans to move against the remaining dual school systems in the South by relying on court orders and the "good faith" efforts of local Southern officials to comply with those orders. In other words, he is abandoning the weapon of cutting off federal funds to non-complying school districts and, in effect, reducing the executive branch's pressure on local school districts to desegregate. This is what has been happening under the Nixon administration; now it is formally declared policy.

Relying on the courts alone to desegregate the public schools means that the process will be slowed. It won't be stopped. Mr. Nixon proudly laid claim to advances in desegregation in the South under his administration. These advances, however, were by and large the result of earlier prodding. The question isn't whether desegregation will proceed, but at what pace.

Plainly, Mr. Nixon will be content with a relatively stately pace.

CHICAGO
Daily Defender

Chicago, Ill., March 30, 1970

The long and tortuous Nixon statement on school desegregation is not an honest attempt at clarification of the befogged school issues. It is a deceptive political document which neither advances the cause of racial school balance nor lessens the emotional resistance to its fulfillment.

The central issue in the whole complex of the school muddle is desegregation. The only way to achieve this objective is by breaking up the all-white and the all-black schools that are widely separated by geography and demography. The process is a simple one: Busing.

The President, however, views this process with alarm. In truth, he makes no convincing plea for integration. He uses the satin slippers of a ballet dancer to tiptoe around the school issue. According to him "integration is no longer seen automatically and necessarily as an unmixed blessing for the Negro, Puerto Rican or Mexican-American child."

He embroiders this indefensible assumption with the statement that "Racial balance has been discovered to be neither a statis nor a finite condition; in many cases it has turned out to be only a way station on the road to resegregation.

The President makes no bones about his opposition to busing as a means of achieving racial balance. His emphasis is on better education for the underprivileged blacks which can be provided at the neighborhood school level. But neighborhood school, which, long ago has been discredited by competent educationists as incompatible with democratic outlook, is a convenient euphemism for segregation either de jure or dé facto.

In short, the crux of the whole Nixon's circuitous logic is that his Administration will not use its police power to enforce the mandates of the courts where compliance becomes a mockery; nor will it alter the systematic erosion of both the spirit and letter of the law on integration.

The best that can be said of the Nixon outline of his policy on the school issue is that it is the classic case of St. George who gives up fighting because there are too many dragons.

The Providence Journal

Providence, R. I., March 29, 1970

Besieged by critics of his civil rights policies throughout most of his time in office, President Nixon has made a commendable effort in his school desegregation statement to clarify a highly complex issue and to set straight the record on where he stands. Even his most determined opponents must credit him for the attempt.

Whether the President has changed any minds is another matter. What emerges from his 8,000-word message is a tone one usually associates with a reasonable man trying to talk sense, engaging in a careful, cautious and somewhat fatherly examination of a national problem that is, of course, highly charged with emotion.

It seems fair to say that anyone interested enough to read the entire message with an open mind and an element of detachment must conclude that Mr. Nixon has achieved partial success in both of his aims: to unravel the legalities involved and to dispel the public's doubt about the White House attitude toward the practicalities of enforcement.

The statement includes an explanation of major court rulings beginning with the 1954 Supreme Court decision in *Brown vs. the Board of Education* and proceeding down to the present. It discusses questions the courts have not spoken on, notably *de facto* segregation—that which is caused by residential patterns. It refers to anti-busing strictures enacted by Congress in the 1960s which, Mr. Nixon says he was advised, "cannot constitutionally be applied to *de jure* (official) segregation."

The statement is most interesting, however, when it touches directly on the position of the chief executive. Several important points become clear:

1. Mr. Nixon is unalterably opposed "to any compulsory busing of pupils beyond normal geographic school zones for the purpose of achieving racial balance."

2. It follows and in effect he so states that he supports the inviolability of the neighborhood school.

3. He will pursue enforcement of court rulings where they leave no doubt as to the means but not beyond. Hence, "federal advice and assistance will be made available on request, but federal officials should not go beyond the requirements of law in attempting to impose their own judgment on the local school district."

While some may applaud the political courage required to make such a comprehensive statement for the record, it is evident the President's dexterity has not deserted him. He has striven for a middle-of-the-road course and in so doing probably has satisfied no one. Certainly he has not extricated himself from controversy nor has he escaped the pitfalls of self-contradiction.

"We are not backing away," he said. "The constitutional mandate will be enforced." Nowhere is there any indication of urgency, however. On the contrary, all signs point to a conciliatory stance and a basic reliance on the courts to bring about desegregation in their own time.

Mr. Nixon points with pride to the gains made in the South in 1969 but ironically it was the determined administrative efforts of the Department of Health, Education and Welfare during the Johnson years that was largely responsible. That course, apparently, has now been set aside.

That Mr. Nixon has pledged 1.5 billion dollars to upgrade schools heavily populated by the disadvantaged is welcome news but one-third will be taken from already undernourished domestic programs; many will wonder if this is not more a symbolic peace offering to alienated black Americans and civil rights advocates in general than a purposeful effort to lessen the deleterious effects of racial isolation.

Clearly Mr. Nixon is committed in principle to ending separate schools for blacks and white, to improving education for all Americans and to healing the North-South divisions brought about by 16 years of footdragging on the desegregation problem.

If there were those who hoped the President would strengthen federal enforcement of the high court's rulings, however, and lash out at the intransigents who espouse continuing delay, they have been sadly disappointed. The President has made it clear that there will be no coercion of Southern segregationists to change their ways. What pressure is applied will come from the courts and if on request the Executive Branch can help, it will do what it can to the letter of the law and no more.

the San Juan Star

San Juan, P. R., March 25, 1970

President Nixon's long-awaited position paper on school segregation, issued Tuesday, was a grab-bag that had something for everyone—particularly the South—while really putting the brakes on the pace of desegregation that began with the historic Supreme Court decision of 1954. The President may claim that he is only reating to the supposed "realities" of today, but he is also building a solid political base in the South. We hope the President is not being derelict in his very real responsibilities to provide moral leadership for the country.

When Nixon revealed Tuesday that he is sharply limiting the types of school segregation he will act against, such a move can be interpreted as moving back the clock. When Nixon also de-emphasized —and criticized by implication — the role of federal enforcement offiers. in favor of new reliance on good faith efforts by local officials to end school discrimination, it can be seen as another administration effort to turn back the clock. And when Nixon can assert that schools have been wrongly burdened with the major role in creating a multiracial society, he is not really grasping the complexity of the racial situation.

To his credit, however, Nixon did reiterate existing doctrine that segregation resulting from past law or official action "must be eliminated at once." But as to the more subtle forms of discrimination, Nixon's statement left much to be desired.

THE MIAMI NEWS

Miami, Fla., March 25, 1970

"There is a constitutional mandate that dual school systems and other forms of de jure segregation be eliminated totally."

If President Nixon had permitted his policy on school desegregation to rest on that statement, he would have done much to end the confusion and frustration that attends the question of quality education for children of all races.

Instead he surrounded that central declaration with an elaborate rationalization against busing — a cop out, the youngsters would call it, in which the rights of the black minority were traded off to quiet the protests of the no longer silent majority.

"But within the framework of that requirement," Mr. Nixon said of the constitutional mandate, "an area of flexibility — a rule of reason — exists, in which school boards, acting in good faith, can formulate plans of desegregation which best suit needs of their own localities."

Well, the courts and the federal government have been intervening for 15 years — since the Brown decision — because school boards have lacked the political courage to act in good faith.

The President's rosy statistic — that in the past year the number of black children attending Southern schools held to be in compliance with the law has doubled — was not achieved through the good faith of school boards, but through the intervention of the federal courts and the Department of Health Education and Welfare.

Now Mr. Nixon intends to soften that intervention. We can only imagine what this will do to the spirit of those school boards and other officials who have crawled out on a limb to comply with the law as it had been interpreted until yesterday.

More important, how will it affect those Negroes who have been urging their people to be patient, on the grounds that the law was finally working in their favor?

The Greenville News

Greenville, S. C., March 25, 1970

First news reports of President Nixon's 10,000-word policy statement on public school desegregation are disquieting to those who had hoped to see emergence of a single, clear national policy on school integration.

Coupled with the Nixon administration's Justice Department threat to initiate statewide legal action against South Carolina and other Southern states the President's policy statement constitutes what amounts to continuation of one set of rules for the South, another for the rest of the nation.

Perhaps a close study of the document, when it is available, will erase that fear. But at this writing it appears the President has fallen into the trap of condemning in de jure (or legalistic) fashion the dual system of integration policy while accepting it de facto (in fact).

Mr. Nixon, who took a single system stance during his campaign by coming out for freedom of choice everywhere, apparently has abandoned that concept, accepting the view that the Supreme Court has outlawed freedom of choice if it does not produce an acceptable degree of school integration. He still objects to massive busing of pupils in order to achieve racial balance in schools and generally favors the neighborhood school concept.

That's fairly acceptable as a national policy, if applied throughout the 50 states. But the President did not stop there.

Although pledging to end hypocrisy and insisting that the "law of the land" be applied equally, North and South, Mr. Nixon accepted the basically hyprocritical and unequal idea of separating de jure segregation and de facto segregation in schools.

It sounds good to say, as Mr. Nixon did, that de jure segregation exists in the North as well as in the South and that de facto segregation exists North and South. It also sounds good to say that the federal government should attack de jure segregation, North and South, and should not move against de facto segregation anywhere.

In actuality, however, that is mere rhetoric and de facto acceptance of hypocrisy. It has been assumed by the courts that de jure segregation still exists almost everywhere in the South because Southern states once had and enforced segregation laws. But de jure segregation is almost impossible to prove in the North where hyprocrisy long has prevailed in race relations and where de facto segregation now is much worse than the segregation remaining in the South.

In effect, all Southern school districts, especially rural and small town areas which predominate in South Carolina and most other Southern states, remain wide open to administrative and judicial harrassment, while most areas in the North, where actual segregation exists because of housing patterns, are protected from federal force.

It may be that Greenville County can get some slight relief under the Nixon policy from the many difficulties involved in the 80-20 integration plan now in effect in schools here. But that's for the courts, not the administration, to determine.

Meanwhile, most of South Carolina's school districts, including quite a few in the Piedmont region, are subject to massive change in September, while most areas of the North will continue to go Scot-free.

This is not what harrassed South Carolinians, who gave their electoral votes to Mr. Nixon, expected. It appears to be putting into actual practice what a high-ranking White House aide supposedly said: the administration does a lot of talking for the benefit of conservatives, but its actions suit the liberals.

NIXON INSTRUCTS RICHARDSON, MITCHELL: 'HOLD BUSING TO THE MINIMUM REQUIRED'

Less than four months after the Supreme Court had ruled busing constitutional, and while many Southern school systems under court orders were preparing to implement extensive busing plans, President Nixon issued a strong statement *against* busing. Disavowing a plan drawn up by the Department of Health, Education and Welfare for the desegregation of schools in Austin, Tex., Nixon said Aug. 3: "I am against busing as that term is commonly used in school desegregation cases. I have consistently opposed the busing of our nation's schoolchildren to achieve a racial balance, and I am opposed to the busing of children simply for the sake of busing."

Nixon directed HEW Secretary Elliot Richardson and Attorney General John Mitchell to "work with individual school districts to hold busing to the minimum required by law." He instructed Richardson to submit to Congress an amendment to the Emergency School Assistance Act that would "expressly prohibit" using any of the act's $1.5 billion to acquire buses. At the same time, however, the President insisted that his Administration would enforce court-ordered busing. Therefore, he said, the Justice Department would appeal on "limited constitutional grounds" the ruling by federal district judge Jack Roberts in Austin rejecting the HEW plan in favor of an Austin school board proposal to bus pupils periodically to special centers for fine arts, social sciences, avocations and science.

Later, Nixon reinforced his anti-busing stand by warning officials in HEW and the Justice Department that they risked losing their jobs if they sought to impose extensive busing. Nixon's warning was made public Aug. 11 by press secretary Ronald Ziegler, who said that "those who are not responsive [to the Presidential directive] will find themselves involved in other assignments or quite possibly in assignments other than the federal government." According to Ziegler, the Administration did not object to busing plans drawn up by local school officials and would enforce any direct court orders requiring widespread busing.

St. Louis Globe-Democrat

St. Louis, Mo., August 5, 1971

President Nixon has moved to blunt any move by the Department of Health, Education and Welfare to greatly expand busing to achieve school desegregation.

He said the HEW's plan for desegregating Austin (Tex.) schools (a plan that was rejected by the Austin District Court) went too far. The plan had been interpreted to call for busing as many as 89 per cent of the district's students.

But in deference to the Supreme Court, the President said he supports the high court's decision this spring that gave district courts the power to use busing as a tool in desegregating schools.

*   *   *

To brake what appears to be a drive by some officials in HEW, the Justice Department and other federal agencies to expand the use of busing, Mr. Nixon called on the Attorney General and the secretary of HEW to hold busing "to the minimum required by law" in desegregating schools.

Further, he asked HEW Secretary Elliot L. Richardson to submit to Congress an amendment to the Emergency School Assistance Act that would bar the use of its funds for busing.

To reinforce his opposition Mr. Nixon said

"I have consistently opposed the busing of our nation's school children to achieve a racial balance and I am opposed to the busing of children simply for the sake of busing."

But again in recognition of the Supreme Court's stand, Mr. Nixon said that while the repudiated HEW plan for Austin called for excessive busing, the District Court's proposal called for less than was indicated by the Supreme Court.

*   *   *

Thus President Nixon is going about as far as he can in opposing busing without bringing on a confrontation with the Supreme Court. As a lawyer, the President is profoundly aware of the fact that he must abide by the Supreme Court's rulings.

As President he also knows he has the right and duty to use his office to prevent abuse and misinterpretation of the high court's decisions.

The great majority of Americans—black and white — perhaps 80 per cent — are opposed to school busing to achieve desegregation. They will applaud Mr. Nixon's timely remarks. For without a firm hand, busing easily could get out of control. The President wisely has acted before this could happen.

HOUSTON CHRONICLE

Houston, Tex., August 5, 1971

The ultimate consequences of the decision by the U.S. Department of Justice to appeal the ruling in the Austin school desegregation case cannot be foretold by anyone.

When the case is reviewed by the Fifth Circuit Court of Appeals, the integration plan could be upheld, scaled down or expanded. The possibility of it being expanded has undoubtedly touched off criticism of the administration.

However, President Richard Nixon's statement about the decision to appeal made the aims of the administration fairly clear. Not only in the Austin case but about integration policy nationwide.

The President promised that he will stand for no more busing of schoolchildren than the minimum required by law. To this end, he wants to insure that no federal funds appropriated for easing the task of desegregation will be used for busing.

Also, Nixon said that the appeal will not support a massive busing plan for Austin schools that was drafted and originally urged by the Department of Health, Education and Welfare.

U.S. District Judge Jack B. Roberts of Austin rejected the HEW plan in his decision and adopted the local school board plan. Thus, under Judge Roberts' ruling, neighborhood schools would be retained at the elementary level but pupils in 40 of the 55 schools would be bused for a part of each day, during one week out of four, to centers for intercultural learning. In effect, students at the elementary level would be integrated about 25 percent of the time. On the secondary level, a junior high and a senior high, both predominantly black, would be closed and students assigned to other schools.

The HEW plan would have a major impact on neighborhood schools. Schools would have been paired and pupils would have been shifted between schools in a massive busing program. The President apparently disavowed this plan Tuesday.

He asserted:

"I am against busing as that term is commonly used in school desegregation cases. I have consistently opposed the busing of our nation's schoolchildren to achieve a racial balance, and I am opposed to the busing of children simply for the sake of busing."

This seems to make the President's intent clear. But the Austin case, expected to be a precedent followed in other areas, will not be decided for some time. Only then will the public know what the pattern will be.

THE COMMERCIAL APPEAL

Memphis, Tenn., August 5, 1971

PRESIDENT NIXON'S statement against busing in the Austin, Texas, school case will be interpreted as a major change in the administration's desegregation policy. In a limited sense this may be true. But the administration is certainly not going to oppose desegregation rulings of the United States Supreme Court.

In March, 1970, the President said that the neighborhood school concept should be the basis for desegregation plans, and that "transportation of pupils beyond normal geographic school zones for the purpose of achieving racial balance will not be required."

After the Supreme Court's "busing decision" last April, the administration was forced to relent on its categorical defense of neighborhood schools. The breakup of such schools was required by the high court to eliminate every vestige of state-imposed segregation. And busing was approved as one method for achieving this goal.

THE PRESIDENT has not reverted to his March, 1970, position. In reference to the Austin case, he said he was opposed to busing as a means of creating racial balance. Furthermore, he said, the administration would work with local school systems to hold busing to the minimum required by law.

Clearly, busing that is necessary to meet the desegregation standards set by the Supreme Court will be supported. There is a great deal of difference between "racial balance" and "desegregation."

"Balance" means that every school in a system will have a white-black ratio that is the same as or nearly the same as the white-black ratio in the whole system. The Supreme Court did not say that "balance" or "racial ratios" were required. Even the existence of some all-black and all-white schools was not necessarily a constitutional violation, the court said.

The administration's commitment to enforcing the law was demonstrated by its announced intention to appeal the lower-court ruling in the Austin case. The federal judge approved a school board plan that would have substituted academic and cultural exchange projects for desegregation through pupil assignment. Atty. Gen. John Mitchell advised the President that the plan was not consistent with the Supreme Court's April decision.

What occurred in Austin represents a special set of circumstances. It would be difficult to apply the President's remarks to different circumstances, except for his general objection to busing for balance.

In what was its first interpretation of the Supreme Court's decision, the Department of Health, Education and Welfare proposed a busing plan that would establish racial balance in every Austin school. The lower court rejected the proposal. The administration has also done so. But this does not mean that the administration will not support some busing.

THE DIFFERENCE is one of degree, not kind. Few balance plans have been proposed. The busing plan for Charlotte-Mecklenburg, which was one of the cases that the Supreme Court ruled on in April, did not involve balance.

Another development will be cited, perhaps unfairly, as a mark of the President's retrenchment on desegregation. He announced that the administration will seek to prevent any funds of the Emergency School Assistance Act from being used to buy buses.

The act was designed to help school systems desegregate—to smooth the way, as it were. It was supposed to finance such programs as teacher training, curriculum revision and special biracial activities. The possibility that the act might finance buses was brought up speculatively after the Supreme Court ruled that busing was a legitimate desegregation technique. The President's announcement can be construed as an attempt to preserve the original intent of the act.

ONE OF THE continuing sources of confusion and dispute over school desegregation and the administration's policies is the failure to define terms.

When the President says he is opposed to busing for balance, he is not saying that he is opposed to all busing or that the administration will resist the busing needed to desegregate formerly dual school systems. The President is not fighting the Supreme Court. He specifically said that "the executive branch will continue to enforce the orders of the court." All he seems to be asking for is a reasonable approach, within the limits of the law, to a complex problem.

The Washington Post

Times Herald

Washington, D.C., August 7, 1971

"Watch what we do," the Attorney General suggested some while ago in relation to the administration's enforcement of civil rights law. Like others who accepted Mr. Mitchell's invitation, we found ourselves wishing by this week that we had remembered to bring along the dramamine. For the second time now, in an important school desegregation case (Austin, Texas), the administration, having raised hopes on one side and hackles on the other, and having wasted money, time, and political capital, has summarily disavowed its own earlier position and come into court, as it were, against itself. And, should the Legal Defense Fund decide to pursue the matter, for the second time the administration may also find itself in court defending against pressures to implement desegregation schemes it dreamed up and sought to enforce in the first place.

The only consistency in these affairs has been their pattern. In the beginning there was the confusion over "guidelines" and HEW's willingness to cut off funds from Southern school districts that declined to comply with the law. For our part, rather naively, we at first went along with the administration's ardent professions of earnest intent —until the whole HEW civil rights enforcement program seemed to come crashing down. Never mind: we were subsequently invited to observe the tough desegregation plans being quietly devised by HEW and promoted in the federal courts by Justice. So we did. And that was encouraging too— until Justice switched sides and came into court seeking to stall the plans HEW had devised for a number of Mississippi school districts. That was the momentous episode which led to the spectacle of the Assistant Attorney General for Civil Rights arguing on the "anti" side of a civil rights case before the Supreme Court, ending in the court's unanimous rejection of his plea—the do-it-now school desegregation order of October, 1969. The pattern was repeated after the Supreme Court's recent busing decision in the Swann case, when the administration *went out of its way* to implement that decision with the comprehensive and unequivocal plans it sought to impose on Austin and Nashville. Those of us who perceived and hailed another profound change of heart within the administration are back in our familiar posture, having once again played Charlie Brown to the administration's Lucy at kickoff time.

The administration as Lucy holding the ball— that is the operative image and the only one that will do for the continuing saga of civil rights enforcement in the schools since early 1969. The Austin plan, which Mr. Nixon has now publicly repudiated, was drawn up at HEW and approved by the Attorney General. Similarly, the Senate-passed desegregation legislation to which Mr. Nixon would now add a disabling anti-busing rider, was worked out with the help and concurrence of officials in his administration who seemed to be acting in his name. Whatever anyone may think of busing schemes in general or the Austin plan in particular, it should not be hard to agree that this style and pattern of performance is a wholly reckless way of dealing with school systems, school children and local officials who are trying in good faith to figure out what the administration wants and/or requires of them—trying to make their plans and raise their funds and prepare the public for acceptance of whatever rearrangements must be made. Nor can this dizzying show of inconstancy and indecision be expected to do much for the credibility of those members of the administration who have cooked up and negotiated and supported these plans and moves that are so lightly discarded. If you were a legislator in the capital or a school board official in an affected district or a federal judge trying to resolve a dispute, with whom in the administration would you be able to deal confidently on these matters? How seriously would you take any given profession of intent or statement of position at any given time? Of all the oddity and mystery surrounding the present affair, the most striking is that which concerns Mr. Nixon's tough and able Secretary of HEW, Elliot Richardson. We persist in believing that this is not the role he envisaged for himself or for his department or for his staff which has been so suddenly and needlessly humiliated.

ST. LOUIS POST-DISPATCH

St. Louis, Mo.
August 5, 1971

President Nixon's statement on the Austin, Tex., school case represents the most startling retreat of the several this Administration has conducted on civil rights policy.

The Austin case involves bussing of school children to educational centers. Mr. Nixon said of it that he had "consistently opposed the bussing of our nation's school children to achieve a racial balance, and I am opposed to the bussing of children simply for the sake of bussing."

This statement is doubly irrelevant to the Austin issue. Nobody has proposed bussing merely for the sake of bussing, of course, and nobody has proposed it to achieve racial balance, if that means some sort of 50-50 or proportionate balance. Mr. Nixon's own Department of Health, Education and Welfare had planned for bussing simply to achieve an adequate measure of desegregation.

Last April the United States Supreme Court ruled that it was entirely proper to use bussing as a means of desegregation. The Austin school district responded with a bussing plan whose net result would have been racial mixing in school "clusters" but during only one week out of four. This was so insufficient that HEW submitted a counter plan dividing 30 schools into six clusters and assigning pupils to mixed schools on a permanent basis.

Even now Justice Department officials say the HEW plan would not achieve full integration, and another Administration official concedes that it is impossible to integrate Austin schools without bussing. Yet Mr. Nixon has ordered the Justice Department to repudiate the HEW plan in appealing a lower court decision against it.

This leaves the Justice Department in a position of defending and rejecting an integration plan at the same time, which is a position of total confusion. Evidently Mr. Nixon hopes the appeals court will agree to something more in the way of bussing than the original Austin plan but something less than the plan arranged by his own Administration's staff. The confusion can only be clarified by the appeals court.

But the President left little doubt as to where he stands personally. He suggested an amendment to the proposed Emergency School Assistance Act to prohibit use of funds for bussing. The entire purpose of the act would be to give financial aid to school districts attempting integration, yet the Administration would deny them help for one of the most essential means of reaching that goal.

Reporters asked a White House aid if Mr. Nixon also opposes the kind of bussing that has for so long been used to keep school districts totally segregated. There was no answer. The Administration is standing on Mr. Nixon's statement that it will "continue to enforce the orders of the court."

But how? That is the question when the President challenges the intent of the high courts orders, rebukes one of his own departments for attempting to carry out those orders, and opposes the use of busses going toward integration when silent about those going in the other direction.

CHICAGO Sun-Times

Chicago, Ill., August 5, 1971

President Nixon's rejection of his own administration's plan for pupil busing in Austin, Tex., is a harshly political act. He has for all practical purposes countermanded the U.S. Supreme Court ruling that it is proper and wise to achieve racial balance in schools through busing. We fail to see how he has helped the cause of children for whom classroom desegregation is equatable with education salvation.

President Nixon pledged during his tours of the hustings in 1968 to oppose forced busing, and he now has chosen a most unfortunate means of keeping a campaign promise that should never have been made. Specifically, he has disavowed a desegregation program for the Austin school system which was devised by the Department of Health, Education and Welfare as the first, and t h e r e f o r e showcase, response to the Supreme Court decision. A lower court already has ruled against the HEW plan, and the President rightly should be upholding the integrity of his administration in the fight against school segregation. Instead, he has instructed the Justice Department to pursue the case only in order to seek a minimal compromise.

Busing is not an all-purpose tool for prying communities loose from the tar pits of segregation. It may not work at all in some communities. In others, such as Chicago, it has not been used as it should have been. Yet, busing can be a valuable adjunct to citywide integration plans and there are areas in which it has worked and worked well. It should not be rejected out of hand, any more than should the traditional busing of white pupils in both rural and urban areas.

The President has allowed his personal antagonism toward busing and his political debts to go slow conservatives to interfere with the national drive for school desegregation. He may have gained political clout in some quarters, but he surely has caused a counterbalancing consternation in others. If the President does not want to help communities upgrade their schools, he should not interpose himself between the communities and those who want to help them.

The Detroit News

Detroit, Mich., August 5, 1971

Although President Nixon remained consistent with himself, his a d m i n i s t r a t i o n presented an appearance of disarray this week on the question of school bussing.

The President's disavowal of a proposal advanced by his own Department of Health, Education and Welfare suggests that the left hand did not know what the right hand was doing — not unusual in government, but disconcerting where a delicate issue such as school desegregation is concerned.

By way of background:

The U.S. Supreme Court last April ordered as much school desegregation as possible and the use of a reasonable d e g r e e of bussing to achieve it. The Austin, Tex., school district asked HEW for a plan. HEW proposed extensive crosstown bussing, and Austin countered with an alternative involving but occasional bussing. A district judge ruled in favor of the Austin school board.

This week the P r e s i d e n t announced that the Justice Department will appeal — not to impose the HEW plan, but because the Austin board's plan fails to meet the requirements laid down by the U.S. Supreme Court. In fact, said the President, "In the process of the appeal, the Justice Department will disavow that plan on behalf of the government."

Mr. Nixon repeated his personal opposition to the concept of bussing, recommended against spending federal funds on it and instructed the attorney general and HEW Secretary Elliot Richardson to work with individual school districts to "hold bussing to the minimum required by law."

None of these statements represented a retreat from the administration's fundamental opposition to segregation. They bolstered the policy, which incidentally has proven highly productive, of achieving desegregation by firm but moderate measures and without creating social ills as severe as the original complaint.

Mr. Nixon's e s s e n t i a l policy makes good sense. It also makes good politics — but only if he manages to maintain his distinctions.

If it is clear that he favors desegregation but with a minimum of bussing as required by law, he will carry with him many citizens of good faith, black and white. For bussing, in itself, is not in the last analysis a racial issue, though some of the more militant libertarians try to make it so.

If he seems, however, to be first on one side and then on another, if, while he is appealing to moderates, HEW seems to be tossing a sop to someone else, the public will lose confidence.

In short, the administration must be unified and consistent in word and deed in order to maintain respect. Mr. Nixon, meet Mr. Richardson.

Richmond Times-Dispatch

Richmond, Va., August 7, 1971

President Nixon's pitiful attempts to articulate a policy on busing bring to mind an old high-school football cheer. To rephrase it into the political context: "Lean to the left! Lean to the right! Stand up! Sit down! Don't fight! Don't fight! Don't fight!"

The Department of Health, Education, and Welfare (HEW), reportedly with the White House's knowledge, proposes the massive busing of children in Austin, Texas, to achieve an exact 65-20-15 ratio of whites-to-chicanos - to - blacks in each school. Lean to the left!

Citing the injurious effects of mass busing, U.S. District Judge Jack Roberts rejects the HEW scheme in favor of the Austin school board's "learning center" alternative – whereupon Mr. Nixon vigorously repudiates the HEW plan and denounces "busing simply for the sake of busing." Lean to the right!

But Mr. Nixon's Justice Department will appeal Judge Roberts' decision because it allegedly doesn't call for enough busing to fulfill Supreme Court guidelines. Lean to the left!

But Mr. Nixon has ordered HEW to submit an amendment to the $1.5 billion Emergency School Assistance Act to prohibit use of federal funds to help purchase buses for the busing his federal agencies promote. Lean to the right!

Stand up! Sit down! Is anybody happy? Is everybody dizzy?

The most charitable thing that can be said of Mr. Nixon's zig-zag course on busing is that he is trying to stake out a safe political middle ground from which to weather the storms of discontent. But in trying to placate everyone, he is pleasing nobody. Pompous liberals like Sens. Walter Mondale (D-Minn.) and Jacob Javits (R-N.Y.), who want every child in the South force-bused 50 miles a day if necessary so long as not a single pupil in their own states is affected, are furious because Mr. Nixon won't go for 65-20-15 or bust in Austin. Conservative Sen. John Tower (R-Texas), a Nixon Administration stalwart on many issues, is livid because the President will try to overturn the moderate decision of Judge Roberts.

If the President is going to exert leadership in saving urban public schools from the disrupting effects of pell-mell forced busing, it is high time he stopped trying to be on both sides of this issue. Mr. Nixon wishes to "minimize" busing? Fine. Then he could have made a contribution to sanity in Austin by instructing the Justice Department not to appeal Judge Roberts' wise and compassionate decision. In its opinion last April, the Supreme Court said objections to busing may have validity when a scheme risks the health of children or impinges upon the educational process. Is it not a point worth fighting for that massive urban busing has precisely those drawbacks?

As a practical matter, Mr. Nixon's latest circumlocution will probably have no effect on cities, like Richmond, which are already under court-ordered busing plans for this fall. But it will matter very much what position the President takes after next month's opening, for the Supreme Court decision clearly indicated that compulsory busing need not be a forever thing.

"Neither school authorities nor district courts," the high court said, "are constitutionally required to make year by year adjustments of the racial composition of student bodies once the affirmative duty to desegregate has been accomplished and racial discrimination through official action is eliminated from the system."

The hour is fast fading, if it has not already passed, that it can be argued the South has an illegal "dual system" while the North does not. If fact, government statistics show that the South is already far ahead of the North in actual desegregation. The time is now for President Nixon to develop a coherent national alternative to forced busing - one that ensures education opportunity for all families and denies freedom to none; one that treats all regions of the nation exactly alike. This will require a leader who will stand up, not sit down, and fight unswervingly for principles that are right.

Newsday

Long Island, N.Y., August 5, 1971

Although for many years busing has been as common to the educational experience of rural and suburban children as stickball in the schoolyard is to city kids, the idea of sending a child to class on a bus somehow becomes diabolical when the issue at hand is integration.

Sharing in this delusion are current White House policymakers, and, most notably, the President, himself, who this week issued a broadside against busing for racial purposes.

Despite a recent Supreme Court ruling that permits busing to overcome patterns of segregation, President Nixon has seen fit to take a hard line. "I have consistently opposed the busing of our nation's schoolchildren to achieve racial balance," he said, "and I am opposed to the busing of children simply for the sake of busing."

Since school boards rarely devise busing plans merely to acquaint children with the wonders of motorized transportation, the last half of Mr. Nixon's statement seems no more than a bit of political theatrics for the benefit of the dissident right. The first part is more distressing since it suggests a close-minded and unreasonable position on a matter of great public interest.

Classroom integration is a long-overdue and necessary means of allowing America's disparate peoples to finally get together. Perhaps the distance between us is not best traveled by bus. But better that way than not at all.

St. Petersburg Times

St. Petersburg, Fla., August 5, 1971

In an unscrupulous performance Tuesday, President Nixon turned Wallace-like and played politics again with the nation's single most valuable resource — it's public schools.

Yet, for Pinellas County and other school districts across the South, Mr. Nixon's equivocal, vote-hunting statement on busing to achieve desegregated schools changes nothing.

After seeking to delude unwary parents by delivering himself of such pieties as "I am opposed to the busing of children simply for the sake of busing," Mr. Nixon turned around and said, "I have instructed the attorney general and the secretary of Health, Education and Welfare that they are to work with individual school districts to hold busing to the minimum required by law."

The minimum required by law is the amount of busing it takes to desegregate the schools. No one wants anything more. Until citizens accept open housing and integrated neighborhoods, busing is the only practical way to end illegal school segregation.

Mr. Nixon's pandering to the lowest political denominator included prohibiting the use of federal emergency desegregation funds for busing. That will not stop busing, of course. It only puts the full burden of costs on local districts.

Mr. Nixon, Rep. Bill Young, many Pinellas anti-busing leaders and some state officials seek to twist school issues to advance their own political ambitions. Whether they succeed or not, their capacity for ethical leadership is questioned.

The Philadelphia Inquirer

Philadelphia, Pa., August 5, 1971

President Nixon's statement in opposition to busing as a means of integrating public schools presents a sensible point of view and a realistic national policy.

If there is one thing that black and white parents seem to agree on, in both the North and the South, it is that they don't want their children hauled out of their neighborhoods to distant schools when an equally good or better school is available closer to home.

"I am against busing as that term is commonly used in school desegregation cases," Mr. Nixon said. "I have consistently opposed the busing of our nation's school children to achieve a racial balance, and I am opposed to the busing of children simply for the sake of busing. Further, while the executive branch will continue to enforce the orders of the court, including court-ordered busing, I have instructed the attorney general and the secretary of health, education and welfare that they are to work with individual school districts to hold busing to the minimum required by law."

★ ★ ★

Carrying out court orders is essential, of course, but there has never been a Supreme Court decision requiring busing to end de facto segregation in public schools resulting from housing patterns. And in de jure segregation cases in the South, where separate schools for blacks and whites had been maintained by state law, court orders have dealt with integration plans in specific cities without defining clearly a set of guidelines for practical application elsewhere.

The decision last April upholding a busing plan for the Charlotte-Mecklenburg school district in North Carolina is generally considered to be the Supreme Court's most definitive pronouncement on busing but, for schools other than those in the Charlotte-Mecklenburg district, the court left unanswered more questions than it answered.

★ ★ ★

As the court candidly conceded in that decision, "No rigid guidelines as to student transportation can be given for application to the infinite variety of problems presented in thousands of situations."

And the court said in the same decision: "An objection to transportation of students may have validity when the time or distance of travel is so great as to risk either the health of the children or significantly impinge on the educational process."

At a time when public schools almost everywhere are in financial trouble, diverting funds to massive busing hardly would be consistent with the goal of quality education for all pupils regardless of race.

This does not mean that nothing can be done to combat racial segregation in public schools. Gerrymandered school districts drawn to promote segregation should be revised wherever they exist. Site selection for new schools can encourage integration. And effective moves to end racial discrimination in housing will help to reduce segregation in the classrooms.

But busing isn't the answer. Enduring solutions to racial problems cannot be found by pretending that it is.

The Greenville News

Greenville, S.C., August 8, 1971

President Nixon's recent outspoken stand against using federal funds to transport school children in order to racially balance schools merely serves to show the depth of the school busing issue all across the nation.

On the one hand is the argument, in many cases backed up by federal court orders, that cross-busing of students is necessary to break up dual school systems, especially in the South.

On the other hand is broad, deep public resentment against breaking up neighborhood school patterns and transporting pupils many miles in order to achieve racial "desegregation," "integration" or "balancing," however it may be put. That resentment is nationwide. It probably is as strong in the North, Midwest and Far West as in Dixie.

The issue cannot help but figure in next year's national elections. It affects too many people in their own backyards to be ignored by public officials.

A government simply cannot start messing around with people's children without kicking up a real political donnybrook. No amount of rationalization or explanation can obscure the hard fact that busing is a drastic form of interference with the lives of many children and many families — and people don't like it.

Raising the money issue, however, does put many school districts in worse position than before. Quite a few Southern districts, Greenville included, are under court orders which require in one way or another, considerable busing of pupils. Denial of federal funds to help defray the extra cost of extra busing won't change those orders one bit. Neither Congress nor the President can "repeal" or "revoke" a court order. Congress can forbid spending federal money on busing, however.

But that would serve only to complicate the problem for those school districts under court orders to bus pupils. It would deny them a source of much-needed funds to carry out the onerous task of busing under court order.

The President's opposition to use of federal funds for busing could tend to prevent implementation of voluntary busing plans in areas outside Dixie, which are not under the Supreme Court's edict to dismantle so-called "de jure" segregated school systems.

Therefore, it is not true that Mr. Nixon's anti-busing stand is part of a "Southern political strategy." If anything it is aimed squarely at the segregated suburbs of the huge Northern, Midwestern and Western big city regions.

His stand helps those areas maintain segregated schools, but does absolutely nothing to change the situation in the South.

TULSA DAILY WORLD

Tulsa, Okla., August 5, 1971

WE CAN'T blame school officials in Tulsa and elsewhere for being confused and upset over the NIXON Administration's fuzzy, opposite-direction guidance on school busing.

PRESIDENT NIXON himself only added to the mixup Tuesday with his latest pronouncement, asking Congress to stop any use of Federal emergency desegregation funds for busing school children. The PRESIDENT is sticking to his announced opposition to busing for the sake of desegregation—but that hardly squares with his Administration's push to achieve racially mixed schools.

Dr. GORDON CAWELTI, Tulsa School Superintendent, stated the problem succinctly: "We can't have one branch of the nation's Government saying, 'integrate your schools' and another branch making it virtually impossible to do so."

The Federal Judiciary, of course, is the branch that keeps the loaded gun pointed at the schools, forcing them to integrate—with pressure coming from two Executive Departments, JUSTICE and HEALTH, EDUCATION AND WELFARE.

We have seen that pressure first-hand in Tulsa, just as it has been felt at Austin, Texas, and at Nashville, Tenn., where the Administration has been a prime force in promoting both desegregation of schools and the busing that is necessary to accomplish it.

The PRESIDENT is disavowing his own HEW Department's plan in Austin, stating that the Administration will "hold busing to the minimum required by law." Who knows what that is?

Even Sen. JOHN TOWER of Texas, a down-the-line NIXON supporter, had to turn against the PRESIDENT publicly this time, saying Mr. NIXON apparently "does not really oppose forced busing or he lacks the resolve necessary to control those who pursue it in his name."

Mr. NIXON appears to be trying to walk down a line so flimsy and thin that he cannot keep balanced between politics and civil rights.

Following a U.S. SUPREME COURT pressing for faster desegregation, especially in the South, JUSTICE and HEW have been insisting on greater racial mixing in schools which can hardly come about without busing. As DAVID FIST, attorney for the Tulsa School Board, says, "the plain fact of the matter is that to integrate is to bus."

We can understand Mr. NIXON'S desire to have it both ways, but that doesn't seem possible now. His present stance is going to wind up satisfying nobody—and confusing everyone.

THE STATES-ITEM

New Orleans, La., August 13, 1971

It is disappointing to see President Richard M. Nixon use the emotional issue of busing for political purposes. It demeans the office of the Presidency.

Mr. Nixon is using the busing issue — or to be more exact, making an issue where there is none — just as he has done with housing.

No one has advocated "the busing of children simply for the sake of busing," as the President suggests. In announcing himself against "forced integration" of the suburbs, Mr. Nixon also created his own straw man to knock over. No national figure that we know of has proposed forced integration of the suburbs; but there is the Fair Housing Act of 1968 which entitles any American to purchase federally assisted housing in the suburbs as elsewhere.

The real effect of Mr. Nixon's opposition to the straw man of "forced integration" is to discourage federal officials from enforcing the fair housing law, thus permitting discrimination in federally supported housing to exist.

Mr. Nixon is using the same strategy on the busing issue, only he has gone even further to openly intimidate federal officials who might use busing as the most effective means of eliminating de facto segregation of public schools.

Last spring, the U. S. Supreme Court approved busing as a necessary means of desegregation, but left it to federal district courts to decide when busing would be required in specific situations.

In publicly speaking against a lower court ruling in an Austin, Tex., case, Mr. Nixon said the Supreme Court ruling of last spring would be enforced only "to the minimum required by law." Mr. Nixon also has sought to amend his own $1.5 billion education bill to withhold federal money in cases where busing is being used.

To cap it off, the White House this week threatened to transfer federal bureaucrats who enforce busing except as a last resort. Taken on its face, that sounds innocent enough. But the practical effect is to intimidate federal employes into steering clear of busing altogether, even in cases where it is the only means of eliminating de facto segregation. The effect also is to undercut the Supreme Court ruling that busing is a necessary instrument of desegregation in some cases. The overall effect is to encourage the continuation of defacto segregation and the hopes of those who would keep blacks in second-class status.

We are not for busing in all cases; but we do believe the President of the United States, especially one who pledged to "bring us together," should not undercut federal law and play upon the fears of the people to further his own political career.

Chicago Tribune

Chicago, Ill., August 15, 1971

President Nixon's stand against multiplying busing of school children to achieve racial balance should be entirely clear to everyone by now. He has stated it and restated it, and his press secretary, Ronald L. Ziegler, has announced that workers in the executive branch of the federal government who are not "responsive" to the President's policy on busing will soon be "in other assignments."

The reasons for the policy are less clearly understood than the policy itself. Some people on both sides of the issue may think that the President's policy implies unhappiness or conflict with the basic Supreme Court decision [Brown vs. Topeka, 1954] which struck down deliberate de jure racial segregation in the public schools. They may think that those who oppose massive busing programs all want to cling to patterns of racial isolation. But there are many cogent arguments against mass busing that are entirely free of racial prejudice.

Busing programs take time, money and energy that might be better devoted to education than to travel back and forth. Even more relevant to the goal of diminishing racial isolation in America, school busing programs have repeatedly elicited more backlash than progress. Widely resented, they increase rather than diminish impulses to desert the public schools, flee to suburbs, or both. They incur widespread disapproval from both whites and blacks. A serious case can be made that school busing leads not to desegregation but to resegregation.

Rep. Roman Pucinski of Chicago, chairman of the House Subcommittee on General Education, made this case in the House on Aug. 4. Pucinski cited two recent federal court rulings, one in Atlanta and one in Austin, in which the judges held that busing programs were not necessary in order for a city to have a genuinely "unitary" public school system. Pucinski hopes that other federal courts, which in a number of instances have ordered busing, will likewise conclude that busing is not required.

There is and always has been a vital distinction between de jure and de facto racial segregation in public schools. The old practice of busing pupils away from the nearest public school to an all-white or an all-black school deserved to be struck down. It has been struck down. The spectacle of governors standing in the doors of state universities saying to all black citizens of their states, "You may not enter here," was unworthy of this country and its Constitution. But it does not follow that every public school either should or can deliver any prescribed racial mix. It is wholly reasonable to think that trying to do so by busing will augment rather than diminish racial prejudice and isolation. It will certainly deflect resources badly needed for instruction into controversial transportation programs.

THE TRIBUNE, no less than President Nixon, has long been a consistent critic of massive busing programs intended to reduce the de facto racial segregation of school children. The time spent in semantic efforts to show that he has been inconsistent or to exaggerate his difference with the Supreme Court, which has never ruled that busing is mandatory, would be better spent on plans to improve the quality of education in the increasing number of schools that are being integrated, with or without busing.

Arkansas 🦅 Gazette.

Little Rock, Ark., August 5, 1971

AFTER AN interlude in which the emphasis was on foreign policy, especially China policy, Richard Nixon is back down to earth and once again talking about "busing" to achieve racial balance. Mr. Nixon is never more shameless in his cynical domestic performance than in his recurrent efforts to undermine both the due process of school integration and the orderly compliance with decisions of the U.S. Supreme Court.

In his latest outing on the segregation issue, the President has (1.) renounced an HEW "busing" plan for Austin, Tex., even though the Justice Department approved the selfsame plan at the outset, and (2.) solemnly urged Congress anew not to provide any transportation money in special school-aid appropriations for the integrating South. He went on to reiterate—

"I have consistently opposed the busing of our nation's school children to achieve a racial balance, and I am opposed to the busing of children simply for the sake of busing."

In a limited, specific context, the President's latest pronouncements in the two matters involving "busing" will hardly have much impact. On the first issue, Austin will still have to find an integration plan that is acceptable to the courts, even if the particular HEW plan is not adopted. And, as for the special federal funds for newly-integrated schools, only a very small percentage of such funds has been used for bus transportation anyway.

It is the spirit, the broad intent, of what Mr. Nixon has said in this latest comment that is so contemptible.

He knows that the United States Supreme Court, unanimously, with the concurrence of Mr. Nixon's own nominees to the Court, has affirmed the use of busing to eliminate racially identifiable schools. The issue, as a matter of law, is settled. And when Mr. Nixon agitates the issue, from the heights of the office he holds, he does nothing but to make the process of transition and of obedience to law all the more difficult and traumatic.

If the Congress, in its turn, goes along with the prohibition against use of special integration funds for "busing," it means nothing except that the individual school districts will have to appropriate for "busing," as required, from their own funds.

What Richard Nixon is up to, of course, is simply the election politics that motivates him in this as in all issues. It is the "Southern strategy" still in force, just as it always has been and presumably will be in force until one fine day when Mr. Nixon leaves office.

In the current application Nixon's demagogy will simply make it somewhat harder for all of us in the South to make the last step in moving from a dual school system to a single system. The truth is simply that Richard Nixon is a sort of scrubbed-up Faubus, perhaps not ready to call out troops against the courts and the law but perfectly ready to inflame public opinion against the courts and the law, for no purpose except his own obsessive ambition to stay in power.

THE INDIANAPOLIS NEWS
Indianapolis, Ind., August 7, 1971

President Nixon's rhetorical opposition to busing, voiced again this week, bears close examination.

Repudiating a plan drawn up by the U.S. Department of Health, Education and Welfare that would have required citywide busing in Austin, Texas, Nixon said he opposes "busing of children simply for the sake of busing."

The President said: "I am against busing as that term is commonly used in school desegregation cases. I have consistently opposed the busing of our school children to achieve a racial balance, and I am opposed to the busing of children simply for the sake of busing."

Actions not words, however, are the clearest indication of the administration's position, and here the record is perfectly clear. Nixon's HEW prepared the Austin plan. Nixon's Justice Department prosecuted the Austin school system. And when a Federal district court judge ruled in Austin's favor and threw out HEW's busing plan, Nixon's Justice Department appealed the decision.

Although the President has repudiated this particular plan, Austin still faces Federal efforts to impose busing. The administration's actions led Texas Republican Sen. John Tower to conclude: "It appears that he [Nixon] does not really oppose forced busing or that he lacks the resolve necessary to control those who pursue it in his name."

A similar pattern is evident here in Indiana where the Justice Department pursued legal proceedings against the Indianapolis school system and HEW is now pressuring Evansville schools to accept racial balance plans.

In view of this evidence, the President's stated opposition to busing seems empty indeed. His performance on this issue tends to confirm Sen. Hugh Scott's observation, voiced with approval, that in this administration conservatives get the words and liberals the action.

THE MILWAUKEE JOURNAL
Milwaukee, Wis., August 6, 1971

President Nixon continues to court votes from those who oppose school integration, especially where bussing is involved. His remarkable repudiation of his own administration's stand regarding schools in Austin, Tex., is an obvious attempt to assure racial bigots that he has no intention of enforcing the law on this point any more than is absolutely necessary.

After the US Supreme Court ruled in April that bussing was constitutional, and sometimes necessary to eliminate segregation, the Health, Education and Welfare Department submitted an extensive bussing plan to integrate Austin schools. The plan was rejected by a federal district court, which approved instead a much more limited plan offered by Austin school officials. The Justice Department concluded that the Austin plan was inconsistent with the Supreme Court ruling and decided that it had to appeal the district court decision.

Rather than simply letting the Justice Department file the appeal, Nixon entered the picture personally. He announced that the appeal would be "on limited constitutional grounds" only and asserted that it was not being done for the purpose of pushing the HEW integration plan.

"In the process of the appeal, the Justice Department will disavow that plan on behalf of the government," the president said.

Further, Nixon asked Congress to prohibit use of emergency school desegregation funds for bussing. And he repeated his own personal opposition to "bussing of our nation's school children to achieve racial balance," a revealing point of information perhaps but irrelevant in that no one is suggesting such sweeping action.

Thus we do not merely have Richard Nixon differing personally with a Supreme Court decision. We have the calculated thrust of the full moral force of the president of the United States against what has been declared by the Supreme Court to be the law of the land.

It remains to be seen whether Nixon's working both sides of the street will convince anyone. He certainly has done nothing here to impress those who favor integration. Yet Sen. John Tower (R-Tex.) attacked the decision to appeal the Austin case, saying that either Nixon "does not really oppose forced bussing, or he lacks the resolve necessary to control those who pursue it in his name." Austin's school superintendent said: "Man in White House speaks with forked tongue."

In all his smart political maneuvering, Nixon may have outsmarted himself. As he has in some other fields, the president may only have made enemies in both camps.

THE ATLANTA CONSTITUTION
Atlanta, Ga., August 13, 1971

School busing itself is nothing new in the South. Most of our Southern school systems have owned school buses for years (Atlanta, incidentally, being an exception). Black citizens have pointed out, quilte accurately that white parents never expressed much concern about busing when the sometimes long bus route involved taking white pupils to all-white schools and black pupils to all-black schools.

The very word "busing" has become a scare word to many people in connection with school desegregation. It seems to bear enormous emotional impact. And, as a scare word, it is used and misused, often by politicians.

But that isn't what is meant by busing as scare word.

In fact, we doubt if either white or black parents have much concern about their children simply riding school buses to school. That's an ordinary enough sort of thing.

The scare word part is the idea of what is sometimes called "massive busing" to achieve a certain racial balance in every school in a given school system.

There are serious people who seriously advocate the idea. In Atlanta, the National Association for the Advancement of Colored People has gone into federal court to urge that the Atlanta school system be forced to undertake this kind of busing plan.

To their great credit, federal district judges here refused to order such a plan. The courts certainly have no intention of upholding any form of racial discrimination in the public schools. But the Atlanta schools today made up of predominantly white or predominantly black students are that way because of residential patterns.

There's simply no way to say to any given parent that he or she *has* to live in a particular school district, Atlanta or anywhere else. The NAACP federal court appeal is self-defeating. It is probably no exaggeration to say a majority of white parents here would move or place their children in private schools if the NAACP won its suit.

Meanwhile, the politicians do their cynical best to exploit the issues for votes.

President Richard Nixon is the latest example, as he publicly speaks out against widespread busing as a means of desegregation in Southern cities. We agree with Nixon's stated view. Trouble is, Nixon has been on every conceivable side of the school desegregation issue. If the political winds change, it's likely that his view will change too.

One of the reasons for the current discontent in many Southern communities is Nixon's exploitation of school desegregation in his 1968 campaign. In effect, Nixon promised to slow down desegregation. As Sen. David Gambrell commented one day this week, "The peope are disappointed and frustrated by the way things have turned out against what they have been promised."

The issue of "busing" as scare word needs to be laid to rest. We would hope the federal courts do so as soon as possible.

The Dallas Morning News
Dallas, Tex., August 5, 1971

THE PRESIDENT'S declaration that he is opposed to the busing that his HEW people are selling is not likely to mollify the people who are on the receiving end.

To many Americans this is about as convincing as a president of an auto manufacturing firm claiming he doesn't like the kind of cars his factories are making but that he can't do anything about it.

Has our system gone so far out of kilter that it only gives us what we don't want? The people do not want busing for racial balance and have said so at every opportunity from opinion polls to elections. The Congress doesn't want busing and has expressly prohibited the use of federal funds for that purpose. Now comes the chief executive saying, once again:

"I HAVE consistently opposed the busing of our nation's schoolchildren to achieve a racial balance, and I am opposed to the busing of children simply for the sake of busing."

That sounds fine, but it is small relief to the people in Oak Cliff who are faced with the prospect of having to practice what the President is preaching against. And the irate citizens here have plenty of company in communities from coast to coast.

On the face of it, the whole concept of busing for racial balance has few supporters outside of the judiciary and the federal bureaucracy. Yet next fall, thousands of American youngsters are going to be going off to school aboard those buses that are deplored and disavowed by officials and citizens alike. Why?

If democracy is self-rule by the people, why can't the people get the system to respond to their wishes? If the elected representatives oppose busing, why are the career bureaucrats still pushing for it at the operating level?

At the present time, the basis for giving the people what they do not want is the recent Supreme Court decision that busing is acceptable constitutionally. In the local case, Judge Taylor softened the impact of the requirements set by the Supreme Court by exempting the neighborhood elementary schools and by including provisions for some flexibility in cases of special hardships.

Yet even this compromise measure leaves older Oak Cliff children facing the problems of busing and their parents are up in arms. As past evidence has shown, the opposition to busing seems to range over the spectrum, blacks and whites, liberals and conservatives, Republicans and Democrats.

This opposition throughout the nation has been unable to find an effective voice, despite the fact that it is the majority. Laws have been passed by Congress, but ignored by the bureaucracy. Executive orders and statements in opposition have been proclaimed and the busing goes on.

BUT THERE is still an avenue open to the majority who oppose busing and seek legal relief from it: A constitutional amendment.

The Supreme Court has interpreted the Constitution to say that racial balancing via the school bus is constitutional. The majority, if it so desires, can demand that the Constitution be amended to eliminate that interpretation.

It is a drastic step, but since all other attempts to gain a voice for the majority have failed, it may be the only way to make government respond to the wishes of the governed.

PORTLAND EVENING EXPRESS
Portland, Me., August 10, 1971

The Nixon Administration has long displayed an ambivalent attitude on the issue of racial bias, and last week the President gave new reasons for blacks to distrust the good faith of the White House in the integration of public schools.

The Supreme Court has already upheld the use of busing to desegregate schools, and within a month after the court's decision the Department of Health, Education and Welfare utilized it to recommend to a district court in Austin, Texas, its approval of "extensive" busing of Negro and Mexican children to integrate the city's schools.

But now Mr. Nixon has disavowed the plan by HEW, and has directed the attorney general and HEW Sec. Elliot L. Richardson to "work with individual school districts to hold busing to the minimum required by law . . ."

If this is not defiance of the court's dictum, it is close to it, and the order will stimulate hostility in the South to the busing of school pupils in the interests of desegregation.

Mr. Nixon almost seems to feel that the bus transportation of students is novel and questionable, when as a matter of fact millions of boys and girls are bused to school every day. He ignores what is also patently true, that hundreds of school districts in the South have revised their earlier racial bias practices and are now busing white and black pupils to racially mixed schools. It is the holdouts that are affected by the Supreme Court, and now Mr. Nixon unwisely is upholding their resistance.

ANTI-BUSING AMENDMENTS PASSED BY NORTH-SOUTH HOUSE COALITION

Northern liberals joined Republicans and Southerners in the House Nov. 5 in the most overwhelming display of opposition to the policy of busing children for purposes of racial integration since the Supreme Court ruled busing constitutional last April. The opposition was manifested in the form of three amendments to President Nixon's proposal to spend $1.5 billion over the next two years to help communities in desegregating schools. The bill and its amendments were part of a $23 billion higher education bill passed 332–38. The vote came five days after a Gallup Poll reported 76% of the public opposed to busing. The key anti-busing amendment would prohibit the use of any of the funds for buses, drivers or any other cost of transporting children out of their neighborhood schools. It passed 233–124. Another amendment would not allow federal court orders requiring busing to go into effect until all appeals had been exhausted or until the time for appeal had passed. A third amendment, adopted by a vote of 231–136, would forbid U.S. education officials from requiring, or even encouraging, communities to institute busing plans.

St. Louis Globe-Democrat
St. Louis, Mo., November 8, 1971

The U.S. House, reflecting overwhelming national opposition to busing, has acted to prohibit use of federal school aid funds for busing school children to achieve desegregation.

It also passed by wide margins amendments to the $24 billion, five-year aid-to-education authorization bill that would prohibit the federal government from requiring that a state spend its own funds for busing and to delay any court-ordered busing plan until all appeals are exhausted.

This was a direct slap at the Department of Health, Education and Welfare and at federal judges who have been implementing HEW's far-out busing plans in many cities around the country.

Americans by a margin of more than 3 to 1 oppose busing. The House commendably has taken the stand the great majority of citizens wanted, a stand supported by blacks and whites.

This would be an appropriate time for President Nixon to ask for the resignation of HEW Secretary Elliot L. Richardson whose department is chiefly responsible for the school busing mess.

This is a perfect example of how federal bureaucrats sometimes are totally out of touch with the public and how they try to impose their own ultra-liberal concepts on the nation.

This massive busing proposal really backfired. Parents all over the country are up in arms about busing plans that take their children out of their neighborhoods to distant schools just to please some bureaucrat, judge or school official playing numbers games with school youngsters.

President Nixon has repeatedly expressed disapproval of this all-out busing to achieve artificial integration. And yet it has happened all around the country.

The blame therefore has to lie principally with the HEW which has been going on its own in this matter. Secretary Richardson has to bear the responsibility for what has happened. He should either step down or be fired.

The Senate version of the school aid bill has no prohibitions against busing. But if Senators take a sounding of public opinion they will quickly learn that their constituents want the House curbs on busing made into law.

THE ROANOKE TIMES
Roanoke, Va., November 9, 1971

The anti-busing amendments added by the House to the federal aid to education bill reflect the changing temper of the times. They show Northern Congressmen, who once took a holier-than-thou attitude on racial problems, caught in the same discontent which besets the South and changing their voting habits. Most acutely, they show how far the nation is from a good solution to integrating schools.

One arm of the government—the federal courts—is telling localities they must use buses to an abnormal degree to achieve racial balance in schools. Despite all the talk about a more conservative Supreme Court, the tribunal just recently refused to hear appeals from Winston-Salem, N.C., and from Pontiac, Mich. school boards. The effect was to continue the massive busing orders.

At the same time another arm of the government, the legislative branch, while willing to help finance some of the extra costs of de-segregation, flatly bans use of these funds for busing. Thus the burden falls on the localities.

Rep. Shirley Chisholm, D-N.Y., was justified in charging hypocrisy. The white communities didn't object to busing in the days of segregation. Today there are selective and excellent private day schools to which parents gladly bus their children at considerable distances. Opposition to massive busing, frequently stated on this page, is not candid if it does not admit an element of hypocrisy.

Do two wrongs make a right? Was the purpose of the Brown decision it, to take revenge on a set of sion of 1954, and those trying to im-children not involved in the original mistake? The purpose of the Brown decision and the worthwhile actions taken following it was to improve the Negro child's education, to which desegregation was a means and not the primary goal itself.

The same newspaper that carried news of the anti-busing amendments quoted the mayor of Pontiac as being resigned to the re-segregation of the races in Pontiac as forced busing causes the whites to leave the central city. That has happened in Washington, D.C., and in other Northern cities. It is happening fast in Richmond and Norfolk, Va., and in Atlanta, Ga.—cities which until forced busing were making remarkable progress in integrating the schools.

When Mrs. Chisholm and Rep. August F. Hawkins, D-Calif., support a course of action that leads to a re-segregation of the schools they are open also to a charge of hypocrisy. Perhaps there is some virtue in dropping the name-calling and concentrating on what ought to be done. For the time being, at least, the nation seems to have lost its way.

SUN-TIMES

Chicago, Ill., November 6, 1971

The U.S. House of Representatives in a middle-of-the-night vote took a stand against school busing that is clearly a vote against racial desegregation in the nation's classrooms. As such it was a disgraceful exhibition of racism and demagoguery compounded by a denial of full debate on an issue of fundamental importance.

The action came on an amendment to a bill that is supposed to ease the task of desegregation by providing $1.5 billion in federal funds to help schools make necessary changes. The amendment would ban the federal government from using its own funds for busing to overcome segregation or requiring a state to use its funds.

The issue was well stated by Rep. Augustus F. Hawkins (D-Calif): "Busing is not the issue. It is desegregation. Those who are opposing busing are really opposing the integration of the schools."

Busing is an old and traditional method of getting children to their schools. It is a commonplace in rural America and it is a commonsight in big cities where schools are becoming regional and children are bused to them as a matter of convenience and safety for them and the community.

Busing has, in fact, been used in the past to get black and Mexican-American children to black schools (going past white schools) as pointed out by Rep. Shirley Chisolm (D-N.Y.) who charged whites with hypocrisy. But now that busing is being used to promote integration it has suddenly become a wrongful practice in the eyes of those who want to defy and avoid the Supreme Court dictate that public schools provide integrated education.

It should be noted that the Senate has passed a similar school aid bill without restrictions on busing. But the House was caught up in what seemed an emotional frenzy.

Debate was limited to 30 seconds for each member. There were frequent cries of "Vote!" "Vote!" drowning out remarks of speakers. The vote was 233 for the restriction, 124 against with 74 not voting and 4 vacancies.

The Illinois delegation at least voted a majority of its votes against the proposal but we cannot be too proud of its count. Eleven voted against it, eight for it and four did not vote. Those in favor were accused by Clarence J. Mitchell, chief civil rights lobbyist for the NAACP as being are promoters of discord. For the record they are:

Republicans: Arends, Collier, Crane, Michel, Shipley, Springer.

Democrats: Klucsynski, Pucinski.

Those with the courage to resist the hysteria and vote no are:

Republicans: Anderson, Derwinski, Erlenborn, McClory.

Democrats: Annunzio, Collins, Mikva, Murphy, Price, Rostenkowski, Yates.

Findley, Gray, Metcalfe and Railsback did not vote.

The vote is not and should not be the final verdict on the matter. When a conference committee meets to resolve the differences between the Senate and the House version, we hope the stigma of racism will be erased by eliminating this disgraceful Huose performance.

Richmond Times-Dispatch

Richmond, Va., November 10, 1971

The House of Representatives' recent decisive vote against busing was an encouraging development, but it is not likely to inspire a wave of victory celebrations by friends of public education. Realists will remember that Congress has previously expressed opposition to busing, to no avail. So has President Nixon. So have numerous governors, educators and other responsible leaders. Fueled by federal court decisions and directives from the Department of Health, Education and Welfare, the buses roll on, despite mounting evidence that they are carrying public schools in some communities to the brink of ruin.

But while the House's action is not likely to put an end to forced busing, it may mark the beginning of a more effective campaign against this despised and destructive practice. For the decision represented more than another protest from Southern foes of busing. Those who voted for the antibusing amendments to the higher education bill included Northern liberals as well as Southern conservatives. One of the most impressive objections to busing came from Rep. Edith Green of Oregon, who is considered by some to be the House's foremost expert on education.

"We cannot go back 100 years to make up for the errors of our ancestors," she told the House. "The evidence is very strong that busing is not the answer to our school problems....I never bought a home without looking first to find out about the schools my boys would attend. Now, the federal government is reaching its long arm in and telling me I can't send them to that school. And that's going too far."

If enough Edith Greens speak out against busing, federal course and federal agencies that promote the practice might be persuaded to recognize it for the ruinous policy that it is. Congress itself might be inspired by such voices to approve the proposed Constitutional amendment that would prohibit busing for racial purposes. Then public schools could proceed with their paramount task, which is to provide the best possible education to all children, black and white.

Indeed, the essential aim of the education bill to which the House added the antibusing rider is to enable public education to improve its performance. The bill would provide $1.5 billion in emergency funds for such purposes as hiring specialists to work with children with educational deficiencies, adding more members of racial minority groups to educational staffs, launching programs designed to improve the academic achievement of children in racially isolated schools, remodeling old school buildings and installing modern equipment. Constructive measures like these would do more to improve the quality of public education than all of the buses in the land.

THE MILWAUKEE JOURNAL

Milwaukee, Wis., November 10, 1971

What started out last year as a Nixon administration bill designed to help school districts pay the cost of racial desegregation is winding up — with a strong push from President Nixon himself — as a fraudulent measure that instead would make desegregation more difficult.

The House, panicked by an angry cry of bigotry across the land, crippled the desegregation aid measure by loading it with provisions against bussing of pupils. Desegregation, of course, can best be accomplished through a variety of means in combination — not just by bussing. But bussing is an important part of many plans, especially in big cities.

The hypocrisy of it is clear. Nearly 40% of the nation's school-children are regularly bussed anyway, without any great national outcry, certainly without any congressional action to stop it. It is not bussing that "bussing opponents" fear; it is racial integration of the schools at the end of the bus ride.

A desegregation aid bill that withholds federal aid for the most costly aspect of desegregation is a sham on the face of it. It also is grossly unfair to school districts that are being ordered, quite constitutionally, by the judicial arm of that same federal government, to desegregate.

The Senate has already passed the aid measure without restrictions on bussing. Senators should stand firm against the House's shocking abandonment of reason and principle.

Minneapolis Tribune

Minneapolis, Minn., November 12, 1971

Consider the contrast. In Washington, the House of Representatives by large margins passed amendments designed to prevent the busing of school children for racial integration. In Minnesota, the state Board of Education moved toward the adoption of rules to require school desegregation in Minneapolis and St. Paul. The difference is in leadership.

The House is responding to election results and opinion surveys that show strong opposition to such school busing. The Board of Education is holding firm on the position that the issue is not busing, but educationally and socially harmful patterns of racial imbalance.

Columnist Carl T. Rowan exposed the cynicism in the House votes. Rowan noted that the House-passed bar on use of federal funds for desegregation busing won't stop the busing. School districts under court orders will simply be forced to use local money for busing and replace the local funds with federal payments. Rowan also contends that Congress does not have the power to keep court orders on busing from going into effect.

The sad result of such House action and of the anti-busing statements by President Nixon is the feeding of opposition to school integration. That opposition in the long run is most likely to be futile, because the courts from the lowest to the highest are calling for an end to the destructive separation of races in the schools. That opposition also is destructive in itself because it embroils school systems in endless controversy, delaying other efforts to improve educational programs.

The American public will respond affirmatively to positive leadership. That was proven when the people reversed themselves and supported United Nations membership for the People's Republic of China after President Nixon led the way with overtures to improve U.S.-China relationships. This is being proven at the local level in the continuing citizen effort to make the Minneapolis Hale-Field pairing program work (it does involve busing). Said one parent: "Fighting old battles is a waste of time. The PTA should be working now to make the most of the chance for quality education."

THE POST-TRIBUNE

Gary, Ind., November 9, 1971

The House appears to have grabbed one of the less exemplary pages from the book of the U.S. Senate in opting for legislation by stampede.

That's about the only excuse for, and the kindest thing which can be said about, last Thursday's mad — well, at least angry — pell mell action in voting a series of anti-busing amendments to a $21.7 billion education appropriations bill.

It's the same way the Senate acted in killing the foreign aid bill. We agreed with President Nixon in calling that Senate action "highly irresponsible." We say the same thing, though with less chance of presidential accord, about the House.

We recognize that busing is a highly controversial tool when used to effect school racial integration — though that was not always so obviously the case when racial segregation was involved as Rep. Shirley Chisolm remarked in asking her fellow House members: "Where were you when the buses were carrying black and Mexican-American children past your white schools to dilapidated schools?"

We further regard busing as far from the only answer, and one preferably used only as sort of a last resort, for we still see considerable merit in arguments for neighborhood schools despite the hypocrisy with which that concept is so often advanced.

To rule busing out entirely, though, as would the House-adopted amendments barring use of any federal funds for integration busing or barring federal officials from ordering use of state and local funds for the same purpose, is to sut the door on a remedy which we still believe may sometimes be effectively used. Further, while we don't at this writing have access to all the technicalities, the action would seem to throw a new burden on those areas, such as that around Charlotte, N.C., which already have opted for desegregation primarily through massive busing.

Further, the amendment which would delay a court-ordered busing plan until all avenues of judicial appeal had been exhausted would carry to an absurd extreme the Supreme Court's 1954 dictum on "all deliberate speed" in efforts to do away with school segregation.

The House anti-busing amendments were passed by the same sort of strange and unlasting coalition which showed up in the Senate on foreign aid. Blatant hypocrisy showed through the considerable support of the changes as Northern liberals, who had fought such amendments when only the South was involved, now joined grinning Dixiecrats in the anti-busing drive.

Whether the amendments stand could be subject to future votes. We hope that's the case. We could understand some efforts at limiting use of the busing tool, but we think throwing it away entirely is a mistake which can handicap schools for years.

LEDGER-STAR

Norfolk, Va., November 10, 1971

The upshot of all the House maneuvering on the use of federal funds to assist in desegregating public schools was one of the strongest national protests yet against the busing of pupils to achieve racial balance in the schools. It bespoke on a national scale the same kind of concern voiced this week by Virginia's Governor Holton at the Southern Governors' Conference in Atlanta. He pointed out that 14,000 to 15,000 Virginia students had left the public schools on account of busing.

There had been attempts to deal with the funding bill in such a way that various Representatives could escape the embarrassment of an actual vote. But balloting on the straight-out question of busing money finally came anyhow, and the result was pretty much in tune with the growing dismay of the country itself over the disruptive nonsense of cross-town switching of students. For even though many of the communities under busing orders could well use the money, the issue as it emerged in the debate was whether Congress should encourage busing by making the cost less burdensome. The verdict was a solid no: Federal funds are not to be used to pay for busing, the House insisted, raising the prospect of a long, tough wrangle in the House-Senate conference.

And to make the point even plainer, the Representatives also (1) voted 235-to-125 that no federal court busing order should go into effect until appeals have been exhausted or the time for them had elapsed, and (2) forbade members of the executive branch to encourage localities in the use of local or state funds for busing.

As a practical matter, such action may offer no great physical impediment to the courts, if the judiciary remains determined to impose busing plans no-matter-what.

But the lower chamber decisions constitute an impressive assertion of sentiment. And any organism of government which consistently attempts to override such a sense of the people weakens the whole structure, and cannot ignore for very long the damage it is doing.

Detroit Free Press

Detroit, Mich., November 4, 1971

CONGRESS is caught in a trap in handling the school desegregation issue: It cannot stop court-ordered busing by denying federal aid, but to grant such aid may be read by the public as sanction of busing.

So the House voted Monday against approving a program of $1.5 billion in aid to districts ordered to desegregate. If the position holds, Congress will have said to the districts that they cannot have money to do what they are going to have to do anyhow.

Congress is not being straightforward in this. Many districts, however much they dislike the idea of busing, urgently need outside help to pay the cost of complying with court orders. Many of them would gladly support constitutional amendments or other efforts to prevent busing. But they can take no comfort in a gesture that will deprive them of money to carry on after court orders come down.

There are other issues involved for instance, serious concern about how the money will be administered and what will be required of applicants. Detroit was recently denied funds from a similar, interim program because its faculty, though thoroughly integrated overall, does not have the same black-white ratio in every one of the city's schools. Should the aid be dispensed on so narrow a basis?

Trying to deal with the busing issue today is like trying to package smoke. The best Congress can do now is try not to take refuge in empty gesture while pushing for court tests.

In such a time as this, a lot of silly things are going to be done and said. One of the silliest would be for Congress to insist on denying schools funds to do what they cannot avoid doing.

The Dallas Times Herald

Dallas, Tex., November 7, 1971

IN VOTING decisively on various antibusing amendments to an education bill, the U.S. House of Representatives recognized that requiring children to be transported for the purpose of racial balance is widely unpopular and needs to be halted.

The House adopted one amendment which would allow schools, if they chose, not to carry out a busing order of a lower court until all appeals to higher courts were exhausted. This measure, if concurred in by the Senate, would not prevent eventual implementation of busing orders, but it would delay action.

During such a delay—which could ease Dallas' desegregation problems if the Fifth Court of Appeals orders massive busing here—two things might happen: the antibusing amendment to the U.S. Constitution might be voted in and the new judges on the Supreme Court might help overturn some of the racial balance and busing guidelines.

We think it is unfortunate that the House also prohibited the use of federal funds to pay the costs of court-ordered busing. Communities caught in the trauma of busing at present have no alternative but to spend the money to obey court orders.

Withholding of federal funds simply puts the burden on defenseless local taxpayers.

The key question arising out of the latest House action is why its members, who have now indicated their opposition to forced busing, cannot use their voting strength to obtain approval of the antibusing amendment. In the final analysis, the amendment is the only certain remedy for the busing controversy.

The Washington Post
Times Herald

Washington, D.C., November 7, 1971

When the effort to pass the President's emergency education act foundered so ignominiously in the House last Monday, it became plain to the bill's sponsors that on a third and last try later in the week they would have to add some so-called "anti-busing" sweeteners. The bill itself, of course, neither authorized nor prohibited busing. It merely acknowledged that desegregation of the nation's public schools—by court order, statute and voluntary action—was a phenomenon very much with us and one that entailed additional expenses for the districts involved; so the measure was devised to provide $1.5 billion over two years time in federal assistance to desegregating school districts. With administration support, some qualifying "antibusing" measures were added to this basic package before it was re-introduced as an amendment to the higher education bill on Thursday night. The key qualifier read as follows:

"No funds appropriated pursuant to this title may be used to acquire or pay for the use of equipment for the purpose of transporting children to or from any school, or otherwise to pay any part of the cost of any such transportation."

The effect of this addition (which was adopted when the House finally passed the bill) was twofold: 1) it made a lot of people feel better, and 2) it made the bill of somewhat less use and value to those school districts whose officials may have been as "anti-busing" as the Congress, but who were faced with the obligation to implement court-ordered busing schemes. As Rep. Quie observed in connection with some other "anti-busing" measures adopted that night:

"...let us be rational about this: There are times when the federal government has said to the schools that you must bus. That was the situation in the Swann [Supreme Court] decision. Now the President has said let us provide $1.5 billion in order to help out some of the school districts who are or will be desegregating. So the federal government says to some schools you must bus, and the federal government says here is $1.5 billion, but you cannot bus with this money even [though] it told them they must."

This confusion of a prohibition on the purchase of buses with a prohibition on busing was given a breathtaking extension in an amendment (also passed) by Rep. Ashbrook which forbids the use of *any* congressionally appropriated funds for desegregation busing programs—not just the funds that might be appropriated under the emergency education act.

Rep. Edith Green proposed an amendment which was also accepted that does not rest on this confusion. On the contrary it represents an effort to limit what the Department of Health, Education and Welfare and possibly also the Justice Department are allowed to do in terms of bringing school districts into compliance with court-developed desegregation standards. It has, in that sense, the potentially of being a *real* anti-busing measure. For it would forbid executive branch officials to "urge, persuade, induce or require any local education agency, or any private nonprofit agency, institution, or organization, to use any funds derived from any state or local sources for any purpose for which federal funds appropriated to carry out any applicable progam may not be used . . ." Since "busing" would be just such a purpose for which funds could not be used, her amendment could have the effect of severely curtailing the federal government's capacity to implement the terms of the Civil Rights Act of 1964. HEW probably could not cut off aid from numerous noncomplying school districts under its terms; Justice possibly could not go into court seeking to enforce standards that the judiciary had established.

We say "probably" and "possibly" because the full implication of this amendment—far and away the most serious adopted Thursday night—and some other amendments designed to contain the impact of court orders have yet to be analyzed fully. Moreover, it is far from certain that some of the rougher measures can be expected to survive a Senate-House conference. What is clear is that the House has given very peculiar and self-contradictory vent to its emotions: as of Thursday evening it had passed a big money bill meant to acknowledge and ease the way to school desegregation around the country and simultaneously passed a collection of measures meant to stop desegregation in its tracks.

Federal Government Policies: 1972-73

The Administration

Nixon asks Congress to act. President Nixon called upon Congress, in his State of the Union address Jan. 20, to exhibit "high statesmanship" and enact his legislative proposals despite the political pressures of a presidential election year.

"There are great national problems that are so vital that they transcend partisanship," he said. "And so let us have our debates, let us have our honest differences but let us join in keeping the national interest first."

Nixon again said he was against "unnecessary busing" for the "sole" purpose of achieving an "arbitrary racial balance." He said that federal spending for civil rights purposes would be up 25% in 1972.

Nixon holds news conference. President Nixon summoned White House correspondents to his office Feb. 10 for an informal news conference to discuss arrangements for his trip to China. However, questions at the impromptu conference covered both foreign and domestic issues.

Nixon said he had ordered a study to determine whether a constitutional amendment or legislation was needed to make the federal courts desist from issuing further busing orders for purposes of racial integration.

Once again, Nixon said he opposed busing for the purpose of racial integration. He said, however, that if the courts "acting under the Constitution, decide that the views I have held are unconstitutional, I, of course, will have to follow the courts."

Nixon also said he had asked Sens. William Brock (R, Tenn.) and Howard Baker (R, Tenn.) and Rep. Norman F. Lent (R, N.Y.) to the White House to discuss their proposed amendment to block further busing.

Nixon promises plan. Nixon's pledge came in a Feb. 14 White House meeting with Congressional busing foes. Among the possible measures discussed at the meeting were a constitutional amendment, Justice Department intervention in court suits, and legislation to discourage busing. The Senate was expected to begin debate soon on a bill to aid desegregated schools, to which the House had added antibusing provisions. These were opposed Jan. 23 by Senate Majority Leader Mike Mansfield (D, Mont.) and Minority Leader Hugh Scott (R, Pa.).

Reporting on the meeting, White House Press Secretary Ronald L. Ziegler said that after the President's return from China Feb. 28, he would receive recommendations on the problem from a panel consisting of Health, Education and Welfare Secretary Elliot Richardson, outgoing Attorney General John Mitchell and George P. Shultz, director of the Office of Management and Budget. Ziegler said outside authorities would also be consulted, including Yale University law professor Alexander M. Bickel.

Sen. Howard H. Baker Jr. (R, Tenn.), one of the participants in the meeting, said Feb. 14 that "in the relatively near future—in a matter of weeks—the products of this meeting will be fully visible within the Administration and to the public. We are about to see an end to the problem of busing as we now know it and as it is required by district courts in some jurisdictions." But Rep. Norman F. Lent (R, N.Y.), also at the meeting, said "we will not know what the answer is until well after the President returns from China." (Rep. John M. Ashbrook [R, Ohio], Nixon's conservative opponent for the Republican presidential nomination, was not at the meeting and called the Nixon pledge "another step—sideways—on the busing issue.")

Those present in addition to Baker and Lent were Sens. Robert P. Griffin (R, Mich.), John G. Tower (R, Tex.), William E. Brock 3rd (R, Tenn.) and Harry F. Byrd Jr. (Ind, Va.), and Reps. Tom Steed (D, Okla.) and Thomas N. Downing (D, Va.), as well as Administration aides.

Senator Jackson

Jackson offers amendment. Sen. Henry M. Jackson (D, Wash.) offered a proposal for a constitutional amendment at a news conference Feb. 14. The proposal began,

"No person shall be denied the freedom of choice and the right to have his or her children attend their neighborhood public school."

The amendment would guarantee "the right to equal educational opportunity in the nation's schools," which right "shall not be abridged by economic discrimination in the allocation of the financial resources available to education authorities." Jackson also introduced legislation to guarantee equal allocation of state tax resources for education, and to raise federal contributions to $16 billion annually in five years.

The senator, who had in the past supported civil rights legislation, was in the midst of a crucial Florida primary campaign, in which the busing issue had been introduced by Alabama Gov. George C. Wallace. A bill had been passed in Florida Feb. 13 which placed the busing question on the primary ballot: "Do you favor an amendment to the U.S. Constitution that would prohibit forced busing and guarantee the right of each student to attend the appropriate public school nearest his home?"

The Congress

House developments. In the House, Rep. Emanuel Celler (D, N.Y.) announced Jan. 26 that he would convene Judiciary Committee hearings March 1 to consider the various antibusing constitutional amendments submitted.

The previous day, House Republican Leader Gerald Ford (Mich.) had added his name to a petition to discharge from that committee Rep. Lent's amendment, which read: "No public school student shall, because of his race, creed or color, be assigned to or required to attend a particular school."

The petition had reportedly obtained 143 of the required 218 signatures by Feb. 14, most of them Southerners or northern Republicans. Similar amendments had been introduced in the Senate, where prospects of two-thirds passage were considered weak without substantial defections from northern Democratic ranks.

Others comment. Among others commenting on the issues, Vice President

A Agnew, Mansfield and Scott all opposed the constitutional amendment procedure.

Agnew, in a television interview taped Feb. 7 and broadcast Feb. 15, said "these things are capable of being handled within the normal statutory framework" and criticized what he thought was "a Pavlovian reaction" to use the amendment procedure whenever controversial issues arose.

B Scott and Mansfield both indicated Feb. 15 that the issue would probably be dealt with by statutory legislation in the current session of Congress, and Scott said an amendment passed under "great emotional stress" would be unwise.

Senate votes compromise. The Senate Feb. 24 approved a legislative compromise on busing of schoolchildren to achieve racial integration, while the Nixon Administration continued to work out a position and a Richmond, Va. C antibusing motorcade descended on Washington.

The Senate plan, offered by party leaders Mike Mansfield (D, Mont.) and Hugh Scott (R, Pa.) was in the form of three amendments to a combined higher education and desegregation aid bill, and was designed to put an outer limit on the use of busing, yet retain it as a desegregation tool in some cases.

D The amendments were passed by votes of 51–37, 50–38 and 79–9, the negative votes coming mostly from Southerners and conservative Republicans. Senate leaders hoped the new plan would head off a drive for more sweeping legislative or constitutional busing curbs.

The first provision would bar the use of federal funds for busing unless voluntarily requested by "local school officials."

E The second provision would prohibit federal aides from requiring or encouraging local officials to bus children "where the time or distance of travel is so great as to risk the health" or education of the child, or where the receiving school was "substantially inferior" to the neighborhood school. The provision would thus adopt as federal regulation the guidelines issued by the Supreme Court in its April 1971 Charlotte, N.C. desegre-F gation decision. A third provision would delay enforcement of court-ordered busing pending all appeals, but only in cases crossing local district lines, and only until June 30, 1973.

Senate leaders had agreed to a final vote on the combined education bill by March 1, precluding a filibuster by civil rights proponents. Busing opponents were planning to offer far more stringent legislative amendments.

G Health, Education and Welfare Secretary Elliot Richardson, a member of the panel named by President Nixon to recommend an Administration desegregation policy, said Feb. 16 that the constitutional amendments suggested up to that time could "have the effect of actually undercutting and rolling back the

measures that have been taken to dismantle dual school systems" without regard to busing.

The Washington Post reported Feb. 19 that the panel was also considering proposals for national reform of school finances and guarantees of quality education that might help defuse the racial aspects of the issue.

The Feb. 17 Richmond-Washington motorcade included about 3,300 cars from suburban areas around Richmond, protesting a court-ordered merger of urban and suburban school districts. The motorcade was preceded at the Capitol by 15 Virginia state legislators lobbying for passage of a constitutional amendment prohibiting busing.

Senate action. The Senate, by a vote of 88–6, passed and sent to a House-Senate conference March 1 the combined higher education and desegregation aid bill.

After accepting the busing compromise offered by party leaders Mike Mansfield (D, Mont.) and Hugh Scott (R, Pa.) Feb. 24, the Senate reversed itself the next day by accepting a stringent provision sponsored by Minority Whip Robert P. Griffin (Mich.) by a 43–40 margin. Griffin's proposal was a direct challenge to the federal courts, all of whom would have been denied "jurisdiction to make any decision, enter any judgement or issue any order the effect of which would be to require that pupils be transported to or from school on the basis of their race, color, religion, or national origin."

Opponents charged the provision overstepped the constitutional powers of Congress, and even Griffin indicated doubts it would be upheld by the courts, hoping it would at least put pressure on the Supreme Court to moderate desegregation programs.

Among the large number of absentees for the roll call vote were four pro-civil rights Democratic presidential candidates—Hubert Humphrey, announced as paired against Griffin's measure, Edmund Muskie, George McGovern and Vance Hartke. Defections by Democratic Sens. William Proxmire (Wis.), Robert Byrd (W. Va.) and Jennings Randolph (W. Va.), all of whom had backed the leadership compromise, tipped the balance in favor of Griffin's proposal.

Following the vote, Mansfield contacted all Democratic senators Feb. 26 to muster attendance for a reconsideration.

With only three senators absent Feb. 29 (Hartke, ailing Sen. Karl Mundt [R, S.D.] and presidential contender Henry Jackson [D, Wash.]), the Griffin amendment was deleted by a 50–47 vote, and the leadership provisions retained by 63–34 and 66–29 votes, with Humphrey, Muskie and McGovern voting with the majority. Jackson, who favored an antibusing constitutional amendment, said in Florida Feb. 29 that both legislative proposals were only "cosmetic solutions for politicians," and that "the issue must be

taken to the people before action will be taken in Congress."

A proposal by Sen. Abraham Ribicoff (D, Conn.) for a 10-year integration plan was defeated 65–29. It would have required minority representation in all schools in a metropolitan area equal to at least one half the minority proportion in the district as a whole.

Busing foes came within one vote of reviving Griffin's proposal March 1, in a version offered by Sen. Robert Dole (R, Kan.). Vice President Agnew, presiding over the 48–47 vote, did not disclose whether he would have broken a tie.

Differences to be ironed out in the House-Senate conference included a Senate provision that the $1.5 million in desegregation aid approved by both houses be spent only in districts maintaining at least one "stable, quality, integrated school." Also in dispute were Senate approval of federal funds for busing if voluntarily requested, and a House provision staying all court busing orders until appeals were exhausted. The Senate set a June 30, 1973 cutoff date for the stays, and limited them to interdistrict busing.

House holds hearings. The Rev. Theodore M. Hesburgh, chairman of the U.S. Commission on Civil Rights, took a strong stand against all the restrictive proposals March 1, testifying in the third day of House Judiciary Committee hearings.

Hesburgh said an antibusing amendment "would undermine what progress we have made in race relations, both in our schools and in society as a whole," and called the version presented by Rep. Norman Lent (R, N.Y.) "fundamentally antiblack." He said a Commission survey had found that busing programs in cities such as Pontiac, Mich. and Charlotte, N.C. were working relatively smoothly, but two Charlotte school board members who also testified said their system was "torn in rebellion."

The first two days of hearings, begun Feb. 28 and expected to last at least three weeks, pitted supporters of the 30 proposed amendments against committee chairman Emanuel Celler (N.Y.) and ranking Republican William M. McCulloch (O.), longtime champions of civil rights legislation.

Celler said the busing debate constituted a national "crisis." He said Feb. 28 that "to favor or oppose the busing of schoolchildren as an abstract matter serves no useful purpose," quoting the Supreme Court in the *Swann* case that "bus transportation has been an integral part of the public education system for years." He said about 40% of all public school students were currently bused to school.

McCulloch warned the same day against amending the Constitution "to change a practice which is itself only temporary." He deplored "inflammatory" and "irresponsible" statements against court rulings, which he said had all been "predicated on a finding that the Constitution has been violated by agents of the state discriminating on the basis of race."

But busing foes, mostly supporting Lent's amendment, said that nothing short of an amendment could affect court decisions which in Lent's words March 1 were "making a complete shambles of the nation's public school systems."

Attorney General Mitchell

Mitchell favors legislation. John N. Mitchell, on his last day as attorney general March 1 before assuming direction of President Nixon's re-election campaign, said he would advise Nixon to eschew a constitutional amendment, favoring instead a legislative approach, which he said could be effected more quickly and would be legally sounder.

Mitchell, who had been appointed to a Cabinet-level committee to recommend an Administration integration policy suggested a law delaying court busing orders pending Supreme Court appeals or further Congressional action.

A group of 40 black senior civil service and appointed officials, organized as the "Black Council," told the Cabinet committee it opposed either legislative or constitutional busing curbs, according to Council chairman Samuel C. Jackson, assistant secretary of housing and urban development Feb. 26. The group promised to present its own proposals "to limit excessive busing" in a private memorandum to Nixon and the Cabinet committee.

Executive Agency

Commission asks states to assume full costs. The President's Commission on School Finance submitted a 147-page report to President Nixon March 6 recommending that the states assume nearly all the costs of public elementary and secondary education, to relieve localities of the growing property tax burden and to guarantee equal educational opportunities within each state.

On the volatile integration issue, the commission supported redistricting to achieve racial and economic diversity, even if this "may require, in some situations, the use of buses." "However," the report continued, "busing to produce a uniform racial ratio in all the schools of a district may not be the best procedure."

The House

House bars busing compromise. The House, by a 272–139 vote March 8, instructed its representatives to the House-Senate conference on the higher education authorization bill to "insist" on retaining the House's provisions curbing the use of busing for school desegregation.

Although the instruction was not legally binding, it put the conferees on notice that a compromise bill might be rejected. It was the first time since 1970 that the House had specifically barred a conference compromise.

The House provisions would deny federal funds for busing for desegregation, prevent federal officials from encouraging busing, and stay all court busing orders until all judicial appeals had been exhausted. The Senate had defeated an even stronger provision by one vote March 1, approving instead a group of provisions that would allow federal funds for busing if requested by local authorities, prevent federal officials from encouraging busing only if it would risk physical or educational harm to children, and delay court busing rulings only where more than one district was involved, and then only until June 30, 1973.

Supporters of the latest House move noted that most of the conferees, drawn from the liberal Education and Labor Committee, had voted against the antibusing amendments to the bill, which had been adopted by nearly 2–1 margins Nov. 5, 1971.

Nixon's Messages

TV address on busing. President Nixon ended several weeks of Administration discussions with a nationwide television and radio address to explain his position March 16, two days after Florida voters overwhelmingly approved a straw ballot proposing an antibusing amendment to the Constitution.

In his address, Nixon said he was acting to enforce his "well known" position, expressed "scores of times over many years" against "busing for the purpose of achieving racial balance." Urgent action was necessary because in several cases the "courts have gone too far," creating "confusion and contradiction in the law; anger, fear and turmoil in local communities," and "agonized concern" among parents "for the education and safety of their children."

The President repeatedly claimed support for his position among blacks as well as whites, since, he said, "the great majority of Americans—white and black" opposed busing children out of their own neighborhoods.

Nixon cited "thousands of letters" he had received from all sections of the country complaining of inconvenience, fear and frustration, including the loss of children bused out of poor neighborhoods of "the extra personal attention and financial support in his school that we know can make all the difference."

To meet these complaints, the President promised to offer legislation, order "all agencies and departments of the federal government at every level to carry out the spirit as well as the letter" of his position, and direct the Justice Department to intervene where lower courts had "gone beyond the Supreme Court requirements in ordering busing." He urged listeners to drum up Congressional support for his proposals.

The President also called for a new commitment that "the children currently attending the poorest schools in our cities and rural areas be provided with education equal to that of good schools in their communities."

Message to Congress. Nixon asserted in his Mar. 17 message that dismantling of "the old dual-school system in those areas where it existed" was "substantially completed." Therefore, efforts to meet the "constitutional mandate" laid down in the 1954 Supreme Court's *Brown v. Board of Education* desegregation ruling, which Nixon defined as a requirement "that no child should be denied equal educational opportunity," should "now focus much more specifically on education: on assuring that the opportunity is not only equal but adequate, and that in those remaining cases in which desegregation has not yet been completed it be achieved with a greater sensitivity to educational needs."

Nixon approached the busing issue from that emphasis on education rather than desegregation:

"In the furor over busing, it has become all too easy to forget what busing is supposed to be designed to achieve: equality of educational opportunity for all Americans."

The President conceded that some opponents of busing were motivated by racial prejudice, but claimed that "most people, including large and increasing numbers of blacks and other minorities, oppose it for reasons that have little or nothing to do with race. It would compound an injustice to persist in massive busing simply because some people oppose it for the wrong reasons."

In many communities, Nixon said, busing was seen as "a symbol of helplessness, frustration and outrage," as parents were denied the right to choose their children's school, were forced to suffer inconvenience, and felt they were subjected to "social engineering on an abstract basis."

Among black parents, the President contended that the "principal emphasis" of the concern for quality education had shifted from desegregation, and now rested on "improving schools, on convenience, on the chance for parental involvement—in short, on the same concerns that motivate white parents—and in many communities, on securing a greater measure of control over schools that serve primarily minority-group communities."

In addition, Nixon charged that advocates of "system-wide racial balance" would condemn blacks to a permanent "minority status" in most schools, which would be "run by whites and dominated by whites," while those black students in densely populated central cities could never be reached by busing plans in any case.

One of the "historical" factors leading courts to order large-scale busing, Nixon wrote, had been "community resistance" [in the South, which Nixon avoided naming in the message] against a unitary school system, which the courts "sometimes saw as delay or evasion." But "the past three years" had brought "phenomenal" progress toward unitary systems and toward a "new climate of acceptance of the basic constitutional doctrine."

The President called this "a new element of great importance: for the greater the elements of basic good faith, of desire to make the system work, the less need or justification there is for extreme remedies rooted in coercion."

Finally, Nixon implied that plans for massive busing imposed over community resistance would not be likely to achieve their objectives. The schools, he believed, should assume a more modest burden, since they could not by themselves bring about "the kind of multiracial society which the adult community has failed to achieve for itself," and might only risk imposing "lasting psychic injury" on children by trying.

Without Congressional intervention, the President warned, busing would continue to be ordered by some courts to a degree "far beyond what most people would consider reasonable" and beyond Supreme Court requirements. He cited a "maze of differing and sometimes inconsistent orders" which have caused "uncertainty" and "vastly unequal treatment among regions" and districts.

As authority for Congressional action to substitute "statutory law" for "case law" as a guide to the courts, Nixon cited the enforcement clause of the 14th Amendment (the basis for desegregation rulings). The clause gives Congress "power to enforce, by appropriate legislation, the provisions" of the amendment.

Besides, Nixon wrote, "the educational, financial and social complexities of this issue are not, and are not properly, susceptible of solution by individual courts alone or even by the Supreme Court alone."

The President's legislative program consisted of two separate bills. The first, on which he requested immediate action, would impose a temporary freeze on all new busing orders by federal courts, "while the Congress considers alternative means of enforcing 14th Amendment rights." The second, an "Equal Educational Opportunities Act," would specify those alternative means, and would attempt through federal aid to improve education for poor and minority children.

Busing moratorium. The Student Transportation Moratorium Act would prohibit all new court busing orders immediately on passage until July 1, 1973, or until Congress passed appropriate legislation, but "would not put a stop to desegregation cases." Where "lower courts have gone beyond the Supreme Court" in ordering massive busing, Nixon promised "intervention by the Justice Department in selected cases."

This "unusual procedure" by Congress would provide a "calm and thoughtful" atmosphere for further deliberation, and would "relieve the pressure on the Congress to act on the long-range legislation without full and adequate consideration." Since Nixon found it "abundantly clear" from "the upwelling of sentiment" against busing that some curb was inevitable, he asked that "while the matter is being considered in Congress" the courts should "not speed further along a course that is likely to be changed."

A constitutional amendment, Nixon warned, would need two-thirds passage in both houses and ratification by three fourths of the states, a long and unsure process. Only legislation, he added, could supply the necessary "precision and detail" and allow a "balanced, comprehensive approach."

Congressional action begun. Senate and House committees began scheduling hearings on the President's proposals March 17, amid reports that the Administration hoped to attach the busing moratorium to the higher education bill in a Senate-House Conference. Both the Senate and House versions of the bill had included various measures to curb busing short of a moratorium. Senate leaders Mike Mansfield (D, Mont.) and Hugh Scott (R, Pa.) both suggested March 18 that the conference consider the President's proposal.

The proposals ran into opposition from Democratic committee chairmen whose committees would normally handle them. Chairman Carl D. Perkins (D, Ky.) of the House Education and Labor Committee March 22 called Nixon's plan "superficial, confusing and unnecessary," and submitted instead his own bill for $2.5 billion in additional Title I appropriations.

Rep. Emanuel Celler (D, N.Y.), chairman of the House Judiciary Committee called the moratorium "an unconstitutional interference with the judicial power." His Senate counterpart, James Eastland (D, Miss.) said March 20 that the moratorium would allow "separate but equal schools in the North," yet ignore substantial busing already ordered in the South.

Among other congressmen commenting, Sen. Edward Kennedy said Nixon's two proposed bills "would combine to perpetuate segregated educational systems where they may continue to exist." Kennedy said busing was often "the only possible device to end outright segregation."

Candidates react. Nixon's message was roundly criticized by all the leading Democratic presidential candidates, although Sen. Hubert Humphrey at first claimed the President had adopted his own views.

Humphrey said March 17 of Nixon's TV address that "at long last the President has been able to get his finger up in the air and sense what's going on and has decided that he would say amen to some of the things that some of the rest of us have been trying to do."

But after reading "the fine print" of the message to Congress, Humphrey said in Milwaukee March 20, he decided the proposals were "insufficient in the amount of aid needed for our children, deceptive," and "insensitive to the laws and the Constitution."

Sen. Edmund Muskie, campaigning in Illinois March 17, repeated his view that busing for desegregation "has value if used with common sense," while Sen. George McGovern, Rep. Shirley Chisholm and New York Mayor John Lindsay sharply criticized the President's stand, which McGovern called "a frantic effort to capitalize on this emotional issue" in order to distract attention from Vietnam, taxes and unemployment. Mrs. Chisholm said Nixon had shown "final evidence of his desire to shut the door to real equality," and Lindsay called the proposals a "cave-in" to the views of Alabama Gov. George Wallace.

Sen. Henry M. Jackson, who had favored an antibusing constitutional amendment, called Nixon's plan "intellectually dishonest" and "an attack on the Bill of Rights itself."

Alabama Gov. George Wallace said March 17 that the President didn't go far enough in his proposals. He said Nixon should use his executive powers to instruct the Justice Department to reopen all schools under a freedom of choice plan. "People want action now and not talk," Wallace said.

Rehnquist drafted antibusing plan. Supreme Court Justice William H. Rehnquist was reported to have prepared for the White House in March 1970 two memorandums proposing a constitutional amendment prohibiting the busing of schoolchildren for purposes of racial integration, according to the New York Times March 16.

At that time, Rehnquist was an assistant attorney general in the Justice Department.

The Times said it had obtained the two Rehnquist memorandums, which it said were dated March 3 and March 5, 1970.

According to the newspaper, Rehnquist had prepared his antibusing amendment at the request of the White House. He was not the only Nixon Administration official to be asked for a proposal. The White House was said to have sent written requests to various departments and specialists within the Justice Department and Department of Health, Education and Welfare for "thinking" on the busing question.

Rehnquist's amendment, if enacted, would have prevented any forced busing to achieve racial balance in a given school district. It would have permitted, however, the busing of students who voluntarily chose to be bused to other schools within their districts even if the purposes were for increasing racial integration.

That option has come to be known as one of several "freedom of choice" plans.

Rehnquist's amendment would have prohibited school districts from denying freedom of choice to blacks or any other group of students except on grounds of school capacity, absence of transportation or other "nonracial consideration."

Nixon holds news conference. President Nixon held an impromptu, untelevised news conference in his office March 24. The President discussed his school busing proposals.

On his proposed legislation to have a moratorium on school busing and to apply more funds to black schools, the President made several points. Congress had the power under the Constitution "to set up the remedies to accomplish the right of equal protection of the law." And while he agreed with the Supreme Court's position "that legally segregated education was inherently inferior education," the question was:

"How do we desegregate and thereby get better education?" Busing "for the purpose of achieving racial balance not only does not produce superior education," he said, "it results in even more inferior education."

Therefore, his proposals dealt with the issue "by saying we can and should have desegregation but we should not compound the evil of a dual school system, of legal segregation, by using a remedy which makes it even worse."

In his opinion, a moratorium on busing was constitutional and the court would so hold because "it deals with a remedy and not a right."

Even if a course of maximum busing were pursued, Nixon said, "it would still leave the vast majority of black schoolchildren living in central cities going to what are basically inferior schools."

Concerning his other proposal to provide $300 per pupil for the purpose of improving inferior schools, Nixon said studies indicated that it took at least that amount to make such a "critical mass approach" effective.

He also gave assurance, since the matter had been raised, that there was "a great deal of new money in this program." Congress had not enacted his previous request for $1 billion in emergency school aid funds that was to go into his new program, Nixon said, and his recent request spanned a four-year period, not one year.

In general, his Administration had made "great progress in desegregation," Nixon said. "There are more black students that go to majority white schools in the South than in the North at the present time. The dual school system has been virtually eliminated."

He told the newsmen, "we cannot put the primary burden for breaking up these patterns [of inner-city segregation] on the educational system . . . Whenever a device is used to desegregate which results in inferior education, we are doing a grave disservice to the blacks who are supposed to be helped."

Executive Agencies

U.S. enters 2 cases, bars Md. fund cut. In line with President Nixon's new school desegregation policies, the Justice Department asked to intervene in two appeals against court-ordered busing plans in Virginia March 31 and Tennessee April 10. Meanwhile, the Department of Health, Education and Welfare (HEW) said March 22 that it would suspend a threatened fund cutoff to Prince Georges County, Maryland schools, at least until Congress acted on Nixon's proposals.

In the Richmond case, in which U.S. District Court Judge Robert R. Merhige had ordered a merger of city and suburb school districts, the Justice Department asked the U.S. Court of Appeals for the 4th Circuit to accept a friend-of-the-court brief in the Richmond School Board's appeal since "the outcome of this case will affect" the government's desegregation "enforcement responsibilities."

Administration enters 3 more cases. The Justice Department sought to intervene in three more pending court desegregation cases in Dallas April 14, Oklahoma City April 27 and in Fort Worth April 28. They were the fourth, fifth and sixth such moves since Nixon announced his new policy March 16.

In the Dallas case, the Department asked the 5th U.S. Circuit Court of Appeals in New Orleans to consider the guidelines recommended by President Nixon's proposed Equal Educational Opportunities Act, which would bar any further elementary school busing for integration and use busing only as a last resort in other schools.

The department asked the 10th U.S. Circuit Court of Appeals in Denver to accept a brief in favor of the Oklahoma City School Board appeal of a federal district court order requiring increased busing. The brief asked the court either to delay a decision until the Supreme Court ruled on a similar Denver case, or to order the district court to reconsider whether some school segregation had been caused by changing neighborhood racial composition rather than by government discrimination.

In the Fort Worth case, the department asked to intervene in an appeal brought in the 5th U.S. Circuit Court of Appeals by black parents objecting to a federal district court desegregation plan.

Low busing costs cited. U.S. Civil Rights Commission Vice Chairman Stephen Horn, testifying April 11 against President Nixon's antibusing proposals at the House Education and Labor Committee, said a study of school busing costs by the Department of Transportation showed that only $2 million was spent nationally on additional busing for desegregation in 1971.

Total costs of public school busing rose $200 million in the year to $1.7 billion. About 95% of the increase was caused by population growth, 3% by school centralization and the remaining 1% by safety, desegregation and other purposes. Increased busing for desegregation in some areas was offset by decreased busing in Southern districts when dual systems were dismantled.

Horn said the $2 million, compared with total national elementary and secondary public education costs of $45 billion, "does not constitute a depletion of education resources," as Nixon, in his message to Congress, had claimed was the case in some districts.

The Administration

Kleindienst, Richardson differ. Acting Attorney General Richard G. Kleindienst told the House Judiciary Committee April 12 that President Nixon's proposed legislation to limit court ordered school busing for integration would allow for reopening all previous school desegregation cases, whether or not busing had been involved. Health, Education and Welfare Secretary Elliot L. Richardson had told the Senate Education Subcommittee March 24 that "an outside range" of 100 cases, in which new busing had been ordered within the past year, might be reopened as a result of the law.

Kleindienst based his view on a provision proposing that "on application of an educational agency, court orders or desegregation plans under Title 6 of the Civil Rights Act of 1964 in effect on the date of enactment of this act and intended to end segregation of students on the basis of race, color or national origin shall be reopened and modified to comply with the provisions of this act."

Kleindienst called the reopening provision the legislation's "great redeeming feature," since all districts could then conform to a "national standard." Southern congressmen had complained that a moratorium on new busing orders would allow Northern districts to escape the remedies already imposed in some Southern districts, where litigation had begun much earlier.

Richardson, on the other hand, specifically denied that "a wholesale reopening of desegregation cases" would occur, and stressed that "litigation and administrative action" to promote desegregation could continue under the proposed busing moratorium provided no "new or different" busing were ordered.

A *Administration dissent aired.* In two separate moves April 25 and 26, two thirds of the Justice Department's civil rights lawyers and the chief black office-holders of the Nixon Administration expressed strong reservations about the Administration's proposals to curb the use of busing for school integration.

A letter signed by 95 of the 148 lawyers in the Justice Department's Civil Rights Division and sent to Con-

B gressional leaders and committees April 25 opposed any legislation "which would limit the power of federal courts to remedy, through busing, the unconstitutional segregation of public school children." The letter did not specifically cite Nixon's proposals. The signers called such legislation of doubtful constitutionality, and inconsistent "with our national commitment to racial equality."

C Ten black lawyers in the department, seven of whom signed the letter to Congress, issued a separate public statement calling the busing issue a "sham" that could undo "much of the progress that has been made in the desegregation area in recent years."

Acting Attorney General Richard Kleindienst responded to the statements April 25 by suggesting that the lawyers resign if the bills were passed

D and if the lawyers could not in conscience enforce them.

The White House released a report April 26 by the Council of Black Appointees criticizing the proposed bills and the intervention by the Justice Department in pending desegregation cases. The Council called for changes in the bills to allow greater flexibility by courts in drawing up desegregation plans. The report said that intervention

E in the court cases had had "a chilling effect on black people," who believed the federal government had decided to use its power and influence to aid "those who stand in opposition to the constitutional rights of minority school-children."

Nixon would back amendment. White House Press Secretary Ronald L. Ziegler reported April 29 that President Nixon

F would support an antibusing constitutional amendment if Congress failed to act on proposed legislative busing curbs. Ziegler did not indicate how long Nixon would wait for Congressional action.

The Congress

Conferees vote busing compromise. A House-Senate conference committee approved an omnibus higher education-

G desegregation aid bill May 17 after narrowly accepting compromise provisions to limit the use of busing for school desegregation.

The busing provision would delay all new court busing orders until appeals had been exhausted, or until Jan. 1,

1974. The House bill had set no deadline, while the Senate bill had limited the delays to cases crossing local district lines and to June 30, 1973.

Federal funds could not be used to finance busing for desegregation unless requested by local authorities, nor could federal officials order or encourage districts to spend state or local funds for busing, in cases in which busing endangered pupils' health or education, "unless constitutionally required." This was similar to provisions in the Senate bill, but milder than the House bill's total prohibition against federal funds or encouragement for busing.

Passage of the bill, which included major new programs of aid to colleges and needy college students, was endangered by opposition from House members to any watering down of their tough antibusing provisions. The House had voted May 11 a second time by a 275–124 vote to instruct its conferees not to compromise on the issue.

Rep. Edith Green (D, Ore.), who had helped write the education provisions, refused to sign the conference report, saying the "integrity of the House" was at stake. Sens. Jacob Javits (R, N.Y.) and Walter Mondale (D, Minn.) did not sign the report, which they thought had gone too far in restricting the courts. The final vote on busing in conference had been 11–9 among representatives and 7–5 among senators in favor of the compromise, according to conference committee chairman Rep. Carl Perkins (D, Ky.).

Later May 17 House Democrats defeated in caucus by a 125–87 vote a resolution backed by Joe Waggoner Jr. (La.), which would have put Democrats on record against busing, and would have instructed Democrats on the Judiciary and Education Committees to report out antibusing legislation and an antibusing constitutional amendment. Rep. Emanuel Celler (D, N.Y.) announced May 10 that he would hold only two more subcommittee hearings on proposed legislative and constitutional antibusing proposals.

Senate approves antibusing bill. The Senate approved and sent to the House the final version of the combined higher education-desegregation aid bill, with its compromise antibusing provisions, by a 63–15 vote May 24.

Voting against the bill were a few Northern liberals led by Sens. Jacob Javits (R, N.Y.) and Walter Mondale (D, Minn.), who objected to the provisions limiting the use of busing for school integration. Liberals had succeeded by a 44–26 vote the previous day in tabling a motion by Minority Whip Robert Griffin (Mich.) to send the bill back to conference with instructions to accept the tougher House antibusing provisions.

Sens. Hubert Humphrey (D, Minn.) and George McGovern (D, S.D.), both campaigning in the California presidential primary, announced they would have voted for the bill.

President Nixon's chief assistant for domestic affairs John Ehrlichman said May 19 that Nixon believed the compromise busing provisions fell "far short" of his own proposed bills, and were "no substitute for the necessary busing legislation." Ehrlichman noted that the compromise would only delay court ordered busing until appeals had been exhausted, which would already have happened in some districts by fall. In addition, he said, the bill set no "final, clear public policy" on busing limits when it expired Jan. 1, 1974.

Critical Republican votes for House passage of the compromise bill reportedly depended on whether Education and Labor Committee chairman Carl Perkins (D, Ky.) would agree to report out Nixon's two antibusing bills.

Congress clears antibusing bill. The House approved and sent to President Nixon June 8 a combined higher education-integration aid bill with three moderate antibusing provisions. The vote was 218–180.

A majority of Democrats and Republicans accepted the conference committee's busing compromise despite two earlier House votes instructing the conferees not to water down the tougher provisions approved by the House.

Voting against the measure were foes of busing who thought the compromise gave only an "illusion of relief," in the words of Rep. Edith Green (D, Ore.); also in opposition were liberals, including members of the Congressional Black Caucus, who questioned the constitutionality and segregationist implications of the provision limiting court desegregation powers.

The bill would stay all court ordered busing for integration until all appeals were exhausted or until Jan. 1, 1974. (The Supreme Court had ruled in 1969 that busing had to be implemented immediately when ordered by a federal district court.)

Federal funds could be used for busing only if requested by a community, and only if no risk to pupil health, safety or education was involved. Federal officials could not require or encourage local busing "unless constitutionally required."

The desegregation aid provision would authorize $2 billion over two years to school districts in the process of desegregation. Of these funds, 4% would be earmarked for bilingual programs, 3% for educational television and 5% for metropolitan area education plans, which could be implemented only if two thirds of the districts in an area approved them.

Though President Nixon had criticized the antibusing provisions as inadequate,

Health, Education and Welfare Secretary Elliot Richardson said June 8 that the bill "embodies the heart of President Nixon's higher education initiatives."

The Administration

Administration sees moratorium effect. The Justice Department issued a statement April 29 listing 157 school districts in 25 states that could be affected by the Administration's proposed busing moratorium and integration guideline bills.

According to the department, at least 45 districts involved in some stage of litigation or administrative action would be covered by the moratorium, and at least 112 others had implemented or were under orders to implement desegregation plans since the Supreme Court decision in the 1971 *Swann* case, which found busing to be a constitutional remedy for segregation.

The statement also listed 20 districts as examples of desegregation plans involving racial balance. The Administration's proposal would exclude racial balance as a goal requiring desegregation moves.

Southern congressmen had criticized the moratorium proposal as irrelevant to their region, most of whose districts had already implemented court-ordered integration plans, and the list was seen as an attempt to meet their objection, since most of the districts listed were in the South.

Stephen Horn, vice chairman of the U.S. Commission on Civil Rights, said May 10 that the list had been "grossly misleading" concerning racial balance. His own survey found that only 11 of the 20 districts had racially balanced enrollments, and only half of those had achieved the balance by increased busing.

Nixon criticizes Detroit order. President Nixon June 22 expressed complete disagreement with the recent federal court decision ordering 310,000 students in the Detroit metropolitan area bused to achieve racial integration, and reiterated his appeal for Congressional action on his antibusing legislative proposals.

In a White House press conference, Nixon called the Detroit order "perhaps the most flagrant example that we have of all the busing decisions, moving against all the principles that I, at least, believe should be applied in this area. It completely rejects the neighborhood school districts, including the busing of kindergarten children, up to an hour and a half a day, and it puts the objective of some kind of racial balance or of attempting to achieve some kind of racial balance above that of superior education or quality education for all."

The antibusing provision included in the higher education bill approved by Congress was inadequate, Nixon said, because "from a legal standpoint

it is so vague." He said Attorney General Richard Kleindienst doubted whether the bill could apply to the Detroit situation.

The bill would delay the implementation of court busing orders until all appeals were exhausted or until Jan. 1, 1974. Nixon's proposals, which he said would cover the Detroit case, would bar courts from issuing any new busing decisions until July 1, 1973, and would set strict antibusing guidelines for any subsequent court desegregation orders.

Nixon said he had not yet decided whether to sign the higher education bill, but implied that his decision would be affected by the "doubtful" prospects of Congressional passage of his own proposals, and by pressures from senators who believed the bill already passed would provide some relief for their constitutents.

In answer to another question, Nixon said he continued to favor the legislative approach rather than a constitutional amendment on the issue, but added that if Congress failed to pass his proposals, then an amendment would be "the only recourse left."

Nixon signs busing, education bill. President Nixon signed into law June 23 the higher education-desegregation aid bill, while criticizing its anti-busing provisions as an "inadequate, misleading and entirely unsatisfactory" response to "one of the burning social issues of the past decade."

Nixon noted that the bill's moratorium on court busing orders was only temporary, while his own proposals had included a set of uniform national guidelines for any future desegregation orders, with a permanent ban on most busing for integration. Furthermore, Nixon said, the bill's language only barred orders requiring busing "for the purpose of achieving a balance among students with respect to race," and he predicted that "an adroit order-drafter may be able to prevent any effective application of this law."

Nixon said he would have vetoed the busing provisions if they had not been attached to the higher education-desegregation aid bill, which incorporated several Administration proposals.

Presidential domestic adviser John Ehrlichman said at a news conference the same day that Nixon would "go to the people" to seek an antibusing constitutional amendment if Congress failed to pass his proposals.

Rep. Carl Perkins (D, Ky.), whose House-Senate conference committee had drafted the final bill, said June 23 that the busing provisions would "bring uniformity of legal procedures on this issue for the first time," and said Nixon "just wants to keep the busing issue alive. He played politics with it as far as he could and he's still trying to keep it up."

The higher education provisions would provide funds for nearly all colleges and

universities in the country and to all needy college students, bar most discrimination against women in education and encourage educational research.

Black Caucus

Black caucus lists demands. The Congressional Black Caucus issued a list of "non-negotiable" demands in Washington June 1 that it planned to present for adoption by the Democratic Platform Committee as a prerequisite for its support of the Democratic presidential candidate.

The demands included full employment and a guaranteed family income plan with a $6,500 floor for a family of four, immediate withdrawal from Indochina, an increase in aid to black Africa, withdrawal of support to Portugal and closing of the U.S. embassy in South Africa.

The demands also included increased aid to and more black control of education, and compliance with Supreme Court busing decisions.

Executive Agencies

Boston bias hearing set. U.S. Office for Civil Rights Director J. Stanley Pottinger notified the Boston school superintendent June 2 that a federal hearing examiner would be appointed to hear evidence that the Boston School Committee had maintained a racially segregated system. It was the first noncompliance action under federal civil rights laws against a large Northern city.

Pottinger wrote Superintendent William H. Ohrenberger that "efforts by the staff of this office to secure your compliance by voluntary means have not been successful." The system could lose $10 million annually in federal aid if charges of discrimination were upheld.

Boston was accused of maintaining two types of intermediate school grade structures (grades 6–8 and 7–9) fed by two systems of primary schools which had markedly different racial compositions. Pottinger also charged that some black students were bused past white schools, and that the system did nothing about under-enrollment of Spanish-speaking children.

Nixon to use busing bill. President Nixon said in a letter released June 29 that he had instructed the Justice Department to "make full use" of the antibusing provisions in the higher education bill, which he had criticized as inadequate.

In a letter to Rep. William S. Broomfield (R, Mich.), who had sponsored the provision delaying court school busing orders and urged Nixon to apply it to the pending Detroit case, the President wrote that "notwithstanding real concerns of the department as to the efficacy

A of that provision in the Detroit situation," he had ordered the Justice Department to attempt to obtain a stay of the order mandating busing for the entire Detroit metropolitan area. Nixon said his criticism of the measure was partly aimed at securing passage of his own antibusing proposals.

The Congress

B
Judiciary Committee curb. The House Rules Committee decided Aug. 1 by a 9–6 vote to discharge the Judiciary Committee from further responsibility for a proposed antibusing constitutional amendment, which the committee had had under consideration for over a year. The amendment was sent to the floor, where it was opposed by Democratic leaders Carl Albert and Hale Boggs. It **C** was only the fifth bill in 20 years to be so treated.

House bars court busing plans. The House passed legislation Aug. 18 which would bar court-ordered busing across school district boundaries for the purposes of school integration. The bill, sponsored by Rep. Albert H. Quie (R, Minn.), retained the major provisions of the President's March 17 antibusing **D** proposal.

The bill preserved the sanctity of existing school district boundaries, at issue in Detroit and Richmond court rulings, unless the districts were "drawn for the purpose and had the effect" of segregation.

The 282–102 vote followed nearly 12 hours of debate. An amendment offered by Rep. Edith Green (D, Ore.) and passed 246–142, would permit the reopening of court-settled desegregation **E** suits, most of them in the South, to determine whether the court rulings conformed with the new legislation. HEW Secretary Elliot L. Richardson estimated that as many as 100 court cases could be subject to review under the bill, the New York Times reported Aug. 18.

The original bill would have barred only the busing of elementary school students but another amendment offered **F** by Rep. Green was passed by the House extending the busing curb to all students.

The House-passed busing curb would permit the continued pairing of schools, an action in which selected grades of predominantly white schools were combined with grades in nearby black schools. A stronger antibusing proposal, offered by Detroit Rep. James G. O'Hara (D, Mich.), would have barred all court-ordered busing, including the pairing concept. That measure was defeated **G** 211–174 Aug. 17.

Also defeated was an amendment by Rep. Augustus F. Hawkins (D, Calif.) that would have added $1.5 billion annually to funds for educating disadvantaged students.

The bill had passed the House Rules Committee Aug. 10 on a 10–5 vote after the Education and Labor Committee reported out the measure 21–16 on Aug. 8.

The Rules Committee refused to take any action to release the President's busing moratorium bill from the Judiciary Committee. The House-passed bill would supersede the moratorium measure in any case. The Administration had sought passage of the stopgap moratorium, however, in case the stronger antibusing bill stalled in the Senate.

In debate Aug. 17, Rep. Parren J. Mitchell (D, Md.), a black Congressman, warned supporters of the antibusing bill that "you are setting the stage for the second post-Reconstruction era in this nation."

Rep. William M. Colmer (D, Miss.) reminded his Northern colleagues that the busing issue had become a national one and was no longer confined to the South. "The chickens have come home to roost," Colmer said, alluding to widespread antibusing sentiment.

Rep. Shirley Chisholm (D, N.Y.) said, "The victim—the American child—has been knocked down," referring to an earlier and more moderate antibusing bill passed by Congress and signed by the President June 23. "Must he be kicked, also?" she asked.

Antibusing bill dies. The Senate failed for the third time Oct. 12 to end a filibuster by Northern liberals against a House-passed bill to limit school busing for integration. It put to rest for the session President Nixon's program to deal with school integration.

The bill would have prohibited federal courts and executive departments from ordering the assignment of elementary or secondary school students to any school other than the school within his district "closest or next closest" to his home, unless district lines had been drawn for deliberate segregation purposes. The bill would have prohibited all federally-ordered crosstown or interdistrict busing, although permitting school pairings.

Districts already operating under desegregation orders could have reopened their cases in the courts to conform with the bill's criteria. A less specific antibusing provision had been enacted in June as part of a higher education bill, but had not prevented most court busing orders from taking effect.

The Senate began debate on the bill Oct. 6, after Sen. James B. Allen (D, Ala.) had succeeded through parliamentary maneuvers to get the House bill directly on the floor without committee consideration. Supporters claimed the backing of a majority of Americans; while opponents, seeking to block passage by extended debate in the last scheduled week of the 92nd Congress, charged the bill would have unconstitutionally interfered with court powers to enforce civil rights and would have undone recent progress in desegregation.

Cloture motions were defeated Oct. 10 by a 45–37 vote, Oct. 11 by a 49–39 vote and Oct. 12 by a 49–38 vote, nine short of the necessary two-thirds of those present and voting. The Senate then agreed by a 50–26 vote to go on to other legislation.

In the third cloture vote, Sen. J. William Fulbright (D, Ark.) was the only Southerner to vote against cloture. Allen and Sen. John McClellan (D, Ark.) cast the first votes for cloture in their Senate careers, while many Northern opponents of past filibusters against civil rights bills voted not to end debate on the antibusing bill.

Proponents of the measure promised to revive antibusing legislation in the new Congress, as did Nixon in an Oct. 5 news conference. Nixon met with five antibusing senators Oct. 10. Afterwards, Sen. Howard H. Baker Jr. (R, Tenn.) said Nixon "fully supports our efforts to pass this particular bill." The House bill had been stronger than Nixon's March proposal, in covering secondary as well as primary schools and in ruling out long distance busing even as a last resort.

Sen. George McGovern (D, S.D.), Democratic presidential candidate, was announced Oct. 11 as opposed to cloture, although he was not present for any of the votes.

The Administration

Nixon holds news conference. President Nixon responded to Sen. George McGovern's charges of corruption in his administration at a surprise news conference in his office Oct. 5. Nixon said he would pursue in the next Congress if necessary his fight for antibusing legislation.

He assigned it "the highest priority. If he could not get legislation on the issue, he said, "then we would have to move on the constitutional amendment front." However, he said he thought the new Congress "might be very much more responsive on this issue after they have found out what people think in the hustings."

Hesburgh asked to quit rights post. The resignation of the Rev. Theodore M. Hesburgh as chairman of the Commission on Civil Rights was announced by the White House Nov. 16. Assistant White House Press Secretary Gerald L. Warren related the resignation, which he said had been requested by the White House staff, to a remark attributed to Hesburgh during the presidential campaign to the effect that he would resign if President Nixon were reelected.

An outspoken opponent of the President's busing policy, Hesburgh had remarked during the recent election campaign that school busing was "the most phony issue in the country."

1973

Executive Agencies

Weinberger testifies on busing. Caspar Weinberger told the Senate Finance Committee at his confirmation hearing Jan. 11 that he would not invoke executive privilege to avoid testimony before Congress as secretary of health, education and welfare.

Weinberger also answered a direct question by Sen. Harry F. Byrd Jr. (Independent, Va.) whether he favored or opposed "compulsory busing to achieve an artificial racial balance in schools." "I oppose that, as does the President," he replied. There were "other ways" to achieve integrated education, he said.

U.S. unit scores Administration. The U.S. Commission on Civil Rights charged in the fourth of a series of reports to Congress Feb. 9 that most federal agencies were failing to enforce adequately the nation's civil rights laws, and lacked commitment or leadership to change the situation.

The commission laid much of the responsibility for the government's poor record on a lack of "Presidential leadership." It predicted that without such leadership "a steady erosion of the progress toward equal rights" would take place, because of the historically crucial role of the President as a moral and political leader. The Administration had "no government-wide plan for civil rights enforcement," the report charged, and even agencies with related civil rights responsibilities, such as the Civil Service Commission, the Equal Employment Opportunity Commission (EEOC) and the Office of Federal Contract Compliance (OFCC), did not work together effectively.

The 425-page report by the independent, Congressionally created agency was the last prepared under the direction of the Rev. Theodore M. Hesburgh, who had resigned in November.

Even when civil rights agencies recognized their duties and initiated action, the report said, "enforcement proceeds at a snail's pace." The commission warned that "the long-term stability of this nation demands an end to discrimination."

With respect to school integration, the report said the Administration's decision to stop the cutoff of funds for uncooperative districts in favor of voluntary negotiations had not brought greater compliance, especially since the Department of Health, Education and Welfare (HEW) did not require the use of "all available techniques" of desegregation, including "transportation."

State of the Union Message

Spirit of bipartisanship sought. President Nixon sent Congress Sept. 10 his seventh State of the Union message in 1973 to "refocus attention" on more than 50 legislative measures he had proposed previously in the year.

He took occasion to restate his opposition to compulsory busing for the purpose of achieving racial balance and to call for "effective and reasonable curbs on busing in a way which would aid rather than challenge the courts."

The Congress

Ford completes testimony. House GOP Leader Gerald R. Ford completed his testimony before the Senate Rules Committee Nov. 5 with "high marks."

Ford opposed forced busing of school children to attain racial balance, but favored "compensatory education" for the disadvantaged.

Helms amendment tabled. Sen. Jesse Helms' (R, N.C.) amendment that would have banned school busing to achieve racial integration was tabled, and thus killed Nov. 19 on a 48–39 vote.

A

B

C

D

CONTROVERSY OVER BUSING HEATS UP DURING FEBRUARY

The controversy over school busing heated up during the month of February. These were the latest developments:

■ On Jan. 26, Rep. Emanuel Celler (D, N.Y.) announced that he would convene Judiciary Committee hearings March 1 to consider various anti-busing amendments proposed in the House. Principal among these was a constitutional amendment sponsored by Rep. Norman F. Lent (R, N.Y.) which read: "No public school student shall, because of race, creed or color, be assigned to or required to attend a particular school."

■ On Feb. 10, President Nixon in a news conference once again said he opposed busing for the purpose of racial integration. He also said he had ordered a study to determine whether a constitutional amendment or federal legislation was needed to make the federal courts desist from issuing further busing orders for purposes of racial integration. In a meeting with anti-busing members of Congress Feb. 14, Nixon reaffirmed his decision "not to leave the situation as it is" in regard to busing.

Detroit Free Press

Detroit, Mich., February 13, 1972

IF THE American people are as solidly opposed to busing to achieve integration as most surveys say they are, they can end it, and there is no inherent power in the Supreme Court that can prevent them from doing so.

The people in the United States are, after all, sovereign. If the people in their wisdom chose to abolish the Bill of Rights, they have that power. All the Constitution does is give us some guidelines for our society that we cannot change capriciously. We can change the Constitution, though.

Unlike the phony state constitutional amendments on busing, then, the attempt to amend the federal Constitution has to be dealt with on its merits. It ought to be subjected to some fundamental questions, for we live with constitutional amendments for a long time.

The amendment that a number of members of Congress propose, and that President Nixon is considering, would add the following language to the U.S. Constitution: "No public school student shall, because of his race, creed or color, be assigned or required to attend a particular school." It is aimed at what its backers consider a kind of reverse racism—that is, the assignment of pupils to achieve racial balance.

The amendment would presumably prevent both busing within a district, as in Charlotte, N.C., or in Pontiac, and busing among districts, which a federal judge has ordered in Richmond, Va., and which Judge Stephen Roth is considering for metropolitan Detroit. School boards would then be unable to draw school attendance boundaries or make school assignments in such a way as to promote either segregation *or* integration.

Before the people of the United States write such a restriction into their basic law, they must satisfy themselves on several questions: Is it only cross-district busing that has set off this clamor and, if so, is that specter real? Is it wise to ban any and all efforts to achieve racial balance within a district? Are there other unfortunate side effects that ought to be weighed? And finally, will such an amendment be read as a sign that the United States is abandoning its long effort to end discrimination in education?

Busing is, at best, an imperfect tool, and unless it becomes more widely accepted it may indeed be counter-productive. There is something obnoxious about any kind of quota system, and it has been with great reluctance that some such quotas have been sanctioned.

But the attempt to end the inequality in American life must not stop now, and if busing is to be banned, some other means will have to be found to carry on the equalization effort. Education is plainly not equal in the Detroit metropolitan area. We are not sure it ever will be equal until all of us take seriously the quality of education available in every district and every school.

The idea of amending the federal Constitution, then, ought to be subjected to the most searching inquiry and debate. There can be no doubt that the proposed amendment is a good election-year gimmick. There is real doubt that it is good long-term policy.

Los Angeles Times

Los Angeles, Calif., February 13, 1972

This nation, which won its independence from colonial rule nearly two centuries ago, was founded upon the principle of equality. But the perceptions that early Americans held of equality were limited.

Servants were indentured; other workers had few rights; women were chattels; some of the most eloquent of the founding fathers saw no inconsistency in denouncing tyranny and keeping slaves

Still, the Constitution and the Bill of Rights were documents that never ceased to exert their powerful appeal to the minds and emotions of the people. As the nation spread westward across the continent, its consciousness grew to comprehend the need for the expansion of liberty. The Civil War decided for that time that this nation "conceived in liberty and dedicated to the proposition that all men are created equal" would endure.

Emancipation of the blacks was short-lived. They were free by law only. In reality, they were not, but the struggle continued, and 89 years after Lincoln's address on the battlefield of Gettysburg, the Supreme Court of the United States reflected the stirring consciousness of the nation.

The court in 1954 unanimously held that segregation of white and black children in the public schools is unconstitutional. The separate but equal doctrine was declared to be what everybody knew it was all along: separate but unequal. The law subjected black children to discrimination and condemned them to inferior education.

The flow of orders from the courts began rapidly to eliminate official segregation in the South, particularly in small-town and rural schools. When the South resisted integration, the North reacted angrily. But what appeared in that era to be the great obstacle to school integration, legal segregation in the South, has taken on a new form in the 1970s: de facto segregation in the large cities and Northern resistance to change.

De facto segregation, based not on law, but on residential patterns, also in part a result of discrimination, is the problem now. Various methods have been proposed to deal with it. Among these, bussing is one, not the only one, but by far the most controversial. Yet bussing in varying degrees must be used to implement integration in some situations.

In the face of this, and in an election year, President Nixon has chosen not only to reiterate his long-standing opposition to bussing "for purposes of racial balance" in the schools, but to announce his support of a constitutional amendment to bar bussing, if legislation cannot achieve that purpose.

Bussing is widely unpopular, but today's realities dictate that some bussing is necessary unless we are prepared to accept de facto segregation as an insuperable barrier to integration. The Supreme Court last April, in overturning an antibussing law in North Carolina, ruled that it "would deprive school authorities of the one tool absolutely essential to the fulfillment of their constitutional obligation to eliminate dual school systems."

President Nixon apparently is willing to risk this. In the short run, his action will stimulate popular response. But the struggle for equality will go on after the November election, and history will not look kindly upon a President who failed to give leadership on so vital an issue when that leadership was so urgently needed.

The Oregonian

Portland, Ore., February 13, 1972

President Nixon some time ago made clear his opposition to forced busing for the purpose of racial balance in the schools. In Thursday's press conference, he for the first time revealed what he proposed to do about it. He told reporters he had ordered a study to determine whether a constitutional amendment or legislation is needed to stop the trend of federal court decisions commanding such busing.

There is a risk in any such legislation, especially a constitutional amendment. Mr. Nixon Thursday reiterated his support of "local control of local schools." A federal restriction on any busing for racial mixture in the classrooms would certainly conflict with such control.

Presumably what Mr. Nixon wants to halt, as do many responsible critics of massive busing programs, including Oregon's Rep. Edith Green, is the requirement for busing in such a degree as to interfere with the education of the children involved and to absorb unreasonable amounts of pupils' time and school districts' resources. On the other hand, districts should be free to use buses to the benefit of pupils, both white and non-white, as is now done in the Portland metropolitan area and in many other areas around the nation.

A federal edict against any busing related to integration would be as bad as a federal edict requiring massive busing programs to reach strict racial quotas.

Arkansas Gazette.

Little Rock, Ark., February 13, 1972

IT IS ONLY about nine months until the election and the odds on President Nixon's re-election can hardly be much better (for him) than even. In spite of all the advantages of the incumbent president, Mr. Nixon has to overcome liabilities ranging from the minority status of the Republican Party to the continuing discontent with high unemployment and inflation—not to mention the American people's constant refusal to warm up to the Nixon personality in the way that they warmed up to General Eisenhower and John F. Kennedy.

Both of the leading pollsters, Harris and Gallup, have President Nixon and Senator Ed Muskie, the Democratic front-runner, about even in the last tests of popular opinion.

Clearly what Mr. Nixon needs for his re-election campaign is a live prejudicial issue to exploit and make people forget about the cost of living and about captive pilots in Indochina. The issue of Mr. Nixon's choice is now coming into full view and it is, of course, the "busing" issue, just as Washington columnists have been hearing it would be from inside sources.

Mr. Nixon announced last week that he had ordered a study to determine if a constitutional amendment is needed to prohibit busing for racial balance in the public chools. At the same time he reiterated his stand four-square for the "neighborhood school" and "local control" of the schools, as well as his opposition to busing for balance. All the worn euphemisms were there, drawn up in line, and all of us know what they mean: the "neighborhood" school is the segregated school of the white suburb or the black ghetto, and "local control" in its turn is all the segregationists have ever wanted, or needed, to accomplish their purpose.

What we may all count upon, for sure, is a Nixon campaign to dramatize the busing controversy, inflame the prejudices that go with it, and give Mr. Nixon an issue on which to ride toward a second term. The Nixon strategy may employ a court suit to try to win some secondary point in the Supreme Court (the primary issue has already been adjudged, u n a n i m o u s l y, with Nixon's "own" Chief Justice writing the opinion). Or it might employ legislation in Congress, or a constitutional amendment, or some combination of the three devices.

The worst of the alternates would be the constitutional amendment route. This is the one that would do the most damage to the Republic and to its Constitution, and it is the route which, perhaps naively, we would hope that Nixon does not take.

The busing amendment which is now in Congress, at the moment bottled up in committees, is fully as capricious and unworthy of the American Constitution as the notorious "prayer" amendment, which was finally laid to its unlamented rest in Congress last fall. Our national Constitution is the greatest charter for government in the world, especially for its Bill of Rights. What an adornment is proposed by the anti-busing spokesmen in Congress, who would add to the eternal verities of the charter a provision that pupils may not be assigned to one school or another under certain conditions and circumstances!

If it were not for such a malicious purpose, the amendment would be purely frivolous; in better times it would have been laughed out of the Congress before now.

We do not discount Nixon's chances for making votes in the middle class white suburbs on the busing issue. Mr. Nixon has pretty well written off the poor and the black anyway, and he knows that great numbers of people in the suburbs and exurbs are prone to get excited about busing, without admitting to themselves that what they are really excited about is integration. Nixon knows the code. And he knows, too, that in any event the majority in middle class surburbia does not want to suffer any personal inconvenience in working out the national racial problems.

What will be critical will be whether enough people in white suburbia, throughout the country, get more excited about busing than about inflation and Vietnam and crime and pollution, and all the rest of it. There is no way of knowing how the President's demagoguery will pan out. The voters are often unpredictable and fiercely irrational: For example, in Florida there is the prospect now that in a big field of Democratic presidential candidates George Wallace will lead the ticket, running wild against busing, and yet in the same state Governor Reubin Askew, who discusses busing honestly and fairly, is reported to be at a crest of popularity.

We make no predictions. Except that Nixon will work the busing question, shamelessly, for all that it's worth. As we have said, he needs a prejudicial, inflammatory issue, and his old favorite, anti-Communism, will hardly ride this time around. There is, after all, a vast disenchantment with our anti-Communist adventure in Vietnam which has been so frightfully costly in blood and treasure. And Mr. Nixon himself is about to embark on his pilgrimage to Peking, although, just for precaution, we would observe that it would not necessarily be surprising if Richard Nixon opened the window to Communist China in February and turned up on the hustings in October denouncing the perfidious, godless Reds.

Mr. Nixon needs a new mount to ride in a campaign that could easily turn either way, hinging on any number of unpredictables. And if anti-Communism is out of style, there is another old favorite, racial prejudice (now called busing), that he hopes will serve just as well.

The Washington Post

Times Herald

Washington, D.C., February 13, 1972

At his press conference the other day, Mr. Nixon signaled that yet another of those fasten-your-seat-belt episodes may be about to occur regarding the administration's position on school desegregation. In the past—as we, George Wallace and a number of similarly incompatible observers have noted—these affairs have tended to leave the steady course of actual school desegregation pretty much intact. Indeed, periodically the administration itself issues documents that comprise a proud accounting of how much school desegregation it has managed to bring about in the past three years, documents that take credit for precisely the kinds of school desegregation measures (busing and the rest) that it inveighs against on the public record on other days of the week.

Evidently these lists of accomplishments are meant to demonstrate the political and practical wisdom of the "watch what we do, not what we say" strategy. And they are also presumably meant to justify the administration's exploitation of the hopes and needs and expectations of many of those most deeply involved—the resisters who have been promised what cannot be given, the school board and other community figures who are hard pressed to gain public support for court-ordered plans because of false expectations raised by administration rhetoric, the children themselves and especially the minority children whose genuine problems and genuine interests tend to be overlooked in the course of the insulting and insensitive political skirmishing indulged in by their elders. We have

never found all this to be an inconsequential price to pay. Thus, it is without much relish that we observe of Mr. Nixon's latest move—his announcement that he will now entertain the idea of supporting the drive for a constitutional amendment to stop busing—that the *best* that can be hoped for it is that it will end up representing just such another feinting and insubstantial maneuver.

The President has explained that he favors "local control of local schools" and opposes busing "for the purpose of racial balance" and that since some lower courts "seem to differ from those views" the constitutional amendment procedure may be the only recourse. But he must know that the Supreme Court has never authorized or even ruled on busing "for the purpose of racial balance," that it has strongly hinted its opposition to such busing, that it has very clearly authorized busing and similar measures *only* for the purpose of overcoming the effects of officially intended racial segregation, and that the lower courts which have been handing down busing orders have been doing so on the same stated grounds. To enact an amendment such as that currently favored by supporters of the move on the Hill could therefore hardly have much effect on a practice that does not even exist and one which the Supreme Court seems unlikely to endorse. What it actually *could* do is throw into new and terribly disruptive litigation much of the progress and achievement the Nixon administration claims for itself, much of the hard-won success in desegregating school systems formerly segregated

by law; at worst it could amount to an effective repeal of the Fourteenth Amendment where the schools are concerned.

Mr. Nixon indicated, in announcing his new hospitality to the amendment tactic, that he had not decided whether to press for legislative, as distinct from constitutional, action or what kind of constitutional amendment he might favor if he finally decides upon his course. Doubtless we shall know more when he has completed his meeting Monday with the congressional sponsors of the drive to amend the constitution, and it is possible that some variation of their preferred amendments will emerge, that a "compromise" version will be put forth if he decides to take this path. But we can see no real good coming from it, since it seems that the President must either favor a sham amendment to end a practice that is not taking place (thereby disappointing its supporters) or an amendment that could have a real and chaotic impact on the orderly desegregation that has already occurred in the South. Is this, as the administration wiseacres would have us believe, really so awfully clever? Is it—to cite the most cynical rationale—such a good idea to score points for opposition to busing in the knowledge that the Senate will probably not muster the necessary two-thirds vote for passage? What, to follow that up, is so politically attractive about forcing a lot of Republican senators to a vote they don't want to take on a questionable proposition of this kind? We do not believe that anyone, including Mr. Nixon, can win by pursuing this maneuver. We think he is playing with fire.

Washington, D.C., February 15, 1972

"Absent a constitutional violation there would be no basis for judicially ordering assignment of students on a racial basis. All things being equal, with no history of discrimination, it might well be desirable to assign pupils to schools nearest their homes. But all things are not equal in a system that has been deliberately constructed and maintained to enforce racial segregation. The remedy for such segregation may be administratively awkward, inconvenient and even bizarre in some situations and may impose burdens on some; but all awkwardness and inconvenience cannot be avoided in the interim period when remedial adjustments are being made to eliminate the dual school system."

The quotation comes from Chief Justice Burger, not exactly a flaming radiclib, who wrote the decision for a unanimous Supreme Court in last spring's so-called "busing" case—Swann versus the Charlotte-Mecklenburg (N.C.) Board of Education. The Chief Justice's remarks are worth pondering because they shed some needed light on a subject that has been grossly distorted in our political discourse. First, they remind of the all but forgotten fact that where large scale busing has been ordered by federal courts, it has not been ordered for the purpose of achieving some arbitrary or desired "racial balance," but rather as an interim remedy for some previous constitutional violation, as a tool for helping eliminate dual school systems in districts where schools have formerly been segregated by official intent. Generally, busing has only been ordered by the courts in the face of local obduracy and refusal to formulate adequate plans to desegregate local school systems.

Busing can be messy—very messy—as the Chief

Justice allows. It can also be (and here and there has been) badly invoked by the courts, for it is neither the ultimate nor the exclusive remedy for overcoming the effects of past official, intentional discrimination. In other words, busing is not "the" remedy, but "a" remedy available in such cases. It has worked better and worse in different districts, and in some districts where the resistance has been strongest courts have found that the busing ordered for purposes of eliminating racial segregation has actually been less extensive and less extreme than the amount of normal busing it would replace. The Supreme Court found this to be true of the Swann case, for example. As Chief Justice Burger wrote:

"This [proposed] system compares favorably with the transportation plan previously operated in Charlotte. . . . In these circumstances, we find no basis for holding that the local school authorities may not be required to employ bus transportation as one tool of school desegregation. Desegregation plans cannot be limited to the walk-in school."

All this is by way of preface to commenting on the latest developments in the emerging argument over whether there should be a constitutional amendment to prohibit busing of students for racial reasons. It is, we believe, no endorsement of all-out, comprehensive busing programs in every affected district in the country to observe that the argument for its use in certain situations as set forth by the Chief Justice, seems to us to provide the framework of a rather compelling case against a constitutional prohibition of busing. This, in turn, leads us to view Monday's events as something of a bad news/good news story. First, as they say, the bad news. It is that Senator Jackson

has unveiled a proposed constitutional anti-busing amendment of his own. The senator presented it in connection with a legislative program and another article to his amendment relating to the improvement of educational opportunity—to which we shall return another time. His anti-busing proposal reads as follows:

"No person shall be denied the freedom of choice and the right to have his or her children attend their neighborhood public school."

The language—"freedom of choice"—is an unfortunate echo of the slogan of Southern resistance ("freedom of choice" as a subterfuge for maintaining segregated systems was struck down by the Court in 1968), and—more to the point— it is plain that this simple language, if incorporated into the constitution could have the effect of reopening litigation likely to undo the massive progress already made throughout the South in dismantling dual school systems.

The good news is that, at least for the time being, President Nixon has declined to support the growing movement for a constitutional amendment on this subject in Congress. Evidently Mr. Nixon means to study the matter further, and he has not foreclosed the possibility. Neither do we know as yet what form his legislative and administrative actions (via Justice Department suits) will take. It is enough now to express satisfaction that the President apparently has not yielded to pressures to join this deceptively simple seeming drive. We remain convinced that there is no such route available that could put a crimp in certain selected court-ordered busing programs without opening a Pandora's box of relitigation and regression so far as the South's hard won achievement of school desegregation is concerned.

The Pittsburgh Press

Pittsburgh, Pa., February 12, 1972

Demands for an antibusing amendment to the U. S. Constitution have g r o w n louder since a federal judge issued a decree last month ordering the Richmond school system to desegregate by merging with two suburban counties.

A proposed amendment in the House now has the backing of Republican leader Gerald R. Ford of Michigan. President Nixon has indicated he intends to take a stronger stand against busing — either by supporting a constitutional amendment or antibusing legislation.

Sen. Sam J. Ervin Jr., D-N. C., and others in both the House and Senate are hoping to forbid busing by law, either by cutting off all federal funds or by barring federal courts from ordering b u s i n g to achieve racial balance.

Popular as these moves may be, they raise fundamental questions about the relationship between the courts, the Constitution and Congress. For example:

✔ Should a document as broad and enduring as the Constitution include a section on how children should be assigned or transported to schools? Probably m o s t Americans whatever their views on busing, would prefer to deal with the problem another way.

✔ What sense does it make for one branch of government (the courts) to order a school district to bus pupils, and then for another branch (Congress) to deny funds for compliance? None.

Some judges, as Chief Justice Warren E. Burger suggested last summer, seem to have gone overboard on busing, an expensive and disruptive technique that should be used as sparingly as possible. This should be corrected — by the Supreme Court, if necessary.

The Supreme Court, perhaps in a Denver case it has agreed to hear, may clear up much of the confusion by setting down some reasonable restraints on how busing is to be used.

This may not be as simple as a congressional resolution, or as dramatic as a constitutional amendment, but it puts the busing issue where it rightly belongs, and where it most effectively can be handled in accordance with local circumstances and problems.

The Dallas Morning News

Dallas, Tex., February 12, 1972

ALMOST CASUALLY, President Nixon has announced what is undoubtedly a deeply considered political commitment: He has decided to throw his weight behind the snowballing movement to halt busing solely for racial balance in the schools.

His decision to talk with the sponsors of an antibusing amendment now circulating in Congress could speedily tip the scales toward adoption. And there is no way he can turn back.

Nixon chose a veiled way of announcing his decision to quit talking about the desirability of the neighborhood school and start doing something about it. He had his reasons.

His support of the neighborhood school and opposition to busing is well known, he says, but it "seems" that some court decisions aren't in agreement with his views. Therefore, he is ordering a study to decide whether a simple federal law or a constitutional amendment will do the best job of ending busing.

THE STUDY isn't necessary. Only a constitutional amendment can do the job. As for the apparent difference he claims to see now between his views and that of the courts, that difference has been as plain as daylight ever since the Supreme Court many months ago blessed busing as one way to achieve racial balance.

That busing decision put Nixon on notice that his personal support of the neighborhood school—repeated so many times publicly—could be just as unconstitutional as anybody else's, depending on the individual case.

It has taken him these many months to make up his mind to try and overturn the court, if possible. The widespread support of the antibusing amendment in Congress undoubtedly helped him decide to do so.

HIS DECISION to take the big step is far from casual. It is political in the deepest sense—a huge majority of the voters think as he does—and a later reversal would be ruinous. He can no longer risk the charge of doubletalk.

Many have not understood that —whatever his own feelings—a president must uphold the Constitution and the court, meaning that ' e could not overturn what had been done. But he could oppose it publicly —and that is what he has now belatedly decided to do.

He is pretending to be only answering a new challenge to his old views. Why the pretense is necessary is politically plain—but, still, better late than never. The real Nixon now has stood up. It is hard to see how he can sit down again on the busing issue.

Richmond Times-Dispatch

Richmond, Va., February 13, 1972

One of the most encouraging recent developments in the antibusing crusade was President Nixon's announcement that he is searching for an effective way to counter the iniquitous efforts of federal courts to promote school integration by transporting children from here to Timbuktu. So far, the antibusing movement has suffered from a lack of vigorous leadership from powerful and respected national and state public officials, and Mr. Nixon s apparent promise to march in the vanguard is, therefore, reassuring.

Many sincere and competent citizens have emerged as leaders of local antibusing organizations.

But most of these men and women lack the time, the resources and the stature to unify the movement on a state or national basis and to provide it with influential, prestigious and constructive direction. Leadership, of one kind or another, the movement will have, however; and if men like Mr. Nixon and Gov. Linwood Holton, both of whom have denounced busing, do nothing more than deplore it verbally, demagogic politicians will move in to exploit the emotional aspects of the controversy. Already there is evidence that rabble-rousers are beginning to fill the leadership vacuum in Virginia.

It is impossible, of course, to squeeze all emotion from the busing issue, for when the welfare of their children is threatened, parents naturally and understandably react emotionally. But busing also can be fought on practical and legal grounds, and foes of busing must make certain that their cries of anguish and anger do not blot out the voices of reason. Moreover, the fight against busing must be viewed not as a negative movement but as a positive, constructive campaign to promote educational progress. Efforts to preserve locally controlled neighborhood schools must be accompanied by a firm commitment to educational equality and excellence.

Should the neighborhood school concept triumph, society must not repeat the tragic mistake of neglecting the educational needs of the black child, as it often did during the era of state-imposed segregation.

Opposition to busing as a device to promote racial balance in public schools is developing throughout the nation. Critics include public figures of all political hues, including left-wingers like Dr. Benjamin Spock, and parents of nearly all creeds and colors. An evil so thoroughly despised is bound to be vincible, if some responsible official will but rally the troops, pick up the lance and lead the attack.

The Charlotte Observer

Charlotte, N.C., February 8, 1972

The anti-busing amendment pending in Congress is a remarkable example of confusion and dishonesty. Behind it are demagogic motivations in an election year. Before it, if it should become a part of the Constitution, are effects which no one can foresee. In fact, its sponsors, unwilling to admit their motivations, have wrapped them in so much disguise that they may have defeated their own purposes.

What does it do? The version sponsored by a large body of anti-busing congressmen says this:

"No public school student shall, because of his race, creed or color, be assigned to or required to attend a particular school."

The sponsors of this proposal, seeking to profit from widespread public confusion about school desegregation, are being demagogic in the basic sense. They hope to win votes not by explaining the issue or taking an honest position on it but by riding the crest of an emotional wave — and adding to the emotionalism. They contribute nothing to reasoned consideration of a very serious matter.

The truth is that the sponsors want people to think they are stopping busing, and they are not. They want people to think the courts have been willy-nilly assigning students by race without regard to constitutional requirements, and that is untrue. And those among them who are not old-line segregationists want the moderate, middle-of-the-road voters to think their purpose is not segregation but a reasonable approach to desegregation, a proposition which is either fuzzy-minded or altogether cynical.

We do not oppose this amendment on grounds that any kind of busing plan anywhere is workable or desirable. We oppose it because the proposed amendment ignores the facts of school segregation, constitutional law and educational quality.

Over a period of decades governmental policy —in housing loans, public housing construction and a variety of other fields — has built ghettoes and created segregated schools. To say now that government has no obligation to undo that wrong would be to ignore the Constitution's "equal protection" requirement in the Fourteenth Amendment. Why not an honest amendment, then, to repeal the Fourteenth Amendment?

Because sponsors of the amendment have chosen sophistry over reason, they do not propose that. They ask for a basic tampering with the Constitution, but in slippery fashion they propose wording that will generate confusion and uncertain results. Court desegregation plans do not now assign a student to a school simply "because of his race, creed or color," though the amendment's sponsors would have us believe that. Instead, the courts call for assignments that would break down dual school systems unconstitutionally created by government policy. If those illegal systems are broken down and new segregation is not created by policy, the Supreme Court emphasized in its Charlotte decision, race is no longer a factor in school assignments.

Since the highest court has unanimously said that — even before President Nixon's appointment of more conservative justices — why should it be said in an amendment ostensibly changing the U.S. Constitution?

Professor William Van Alstyne of Duke University's law school, a widely recognized authority on constitutional law, has testified that the amendment "is in fact exceedingly unlikely to have any effect upon the authority of a federal court to require pupil assignments to schools other than those within their neighborhoods." But, he notes, passage of the amendment would place in the Constitution — a document which we believe should never be tampered with on the basis of the emotionalism of the moment — a provision representing the dishonesty of congressmen seeking reelection.

If the country really wants to freeze the courts out of the business of interpreting the Constitution insofar as it applies to "equal protection," let Congress say that clearly and then we can debate whether we want to change a basic part of our form of government. We hold to the conservative position in this case: the position that the nation should move very slowly indeed to change its basic forms of government, and the position that it should not do so with a confused proposal directed toward the next election.

THE ARIZONA REPUBLIC

Phoenix, Ariz., February 9, 1972

The Senate Education Committee predictably approved an anti-busing resolution, urging Congress to propose a constitutional amendment that would prohibit transportation of school children to public schools out of their neighborhoods just to achieve an arbitrary racial balance.

There would be little reason for the resolution if not for its significance as a testimonial against the busing concept that has been forced on public schools by federal courts. But that alone is important, because it obviously represents the sentiment of almost all Arizonans.

And in order to help stop this draconian f e d e r a l interference with local schools, the legislature should give congressional proponents of such an a m e n d m e n t (which has been introduced in the past two sessions of Congress) all possible support to convince uncommitted legislators to vote for its passage.

There is no doubt that the overwhelming majority of people oppose busing. The latest Gallup Poll on the subject, taken last September, showed that only 18 per cent of all Americans favor busing. And among the individual groups polled (Gallup surveyed 13 groups, breaking the poll down into categories of age, race, education, and political affiliation), the largest percentage in favor of busing (those under 30 years of age, 26 per cent of whom approved) was still a significant minority within that group.

Leaders of Washington's liberal establishment — some of them Democratic presidential candidates—have been the most vociferous in their demands that busing be implemented on a large scale to create immediate racial balance in public schools across the country. Sen. George McGovern, for e x a m p l e, blasted President Nixon for his opposition to compulsory busing, and declared: "The President has encouraged massive evasion of and contempt for the law."

But the record clearly shows their pro-busing fervor to be nothing but ideological hypocrisy. Mike Wallace, host of CBS' "Sixty Minutes," cut through the rhetoric to demonstrate that almost all Washington - based pro-busing enthusiasts avoid Washington public schools like the plague, and send their children to private schools where they will never be affected by their parents' social engineering.

The children of Sens. George McGovern, Edmund Muskie, Ted Kennedy, Birch Bayh, and Philip Hart, Rep. Donald Fraser, Washington Mayor Walter Washington, Supreme Court Justice Thurgood Marshall, and liberal journalists Tom Wicker, Phil Geyelin, Benjamin Bradlee, and Nicholas Von Hoffman all attend high-fee private schools in suburban Washington.

Washington Post columnist Von Hoffman, one of the nation's most liberal newsmen, said he only supports busing symbolically. "Nobody wants to make his children pay for his own social philosophy," he frankly declared.

Interestingly enough, U.S. District Court Judge Robert R. Merhige, who ordered Virginia school children bused from Henrico and Chesterfield counties across political boundaries into the nearby City of Richmond, is himself one of those parents who will never personally suffer from the doctrinaire racism of his recent decree.

Like so many busing proponents he sends his young son to a private school for well-heeled Richmond suburbanites. And that school itself has a racial imbalance resulting from de facto segregation — something he has declared unconstitutional for parents whose children attend neighborhood public schools that similarly reflect the racial and ethnic composition of their neighborhood.

SCHOOL BUSING: VOLATILE POLITICAL ISSUE

The question of busing school children to achieve racial balance was rapidly emerging as the most volatile political issue of the year. Fostered by President Nixon, opposition to "forced busing" appeared to be on the verge of becoming a respectable stand in the U.S. The latter part of February saw busing foes gain support in state capitals and city halls, both North and South; among the presidential candidates campaigning in Florida for the March 14 primary; and in Congress, where at least 30 bills and several constitutional amendments had been introduced to ban school busing.

These were the major developments:

■ President Nixon asked a cabinet-level committee to study the busing problem and report to him after his return from China. Among those on the panel were Health, Education and Welfare Secretary Elliot Richardson and outgoing Attorney General John Mitchell. Outside experts were to be consulted, including Yale University law professor Alexander M. Bickel. Prof. Bickel was co-author with Rep. Richardson Preyer (D, N.C.) of a two-year-old bill that would have allowed for voluntary, federally-financed busing to high-powered schools enriched with federally-funded programs to improve education for whites and blacks. (The Preyer legislation was never acted upon, but a revised bill was submitted by the congressman in the House March 2.)

■ In the midst of the Florida primary campaign in which the busing issue had been introduced by Alabama Gov. George Wallace, presidential contender Sen. Henry Jackson (D, Wash.) proposed a constitutional amendment to curb busing that led off with the ringing declaration: "No person shall be denied the freedom of choice and the right to have his or her children attend their neighborhood public school." Florida Gov. Reubin Askew, meanwhile, fought a lonely battle to halt the antibusing movement in his state. He called school busing a "neces-

sary evil" and insisted on submitting the issue to Florida voters in a referendum.

■ Among the foes of a constitutional amendment was—surprisingly—Vice President Agnew, who said "these things are capable of being handled within the normal statutory framework"; also George Meany, who accused antibusing champions including the White House of stirring up a "divisive political issue"; HEW Secretary Richardson, who said that constitutional amendments could "have the effect of actually undercutting and rolling back the measures that have been taken to dismantle dual school systems"; and Walter Mondale (D, Minn.), who opened Senate debate with a stirring speech Feb. 18 in which he declared: "Every reasonable effort must be made to overcome the results of officially approved school segregation . . . and reasonable transportation will be required where necessary to defeat the results of racially discriminatory student assignment policies."

■ In the Senate, a compromise plan by Majority Leader Mike Mansfield and Minority Leader Hugh Scott was approved Feb. 24. The legislation, attached to a combined higher education and desegregation aid bill, put a limit on the use of busing while retaining it as a desegregation tool in some cases. One day later, however, the Senate reversed itself, accepting a stringent provision sponsored by Minority Whip Robert Griffin (Mich.) which denied all federal courts the "jurisdiction to make any decision, enter any judgment, or issue any order the effect of which would be to require that pupils be transported to or from school on the basis of their race, color, religion or national origin." Since the proposal was passed by only three votes, 43-40, Mansfield called back the many absentee senators, among whom were four pro-civil rights Democratic presidential candidates—Hubert Humphrey, Edmund Muskie, George McGovern and Vance Hartke. On Feb. 29 the Griffin measure was defeated by a vote of 50-47 and the Mansfield-Scott provisions were adopted.

The Sun Reporter

San Francisco, Calif., February 19, 1972

"I do solemnly swear that I will faithfully execute the office of President of the United States, and will to the best of my ability preserve, protect and defend the Constitution of the United States."

This is the oath that Richard Milhouse Nixon, 37th President of the United States of America, took January 20, 1969. Since occupying the White House, Nixon has used every opportunity to coerce the Supreme Court, to cajole the Legislative branch, and to develop his personal antagonism to the U.S. Supreme Court's decision that busing of school children is an accepted means by which the constitutional rights of racial minorities to obtain equal public education is to be secured.

Never before has the prestigious office of the presidency been used for a continuing campaign of intimidation against the other two branches of the federal government, and never before has a President suggested that Supreme Court decisions which are unpopular need not be enforced by the executive branch of the government nor obeyed by the citizenry.

Nixon, nationally, and Alioto, locally, through their busing gyrations are saying that in their view ours is a nation of laws and not men -- only when the courts interpret the law in a manner which agrees with their personal prejudices.

How can one bound by oath, urge the Congress or the nation to adopt a constitutional amendment which implants into that document prohibitions against Supreme Court decisions which guarantee constitutional rights? We have no doubt that in a society sick with racism the White majority is antagonistic to busing. But for the President of the United States to suggest that we yield on enforcement of constitutional rights to satisfy racism literally destroys a cornerstone of the Republic. Should this Nixon constitutional amendment be passed by the Congress and adopted by the states, Blacks and other racial minorities would have no further recourse than to conclude that this nation in fact is unalterably opposed to the establishment of a society based upon equality, cleansed of racism. How then could Blacks, ignore the admonition over the gates of Hell in Dante's Inferno: "Abandon hope, all ye who enter here!"

The Detroit News

Detroit, Mich., February 16, 1972

Millions of families worried about massive, cross-district bussing are reassured by President Nixon's pledge to counter the wave of court decisions requiring this technique of school integration. We welcome the President's action and we concur in the moderate, thoughtful position he has taken.

Rather than immediately embrace a constitutional amendment to stop bussing, President Nixon promised to study less drastic but possibly equally effective alternatives. For example, in the Detroit case, the whole premise of a remedial bussing plan for racial integration is Judge Stephen Roth's finding of de jure segregation in the city schools. Many would argue the pattern of segregation in Detroit arises solely from housing patterns which have been and are changing. This segregation is de facto, not de jure.

In this and similar cases, constructive intervention by the Justice Department might lead to a clear-cut Supreme Court decision that draws a more careful line between de jure and de facto segregation and the remedies that may or may not be required.

It may a l s o be possible to halt massive, cross-district bussing by legislation t h a t distinguishes between the law of the land — which forbids deliberate, officially sanctioned segregation — and a mandatory responsibility to integrate. Certainly no city or school district can legally bus children to keep them racially separate. That need not mean, however, that a city or school district is duty-bound to bus children to keep them racially mixed. Legislation, upheld by the Supreme Court, could clarify this point.

If court case intervention or new legislation could solve the problem, it would be preferable to a constitutional amendment. That document is too important to be changed casually. The amendment process should be used only if that is the sole means of reflecting the will of the majority. Until the study of legal alternatives commissioned by the President is completed, no one really knows whether a constitutional amendment is required.

We note, however, that efforts of congressmen such as Michigan Republican Senator Robert Griffin to amend the Constitution and take other steps to curb court-ordered bussing have been instrumental in bringing public o p p o s i t i o n into focus. Without strong leadership, the issue could have produced extreme, destructive and ineffective anti-bussing efforts. It took the professionalism of Senator Griffin and others to involve the President directly. In turn, the President now offers the public the best hope of finding the best means to stop the massive bussing schemes.

Again, we point out that anti-bussing sentiment is not a new racism. Despite lingering personal prejudices of both races, the acceptance of integration has come a long way and will go further. However, the contribution massive forced bussing may have made toward this goal is miniscule compared to the cost, disruption and inefficiency of such plans.

The neighborhood school, particularly defined in terms of a neighborhood of open housing and a school of good quality, is important and valuable to the public. That is why the public must and will support programs to make that kind of neighborhood school available to everyone but will not support the bussing technique.

The San Diego Union

San Diego, Calif., February 16, 1972

The busing of school children to achieve a predetermined ethnic mix has been a vexing national problem for several years, but there can be no doubt that the issue now is narrowing to a decision.

More than 30 measures have been introduced in Congress seeking a constitutional amendment to prohibit busing when ethnic proportions in schools are not established by public policy. The Administration also is making it clear that it intends to press for a resolution of the problem.

Unfortunately, as in most issues surrounded by intense emotion, much of the dialogue has not been germane to the controversy over recent court decisions requiring children to be bused across city boundaries even when there is no public policy of discrimination.

It is not a matter, as some suggest, of which presidential aspirant among the Democrats sends his children to private school while he advocates busing — although that hypocrisy speaks for itself. It is not a problem of inadequate enforcement of constitutional provisions requiring equality before the law. All responsible persons favor that. It is not even an issue of unequal financing of schools, and thus presumably inferior educational opportunities. These are soluble problems.

It is not even a racial matter.

Instead, the current busing controversy makes it plain that America has reached a crossroad — the basic question of whether or not education will remain a local, neighborhood matter. In this regard, we should be speaking now of our aspirations in education; of whether we want families to be close to the schools and teachers; of whether we want mothers and fathers to be included in the formal educational experience.

We also should be speaking of whether Americans have a right to choose the neighborhoods in which they want to live — a choice that often is determined by the number and quality of the schools available.

To the extent that these questions have been discussed, it is apparent that Americans, black, white, brown and yellow, have opted for the historic neighborhood concept. Citizens of all colors are raising their voices to oppose busing if no public policy of segregation exists. Polls as well as the strong support for an anti-busing amendment also reflect the public mood.

Under these circumstances, it is plain that the cause of education would best be served by whatever act of Congress it takes to convince the courts that they are not reflecting the public will when they order transportation of children simply to achieve some sort of artificial statistical harmony.

CHICAGO DAILY NEWS

Chicago, Ill., February 17, 1972

In setting up a Cabinet committee to advise him on the issue of school busing, President Nixon appears to be backing away from the idea of a constitutional amendment to restrict busing. If so, he's on the right track, for amending the Constitution would be the worst way of dealing with this complex and thorny problem.

It's a problem that won't vanish soon, and it threatens to become a major issue in the political campaign, fanned especially by George Wallace but helped along by dozens of others. Nor is it an issue confined to the South. Sen. Henry Jackson (D-Wash.) is the only Democratic presidential aspirant except for Wallace to advance an amendment of his own, but congressmen of both parties and from widely scattered parts of the country have joined the parade. The House Judiciary Committee will open hearings March 1 on dozens of amendments already offered.

President Nixon has left no doubt that he believes the courts have gone too far in ordering busing for racial balance, and there isn't much question that this is a popular view. Even strong proponents of school integration by every feasible means have been appalled by some rulings that seem to demand transfers on such a scale that children would spend as much time aboard criss-crossing fleets of buses as they would in school.

But a flat constitutional ban is no way to deal with a problem that is essentially local and varies from one city or school district to the next. And almost any such ban would halt or reverse the slow but steady progress made since the Supreme Court's historic school desegregation decision of 1954. If better guidelines are needed to keep busing within reasonable bounds — and we are inclined to think they are — they should come either from the Supreme Court or through legislation broad enough to be applicable on a national scale.

Even if it could be divorced from the racial issue, school busing would remain a touchy subject. No parent enjoys seeing his child exposed to the hazards of highway or city traffic if it can be avoided. It has been accepted in rural areas because it became the means to consolidate schools and provide a better education, but it isn't likely to meet the same acceptance when there is a school within walking distance.

Obviously, race enters hugely into the whole busing controversy, so the simple merits of neighborhood schooling and busing where necessary cannot be discussed dispassionately. One who opposes busing becomes a segregationist, and proof of good intent for integration requires unstinting support for busing. This would appear to be the only rationale behind some lower court orders prescribing set racial mixes that cannot be achieved without moving thousands of children daily out of their home neighborhoods.

It is all too evident that some school districts in the South used busing to preserve segregation, and that busing to break up that system imposes no greater hardship. It should also be evident that many communities can achieve good racial balance and good education at the same time by limited busing — Evanston is a prime example. But to cite either example merely confirms the fact that both the problem and its solution are highly localized; what works in one place may not work in another, and to say that busing is right or wrong for the whole country approaches the ridiculous.

The main issue continues to be promoting better education for the children. That aim should not be clouded by ideological stances pro or anti busing, or by using children as pawns in the furtherance of the arguments. And most particularly, the aim should not be lost by driving the school bus in among the basic principles of the U.S. Constitution.

THE SUN

Baltimore, Md., February 16, 1972

Obviously busing is a major political issue. It is showing signs of becoming such an emotional issue that good sense, good manners and orderly process are in danger of being left behind. Therefore, we were pleased to see that Vice President Agnew was willing to speak out forthrightly against the nonsensical idea of amending the Constitution to deal with the problem. We trust that President Nixon will, too, when he has his China visit behind him. It is unfortunate that Mr. Nixon has left the impression that he is even considering supporting such an inappropriate approach to the problem. Meanwhile, it ought not be ignored that there are many people who still believe in busing within the framework of better education, and better and fairer educational opportunities, for all children. Thus:

The next president of the American Bar Association is Chesterfield Smith, from Polk County, Fla., in the heart of the backlash country. Polk voted for Wallace in '68 and Goldwater in '64. But Mr. Smith says he believes busing of school children is a "necessary evil" to overcome the problems caused by years of segregated schools. That is hardly a popular view in Florida or in Maryland or in Michigan, but it is important to remember that a great many public leaders like Mr. Smith are still trying to talk sense to the American people about this increasingly emotion-laden issue. The governor of Mr. Smith's state, Reuben Askew, is another individual who says publicly that some busing is desirable—or at least necessary—in the present circumstances.

These are a couple of the very few straws in the fierce anti-busing wind, it is true, but it is also true that in part because of busing, school desegregation is now proceeding apace in Florida and other Southern states. Hillsborough County (Tampa), which adjoins Polk, has put a "massive" busing plan in operation without the sort of turmoil being predicted in other places. (Hillsborough has half again the area of Richmond, Chesterfield and Henrico counties in Virginia, where a court's order for busing has created such a stir.) The record in the South as a whole shows a dramatic decrease in the number of schools with nearly all black student bodies. In the North, meanwhile, the number of such schools is increasing.

In New York state, for example, the number of schools with 90 per cent or more minority enrollment rose from about 45 per cent to about 50 per cent from 1968 to 1970. This finding and others about the schools there have led a special study commission appointed by the governor to recommend that busing be used to break up such concentrations. Not only is integrated education better education the panel concluded, but it is also a major tool to keep America from "going down the apartheid road," as one member put it.

Busing isn't the only answer to the problem. In some communities it isn't an answer at all. But it is one answer in many situations, and the only answer in some.

Daily Defender

CHICAGO

Chicago, Ill., February 17, 1972

It can scarcely be doubted now, if there ever was a doubt before, that President Nixon's racial antipathy is reflected in his unflagging desire to scuttle school busing at all costs. Not satisfied with giving unbounded endorsement to the members of Congress who are pressing for passage of a proposal that would outlaw the mechanism by which school ethnic balance would be hastened, the President is exploring feverishly legislative or constitutional device that would best put to rest the controversial school issue.

He has ordered a study with a view to determining if a change in the Constitution is needed to overcome federal court rulings that require crosstown busing to avoid concentration of black pupils in inner city classrooms.

Some Republicans who share Mr. Nixon's racialist views believe a Presidential endorsement of an anti-busing amendment would bring plenty of political dividends in the November elections. And that's precisely why Mr. Nixon is leaving no stone unturned in the quest for a procedure to end busing, thus voiding all previous federal court actions to do away with school racial imbalance.

The President is playing politics with an issue with which is bound up not only the education of the underprivileged, the black minority, but the moral principle of equality of opportunity which is essential to the preservation of democracy.

Whoever is against busing is ipso facto against integration. In this context Mr. Nixon and Alabama Gov. Wallace sleep in the same bed. Neither has shown much enthusiasm for the 1954 landmark school decision. Both would overrule the Supreme Court if the Constitution had granted them that power.

Pittsburgh Post-Gazette

Pittsburgh, Pa., February 16, 1972

IT WOULD be hard to conceive of anything more divisive — and regressive to civil rights — than the full-scale and highly emotional national debate that would attend an effort to amend the constitution to forbid busing of children outside their school districts. Such an effort might well cripple the considerable progress toward racial integration made in this country since World War II.

We think, therefore, that it is unwise of the President even to entertain such proposals or to lend encouragement to their sponsors.

Mr. Nixon and the Congress would be much better advised to seek a solution to this vexatious issue through existing or additional laws and the interpretation of the laws by the courts. School attendance is not the sort of question that should be embedded in the federal constitu-

tion. This is a matter best handled at the school district level, taking advantage of such good will and cooperation as may still exist.

* * *

The courts got into this because of questions of inequality of educational opportunity, and busing has become one of the tools used in the search for answers.

It is possible that the Supreme Court will point the way to an acceptable solution in a Denver case which it has agreed to hear. Certainly there is no reason to get started on anything so drastic as a constitutional amendment until the high court has ruled.

* * *

The busing issue has hit millions of Americans in the pits of their stomachs. We can appreciate the resistance of parents who have chosen a neighborhood at least in part because of its schools and then are told

that their children must be bused out of the neighborhood to achieve racial balance or for any other reason. Nor are whites the only Americans disturbed. Many blacks also oppose busing for various reasons, not the least of them the insulting implication that their children can't be educated except in proximity to more affluent whites.

And of course both black and white parents have reason to resent the blatant political opportunism of officeholders and candidates who advocate busing but have no idea of putting their own children in public schools to and from which they might be bused.

For those and other considerations, this is the most explosive domestic issue in American life. It would be a good idea to cool it through rational approaches rather than to inflame it through an attempt to amend the constitution.

The Afro American

Baltimore, Md., February 19, 1972

President Nixon comes close to openly encouraging defiance of the law in his questionable statements and actions that fly directly in the face of Supreme Court rulings on busing as a desegregation tool.

Despite the Supreme Court's clear decision that busing of pupils is a legitimate and necessary tool to be used in desegregating schools, a tool the Supreme Court declares supersedes considerations of neighborhood

or nearby schools, President Nixon continues to worm his political way into the emotional hearts of anti-busing voters by seeming to offer them a way out.

His latest low-level ploy is to entertain and encourage groups interested in having Congress pass an amendment to the Constitution that would prevent busing to bring about racial balance in schools. Would that

amendment repeal any other? And what if it conflicts with another?

No more despicable position can be taken by any leader than one in which he goes to great length to incur political favors at the expense of the welfare of the nation.

If busing of students to increase educational goals is a legally necessary tool, then the President of the United States should put aside his

personal views and ambitions and practice some of the "law and order" he uses as another of his vestful of political gambits.

It serves no useful purpose to have the President of this country spending huge sums and playing at summitry in the name of world peace while contributing to the destruction of the homebase of U.S. strength for selfish reasons.

The New York Times

New York, N.Y., February 17, 1972

President Nixon has obviously seized on school busing as a political issue during this election year. Regrettably, Senator Henry M. Jackson has chosen to join Mr. Nixon in this callous exploitation of the voters' ignorance and fear.

School integration is, even under most favorable conditions, a difficult goal and a delicate process. The current debate—if the busing arguments can be so dignified—obscures the real problems and legitimate ways of dealing with them. Busing is falsely portrayed as the principal device for school desegregation; and the impression is created that nothing short of a Constitutional amendment or a legislative prohibition can prevent the Supreme Court from ordering millions of children to be transported over long distances in order to create a "racial balance" in the nation's schools.

This picture is a divisive distortion of the facts. In a unanimous ruling based on an opinion written by Chief Justice Warren E. Burger, the Supreme Court last April did uphold the constitutionality of busing as a means of dismantling dual school systems; but the Court also made it clear that it had neither mandated nor considered desirable the establishment of any "fixed mathematical norms" or rigid racial balance. The issue, as the Chief Justice saw it, was simply that the local school board had "totally defaulted in its acknowledged duty to come forward with an acceptable plan. . . ."

The present drummed-up hysteria creates the impression that a constitutional or legislative wall is needed to protect the schools against wholesale court-ordered busing. The Burger ruling, in fact, actually stated that in the absence of a history of discrimination, "it might well be desirable to assign pupils to schools nearest their homes." The opinion explicitly questioned the wisdom and propriety of transporting children over long distances—as many children had in fact been transported in order to *avoid* integration.

Such objections to long-distance busing, with its inconvenience, dislocation and high cost in time and money, are thoroughly well-founded. Furthermore, it is undesirable and impracticable to transport children of more favored socio-economic backgrounds, regardless of color, into schools located in poverty neighborhoods.

But with few exceptions—and those generally provoked by long-term local intransigence—this has not been the issue in the courts. Two-thirds of all the nation's public school pupils ride to school, and 18 million do so by school bus. The bus has been the indispensable instrument of school consolidation, which educators consider crucial to improved educational quality.

The recent Federal court order to merge Richmond with two adjoining suburban school systems emphasized that in this case district lines had been gerrymandered to prevent desegregation. The effect of the required merger could well be to reduce rather than to increase busing—further proof that busing is a political red herring rather than a central issue.

President Nixon—and any candidates of either party who may be tempted to seek votes by inflaming irrational anti-busing sentiments—may pretend that they are only trying to prevent excessive busing. In fact, they are creating a political code word to rally those who want to scuttle desegregation. Let the President and the other candidates instead put forth rational and constructive proposals to end official segregation and to promote, wherever possible, harmonious and educationally sound integration.

It is a mockery of the Constitution to seek to abuse it as a school transportation manual which specifies who may or may not ride to school. It is hypocrisy for the Administration to pretend that it is underwriting accelerated school desegregation, when the President at the same time encourages Southern strategists to create legal and psychological roadblocks to effective integration.

Richmond Times-Dispatch

Richmond, Va., February 13, 1972

Lack of leadership is not the antibusing crusade's only problem. It suffers, too, as a result of the despicable double standards that some influential commentators apply in sanctimoniously analyzing the issue.

Consider, for example, the bald hypocrisy of The New York Times. Recently, that newspaper editorially applauded the Richmond school consolidation decision of U.S. District Judge Robert R. Merhige Jr., a decision calling for the busing of large numbers of children, prescribing quotas designed to achieve racial balance in public schools and ordering the racial composition of each school's faculty to reflect, generally, the racial composition of the total faculty of the entire consolidated system.

Now, if the Times considers busing and racial quotas desirable for Richmond area schools, it surely considers busing and racial quotas desirable for New York City schools, right? Wrong. When a special study commission proposed such integration devices for New York last week, the Times objected. Controversial and unrealistic, the Times called the proposals, adding:

The key to the proposed approach is to create a strict ethnic balance that approximates the racial pattern of total pupil population. In New York City, where the white enrollment now constitutes less than 40 per cent, this would mean that a white minority of roughly that proportion would have to be maintained in every school. Such a redistribution could be accomplished only by either transporting large numbers of white children into the presently predominantly black schools or by phasing out all schools in such areas. Both approaches would run into massive opposition on the part of black as well as white parents.

Equally questionable is the commission's proposal to bring about an ethnic balance among each system's teachers and administrators to reflect the racial profile of the total population. We have long urged effective measures to train and recruit greater numbers of educators among the minorities, along with elimination of licensing procedures which result in racial discrimination. But to impose a relatively rigid ethnic balance is to mandate a quota system with its inherent discriminatory and divisive consequences.

Well, trot out the cliches: It depends on whose ox is being gored, the shoe is on the other foot, what's sauce for the goose is sauce for the gander, turn about is fair play and tit for tat. Obviously, the Times has no strong convictions about busing and racial quotas. It favors busing and quotas for the South but not, perish the thought, for Fun City. Unfortunately, many of the nation's decision-makers read, and possibly often heed, the Times. If it ignores the contradiction in its views, they may ignore the contradiction too. And the antibusing crusade will suffer.

THE PLAIN DEALER

Cleveland, Ohio, February 16, 1972

Amending the U.S. Constitution would be the wrong approach to solving the school busing issue.

We find ourselves in agreement with Vice President Spiro T. Agnew in his opposition to amending the Constitution to prevent busing school children for integration purposes.

"I don't favor a constitutional amendment because I think it fuzzes and obfuscates the entire issue," the vice president said in a television interview.

"I think these things are capable of being handled within the normal statutory framework and constitutional framework of our existing Constitution."

Although President Nixon has yet to commit himself on the problem, other than to make clear his opposition to mass busing, we hope he will follow the vice president's lead.

The President was under considerable pressure earlier this week from a coalition of congressmen, mostly southerners or northern representatives from areas where busing has been vigorously fought, to endorse a constitutional amendment.

Instead, the President asked a cabinet-level committee to consider all alternatives and report to him after he returns from China at the end of the month.

Hopefully, this cooling-off period will allow a calmer approach to busing than has been heard in recent days. The issue has snowballed because of the presidential primary in Florida next month where a straw vote on busing is also on the ballot. The primary is important because it is one of the first in the nation.

Gov. George C. Wallace of Alabama, who is expected to do well in the Florida Democratic presidential primary, has proposed a constitutional amendment on busing.

Sen. Henry M. Jackson, D-Wash., who needs a strong Florida showing to maintain his presidential campaign, has suggested a dual amendment not only to ban busing but to increase money aid to equalize disadvantaged schools.

Ironically, the emotional nature of the busing issue, in part brought into national focus by recent court decisions, has overshadowed the school financing crisis, also made a national issue by courts, which in several states have ruled that school financing based on property taxes penalizes pupils in poor communities.

As well as being an emotional issue, busing also is basically a temporary issue. It is these factors that cause us to urge restraint. Busing is not all bad and can be a useful integration tool, as citizens of Shaker Heights can attest to through their voluntary school busing program. A constitutional amendment would straitjacket integration throughout the nation, in effect revising a national goal.

As difficult as it is to amend the Constitution, it is just as difficult to rescind the amendment later, as the nation learned from the Prohibition experiment.

It would be far, far better for the nation to resolve this crisis another way.

THE WALL STREET JOURNAL.

New York, N.Y., February 16, 1972

In principle we find much to be said for a constitutional amendment outlawing the use of racial quotas in schools and elsewhere, and in the end that step may yet prove necessary. Yet we are given pause by the timing of, and in some cases the spirit behind, the anti-busing amendments now offered in Congress.

President Nixon apparently has pledged to put the administration's weight behind the movement against busing to achieve racial balance, and is now considering whether a constitutional amendment is the best method of doing so. Alternatives include supporting anti-busing legislation or directing the Justice Department to intervene in court suits on behalf of the anti-busing position.

We find it hard to fault the administration for wanting to do something to recognize the growing public opposition to busing for racial balance. Public opinion polls find the overwhelming majority of whites and about half the blacks oppose any such step. Nor, when the issue actually arises, is this a passive opposition; people are quite prepared to get excited about matters touching their children. If the courts actually do order extensive busing throughout the nation, the reaction could well be strong enough to stop the civil rights revolution in its tracks—in fact, this is the one thing we can see that might do that.

The realistic way to frame the problem is not in terms of stopping the reaction against busing, an impossible task, but in terms of channeling it in reasonably healthy directions. This means that if the administration is to take an anti-busing initiative, the important thing is to shape it in a way that is intellectually and morally respectable.

Among the distinctions this requires is a sense of what is constitutional timber and what is not. The mechanics of busing or attendance zones or school financing, these are not matters a sensible nation deals with through constitutional amendments. But underneath the "busing" debate, and underneath the court decisions requiring busing, there is an issue of truly constitutional sweep: whether government policy ought to be color-blind, or ought to require some form of racial quota.

On this issue the high ground belongs, at least as a matter of logic, to the "anti-busing" side. Certainly the higher ideal is a state where pluralistic racial and ethnic groups coexist under a law that takes no formal notice of their differences. Far higher than the "ideal" of a state that parcels out members of a racial group by quotas, with the ultimate implication that the misery of their company must be spread.

Clearly it is the pluralistic-color-blind state that we should ultimately be trying to create. That's why it's possible to conceive of an entirely respectable "anti-busing" position. That is also why, if the courts actually do follow the recent drift of their logic to the conclusion that the Constitution requires at least loose racial quotas, it's possible to conceive of a constitutional amendment writing the colorblind position into the highest law.

But yet, matters of logic do not always prevail, and in the current context it's doubtful that an anti-quota amendment could in fact claim the high ground it deserves. Much of the support for anti-busing amendments arises from segregationist sentiments, and unfortunately the administration has nothing like the kind of rapport with blacks that might offset this taint. This is of course not a very powerful argument—that we should not do the right thing because it would not *seem* to be the right thing—and thee courts may yet make it necessary to set such considerations aside.

As a practical matter, though, President Nixon's appointments have created a new Supreme Court, and even without that the Supreme Court far more than lower courts has usually been sensitive to developments such as the rising public opposition to busing. Also as a practical matter, the kind of loose quotas and extensive busing used to remedy *de jure* segregation in the South have obviously been useful tools for breaking the recalcitrant resistance to integration there. It's hard to condemn them so long as they can be seen as temporary and exceptional expedients, not the permanent rule by which this nation will deal with racial division.

So perhaps the administration would be wise to wait, not necessarily long but at least for a year or two, before it lends its support to anything so drastic as a constitutional amendment. The best source of a respectable "anti-busing" rationale, one that both preserves the ideal of racial justice and avoids the impasse into which the issue seems to be headed, would be the courts themselves.

The News American

Baltimore, Md., February 17, 1972

A BLOCKBUSTER federal court decision early last month, coupled with the pressures of an impending national election, give every indication that 1972 will be a year of crucial decision on the bitterly-divisive social problem of school busing.

The long-festering controversy erupted with new virulence when a Virginia district judge ruled, in effect, that busing to achieve racial balance should join city and suburban school districts. This was simply too much for many voters determined to maintain their social and economic exclusiveness.

As a result of their indignant flood of protests, nearly 30 congressmen to date have introduced some form of anti-busing legislation, including proposals for a constitutional amendment. This week their general aims were formally backed by President Nixon, who promised personal action.

The President, long known to favor the principle of neighborhood schools, undoubtedly was stirred in part by political considerations. Alabama Gov. George Wallace, for example, has been making considerable campaign hay out of his anti-busing platform in the Florida Democratic primary.

What the President proposes to do to halt the forced busing of school children will not be announced for some time, but definitely before the November election. Meanwhile we think he has gone on too strong in this issue.

He can properly criticize the wisdom of the law, but as the chief defender of law it strikes us as unseemingly for him to lead a battle against it.

This is a study in moral values almost as controversial as school busing itself — an issue which more than a decade of heated argument has failed to resolve. It is no longer the right of minorities to equal education opportunities which is being challenged. It is and has been the Supreme Court rulings which disrupt chosen life styles which are the target.

We offer no definitive solution here. At base it is a problem of law which only lawyers and lawmakers are qualified to handle. Pending the action which seems inevitable this year, however, we find ourselves in general agreement with this view expressed by Sen. Henry M. Jackson (D.-Mich.):

"Every parent should have the right of freedom of choice and the right to have his or her children attend their local neighborhood school."

The Providence Journal

Providence, R.I., February 18, 1972

The mounting pseudo crisis over school busing to achieve desegregation — bordering on public and political hysteria — has been touted for some time as possibly the Number One domestic issue in the 1972 presidential campaign. Recent events leave little doubt that that message has reached every incumbent and aspiring officeholder at every level of government and that the race to outdistance the competition in support of anti-busing forces is well under way.

What caused the crisis?

When President Nixon took office, the Department of Health, Education and Welfare was still pressuring Southern school districts to desegregate, threatening to withhold federal funds from those that failed to follow guidelines. Then came the administration's Southern strategy, designed to counter stinging criticism on the right from George Wallace and those who share his racial views. The President, on record as opposed to busing to achieve racial balance, found himself obliged to repeat his stand on numerous occasions as an apparent conflict arose between the White House and the courts.

In a detailed document, Mr. Nixon outlined his administration's policy hoping to clear up confusion. It was, essentially, that the government would take no affirmative action to force school desegregation beyond what was ordered by the courts but that court orders would be enforced.

That policy has failed to slow the pace of compliance with the 1954 Supreme Court ruling, despite the President's warning last summer that government officials must limit the scope of busing or lose their jobs. In fact, the pace has quickened as federal judges ruled in case after case that busing plans must be implemented to achieve equal educational opportunity, even if it means adopting metropolitan plans as in the case of Richmond, Va., involving two suburban counties.

With Supreme Court sanction for busing "unless the time or distance is so great as to risk either the health of the children or significantly impinge on the educational process," the administration became caught in a political dilemma. It could tacitly accept the court rulings, inadvertently strengthening the anti-busing forces led by George Wallace, or it could take some action sufficiently dramatic to undercut Mr. Wallace and to neutralize the issue prior to the presidential election campaign.

At Monday's meeting with anti-busing leaders, Mr. Nixon promised something would be done, named a Cabinet committee to plot a course, and said a decision would be reached after his return from the China visit.

At the center of all the hustle and bustle are the various proposals in Congress to amend the Constitution to prohibit busing to achieve racial balance. They are straws being seized in desperation. They are seen by some as the easy answer to restoring the concept of neighborhood school and local control.

One wonders, however, how the moral validity of the Supreme Court's 17-year-old ruling against dual school systems for blacks and whites became lost in the shuffle. One wonders how many who are fighting to preserve their neighborhood schools are masking their fear of and hostility toward racial integration. In all the years that busing was used widely and when one major effect was to preserve segregation, in the North as well as South, there were no cries of pain or anguish. With the situation reversed and the courts pressing hard for equality, all hell has broken loose.

In terms of the basic justice of our system and integrity of our lawmakers, a constitutional amendment stands little chance of adoption. Such a threat to all that has been accomplished in behalf of race equality and harmony in this country is beyond reason. The present crisis stirred by those who would turn back the clock is in reality no crisis at all. It is a kind of mass hysteria induced for a purpose by those who would stop the civil rights movement in its tracks, and it ought to be recognized and labeled as such.

The Virginian-Pilot

Norfolk, Va., February 16, 1972

The Busing Bugaboo

President Nixon understandably stopped far short of endorsing a Constitutional amendment to bar mandatory school busing in his remarkable meeting on the question. It is unlikely that the necessary two-thirds of the Senate would approve such an amendment. As emotional as busing has become, and as politically inviting, it does not merit a place in the Nation's basic law—and n e i t h e r Senator Henry M. Jackson's Presidential-campaign amendment nor the Congressional movement paralleling it, with which the President flirted, raise busing above relative triviality. Finally, Mr. Nixon all along has encouraged ambivalence in his Administration in civil-rights affairs; his familiar odes to the neighborhood school u s u a l l y have been drowned out by desegregation statistics issued by the Department of Health, Education, and Welfare.

If, h o w e v e r, the President is ready to put a c t i o n where his mouth is, legislation to tame the busing bugaboo—to reduce busing to its logical place in a national good-school program—is available in the bill that Representative Richardson Preyer of North Carolina wrote in collaboration with Professor Alexander B i c k e l. There is some reason to believe Mr. Nixon through several Cabinet advisers will e n d o r s e the Preyer plan—which, ironically, has been available for more than a year, shunned by civil rightists for its deemphasis of race and by segregationists for its good sense.

An alternative that Mr. Nixon might choose to fulfill his pledge to change "the busing s i t u a t i o n" would be to jam the Justice De

partment deeper i n t o desegregation cases pending in the Federal c o u r t s, the Richmond-suburban counties case in particular. That might not be enough just now, the political season being what it is. The plenitude of a m i c u s curiae briefs in the most recent major busing case, the Charlotte one of last April, is evidence enough that the Court is only so amenable to unsolicited advice.

Chief Justice Burger wrote the Charlotte decision. In it he said busing is a suitable tool for dismantling "deliberately constructed and maintained . . . segregation . . . in the interim period when remedial adjustments are being made to eliminate the dual school system." But the Chief Justice failed to define "interim period." More to the point just now, he did not specify the boundaries of a school system.

Judge Robert R. Merhige Jr. in his Richmond-Henrico-Chesterfield decision filled the latter gap. The system, he said in effect, encompasses a metropolitan area. If the inner city's schools are desegregated, only then to be abandoned by white residents m o v i n g into the suburbs and reentering a segregated arrangement, the law demands that the city and suburban school divisions be merged into a single system, with the desegregating process renewed.

That, it seems to us, is an exercise in pure logic. Judge Merhige identified an e s c a p e route from court-ordered desegregation a n d blocked it. To achieve full desegregation in the extended school system, he called for extended busing. And inasmuch as he viewed the suburban route to segregation as officially sponsored, he labeled the

practice *de jure*—by law—outlawry. That is what is behind the fuss to which the President, Senator Jackson, *et al.* are so sensitive these days.

The Supreme Court is going to have to step forward with Judge Merhige or step back. The Burger decision in the Charlotte case, like a child's last-year suit, has been outgrown. For Judge Merhige has raised the proposition that courts should order desegregation beyond the South and throughout the land. Mr. Burger stuck to the South.

H o w e v e r the Supreme Court moves, many of the schools subject to its order will remain in or enter a state of confusion. For if anything in public school affairs now is obvious, it is that the courts are not, and never have been, the proper agency for administering educational affairs.

The Jackson and kindred amendments, meanwhile, would encourage a return to the old separate-but-equal philosophy. The Senator denies it, but unconvincingly. And anyway, *busing* and *neighborhood schools* simply are not words to be inserted into the Constitution of the United States of America.

So we hope, and hope very much, that Mr. Nixon will support the Preyer bill. Congress, we hope still more, will pass it. The Preyer bill embraces the national c o m m i t-ment to desegregation and concentrates on superior instruction. It would seek to do what the Founding Fathers surely would have approved: to reinforce in the conduct of education the equality of individuals by assuming and practicing equality, rather than by proclaiming equality with appearances.

Echoes and Ghosts

Even as President N i x o n was meeting in Washington with Con-g r e s s i o n a l foes of busing, the House of Delegates in Richmond was adopting a resolution aimed at creating a Virginia Legislative Commission o n Neighborhood Schools to preach antibusing efforts among the 50 states. Echoes and ghosts of Massive Resistance must haunt veteran Delegates viewing t h e resolution's declaration: "The Federal Judiciary has abused its power and abrogated the rights of the several states by promulgating, upholding, and enforcing Federal guidelines which have no Constitutional basis . . ."

Events of the late 1950s also have parallels in what goes on outside the State House in Capitol Square. Last week, addressing an antibus-

ing rally of 3,000 at the Bell Tower, Richmond Councilman Howard Carwile called Governor Holton a "gutless, spineless, no-good Governor" and added, "When I think of that man, I think of euthanasia." The rally's sponsors delivered an "ultimatum" that Mr. Holton "immediately take a stand in opposition to consolidation and f o r c e d busing."

To the ultimatum, Mr. Holton replied calmly that although he is opposed to the principle of busing, he has a duty to provide the leadership to comply with the Virginia Constitution's mandate for h i g h-quality education for every child. He invited the bearers of the ultimatum to join him in insuring t h a t the children's education is

continued "in an atmosphere of reasonableness."

And to the Councilman's tirade, the Governor said, "I understand that I'm the focal point and I think that particularly for one in public life, people are going to say extreme things about him . . . But the real leadership and the real basic individual in our society is offended by that type of attack. You just have to grin and bear it."

Busy passing resolutions for a national campaign, none of the real leadership in the House had expressed any offense at the Councilman's demagoguery. But then, perhaps the Delegates felt that the Governor's good sense was his own best defense.

The Chattanooga Times

Chattanooga, Tenn., February 18, 1972

Out of President Nixon's recent comments on the school busing problem, there came an expression on the way our system works, the clarity of which should be lost on no one.

Mr. Nixon said that he personally was against the busing of school children to achieve racial balance, a view to which he is entitled, of course, and in which he is honestly joined by a great many other Americans.

But then he went on to say:

"If the courts, acting under the Constitution, decide that the views that I have held are unconstitutional, I, of course, will have to follow the courts."

If he or others want the situation changed, he said, they must decide whether it can be accomplished by legislation or by constitutional amendment.

Nothing could be clearer. If the President of the United States is bound by the decisions of the courts, then so is every other citizen of the country, until the basis for legal determination is altered.

OREGON JOURNAL

Portland, Ore., February 16, 1972

There ought to be a better way to resolve the school busing issue than through a proposed constitutional amendment.

President Nixon, who opposes forced busing to achieve racial balance, has discussed with key congressmen the possibility of an amendment that would have the effect of countermanding present court orders on busing.

No such proposal could be pushed through the Congress without the kind of fight that would divert that body from other important business.

And if it were to be passed, it would prohibit kinds and degrees of busing that are desirable.

The chief opposition to busing is not to the principle but to extreme practices which have been ordered by some courts without taking into account such other factors as cost or the disruptive effect on the child of excessive travel time.

The chief wrong is the assumption that a certain mathematical balance between races has to be achieved. Desegregation plans ought to be flexible enough to take into account local situations which differ greatly from place to place.

Any fixed ratio is arbitrary. Proof is lacking that any particular mix has better educational value than another.

The courts ought to be able to produce a master plan under which desegregation criteria could be met, through busing or other means, but which would not require unreasonable and costly transfers of students over long distances.

Let's not try to veto busing **per se** through the Constitution.

THE ROANOKE TIMES

Roanoke, Va., February 17, 1972

President Nixon's promise to intervene in some manner in the controversy over massive busing in school desegregation can be an encouraging sign. One of the tragedies of the past decade or longer is that the federal courts alone have had to struggle with the problem. Although the Congress has the duty to enforce the Fourteenth Amendment, and the Supreme Court decisions of 1954 and 1955 pursuant to it, it has been reluctant to act. Presidents have been reluctant to suggest how Congress may act.

A result of the congressional vacuum and the courts' lonely battle is that the desegregation d o c t r i n e seems to have come full circle. From the 1955 simple admonition *not* to assign children to schools for reasons of race, the doctrine now seems to read the authorities *must* assign children to schools for reasons of race. Not only must authorities use race as a basis of school assignments, they must seek certain racial ratios in **each** school.

Further, they must employ buses to **a** remarkable degree in dispatching children to schools on the basis of race. That is the way current doctrine—including the latest opinion by Chief Justice Warren Burger in the Swann, or Charlotte, N.C., case—seems to read.

Federal District Judge Robert R. Merhige Jr., in his celebrated Richmond area decision, simply carried Chief Justice Burger's logic a little bit farther: Three separate school systems must be merged so that children can be dispatched and bused to schools on the basis of their race, he said.

If the President's deliberations are to be meaningful, he and his advisers might ask themselves how the federal judges managed to swing 180 degrees in 17 years? If they will trace each case and each decision, they will find entirely too many instances—an almost universal situation—of cases based on bad faith, on negative efforts to defy the 1954 and 1955 d e c i s i o n s. In each effort to c h e c k m a t e defiance, the federal courts moved further and further from the original decisions.

What has been needed, and is now needed, is affirmative action by Congress to replace the negative attitudes confronting the courts. One instrument is at hand, called "The National School Desegregation Act of 1970." It was prepared with the aid of a recognized expert in constitutional law, Alexander Bickel, of Yale. It places the emphasis on the neighborhood school but permits transfers out of the neighborhood school under certain circumstances. It recognizes that even with a national policy of fairness there will be schools in which children of one race may be concentrated; but in such cases it requires that equal standards be maintained.

In brief, the bill would put into effect the 1954 and 1955 decisions without the distortions forced by defiance.

The bill, once sponsored by Rep. Richardson Preyer, of Greensboro, and Sen. William B. Spong, of Virginia, was shot down from the right and left. It remains the sanest legislative approach that has yet come forth for a complex problem. The President, of course, could go for the quick, easy and negative solution of a constitutional amendment. But the quick, the easy and the negative routes so far have led only to today's unhappy predicament. The choice for the President on this question is whether to be a statesman looking for a long-range answer or a politician looking for the quick and easy one, no matter what consequences come after the election.

The Miami Herald

Miami, Fla., February 24, 1972

SINCERE opponents of so-called "forced busing" to achieve racial integration in Florida schools can demonstrate that fact by voting also for an amendment to the March 14 straw poll designed by Gov. Askew and accepted by the State Legislature.

It would set forth as an article of faith that the voter favors "an equal opportunity for quality education for all children regardless of race, creed, color or place of residence and opposes a return to the dual system of public schools."

This was the Governor's price for signing the bill rather than vetoing it and presenting a state already troubled with dissension one more political confrontation. Call it what you will, but this to us is statesmanship.

Gov. Askew also wants the Republican sponsors of the straw poll to further amend the busing question by striking out the word "forced," which is mean-ingless when you come to think of the semantics, and substitute "busing solely to achieve a racial balance." According to reports yesterday they agreed to do this.

Along with the Governor we do not believe that Florida is a "racist" state but one perplexed by a tool — busing — employed by the courts to effect integration. Some 42 per cent of all American school children ride buses to school, a minority of them for reasons of integration. Busing in fact goes back to a Massachusetts law of 1869 (horse-drawn vehicles presumably were used) which gradually was adopted by all the states. Many were bused to preserve the dual system which the Supreme Court found in 1954 to be in violation of the Constitution.

Three things strike us as pertinent to the issue in Tallahassee today and at the polls next month.

First, in Gov. Askew's words, equal opportunity is "not a question of trans-portation. It's a question of justice." For the last 18 years the law of the land has been made perfectly clear in dozens, even hundreds, of court decisions.

Second, courts have not been unsympathetic to those who feel aggrieved. It seems to be forgotten that the celebrated busing case of Swann v. Charlotte-Mecklenburg found the Supreme Court saying last spring that busing was proper unless "the time or distance is so great as to risk either the health of the children or significantly impinge on the educational process."

Third and finally, a straw vote has no force of law and may only delude anxious persons who are led to believe that it has. If the Constitution is to be amended it can be done by historic processes, and preferably not in the heat of an election year when emotions may be exploited to the detriment of stable government and equal justice under law.

The Washington Post
Times Herald

Washington, D.C., February 24, 1972

The Busing Debate Begins in the Senate

"SEC. 1819. (a) No person shall be refused admission into or be excluded from any public school in any State on account of race, creed, color, or national origin."

The dictum is compelling. The NAACP Legal Defense Fund put in some fifteen years arguing those civil rights cases that culminated in the Supreme Court's ruling to the same effect in the 1954 *Brown* decision. And in the eighteen years that have passed since then, Congress, the executive branch, the courts and a variety of civil rights groups have expended a good deal of energy and time in an effort to oblige the patrons of Jim Crow schools in the South to accept it. But this has not been easy, owing in large part to the determined step-by-step resistance of such Southern political leaders as Senators Ervin, Ellender, Eastland, Jordan, Long, McClellan, Sparkman, Stennis, Talmadge and Thurmond. Now we find the names of all these men who have done so much to prevent the orderly fulfillment of this equitable proposition adorning a Senate amendment from which the language cited above was taken—"No person shall be . . . excluded from any public school . . . on account of race . . ." How different things might have been, how much happier recent Southern history, how much less disruptive those integration orders the courts have imposed as a resort, had all or any of them responded to this call for simple justice when it mattered.

For you must not suppose that this language represents some change of heart or change of ways on the part of those senators who are sponsoring this and variety of similarly high sounding amendments to the education bills now before the Senate. Rather it represents raw cynicism, an attempt to turn the equity of the principle against itself by using language to subvert its own meaning. This is how the maneuver is meant to work: the courts have outlawed dual school systems based on racial classifications of students; in the face of persistent footdragging and obstruction on the part of much of Southern officialdom charged with dismantling the segregated system, the courts and the executive branch (acting under the Civil Rights law of 1964) have been obliged to compel that dismantling on their own; so now the resisters are attacking these efforts at integration on the grounds that they (necessarily) take account of race, and race—thanks to *Brown* — is no longer a legitimate criterion for the assignment of students. If you understand that maneuver, you will be able to understand why much of the Senate effort, in the next several days, to turn back the progress that has been made in dismantling dual school systems is going to read like a civil rights brief.

We dwell on this not because the Southerners have a corner on cynicism and sham in this department—far from it—but because it is one of the more important confusions that is going to mark the debate now under way. That debate concerns the disposition of the bill to spend a billion and a half dollars over two years in assisting school dis-tricts that are caught up in the toils and expenses of desegregation. Because the parliamentary situation in which this bill is being discussed is even more complex than usual, because of the volatility of the issue and because legislative amendments do not have the force of those other amendments—constitutional—now being promoted, the debate is bound to be perplexing and misleading.

Maybe no program would be sufficient to identify the players in this game, let alone to untangle their intentions. The Senate leadership proposal, which has just been unveiled, for example, requires separate discussion because it appears to combine numerous better and worse features of the legislative effort on this subject. But as a general guide, there are a few things to keep in mind. One is that much of the most regressive legislation is going to sound positively libertarian in nature. Another is that a great deal of what is being proposed by some of the "anti-busers" is clearly unconstitutional. There is also the fact that certain seeming "anti-busing" votes will not be votes to terminate busing, only be votes to terminate aid to districts required to bus. Finally, from the segregationists who will be denying any attempt to roll back the progress already made to the integrationists who will be looking for a vote that seems to be "anti-busing" but actually does small harm to the desegregation now under way, you can rest assured that very few senators will be willing to acknowledge what their intent really is. You can rest assured, that is, if you find that either restful or assuring in the Senate of the United States.

The Dallas Morning News

Dallas, Tex., February 25, 1972

The country has been through this hypocrisy before, but the Senate leadership has teamed with liberals to push a measure that would limit school busing by law instead of by constitutional amendment.

A hodgepodge called the Mansfield-Scott amendment would, they think, take the public heat off the busing issue and also give liberals a chance to pretend they oppose busing.

The amendment (tacked onto the higher education bill) would ban any busing harmful to health or the educational process and would excuse any school district from spending its own or federal money for busing unless it wanted to. The federal bureaucracy would be prohibited (ha!) from forcing a district to do so.

What it all boils down to is that these limitations would stand until some federal court decided otherwise—or until the Department of Health, Education and Welfare found means to circumvent them.

That's what happened to the Civil Rights Act of 1964, which expressly forbade busing for balance. A new prohibition would have even less effect, now that the Supreme Court itself has made busing constitutional. Congress may propose but the courts dispose.

Unless, that is, Congress either votes to take busing out of federal court jurisdiction or goes ahead and gives the states an antibusing constitutional amendment to vote on.

This is what the Senate leadership and the liberals are out to stop—by defusing the public clamor with the Mansfield-Scott amendment. The public should know it is an empty exercise.

THE RICHMOND NEWS LEADER

Richmond, Va., February 25, 1972

Two hundred years ago the French philosopher Jean Jacques Rousseau propounded his theory that in every society there is an abiding consensus on every major issue; societies simply need the right sorts of persons to interpret the General Will, and to implement it. Since Rousseau's time, the General Will has been perhaps the dominant theory of free society. But yesterday the United States Senate showed just how wrong Rousseau's theory can be.

Compulsory busing is probably the hottest domestic issue of the past 25 years. Public sentiment seems so weighted against compulsory busing that finding persons who support it is rather like finding persons who support infanticide: There are some, but not many. Yet yesterday, when the Senate finally got around to interpreting and implementing the General Will on the matter of compulsory busing, the Senate did practically nothing. Instead of whacking the ball over the fence, as the fans were demanding, the Senate hit a pitiful dribbler past the pitcher, and barely made it to first base.

The Senate approved a measure co-sponsored by Democratic Majority Leader Mike Mansfield and Republican Minority Leader Hugh Scott. In effect, the measure would seek to prevent the use of Federal funds for busing when the time or distance would be sufficiently long that busing might threaten the health of the children or possibly impinge on the educational process. The measure would prevent Federal officials from requiring the busing of a child to a school where the opportunities "will be substantially less than those offered at the school to which such student would otherwise be assigned." But, in the words of Senator Scott, the measure would permit "the interposition of the courts when that is necessary to carry out desegregation required by the Constitution."

Southern Senators did not support the measure because they properly understand it to be a piece of legislative mush. It would do almost nothing at all. It would not diminish the fears of anxious students and parents. It would not lift the heavy yoke of compulsory busing under which the South labors now. It would not heal the sores that compulsory busing has opened on the body politic. The Federal courts have given us compulsory busing, and the Mansfield-Scott provision would do nothing to compel the courts to cease and desist. This measure was shoved through the Senate by the same people who told us it would be impossible to write a constitutional amendment that would effectively constrict the Federal courts. It is difficult to comprehend why the courts could be expected to be more inhibited by mealy legislation than by a constitutional amendment: The courts were not at all inhibited by the unequivocal anti-busing language in the Civil Rights Act of 1964.

The Mansfield-Scott provision is brought to you by people who are not particularly averse to the assignment of a child to a school solely because his skin is black or white. The provision is dubbed a "compromise" measure, yet no conscientious parent will tolerate "compromise" in matters of principle that profoundly affect his child. The Senate is not done with the question of compulsory busing; the next few days of debate may give parents and children who have suffered under compulsory busing the relief that they seek. But do not swoon with optimism over the prospect that the Senate will grant such relief. Ours is a free society, and that is one of our fundamental qualities. But implicit in that quality is the defect that deliberative bodies such as the United States Senate are dreadfully slow at interpreting and implementing the General Will—if they implement it at all. Meanwhile, the wrongs persist, and the disintegration of the public order goes on.

Herald News

Fall River, Mass., February 26, 1972

The compromise busing plan offered by Senate leaders is bound to be attacked on the grounds that it limits busing to places where it is specifically requested by the local government. Furthermore it prohibits busing where the health of the children would be affected by it or when it might retard their education. In other words, it hedges busing around with so many restrictions that it almost makes it a dead issue. Advocates of busing will not call the Senate's plan a compromise; they will call it abolition under another name.

They will not, however, be altogether right. In the first place, given the extent of the opposition in the Senate to any form of busing, the plan now suggested is probably the only one that had a chance of being passed. And it does preserve busing as a principle as well as a practical fact in localities where the governing body wants it.

Since a sizeable number of senators simply want to abolish it, the originators of the present plan have every right to call it a compromise. They have done their best to please both camps. The chances are they will please neither, but that, traditionally, is the fate of those that steer a middle course.

The trouble all along with busing is that it was admirable in theory but notoriously weak in practice. And when it comes to issues affecting their children, most Americans are unwilling to tolerate expedients that don't work. The Senate compromise proposal makes busing available in situations where it has a chance to function effectively. That may not be as much as its proponents wish, but it is still a great deal.

Tulsa, Okla., February 28, 1972

A VOTE in the U.S. Senate last week points up the importance of the absenteeism that has plagued that lawmaking body in recent months.

The issue was a proposal by Sen. ROBERT GRIFFIN of Michigan to bar Courts from ordering school busing for racial purposes. It also would prohibit Federal officials from withholding or threatening to hold back Government funds as a weapon to force busing for desegregation.

The GRIFFIN Amendment was adopted by a 43-40 vote, on a highly controversial and significant public issue. The point is this: Seventeen Senate votes were not cast, among them the votes of five Democratic members who were out running for PRESIDENT.

All five of the absentee PRESIDENTIAL candidates have indicated they oppose the GRIFFIN plan—but they weren't on hand to keep it from passing.

That could be either a blessing or a curse, depending on how one views the amendment. In fact, a later vote may be forced in which the 43-40 tally could be reversed.

But absenteeism itself has become such a problem that Sen. MIKE MANSFIELD, the Majority leader, has publicly chided members of his own party for not attending to Senate business.

And Sen. MARGARET CHASE SMITH introduced a bill requiring lawmakers to make 60 per cent of the roll calls or forfeit their seats.

All this is not going to keep members of Congress from running for PRESIDENT—nor should it. But somehow they and the other absentees are going to have to arrange to be on hand for important votes—or Congress will be run increasingly by default.

LEDGER-STAR

Norfolk, Va., February 28, 1972

The busing controversy is not likely to be resolved either through Senator Griffin's amendment to take away from the federal courts the power to issue busing orders or through the bipartisan compromise bill adopted earlier by the Senate.

At least these particular approaches are not likely to bring the results sought by the objectors to busing, which would surely include much of the busing-affected or threatened citizenry at this point.

The attempt to simply deny, by legislation, a power the courts have been exercising is the more dubious of the two propositions. For the courts, if they insist that busing is necessary to dismantle some dual school system, would certainly challenge the law on the basis that the court proceeding is in pursuit of a Constitutional principle and that legislation cannot change matters.

Larger hopes, then, may attach to the Mansfield-Scott bipartisan proposal, which would restrict busing's scope by the use of Congress' funding powers. The doing of certain things with federal money—as in busing for a distance which risks a child's health—would be prohibited. But in general this compromise plan would not attempt to interfere with the courts' action to enforce Constitutional compliance. It was this latter which attracted some liberal support for passage, along with the prospect of perhaps defusing the issue.

But even here, there is great weakness when it comes to any positive impact on the situation as it has developed under increasing court management of the Southern school systems and as the process threatens to affect the North and its *de facto* segregation.

And again, the problem is that the federal courts can argue a Constitutional mandate for what they are doing and go right on doing it. If that is the courts' choice, who is to say they won't prevail—just as they have all along? The first letter in today's Open Forum deals with this point, too.

So if there is anything useful in the Senate debate and actions of recent days, it lies in the demonstration of just how all-pervading the nation's concern has become. So all-pervading, in fact, that even some of busing's liberal advocates are drawn into support of steps with a nominal anti-busing label.

How such demonstrable concern can eventually be made effective remains a question. There is a possibility, of course, that the judiciary itself will rein in from some of the more flagrant absurdities. But that the country is in a mood to press ever harder for a turnaround by one means or another can scarcely be doubted.

THE DAILY OKLAHOMAN

Oklahoma City, Okla., February 21, 1972

IN view of its earlier position supporting the toothless Mansfield-Scott amendment, the Senate wasn't expected to do anything effective this year about the red-hot school busing issue.

But in a 43-40 squeaker, it quickly dropped a bombshell on the whole desegregation effort by approving a proposal by Sen. Robert P. Griffin, R-Mich., to strip the federal courts of the power to issue busing orders.

The Griffin amendment to a pending educational fund bill relies on Article 111, Section 2, of the Constitution, which empowers Congress to limit the appellate jurisdiction of the U.S. Supreme Court. Opponents say that if the amendment becomes law, the Supreme Court will throw it out because it conflicts with the 14th Amendment's equal protection clause. That's entirely conceivable, since the courts increasingly are making the equal protection clause the only operative part of the Constitution.

But it's conceivable also that the presumably less "activist" Burger Court would welcome any congressional action that extricated it from the deepening desegregation quagmire. It's conceivable further that many senators who voted in favor of the Griffin amendment were doing so to establish voting records pleasing to their constituents and will return to the Mansfield-Scott version.

Final Senate acceptance of the Griffin amendment and subsequent House concurrence would present President Nixon with a difficult choice in an election year. He is committed to effective action on the busing issue, and a veto would place him in grave jeopardy. His approval, on the other hand would go far toward dismantling the desegregation effort.

The Senate-approved Mansfield-Scott amendment, which purports to limit busing, is largely window dressing aimed at appeasing overwhelming public sentiment while actually placing few or no restraints on the courts. Its co-authors are Senate Democratic leader Mike Mansfield of Montana and Republican leader Hugh Scott of Pennsylvania, both of whom lean to the "liberal" side of most issues.

The amendment doesn't reach the basic issue which is the arrogation by the federal judiciary of school administrative functions properly within the purview of the people's elected representatives on the boards. The federal judiciary has usurped a political function while enjoying lifetime immunity from the usual political processes.

The amendment would bar the use of federal funds to carry out racial desegregation except on the written request of local school officials, and it would prohibit the courts or federal officials from ordering local officials to make such a request. The withholding of federal funds not formally requested in writing would amount only to further coercion of the local districts.

Similarly fraudulent is a provision stating that federal funds can't be used for busing when the time or distance of travel is so great as to risk the health of the children or significantly impinge on the educational process. But who is to be the judge in these matters? Not the parents who have the deepest involvement—emotionally, financially and in all other respects. Not their elected representatives on the school boards. As in all other aspects of desegregation, the final judgments would rest with the courts.

Sponsors of the amendment say parts of it were patterned after last year's Supreme Court decision in the Charlotte-Mecklenburg case. But this ruling was so obscure and hedged about that Chief Justice Warren Burger was obliged subsequently to admonish his brethren in the lower courts no to go beyond its intent.

The Mansfield-Scott amendment would order federal officials to refrain from inducing local officials to use state or local funds for busing unless constitutionally required. What's "constitutionally required" is always a subjective judgment for the courts to make, since the Constitution itself doesn't contain a word about public schools.

SENATE PASSES EDUCATION ACT; HOUSE BARS BUSING COMPROMISE

On March 1 the Senate by a roll-call vote of 88–6 approved a combined higher education and desegregation bill including the Mansfield-Scott provisions only moderately restricting the future use of busing and sent it to a House-Senate conference. One week later, in an unusual action, the House instructed its conferees to "insist" on keeping intact its strongly worded anti-busing amendments adopted in November 1971. The House vote March 8 was 272–139. Although the instruction was not legally binding, it put the conferees on notice that a compromise bill might be rejected. It was the first time since 1970 that the House had specifically barred a conference compromise.

THE  SUN

Baltimore, Md., March 2, 1972

The Senate has adopted a cool and calm busing amendment to the education bill. If there has to be an amendment this is certainly better than the straitjacketing one proposed by Senator Griffin of Michigan, which would have in effect outlawed all mandatory busing. The language the Senate approved (after specifically rejecting the Griffin language) allows courts and local school agencies the freedom they need to deal with school desegregation. In many cases busing is the only way desegregation can proceed, and the Senate recognized this.

Attempts by some critics of the Senate action to cast this issue as a liberal versus conservative one are feeble. The Senate incorporated language in its bill that is a direct quotation from the Supreme Court decision written by Chief Justice Warren Burger, who is, of course, a celebrated conservative and strict constructionist. That language forbids bus trips that are so long that they will cause educational or health hardships.

The Senate vote was both heart-ening and troublesome. It was heartening because it displayed good sense by an overwhelming majority of senators from outside the South. Much progress has been made in deed and thought in the South, but politicians there are still captive to inflamatory issues concerning race. None voted for busing. But non-Southerners voted for it by 51 to 24. One troublesome aspect of the vote was the portent that the political parties may be dividing up on the race issue. Non-Southern Democrats voted 31-5 against the Griffin plan, but non-Southern Republicans were 20-19 for, a sad situation. Worse, the trend in the North seems to be clear: last year an anti-busing proposal received only 35 votes, but this year it received 47.

Perhaps the major reason public opinion is carrying senators in this direction is that so few national leaders have been willing to explain to people just exactly what is involved in the busing issue. The opponents of busing, and the George Wallace type opponents at that, have dominated the debate. Thus many people do not understand what is truly involved.

OKLAHOMA CITY TIMES

Oklahoma City, Okla., March 1, 1972

MEMBERS of Congress sometimes tell the home folks that on this or that question, their single votes would not have been decisive in any case, so it was only good politics to trade with other members for a future bit of needed support. There is enough truth in that to make the story acceptable, even if not palatable, to the voters.

But there are times when one or two votes are decisive. A case in point occurred Tuesday, when the votes of Oklahoma's two senators changed the outcome on a tally of great interest to the people of Oklahoma.

BEFORE the Senate was a bill governing aid to higher education and school desegregation. Sen. Griffin of Michigan had introduced an amendment earlier which would remove the busing cases from the jurisdiction of the federal courts. Under the U. S. Constitution, Congress is to set the limits of federal court jurisdiction. An act of Congress is considered the quickest and legally the best way to handle this hot issue. An amendment to the Constitution itself would not only further encumber that document, but would require approval by two-thirds votes in both the House and the Senate, and then ratification by the legislatures of two-thirds of the 50 states. It would be a slow process. The issue is pressing now.

The Senate adopted the Griffin rider last Friday by a 43-40 vote. A number of liberals who were out of town were rounded up and Tuesday, on a second consideration, the Senate reversed its stand, and took out the Griffin amendment by a vote of 50-47. Both Oklahoma senators voted to kill the Griffin limitation on the federal courts.

THERE is no hotter issue in Oklahoma today than the power presently wielded by the federal courts over our local school systems. Sentiment is overwhelmingly in favor of removing the school question from the federal courts. Yet, ironically, when it came to a really decisive vote, the vote of the Oklahoma senators was decisive—in favor of the courts.

If both Sen. Fred Harris and Sen. Henry Bellmon had voted in favor of the Griffin rider, it would have remained in the bill. The vote would have been 49-48 in favor of its retention. Sen. Harris has removed himself from the re-election picture, and is presumaby free of home state pressures. Sen. Bellmon will remain in the Senate, and does not face the voters in this year's elections. He can expect that his stand on this question will come back to haunt him during future campaigns, however.

The school busing issue is not likely to be laid to rest this year. It will remain a political hot potato for some time.

THE ROANOKE TIMES

Roanoke, Va., March 2, 1972

That platoon of senators out campaigning for the Democratic presidential nomination is open to criticism for neglecting Senate business. But when the roll was called up yonder Tuesday on a pivotal issue—how Congress shall react to school busing for desegregation—most of the absentees were back in Washington. And their votes turned the tide against the retrogressive Griffin amendment.

By their votes, Sens. Edmund Muskie, George McGovern and Hubert Humphrey said that—while they may deplore the ill effects that come with some massive busing plans—they are not ready to repudiate the commitment to equitable education made by the Supreme Court 18 years ago. Nor, it seems, are these presidential hopefuls prepared to make a little cheap political hay at the expense of the federal court system.

Two other campaigning senators, Henry Jackson and Vance Hartke, did not return for the vote. What this says about their attitudes on busing may not be clear, but it suggests something about where they think their chief duty lies.

The Washington Post

Times Herald

Washington, D.C., March 2, 1972

It was quite a show in the United States Senate yesterday—and over the past week for that matter. A parliamentary situation at least as complex as any in recent memory, a series of close and critical votes contradicting and reversing one another, Senator Mansfield as Mr. Keen, Tracer of Lost Persons, collecting and then misplacing and then retrieving the majority required to stop the pernicious Griffin amendment—all this was part of the fun. Over it, at critical moments, there hovered the mysterious presence of the Vice President who was in place to break any possible tie votes, to reveal what the administration really had in mind behind its "benevolent neutrality" stance on an amendment designed to strip the courts of their power to remedy constitutional violations. And there was cliffhanging drama too. Two o'clock Wednesday afternoon had been the agreed-upon deadline for introduction of amendments before final floor action on the whole bill. At five minutes of two, Senator Dole suddenly reintroduced the Griffin amendment, which had been beaten back the day before: this time it was defeated by a single vote—48 to 47.

There are a number of general conclusions to be reached about all this, and the first is that the episode came out well. Which leads directly to our second observation, namely, that the skirmishing has only begun. We will be treated soon to a heightened debate over the numerous constitutional amendments under discussion, the administration has promised—or threatened, it's not quite clear which—to unveil a new view on the issue soon, and the legislation that was passed in the Senate yesterday will now go to conference with the House. That conference is unlikely to be tranquil. The House version of the legislation in question—a 2-year $1.5 billion program of aid to desegregating schools—has been embellished with a number of restrictive and regressive amendments concerning desegregation that will be the object of much contention. The Senate, owing to its action in rejecting the Griffin amendment and in maintaining its much wiser version of the emergency aid bill, comes into conference in a far better position than seemed likely earlier in the week. Had the Griffin amendment been permitted to stand, the character of the final legislation would have been a foregone conclusion. Now there is at least a chance in conference to undo what the House has done.

This chance is owing to the persistence and political courage of a number of men. Senators Mansfield, Scott, Mondale and Javits were largely responsible for the result. Senators Humphrey, Muskie and McGovern, having lamentably missed the original Friday vote on the Griffin amendment, showed more than an earnest of good faith in breaking up their primary campaign schedules and returning not just to vote on Tuesday but to stick around through the Wednesday deadline to make sure the thing didn't get away again. The failure of the Dole-Griffin five-minutes-of-two caper demonstrates that their presence made the difference—at some cost, no doubt, to their own campaigns. They are to be commended and so are such senators as, for example, Mr. Bellmon of Oklahoma who voted courage and sense throughout the week, despite a political atmosphere at home that would argue to many an opposite course.

The best that can be said for the Nixon administration, with its seemingly endless capacity for exploiting and making this national problem worse, is that it didn't leap openly into the fight. Senators Hartke and Jackson, on the other hand, out there campaigning for the most responsible office in the land, didn't leap into the fight either—although they should have. Both candidates preferred to remain with their campaign schedules, even though the votes were bound to be close and hard to predict. Senator Jackson, who has lately put forth his own constitutional amendment which would roll back Supreme Court decisions dating to 1968 and which would open much more than the busing cases, was in Florida. Senator Hartke was up in New Hampshire. They were telling the folks why they should be President.

The Chattanooga Times

Chattanooga, Tenn., March 2, 1972

The Senate's overwhelming acceptance of the Mansfield-Scott plan to limit but not frustrate busing when necessary to rectify racial imbalances in local schools was an important step toward bringing reason to bear on a highly emotional problem. It could well prevent far more stringent actions the nation would long regret.

No less important when regarded as a fundamental issue, however, was at least the tentative defeat of the Griffin amendment to the same omnibus aid to education bills. The measure would have denied federal courts jurisdictional authority to order busing in school integration cases.

The Mansfield-Scott bill, sponsored by the majority and minority leaders of the Senate, would prohibit the use of federal funds for busing unless requested by a local school board carrying out a court-ordered or a voluntary desegregation plan. At the same time, it would discourage federal agencies from demanding or even specifically encouraging busing to achieve segregation, while recognizing that such a program was a permissible instrument for reaching the latter legal goal.

Its passage by a lopsided vote indicated it represented a reasonable and acceptable compromise among the various views of senators, troubled in their own minds as to the wisdom and feasibility of massive busing programs. Advocates predicted it would lessen the pressure for an anti-busing amendment to the Constitution. This would impose a legalistic rigidity and an absence of alternatives in an area where the greatest flexibility is required.

Somewhat the same principle is at stake in the Griffin measure. Congress has the power to fix the jurisdiction of federal courts, authority granted it by the Constitution to help assure the lasting co-equality of the three branches of government. When that power is employed in effect to prevent aggrieved parties from seeking judicial redress from what may be merely contemporary legislative policy, however, it is grievously abused.

The Constitution should remain as nearly as possible the statement of broad principles by which the American people agree to govern themselves, rather than a collection of specific directives best left to the legislative process. There are exceptions, but the intent is clearly established by the frequent repetition of the clause accompanying a constitutional provision: "The Congress shall have power to enforce this article by appropriate legislation."

So be it in the instance of busing, a matter for administration action under legislative guidelines and judicial interpretation of the right of every person to equal protection of the laws.

CHICAGO DAILY NEWS

Chicago, Ill., March 2, 1972

In a tardy onset of good sense, the Senate has backed away from an extreme position on school busing. The reversal of its own previous stand properly took the issue back out of the ideological area and put the emphasis where it belongs — on the best interests and greatest convenience of the children.

The amendment the Senate had earlier narrowly voted into the $23-billion higher education bill would have barred federal courts from issuing racially related busing orders. One result would almost surely have been to present the Supreme Court with a new and highly emotional issue in the race area — whether to accept Congress' mandate or defy it in defense of its own interpretation of the 14th Amendment. To moderates seeking to defuse the already supercharged issue, this seemed to be one battle that the nation could well be spared.

Moreover — as we observed the other day — a flat ban on busing to achieve integration would be a dangerous way to approach a problem that is essentially local and varies in nature and intensity from one community to the next.

A far more sensible approach is the one adopted after the Griffin amendment was rejected. This is a proposal offered by Democratic Leader Mike Mansfield and Republican Leader Hugh Scott banning federal funds for racial-balance busing unless local school officials requested such money of their own free will. It would also ban money to bus children over unusual distances or to schools inferior to those in their own neighborhoods. Under the proposal, court orders to bus children out of their districts would be held up until all appeals had been exhausted.

The Senate compromise still must be reconciled with tougher anti-busing measures tacked onto the education bill in the House, but it is to be hoped that the thorough airing the question got in the Senate will enable the Senate view to prevail.

It seems to us that this proposal takes an intelligent middle course, respecting the principle of desegregation while avoiding flat-out rigidity on the busing issue.

In so doing, it serves the main aim of getting on with the job of educating children — an objective too often obscured by the sound and fury surrounding the racial turmoil. Busing will still be an instrument available to oppose deliberate segregation. Local authorities will maintain a certain flexibility to suit policy to local circumstances. Both Congress and the Supreme Court will be free to watch developments and devise such further guidelines as may be required. And meanwhile, we can hope, the nation will have one less bone of contention to chew on in an era amply strewn with such bones.

The Courier-Journal

Louisville, Ky., March 3, 1972

JUST HOW STRONG the emotional tide that has washed over the busing issue has become is made apparent by the Senate's narrow vote on the down-but-not-out Griffin Rider. This amendment to the pioneering, $23 billion higher education aid bill, adopted on a 43-to-40 count last Thursday, dropped in a 50-to-47 showdown on Tuesday and voted down again 48 to 47 on Wednesday, is nothing but an ill-disguised attempt to turn the clock back to 1954.

But, then, that is what the whole busing issue, when you get right down to it, is all about anyway, isn't it?

Of course, the reality is seldom couched in such blunt terms. Nonetheless, that would have been the effect of the proposal offered by Michigan's Senator Griffin that would have stripped the courts of the right to. order transportation of pupils "on the basis of their race, color, religion, or national origin."

The only circumstances under which the Supreme Court has authorized such orders have been those designed in some situations to remove the vestiges of the *de jure* segregation that existed both before and for years after its historic 1954 Brown decision. It has not yet directly touched upon those *de facto* situations that result from neighborhood housing patterns.

This simple truth has not prevented the great clamor that has brought us to the point where even the President of these United States, who is supposed to provide moral leadership, is willing to play fast and loose with the facts in order to gain political

capital. To see him and some of his would-be successors willing to stoop to talk of cluttering up the U.S. Constitution with an amendment worded similarly to Griffin's proposal is disgraceful. Equally as disgraceful is the sanctimony of Indiana's Senator Hartke, one of those aspirants for the nation's highest office, who spanks the administration's position while ducking the duty of taking a position himself.

Issue now goes to conference

Senator Hartke is not alone. That most of his colleagues find the issue distasteful is evidenced by their adoption of the Mansfield-Scott rider that would put mild restraints upon busing. It is a political placebo, designed to defuse the issue and get them off the hook with their constituents by appearing to oppose busing without really doing anything about it.

Even that does not get the issue off their backs. The fight now shifts to the House-Senate conference committee that must reconcile the differences in the two chambers' versions of the measure. Among those differences are the much more sweeping busing curbs voted in the House.

Amid all the great waves, voices of reason and caution have emerged infrequently. Senator Mondale of Minnesota is one such voice, with his view that integrated education can mean a better education for all and that

busing is one way to achieve it. Mayor Lindsay of New York is another, having told the Florida legislature what it did not want to hear—that busing's foes were out to block racial integration.

Housing patterns at fault

Likewise, Florida's Governor Askew confessed his own dislike for busing but defended it as a "temporary measure to try to put us on the road to . . . equal opportunity." Then he got to the real root.

The solution, he said in one of the most courageous speeches by a Southern governor in decades, lies in changed housing patterns and upgraded schools "so that busing then will become unnecessary." This has been the missing element in the debate—the point at which so many of our so-called leaders have failed in their responsibility.

If they want to take a reasoned stand against busing, they must talk of the alternatives, of ending the condition that makes busing necessary. They must face up to the morality of sanctioning the continuation of a divided society and all the evils that go along with it.

The thundering silence along those lines is proof, we submit, that the real design of the anti-busing adherents is to turn back the clock. They are agitating because they look through a one-way glass, seeing busing as purely a political matter. It is not. It is a moral issue that will not go away until it is recognized and dealt with as such.

Detroit Free Press

Detroit, Mich., March 13, 1972

THE MOOD and motive of the House were obvious as its members prepared to vote on whether they would compromise with the Senate on legislation to restrict the use of busing to achieve school desegregation.

The House restrictions were in the form of amendments to the $20 billion higher education bill, and were considerably stronger than the Senate's. They may, in fact, be unconstitutional. But the mood and the motive were important.

They were summed up by Rep. Joe D. Waggoner of Louisiana: "This is a vote the people of the country are going to look at."

Whereupon the House voted, 272-139, to instruct its members to remain firm when they meet with the Senate to work out compromises. The vote doesn't quite have the force of law, but its one-sidedness was a strong indication that the House would reject a compromise that did not include its own strong, anti-busing amendments.

In the Michigan delegation, 10 of the 12 Republicans voted to stick with the tough House version. Rep. Donald Riegle didn't vote. The sole exception was Rep. Phil Ruppe.

Of the seven Democrats, five voted with the majority. The two exceptions were Reps. Conyers and Diggs, both black.

The vote means that the House is willing to throw the baby out with the bath water. The anti-busing amendments are minor nuisances compared to the education bill itself, which is probably the most significant higher education measure since World War II's GI Bill.

For the first time, direct and unrestricted grants would be given to the nation's colleges and universities. For the first time, direct and hefty tax deductions would be allowed families with students in college.

But, as Joe Waggoner implied, the politicians are far more hung up over how students get to their education than over what kind and quality of education they get. To borrow a classic, the House members wrestled with their consciences—and won.

Much as we dislike the idea of busing, and much as we doubt whether it offers any long-range answers, it must be said that the strong House version of the anti-busing amendments is at least unfair. Some experts also say unconstitutional.

The House version, for instance, would prohibit the use of federal funds to pay for busing. Yet it is federal courts, operating under the same Constitution, which ordered local school districts to spend money on busing.

And the House version also delays all court-ordered busing until all appeals are exhausted. This is an unwarranted interference in the judicial process which badly abuses the constitutional separation of powers.

Far worse, neither the House bill nor the Senate version gets to the real problems. One is whether it is national policy to "desegregate," that is, to eliminate compulsory segregation, or whether it is national policy to "integrate," that is, to force a racial balance.

The other is whether it is national policy to achieve equal education for all children, which includes, to our mind, a complete revamping of the method of financing education as a beginning, or to use school buses and other gimmicks as substitutes.

To us, the Supreme Court answered the first question in 1954 when it decided that no state could deny to any person, on account of race, the right to attend any schools the state maintains. This means desegregation.

The second question is decided, less directly but not less clearly, each time the court upholds the 14th Amendment that no state may deny to any citizen "the equal protection of the laws." Four state supreme courts have decided specifically that this means our present system of financing is unconstitutional. Other states, including Michigan, are in the process of deciding the same thing.

Neither problem has been faced by the House in its vote. Nor, for that matter, by the Senate. And certainly nothing is achieved by allowing a minor squabble over a yellow bus to kill a landmark bill that would help achieve both quality and equality.

THE DAILY OKLAHOMAN

Oklahoma City, Okla., March 10, 1972

ON any explosive issue such as school busing, the House ordinarily is far more responsive than the Senate to what it thinks the people want.

The reason is simple. Representatives run for office every two years, whereas senators enjoy six-year terms and therefore can afford the occasional luxury of putting their own convictions ahead of those of their constituents.

That's why the House is taking a tougher stand than the Senate against the use of busing in court-ordered school desegregation. It has instructed its conferees on a Senate-House conference committee to be uncompromising in their support of the anti-busing amendments the House attached to a pending $20 billion bill for higher education and school desegregation.

Thus it's conceivable that busing, which is done in the name of "quality education" for all pupils, could become the focal point of a congressional stalemate threatening education with a $20 billion loss of federal funds.

The Senate's less r e s t r i c t i v e Scott-Mansfield amendment would forbid the use of federal funds for busing unless school officials voluntarily made a written request for the money. The only effect of this provision would be to force financially-plagued school districts to certify in writing their acceptance of court-ordered busing by asking for federal money to implement it.

The Scott-Mansfield amendment would prohibit busing that would be harmful to the health or safety of children or would place them in schools inferior to those nearest their homes. It would bar federal employees from ordering the use of state and local funds for busing "unless constitutionally required," and it would delay court-ordered busing across district lines pending the outcome of appeals.

These provisions largely "waffle" the issue, something co-author Hugh Scott, R-Pa., said Congress would do in view of the approaching election. They leave most of the final judgments to the courts which are making busing necessary in the first place. The only limiting Senate provision is the proposed delay of busing across district lines pending appeal. That could tie up early implementation of the order by U. S. District Judge Robert R. Merhige Jr., consolidating the largely black Richmond, Va., school district with the largely white districts of adjoining Henrico and Chesterfield Counties.

One of the House amendments would delay any form of court-ordered busing until all appeals had been exhausted. That amendment would be much wider in its applications, affecting Oklahoma City's situation among others. Another House amendment would prohibit the use of federal funds to pay for busing. But of course the denial of federal funds wouldn't reverse a busing order, and the practical effect would be to force school districts either to raise taxes or to spend for transportation money that otherwise would be available for improving the "quality" of education. Another largely empty House gesture is a provision forbidding federal officials from encouraging communities to use their own funds for transporting students as a means of desegregation.

Still to be heard from on the busing question is President Nixon, who is in much the same position politically this year as a House member seeking re-election. He has said that he opposes busing to achieve "racial balance," and that the present situation can't be left unchanged. He could be in trouble if the course he advocates promises to have no more practical effect than the relatively mild congressional measures.

The New York Times

New York, N.Y., March 10, 1972

The majority of the House has voted to ram its extreme anti-busing position down the Senate's throat. By instructing its conferees to "insist" that these uncompromising anti-busing amendments must remain unchanged, the House has resorted to the device of nonnegotiable demands that used to be considered a mark of radical adolescence.

At stake in this maneuver is the higher education aid bill, to which the public school desegregation-assistance measure and the anti-busing amendments were incongruously attached. At a time when the nation's colleges and universities are in unprecedented fiscal difficulty, the House ultimatum creates extraordinary pressure for action at almost any price. The anti-busing forces and those who want to exploit the issue in the hustings know, of course, that the importance of the aid-to-education measure they are holding hostage increases the chances that the ransom may be paid.

Such a surrender would be a grave error. The House anti-busing amendments are segregationist in intent and in effect. They would bar expenditure of Federal funds for busing even where this integration device was favored by the local community. They would encourage lengthy litigation in the courts. Aid to higher education must not be bought at the cost of such a sell-out.

The Senate amendment is a rational effort to prevent excessive busing without sabotaging the cause of school integration. Liberals and moderates in both houses, as well as the country's university leadership, can accept it in good conscience. A determined campaign to force the House to reconsider its arbitrary move to block a compromise is the honorable way to save the urgently needed aid to higher education.

The Providence Journal

Providence, R.I., March 11, 1972

Spurred on by the leadership of the Southern bloc, the U.S. House of Representatives has brought the school busing issue to a new impasse and placed in jeopardy the 20-billion-dollar aid bill for higher education.

By forcing its conference committee to take an uncompromising stand on busing, the House has catapulted this highly emotional, politically explosive issue back into the news. How it can be resolved now without some flexibility in either the House or Senate is anybody's guess.

Before the House voted to stand fast on its position—virtually to stop all busing for desegregation purposes—Rep. Joe D. Waggoner Jr., D-La, orchestrated the fears of House members. "You cannot vote for the motion to table," he said, "without telling your constituents, 'I like busing. I want some more.' This is a vote the people of the country are going to look at."

Fortunately, conference committees seldom are instructed not to compromise, since it is their function to settle differences between House and Senate versions of a given bill, and normally it is only through compromise that a settlement is reached.

But so gun-shy over busing has the Congress become, with a presidential policy statement in preparation for release following next week's Florida primary, that unusual departures are not really surprising. It may be that House strategy is to delay settlement until the President's stand is clear, in the belief that he will back the stricter House curbs. That such maneuvering might be carried too far, however, and endanger passage of the higher education bill offers reason for worry.

The busing issue is not really what opponents of busing would make it seem—a substantive matter that can be argued rationally on its own merits. Essentially, it is a device to advance the aims of those who oppose desegregated schools and are fighting to preserve the de facto segregation of neighborhood schools. It is a disguise to cover such motives for many in respectable robes and bring 17 years of progress toward unitary school systems to an abrupt halt.

If Congress allows itself to be used for this purpose out of fear of the electorate and offers as an alternative to busing greater efforts to improve the quality of predominantly black schools, then it will be saying that the 1954 Supreme Court ruling rejecting the doctrine of "separate but equal" is meaningless rhetoric which this country is free to disregard.

THE BLADE

Toledo, Ohio, March 13, 1972

THE nimble footwork being displayed by so many politicians clearly demonstrates how sensitive an issue the bussing of children to promote integration has become in this election year. The Senate, in a teeter-totter, first accepted, then softened a tough anti-bussing bill approved by the House, reversing itself largely because its touring presidential candidates missed the first vote but heeded a summons back for the second. These same candidates, with one exception, have been campaigning in Florida while trying to avoid flat declarations either for or against bussing by constantly stressing the need for "quality education," today's catch-phrase.

President Nixon, too, has engaged in some extraordinary maneuvering. He has expressed himself as unhappy with bussing but has held off saying what he would do about it. Now, he says, his announcement will be made after Florida's primary on Tuesday, where a referendum on bussing has upstaged the presidential primary in voter interest. The White House explanation is that he does not want to influence the balloting, although some suspicious souls suggest that he really does not want to intrude on Alabama Gov. George Wallace's campaign—based chiefly on opposition to bussing — in the belief that a strong Wallace victory will contribute to Democratic disarray. As it stands, Mr. Wallace and Sen. Henry Jackson of Washington are the only candidates who have taken forthright stand on the volatile issue.

The latest development came last week in the House, which reiterated its demands for a tough line by a margin of almost 2-1 and told its conferees not to bow to the Senate's softer views. The House would prohibit the use of federal funds for bussing, would fight the matter in the courts until and unless all appeals processes were exhausted, and would limit federal authority to force the use of state and local funds. The Senate watered down such a tough approach with amendments.

There is some sentiment for a constitutional amendment which hopefully would take the whole dispute out of the hands of the federal courts. Some senators, in particular, feel that this would take them off the hook Whether President Nixon is willing to go this far remains to be seen. We concur in the view that all other legal and legislative remedies should be tried first.

BUSING HALT, SCHOOL AID SOUGHT IN NIXON MESSAGE TO CONGRESS

President Nixon appeared on national television March 16 to explain his administration's policy on the controversy over busing. Nixon's speech came two days after the Florida primary in which the voters had demonstrated their opposition to busing. In his address, which preceded a formal message delivered to Congress the next day, Nixon announced that he would seek a Congressional "moratorium" on all new court-ordered busing while simultaneously asking Congress for more federal school aid to go to the predominantly black urban schools.

The Cincinnati Post

TIMES ✈ STAR

Cincinnati, Ohio, March 18, 1972

We have the sinking feeling, after hearing President Nixon's "antibusing" speech Thursday night, that in Election Year 1972 the school busing issue is going to be blown up out of proportion. At a time when the nation needs repeated appeals to its best instincts, in order to get closer to the goal of racial harmony, it looks as though we are in for repeated appeals to our worst fears, with the potential for a damaging round of divisiveness and retrogression.

President Nixon's policy may have been weeks in the making, but it is significant that it was announced just two days after the victory of longtime segregationist George Wallace in the Florida primary. Yesterday, Governor Wallace warmly congratulated the President, and wished only that he would go further.

Nixon's chief proposal was that the Congress pass a law barring all federal courts from ordering any further school busing at least until July 1, 1973. There are two things seriously wrong with this proposal:

First, it infringes upon the integrity and independence of our courts. The U. S. Constitution, in order to secure a system of checks and balances, set up a triangular form of government: Executive, Legislative and Judicial. For the President to now sick the Congress upon the courts, with the aim of barring the courts from performing their constitutional-granted judicial functions, is an alarming proposition. It is ironic that it comes from a President who has hailed himself as a defender of a "strict constructionist" attitude toward the U. S. Constitution.

There are two major obstacles the President would have to overcome before his proposal would take effect, thank heavens. First, the Congress could refuse to bow to his wishes, and not pass the antibusing legislation he asked for.. Moreover, even if the Congress were to lose its wits and pass such legislation, the honorable judges could ignore it, on grounds of unconstitutional infringement on its role.

The other disappointing aspect of the President's policy was the election year rhetoric, the cold lawyer's brief, the carping cuts at anonymous "extreme social planners." To us, this sounded like an abdication from the moral leadership the nation needs in the highly emotional, agonizing complex yet transcendentally important issue of how we educate our youngsters and see them grow up in a harmonious society that does not suffer from the racial discrimination and discord that haunts our lives today.

Let us try to put busing in perspective. The U. S. Supreme Court in 1954 ruled that racial segregation in schools was illegal. In the slow process of repealing racial segregation, the school bus—a device that for years had been used to assure segregation—was put in reverse and used as a means to undo segregation. Or at least in the South. The present uproar is caused by Northern and Western resistance to busing to end segregation or as opponents put it, "forced busing to achieve racial balance."

Nobody with any concern about children—white, black or yellow—(and we include ourselves) can be in favor of any busing schedule that places undue hardship or fatigue upon students. To quote the words of Sen. Walter F. Mondale of Minnesota, "In itself, busing can be either helpful or harmful. It can be the safest, most reasonable way for children to reach integrated schools of high quality. Or it can be used to uproot stable communities and destroy the one chance that parents have to provide the best for their children." Busing is but one tool for achieving racial desegregation in the public schools.

Which leads us to a final point: The furor over school busing is largely the work of politicians and parents. In city after city, county after county, in the South particularly, but in the North and West too, where school children, from early grades through high school, have been put together on school buses, they seem to have gotten along awfully well.

It's often said the youth of today are the leaders of tomorrow. Perhaps if we listened to our youngsters, and watched them, and asked their advice, we'd find they make good leaders—for today.

The Evening Bulletin

Philadelphia, Pa., March 19, 1972

In his short television speech on school busing Thursday evening, President Nixon said that the question is "How can we end segregation in a way that does not result in more busing?"

The answer, he said, was provided in proposals he was sending to Congress calling for an immediate halt to all new busing orders by the federal courts and the enactment of legislation requiring that every state or locality must grant equal educational opportunity to every person.

In some rather glaring ways, however, Mr. Nixon's long awaited pronouncement fell short of the standard he set for the American people in the handling of the emotion-charged busing issue.

It is indeed a test of their character, responsibility and decency. And this means that it is a moral problem as well as an educational one. But Mr. Nixon chose to dwell most on the evils of busing. He did not give equal time to the evils of segregation.

In offering improvement of poor schools as the proper alternative to busing he conspicuously failed in his TV speech to call on the American people to break down the walls of prejudice behind which the most improved schools for the blacks could be left segregated and so unequal. He did not issue any ringing appeal to the white suburbs to join in breaking the housing patterns that are so large a part of school segregation.

Mr. Nixon, in short, did not offer the strong moral leadership for which even some of the most cynical Americans in their hearts look to their President when they are deeply troubled. Instead, his was a political address tailored principally to the worry and fear that busing for racial purposes causes American parents, both black and white. He did not lift us up to see the problem in its entirety; he presented us with a "solution" which was a common denominator of the public opinion polls.

• • •

Mr. Nixon is profoundly right, of course, in rejecting as a "vicious libel" any assertion that the concern of parents over busing is simply concealed racism and resistance to desegregation. That racism is behind the thinking of some, he acknowledges. But the extent of the antibus feeling throughout the country clearly indicates that concern for the well-being of the children themselves is its principal basis.

But if Mr. Nixon rightly recognizes this, and if his own opposition to busing is long-established, he has nonetheless catered to emotion rather than clarified the basic issues. He professes to walk the middle road between "extremists who oppose busing for the wrong reasons" and "the extreme social planners who insist on more busing even at the cost of better education." Yet in so doing he conveys the unmistakable impression of trying to edge Alabama Governor George Wallace out of his place at the head of the antibusing parade while avoiding any taint of the bigoted image associated with some of Mr. Wallace's supporters.

The result is that his own stand is fuzzy.

His only criticism of a constitutional amendment to stop busing is that it would take too long, not, as many conservatives feel, that this would trivialize and injure that basic American document.

His advocacy of a legislative moratorium on new busing orders by the courts while Congress considers alternative approaches is another version of efforts in Congress to achieve a breathing spell. But it is not quite the clear-cut stop-busing-now action that Mr. Nixon managed to imply in his TV speech. Indeed, his far less simplistic message to Congress which followed indicated that there is a place for some new busing in the future although as a last, temporary resort hedged about with restrictions.

His call for directing $2.5 billion next year "mainly" toward improving the education of children from poor families is not quite the breakthrough he suggests. It avoids some of the thorny education problems which arise when even a "good" slum neighborhood school is surrounded by a racial slum neighborhood.

In his message to Congress, the President spoke proudly of his administration's achievements against discrimination in housing, jobs, schools and other areas. He said firmly that they would continue. But because he dwelled so much on the evils of busing in his address to the people and said so little about what is required of Americans to end the evils of segregation, he unfortunately left himself open to serious criticism.

• • •

Despite his assertions to the contrary, and despite the undeniable need to concentrate on quality education and to involve the legislative branch of government in untangling the present muddle, he may well have weakened to an appreciable degree our national commitment to equal justice for all under the Constitution.

In the context of this campaign year, and as desegregation problems loom ever larger and in a more complex form outside the South, it may fairly be asked whether Mr. Nixon was more interested in defusing the busing issue or in appropriating it.

The Dallas Morning News

Dallas, Tex., March 18, 1972

THERE ARE MANY things about the President's message on busing that are not perfectly clear.

We hesitate to raise any questions about this apparent plan, for the President has indicated that anyone who is not satisfied with it is an extremist of the right or left.

The President said that he is against busing for balance. Then he declared that the lower courts have gone too far in forcing busing.

"The decisions have left in their wake confusion and contradiction in the law—anger, fear and turmoil in local communities and worst of all agonized concern among hundreds of thousands of parents for the education and safety of their children who have been forced by court order to be bused miles away from their neighborhood schools."

HAVING NOTED these results, the President put the entire emphasis on limiting future damage, rather than suggesting ways to repair the damage that such busing plans have already done. His plan is aimed at halting "all new busing orders," but there are only faint suggestions of relief for the dozens of school districts already suffering under court orders to bus.

Having acknowledged that busing plans are creating anger, fear and turmoil in local communities, the President merely declared that there must be no more such disasters. While this may reassure those who have not yet seen their children ordered onto the buses for racial balance, it is small comfort for those already afflicted.

The dozens of cities whose citizens see resegregation, disruption and violence steadily corroding their public school system are apparently to be left as is, presumably as a sop to the pro-busing progressives.

The majority not yet bused must be protected, but the minority who are being bused must work out their problems as best they can.

The awkward insertion of the word "more" in the President's summary remark appears to be most significant:

"I believe that the majority of Americans of all races want more busing stopped and better education started."

Is the President hedging his moral bet here? If busing children solely for the purpose of pigment-mixing is wrong, isn't the practice of busing now at least as wrong as is the prospect of busing tomorrow? Though it is undeniably politic to reassure the majority who fear that their children will become the planners' guinea pigs tomorrow, what about the minority whose children are being used for that purpose today?

The President pointed out that "there are right reasons for opposing busing, and there are wrong reasons."

He's undoubtedly correct. There are also right reasons for proposing remedies, and there are wrong reasons.

THE RIGHT reasons, it seems to us, are to halt a practice that does not work, that wastes money and effort better spent on education and that provokes vigorous opposition of the vast majority of Americans. The wrong reasons have to do with getting an incumbent through November unscathed.

It may be extremist to think such thoughts, but the President's plan leaves some question as to its true purpose. Is it being advanced to stop busing problems—or to stop Wallace problems?

The Charlotte Observer

Charlotte, N. C., March 19, 1972

President Nixon's proposals on school desegregation prove again what a political master he is. With the skillful precision of a master mechanic, he has put together just the right phrases and the exact degree of quietly modulated emotional appeal to persuade many people that he is standing firmly in the path of the school bus.

What he is doing is apparently intended to help Republican candidates in the South in one way while helping those outside the South in quite another.

In the South, the party's candidates for Congress and the Senate can hail the President's position as their own. Thus they need not be as evasive as they otherwise might have been about whether they support George Wallace on busing and about what they themselves would do: They can simply say they support Mr. Nixon's anti-busing efforts in Congress. And since he did not close the door on supporting a constitutional amendment against busing, they can add that to their own promises.

Outside the South, Mr. Nixon's careful use of the race issue may help the party in a different way. After all, what he proposes — even if it could achieve what he wants people to think it can achieve — would apply principally to non-Southern cities. He proposes nothing that would reduce busing in Southern cities such as Charlotte that already have large-scale busing. Mainly, he holds out the promise that large Northern cities will not have to do the same thing. Thus, there is a kind of Northern and Western Strategy in this. He is suggesting that while Charlotte buses, Detroit and Denver need not. That may be very beneficial to his candidacy, and other GOP candidacies, outside the South.

The big political question in this very political approach to education is whether Mr. Nixon can make the spell he is casting last until election day. He is running some risk that his proposals will be exposed before then as a wasteful sham. But his political instincts usually are good; and even though he has been rushed into this earlier than he might have liked, he may be able to make the spell last just long enough.

A 'Moratorium'

His principal legislative proposal is for a "moratorium on new busing." The only constitutional way to prevent the courts from ordering the use of buses in some desegregation plans would be by passage of a constitutional amendment which in effect limits the meaning of the Fourteenth Amendment's "equal protection" clause. But Mr. Nixon is maintaining it can be done by congressional act. Ironically, he claims this is possible under that same Fourteenth Amendment, which gives Congress the right to enact laws to enforce the "equal protection" guarantees.

If Congress approves of this proposal by the President, months probably will have to pass before the laws enacted are finally declared unconstitutional by the Supreme Court. By then, the election might be over. But if the decision came before the election, Mr. Nixon still could say he had fought hard to stop the school bus, and many people could be persuaded.

Is it possible that the changing Supreme Court, headed by a Nixon appointee, would uphold this flimsy approach? Chief Justice Warren Burger is a conservative, but he is neither a constitutional ignoramus nor, we think, someone who would happily be a political patsy for the man who appointed him. For him, Mr. Burger, it would mean seriously compromising the court's independence by accepting executive and legislative supremacy over the judiciary. We cannot believe that any chief justice would want to preside over such a destruction of the "divided powers" principle that has always been the bedrock of our form of government.

Ghetto Schools

Mr. Nixon's proposal for $2.5 billion to improve schools with large numbers of poor children, such as those in urban ghettos, has not been sufficiently detailed to permit final judgment. The figure in itself is a dramatic but questionable one, since much of this money apparently would come from existing funds, some of which serve the same purpose.

This proposal seems to be grounded in faith that "compensatory education" is a working proposition. But a recent study by the Department of Health, Education and Welfare showed that of about 1,200 projects funded by $1 billion in annual spending under Title I (a program to help academic schools with low-income children), only a dozen produced significant improvement for the children. Other studies are showing the same thing.

We believe there are urban situations in which busing is an impractical solution. If federal money is carefully aimed at those situations, and carefully used, that can be useful. But the danger is that politicians will ignore educational facts and attempt to substitute "compensatory education" approaches for integration in situations where integration IS achievable. Mr. Nixon's approach smacks of that.

The President's words Thursday night at times artfully confused the issues. He spoke of "massive busing to achieve racial balance," busing "just to achieve some social planner's concept" and busing "at the cost of better education." He depicted a nation beset by a new peril ominously bearing down on all fronts, with conniving courts as the villains.

Yet the very protections he wants the public to think he is providing have been provided already by the Supreme Court itself. He carefully avoided a direct attack on the Supreme Court, limiting his comments to suggestions that lower courts have been going too far with busing. In fact, that may be so in some cases; but those cases are decided finally by the Supreme Court.

And what has it said? It already has declared, unanimously, that no one has a constitutional right to attend a racially balanced school; that busing is not required when it damages the educational process; and that school systems cannot be expected to correct all the racial ills of the country.

We should take note of some of the words in the Swann case, involving Charlotte-Mecklenburg, the most important decision yet on busing.

About busing itself: "An objection to transportation of students may have validity when the time or distance of travel is so great as to risk either the health of the children or significantly impinge on the educational process." (The court decided that the time and distances were not too great in Charlotte; it may find they are too great in Detroit.)

On racial balance: "If we were to read the holding of the District Court to require, as a matter of substantive constitutional right, any particular degree of racial balance or mixing, that approach would be disapproved and we would be obliged to reverse. The constitutional command to desegregate schools does not mean that every school in every community must reflect the racial composition of the school system as a whole."

On one-race schools: The court said it is not necessarily unconstitutional for a school system to operate "a small number of one-race, or virtually one-race, schools" if that did not result from "present or past discrimination" by school officials.

Hysteria Or Effort

Those are the words of the court on some of the subjects Mr. Nixon dealt with so loosely. We find them reasonable. We believe a lower court may go further than is desirable in ordering busing; but it appears that the Supreme Court itself is standing by watchfully to prevent that when it happens.

The anguish which many people feel about busing is understandable, we think, but not always well grounded. When school systems have made sudden changes without much advance preparation, as in Charlotte, many inconveniences and inequities have resulted; we thoroughly sympathize with the parents and children involved.

But the answer, we think, lies in a community's calm efforts to create quality integrated schools by providing the necessary resources and public support. That means better administrators and teachers, better facilities, more imaginative programs, safer vehicles.

The solutions should be encouraged too, by the President of the United States. We do not believe President Nixon is providing that kind of leadership.

BUFFALO EVENING NEWS

Buffalo, N.Y., March 30, 1972

In his recent call for a moratorium on new federal court bussing orders, President Nixon left us with two impressions that close reading of his actual proposed legislation have since corrected.

One was his indication that his main quarrel was not with the Supreme Court but with lower courts which "have gone too far." This led us to assume, hopefully, that the moratorium would apply only to the latter until the Supreme Court could decide the constitutional issues already pending. But such is not the case. The moratorium bill applies to ALL federal courts, Supreme as well as lower, and the clear intent is to have it end not with a Supreme Court clarification but with a pre-emption of the entire issue by congressional statute.

This we find hard to reconcile with the concept of an independent judiciary, rather than Congress or President, having the final say on basic constitutional interpretations. Mr. Nixon conceded in his last news conference that "lawyers will disagree" on whether his proposed moratorium is constitutional; he merely adds that the Supreme Court will decide and he thinks it will decide for him. But whether it does or not, we cannot believe it is either a necessary or a healthy precedent to force such fundamental confrontations between the legislative and judicial power.

Our own expectation, as we have said on two recent occasions, is that the Supreme Court as now constituted will probably, if it gets the chance, write a rule of reason on the Denver, Richmond and other pending cases that may cool the bussing issue. Only if it fails to do so should such drastic remedies as a constitutional amendment be considered.

The other point on which the text of the proposed administration legislation has caused us to change our first impression of what the President sought concerns the status of federal court bussing orders already in effect. From his repeated emphasis on halting "new bussing orders," we had assumed that he did not propose wiping out existing orders. But Sec. 406 of his proposed Equal Educational Opportunities Act specifically directs that any such "court orders in effect on the date of enactment of this act . . . shall be reopened and modified" if a local educational agency so requests.

Ironically, this would mean that the only kind of mandatory bussing for which the President's proposals intend no relief whatever is the very kind of state-ordered rather than federal-court ordered massive bussing for racial balance which the Buffalo city school system now faces in its confrontation with State Commissioner Nyquist.

There is much in the Nixon Equal Educational Opportunities bill which we welcome—and much that belies the cry of many critics that he would revert to a standard of "separate but equal." But on bussing itself, we have to conclude that: (1) while giving no relief for the situation faced in Buffalo, the Nixon bill provides too much relief for some recently desegregated southern districts which once used bussing to segregate the races but now balk at using even less of it to maintain integrated schools; and (2) its effort to pre-empt a portion of the Supreme Court's jurisdiction, even if its questionable constitutionality is upheld, seems both unnecessary and imprudent.

The appropriate remedy for any truly intolerable Supreme Court decision remains, as always, a constitutional amendment. But if it is not yet time to consider that, it also is not yet time for the in-some-ways more drastic approach of curbing the Supreme Court's fundamental powers. So we come back to our first reaction to the Nixon bussing message: While we would welcome a moratorium on further bussing orders, at both the state and federal levels, what is most needed now is some time-buying until the Supreme Court can cool the issue, as we would hope its next decisions may do.

THE COMMERCIAL APPEAL

Memphis, Tenn., March 18, 1972

PRESIDENT NIXON told the American people Thursday night that he will try to stop forced busing of school children. His televised message was full of high-flown rhetoric, as if he were trying to prove that George Wallace's Florida victory was nothing for Republicans to worry about. But in addition to telling the opponents of busing what they wanted to hear in political melodrama, the President unquestionably reflected the feelings of most Americans.

The real issue is not the election campaign of Richard Nixon. It is the grass-roots, nationwide resistance to what the President called "the busing of school children away from their own neighborhoods for the purpose of achieving racial balance."

THE SERIOUS business of education has suffered enough from the polarization created by the busing issue. The nation needs to solve the problem so that children can go to school without the threat of continual disruptions in school assignments, echoes of adult confrontations ringing in their ears, and the damaging example of disrespect for the law.

If the current trend of court decisions on school desegregation continues, the public schools might remain in a state of confusion and conflict for years. The President offered a two-fold program to prevent this from happening and to help the schools perform their educational service better than they ever have.

First, he called for a moratorium on busing orders. Second, he recommended the Equal Educational Opportunities Act of 1972, which would funnel 2.5 billion dollars a year into poverty area schools to make them as good as any others.

We believe that the President did the right thing in not supporting a constitutional amendment on busing. The Constitution is too great and basic a document to alter for what might be only a temporary problem. Besides, the amendment process is a long one. The best way to control busing is for the United States Supreme Court to clarify its guidelines. The next best way is through national legislation.

But the President's alternative raises two major questions: Even if Congress passes such a controversial measure, will the Supreme Court accept it as constitutional, and can the President deliver on his very ambitious promises of equal educational opportunities?

Constitutional experts disagree about how much Congress can limit the powers of the federal courts. It is highly questionable, however, that the Supreme Court would permit some of its most important decisions in the last several years to be rolled back by legislative fiat. Those decisions were meticulously developed to protect rights granted by the Constitution, as the highest court in the land interpreted it.

THE SECOND PART of the President's program — improving poverty-area schools — seems at first sight to offer little that has not already been tried. In 1964, Congress took similar action in Title 1 of the Elementary and Secondary School Act. A billion dollars a year was authorized to upgrade the education of the children of the poor. Much of the money was wasted in bureaucratic mismanagement. Even the dollars that were spent as they were intended to be did not prove educationally effective.

If that effort at compensatory education failed, can the President fare better just by increasing the federal ante? Or will he simply raise false hopes among the poor and disadvantaged, whose frustration might break out into more violence and polarization?

The nation must become committed to making the educational system work well for everyone. It must find practical, effective ways of removing discrimination and of correcting the damage done by past segregation.

Because of the confusion about what is constitutionally required in desegregation cases, the prospects of achieving these goals are not good. The law works slowly. Long before the Supreme Court could issue additional rulings, lower courts might order an array of busing plans. There isn't even any assurance that the Supreme Court could clarify the issues sufficiently to bring peace to the schools. The decisions it hands down in cases on appeal typically deal with specific situations, and are not easily applied to other cases.

THE PRESIDENT'S intent clearly is to head off as much confusion as possible. His directive that the Justice Department intervene in desegregation cases on behalf of school boards has that purpose. He wants to hold the lower courts more tightly to the Supreme Court's guidelines.

Whether his proposals will be successful can't be forecast. But at least he has given Congress the opportunity to once more attack the problems of desegregation and quality education. It is one of the most important jobs Congress will have this year. The 14th Amendment, which is the basis for school desegregation suits, gives Congress the power to set forth how the amendment should be enforced. No effort should be spared to pass legislation that will preserve what is good in America's schools, improve what is bad, and save parents and children from the divisive, disruptive effects of busing.

ST. LOUIS POST-DISPATCH

St. Louis, Mo., March 19, 1972

Richard M. Nixon demeaned the office of the presidency with his appalling speech on bussing and school desegregation. If he was trying to tell some Americans what they wanted to hear, he was also offering a shoddy bill of goods.

In 10 minutes Mr. Nixon tried to restore the "separate but equal" doctrine that it took the Supreme Court a half-century to undo. That is the substance of his proposals for a moratorium on bussing and more emphasis on federal spending to uplift schools in poor neighborhoods.

His righteous protestations about ending segregation and achieving equality of education have nothing to do with his program. The idea of keeping poor and black children where they are and spending more money on their schools was always the contemptible apology for separate but equal education.

It never worked. As the Supreme Court said in its historic 1954 decision, "Separate educational facilities are inherently unequal." This was not legal theory; the court had thorough educational studies to prove it. Today, compensatory education can help poor children, but it will not give them equal education.

In all this unnecessary and politically-inspired furor, the school bus is only an instrument—an instrument for cynical political exploitation on one side, and for ending some forms of school desegregation on the other. We assume it is all right with Mr. Nixon if the bus takes rural and suburban children to better schools; what is not all right is a bus that takes black children out of their ghettos to white schools anywhere.

That kind of proposition is the work, to use Mr. Nixon's words, of "extreme social planners." Including, we suppose, high officials of his own Administration who had planned to help school districts desegregate by bussing.

As for Mr. Nixon's proposal for Congress to order the courts to quit requiring bussing, that is a constitutional monstrosity. Neither Congress nor the President can tell the courts how to interpret the Fourteenth Amendment. While the Amendment gives Congress the power to enforce equal protection of the laws by legislation, Mr. Nixon's idea that Congress can enforce unequal protection is a fantastic sophistry.

Mr. Nixon, however, is not deterred by undue respect for the third branch of government. He is not above arousing popular pressure to intimidate the courts, or even above suggesting that there are ways to get around unpopular laws and constitutional provisions. What a performance for a law and order proponent!

It is not difficult to trace how this whole fictitious issue of the school bus arose to such national prominence. Southern districts had already begun to accommodate themselves to obeying the law and using school busses for integration (rather than segregation) when Mr. Nixon began, last summer, to invoke the horrible possibilities of bussing to achieve "racial balance"—itself a myth of his creation.

The more George Wallace made of the issue, the more Mr. Nixon made of it, and after Florida the cynical search for votes has been intensified. The Administration's political strategy now means assuring white suburbs that school busses will be stopped if they transport blacks.

The tragic part of the Nixon policy is that it could have been otherwise. The President showed what he could do to lead the nation into constructive policy with his China trip. But his separate but equal educational policy rolls history backwards. Mr. Nixon has delivered the most divisive speech of any president on the most divisive issue facing the republic. And this is the man who promised to bring the American people together.

The Boston Globe

Boston, Mass., March 18, 1972

President Richard M. Nixon has, as he likes to say, made one thing perfectly clear in his 15-minute television address Thursday night and in his special message to Congress on Friday. He has adopted the busing issue as a prime vote-getter in his campaign for reelection.

The Southern strategy is in full bloom again. And what is not so clear is where this leaves Alabama Gov. George C. Wallace, who may have thought that he had the issue all to himself. Yet it is becoming quite clear where all this is leaving or could leave the nation—back in 1954, before the US Supreme Court ruled that racial segregation in the public schools is unconstitutional.

The President's action was both political and opportunistic—two adjectives that are not necessarily contradictory. Before the returns from Florida, Mr. Nixon had planned only a written message to Congress on busing. But with Wallace polling 42 percent, and 74 percent of Florida's voters favoring a constitutional amendment to ban school busing, the President changed his mind and took to the airwaves.

It was a blatant piece of free campaigning and the Democrats would do well to demand equal time.

"Busing" has become a code word, and the President surely had to know this and take advantage of it. Forty percent of all schoolchildren in this country are bused every day to regional, parochial or private schools with no protest at all. But when busing for purposes of racial balance is involved, it becomes another matter.

When the President took office he also took a solemn oath to "preserve, protect and defend" the Constitution, which vests in the Supreme Court the judicial power to interpret the Constitution. The Supreme Court has ruled — and unanimously — that busing is one of the tools — not the only tool, but one of them — that may be required to desegregate public schools.

Mr. Nixon has now gone farther than he went last Aug. 3 when he opposed "the busing of our nation's schoolchildren to achieve racial balance," which in itself seemed to call into question the Supreme Court's ruling.

He will now, he says, take action to stop such busing, because "a number of . . . lower Federal courts . . . have gone too far, in some cases beyond the requirements laid down by the Supreme Court in ordering massive busing to achieve racial balance." Doing all this by a constitutional amendment "deserves a thorough consideration by the Congress," he says, but has "a fatal flaw. It takes too long."

And so what he proposes is a law calling "an immediate halt to all new busing orders by Federal courts, a moratorium on new busing." It is bad enough for a Chief Executive to contravene the ruling of our highest court, but in this case he is asking the legislative branch of government to join him in dictating to the third branch established by the Constitution he is sworn to uphold.

And in what case pending in a lower Federal court would he have the Justice Department intervene, not on the side of the Constitution, but on the side of those charged with violating it?

Would it be similar to the case involving Charlotte, N.C., and its surrounding county, decided last April 21 in a unanimous opinion written by Chief Justice Burger? In that case, the decision approved a new busing plan that meant less busing, not more, to achieve racial desegregation. Under the old, dual school busing system, pupils at all grade levels had averaged 15 miles of busing one way, for an hour a trip. Under the new system, an elementary school student would average only seven miles, and not more than 35 minutes.

And it is not alone a matter of how far Congress, already divided, will go on this spurious and divisive question of changing the law of the land. Mr. Nixon says he will have the Justice Department intervene in "selected cases" in which lower courts have exceeded Supreme Court requirements on busing.

Is he not willing to recognize that the final arbiter of lower court decisions that exceed its own is the highest court itself, and that so intervening in the judicial process is to load the judicial dice?

No amount of words, under such attractive headings as "The Equal Educational Opportunities Act of 1972," can hide the terrible injustice of what is being proposed. All in all, it was a demeaning day for our country.

HOUSE-SENATE CONFERENCE REACHES COMPROMISE ON ANTI-BUSING RIDER

A House-Senate conference committee May 17 agreed on compromise legislation as part of the Higher Education Act of 1972 that would delay the implementation of court-ordered school busing until Jan. 1, 1974 or until all new judicial busing orders had been appealed. The busing limitations adopted were weaker than the provisions approved by the House which had set no deadline and the moratorium sought by President Nixon, but firmer than Senate proposals which had limited delays to cross-district busing until July 1973. The compromise came despite a 275–124 House vote May 11 calling upon its conferees for the second time this year to make no concessions on the House version.

The Evening Star

Washington, D.C., May 22, 1972

An $18.5 billion higher education bill, the most far-reaching measure of its kind in modern history, is coming down the homestretch in Congress. And yet, because of the extraordinary emotionalism generated by several amendments on busing and desegregation, it is in danger of falling flat on its face. That must not be permitted to happen.

The way those busing amendments became attached to the bill is itself testimony to the irrational way Washington politics can work, especially in an election year. First came a decision to use the larger measure as a vehicle for President Nixon's long-stalled plan to assist school districts that are desegregating. That opened the way for anti-busing legislators to attach restrictive riders. It has been a bloody battle ever since.

Now the legislation has cleared a House-Senate conference committee. Without getting into their merits, it is enough to say that the busing amendments now represent about the best possible compromise between the very tough provisions the House had written and the more moderate Senate provisions. But many liberals are unhappy with the product. So are conservatives, especially in the House, which twice had ordered its conferees into a no-retreat, no-compromise stance. Representative Edith Green and others among them now are threatening to lead a fight to defeat the compromise, a move that if successful would doom the entire legislation.

Although some of this pressure reflects nothing more than pique and traditional House-Senate rivalry, the rest stems directly from rising resentment among voters toward ever-expanding court-ordered busing schemes. Yet in the larger context of this controversy, the amendments to the higher education bill do not mean very much. President Nixon, with his March proposal to freeze federal court busing orders, has gone well beyond them.

In recent days, White House aides have gone out of their way to downgrade the busing sections of the higher education bill, even to the extent of implying the President might veto the bill. This should be seen as part of a complex and somewhat risky political ploy in which the White House is saying, especially to Representative Perkins: You get our strong busing bill out of committee, and we'll help you pass that higher education bill. Apart from the pressure tactics, we believe Perkins' Education and Labor Committee, and Congress as a whole, should get moving on the President's recommendations.

Until that happens, and regardless of what happens to the busing amendments now in question, school officials and others across the country have little way of knowing what federal policy is, or where it is going. This was illustrated dramatically last Wednesday by a hearing examiner's ruling on the Department of Health, Education and Welfare's longstanding insistence that Prince Georges County produce a plan to further desegregate its schools. The picture has become "clouded," said the examiner, and he placed the burden on HEW to show what needs to be done, and how.

Meanwhile, the higher education bill awaits final action. It provides operating subsidies to colleges and universities, many of them now in desperate financial straits. It would create new and expanded forms of federal scholarships and loans. Not least, it would establish a National Institute of Education, capable of raising research in education from its current low level of visibility and support. Clearly, this is legislation that must be rescued from jeopardy.

THE COMMERCIAL APPEAL

Memphis, Tenn., May 19, 1972

THE ANTI-BUSING legislation approved by Senate-House conferees does not appear to have much chance of affecting most school-desegregation plans ordered by federal courts, even if it survives strong opposition in the House. The best hope of anti-busing forces is still the administration proposal for a moratorium on all busing. That bill is hung up in committee.

The very weakness of the conferees' legislation may kill it. Last week the House voted overwhelmingly to tell its conferees not to compromise. But they did.

Under the compromise, court orders for busing to achieve racial balance would be prohibited until all appeals to higher courts had been exhausted. The critical words in this proposal are "to achieve racial balance." What court has done that?

In upholding the Charlotte-Mecklenburg busing order, the United States Supreme Court said balance was not required by the Constitution. But the court ruled that the extensive busing in the North Carolina plan was designed to eliminate the vestiges of segregation, which is a constitutional requirement. It can be argued that most desegregation orders, even those with considerable busing, meet the high court's guidelines.

The compromise also would prohibit busing of children to "substantially inferior" schools or if there would be a hazard to health or safety. How would schools be evaluated? Since the purpose of desegregation is to improve educational opportunities, it would seem impossible to judge an integrated school before the fact. As for busing that harmed health or safety, the Supreme Court already has ruled against that.

In contrast, the President's proposal sets forth specific standards for the courts to follow in pursuing the goal of desegregation. Busing, which would have the lowest priority, would be banned for elementary school children and severely limited for students in higher grades. All new busing would be stopped for 18 months while Congress and the courts developed the new approach to desegregation.

SERIOUS constitutional questions have been raised about the President's bill. Among them is whether Congress can prevent the federal courts from providing remedies when local or state governments have been found guilty of unconstitutional actions.

But the bill deals more directly with the issues that have troubled most Americans. If the bill were released from committee and brought to the floors of both houses for debate, perhaps those issues could be clarified. At least that would be bet er than the passage of a weak, possibly ineffective measure open to widely different interpretations.

St. Louis Globe-Democrat
St. Louis, Mo., May 24, 1972

The hard-won antibusing compromise amendment to a $20 billion federal aid to higher education bill, reached in a lengthy bargaining session which climaxed several weeks of negotiations by House and Senate conferees, faces perhaps an even more bitter fight on the House and Senate floors. This was predictable.

Battle lines were drawn almost before the ink was dry on the compromise plan, which squeaked through the conference committee by a very narrow margin. Opponents of forced busing attacked the plan as being too weak; backers of busing assailed the compromise agreement as going too far.

Essentially, what the antibusing measure provides is an 18-month moratorium on court-ordered busing to achieve integration. During this time no federal court order requiring the transfer or transportation of pupils to overcome racial imbalance in public schools could become effective until all appeals had been exhausted.

The moratorium and a limited ban on the use of federal funds for busing were attached to the landmark higher education bill, which for the first time authorizes direct federal aid for private as well as public colleges and universities and establishes a comprehensive new program of federal aid for poor and needy students.

The $20 billion educational package allots $18.5 billion in federal money for institutions of higher learning, with $1.5 billion provided for helping communities in the process of desegregation.

No less historic than the higher education bill is the busing issue itself. If not the major issue, it is the most emotional political issue in the presidential campaign.

George Wallace's solid victory in the Democratic primary in Michigan, where the busing controversy is heated, can be attributed in large part to his firm antibusing stand.

His liberal Democratic opponents support the busing concept in general as a way to end segregation.

The compromise worked out by House-Senate conferees is certainly not the final answer to the busing question. It provides, at best, a year-and-a-half delay in which Congress could attempt to write clear legislation to guide courts in school desegregation cases.

An apparent weak point in the amendment is that it does not prevent any new busing orders — as a plan backed by President Nixon had proposed — while Congress is trying to draw up a new set of ground rules.

This means that despite the restrictions the busing controversy could continue to occupy the courts with appeals of busing orders even while the moratorium is in effect.

But overall, the compromise plan is probably all that could be expected to get through a Democratic Congress, which has balked at placing any controls on court-ordered busing.

While the amendment appears largely another stopgap measure, it at least could have the desirable affect of slowing down a trend which has been wrong and irrational from the beginning. Forced busing is not and never has been the route to better education, which in both theory and practice is what it's all about.

The higher education bill should be approved because of the sound assistance to education it provides, and the antibusing amendment along with it because it seems the best measure of its type achievable in an election year. It would at least buy some time during which reason might prevail.

Detroit Free Press
Detroit, Mich., May 21, 1972

THE CASE for Congress to accept the busing moratorium compromise attached to the higher education bill is overwhelming

In strictly pragmatic terms, it is the only way to speed passage of the bill, which is itself one of the most important pieces of education legislation in several years. Basically, it would entitle every college-age youth to a grant of up to $1,400 to attend the college of his choice. The amount would be reduced gradually until it disappeared at the $13,000 income level.

In addition, the bill continues and broadens existing programs for aid to higher education. For many families, the bill could mean marked improvement in the opportunity to give children a higher education. And because the federal government would provide an additional "cost-of-education" grant to institutions that accept the federal scholarship students, schools would have an incentive to recruit applicants from less-affluent families.

Despite such attractions, the bill has been tied up in conference in a dispute over the anti-busing riders. The bill approved by the Senate-House conference committee last week would provide for an 18-month moratorium to the end of 1973 on any new court-ordered busing to achieve racial balance for which appeals have not been completed.

This proposal, unlike President Nixon's proposed moratorium, does not represent a frontal assault on the authority of the courts and the Constitution. Because it is qualified it would simply provide breathing space while the question of cross-district busing, particularly, is settled in the courts.

As such, the proposal will not satisfy those who are ready to plow ahead with a full-scale attack on the courts on the basis of what might happen. It is, however, a reasonable step to assure that schools will not be forced to act before the Supreme Court has settled the issue of busing. A consensus probably exists in Congress for going this far to accommodate the intense feelings over busing, but insistence on any more extreme measure is likely to result only in stalemate.

Meanwhile, the higher education bill with all its important benefits for schools and students will have been endangered to no good end. The proposal for a limited moratorium is the best means at hand for dealing with the busing controversy without provoking a constitutional crisis and or forestalling all hope of further desegregation.

THE RICHMOND NEWS LEADER
Richmond, Va., May 19, 1972

As a camel might be described as a horse made by committee, so the compromise anti-busing provision worked out by the House-Senate Conference committee is far from what it ought to be. In unprecedented votes, the whole House twice instructed its conferees not to accept a dilution of House-passed anti-busing measures. Yet the House conferees went into their huddle with their counterparts from the Senate, and behold! The House now has been offered an anti-busing provision that would do practically nothing to halt busing.

The whole House must hold fast. Throughout the land, opposition to compulsory busing continues to mount. Parents and children have been anxiously awaiting definitive congressional action to prevent compulsory busing, but Congress has diddled and dawdled and now come forward with a recommended provision that is so full of oatmeal and mashed potatoes, the public cannot possibly force it down. It is congressional performances such as this that undermine public confidence in the ability of our Federal institutions to function in behalf of the public good.

The matter of compulsory busing is attached to the $18.5 billion education bill that would be bad enough without the useless anti-busing provision. The education bill would federalize public education in the United States to a degree undreamed of even five years ago. If the education bill fails because of the fight over the anti-busing rider, then very well: The public will not suffer. The so-called anti-busing provision that has emerged from the House-Senate Conference is an insult to the American people. In their arrogance, the conferees have refused to do what the public has demanded they do; thereby the conferees have abrogated their public trust. The whole House ought to throw out the House-Senate Conference's useless compromise on compulsory busing, and it should sit on the education bill until a satisfactory anti-busing provision issues forth.

This is a matter of principle. It is a matter on which public consensus is clear, a matter on which consensus comes as close to unanimity as consensus ever does in a free republic. On such matters there can be no satisfactory compromise. The House must hold fast. It must.

The Washington Post
Times Herald
Washington, D.C., May 30, 1972

There are several things to be said about the school desegregation provisions that have been stuck onto the $19 billion higher education bill that recently came out of conference and which the Senate has now passed. Those provisions include the $2 billion, two-year program of emergency aid to desegregating schools, which was first requested by the administration—in rather different form—in 1970. They also include a string of "anti-busing" amendments. Of these, the one which has rightly inspired most controversy is an amendment granting temporary stays of district court-ordered desegregation plans until the affected school system has exhausted its appeals to higher courts. Once the appeals process is complete and provided the lower court ruling has not been overturned. the plan will have to be put into effect.

The amendment in question unfortunately is broader in scope than is the administration's proposed moratorium on busing, since it includes not just transportation but "transfer" of students within its terms. However, on what strikes us as the critical difference between the two, the administration proposal is materially worse, for it would forbid the implementation of new busing orders until a fixed date—no matter *what* the higher courts, including the Supreme Court, said in the meantime. Thus although the administration's proposal has an earlier cutoff date than the amendment in the conferees bill—July 1, 1973, as against January 1, 1974—it is self-evidently a far more questionable proposition, constitutionally speaking. It would simply forbid the carrying out of federal court orders until such time as the Congress felt like it, while under the Senate-House conferee's proposal those orders would merely be stayed until the federal judiciary had given its final order.

We say "merely" not because we think the issue raised by the conferee's proposal is trivial or harmless or without consequence, but rather to make the point that in relation to what the President has been seeking, this amendment does less obvious damage to the process of fulfilling constitutional commands. That is one of the observations that can be made concerning the whole "anti-busing" package that has been added to the higher education bill: it is not good; it is mean spirited and extremely poor public policy—but it does not incorporate the most vicious and dangerous features of the program Mr. Nixon proposed this spring. Indeed, regrettable as the conferees' restrictive package is, its enactment could have the effect of warding off Mr. Nixon's far more irresponsible proposals. Moreover, little as we like the idea of Congress' arrogating to itself the federal judiciary's authority to grant or deny stays while cases are on appeal, it is a fact that in a number of complex, inter-district cases the congressional dictum might only have the effect of doing what federal courts themselves have done and continue to do: stay implementation orders during appeal. The congressional dictum would have that effect, that is, so long as it was permitted to stand by the courts—there is at least a chance that this bit of congressional power-grabbing, if enacted, would subsequently be declared unconstitutional itself.

If this and the other "anti-busing" measures appended to the larger legislation were scheduled to be voted up or down on their own, we would have no trouble recommending a vote against them. As it is, however, they (1) cannot be separated from the higher education and school desegregation money bills to which they are attached and (2) would be far more likely to be resurrected and passed separately this summer than the worthy legislation they amend if the whole higher education bill were to be killed on their account. Thus, a vote to defeat the omnibus bill by way of defeating the "anti-busing" measures could easily guarantee the survival of the worst part of the bill and the death of its better features.

We believe the question is a tactical one, and while we fully appreciate the reasoning behind the opposition of a number of liberal senators and an impressive array of civil rights leaders, it is our reluctant judgment that the omnibus bill should be passed. We have expressed in this space our reasons for believing that the higher education bill to which these amendments are attached is one of the most important and commendable pieces of legislation to come before the Congress in a long while. We do not think it should be sacrificed in an effort to stop the "anti-busing" provisions of the bill—when the effort, almost by definition, cannot succeed in the Congress this year and when its ultimate consequence would quite likely be the enactment of far more regressive anti-civil rights legislation.

The Boston Globe
Boston, Mass., May 26, 1972

For raw politics at its most unconscionable, one has to look no further than the omnibus higher education bill approved by the United States Senate Wednesday after its earlier approval by a Senate-House conference committee. The bill is a prime example of what can be accomplished when devious men deliberately set out to fool not just some of the people some of the time but all of the people all of the time.

As the bill was first conceived by Sen. Claiborne Pell (D-R.I.), it was a superb measure authorizing expenditures of $18.5 billion to $21.5 billion over three years for sundry programs in support of higher education, programs that included basic $1400 annual grants to students who, on their own, would be denied the college and university training without which the nation would be deprived of their native talents as teachers, scientists, physicians, whatnot. It also provided assistance to financially distressed colleges and universities, set up a National Institute of Education, established a new program for the education of Indians and extended present Federal vocational programs for another year. In its original form, it was precisely what Sen. Jacob K. Javits (R-N.Y.) called it, "a landmark piece of legislation."

Then entered the White House (Globe editorial, May 18) and Senate and House segregationists with their antibusing amendments. The bill was metamorphosed overnight into what a disgusted Mr. Javits properly identified as "the clod in the buttermilk — a clear and unconstitutional repudiation of racial equality."

Segregationists are as entitled as are integrationists to their day in court, or in Congress. One wishes, however, that they had the courage to face the issue squarely, rather than covertly, as in this instance, by attaching antibusing amendments to an otherwise superb bill to which the amendments are germane only to the questionable degree that the financial problems of college and university students can be related to the difficulties that children experience in traveling between their homes and the secondary and elementary schools. The 63 to 15 vote by which the conferees' report passed the Senate indicates nothing short of contrived confusion — as is true of the whole busing issue.

The bill now goes to the House, where its fate is uncertain. This is for the ironic reason that even President Nixon, who helped contrive its key and probably unconstitutional antibusing amendment, does not now believe it is strong enough. It stays court-ordered busing until Dec. 31, 1973, or until all appeals have been exhausted. Mr. Nixon, according to White House aide John Ehrlichman, wants a flat moratorium until the middle of 1973. At that time, providing he is re-elected, he will ask Congress for a law "establishing precise nationwide standards governing the busing of school children."

This would at least provide an opportunity for separating the segregationists from the integrationists. As it is now, confusion, contrived and rampant, is the order of the day. A sensible out would be the defeat of the hodge-podge now up for House consideration and enactment of a straightforward higher education measure. Mr. Nixon's repressive proposal — a fitting occasion for the segregationists to put themselves on the record indelibly and for all to see—should be dealt with separately.

The Virginian-Pilot
Norfolk, Va., May 19, 1972

Whether the antibusing compromise in the omnibus higher-education bill meets the House's demand for toughness is but one of the questions hovering over the Senate-House conference committee's handiwork. Chairman Carl D. Perkins (D-Ky.) of the House Labor and Education Committee, who headed the conference, claims it does; Representative Edith Green (D-Ore.), a principal sponsor of the original House education measure and the antibusing appendage, doesn't agree. Meanwhile, liberals among the Senate conferees, including Senators Jacob K. Javits (R-N.Y.) and Walter F. Mondale (D-Minn.), remain committed to all the soft language that passed the upper house.

It has been the House's notion that the way to discourage busing is to ban, flat-out, Federal funds to pay for it. That was written into the House amendment and twice reinforced by House votes instructing the conferees to hold fast. The Senate, on the other hand, called for a denial of Federal funds for busing *except when local school officials ask for them in writing.* Under the conference compromise, Federal money could be used for busing if sought by local officials and Federal officials could encourage busing under the Civil Rights Act of 1964, although pupils could not be ordered bused to inferior schools or at hazard to their health; but busing orders by lower courts would be suspended until appeals have been exhausted or until January 1, 1974—the Nixon moratorium proposal.

The House conferees were wise to accept the Senate's thaw on Federal busing money, and the House itself ought to go along with them. Norfolk's plight tells why. Not only have Federal courts ordered extensive busing here; they also have ruled that the City must foot the busing bill. Why shouldn't Norfolk school officials be allowed to request and receive Federal funds to pay for the Federally required busing? Why should the Government in any case be prohibited from paying for busing it demands?

There is another reason why Congress should adopt the conference report. The $18.5 billion basic bill would rescue colleges and universities from financial disaster and help students with subsidies and loans, as well as create a national agency to conduct research in education much as the National Institutes for Health do in their field; also, it would authorize $1.5 billion for President Nixon's project to help communities meet the nonbusing expenses of desegregation. These are positive programs, and they deserve enactment now.

ST. LOUIS POST-DISPATCH
St. Louis, Mo., May 27, 1972

Were it not so probable that the antibusing provisions of the aid to higher education bill will not pass constitutional muster and were colleges and universities not in such desperate straits for financial assistance, we would strongly urge the House to reject the measure which the Senate has just approved. As it is, one can make, although without much enthusiasm, a case for passage notwithstanding the fact that any antibusing legislation must be regarded as a highly unfortunate symbol of a weakening of Congress's commitment to the national goal of racial integration.

The bill, which would authorize 18.5 billion dollars over three years, would for the first time provide direct federal operating subsidies to institutions of higher learning and it would provide "basic education grants" to any qualified student who lacked money to attend college. The recently revealed financial crisis at New York University graphically illustrates why such aid is needed. NYU, the largest private university in the state, is expected to run a $15,000,000 deficit this year and a special task force has recommended a drastic reduction in faculty and educational programs, including the closing of the Graduate School of Social Work. The antibusing provisions would prevent court busing orders from going into effect until all appeals have been exhausted. Although deplorable, the provisions are less drastic than the ones originally approved by the House, which would have prohibited federal officials from withholding funds to school districts which did not carry out desegregation plans involving busing.

The Administration criticized the version passed by the Senate as being too weak, which can only be interpreted as further evidence of its election year surrender of decent principles to political expediency.

On its face, the attempt by Congress to restrict the courts appears plainly illegal, especially as court decisions pertaining to desegregation are based on interpretations of the Constitution. So there is serious doubt whether the antibusing provisions will be allowed by the courts to stand. The higher education bill may be remembered as a milestone in Government responsibility to institutions of learning and their students; it is more likely, however, that it may go down in history as the occasion in which Congress lost its courage and its will and turned its back upon millions of black school children.

Pittsburgh Post-Gazette
Pittsburgh, Pa., May 29, 1972

ONE CONGRESSMAN, with perhaps only slight exaggeration, described the 1972 higher-education bill as "the most significant advance in the history of federal support for higher education since the Land Grant College Act was signed by President Lincoln."

Yet, as a sign of the times, the press generally greeted the bill as an anti-busing compromise because of a rider which would prevent court-busing orders from taking effect until all appeals had been exhausted. The measure, passed by the Senate, is now before the House.

Much more importantly, the bill opens doors to more U.S. students and offers more equality of educational opportunity than ever before. It will mean that any student admitted to an accredited college or university is entitled to a federal grant based solely on his need ($1,400, less what his family could reasonably be expected to contribute, with the total not to exceed 60 per cent of his educational costs).

Unlike other federal programs (which are also to be retained), these grants go directly to needy students rather than to the states first and then to colleges. They thus will not be treated differently at different universities. Today, the particular college to which a student happens to apply and the whims of its student-aid officer often determine the amount, if any, of his aid. This uncertainty keeps many qualified but needy students out of college.

A second landmark feature of this $18.5-billion aid bill is its authorizing direct federal grants to colleges and universities for operating purposes — the first such grants ever — which the institutions may generally spend as they see fit. It thus recognizes that if the government is to encourage more students through aid, it must also help institutions cover resultant, added operating costs.

This omnibus education bill goes a long way toward establishing, in the economic sense, a classless society in higher education. Therefore, we urge its passage by a Congress whose members, we suspect, believe as we do that education is America's most vital resource.

Orlando Sentinel

Orlando, Fla., May 27, 1972

CONGRESS, IN considering and writing legislation on busing of elementary students, has created an omnibus bill running far afield of the busing issue.

The bill c o m b i n e s federal operating subsidies to colleges with outright grants to college students.

Monies would go to institutions of higher learning, based on the number of students enrolled who receive federal scholarships or loans, with no strings attached.

✿ ✿ ✿

HIGHER INSTITUTIONS should be held accountable for financial operations before any federal money is handed over. The proposal is the first-ever program of general federal aid for all colleges and universities — and without controls the potential is great for waste and mismanagement.

The student assistance program would be a new approach under which every student is eligible for a basic annual $1,400 stipend, minus his expected family contribution.

How anyone could expect such a plan to work fairly and equitably is a prime and unanswerable question,

Heretofore the government has provided loans, rather than grants, to students. The present loan system not only is cheaper but actually makes financing available to more students.

It certainly attracts the more serious student, since the recipient knows he must pay back an obligation.

✿ ✿ ✿

NOW THAT it has been approved by the Senate, the bill goes to the House for final congressional action next week.

There may yet be time, though it is doubtful, for sound-thinking legislators to apply a little logic and make commonsense changes,

We may be stuck with a bad law, though, because under the rules at this stage of the game both houses must consider the entire legislative package without changes.

The Topeka Daily Capital

Topeka, Kans., May 28, 1972

The U.S. House of Representatives should act to remedy a serious mistake made by the Senate last week when it passed a giant give-away, which supporters called a "far-reaching, landmark higher education bill."

Most stories about the act have concerned antibusing riders attached to it. Controversy over these has slowed the measure's progress through Congress. That is well.

The busing argument has obscured features of the bill which are foolhardy. The House should consider these very carefully — and then reject them.

The bill deserves defeat as a three-year $21.3 billion spending spree.

It would guarantee every eligible college or university student a basic $1,400 annual grant — less any funds contributed by his family. Over the three years of the life of the bill, each student could cost the taxpayers up to $4,200 — depending on how much responsibility the student and parents assume for his education. If the system were continued, the full four years could cost $5,600.

This money is not a loan, to be repaid when the student completes his education; it is a gift.

It is estimated the gifts and other student aid would cost $7.5 billion over the three years. In addition the bill would continue a student loan program.

For the first time, the bill authorizes direct federal aid to private and public colleges and universities.

Officials of Harvard, Yale, Columbia, Stanford and other prestige institutions were told by a congressman they must work hard for the act's passage. There's money in the bill for these large institutions.

The massive college aid would come at a time when it has been shown that a college diploma is not an automatic passport to a job. The government would encourage more students to attend college when some people have begun to doubt that all youths should attend.

There seems to have been no great public clamor for such a bill. The measure was the result of a sustained lobbying campaign by educators.

The governmental policy and philosophy illustrated here should come to a screeching halt.

Here's the way the "gimmee bill" program works: Congress responds to cries of lobbyists and governmental spenders by authorizing massive expenditures of public funds. These funds are turned over to the spenders; taxpayers are told how much Congress has provided in public grants and aid. The local governments and educational institutions use the funds with no regard for the wishes of local taxpayers. With all that federal money coming in, these spenders can ignore voters and taxpaying citizens.

The system encourages waste and governmental i n e f f i c i e n c y . The spending and waste are paid for by ordinary citizens — in the form of federal taxes — or in the costs of inflation induced by government deficit spending.

This isn't government of, by and for the people. It is taxation of the people, by Congress and for big spenders.

It isn't quite taxation without representation — but the representation is very indirect.

The education bill is hailed as far-reaching, but the truth is Congress has over-reached itself in spending our money. If it is a "landmark" bill, it marks a land into which the government should travel no farther.

The House should say "no" to this government "give-away," which really is a "take-away" of citizens tax money.

The New York Times

New York, N.Y., May 19, 1972

The omnibus higher education bill is far more than emergency first aid. Its aim is to establish a new pattern of Federal support without allowing the Government to interfere with the universities' independence.

In its key provision, the bill provides a $1,400 annual subsidy to which every college-age youth is theoretically entitled—minus the amount the family can reasonably be expected to cover. In practice, this would mean that students from homes with incomes in the neighborhood of $4,500 a year would collect the full "entitlement." This contribution would be reduced gradually until it disappears at approximately the $13,000 income level. In addition, existing direct grants, loans and work-study aid would be continued and could be added to the basic allowance, according to the need.

At the same time, a college would collect "cost of education" grants computed on the number of the federally aided students it enrolls. This aid would be augmented by direct grants for each graduate student, the most costly level of higher education.

The approach is revolutionary because it offers students, regardless of their economic condition, maximum choice of campuses, without the need to apply hat-in-hand. Since the colleges would thus be competing for students who, though not affluent, would bring with them a Federal reward to the institution, there would be a premium on social responsibility in opening up expanded educational opportunity for needy students. And if students invest their allowance in seeking quality education, there will be pressure on the institutions for continuous self-improvement.

The conferees have wisely rejected across-the-board handouts despite their short-range appeal at a time of great fiscal need. They responded instead to the particularly acute crisis among the private colleges and universities by projecting that 39 per cent of the allocations would go to these institutions, even though they enroll only about 26 per cent of the nation's students.

Unless this measure is passed now, it is unlikely to be revived next year when the elementary and secondary schools will move to the forefront of Congressional attention. Meanwhile opportunities would close for many students caught between recession and inflation, while the disastrous academic depression could easily lead to the collapse of some colleges and to a decline in quality for most others.

This—and not the extraneous anti-busing controversy —is the real issue. Congress, by its response, can affect the fate of American higher education for generations to come.

HOUSE PASSES ANTI-BUSING LAW; BILL CONFORMS TO NIXON'S PLANS

The House Aug. 18 voted 282–102 to bar court-ordered busing across school district boundaries for the purpose of racial integration. The vote on a bill sponsored by Rep. Albert H. Quie (R, Minn.) retained the major provisions of President Nixon's March 17 anti-busing proposal. The bill preserved existing school district boundaries, at issue in Detroit and Richmond court rulings, unless the districts were "drawn for the purpose and had the effect" of segregation.

Attached to the bill was an amendment sponsored by Rep. Edith Green (D, Ore.) which would permit the reopening of an estimated 100 court-settled desegregation suits, most of them in the South, to determine whether the court rulings conformed with the new legislation. The amendment passed 246–142. (The House also passed another amendment proposed by Rep. Green that extended the coverage of the legislation from elementary school students to all students.)

Chicago Daily Defender
Chicago, Ill., August 22, 1972

The shocking action of the House in passing the long-awaited anti-busing bill is probably one of the most reprehensible racist acts ever undertaken by a contemporary legislative body. A provision was adopted declaring it to be the policy of Congress that "the neighborhood school is the appropriate basis for determining public school assignments."

This in effect, puts the House on record as favoring an end to cross-town or long-distance busing such as the courts have ordered to achieve school desegregation. The legislation, for the first time, defines who can or cannot be ordered by the courts to go to school outside his or her neighborhood.

This grotesque emasculation of the judiciary has no parallel in American history. We believe with Rep. Emmnauel Celler of Brooklyn that the bill is unconstitutional and a political ploy to achieve short-term political gain by rolling back progress so painfully won. It would roll back the clock on civil rights advances of the past two decades.

The evidence is strong that desegregation improves the academic achievement of black children. The evidence is even stronger that white children fail to suffer any learning disadvantage from desegregation.

Should the Senate concur with the outrageous provisions of the House bill, that will wipe out all the gains made under the 1954 landmark decision on school desegregation. The whole struggle would have to be reenacted all over again.

Richmond Times-Dispatch
Richmond, Va., August 26, 1972

The House of Representatives is more responsive to the changing will of the people than is the Senate. Every two years, a House member must go back to his home district, and, if he desires re-election, give his constituents an acceptable accounting of his legislative record. In this Presidential election year, all 435 House seats are on the line.

Thus, the 282 to 102 vote in the House for a strong prohibition against racially-motivated forced busing was an excellent demonstration of majority American sentiment on this important school issue.

Unfortunately, pundits are predicting already that, despite its nearly 3 to 1 margin of approval in the House, the legislation will receive the cold shoulder in the Senate. Only one-third of the Senators are running for renewal of their six-year terms this year and large sections of the nation remain unaffected by compulsory busing. So, the thinking goes, many Senators can safely ignore the cries of anguished citizens where busing is an issue, and just ride with the status quo.

Let us hope and pray that a majority of U. S. Senators take a loftier view of their public responsibilities than that! From Florida to Michigan, from Virginia to California, the desire of the public has been made manifest again and again in elections and in polls: The people want freedom and fairness in education; they want nothing to do with assignment of children solely on the basis of their race either for racial balance or segregation.

The House-passed bill would allow communities such as Richmond which are already under busing orders to go back into court and seek a variety of freer, more humanistic routes to good education than racial busing. A principal architect of the House measure, it should be noted, was Rep. Edith Green (D-Ore.) who very likely has done more in the cause of improved education over the years than any other member of Congress. Mrs. Green typifies tne genuine, non-racist concern of Americans who want to preserve and strengthen the public schools. Can the Senate afford to continue to ignore such voices as these? If so, we suspect that, in time, the Senators will find that it will be they themselves who will be ignored—by the voters in their states.

THE ARIZONA REPUBLIC
Phoenix, Ariz., August 19, 1972

The NAACP and some other black groups frequently criticize President Nixon for his stand against busing as a means of integrating schools. We have long held to the belief that the average American, whether white, brown or black, is even more opposed to busing than the President.

Thursday's vote in the House of Representatives bears out this opinion. After approving a series of amendments that went beyond President Nixon's recommendations, the House passed an anti-busing bill by the overwhelming vote of 282 to 102. Since the Democrats are in the majority in the House, it is evident that a good many Democrats joined Republicans in an effort to ban busing.

The bill, as passed by the House, stipulates that a student can be bused only as a last resort after the failure of such other desegregation measures as changing attendance zones, pairing black and white neighborhood schools, building new schools, and allowing students freedom of choice as to schools. When busing is used under this bill, a child can be bused past only one school house. Finally, the bill provides that wherever a court has ordered busing, the order can be challenged and a new court hearing obtained.

There is some doubt as to whether the Senate, which is not subject to the same local pressures as the House, will pass the bill in its present form. There also is some doubt as to whether the Supreme Court will uphold the constitutionality of the measure if it is enacted into law.

But there is no doubt that the vast majority of representatives, and we believe the vast majority of Americans, think it is silly to bus children across town, for an hour or more a day, in order to fulfill some sociologist's dream of racial balance.

The important thing is to give a child a good education in his own neighborhood. An hour in a decent classroom with a good teacher will do far more for a child than an hour in a bus heading for a different part of town.

THE DALLAS TIMES HERALD
Dallas, Tex., August 20, 1972

IN THEORY, it is the House of Representatives that first reflects shifts in public sentiment. This is because House members, who represent relatively small constituencies and must run for re-election every two years, are "closest to the people."

If the theory is correct—and experience shows there is much to be said for it—then opposition to racial-balance busing is mounting faster than most of us had dared hope it would.

House members the other day voted by overwhelming margins—the adjective is altogether appropriate—to ban cross-town busing and to allow the reopening of court orders that mandate such busing.

The vote on the busing ban was 178 to 88. The order reopener won by 246 to 142. And the bill that embodies the two provisions passed 282-102.

The House has long been registering its opposition to busing. But these are the strongest curbs it has yet voted—stronger, even, than President Nixon had requested. That they should have passed by such lopsided margins is evidence of the antipathy busing nowadays arouses—not just south of Mason-Dixon, but in Michigan, California, Indiana, Pennsylvania. Since federal judges started ordering busing "up North," a lot of Northerners have come to realize that Southerners have some valid objections to the whole concept of forced transportation.

Of course the polls have for some time been mirroring such sentiment. But it is one thing to oppose busing in principle—quite another to complain to one's congressman about it. Evidently, a lot of Americans have been doing a lot of complaining.

The busing bill goes now to the Senate, where its future is dim. The upper chamber has consistently refused to enact busing legislation. That may be on account of theory also: Since senators represent entire states and run only every six years, they are less responsive, as a rule, to a popular hue and cry.

Even so, the House vote has to be regarded as distinctly encouraging. Clearly, the pressure is building. The folks back home are letting it be known they see no sense in busing children miles from their homes for no better purpose than "racial balance."

In the end, mere legislation, even if passed by both House and Senate, is not likely to solve the problem. The U.S. Supreme Court, which appropriated the power in 1803, is capable of annulling any act of Congress.

The best safeguard against that fate's befalling antibusing legislation is passage of an antibusing constitutional amendment. And by a not-so-strange coincidence, such an amendment is due to come up soon before the House.

As with antibusing legislation, there appears virtually no chance of getting an amendment through the Senate this year. But one shouldn't lose hope. The times, they are changing—and as they change, so do the people's representatives.

The Detroit News
Detroit, Mich., August 21, 1972

By a wide margin, the House has passed a strict anti-bussing bill. But it would be a grave mistake to believe that because the measure has passed one of the two congressional bodies it is half-way toward becoming federal law. A tough battle in the Senate and review by the Supreme Court are inevitable. The odds favor some weakening of the bill if it does win Senate passage and the reaction of the Supreme Court is an open question.

The House bill pleases bussing opponents in both the North and the South. It incorporates a total ban against cross-district bussing. Then the bill limits intradistrict bussing to a "last resort" remedy after intermediate steps have been exhausted. The scope of intradistrict bussing would permit bussing only to the closest or next closest school. These restrictions would apply from first grade through high school. Previous court-ordered bussing plans could be reopened and revised if the plans exceed limitations in the bill.

Although the bill goes beyond the March 17 proposals of President Nixon, the House did include money for the upgrading of the poorest schools: a billion dollar two-year fund would be available to improve the quality of education.

The Senate, of course, is more liberal than the House and only one-third of its membership must go to the voters for reelection this year. Political observers believe the lack of public pressure on "secure" senators will prevent the bill from being passed in its present form. In Michigan, for example, where bussing is a key issue, Senator Griffin would support anti-bussing legislation but Senator Hart has indicated strong opposition.

However, if we assume Senate passage of some kind of bill and subsequent compromise with the House, the public would soon find its anti-bussing legislation on the way to a Supreme Court test.

Those who believe the bill would be unconstitutional pin their major argument on the impropriety of limiting those courts seeking to remedy violation of the constitutional right of equal education. But in a sense, this argument is premature.

So far, the Supreme Court has not broadened the definition of de jure segregation to include de facto segregation, as some of the lower courts seem to be doing. Nor has the Supreme Court ruled on the legality of cross-district bussing remedies regardless of suburban culpability.

Nor has the Supreme Court demanded massive bussing to achieve racial balance as a goal separate from undoing the effect of official segregation

Questions of constitutionality are often raised as if they bolstered only the pro-bussing case. But the majority of people who oppose bussing are also proected by the same Constitution and the Supreme Court could well recognize this by overturning the "new wave" of bussing orders even if the House bill were found unconstitutional.

THE SUN
Baltimore, Md., August 19, 1972

A number of civil rights advocates charge that the bill the House of Representatives has just passed is not anti-busing but anti-desegregation. The charge is correct. No one can say for sure if the *intent* of all the members who voted for the bill was to stop desegregation and roll it back, but one can say for sure that this would be the effect of such legislation. (*If* it becomes law. The Senate may not pass it. Even if it does, the courts might rule such a law unenforceable. Even the White House has called the House bill unconstitutional.) Consider the two principal parts:

1. The bill outlaws busing beyond the two schools closest to a child's home. Yet the racial residential pattern in big cities is such that in some cases desegregation can only come about by transferring pupils farther than that. Even parents and others who most strenuously object to over-long rides must know that this is an artificial formula.

2. The bill allows settled cases to be reopened, even those, says a Justice Department official, that aren't really busing cases. Obviously what is under attack here is the body of the law and practice that flowed from the original school desegregation decision in 1954.

Undoubtedly a number of representatives voted for the bill just to make a record. Busing has become an emotional issue. Probably many representatives who voted for this bill are as anxious that it not become law as those who voted against it. But sympathy for their plight would be misplaced. It is the constant giving in to such pressure that has allowed the issue to flower into such an ugly bloom.

People of good will who do not want to see a halt to the progress of the 1950's and 1960's—progress made at an enormous price—will be hoping that the Senate can resist the emotional pressure. The day may come when new national laws are needed to deal with the transportation of school children. But that time is not now. No one knows for sure what the existing law is. The Supreme Court is expected to clarify the matter during its next term. Obviously Congress ought to wait till then.

The New York Times
New York, N.Y., August 21, 1972

The House of Representatives, by a vote of 282 to 102, has passed an antibusing bill that would literally turn back the clock of history. The measure not only prohibits virtually all busing for purposes of desegregation, regardless of the pupils' age or grade; it also permits the reopening of previously settled cases involving court-ordered desegregation.

The bill is clearly segregationist in intent and potential impact. The House appears to have been determined to do as much mischief as possible by catering to the country's lowest political instincts, in total disregard of the rights of black children.

As originally approved by the House Education and Labor Committee, the measure was bad enough, but at least it exempted secondary schools from the busing ban. The House bill is infinitely worse because it would restrict busing even of high school students, most of whom have always been transported to school. Moreover, it threatens to wipe out earlier desegregation gains.

Although many Senators have in recent months also been giving in to the lure of expediency, the Senate has thus far held the line against the segregationist onslaught. This bill provides a crucial test of the Senate's resolve. It would be a tragedy if it now surrendered to the Administration's divisive antibusing gamesmanship.

OREGON JOURNAL

Portland. Ore., August 19, 1972

Extreme positions taken by some federal courts on busing admittedly have created chaos in a few school districts.

In some instances, the lower courts have gone far beyond the requirements of U.S. Supreme Court decisions on desegregation by imposing unrealistic and costly busing patterns.

Now the House of Representatives has overreacted to what the courts have done by enacting a tough anti-busing bill which would not only void some of the extreme busing plans but would deny the use of busing as a desegregation tool in situations where it would be useful and desirable.

A comparatively mild anti-busing bill offered by the Nixon administration has been loaded with amendments, a key one submitted by Oregon's Rep. Edith Green, which fall short of banning busing for desegregation purposes altogether.

While many opponents of busing, including Rep. Green, see it as purely an educational, not a racial, issue, many black leaders see the House action as an attempt to repeal many of the gains made by minorities over the last 15 years. While minorities themselves are divided on busing, that feeling in itself holds the seeds of danger in the nation's attempt to deal with racial problems.

Some members of the Congress, particularly in the Senate, believe the House bill is unconstitutional and predict rough going for it in the Senate.

Unfortunately, this has become a volatile issue in the country. The majority of the American people are against busing on the scale that some of the courts have required. It is not clear that they favor busing bans as restrictive as those passed by the House.

The Journal consistently has favored the use of busing as one desegregation tool. We have opposed some of the court orders which have forced extreme patterns. We now believe the House has gone too far in its reaction to court rulings. Every effort should be made in the Senate to put the issue in perspective.

Chicago Sun-Times

Chicago, Ill., August 21, 1972

The anti-busing bill approved by the House last week has nothing to do with encouraging equal educational opportunities, although that is its ostensible purpose. It has a great deal to do with politics and is, perhaps, the ultimate in exaggeration of an already sadly overblown political issue.

The question of whether to employ busing as a means of achieving racial balance in public schools should be approached calmly and rationally. Discussion must always begin with the concession that busing is merely a tool, one method of desegregating public schools in compliance with national policy established by the U.S. Supreme Court nearly two decades ago.

The bill passed in the House on Friday, however, is not the result of quiet and reasonable deliberation. It is the outcome of somewhat panicky efforts by members of both political parties to use busing and its attendant racial emotionalism as stairsteps to election or re-election to one public office or another. For example, Rep. James G. O'Hara (D-Mich.), a liberal under strong challenge by an opponent of pupil busing, proposed one of the more extreme anti-busing amendments to the already extreme anti-busing bill. His amendment fortunately was defeated, but he saw to it that the folks back home saw that his heart at last was in the proper place.

By the same token, it is noteworthy that the bill, which goes well beyond the Nixon administration anti-busing bill upon which it was based, was managed on the floor by Rep. Roman C. Pucinski, a Chicago Democrat seeking to wrest a Senate seat from Republican Charles H. Percy, the senior Illinois senator.

The Senate has a duty to reject the bill, for some of its politically inspired provisions are truly disturbing. It would allow reconsideration of school district desegregation orders already in effect and thus would short-circuit years of painstaking American educational progress. Busing, even as a last resort, is limited to busing of a pupil to the school second closest to his home. This could have the effect actually of preventing the busing of minority pupil out of the ghetto. As a sop the bill provides funds for upgrading schools in high-poverty areas and thus endorses the hoary seperate-but-equal concept the Supreme Court sought to bury in its historic 1954 school bias decision.

The measure may be unconstitutional on its face. One Republican said 100 legal scholars had so testified at hearings that the bill was, indeed, unconstitutional, while only one scholar had taken the opposite stand. In addition the bill unnecessarily challenges the powers of the Supreme Court, which has said an anti-busing bill cannot be enacted.

All in all, then it is a bill only for anxious politicians, who have adopted busing as a code word just as the phrase law and order was adopted earlier and the concept distorted. It is a bill that violates common sense, and it should be jettisoned.

The Oregonian

Portland, Ore., August 22, 1972

Historians looking back from a time span of 50 or 100 years at the national furor in the 1970s over busing of school children surely will be amused or amazed. The issue these days has become so embroiled and embittered in emotions and politics that a sensible compromise of views seems unattainable.

But, of course, such conflicts will be resolved by time, experience and development of newer teaching methods. The nation is not going to stand for inferior schools, whether or not caused by segregation, for the rest of time. And the solutions to the critical inadequacy of local financing of education will go hand in hand with resolution of the busing issue.

The House of Representatives doubtless reflected a majority view of the people in voting for the amendments by Rep. Edith Green, D-Ore., Thursday. One would prohibit busing of children except as a last resort for desegregation, and even as a last resort children could not be transported farther than the school second-nearest to their homes. The other would permit school districts in which cross-town or distant busing has been ordered by courts to petition for reopening of the suits and modification of the orders.

The Nixon Administration's request would have allowed cross-town busing for junior high and high school students only as a last resort to end segregation. The Green amendment broadened that. And the other amendment restored the section asked by the President and removed by the House Education Committee permitting reopening of busing court orders.

The use of buses as a tool to achieve better education is as old as buses and it is a useful tool. But the thrust of black and white liberal agitation is to use buses, the cost of which come out of education's funding, for the primary purpose of ending segregation. The courts have supported this view, in line with the U. S. Supreme Court's 1954 decision holding unconstitutional the segregation of black and white school children.

Is it possible to make a distinction between busing for better education and busing for segregation? Certainly, not in all cases, and perhaps in none, because deficiency in educational opportunities goes along with segregation in most cases.

Still, there should be limits to the busing of children, both black and white, not only because long-distance hauling inhibits learning but because parents simply will not stand for it. The House amendment may go too far in limiting busing, even in last resort cases, to the second school from home; it might be as segregated as the nearer school. But there is no benefit to education in spending the money badly needed for teachers, materials, and buildings for long-distance hauling. The key is equality of educational opportunities — a goal not easily achievable in segregated schools.

Philosophizing doesn't do much good in this emotional situation. The Senate probably will knock out the House bill, partly because of politics, but its members should know that the House, at least, has made a sincere effort to meet the desires of a majority of Americans. Unless the Senate has something better to offer, it should go along substantially with the Administration's program.

The Des Moines Register

Des Moines, Iowa, August 23, 1972

More than 40 per cent of America's public school pupils are transported to school by bus, because school officials and parents recognize the obvious good sense of bringing pupils to schools instead of bringing schools to pupils. The U.S. House of Representatives has voted to throw good sense to the wind by insisting that school systems be required to build new schools rather than require youngsters to ride buses to achieve racial desegregation.

The anti-busing bill passed by the House is premised on the belief that Congress knows better than the courts and federal officials concerned with the school situation in each district how to bring about desegregation. The measure lists a series of remedies that must be attempted before busing can be ordered.

Even when busing is allowed as a last resort, the busing can only be to the next nearest school. Among the measures short of busing that must be attempted are the revising of attendance zones and permitting school transfers, in addition to building new schools.

Congress invades the province of the judiciary when it attempts to dictate to judges how to fashion remedies for unconstitutional conduct, and in the process handcuffs the courts. Even if busing is the least expensive and most efficacious way to break up a segregated school system, the courts would be barred from ordering the necessary busing under the House-passed bill.

It would be preferable for locally elected school board members to use their best judgment in devising desegregation plans. The history of school desegregation shows that local officials often refuse to take the necessary action. When this occurs, the courts are the logical agency to step in and see that the right to an equal education is safeguarded.

The House has declared in effect that the courts can't be trusted and congressmen know best how to manage desegregation of schools. The measure would knock into a cocked hat all the desegregation accomplished since 1954 by authorizing the reopening of every case decided since then and the imposition of the congressional remedies.

The irresponsible House-passed bill is proof of the inability of Congress to cope with this issue. Responsibility for this congressional folly, however, must be shared with the President, who had the plan introduced and pushed for its passage.

Iowa Representatives Wiley Mayne, Fred Schwengel, Neal Smith and John Culver deserve commendation for their refusal to go along. We are shamed by having the names of Iowans H. R. Gross, William Scherle and John Kyl associated with the bill's approval by the House.

Rocky Mountain News

Denver, Colo., August 23, 1972

SHORT OF CARVING an 11th Commandment on tablets of stone, the House of Representatives has made it perfectly clear it wants the courts to stop busing school children to achieve racial desegregation.

Before recessing for the Republican convention, the House passed a tough anti-busing bill that would:

● Prohibit all new busing orders, except as a last resort, and even then require that no student be bused beyond "the school closest or next closest" to his home.

● Enable school districts, mostly in the South, to reopen long-settled desegregation cases and reduce the amount of busing required.

If these edicts pass the Senate—which is unlikely—all cross-town busing would be strictly forbidden, and scores of desegregation plans already in effect would be challenged, modified, and, in some cases, overturned.

Basically, this is the anti-busing bill President Nixon proposed last March, and the bill has the same flaws today that it had five months ago.

No matter how unpopular busing may be, Congress is on thin ice when it tries to tell federal judges, who've been struggling with desegregation for 18 years, how to conduct their business.

Judges and school boards should be given the latitude they need to resolve individual cases without relying on a list of "thou shalts" and "thou shalt nots" handed down from Congress.

Nor does it make much sense to reopen old and bitter desegregation arguments that were settled years ago.

Busing is an explosive issue in many communities—the type of issue that demands judicial restraint and makes congressmen stay up half the night passing anti-busing legislation.

But the Supreme Court has said busing is "one tool" of school desegregation. And nothing Congress says or does is likely to deprive judges of the right to use it.

THE DAILY OKLAHOMAN

Oklahoma City, Okla., August 20, 1972

OVERWHELMING House support of a sweeping anti-busing bill does nothing to strengthen the contention of Sen. George McGovern and other integrationists that the issue isn't of great political significance.

Election-year politicking plainly was involved in the thumping vote by which the House sent the bill to an expected burial in the Senate. Some of the House members who voted favorably in order to make a record with their constituents may have reconsidered if they had thought the bill stood any chance of Senate passage. At the same time, the 282-102 favorable vote was an impressive reflection of where the House deemed the overwhelming public sentiment to rest on the issue.

The legislation goes beyond the recommendations President Nixon made last March in calling for a moratorium on new busing orders and a law allowing busing only as a limited last resort for desegregation. The present bill provides that even as a last resort, a child could not be bused farther than the second-nearest school to his home. It provides further that school districts already under desegregation orders could petition to reopen their cases.

The reopening provision was a bid for the support of southern congressmen, most of whom were cool to Mr. Nixon's original proposals, looking upon them as fulfillment of their predictions that busing would be halted when it reached the North.

Those who argue that the issue is exaggerated cite governmental estimates indicating that only 2 to 3 per cent of the more than 18 million pupils using buses are involved in busing for racial purposes.

But of course such estimates would have to be revised sharply upward if racial busing were practiced in all parts of the country on the scale that is contemplated in Oklahoma City and is in effect already in wide areas of the South. Large-scale busing quickly becomes an explosive issue where it is in effect or is in prospect.

As court orders calling for busing were issued in the North and West, congressmen from those parts of the country began joining their southern colleagues in opposition. Typical of the emerging coalition is the Michigan Democratic delegation, five of whose members served districts in Detroit or its suburbs which now are under a federal court order calling for consolidated school administration and area-wide busing.

Members of the Senate are accountable to their constituents only at six-year intervals and are therefore less responsive than the representatives to majority sentiment. But the inertia of the legislative arm and the refusal of the U.S. Supreme Court to define its terms and provide coherent guidelines is permitting all manner of conflicting and often completely impractical lower-court orders to become the "law of the land."

The courts are using such terms as "unitary" and "dual" school systems without defining what they mean. They call for "racial balance" without defining race. The Supreme Court decreed in Brown vs. Board of Education that the assignment of pupils by race was discriminatory and was therefore in violation of the 14th Amendment's equal protection clause. But now the courts are assigning pupils to distant schools precisely on the basis of race, and in the process are doing exactly what the Supreme Court ruled was unconstitutional in 1954.

The chaos the Warren court brought to public education in 1954 will end in the complete dissolution of the public schools unless either Congress or the Supreme Court intervenes soon to restore sanity. The tax bases of inner-city school districts are being eroded by white flight where judges have ordered busing regardless of the consequences. In such places as Richmond and Detroit the judges are ordering consolidations to recapture white taxpayers, but this will result predictably in still more white flight.

The supreme irony is that those who vehemently opposed the assignment of pupils by race 18 years ago are just as vehemently advocating now what they formerly said was unconstitutional.

ANTI-BUSING BILL DIES IN SENATE AS LIBERALS EMPLOY FILIBUSTER

Senate Northern liberals Oct. 12 blocked any possibility of the passage of anti-busing legislation in the current session of Congress when for the third time in three days they succeeded in defeating an attempt to cut off debate on a bill passed in the House Aug. 18. The cloture proposal failed to achieve the necessary two-thirds majority by nine votes. The House-passed bill had incorporated the major provisions of President Nixon's proposed restraints on busing. Specifically, it would have prohibited federal courts from ordering the busing of school students to any school other than the "closest or next closest" to his home, unless district lines deliberately had been drawn for segregationist purposes. Proponents of the defeated legislation promised to revive anti-busing legislation in the new Congress, as did President Nixon during an Oct. 5 news conference.

The Detroit News

Detroit, Mich., October 16, 1972

Although public opposition to bussing is overwhelming, the anti-bussing position has not fared well in the hands of the courts. Nor has its fate improved in Congress. The huge majority of Americans who oppose bussing have been given no remedy.

The House passed an anti-bussing bill, but the Senate filibusted to prevent a vote on the issue. Anti-bussing senators like Michigan's Robert Griffin could not gather enough votes to stop the talkathon. Michigan's Sen. Philip Hart supported the filibuster even though it denied the Senate the opportunity to declare itself on a vital public issue.

Hart, who condemned the filibuster when Southerns used it to deny civil rights to minorities, was one of the Northern liberals who resorted to the same technique to block a vote on the rights of a majority of parents and school children. His position is ironic.

But irony becomes blatant disregard for public opinion if we consider what would have happened if Michigan Atty. Gen. Frank Kelley were Hart's Senate colleague. Kelley says that, if he were elected, he would line up vote for vote with Sen. Hart. That would have put Michigan, faced with some of the worst effects of bussing orders, on record in the Senate as opposing a vote on anti-bussing legislation.

Since Hart would undoubtedly vote against such legislation, he and tag-along Kelley would also record Michigan in favor of bussing. Kelley's promise to lock steps with Hart makes it impossible to believe Kelley really opposes bussing, whatever he says to the contrary.

Despite the damage done by the Senate and the courts, anti-bussing forces still have options available to them. There will be other strong efforts to pass the desired anti-bussing legislation in the next session of Congress. The November election offers the opportunity to tell politicians that bussing opponents are determined to have their views represented in Congress, and especially in the do-nothing Senate. There is also the possibility that the Supreme Court will reverse the "social engineering" of lower courts bent on replacing freedoms with quotas. As a last resort, opponents of bussing can work for constitutional amendment.

In the meantime, however, the people of Michigan are confronted with Sen. Hart doing his best to thwart their will and another would-be senator perhaps planning on doing the same thing despite his amazing ability to talk out of both sides of his mouth. For the people of Michigan, the next obvious step in opposing bussing is to make sure Kelley never takes Sen. Griffin's office.

THE CINCINNATI ENQUIRER

Cincinnati, Ohio, October 24, 1972

LEGISLATION TO CURTAIL massive crosstown busing to achieve racial balance in the nation's schools, despite support of that legislation by President Nixon, a majority of Americans of both races (according to nationwide polls) and probably a majority of both houses of Congress, is now dead.

The death of the bill was symbolic of the performance (if that can be the word for it) of the Democratic-controlled Congress during the entire four years of Mr. Nixon's tenure in the White House. The bill wasn't defeated in a clear-cut contest; it was talked to death, fizzling out after three unsuccessful attempts to get the required two-thirds vote in the Senate to end a filibuster mounted by pro-busing liberals.

Whether the bill should or should not have been enacted is beside the point here. What is important is that busing is an issue of grave concern to most Americans, regardless of whether they are for or against it. Public confidence in the principle that in a republic the government, and the Congress especially, are responsive to the people's views must have been greatly shaken by the Senate's avoidance of the issue. Had there been a straight vote, up or down, the reaction by the defeated side would have been one of loud lamentation—but the issue would have been resolved cleanly, and the American people ultimately would have accepted the verdict. We question whether they will accept the spectacle of seeing the Senate weasel out of a direct grappling with a tough issue.

The busing bill's flameout was not unique. The Senate's recent nondecision on welfare reform was another example. (Although we applaud the outcome—namely, that three competing reform plans will be tested before any one plan is implemented—most indications are that this result came not as a result of deliberation but as a last-minute compromise when none of the plans could muster a majority vote. It was an inadvertence, not a decision.) Other examples include the defeat by default of President Nixon's efforts to make the federal bureaucracy more workable and of major legislation to control strip mining.

The last four years on Capitol Hill have been evidence of Congress' inability or unwillingness to come to grips with the major issues of the day—despite sessions of record length. We hope the effect is not lost on the voters on November 7.

THE WALL STREET JOURNAL.

New York, N.Y., October 11, 1972

This seems to be busing week in Washington, with the Senate debating the latest anti-busing bill and the Supreme Court about to hear arguments on the key Denver school desegregation case. We still hope to see signs, though we do not yet, of a broadening understanding that the key issue in school desegregation has little to do with school buses and everything to do with racial quotas.

The bill before the Senate is a rather silly one, prohibiting courts from ordering any student bused to any school beyond the second nearest his home. Bus rides can of course be a hardship for children, but if limiting the hardship is the purpose of the bill it would make far more sense to set a maximum mileage or time. What a next-nearest-school rule would accomplish is quite beyond us, except to allow legislators to display "anti-busing" votes to their constituents.

In any event, the hardship of bus rides is not the most worrisome thing about the lower court desegregation decisions that have inflamed the busing controversy. In most cases that hardship is no greater than that imposed for other reasons without stirring controversy. The worrisome thing, rather, is the spreading tendency to set quotas, to rule that all schools or most schools must conform to the racial distributions of the district, or the metropolitan area, or whatever strikes the fancy of a particular district judge.

As we hope is becoming clear in the ongoing debate over hiring practices, legally enforced quotas have no place in the American tradition, at least no permanent one. We are not trying to create a society where an individual is judged on the basis of whether he fills a given percentage. We are trying to create a society where an individual is judged as an individual, regardless of membership in any racial or ethnic group.

This is no small matter, and eventually it may have to be dealt with through constitutional amendment.

Amendments have been proposed to specify that no child shall be assigned to any school on the basis of race, creed or national origin. That is something far more worthy of extended Senate debate than anything like the next-nearest rule.

Whether such an amendment will eventually prove necessary depends no little on what happens in the case the Supreme Court takes up this week. The Denver case is the first large-scale busing case from the North to reach the High Court, and if certain arguments are accepted it will set a precedent that could lead to racial quotas and massive busing throughout the land.

The district court held that Denver's minority schools were inferior, that they were inferior because they were segregated, and that the solution was a busing plan to insure they conform to certain percentage racial distributions. The appeals court rejected this sweeping rationale, and its opinion pointed toward eliminating only those few minority schools where past building and attendance-district decisions suggested an intent to preserve black and white schools. The Supreme Court is now asked to reinstate the original opinion.

So the question is clearly joined. Are the courts in the business of redressing demonstrable wrongs? Or are they in the business of remaking society to conform to certain social theories foreign to the American tradition? It's difficult to guess where the Supreme Court will come out on this question. Its own past decisions suggest a wariness of quotas, but also a wariness of ruling against propositions advanced in the name of integration.

We would think it far better if the Supreme Court took the lead in recalling the trend of the law to an open but quotaless society. But that may not happen, and the debaters in the Senate would be wise to lift their sights from petty specifics to the grand constitutional action they may yet be called upon to take.

CHICAGO DAILY NEWS

Chicago, Ill., October 16, 1972

The antibusing bill has been filibustered to death in the Senate, and that's just as well. Busing as an issue has been magnified and distorted throughout the political campaign; a delay in congressional action now should mean that the subject can be taken up in a calmer atmosphere once the inflammatory campaign oratory has died down.

Given the antibusing sentiment in both House and Senate, and the strong backing the bill got from the Nixon administration, some limitation on court-ordered busing is likely to come. But the version that passed the House was overly restrictive to the point that

it might have reversed the trend of desegregation.

Better guidelines on the complex matter of busing are doubtless in order, but when conditions differ so widely from one community to another, some flexibility should be maintained. Neither a flat ban such as the House approved, nor a constitutional ban should be the answer.

The issue will remain alive through the election, and many a congressman's seat may depend on how he deals with it. But we continue to hope that common sense will prevail over the simplistic pro-and-con arguments one hears on the campaign trail.

ARKANSAS DEMOCRAT

Little Rock, Ark., October 17, 1972

As predicted, the busing bill died in the throes of the Senate's adjournment drive. To have this particular bill expire is no great loss; it was perfectly sound when the President introduced it, but the House amended it to the point where it was silly and maybe unconstitutional. But it is a shame that the Congress has failed to take any action on what, to millions of Americans, black and white, is the most pressing problem of the moment.

Those members of the Senate who are opposed to any antibusing measure have scored what we fear may be a decisive victory. The hope for a busing bill in this session hinged on the fact that it was an election year. After those results are in next month, the pressure to do something about busing will be much easier to resist. This is true of the members of Congress as well as the President, even though he has said he would make an antibusing bill the first order of business next year.

The pro-busing filibuster in the Senate last week was a little like a play — the actors knew the outcome but the audience didn't. They even worked it so that there was no roll-call vote on busing. The votes to end debate really aren't an accurate index because some senators, like J. W. Fulbright and, until last week, John McClellan, vote against stopping filibusters as a matter of principle. Obviously, the senators do not feel the urgency about this matter that many of their constitutents do.

In the first place, many of them doubt that the Congress could enact anything that would halt the federal courts' determination to racially balance every school. Secondly, they dread doing anything that might expose them again to the civil rights activists. And last, they are so old or so situated that the problem does not affect them — or the members of the establishment in their home states, who are usually the people they listen to. For them, desegregation also has been solved, either by their children graduating or being put into a private school. Eleven per cent of all the school children in this country are now in private schools.

Maybe some senators are still waiting on deliverance from the Supreme Court. In a short time we will know if there is to be any. The court has before it the Denver case — the first clear-cut case from a non-southern city. The lower court said that Denver schools were inferior because all of them did not have the same percentage of black and white children, so it ordered wholesale busing. The appeals court disagreed, ordering busing only for those schools where injustice had occurred because of drawing boundaries and constructing buildings so as to insure segregated schools. So the Supreme Court will have to decide whether the court's job is to end discrimination by tax-supported institutions, or to remake society according to some idealistic plan with unnatural methods.

We are not very optimistic at this point that relief will come either from the present Supreme Court, the new Congress, or the White House. The only chance may lie in a change in membership in the court. If Mr. Nixon is re-elected, we can be sure that he will appoint a man who does not believe in quotas. One more member of this kind is enough to change the balance and to get the schools back to providing education fulltime.

The Charleston Gazette

Charleston, W. Va., October 11, 1972

If ever there was an emotional issue before Congress, it is the one now being debated in the Senate over a bill to hamstring the federal courts and sharply restrict if not prohibit the use of busing as a tool for school desegregation.

As an indication of how deeply some people are disturbed, this newspaper received a telegram of more than 300 words Tuesday from a woman in Memphis, Tenn., urging support for the antibusing legislation. We have no idea how many other newspapers were sent the same message, but if the distribution was general the cost to "Jane A. Citizen" would be considerable even at night letter rates.

The Senate defeated a motion to shut off debate on the bill Tuesday, and we're sorry to report that Sen. Jennings Randolph voted with the antibusing forces while West Virginia's other senator, Robert C. Byrd, was paired in favor of that position. A similar vote is scheduled for today and perhaps a third for Thursday —and, much as we abhor filibuster tactics, we think the whole country would be better off if the bill were shelved to allow time for emotions to cool and for a test of busing as a means of ending school segregation.

The point is that arguments used by opponents of busing have been fraught with distortions. They give the impression that such busing would be general, whereas only a relatively few school districts would be involved.

"A popular tactic is to denounce busing as "massive" or "forced," despite estimates that busing for the purpose of desegregation accounted for only a very small percentage of total busing—no more than 3 per cent.

The Nixon administration articulated some of the complaints about busing, as reasons for its proposals, in a statement accompanying its antibusing measures sent to Congress last March. Busing, said the administration statement, was widespread, costly, harmful to the educational process and it created unnecessary administrative burdens.

Stephen Horn, vice chairman of the Civil Rights Commission, refuted these charges in testimony before the House Judiciary Committee. He said that population growth accounted for almost all busing and that the cost of busing had held steady at between 3 and 4 per cent of total educational expenditures for 40 years. Horn reminded the committee that HEW Secretary Elliot L. Richardson had told Congress in 1970 that there had been more busing in past years to preserve segregated schools than there was in 1970 to desegregate schools.

"Desegregation," said Horn, "actually can cause many children to spend less time on the bus...because children are no longer bused past one segregated school to get to another, and hence the trip is much shorter." As an example, he cited Georgia, where the number of pupils bused rose to 566,000 in 1971 from 517,000 in 1967, but where the miles logged in a year by Georgia buses dropped to 51.3 million from 54 million.

The Supreme Court approved busing as a means of desegregating schools in a 1971 decision involving the Charlotte-Mecklenburg Board of Education in North Carolina, holding unanimously that "desegregation plans cannot be limited to the walk-in school.." Busing was permissible so long as it did not risk the student's health or impinge on the educational process, the court said. This led to a busing program in the Charlotte-Mecklenburg area, and subsequent reports are that it is working very well.

The House-approved bill now before the Senate not only would make busing for school desegregation a last resort, but would permit busing a child no farther than the next nearest school to his home and would even permit reopening old court orders for school desegregation.

Obviously, this would be the opening wedge for segregationists to turn back the clock on nearly two decades' progress since the Supreme Court's landmark ruling in 1954 that "separate but equal" schools for blacks and whites are unconstitutional.

President Nixon and certain members of Congress have used this emotional issue as a political tool, and in the process have succeeded in sanctioning hysteria and chaos. It remained for Sen. Edward M. Kennedy to bring the question into clear focus when he said the Senate action on the bill "will determine whether this great nation can emerge triumphant on the side of decency and justice for all Americans, or whether America will again slide into the cesspool of racism, inequality and injustice."

Detroit Free Press

Detroit, Mich., October 14, 1972

IN MANY WAYS, the anti-busing debate in the Senate over the last few days has been a charade, and those who participated in it knew it was a charade.

The minority of senators who voted against shutting off the debate were voting to wait until the other shoe has dropped — until the U.S. Supreme Court further defines what the limits of its sanction of busing are. Many of their colleagues who voted the other way also know that it would be a mistake to act hastily, and for this reason they almost seemed to be going through the motions on trying to end the filibuster.

The votes on cloture, then, were not a litmus test of who is pro- and who is antibusing. The sloganeering that has gone on is unfortunate, because the issue is not simplistic. We believe that either the House-passed bill or the constitutional amendment Sen. Robert Griffin favors would be a mistake and undoubtedly premature. Either would tend to provoke a constitutional crisis and to roll back the civil rights gains painfully made over the last few years.

What we must hope for, instead, is that the courts will come up with a workable set of standards for controlling the use of busing or, failing that, that Congress can come up with a more rational approach. We believe that due process will permit us to find an answer to the busing controversy without either ripping up the Constitution or throwing down the gauntlet to the courts.

To say this is to risk being accused of being insensitive to the depths of anxiety that the busing controversy has generated among parents. Not so, not at all. What it is saying is that we must try to look at the problem in its entirety and find ways to insure the safety and well-being of our children without damaging our community in other ways that will last long after we have forgotten about Judge Stephen Roth and his integration orders.

In that context, it will be better if the courts themselves can work out a standard that reasonable men can follow.

LEDGER-STAR

Norfolk, Va., October 13, 1972

Senate opponents of a House-passed bill to limit busing have succeeded in holding off the measure's final consideration. The matter had turned on whether proponents could gather enough votes to invoke cloture, which would cut off debate on the issue. In each of three attempts, the vote for cloture gained majority backing but fell short of the necessary two-thirds.

To be sure, some questions can be raised about the legislation's potential effectiveness. Its constitutionality would doubtless be tested, and the Supreme Court would be placed in the position of considering a statute that, among other things, provided for communities to challenge the court's earlier busing decisions.

Busing remains, however, a source of deep concern among the people. And the large approving vote in the House two months ago was a reflection of this concern. The bill would, for example, hold busing in reserve as a desegregation tool to be used only when other means failed. Another provision would, in any case, limit busing of a child to no farther than the second closest school to his home. Hence, busing would be acknowledged as a last-resort method for eliminating segregated schools, but the long-distance cross-city busing which has upset many parents would be prevented.

In supporting the filibuster cutoff move, Senator Spong spoke of the confusion and bewilderment among the people owing to "conflicting court decisions, various governmental actions and differing pronouncements by governmental officials.

"It is," he continued, "an issue which burdens people, which frightens people, which imposes hardships upon their children and which costs them money. It is a requirement which has been ordered for some, but not for others. It is a matter which the people of this nation expect their representatives to deal with."

This busing bill is only one approach to dealing with the problem. A constitutional amendment would be another, perhaps more effective approach. But in any event the Senate, by using its rules to avoid dealing directly with the issue, has failed to respond to an important public concern.

The Afro American

Baltimore, Md., October 21, 1972

The political and racist trend to turn back the clock on school desegregation, aided and abetted by President Nixon, lost an important round last week when moderates and others concerned about the sanctity of the Constitution defeated an anti-busing bill in the Senate.

At no time since the first hysterics that greeted the Supreme Court's 1954 ruling outlawing racial segregation in public schools, have reactionaries had such influence in governmental places of power.

Even when there were questions about how the Congress eventually would stand on the question, the courts and the executive branch could be counted on to hold fast for the rights of all American citizens as clearly granted in the U.S. Constitution.

No longer is this true on the part of the executive branch. President Nixon has been milking the troublesome school busing issue for every vote he can wring out of it. He has linked hands with the Eastlands and Thurmonds and Wallaces on this issue.

Because he has not yet succeeded completely in putting together a Supreme Court that can be expected to turn its back on the Constitution to carry out majority viewpoints contrary to law, Mr. Nixon has not been able to stop busing.

But he has threatened to seek a constitutional amendment to stop busing to end racial discrimination, in effect, rewriting the constitution to restrict the rights of black citizens to equal protection of the laws.

The filibuster tactics of the moderates who stymied passage in the Senate of the dangerous and clearly unconstitutional anti-busing legislation, is the major hopeful development on the civil rights front to emerge from this Congress. Even the disgraceful public arm-twisting of Mr. Nixon failed to budge the moderates.

Not only did these concerned and dedicated Americans prevent passage of this reactionary proposal, which the House had bought, but they suggested Mr. Nixon will have trouble with his reactionary anti-busing constitutional amendment if it gets to that.

The New York Times

New York, N.Y., October 10, 1972

In an extraordinary maneuver designed to prevent the voices of reason from speaking out against prejudice and political expediency, the antibusing forces in the Senate have moved to limit debate on the House-approved segregationist measure. Not a single word had been spoken on the bill when twenty Senators last week filed a petition for closure.

A two-thirds majority of the Senators voting today thus could end the debate before it ever started. This would bring to a vote an issue that has been totally distorted by President Nixon's cynically irresponsible rhetoric and hopelessly embroiled in the emotions of the election campaign. Such a silencing of the opposition would make a mockery of the Senate's deliberative process.

The antibusing faction evidently realizes that rational discussion is anathema to this legislation. The bill is an abomination—more damaging to the cause of orderly desegregation than President Nixon's own objectionable proposals. It would block integration even in secondary education where there can be no rational defense of the neighborhood school. It would re-open long-settled arguments and roll back desegregation where it has been successfully implemented. It would undermine the authority of the judiciary, including that of the Supreme Court.

To give approval to this bill, under any circumstances, would be a surrender to bigotry. To do so without debate would be an outrageous affront to the democratic process.

© 1972 by The New York Times Company. Reprinted by permission.

The Washington Post

Washington, D.C., October 10, 1972

Today the Senate will vote on a cloture motion to cut off a "filibuster" on the House-passed anti-busing bill. We put the word "filibuster" in quotations, because if this is a tactical talkathon that the bill's opponents are pursuing, it must be one of the shortest in recorded Senate history. The legislation was brought before the Senate on Friday—and the motion to cut off debate was filed the same day. Clearly, what supporters of the House-passed busing bill are after, then, is not the termination of prolonged and dilatory debate, but rather a quick opportunity in the heat of a political year to force a vote on busing and to do so without Senate examination of this particular legislation to which the House added some very far reaching provisions on the floor. These provisions have been studied by neither the House nor the Senate in committee (the bill was put directly on the Senate calendar), and it seems to us doubly necessary, in consequence, that the Senate be given at the very least a reasonable period of time to discuss them. A cloture ruling would prevent such discussion.

Among the provisions of the House-passed bill that demand such scrutiny is one which would permit the reopening of long since closed and completed South-

ern school cases, cases which preceded and had nothing to do with the current furor over court-ordered comprehensive busing in big cities North and South. It could put in train an endless flow of disruptive and harmful relitigation and possibly result in a rollback of court decisions whose fairness and necessity have by now been granted by practically everyone—including many of those who once opposed them.

Another provision which has not been thoroughly studied by either the Senate or the House is that which would permit court-ordered busing, but limit it to the "next nearest" school from that which was being desegregated. What this strange feature could do—and in innumerable cases would—is guarantee that the effects of busing orders be felt only in those poor white "ethnic" areas whose schools have least to offer ghetto children and where racial tensions run the highest. By voting for such a provision, the members of Congress are saying, in effect, that busing is fine so long as it tends to leave the affluent middle-class alone.

Finally, there is a provision authorizing the federal judiciary and the executive branch to compel, as a remedy preferable to busing, the closing down of old schools and the construction of new. Interest-

ingly, when this provision came before the House, an amendment was voted down which would have at least provided some federal funds for districts compelled by the federal government to engage in what could be extremely costly construction. That vote, in our view, offers a pretty fair measure of the degree of sensitivity that prevails in Congress concerning the potential long term effects of this legislation on the districts in question—as distinct from sensitivity toward the political value of an "anti-busing" vote, which the members feel only too keenly.

The provisions cited above in no way exhaust the list of features in the bill which could do with a good deal more reflection on the part of members of the Senate. But they do make a fairly solid case, in our judgment, for—at a minimum—a reasonable period of discussion on the floor. You do not have to be a friend of the filibuster to reach that conclusion, because that is not what is at issue in the couple of days of debate that have taken place on this very complicated and consequential bill. The Senate should resist these premature and politically motivated attempts to silence discussion on such an important issue.

PORTLAND EVENING EXPRESS

Portland, Me., October 13, 1972

Yesterday the Senate set aside one of the most controversial issues to come before it this year, the anti-busing bill sought by the Senate right-wing and the Nixon Administration itself.

Three times the conservatives tried to break a filibuster against the bill by Senate liberals and three times they failed. Now the measure is dead, and it remains to be seen if President Nixon, who no longer needs the support of busing

foes, will try to push through in 1973 the constitutional amendment he has long threatened.

The busing of school pupils is, in large degree, a false issue. Millions of children are bused every day, to consolidated schools that serve a large area. What agitates many voters is not busing itself, but the mixing of races to comply with court injunctions which hold that without busing the Supreme Court's edict in the famous school

segregation cases cannot be upheld.

Busing is not so great an issue in the South as it is in northern cities, where many all-black schools are found in urban centers. Usually the segregation is the result of housing patterns in which most whites have moved into the suburbs. Sometimes it is the result of local and state law; in either case the result has often been that suburban white or nearly white schools

are first-rate while all-black schools are not.

Had the busing bill reached the floor, to be passed, the discredited doctrine of allegedly "separate but equal" schools would have continued. There are also grave doubts as to its constitutionality, and there would have been court tests. On the whole, it is good that the bill lost out, and now the emphasis should turn to making Negro schools as fine as those found outside the ghettos.

New York Post

New York, N.Y., October 14, 1972

Many Americans who read only the headlines or heard only the bulletins may have concluded that the U. S. Senate had opened the door to massive capricious busing of millions of school children. Those anxieties are the cruel consequence of the inflammatory distortions and false alarms in which extreme "anti-busing" legislation has been promoted, with the lamentable encouragement of the President.

In fact what happened is that the Senate voted 59 to 26—after three unsuccessful moves for cloture—to bury a House-approved bill that could be properly called a *re*segregation measure. It would have not only imposed an absurdly rigid (and probably unconstitutional) ban; it would have invited prolonged legal assaults on existing school desegregation programs long ago ratified by the courts. It would have precipitated new strife and turmoil in many areas—especially in the South—where local citizens have joined together in carrying out the peaceful transition projected by the Supreme Court 18 years ago.

This prospect is obviously quite different from the current misconception that a vast new flood of ill-conceived busing expeditions is about to be unleashed. The prevailing standard remains what it was before the House hysteria began. It was stated by Chief Justice Burger— Mr. Nixon's appointee — in an opinion holding that busing plans may be validly challenged "when the time or distance of travel is so great as to risk either the health of the children or significantly impinge on the educational process."

Surely that is a modest rule of reason. It is sad that the doctrine of the "Nixon Court" should become the target of attack by the House Republican leadership and its Southern allies and by Mr. Nixon himself.

The tragic fact is that the politics of discord continues to animate the busing furor. On his trip to Georgia, the President solemnly disclaimed any "Southern strategy" and professed his resolve to seek national unity. But there—as at his recent press conference—he once again assigned high priority to the "anti-busing" crusade. Admittedly it is no longer a predominantly Southern issue; it has become a divisive battle-cry in the North as well. Yet in the real world it affects only a fragment of the populace in areas where segregation has been lawlessly protected.

* * *

We cannot rejoice over the defeat of cloture in the Senate; we have too often been on the other side. It can be justly pointed out, however, that no "extended debate"—the polite word for filibuster—had occurred and that supporters of the bill were obviously trying to stage a stampede amid the general pressure for adjournment. It is hard to avoid the suspicion that at least some of the "anti-busing" agitators were entirely content to lose the vote and retain the issue. The misfortune is that the President has seemed unable to resist similar political temptation, adding new fire to a divisionary, abrasive conflict when a conciliatory, measured voice at the top was so sorely needed.

Chicago Daily Defender

Chicago, Ill., October 19, 1972

Three frenzied attempts to push through a house-passed bill to prevent busing of students were defeated in the Senate by wide margins The bill had the massive backing of President Nixon and a majority of Senators, but Northern liberals of both major parties were able to muster enough votes to stem the tide for at least this session of Congress.

The proposal is one of the most far-reaching and ill-conceived pieces of legislation to come before Congress since Reconstruction. It would bring chaos into the lives of million of Americans who had begun to make their piece with the requirements of the Constitution.

Had the bill passed, it would have removed from the courts the right to assign students to a school other than the one closest to their homes. Perhaps the most sinister aspect of the Nixon-backed legislation is the provision that would enable desegregation suits already settled by the courts to be reopened to insure that they conform to the provisions of the legislation.

That would have turned the clock back on desegregation and nullified all advancement made in blood and tears toward achieving the goal of equal educational opportunity. The sad, if not the saddest aspect of the whole affair is the addition of some black voices to the discordant racist chorus against the achievement of a democratic process.

Despite the collusion of some misguided blacks with paranoic white racists, should the anti-busing proposal ever become the law of the land, it would be the signal for relighting the flames of the unfinished black revolution.

THE CHRISTIAN SCIENCE MONITOR

Boston, Mass., October 16, 1972

While Congress was stalling itself on school busing legislation, the Supreme Court was moving ahead on its effort of nearly two decades to draw the ever finer lines of what is required to desegregate American schools.

It happened on the same day last week. The Senate conceded it could not break a liberal filibuster of an antibusing bill. The measure would have limited busing to neighborhood schools or to second-closest schools, and would have reopened earlier cases in which busing was ordered. It had been passed in the House. The President had backed it. It represented the last possible roadblock Congress could have thrown up against school busing in this session of Congress. In effect, it meant that Congress had decided again not to act.

Meanwhile, the Supreme Court, only a football field distance away from the Senate chamber, was hearing the so-called Denver desegregation case. It marked the first of a series of important cases involving Northern cities the court will take up. In these cases the court will be deciding whether the distinction between de facto and de jure has any legal meaning. It will decide whether school district lines should be disregarded in seeking remedies for racially imbalanced areas — whether suburbs can be made to join with cities in mass desegregation plans.

What Americans witnessed, in the failure of Congress to act on school busing matters and the steady progressive weighing of the issue by the high court, has been typical of this subject all along.

Two decades ago it was the Southerner and the conservative who filibustered to keep Congress from acting in favor of desegregation. Now the tables are turned and it is the liberals who are filibustering to prevent the antibusing majority from limiting desegregation devices. But the result is the same: Congress is unable to rise above its own internal conflict.

Prospects for congressional action to limit busing in its next session are, if anything, dimmer. The election has likely raised antibusing voting power as high as it can get. A new attempt will no doubt be made next session to limit busing. But even a constitutional amendment would have to pass the liberals' filibuster in the Senate — and the liberals' resistance appears deeply planted.

As a practical matter, when the new Congress convenes it will be faced with an altered school busing situation when the Supreme Court rules on the Denver case. In the Denver case, those who brought the suit argue that a *general pattern* of official decisions allowed a segregated situation to develop. If the court upholds this, it could mean a broader definition of infringement of constitutional rights. However, it is the remedy busing, one which would be required in such cases, that most concerns legislators. The court could make things easier for Congress by setting its own limits on busing where the scale of it might be truly massive. But Congress like the rest of the country will have to wait and see.

Some may castigate Congress for its history of inaction on the school desegregation issue, which led the Supreme Court to act in its landmark 1954 decision. But as Congress winds up its business for 1972, the initiative remains the court's.

Federal Government Policies: 1974-75

The House

House OKs aid bill, busing curbs. The House passed by a vote of 380–26 March 27 an elementary and secondary education aid bill with strong anti-busing provisions and extensions of most existing aid programs in modified forms. The aid formulas would authorize almost $21 billion over three years (fiscal 1975–77).

The bill went to the Senate, which was considering a version without busing restrictions and with different aid formulas. An anti-busing bill passed by the House in 1972 had been killed by a Senate filibuster.

The primary busing restriction had been adopted, 293–117, the day before as an amendment almost identical to the 1972 measure. The amendment would permit busing only after other desegregation attempts had been proved ineffective. Even under such circumstances, a student could be bused only to a school "closest or next closest" to his home.

The measure would also permit communities currently under court-ordered busing plans to reopen their court cases if the orders did not conform with the new legislation.

By a vote of 239–168 March 27, the House added a second amendment, by Rep. John M. Ashbrook (R, Ohio), prohibiting the use of federal funds for any form of busing designed to correct racial imbalance.

Nixon supports House bill. President Nixon had supported the House bill in a radio address March 23 as "a step in the right direction toward more community and state control" and threatened to veto a bill such as the measure pending in the Senate.

Nixon stated his opposition to "excessive forced busing" and stressed the importance of "neighborhood schools." Parents were "naturally concerned," he said, when courts imposed busing orders based on "complicated plans drawn up by far-away officials in Washington . . ." In the areas of desegregation and aid funds, Nixon added, federal employes must not be placed "in the role of master social planners."

Democrats rebut Nixon on schools. Democratic Congressional spokesmen on education March 30 sharply criticized President Nixon's positions on both busing for integration and federal aid to schools as divisive and obstructionist. The remarks by Sen. Claiborne Pell (R.I.) and Rep. John Brademas (Ind.) were the Democrats' "equal time" reply to Nixon's March 23 radio address.

Pell accused Nixon of "reopening a painful wound" in calling for strong legislative restrictions on busing (which were passed by the House March 27.) Pell said the existing limited busing restrictions had "worked for the past two years" and should be "left alone."

HEW

Pasadena loses integration funds. The Department of Health, Education and Welfare informed Pasadena, Calif. school officials April 11 that the district had failed to comply with a court-ordered desegregation plan, forcing the department to cut off the city's share of federal integration-aid funds, provided under the Emergency School Aid Act of 1971.

Schools still segregated. In a report marking the 20th anniversary of the Supreme Court decision ordering an end to public school segregation, the Department of Health, Education and Welfare (HEW) said May 17 that based on data compiled in a late 1972 survey, 11.2% of black students attended schools where there were no white children. The report noted that segregation was clearly an urban problem: in 20 large Northern and Southern cities, 25% of the black pupils attended all-black schools.

The survey also found that more than 71% of the public schools in the North had enrollments of more than half black. Comparable figures for other areas were 68% in border states and 53.7% in the South.

The Senate

School aid OKd after busing debate. The Senate, by an 81–5 vote May 20, approved a bill authorizing $25.2 billion over the next four years for elementary and secondary education after a week of debate focusing primarily on busing. The bill's busing provision was not as strict as the one passed by the House, which would go into conference with the Senate on the bill's final provisions.

The Senate version would allow pupils to attend the school "closest or next closest" to their homes with the added specification that the proviso was "not intended to modify or diminish" the authority of the courts "to enforce fully" the Constitution. The amendment, proposed by majority and minority leaders Mike Mansfield (D, Mont.) and Hugh Scott (R, Pa.), was adopted May 16 by a vote of 47–46.

The key vote followed a 47–46 rejection May 15 of an amendment identical to the anti-busing amendment approved by the House. Proposed by Sen. Edward J. Gurney (R, Fla.), it would have barred busing to achieve racial integration to all but the school closest or next closest to a student's home and then only when all other alternatives had been exhausted. It would also have permitted all previous busing litigation to be reopened to comply with the amendment.

In the debate May 16, Senate Republican whip Robert P. Griffin (Mich.) proposed the Gurney amendment without the litigation provision. A motion to table it lost 47–46, but at that point the Scott-Mansfield proposal was offered and adopted.

In other busing decisions, the Senate:

■ Adopted May 15 by a 56–36 vote an amendment by Sen. Birch Bayh (D, Ind.) to bar busing across school district lines without a court finding the lines had been drawn to perpetuate segregation or unless discrimination occurred in each of the districts. The latter would bar busing between two districts if one was in compliance with a court desegregation order and the other was not.

■ Approved by a 71–20 vote May 16 a proposal by Sen. J. Glenn Beall Jr. (R, Md.) to bar implementation of court-ordered busing after the beginning of a school year.

■ Rejected by a 51–41 vote May 16 a proposal by Sen. Sam J. Ervin Jr. (D, N.C.) to bar courts from ordering busing

A to alter racial composition, except for Supreme Court cases of original jurisdiction.

■ Rejected 61–26 May 20 an amendment by Sen. William L. Scott (R, Va.) that would have given jurisdiction on public school problems to the state courts, instead of the federal district courts, with the Supreme Court hearing appeals.

B The Congress

Compromise school aid, bus curbs OKd. A conference committee version of a bill authorizing $25.2 billion over four years in aid to elementary and secondary schools and containing restrictions on busing of students was passed by the Senate on a vote of 81–15 July 24 and by a House vote of 323–83 July 31.

C Busing provisions accepted by the conferees were generally closer to the more lenient Senate bill. The final version prohibited busing for desegregation beyond the school next closest to a student's home, except—as in the Senate bill—when courts determined that more extensive busing was necessary to protect students' constitutional rights.

D The final bill did not include a House provision that would have required the courts to reopen consideration of previous integration orders to bring them into compliance with the bill's restrictions. Under the compromise, parents or school districts could seek reopening of cases only if time or distance traveled would be harmful to students' health or would impair the educational process. A court, however, could terminate existing busing orders if it determined that a district was no longer violating students' rights and was not likely to do so in the future.

E The conferees also accepted Senate amendments prohibiting busing across district lines unless boundaries were found to have been deliberately drawn to foster segregation and prohibiting implementation of integration orders after the beginning of a school year.

The overwhelming vote in the House—where busing opponents had been insisting that the House's stronger restrictions prevail in conference—was attributed to the defusing effect of the Supreme Court's July 25 decision against cross-district busing.

F In the Senate July 24, a last-minute attempt by busing opponents to send the measure back to conference had been narrowly defeated, 55-42.

President signs school bill. President Ford Aug. 21 went to the Department of Health, Education and Welfare (HEW) to **G** sign a major education bill. Ford's signing of the education aid and busing bill at the HEW offices rather than at the White House was regarded as an unusual gesture. Ford said he was not pleased with all elements of the bill, including funding levels and the lack of a provision for automatic re-evaluation of court-ordered bus-

ing, but said he was signing in the "new spirit of cooperation and compromise."

Ford's signing of the education aid and busing bill at the HEW offices rather than at the White House was regarded as an unusual gesture. Ford said he was not pleased with all elements of the bill, including funding levels and the lack of a provision for automatic re-evaluation of court-ordered busing, but said he was signing in the "new spirit of cooperation and compromise."

Justice Department

U.S. drops Pontiac bombing charges. A Justice Department spokesman said Oct. 22 that charges had been dismissed against five men arrested in the 1971 bombing of school buses in Pontiac, Mich. The spokesman indicated that the principal witness against the five men had been severely beaten by another inmate at the federal prison at Terre Haute, Ind. and no longer had the mental capacity to testify.

The Congress

Labor, HEW funds enacted. The fiscal 1975 appropriations bill for the Labor Department and the Health, Education and Welfare Department (HEW) was approved by both houses of Congress Nov. 26 and signed by President Ford Dec. 9. The funds totaled $33,045,856,000, which was $485,239,000 less than the budget request.

The Labor Department's share was $3,356,057,000. HEW received $29,424,170,000, of which $3,629,151,000 was for health programs, $3,240,379,000 for education programs and $22,554,640,000 for welfare programs.

A proscription was written against use of the funds to bus students to achieve racial integration, although few federal funds were used for such purposes.

Busing curb defeated. In the final week of its session, Congress resolved a 2½-month dispute over an amendment prohibiting enforcement of federal anti-discrimination laws in school systems. The amendment, sponsored by Rep. Marjorie S. Holt (R, Md.), was attached to a bill making fiscal 1975–76 supplemental appropriations of $8,659,352,078, more than $5 billion of it for elementary and secondary education programs. Another $2.175 billion was for the community development grant program. The bill was cleared by Congress Dec. 16. President Ford signed it Dec. 27.

The House first approved the Holt amendment by a 220–169 vote Oct. 1. It was dropped in the Senate during the committee stage and rejected on the floor by a 43-36 vote Nov. 19 when it was offered by Sen. Jesse A. Helms (R, N.C.).

A House-Senate conference committee reinstated the amendment after dis-

carding language prohibiting the Health, Education and Welfare Department (HEW) from requiring school districts to keep record files on the basis of race, sex, religion or national origin. As adopted by the conference, the Holt amendment read: "None of these funds shall be used to compel any school system as a condition for receiving grants and other benefits from the appropriations above, to classify teachers or students by race, religion, sex or national origin; or to assign teachers or students to schools, classes or courses for reasons of race, religion, sex or national origin." This was approved by the House by a 212–176 vote Dec. 4.

The Senate retained the amendment after adding 12 words: ". . . except as may be required to enforce non-discrimination provisions of federal law." The nullifying clause was sponsored by Senate Majority Leader Mike Mansfield (D, Mont.) and Minority Leader Hugh Scott (R, Pa.) and supported by HEW and the Justice Department. Sen. James B. Allen (D, Ala.) threatened to filibuster the revision Dec. 11 after his motion to table it was rejected 60–33. A motion to invoke cloture, or limit debate, was adopted Dec. 14 for only the 19th time in Senate history. The vote, requiring a two-thirds majority to carry, was 56–27. The Scott-Mansfield proposal then was approved 55–27.

The House reversed itself on the amendment by approving the nullified version by a 224–136 vote Dec. 16. Then the bill was cleared for the President's signature.

Although busing of students was not mentioned in the amendment, the provision was considered an antibusing stricture in the original version. Holt told the House Dec. 16 the busing issue was "going to destroy our school system" if Congress continued to sanction the "harassment" of local districts. Congress should "spell out what we want," she said, and not leave it up to the courts and HEW.

1975

Civil Rights Commission

U.S. agencies scored on rights effort. A report by the U.S. Commission on Civil Rights, made public Jan. 22, accused the federal government of laxity in enforcement of civil rights laws in education. The 400-page document singled out for criticism the Department of Health, Education and Welfare (HEW), the Internal Revenue Service (IRS) and the Veterans Administration (VA).

In its recommendations to President Ford, the report warned, "We are at a dangerous crossroad in connection with school desegregation. . . . We cannot afford—because of organized resistance in Boston or any other community—to turn back. Extraordinary action is called for. . . ." To insure effective civil rights compliance, the commission said, the President should appoint a White House coordinator of enforcement to bring about "vigorous and effective enforcement of the constitutional mandate to desegregate. . . ."

The commission found that HEW had failed to issue comprehensive guidelines on such matters as busing and city-suburb desegregation because of pending court or Congressional action. "Administrators are entitled to guidelines based on today's law. If the law changes, changes can be made in the guidelines," the report said.

To a large extent, the report contended, HEW had depended too heavily and too long on voluntary compliance "to the virtual exclusion" of the ultimate sanction of cutting off funds. As a result many educational institutions stopped taking government enforcement efforts seriously, the report asserted.

Civil Rights Group sees more busing. The U.S. Commission on Civil Rights, in a report issued March 11, warned that "without positive action, segregation in urban areas, both North and South, appears likely to increase, and urban-suburban racial divisions will be intensified." The group found that one-half of all black schoolchildren are in the nation's largest and most segregated school systems, where black enrollment is rising.

Busing is one solution to the problem, the commission says. "There will continue to be situations when transportation of pupils will be required if the constitutional right to desegregated education is to be implemented. The report notes that less than 4% of busing is for purposes of desegregation; although 43.5% of American children are bused to school.

The Civil Rights Commission urged the federal government to withdraw aid from schools that failed to desegregate voluntarily. Such schools, the report said, should be given 90 days to initiate integration plans before the Department of Health, Education and Welfare began proceedings to end federal financial assistance.

The report said that the percentage of black students attending integrated schools in the South had increased but had remained unchanged in the North. Between 1968 and 1972 the proportion of blacks attending predominantly white schools in the South rose from 19% to 46%. In the North in 1972, 71% of blacks continued to attend predominately black schools. "There appear to be legitimate fears," the report noted, "that the South is in a transitional stage and is moving toward duplication of Northern residential segregation as desegregated schools are undercut by increasingly separated neighborhoods."

Among the report's other recommendations:

■ The Internal Revenue Service should revoke tax exemptions held by private, segregated schools, and the U.S. government should withdraw aid from them.

■ Federal funds should be withheld from school districts failing to meet special needs of non-English-speaking pupils.

■ A national standard, adaptable to local situations, should be formulated to insure that school districts were in compliance with federal desegregation laws. Busing should be a valid instrument of desegregation.

HEW

Judge orders HEW to enforce integration. U.S. District Court Judge John H. Pratt ordered the Department of Health, Education and Welfare (HEW) March 14 to act swiftly to enforce desegregation guidelines in 125 school districts in 16 Southern and Border states. Ruling on a suit by the NAACP Legal Defense and Educational Fund, Inc., Pratt also ordered HEW to move firmly in another 39 school districts whose voluntary desegregation efforts had been unsuccessful.

"There appears to be an overreliance by HEW on the use of voluntary negotiations over protracted time periods and a reluctance in recent years to use the administrative sanction process where school districts are known to be in noncompliance," Pratt said in his ruling.

Pratt's ruling gave HEW 60 days in which to notify each of the 125 districts that it would have to answer the charge that a "substantial" racial disproportion existed in one or more of its schools. The point at which racial imbalance occurred, Pratt's ruling said, was when there was a 20% disproportion between local minority pupils and their percentage for the entire district.

The court also set up a procedure for handling future complaints of noncompliance: HEW would have 90 days to determine if a district was in compliance with the law. When a district was found to be in noncompliance, it would be given an additional 90 days to take voluntary corrective action. If, after 180 days, the district was still in noncompliance, HEW would commence within 30 days enforcement proceedings "through administrative notice of hearing or any other means authorized by law." (Knowledgeable observers noted, however, that a school district could lengthen the enforcement process with court appeals.)

The Congress

23 antibusing proposals are pending in Congress. Eleven constitutional amendments to prohibit busing have been filed in the House and Senate, according to a report in the *Boston Globe* March 31. An additional 12 bills propose to limit the extent of busing for school desegregation purposes. Ranking congressional staff members told the *Globe,* however, that "there is no chance that any of the 23 constitutional amendments and bills affecting school desegregation will be reported out of House or Senate judiciary committees this year."

The constitutional amendments are phrased in terms of prohibiting federal courts and agencies from assigning, transporting and requiring attendance of students on the basis of race, color, creed, sex, religion or national origin.

The following are the proposed antibusing constitutional amendments before the House Judiciary Subcommittee on Civil Rights and Constitutional Rights, listed in order of their House Joint Resolution numbers. The sponsor's name is in parenthesis:

HR No. 2 (Charles Bennett, D-Fla.): No student may be compelled to attend a school except the one closest to his home.

HR-24 (Joe Waggoner, D-La.): Nothing in the Constitution may be used by US officials or court to compel busing or attendance at any but neighborhood schools.

HR-26 (Waggoner): No student shall be assigned or required to attend a school by race, creed or color.

HR-55 (John Flynt, D-Ga.): Each state and state court has sole jurisdiction for public schools.

HR-67 (Dale Milford. D-Tex.): The right to attend nearest school can't be abridged for race, sex, color, religion or national origin.

HR-82 (David Satterfield, D-Va.): No student or teacher may be assigned to a school by race, creed or color.

No. 95 (Ray Roberts, D-Tex.): Parents and local school boards have sole authority to determine which school a child will attend.

No. 162 (Jamie Whitten, D-Miss.): Busing cannot be ordered for an integrated school even if racial balance is lacking.

The following are the bills before the committee calling for antibusing legislation:

H-521 (Marjorie Holt, R-Md.): The effect of court desegregation orders is delayed pending all appeals.

H-1105 (Olin Teague, D-Tex.): A moratorium on student transportation until Congress defines what is required under the 14th Amendment.

H-1134 (Waggoner): Defines "unitary school system" as one with no students excluded for race: also encourages voluntary transfer for racial balance.

H-1304 (Holt): No Federal court may issue an order causing assignment by race, color, religion or national origin.

H-1477 (Roberts): No Federal court may require reassignment by race in a "freedom of choice school system," no funds may be cutoff because of racial composition.

H-1484 (Roberts): Neighborhood school assignment is permitted if not for segregation: racial balance is not required: no court may order transportation beyond nearest school.

H-1576 (John Ashbrook, R-Ohio): No Federal court has jurisdiction to order attendance by race, color, creed, or sex.

H-1950 (W. Henson Moore, R-La.): No Federal court may order transportation by race; desegregation cases may be reopened and may not be executed pending appeals.

H-2675 (Joseph Gaydos, D-Pa.): No busing court orders will be effective until appeals have been decided.

H-2818 (Holt): No Federal court or agency has the power to assign students or teachers by race, religion, sex or national origin and Federal funds cannot be based on such assignments.

H-4253 (M. G. Snyder, R-Ky.): No Federal court has jurisdiction to issue an order leading to transportation on the basis of race, color, religion or national origin.

H-4254 (Snyder): No Federal court has jurisdiction to hear public school cases; that right is reserved to state courts.

The following are proposed antibusing amendments before the Senate Judiciary Subcommittee on Constitutional Amendments:

SR-29 (William Roth, R-Del.): No student may be transported to a school because of race, color, national origin, creed or sex.

SR-40 (William Scott, R-Va.): No student or teacher may be assigned or required to attend a particular school by race, creed or color.

SR-60 (Dewey Bartlett, R-Ok.): No assignment, transfer or compulsory attendance of students because of race, color, creed or national origin.

HOUSE PASSES EDUCATION AID BILL WITH STRONG ANTI-BUSING RIDER

The House passed by a vote of 380–26 March 27 an elementary and secondary education aid bill with strong anti-busing provisions and extensions of most existing aid programs in modified forms. The aid formulas would authorize almost $21 billion over three years (fiscal 1975–77). The bill went to the Senate, which was considering a version without busing restrictions and with different aid formulas. An anti-busing bill passed by the House in 1972 had been killed by a Senate filibuster.

The primary busing restriction had been adopted, 293–117, the day before as an amendment almost identical to the 1972 measure. The amendment would permit busing only after other desegregation attempts had been proved ineffective. Even under such circumstances, a student could be bused only to a school "closest or next closest" to his home. The measure would also permit communities currently under court-ordered busing plans to reopen their court cases if the orders did not conform with the new legislation. By a vote of 239–168 March 27, the House added a second amendment, by Rep. John M. Ashbrook (R, Ohio), prohibiting the use of federal funds for any form of busing designed to correct racial imbalance.

President Nixon had supported the House bill in a radio address March 23 as "a step in the right direction toward more community and state control" and threatened to veto a bill such as the measure pending in the Senate.

THE ATLANTA CONSTITUTION
Atlanta, Ga., March 28, 1974

This newspaper has editorially supported integration of the schools and we still do.

We've supported transfer of students from one school to another as a tactic in achieving a real as opposed to a token integration.

But we feel uneasy about trying to achieve true racial integration and educational equality by transporting children, as if they were shock troops, to areas where the high command feels they are most needed in the effort to win the battle against segregated schools. We have serious doubts about the wisdom and effectiveness of transporting inner city children to the suburbs with the idea that this will provide better schooling for them and will insure a more equitable, just and fair society.

Busing should not be ruled out entirely as a useful measure in achieving an integrated society, but neither should it be depended upon to solve huge and complex social problems by itself.

The U.S. House of Representatives has voted 293 to 117 approval of a school bill amendment to make busing a limited, last resort option in achieving integration of the schools. Busing is not ruled out. But it is recognized as an extreme measure to be resorted to only if all else fails.

It seems to use that this amendment reflects the feeling of the vast majority of Americans. A similar plan was voted past the House two years ago, but failed in the Senate. Back of the present amendment is the dispute over a busing plan involving Detroit, Michigan, which calls for busing acrss school district lines. The amendment provides alternatives that must be tried before busing is resorted to—the alternatives including assignment to neighborhood schools, voluntary transfers, construction or closing of schools and revision of attendance zones.

Those opposing the amendment argue that it is probably unconstitutional. They point to anti-busing measures in the past that have failed in the courts. The constitutionality of the amendment is for the courts to decide, but it is clear that Congress—with heavy pressure from the general public—is seeking to provide legislation that will stand up to challenges in court and at the same time will not impede desegregation. This amendment strikes us as being a reasonable and fair effort in that direction.

THE COMMERCIAL APPEAL
Memphis, Tenn.
March 28, 1974

FOR THE SECOND straight year the U.S. House of Representatives has passed an antibusing amendment to the federal aid-to-education bill. Most Americans, including many blacks, would like to see the amendment become law.

The issue is not one of segregated vs. integrated schools. The amendment would even permit limited busing, as long as a student was not transported farther than the second nearest appropriate school to his home. Pairing and other methods of achieving desegregation would be allowed.

What bothers most parents is the use of massive, crosstown busing. Children should not have to endure long rides to and from school. It may be necessary in rural areas, but that doesn't make it right in and around cities where schools can be built closer together.

Rep. Carl Perkins (D-Ky.), chairman of the House Education and Labor Committee, argued that the problem should be solved by amending the Constitution, not by complicating the education bill. To the contrary, a constitutional change should be avoided if at all possible.

The Constitution derives its strength from timelessness and flexibility. It deals with the basic problems of self-government in such a way as to provide relevant and reliable guidelines when times and political circumstances change. It should not be used to jerry-rig responses to every issue that comes along. Busing, regardless of how strongly many Americans feel about it, is not likely to become one of the continuing controversies of our national life.

Critics of the House amendment say it should not be passed because it is unconstitutional. But not everyone agrees. The way to answer the question is to pass the amendment so it can be tested in the courts. Busing has been required by orders of the federal courts. The orders should and must be obeyed. That doesn't mean, however, that elected representatives of the people can't revise the laws in effect when the orders were handed down.

LAST YEAR THE antibusing fight was ended by a filibuster in the Senate. That tactic was necessary because a majority of the Senate would have voted against busing. Busing is certainly no more popular now than it was then. The overwhelming House vote, 293-117, indicates opposition even from areas of the country that have not been affected by wholesale transfers of students for desegregation purposes.

Congress should follow what is clearly the will of the American people, and try to legislate an end to massive, long-distance busing as a remedy in school desegregation cases.

THE SAGINAW NEWS
Saginaw, Mich., March 31, 1974

The U.S. House held a streak-in the other day for political identity in an election year when it voted overwhelmingly in favor of a federal school aid bill heavily weighted down with antibusing amendments.

From a practical political standpoint that may be the popular thing to do. It is unfortunate all the same and for a number of reasons — not the least of which is the roadblock it erects to swift passage of a multi-billion dollar appropriations bill to meet the needs of elementary, secondary and advanced education over the next four years. Until it is passed, schools and colleges are at loose ends and over a barrel as far as program planning is concerned.

What the House has passed is bound to please the President. The measure contains the provisions Mr. Nixon has wanted for a long time. And Mr. Nixon is hardly alone in this country in opposition to busing as the way to desegregate schools and guarantee every child equal opportunity to quality education.

We number ourselves among those with most serious reservations on cross-district busing from the standpoint of costs, efficiency, management control and reorganization — to say nothing of its dubious potential for achieving its intended purpose. All of this, admittedly, aside from its potential for societal improvement.

This is incidental, however, to the action taken by the House.

About the kindest thing to be said of it is that it is seriously flawed. More bluntly, it is heavy-handed, thoughtless, ill-conceived and marked by a certain amount of arrogance that blurs the distinction between the legislative and judicial branches of government.

At a moment when the U.S. Supreme Court is thoughtfully immersed in the weighing of the Detroit cross-district busing order of Federal District Judge Stephen J. Roth, it's timing is atrocious. Instead of standing back from busing, as it should have done, to await a decision that everybody awaits, the House has plowed on with total irreverence for the right of the court to play its proper role on a question, which at its root, is a constitutional one.

This serious over-step is exceeded only by the House attempt to legislate the federal courts out of the role of decision-making on busing issues and to turn back the clock on others already implemented. The House might just as well attempt to legislate the courts out of cases on housing, public accommodations or anything having to do with constitutional guarantees of equal rights under the law.

The worst part of this legislative assault upon the judicial process as it relates to busing is that it reheats an emotional issue by inviting new challenges where school desegregation projects have already been carried out.

We regret that the House has gone to such lengths to put itself one more time on a collision course with the Senate which has shown somewhat more sensitivity in the past to the fine points of separation of powers. It will oppose this measure as written just as it has before — and on the same grounds — and particularly on that segment of it which contains almost identical language on antibusing provisions that the House has tried to push through previously.

The truly sad part of it is that in tieing a host of antibusing amendments to a bill dealing with federal aid to education, it has mixed apples with oranges in a way that guarantees delay of legislation vital to education. That is hardly in the best interest of education nationwide.

The scenario for rehardening of attitudes has been drafted by the House. The Senate will oppose this measure and the courts will likely ignore its intrusions into territory that properly belongs to the judicial branch on first call.

There is no way to predict precisely what the high court will decide with the Roth decision. We submit, however, that there are a number of questions within the larger question that must be weighed against the Constitution as it is now written and given court interpretation. The court may issue a firm landmark decision. It may send it back for further review as it did in the Denver case. Or it may settle on something in between that attempts to strike a balance on busing. For now, however, that is where the decision belongs.

Later, if the country and the Congress are not satisfied, there is a remedy available. It is an amendment to the Constitution setting prohibitions on busing for purposes intended.

In the meantime Congress owes it to the people and to education in general to get a workable appropriations bill drafted and passed. Long after busing has ceased to be an issue, the obligation to meet education's needs and the needs of the nation's young people will remain.

The Detroit News
Detroit, Mich.
March 29, 1974

Even though the courts have a habit of ignoring anti-bussing measures passed by Congress, the bill approved by the House of Representatives this week served as a timely reminder of public sentiment on the volatile issue of bussing for racial balance.

The reminder comes at a moment when the U.S. Supreme Court is weighing arguments and preparing to hand down a decision in a landmark cross-district bussing case involving Detroit and 52 suburban school districts.

The House overwhelmingly voted to prohibit bussing except as a last resort. If bussing should be absolutely necessary, no student could be bussed beyond a school close to his home.

This measure accurately reflects public opinion. Again and again the opinion polls have shown Americans, black and white, opposed to massive bussing of schoolchildren for purposes of racial integration. The Supreme Court may get the message.

Indeed, the House vote on the anti-bussing bill is perhaps more important as an advisory than as an effective deterrent in its own right. Some judges in lower courts—judges who don't make conclusive and definitive decisions and don't stand continuously in the spotlight of public attention—have ignored the returns as well as anti-bussing legislation previously passed by Congress.

Two years ago, for example, Congress enacted a bussing moratorium which the courts simply ignored or which they shrugged aside as inapplicable. Judge Stephen Roth's bussing juggernaut rolled right up to the doors of the Supreme Court.

If the Supreme Court approves the Roth concept of bussing for integration, where do the foes of bussing go from there?

Should the full Congress fail to pass strong anti-bussing legislation, or should the courts continue to ignore and override such legislation, one final course would remain open: a U.S. constitutional amendment explicitly forbidding bussing.

Let's hope reason prevails so that Americans don't have to resort in desperation to that drastic action.

San Jose Mercury

San Jose, Calif., March 28, 1974

The House of Representatives' overwhelming embrace of an anti-busing amendment to the $15.1 billion school aid bill will probably prove to be an exercise in futility.

In addition to being of dubious constitutionality, the amendment really misses the central point of the busing controversy, which focuses on educational quality and convenience rather than on the racial issue per se.

It is too often overlooked that busing children to schools out of their immediate neighborhood is a means to an end, not an end in itself. The object has been to create racially integrated schools in accordance with the United States Supreme Court finding that segregated schools are constitutionally impermissible, regardless of whether the segregation has been accomplished by law or as a result of economically dictated housing patterns.

The rub has come because a great many parents, of all racial and ethnic backgrounds, prefer the neighborhood school. It is close at hand; the parent can oversee his child's education more easily; the child himself is spared the fatigue of a long bus ride at each end of the school day. These are valid, perhaps even overriding, considerations.

Regrettably, Congress is responding to the politics of the problem rather than the substance of it. Simply prohibiting busing—if in fact that can be done—will not provide first rate neighborhood schools where they are most urgently needed — in low-income.

A more valid approach would seem to require two things essentially. First, there should be totally open enrollment in every school district. That is to say any academically qualified child should be eligible for admission to any school where there is a seat for him and where his parents are willing to take or send him. This would guarantee genuine equality of educational opportunity, provided the second consideration were met adequately.

Second, the state and federal governments—especially the federal—should undertake a massive upgrading of the long-neglected neighborhood schools of the so-called "inner city." This upgrading should extend to faculty as well as physical plant. The pressure for busing would evaporate if all schools in a given district were of good quality and if all schools were open to all children in the district.

In the short run, such an approach might slow down, perhaps even reverse, the middle class flight to the suburbs that has created ethnic ghettoes in the inner cities. In the long haul, better schools are bound to accelerate the upward class mobility of minority group members, thus breaking down patterns of segregated neighborhood housing.

In fact, this latter trend is already apparent in a great many suburban communities. Good inner city schools will help make it happen faster, and when neighborhoods become integrated the busing issue will by definition cease to exist.

The Virginian-Pilot

Norfolk, Va.
March 28, 1974

The Michigan antibusing provision that the House of Representatives passed this week is a word-for-word copy of President Nixon's proposed Equal Education Opportunities Act of 1972, which sank in the Senate after sailing through the House. Back then the House vote was 282 to 102. This time it was 293 to 117. Again, Senate doubts impend.

Michigan, a good Yankee state well disposed toward public education, is politically jittery about busing. A lawsuit to merge Detroit's mostly black school system with 52 mostly white suburban systems is hanging fire in the Supreme Court. Michigan politicians are scrambling to head off any busing that would be necessary to achieve desegregation in the jumbo school district.

They are receiving a lot of Congressional support, as the two House votes show. The Michigan provision bars busing's introduction as a racial-segregation remedy until half a dozen other measures, including rezoning and voluntary pupil transfers, have been tried, and then would limit busing to the school closest or next closest to a pupil's home. A clause angled at the South would authorize the reopening of court cases and desegregation programs under the Civil Rights Act of 1964 to bring them into compliance with the new law.

Regardless of how the Michigan provision fares in the Senate or a House-Senate conference, Mr. Nixon in endorsing it and the House in passing it have sent a message to the Supreme Court. The Court probably will ignore it.

Its Richmond-Henrico-Chesterfield school merger no-decision of last year suggests that its Denver ruling will turn on one Justice's vote—Lewis F. Powell Jr.'s. Being from Richmond, Mr. Powell abstained in that case; the Court then split 4-4, letting stand the Fourth U.S. Circuit Court's antimerger judgment. Detroit merger advocates are relying on Mr. Powell's sentiments for a national school policy to override his antipathy to forced racial balances.

And if, they reason, he joins Chief Justice Warren E. Burger and Justices Harry A. Blackmun and William H. Rehnquist in a segregation-serving opinion, Justice Byron R. White may tip the scales against them by returning to the integration fold from which he has strayed only in the Richmond instance.

Meanwhile, the Michigan provision that the House passed is, as the House well knows, of dubious constitutionality. Also, interdistrict school busing isn't the bugbear that the Honorables and Mr. Nixon would make it out to be. The Detroit busing plan before the Supreme Court would barely extend beyond the current 3 per cent the portion of school busing that desegregation imposes. And while it most clearly would upset countless suburbanites, for good reason or bad, it embraces the only formula anybody has come up with for rescuing inner-city public education.

The State

Columbia, S.C., April 1, 1974

IMPLICIT in John Adams' famous premise that ours is "a government of laws, and not of men" is the assumption that obedience of the law is based upon an understanding of the law.

The thought comes to mind as we contemplate the current flurry in Congress over legislation to limit the busing of school children. This year — as in 1971 and again in 1972 — the thrust is toward restrictions which curtail school busing as a mechanism for achieving racial integration.

The State is persuaded that massive busing for purposes of integration has caused more harm to education than it has corrected. But that is not the point of this particular editorial. What puzzles us is the continuing effort to enact new laws to accomplish what should already have been achieved through existing law.

We refer to the celebrated Civil Rights Act of 1964. When that landmark measure was adopted a decade ago, Congress specifically included a provision to limit school busing except as required to foster purely educational benefits. Lest there by any misunderstanding of the congressional intent, we quote from the act:

"Nothing herein shall empower any official or court of the United States to issue any order seeking to achieve a racial balance in any school by requiring the transportation of pupils or students from one school to another or one school district to another in order to achieve such racial balance, or otherwise enlarge the existing power of the court to insure compliance with constitutional standards."

That language would seem clear enough to the average layman, but it seems to have been over the head of — or rejected out of hand by — the numerous federal judges and bureaucrats who have pressured school authorities into extensive busing programs.

An interesting aspect of the situation is the involvement of President Nixon. Within the last two weeks, he has urged Congress to enact just such curbs on busing as the House of Representatives approved last Wednesday. He had done so before, only to see the ensuing legislation die in the Senate after approval in the House.

Here again is a puzzler. The same Civil Rights Act of 1964 embraces another meaningful provision in Title VI, which relates to all programs receiving federal financial assistance. Obviously, this touches on almost the entire public school structure at all levels, including higher education. But the controls over such programs, with respect to racial matters carry this qualifying sentence:

"No such rule, regulation, or order shall become effective unless and until approved by the President."

If Mr. Nixon has disapproved any regulation aimed at achieving racial balance by busing or otherwise, it has escaped our notice.

One final quote from the Civil Rights Act:

"Nothing contained in this title (on Equal Employment Opportunity) shall be interpreted to require any employer, employment agency, labor organization, or joint labor-management committee. . .to grant preferential treatment to any individual or to any group because of the race, color, religion, sex, or national origin of such individual or group on account of an imbalance which may exist . . ."

Despite that provision, quota systems have been established in both public and private employment which clearly are designed to correct imbalances. Favoring those persons or groups on the short side of the imbalance may or may not be desirable, but nothing in the Civil Rights Act makes it mandatory.

All of which brings us back around to the bills pending in Congress. They may be meritorious in both intent and content, but if they carry no more weight than similar provisions in the Civil Rights Act, their enactment would be another exercise in futility.

LEDGER-STAR

Norfolk, Va., March 29, 1974

The problem with the anti-busing amendment to the House-passed aid-to-education bill does not lie in its purpose. The problem is that this attempt to curb the judiciary via the use of a new law may simply promise more than it can deliver.

Ever since the courts began using the device of pupil-swapping from one neighborhood to another over considerable distances as a desegregation tool, its wrongness has been very clear. The results have included disruptions of family life patterns, fearsome overall costs, danger to the bused young in their long treks in many instances, and a hampering rather than any enhancement of education itself, which is what the schools exist for.

The massive manipulation of student populations, with color used as a criterion instead of being disregarded, has been a disproportionately drastic measure. It has even defeated its own purpose in places, with white flight from busing situations creating resegregated schools and pushing the advocates of busing to consider preposterously enlarged school systems.

★ ★ ★ ★

As to basic public reaction against busing, by all races and in all parts of the country, there isn't much question about what would happen if the issue could somehow be put to a vote.

But to recognize this, to know that any politician has the most potent of vehicles if he promises to do something against busing, is not to argue for such things as the amendment the House has so resoundingly approved.

The hard fact is that the judiciary is in the driver's seat on this question. And it is a very thin theory which postulates that Congress can enact laws curbing actions which the courts adjudge necessary to the implementation of constitutional commands already in existence.

Earlier legislative pronouncements to limit busing have simply been disregarded by the courts, and there is little reason to believe a new effort would fare any better.

★ ★ ★ ★

There may be some faint value in formally asserting the sense of the country, by means of such a legislative message, for the consideration of the courts. But surely the federal bench is not ignorant on that score.

The point is that the American people should not be given the impression that enactment of a bill such as this — if it should survive the rough going predicted in the Senate — will reverse busing requirements already in force and prevent new ones. For the very first fact to face is that it will be the federal judiciary itself which will decide whether the federal judiciary must obey the congressional restraints.

This means that, short of the unlikely step of a constitutional amendment, the chances of turning the busing process around will continue to hinge on the Supreme Court. And the best hope is that the court's improving vision and a truer grasp of the damage done by busing will, soon or late, ease this burden off the backs of the American people.

SENATE PASSES ANTI-BUSING CLAUSE; BROWN-TOPEKA ANNIVERSARY MARKED

The Senate, by an 81–5 vote May 20, approved a bill authorizing $25.2 billion over the next four years for elementary and secondary education after a week of debate focusing primarily on busing. The bill's busing provision was not as strict as one passed by the House, which would go into conference with the Senate on the bill's final provisions. The Senate version would allow pupils to attend the school "closest or next closest" to their homes with the added specification that the proviso was "not intended to modify or diminish" the authority of the courts "to enforce fully" the Constitution. The amendment, proposed by majority and minority leaders Mike Mansfield (D, Mont.) and Hugh Scott (R, Pa.), was adopted May 16 by a vote of 47–46.

The key vote followed a 47–46 rejection May 15 of an amendment identical to the anti-busing amendment approved by the House. Proposed by Sen. Edward J. Gurney (R, Fla.), it would have barred busing to achieve racial integration to all but the school closest or next closest to a student's home and then only when all other alternatives had been exhausted. It would also have permitted all previous busing litigation to be reopened to comply with the amendment. In the debate May 16, Senate Republican whip Robert P. Griffin (Mich.) proposed the Gurney amendment without the litigation provision. A motion to table it lost 47–46, but at that point the Scott-Mansfield proposal was offered and adopted.

In other busing decisions, the Senate:

■ Adopted May 15 by a 56–36 vote an amendment by Sen. Birch Bayh (D, Ind.) to bar busing across school district lines without a court finding the lines had been drawn to perpetuate segregation or unless discrimination occurred in each of the districts.

■ Approved by a 71–20 vote May 16 a proposal by Sen. J. Glenn Beall Jr. (R, Md.) to bar implementation of court-ordered busing after the beginning of a school year.

■ Rejected by a 51–41 vote May 16, a proposal by Sen. Sam J. Ervin Jr. (D, N.C.) to bar courts from ordering busing to alter racial composition, except for Supreme Court cases of original jurisdiction.

■ Rejected 61–26 May 20 an amendment by Sen. William L. Scott (R, Va.) that would have given jurisdiction on public school problems to the state courts, instead of the federal district courts, with the Supreme Court hearing appeals.

The Senate vote on busing came during the week marking the 20th anniversary of the 1954 Supreme Court ruling credited with igniting the modern-day civil rights movement. In that ruling, the Court found that the "separate but equal" educational facilities provided by the Topeka, Kansas Board of Education for black school children were inherently unequal.

THE ARIZONA REPUBLIC
Phoenix, Ariz., May 4, 1974

Rep. Edith Green is a Democrat, a liberal from Oregon. She has been in Congress for 20 years and spent 18 of them on the House Education Committee and has made education her area of special expertise.

In fact, she is known in Congress as "Mrs. Education." She was an early advocate of federal aid to education and still believes in the ideal, although she has admitted that the reality has been a wasteful and maladministered failure.

Mrs. Green is the author of a discharge petition seeking the release from committee of a proposed constitutional amendment banning forced busing of pupils.

Her reason: Busing has no educational or social value. As she pointed out, it threatens to cause educational and social deterioration.

Money is spent on busing, she contends, that could better go for staff, equipment and facilities. In Charlotte, N.C., where a court-ordered busing plan is in effect, it is costing local and state governments $1.6 million a year to operate a bus fleet as compared with transportation costs of $784,000 three years ago.

This cost hike occurred even though the school population dropped by 7,000. Some of the children, Mrs. Green adds, spend 2 hours and 45 minutes a day on a bus, traveling up to 40 miles.

Socially, the effect of busing has been to generate hostility between the races and between parents of all races and the officials responsible for busing:

"Many white and black parents are annoyed by the disruption of their neighborhood schools and incensed by the dreams of those who think that children are merely numbers," she asserts.

In her own district, which she emphasized is close to 80 per cent Democratic and urban, a survey revealed more than 70 per cent support for a constitutional ban on forced busing.

The federal courts have shown that nothing less than a constitutional amendment will have any effect on their decisions to impose a racial calcus on the nation's school children.

Mere acts of Congress have been dismissed as almost unworthy of judicial notice. The only real remedy now lies in discharging the proposed constitutional amendment from committee and getting it to the states for action.

Amsterdam News
New York, N.Y., May 11, 1974

It is ironic that as we mark the 20th anniversary of the 1954 Supreme Court school desegregation decision, there is a determined move in Congress to set the clock back to the segregated status of 1953.

On March 26 of this year the House passed the Esch Amendment by a vote of 293 to 117. It proposes that Congress find as a fact that transportation of students creates serious risks to their health and safety.

2. It holds that assignment of children to public schools on a neighborhood basis is NOT a denial of equal educational opportunity.

3. It would forbid the implementation of any desegregation plans that would require the transportation of any student to a school other than the closest to his residence.

4. It proposes the modification of Title VI of the Civil Rights Act of 1964 which authorizes civil action in Federal Courts for denial of equal educational opportunity.

Another amendment offered by Rep. John M. Ashbrook (R. Ohio) would forbid the expenditure of Federal funds for busing to achieve desegregation.

Comparable amendments are being offered in the Senate. One of them, submitted by Sen. Edward J. Gurney (R. Fla.), would prohibit busing, reopen all court-ordered desegregation plans submitted by the Department of Health, Education and Welfare, and forbid new desegregation orders. The Gurney provision would be substituted for Title VIII of S. 1539 — the Education Amendment Act of 1974.

Demagoguery At Worst

This being an election year, when the Watergate cloud hanging over the landscape sends politicians scurrying for issues to divert the voters' attention from their own credibility problems, busing and school desegregation are sure-fire issues to seize upon and delude the electorate.

It is demagoguery at its worst. Not only is it immoral, it is further damaging to Black and brown children already handicapped by years of being disadvantaged.

It is an intolerable situation that calls for collective action. The member papers of the National Newspaper Publishers Association hereby go on record to say to the Congress of the United States, "Stop playing politics with our children's lives and their welfare."

Those who support such reactionary legislation as the Esch Amendment must be regarded as the enemies of Black and brown children and, indeed, of all children and America itself.

Their actions must be remembered at the polls in November, 1974. Respect for law is just as incumbent upon lawmakers as it is upon ordinary citizens.

The Washington Post
Washington, D.C., May 15, 1974

IN MARCH OF 1972, when Watergate was still a gleam in Gordon Liddy's eye and the Board of Directors (as we now know) had yet to give final approval to his plans, Mr. Nixon unveiled his preposterous "anti-busing" plan. Mr. Ehrlichman, now busy with other matters, did the best a lawyer could do to justify and explain its patent illegalities to the press. And Richard Kleindienst, then Attorney General and nothing if not blunt, happily explained to a committee of Congress that the proposed legislation would authorize the reopening of every school case—North and South—that had been settled since the Supreme Court's original school desegregation decision in 1954.

Since that time we have acquired, for our sins, a much richer context of administration law-breaking and contempt for the commands of the constitution into which to fit this particular exercise in defiance and contempt—from the court-blocked adventures in impoundment of congressionally appropriated funds to the Watergate crimes and improprieties to the sloven procedures for obtaining wiretaps, which has just compelled the Burger Court unanimously to render a decision that will free some 600 persons accused and/or convicted of violating federal criminal statutes. So it is hardly surprising that the administration's proposed monument in the field of desegregation law turned out itself to be a monumental challenge to due process, to the Constitution and to the rule of law. What is surprising and—to put it mildly—distressing, is that two years later the United States is considering commemorating the 20th anniversary of the Supreme Court's 1954 decision by passing this proposal. Today the Senate is scheduled to vote on a House-passed variation of the Nixon administration bill which has been introduced by Senator Edward J. Gurney of Florida as an amendment to an extension of the federal school aid act. And the vote, according to most accounts, is likely to be close.

Everybody, as it seems, is against skullduggery and for the rule of law—except when it is either inconvenient or inexpedient to explain. Thus, legislators who in a nonpolitical year would acknowledge themselves horrified by the reckless sweep of this proposal and acutely aware of the cynicism from which it springs, are counted among those who, for "political" reasons are likely to go over to the side and vote with Mr. Gurney. We refer to the cynicism underlying the effort because for all the chaos and disruption it could bring to settled school systems North and South, the proposal itself would almost undoubtedly be overturned in many of its key parts by the Court, meanwhile creating new and burdensome problems for numerous of those communities whose burdens it purports to relieve.

Consider the bill's provisions. Its list of mandatory remedies that must be invoked before busing can be ordered could cost tax-ridden communities a fortune in the demolition and construction of schools. It is a rich man's bill, in effect providing that any busing which occurs will spare the affluent suburbs and be contained within geographical limits that are likely to result only in sending poor blacks from their own inferior schools to the inferior schools of neighboring poor white children —to communities where racial hostilities and insecurities are keenest. And, above all, it says to black children—to black people generally in this country—that even where a finding has been made of unconstitutional discrimination against them by the state, there will be no remedy in many cases. It is a tribute of sorts to the monstrosity of this concept, in a nation of laws, that back in 1972 even Mr. Ehrlichman had trouble explaining it when pressed.

In the 20 years that have passed since the Supreme Court rendered its original decision in Brown, and in the 10 years that have passed since the Civil Rights Act of 1964 gave that decision heightened impact and authority, there have been some lower court decisions and administrative interpretations that, to our mind, have skewed and distorted the meaning of the law and imposed senseless burdens on communities around the country, so that both blacks and whites have suffered. There have been, in other words, some bad busing decisions and some unreasonable and unsound bureaucratic regulations rendered. It could hardly be otherwise, given both the complexity of the cases and the familiar resistance to reasonable and desirable change that preceded and, in effect, brought on the compulsory programs to which so many now object. But it has been clear for some time now that the Supreme Court was moving carefully and deliberately to refine its position in consonance with the constitutional command that is the bedrock of *Brown* so as to take account of changed circumstances that underlie so many school cases 20 years later. This is as it should be. The question is whether the Senate will wait. The alternative before it today was admirably summed up by William McCulloch, who was ranking Republican member of the House Judiciary Committee, when the Nixon bill first came up two years ago, accompanied by a proposal for a temporary freeze on busing orders:

It is with the deepest regret that I sit here today to listen to a spokesman for the administration asking the Congress to prostitute the courts by obligating them to suspend the equal protection clause so that Congress may debate the merits of further slowing down and perhaps even rolling back desegregation in public schools—What message are we sending to our black people? Is this any way to govern a country?

The Detroit News

Detroit, Mich., May 17, 1974

Twenty years ago today, the U.S. Supreme Court handed down the historic Brown decision outlawing racial segregation in schools. This week, the nation was still debating how to implement that decision reasonably and justly.

Although the U.S. Senate on Wednesday narrowly defeated much-needed legislation to prohibit long-distance bussing of children, the Senate's approval of a companion measure constituted a net gain for justice and good sense.

That gain was probably recognized more readily by citizens of Detroit and its suburbs than by people elsewhere, since the approved proposal goes straight to the heart of the bussing issue as it applies to this metropolitan area.

Under the controversial Roth concept, now before the Supreme Court, schoolchildren would be hauled by bus between Detroit and 52 suburban school districts, although suburban districts have not been found guilty of discrimination.

The provision approved by the Senate prohibits court-ordered bussing between districts unless each school district involved has practiced discrimination or has had its boundaries deliberately drawn for purposes of segregation. That stops in its tracks cross-district bussing as conceived by Federal Judge Stephen Roth.

Bussing foes should temper their joy. First, the differences between Senate and House anti-bussing provisions still must be reconciled in conference. Second, the lower courts have paid small heed to congressional efforts to assume jurisdiction in this issue; they place a very liberal interpretation on their own authority to set the course for school integration.

Detroit and other metropolitan districts threatened with cross-district bussing still must pin their hopes on the Supreme Court, which is expected soon to deliver an opinion in the Detroit case. If the Supreme Court upholds the Roth concept, bussing foes will then test the value of congressional legislation.

One of the deeply interested observers of all the social trauma produced by school bussing is former Chief Justice Earl Warren, who delivered the Brown decision 20 years ago. "Bussing is a tool, not a principle," he said recently. "It has been used by the courts only to remedy the patterns of segregation. It is a device to implement the Brown case."

Unfortunately, the tool creates new wrongs and new turmoil as it imposes staggering new costs on strapped school districts, upsets the concept of local control and ignites new racial discord—without promising any significant educational benefits.

Warren falls back on another dog-eared and fallacious argument when he notes: "We used to bus black children 50 miles to a school when next door to their home was a school they could not attend because it was for whites only."

Such bussing was wrong, of course. But it doesn't make cross-district bussing right—unless Americans are willing to accept, as they never have, the proposition that one evil justifies another evil as its remedy.

The Virginian-Pilot

Norfolk, Va., May 17, 1974

The "ifs" of the Brown decision, handed down 20 years ago today, are legion. A favorite one, which had its reflection in the Senate yesterday, is that if the Supreme Court had ruled simply that the Constitution is color-blind, education would be free of the racial-balance shibboleth—of coerced busing—and much better off. A more intriguing "if" is how schools and society would have fared had Southern states accepted the Court's desegregation order gracefully.

"We conclude that in the field of public education the doctrine of 'separate but equal' has no place," Chief Justice Earl Warren said for a unanimous Court on May 17, 1954. "Separate educational facilities are inherently unequal. . ."

The repudiation of the old Plessy doctrine was clear. Yet the Court was not ready to say how state-required dual school systems were to be dismantled. It called for advice and deliberated a year. Meanwhile, three of the defendant school boards—in Kansas, Delaware, and the District of Columbia—moved to desegregate.

In contrast, the political leaders of the states in the old Confederacy used the year of grace to draft legislative programs of defiance. Virginia achieved preeminence at the dictation of Senator Harry F. Byrd. (Before the decade was out there was proof that under better-spirited leadership the State could have managed integration well enough and avoided the disgrace of such school-closings as Norfolk suffered in 1958-59.)

* * *

The Court's implementing decree, issued on May 31, 1955, charged U.S. District Courts, "because of their proximity to local conditions and the possible need for further hearings," with seeing that the school districts in question made "a prompt and reasonable" start toward compliance and then proceeded "with all deliberate speed" toward its completion. Chief Judge John J. Parker of the Fourth U.S. Circuit Court of Appeals, with headquarters in Richmond, interpreted this as meaning that the Supreme Court had forbidden segregation but had not demanded integration.

But that was not good enough for most of the South, including Virginia. "Never!" was the political watchword here. The vast majority of Southern members of Congress joined Senator Byrd in issuing the "Southern Manifesto" of March 1956 commending "the motives of those states which have declared the intention to resist forced integration by any lawful means" and pledging its signers to work for a reversal of the Brown decision. By the end of that year, the 11 Southern states had passed 106 measures of defiance, and more were to follow.

It was in knocking down those laws that the Federal courts—and Congress—extended the Brown decision far beyond the Parker dictum. The Supreme Court's role was largely passive. The Circuit Courts, particularly the Fifth at New Orleans, carried the load. For the first 15 years after Brown, the school-desegregation pattern was a gradual absorption of black pupils into formerly all-white schools, usually in meager numbers. Only five years ago the Supreme Court mandated into law the proposition that nothing short of a prompt dismantling of dual school systems and their replacement by "unitary" systems would meet the constitutional test. A year earlier it had defined a unitary system (in a Virginia case, Green v. New Kent County) as "one without a 'white' school and a 'Negro' school, but just schools."

Then in April 1971 the Court issued its most important school order since Brown—and perhaps its last unanimous one in a landmark case. Reviewing a suit brought in Charlotte-Mecklenburg County, North Carolina, it found "no basis for holding that the local school authorities may not be required to employ bus transportation as one tool of school desegregation," and added: "Desegregation cannot be limited to walk-in schools."

The Court noted that "18 million of the nation's public school children, approximately 39 per cent, were transported to their schools by bus in 1969-70 in all parts of the country . . ." Surely, it was aware of the unpopularity of forced busing over long distances to achieve racial balances. It held nevertheless that "very limited use of the racial ratio—not as an inflexible requirement, but as a starting point in shaping a remedy—was within . . . equitable discretion." The judgment has been used by lower courts, sometimes to the pain of its author, Chief Justice Warren Burger, as authority for achieving through busing racial balances throughout school districts.

* * *

On this 20th anniversary of Brown, the ruling has been applied almost exclusively to the South. In 1954, unitary school systems were presumed to be standard in all states that did not require separation by statute. Now that concept is in popular disrepute and official doubt. A challenge of it is pending before the Supreme Court in a Detroit case. The Third Circuit Court has ordered that metropolitan Detroit be desegregated through cross-busing among the city's mostly-black school district and 52 mostly-white suburban districts. If the Supreme Court supports the order, Southern-type desegregation at last will reach the North. Also, interdistrict busing presumably will become applicable to all regions.

The Senate on Wednesday rejected by one vote (47-46) a House-passed proposal to bar courts from ordering students bused for desegregation purposes farther than the school next-nearest their home, and to facilitate the reopening of any existing court order requiring busing beyond that. By the same count it approved yesterday a compromise provision to discourage court-ordered busing while, paradoxically allowing judges to enforce the equal-rights amendment—a message to the Supreme Court that the Justices may not find worth reading.

The Nixon Administration, consistent with its professed devotion to neighborhood schools, supported the stronger measure. That and the single-vote margins are good evidence of widespread disenchantment with contrived integration in schools, certainly including its effects on learning. They suggest too a Congressional retreat from the Johnsonian spirit that inspired passage of the Civil Rights Act of 1964 and the Voting Rights Act of 1965—if such suggestion is required. Yet the race revolution that began with Brown, exploded in Little Rock and Montgomery and Oxford and Birmingham and Danville and Detroit and Newark and Watts, and ultimately established first-class citizenship for black people, has succeeded to the point that school affairs are but a detail of it. Indeed, blacks have arrived to where they may differ among themselves as participants in the national debate over forced integration. Black management of black-district schools is as lively an educational topic as school pairings and noncontiguous attendance zones.

* * *

Means of measuring the impact of Brown during these past 20 years are as numerous as the "ifs" inherent in the decision. One of them is the unsuccessful attempt Wednesday by Senator Sam J. Ervin Jr. of North Carolina to legalize freedom-of-choice as a school policy—the right of pupils to attend the school of their choice. The courts long ago rejected that on good evidence that black pupils were intimidated into remaining in black schools; to be legal, the conservative Fourth Circuit Court said in a Charlottesville case, desegregation plans had to be effective.

Senator Ervin offered his amendment to "accomplish what all freedom loving Americans should desire . . ." When he signed Senator Byrd's Southern Manifesto, he hardly could have imagined himself saying that in May 1974.

FORT WORTH STAR-TELEGRAM
Fort Worth, Tex., April 1, 1974

Those who oppose busing for racial balance in the schools shouldn't allow the recent House approval of anti-busing provisions to get their hopes up.

Both the constitutional framework of the busing issue and the history of previous attempts to get anti-busing legislation through Congress diminish the odds that the House proposals will ever have any impact at all on the busing situation.

The House provisions would require the federal courts to try several alternative methods to overcome segregation before ordering busing, then to limit it to the next closest school to the pupil's home. They would also permit school districts now under court busing orders, to have their cases reopened to conform with the new standards. Local school authorities would be prevented from using federal funds to pay any costs of transportation in carrying out a desegregation plan.

Other strong legislative proposals for putting strict limits on busing have not made it into law.

Even energetic administration support and overwhelming House approval wasn't enough to get the last such proposals on the books. One was a 1972 measure that died in the Senate when supporters failed to muster the votes to cut off debate and end a filibuster led by northern Democrats and liberal Republicans. The others were amendments to the Equal Education Opportunities act which were watered down by Senate action.

With emotions generally calmer on the subject now than in 1972 or last year, it's doubtful that stiff busing limitations have even as good a chance in the Senate now as they did in the earlier rounds.

If the legislation did succeed in clearing the Senate hurdle and becoming law, however, it's highly questionable that it would have the intended effect.

In the case of Fort Worth, for example, busing is being carried out under a final court order issued by the Fifth Circuit Court of Appeals. This order, in turn, rests on a foundation of Supreme Court rulings going all the way back to the Brown decision and including a 1971 ruling upholding busing as a means of bringing about desegregation of the schools.

It is doubtful that an existing final court order could be wiped out by statute. Even if that should prove possible, the Supreme Court's decisions making desegregation mandatory and approving busing as a means of accomplishing it would stand in opposition to the new legislation. When tested in the courts, as it certainly would be, the law would in all probability be ruled unconstitutional.

In Senate Judiciary Committee hearings last year, Sen. Herman E. Talmadge, D-Ga., argued that busing for racial balance can't be stopped by the legislative route. The only approach that offers any hope is that of a constitutional amendment.

The wisdom of that conclusion is becoming increasingly obvious.

The most popular of several proposed anti-busing amendments reads: "No public school student shall, because of his race, creed, or color, be assigned to or required to attend a particular school."

By changing the Constitution, such an amendment would take away the basis for court-ordered busing for purposes of integration.

The proposal, however, would require approval by two-thirds of both houses of Congress, then ratification by three-fourths of the states. At the moment, that seems impossible. But the situation could change in the months ahead.

While there's less emotion on the busing issue now than in the past, there's an increase in reasoned opposition to the idea. Much of that opposition comes from black leaders who suspect that busing, which almost invariably puts the black child in school with an overwhelming white majority, is having adverse effects on black children in both scholastic achievement and character development.

Why is Congress still toying with the legislative approach instead of turning to the constitutional amendment? The fact that this is an election year may have some bearing on that.

But as more of the public begins to perceive the fallacies of busing for racial balance, the amendment's chances will improve, and the sooner it happens the better.

ST. LOUIS POST-DISPATCH
St. Louis, Mo., April 3, 1974

The nation now approaches the twentieth anniversary of the historic Supreme Court decision in behalf of equal rights in education and, by extension, in everything else. But how will Congress observe the anniversary?

Congress is considering a bill to prevent busing of school children for the very purpose that the May 1954 Supreme Court decision was delivered: public school desegregation. The House passed the measure by 293 to 112 votes and it is before the Senate, which let a similar proposal die in 1972. Today, however, the Senate faces renewed pressure to take this backward step, urged on by President Nixon.

It is a backward step: the House bill is really intended to stop most future busing of black or white pupils to achieve racial intergration; it would also halt most present busing. But when Mr. Nixon speaks of "excessive, forced busing," he refers to the busing of the 3 per cent of 21,000,000 school children who daily ride school buses in the United States. Only 3 per cent are bused for desegregation purposes.

Can it be that 3 per cent of the busing is excessive and forced but the 97 per cent is not? The kind of leadership the nation is getting on the race issue today is pure political hypocrisy. As Roy Wilkins of the National Association for the Advancement of Colored People has said, "When the busing of white children to maintain segregation was in full swing, it was O.K. Busing has only become an evil since it has been used for desegregation."

No parent, of course, is happy about the prospect of busing small children miles away from the home or neighborhood. But busing has been accepted as an alternative to trying to build good schools for every neighborhood, which would be impracticable. As Mr. Wilkins also observed, busing is simply an interim method of providing equality in school districts in which schools could be made equal only at great expense.

Foes of busing for desegregation purposes often object that it leads to "white flight" and de facto segregated schools. That is what has happened in many cities but it is not the fault of busing. Dr. Kenneth B. Clark has reported that much of the white flight in New York City resulted from too little rather than too much desegregation. Piecemeal desegregation, he noted, had protected some white communities and turned others into new black ghettos.

In 20 years the nation has made considerable progress in legalizing rights that presumably always had been constitutional. In six years the number of children attending all-black schools has been reduced from nearly 40 per cent to 11 per cent. But the figures are misleading; by far the greater part of the desegregation has occurred in the South's traditionally segregated schools. Meanwhile core cities elsewhere have been left in isolation, and their color is black.

Indeed, it is now almost impossible to desegregate city school systems without turning them into totally minority systems. To avoid that the suburbs to which the whites fled have to be brought back into the desegregation effort. Hence the school bus is essential, and also has become the symbol of resistance to desegregation.

We cannot imagine that the Supreme Court, which has already held busing to be an acceptable desegregation device, would accept a congressional limit to its constitutional function. Still it is ironic that the high court might once again be left as a solitary bastion of equal rights because of executive and legislative default. It would be less ironic than tragic if the Congress, with presidential urging, chose the twentieth year of modest progress in national comity to try to retreat to national division.

Daily Defender

CHICAGO

Chicago, Ill.. May 22, 1974

The razor-edge margin by which Sen. Edward J. Gurney's anti-busing amendment was defeated is chilling proof that the poison of racism has not yet been purged out of America's bloodstream. The prospects of reducing school racial imbalance to a bare minimum are bleak after 20 years of court battles, demonstrations and quasi-judicial opinions.

The Gurney amendment would have reduced the authority of the courts in the enforcement of the equal right provision of the fourteenth Amendment. What would have been far more dangerous is the provision in the Senator's proposal which would license the right to reopen litigation on all existing busing orders. Nullification, of course, was the ultimate intent.

This unwarranted intrusion into the conventional judicial process is wholly at variance with normal legal traditions and would open the way for a review of a wide range of racial challenges already settled by the courts.

Perceptive and emotionally balanced Senator Scott of Pennsylvania, who helped draft a compromise, was eminently right when he observed that busing is not a legislative matter but a judicial one.

The House, over populated with unreconstructed and myopic Southerners, by a vote of 293 to 117 adopted a much stronger provision prohibiting federal courts from ordering long-distance busing of school children.

The House version was inspired and sponsored by President Nixon who made anti-busing advocacy a cornerstone in the structure of his monstrous Southern strategy. It is a cynical attempt, as Sen. Edward W. Brooke remarked, "to circumvent the law," toward the achievement of political ends.

The leadership compromise wrought by Mike Mansfield of Montana, the majority leader, and Hugh Scott of Pennsylvania, the minority leader, has weakened the anti-busing language leaving it to the courts to restate their judicial interpretation of the law. The issue is by no means settled beyond the susceptibility of the whims of prejudiced judges. As it stands now, the ultimate fate of the matter rests in the hands of the judges for good or for woe.

Let the people be reminded that elimination of the mechanism to accelerate and implement racial balance in the nation's public schools would in time make the Supreme Court's 1954 desegregation directive only a foot-note to history.

DAYTON DAILY NEWS
Dayton, Ohio, May 26, 1974

President Nixon is placing federal school aid, the rights of black children and a complex major issue in hock to his own political needs.

Compounding the irresponsibility of his gratuitous revival of busing as an emotional issue, Mr. Nixon now says he may veto federal school aid unless the Senate, which has passed a showy but weak anti-busing provision, accepts the reactionary anti-busing position favored by the House.

Mr. Nixon has never been a segregationist. No enthusiast for school integration, still he generally supported it in the past. He never went out of his way to oppose busing, until that became politically expedient, specifically in his "southern strategy" for re-election.

It is now more expedient than ever for Mr. Nixon. Facing an impeachment trial in the Senate, where just 34 senators could spare him from being voted out of office, the President is bidding hard for support by conservative, especially southern senators. His new militancy against busing is not even misguided conviction. It is just cheap demagoguery.

Mr. Nixon is trying to plug the safety valve that for years has allowed congressmen to let off steam about busing but has spared the nation a formal renunciation of school integration and a return to Jim Crow schools. The pattern has been that one chamber, usually the House, would vote some bizarre back-to-segregation law, the other would refuse to go along and both would compromise in favor of responsibility.

That was the set-up again this year — until Mr. Nixon jumped in.

The House did its usual tough act, but the Senate's anti-busing provision, though it would harass integration, basically reaffirmed the goal and acknowledged the right of courts to order busing as a last resort. Chances were that the House would give in. Legislators then could tell the home (white) folks they had tried to stop busing and tell the home (black) folks that they had stopped re-segregation.

No longer content just to show off a little for the racists, however, Mr. Nixon now is trying to force the re-segregation of American — particularly of southern — schools. It is unlikely Congress would be able to override his veto, and in order to continue aid to educaton, it would have to accept the House's anti-busing amendment to the school aid bill.

That amendment is a killer.

It would forbid the courts from ordering busing, the only practical means of achieving integration in many situations. It would permit districts that already are integrated to go to court for cancellation of old busing orders. The first provision would force a dangerous, divisive constitutional clash between the courts and Congress — something the nation hardly needs just now — and the second would put even successfully integrated districts pretty much at the mercy of anti-busing demagogues and mobs.

The President's calculation is that conservative senators would be so grateful to him, and so fearful of their constituencies' gratitude to him, that they wouldn't dare vote for his conviction even if the prosecutors were to spring film of the President sticking up a bank on them.

Mr. Nixon, no idealist, always has trimmed and angled his sails to the prevailing political winds — and never mind which way those might be blowing. In the past, however, he never proposed to stir up a damaging storm and inflict it on the country, just so he could catch a helpful gust. This busing act is his most cynical and irresponsible one yet.

THE SUN
Baltimore, Md., May 18, 1974

School busing is one of the most divisive of national issues, because of its high emotional content, and one that significantly has found Maryland's two members of the United States Senate on opposite sides. The key vote this past week was on the motion to table the amendment proposed by Senator Gurney, a Nixon-flavored Florida Republican, which would have prohibited court-ordered busing of children beyond the "next closest" school to their homes.

Two aspects of the Gurney amendment made it conspicuously wrong, for those who rise above the emotional level to the higher constitutional considerations which are supposed to set the tone for Senate deliberations. For one, the anti-busing amendment in practical application could have had the effect, deliberate or not, of being an anti-desegregation measure, since the "next closest" school might well have the same racial composition as the one a child currently attends. For another, the amendment was a blatant attempt to tie the hands of the courts, contrary to traditional American belief in the sanctity of the judiciary as a branch of government separate and distinct from the legislative branch.

What opponents of busing frequently overlook is that the courts in this country have not ordered school integration purely for the sake of racial balance. They have ordered desegregation, through busing if need be, in cases where it could be demonstrated that deliberate official actions had fostered segregated situations which amounted to a denial of a child's constitutional right to have equal access to a nonsegregated education. A constitutional right is not something that the courts, and certainly not legislative bodies, can limit by saying, you can exercise your constitutional right, but only on foot; or, you may exercise it, but only as far as the next closest school. The courts have to have the freedom and flexibility to approve or devise plans that square fully with the constitutional circumstances, and so far in most instances they have acted sensibly.

On this issue, as we have said, Maryland's two Republican senators were on opposite sides. Although coming up for reelection and in the more vulnerable position, Senator Charles McC. Mathias stood on the high ground with the slim majority of senators who mustered a one-vote margin to kill the Gurney amendment. Senator J. Glenn Beall, Jr., alas, was with those who are willing to ride the anti-busing emotions without regard for the Constitution. It is not hard to determine which is our more courageous senator.

HOLT AMENDMENT ATTEMPTS TO END ASSIGNMENT OF STUDENTS BY RACE

An amendment sponsored by Rep. Marjorie S. Holt (R, Md.) to prohibit use of federal funds for classifying or assigning students to particular schools was rendered meaningless by the Senate Dec. 14. As approved by the House Oct. 1 by a 220–169 vote, the Holt amendment would not allow the Health, Education and Welfare Department (HEW) to require school districts to keep files on the basis of race, sex, religion or national origin. The Senate rejected that version Nov. 19 by a 43–36 vote.

Senators Mike Mansfield (D, Mont.) and Hugh Scott (R, Pa.) sponsored a nullifying clause "... except as may be required to enforce non-discrimination provisions of federal law." The Senate approved the Scott-Mansfield proposal 55–27 Dec. 14, and the House reversed itself, approving the nullified version 224–136 Dec. 16.

The State
Columbia, S.C., December 8, 1974

LITTLE by little, Congress is trying to arrive at some workable arrangement which will prevent racial discrimination in public schools without going overboard in the direction of compulsory race-mixing.

The current effort, of course, is triggered by the vehement — in some cases, the violent — reaction of Northern communities against school busing. Busing itself is not really the problem, although there are legitimate grounds for complaint when youngsters are compelled to ride long distances without any accompanying educational benefit.

The real issue in the busing controversy is the forced transportation of children out of their neighborhood into another in order to achieve the elusive and illusory goal of "racial balance." According to existing (but ignored) law, no such tactics are allowable. Indeed, the Civil Rights Act of 1964 specifically forbids the practice in these words:

"Nothing herein shall empower any official or court of the United States to issue any order seeking to achieve a racial balance in any school by requiring the transportation of pupils or students from one school to another or one school district to another in order to achieve such racial balance . . . ."

In light of the above, one wonders how effective the latest congressional effort will be. That effort, embraced in a House-Senate compromise already accepted by the House, would prohibit the use of federal funds to compel the classification of students (or teachers) by race, religion, sex, or national origin.

What Congress seems to be saying, with mingled concern and confusion, is that school desegregation should be handled in the fashion contemplated by the United States Supreme Court in its landmark decision of 1954. The thrust of that ruling was that race could not be used as a factor in the admission, rejection, or assignment of students.

Since then, however, judicial and bureaucratic zealots have twisted the decision almost 180 degrees. Instead of eliminating race as a factor in school assignment, they have issued orders, adopted policies, and applied pressures which make race the prime consideration in pupil assignment. Instead of becoming color blind, as was implicit in the 1954 decision, enforcement has become increasingly color conscious.

The shame of the situation is that the people of the United States have not been brought into the decision-making. Assuming that the Congress serves officially as a "voice of the people," it is significant that the congressional (popular?) mandate in the Civil Rights Act of 1964 has been flouted by the comparative handful of crusaders who would rework society into conformity with their own notions.

What seems needed is a constitutional amendment which would prohibit discrimination in reverse fully as much as in its original form. In short, the Constitution should say, perhaps in the very language of the Supreme Court in its follow-up decision of 1955, that "racial discrimination in public education is unconstitutional."

ARKANSAS DEMOCRAT
Little Rock, Ark., December 13, 1974

The House is once again on record against busing. This time, the lofty Senate will feel more than the usual pressure to stop ignoring one of the hottest issues in politics. How the Senators perform could have a lot to do with our ending busing for good.

Their own conferees have agreed to a House declaration that the federal government is not to spend any money for new busing. The House has ratified the conference action. If the upper-chambermen follow suit, President Ford will sign with a flourish — and the first blow ever will have been struck against busing.

The House action is different this time around. In the past, the House has several times tried to outlaw busing by law — something it can't do so long as the Supreme Court says busing is constitutional. For that reason, the Senate has either refused to go along or has added such phrases as, "if it is constitutional" or "except when ordered by the courts." These amendments showed up the absurdity of the House action.

But there's no constitutional question involved in what the House aims at doing now: Telling the department of Health, Education and Welfare it is not to spend a penny of a $5.8 billion appropriation on achieving racial balance in the schools.

Time was when HEW would have ignored such an order. Either bus or lose federal education funds was its message in the days when HEW wrote guidelines for mixing and served as an arm-twister for the federal courts. But under Nixon first and now under Ford, HEW has lost its mixing zeal. HEW Director Caspar Weinberger says his agency will obey the new law if it is passed. That is unprecedented.

The bureaucracy is a fourth branch of government. If Congress — which has never done a thing to halt busing — and HEW, which has done everything to promote it, should come over to the side of the anti-busers, a way will be cleared to stop busing altogether.

Congress hasn't the power to stop it, but it can start the process by first chaining HEW — thereby isolating the federal courts as the only pro-busing force in government — and then give that process momentum by authorizing an anti-busing constitutional amendment. The President and the people of the states will do the rest, blacks as well as whites.

It all depends on the Senate. If the Senate blights this promising prospect by refusing to ratify the House action, it should be put on the spot for ignoring the popular will.

The Democratic Congress, the Senate included, is supposed to have a mandate — meaning a popular endorsement by the people to give the people what they want. One of the things they want, in something like a three-fourths or four-fifths majority, is no busing.

The Dallas Morning News
Dallas, Tex., December 6, 1974

THE HOUSE has maneuvered to prevent additional busing for balance. In a 212-to-176 vote, it approved a measure to bar the use of new HEW money for balancing work.

This has produced a few headlines and gives those representatives voting a record busing vote to display in 1976. But the chances that it will actually accomplish anything to stop busing for balance are exceedingly slim. Before the plan can go to the White House, it must be endorsed by the Senate. Considering the past, that seems unlikely.

It also seems unlikely that the three fourths of the population opposed to busing will be very excited by this latest maneuver, unless the Senate does go along.

Americans have seen many of these alleged attempts to remove the hated busing policy, but the buses go right on rolling. The federal judges go right on rearranging the lives of schoolchildren to suit the needs of their own grand design.

There has rarely been an issue in American political life in which the conviction of the majority has been so unmistakable. Time after time, in every poll and election, in every region, among voters of every race, the will of the American people has been firmly expressed on this issue.

It is consistently, overwhelmingly opposed to the practice of busing children back and forth for the sole purpose of meeting some racial formula.

And yet the will of the vast majority has been "overwhelming" only in the figurative sense. Literally and practically, the will of the tiny minority of Americans who favor busing for balance has carried the day again and again. For all of the votes by the people and by the Congress, for all of the one-sided consensus that busing must go, busing stays.

The latest move by the House would, if endorsed by the Senate, tend to discourage busing, though by a roundabout path. And again, that is an extremely large "if."

But it is nevertheless impossible to overlook the fact that a Congress sincerely determined to carry out the will of the people has the power, the right and indeed the duty to stop busing,

once and for all.

The Congress can act on the proposed constitutional amendment that would make school enrollment policies truly color-blind. This resort to the amendment process is, to be sure, a drastic move. But as we have seen, nothing less drastic offers any hope of bringing this elitist game-playing to an end.

The time for striking attitudes, taking roundabout paths and voting for futile half-measures is past. The American people have expressed themselves as clearly as they possibly can: Busing for balance must go.

If a constitutional amendment is what it takes to accomplish this, then a constitutional amendment is what we must have.

MANCHESTER UNION LEADER
Manchester, N.H., December 8, 1974

Congress Wednesday tacked a crippling amendment on a bill to appropriate $8.5 billions financing a grabbag of programs, including Boston Judge Gerrity's ignorant and arrogant ukase commanding 35,000 elementary and high school pupils to be bused forcibly away from their neighborhood schools to achieve racial "integration."

The amendment says no funds may be used in any school district "to classify teachers or students by race, religion, sex or national origin; or to assign teachers or students to schools, classes or courses for reasons of race, religion, sex or national origin."

The amendment was adopted by the House by a vote of 212 to 176 and now goes to the Senate.

It has thrown the Bay State liberal-leftist establishment, from Senator Edward W. Brooke to the Boston Globe, into tizzy.

Although the measure's language plainly knocks U. S. Judge Garrity's ukase into a cocked hat, Boston leftists are dealing with it by declaring simply that it cannot apply to the Boston schools, taking their cue from Sen. Teddy Kennedy's insistence that the move comes "after the fact" of Garrity's order. The Globe, which surely must be one of the most barefaced falsifiers in the history of journalism, puts in two separate headlines its allegation that "Boston Court Order Won't Be affected."

This is crystal ball reading. If the Senate backs the House Boston's forced busing plans certainly will be affected, to the chagrin of Ed Brooke, Ted Kennedy, the Boston Globe, and the "black congressman" who, the Globe reported, protest that "progress against racial and sex discrimination would be impaired."

The Boston Globe
Boston, Mass., December 9, 1974

The amendment to restrict government power to enforce anti-discrimination laws which was passed last Wednesday by the House of Representatives has gathered considerable support, enough to pass by a 36-vote margin, largely because it has mistakenly been perceived as an anti-busing amendment. In fact, should it become law, its application to any current or pending busing plans, including those for Boston, would be unaffected.

The Federal Courts are generally responsible for busing plans to carry out desegregation orders and the Congress has not challenged the courts on this point. An attempt was made earlier in the year to attach an anti-busing curb to the 1974 education amendments but it was neutralized in conference by excluding Federal court-ordered busing from its provisions. What the amendment does threaten, however, is much of the vitality of the Civil Rights Act of 1964, the anti-sex discrimination statutes of the 1972 education amendments, bilingual language and Indian programs and all affirmative action plans.

The original amendment, named after its patron Rep. Marjorie Holt (R-Md.), included a prohibition against compelling school authorities to keep records of the race, sex and national origin of students and teachers. Federal agencies, notably the Department of Health, Education and Welfare, use such records to determine if discrimination exists, and withhold Federal funds where discrimination is found. The record-keeping provision was compromised out of existence by House-Senate conferees after the Senate rejected it 43-36, but the provisions denying the government the power to compel the classification or assignment of students and teachers by race, sex or national origin remain. The language of the amendment is deceptively democratic in tone and, besides its appeal to anti-busing spokesmen

like Sen. Jesse Helms (R-N.C.) who sponsored it on the Senate side first time around, probably got some votes because it was misunderstood as something benign or even positively progressive.

But the Holt amendment would strangle the enforcement power of the Federal government which the Congress, in wiser moments, has conferred. Beyond the strictures on enforcement the legislation also makes it virtually impossible to investigate whether discrimination even exists. If students or teachers cannot be classified as to sex or race, any attempt to determine the existence, or nature or extent of discrimination in a school district or hospital system would be fruitless.

The conference leadership and labor, civil rights and women's groups have joined Sen. Edward W. Brooke (R-Mass.) in trying to neutralize the bad effects of this amendment by adding language that would exempt from its provisions administrative measures that are required to enforce non-discriminatory provisions of Federal law. The parliamentary maneuvering, which will probably begin tomorrow, is complicated, but the fact that this kind of regressive legislation has gotten this far indicates that nothing less than full pressure should be brought to bear to have the Holt amendment killed or effectively modified.

Three Massachusetts representatives, Democrats James Burke and John L. Moakley and Republican Paul Cronin supported the Holt amendment. Democratic Representatives Torbet Macdonald and Harold Donahue missed the voting. Those of their constituents who view race and sex discrimination with disapproval should inform their representatives of their feelings. The Holt amendment deserves to pass into oblivion, not the law books.

THE DALLAS TIMES HERALD

Dallas, Tex., December 6, 1974

THE HOUSE-passed bill denying the use of federal funds to Health Education and Welfare for desegregation programs based principally on busing would apparently have no effect on Dallas, even if it is finally enacted into law.

The anti-busing provision, sponsored by Rep. Marjorie Holt, R-Md., prohibits HEW from compelling school systems getting federal funds "to classify teachers or students by race, religion, sex or national origin, or to assign teachers or students to schools, classes or courses for reasons or race, sex or national origin."

This provision in the bill would n o t affect busing programs now in effect or, as in Dallas, now under the jurisdiction of the courts.

In fact, it apparently would not affect future desegregation suits filed in the courts by individuals or organizations other than HEW.

Thus t h e extent of the impact of the bill, should it become law, is questionable. (The bill now goes to the Senate, where the Holt amendment may well be rejected.)

Even now opinions on the possible effect of the bill vary widely.

HEW Secretary Caspar W. Weinberger said the bill would effectively bar his department from enforcing school desegregation under the 1964 civil rights act.

Rep. Holt on the other hand said that her amendment would not have such sweeping impact, that it is a method of expressing Congress' wish to do away with school busing for desegregation purposes.

In any case, Rep. Holt is right on this latter point. The 212 to 176 vote in the House does express the feeling in the House and the growing feeling in Congress as a whole that busing has failed as a viable tool for desegregating the schools — that a better alternative to busing must be found for that worthy purpose.

ST. LOUIS POST-DISPATCH

St. Louis, Mo., December 8, 1974

Six years have now passed since Congress approved the last major civil rights act, and since the last strong proponent of equal rights under law left the White House. They have been empty years, numbered by efforts to turn back the calendar.

The latest example of looking backward is the 212 to 176 vote of the House for an amendment to prevent schools getting federal funds from being compelled to classify teachers or pupils by race, religion, sex or national origin. Put that way, it almost sounds patriotic. Isn't this nation one that in principle ignores matters of race, religion, origin and sex in law and public affairs?

Yet every American should know that the practice defies the principle, and so does the new House amendment. Its sponsor, Representative Marjorie Holt, Maryland Republican, admits that the measure is a "more sophisticated" effort to stop interracial school busing. So it is, after all, an anti-civil rights measure. But it goes further than the issue of busing.

Government departments generally depend on accurate statistics as to minority groups in preparing desegregation and equal rights cases. Without the facts to demonstrate segregation, the Government could make no case. A coalition of voices for minorities, and for women's rights, pointed that out. So did the Secretary of Health, Education and Welfare, Caspar Weinberger. But the House majority was listening to arguments advanced for nibbling away at past progress.

The minority statistics, for example, and the whole idea of interracial composition, are often equated with the kind of quotas that once were used to keep minorities out of jobs and colleges and even housing. The comparison does not stand up. Statistics can be used one way or another; the fact that they were wrongly used for decades necessitates their use now to repair the damage.

Then it is said, by some scholars as well as politicians, that busing is not a valid instrument for seeking quality education. For a long time it was regarded as just that. Even now, as blacks well know, if busing does not automatically confer better education on their children, it at least places them in schools that the white majority insists should be good schools. But quality education is not the main purpose of desegregation. The purpose is simply to achieve the principle of equal protection of the laws and, as the Supreme Court said so long ago now, segregated schools are unequal.

To many it seems unfortunate that the school system has been made the focus of efforts to wipe out America's longstanding social injustice. Yet there is a reason for that, too. It may be decades before changing housing patterns automatically destroy segregated life in this country. Meanwhile, millions of Americans would grow up in segregated neighborhoods and schools and with segregated attitudes. The first place to nurture the principle of equality is among the young, which is to say, in the schools. Democratic education is not too much to expect in a democracy.

To such expectations the Holt amendment is an abomination, as Representative Bella Abzug of New York said. Yet the most that can be anticipated, probably, is a promised effort by the bipartisan Senate leadership to water the bill down to nothing. In short, the civil rights movement in America is reduced to a rear-guard action. It is no longer boldly advancing. It awaits a rebirth of principle in the nation's leadership to do that.

The Providence Journal

Providence, R.I., December 9, 1974

Surely the U.S. Senate will not be misled into accepting last week's blatant House attempt to block enforcement of existing federal civil rights laws. Indeed, there is some question whether House members understood the full meaning of an amendment sponsored by Rep. Marjorie Holt, R-Md, which would prevent the federal government from collecting school data pertaining to the sex and race of the students and teachers.

The Ford administration, on record as favoring an end to busing for purposes of school desegregation, has urged defeat of the amendment. In fact, the provision would go far beyond the intended aim of its sponsor who said it was a more sophisticated method of expressing Congress' desire to end desegregation busing.

The full implications were not lost on Caspar W. Weinberger, Secretary of Health, Education and Welfare, however. Such a ban, he pointed out, would eliminate HEW's authority to enforce the civil rights laws. In order to ascertain compliance or noncompliance with various laws that prohibit discrimination on the basis of race, national origin, and sex, the department must have data provided by the schools. Without statistics available on the number and ratio of Spanish-speaking students, the law on bilingual education would be virtually meaningless. impunity. Without statistics available on the number and ratio of Spanish-speaking students, the law on bi-lingual education would be virtually meaningless.

The amendment, said Rep. Parren Mitchell, D-Md, would signal the country that Congress sanctions "a policy of apartheid in American schools."

Even the limited interpretation of her proposal given by Representative Holt would constitute intolerable interference with the constitutional rulings of the Supreme Court governing unitary school systems. Obvious to everyone by now must be the frequent lack of an alternative to busing where dual systems continue to exist. In countless cities, if the anti-busing hysteria were translated into a statutory ban, the principle of equal educational opportunity could not long survive.

Over the last few years, the House has written a sorry record where this issue is concerned. It has consistently pandered to the political motives of those who would erase the civil rights progress of the last two decades. Consequently, last week's concession to the backsliders hardly comes as a surprise.

If this monumental blunder is to be averted, however, and if the rights of this country's largest minority as well as those who have been the victims of sex discrimination are to be preserved, the Senate will move swiftly this week to consign this misguided proposal to the one place where it clearly belongs — the scrapheap.

THE MILWAUKEE JOURNAL
Milwaukee, Wisc., December 6, 1974

Another attempt to abandon the nation's constitutional commitment to eliminating racial segregation has made startling progress in Congress. House and Senate conferees have voted a provision into a supplemental appropriations bill that would prevent the federal government from cutting off aid to school districts that disobeyed court orders to desegregate.

The cutoff authority currently is vested in the Department of Health, Education and Welfare by federal civil rights law. While HEW was lax in its enforcement sometimes in the past, it is a logical and important provision for keeping federal agency practice consistent with the Constitution and the intent of a broad range of official public policies.

The provision to destroy HEW's aid cutoff power was authored by Rep. Marjorie Holt (R-Md.). It has now been approved by the House, but earlier had been rejected by the Senate. Responsible senators now will have to perform the distasteful task of killing the whole appropriations bill to keep this atrocious, segregationist amendment from becoming the law of the land.

Daily Defender
Chicago, Ill., December 19, 1974

It was an act of unmitigated wisdom when the Senate blocked an anti-busing filibuster which was mounted by Alabama Senator James B. Allen who is only noted for his anti-black spasm that he falls into whenever the racial question comes up before the Senate.

The Senate pushed its logical course of antiseptic action by voting to nullify a house-passed amendment designed to curb government enforcement of desegregation orders. This is the amendment that segregationist Marjorie E. Holt, a Republican from Maryland, had sponsored to satisfy her constituents.

The district from which she comes has refused categorically to cooperate with federal authorities in an investigation of discrimination in the district public schools. Mrs. Holt's amendment would block action by the government to withhold federal funds from all districts that have desegregated orders.

Opposition to the amendment is based on the certainty that it would nullify Title VI of the Civil Rights Act of 1964, which gives the Department of Health, Education and Welfare the authority to enforce school desegregation orders.

In the battle to block the filibuster and prevent passage of the Holt amendment, Sen. Edward W. Brooke from Massachusetts played a stellar role. Pounding his desk, Brooke asserted that "If we have to stay here until the next Congress comes here on January 14, we will not accept the Holt amendment." The Senate action now goes back to the House for conference where the anti-busing sentiment is strong. What compromise will be reached on the issue is anybody's guess.

TULSA DAILY WORLD
Tulsa, Okla., December 18, 1974

THE BATTLE over forced school busing has been stilled in Congress, but only temporarily. So long as Boston-type resistance to busing continues in either the North or South, the issue will not die in Washington.

Congress' current spearhead against busing is Rep. MARJORIE S. HOLT of Maryland, who twice in the present session has won House votes for her antibusing amendment to an $8.6 billion supplemental appropriations bill.

A Senate filibuster attempt on the issue was headed off by only one vote. Monday Mrs. HOLT's effort finally was beaten back in the House, which is trying to clear its calendar for the year-end recess.

The Maryland Republican says she isn't through.

"I hope we can resume this fight on every education bill in the next session," she told a reporter. "We just ran out of time today."

Her argument is that Congress never intended to sanction forced busing to achieve racial desegregation of public schools. Many would quarrel with her interpretation, but it is true that opinion is sharply divided on how far to pursue this method of integration in the face of passionate resistance in some of the areas most affected.

Civil rights advocates would consider Mrs. HOLT's effort a major step backwards if it should succeed. Opponents of busing would hail it as a return to sanity.

It is a fact that the nation is going to have desegregated schools, one way or another. As a national policy that can hardly be turned back. But the complex means of reaching the goal — the procedure, the timetable and the policing — are still matters of much debate.

Most people would have thought the violence in Boston would be quieted by now — but it is still an ugly reality causing schools to be closed, and every new incident provokes angry reaction on both sides.

Does Mrs. HOLT have the answer? Probably not — but the longer the militants on both sides keep banging away at each other, that much longer will Congress nervously toss this stick of dynamite around, unable to defuse it or guarantee that it won't go off.

THE RICHMOND NEWS LEADER
Richmond, Va., December 16, 1974

The Senate has folded again.

Over the weekend, the Senate stopped a filibuster by Senators opposing compulsory busing, and then proceeded to reject a House-passed amendment to an $8.6 billion supplemental appropriations bill for the Department of Health, Education, and Welfare. Intended to prevent the withholding of federal funds from localities that fail to comply with racial balance plans ordered by the courts, the amendment now goes back to the House.

The House should stand firm. In the words of one news report, "Pressure is on Congress to pass the supplemental money bill before adjournment. Without it, a number of federal agencies will be unable to meet their spending commitments." Which implies that there is more "pressure" on Congress to pass the supplemental funding measure so that Congress can go home, than there is among our federal legislators a sense of commitment to do right by the people of the United States.

Once again, then, the Senate has voted to allow judicial monkeyshines to raise racist dogma to self-destructive heights. Once again, the Senate has voted to allow fundamental assumptions on which this nation was founded to be stealthily repealed. Once again, the Senate has voted to let stand the mischievous dogma that judicial fiat can wash away discriminations of the past by imposing new discriminations now. In short, once again the Senate has shown itself to be out of touch with the people for whom it presumes to speak.

And all this, as compulsory busing proceeds to its ineluctable climax in . . . Boston. What moral gratification there must be among the self-righteous Liberals who reside in Boston's rich suburbs — as the compulsory busing that has come to South Boston continues to rip the city apart. Under the current plan, 18,000 Boston children are being bused. Today, the Boston Schools Committee will unveil its plan for Phase II — a plan demanded by a federal judge — that will require the busing of another 35,000 Boston children next year.

Boston has seen nothing yet. Yet already Boston taxpayers are dispensing $90,000 *per day* in overtime pay for police; special police rifle teams have occupied perches on housing rooftops; the citizenry has endured house-to-house searches by police seeking felons and miscreants. And the irony is obvious. In the 1972 presidential election, Massachusetts was the only state won by George McGovern; at the height of Watergate, many Boston area residents sported bumper stickers reading, "Don't blame me. I'm from Massachusetts." Now one of the most popular bumper stickers in the Boston area reads: "Don't blame me. I'm from Alabama."

These days the public hears a good deal of bemoaning about a lack of leadership in Washington. Usually the moans are directed toward the unelected Ford administration. But the real lack of leadership is on Capitol Hill — as the Senate so amply illustrated over the weekend when it voted once more in favor of judicial usurpation of local prerogative. The House now has an opportunity to set a leadership example: It should refuse to cave in on compulsory busing. It should say to the Senate: "Very well. Either you support the anti-busing amendment to the supplemental funding bill, or HEW goes *un*funded." For standing on principle is what leadership is all about. And the principle of parental prerogative in determining where children will go to school is one of the fundamental principles in the land.

The Senate has folded — again. And again, the House should stand firm.

CIVIL RIGHTS COMMISSION ISSUES DESEGREGATION PROGRESS REPORT

The U.S. Commission on Civil Rights, in a report issued March 11, urged the federal government to withdraw aid from schools that failed to desegregate voluntarily. Such schools, the report said, should be given 90 days to initiate integration plans before the Department of Health, Education and Welfare began proceedings to end federal financial assistance. The recommendation was contained in the commission's report, "Twenty Years after Brown: Equality of Educational Opportunity." It was the second in a series of seven reports commemorating the 1954 Supreme Court decision—*Brown v. Board of Education*—declaring racially separate schools inherently unequal and unconstitutional.

THE CHRISTIAN SCIENCE MONITOR
Boston, Mass., March 13, 1975

Does the United States really want to return to the "separate but equal" doctrine of education that was found unconstitutional by the Supreme Court 20 years ago?

The nation risks lapsing back into that attitude as efforts to comply with the court's desegregation order face new setbacks in a virtual vacuum of presidential leadership on the subject.

Such leadership becomes especially important as controversies over desegregation, notably involving busing, continue in various parts of the country. It seems clear that, whatever specific legal and educational steps are taken, their effectiveness will depend on the degree to which there is a supportive climate of community thought. This is where local leaders need national example and reinforcement in fostering attitudes to uphold the law.

What brings the subject to public attention this week is the coincidence of a sobering report on desegregation coming from the United States Commission on Civil Rights at the same time that the California court of appeal was overturning a 1970 ruling requiring desegregation in the Los Angeles school district.

The new California decision was based on the finding that segregation had not been "intentionally fostered" but rather "ignored." To which the desegregationists reasonably reply that to ignore a wrong is, in a sense, to foster it. In a nation with a wholehearted commitment to desegregation, segregation would not be "ignored."

As this case goes through an inevitable further appeals process, the nation in general ought to heed the warning of the civil rights commission: "Without positive action, segregation in urban areas, both North and South, appears likely to increase, and urban-suburban racial divisions will be intensified."

Such a prospect appears in the perspective of the commission's findings of substantial progress against school segregation in the South and minimal progress in the North. In a previous report this year, the commission pointed to federal agencies that themselves were failing to carry out their responsibilities to promote equal educational opportunity. The commission takes account of the new resistance to desegregation but remains firm against it:

"Although some white segregationists have been joined by some black separatists in a thrust for 'separate but equal' schools, the Supreme Court's finding that separate can never be equal nevertheless remains sound. . . ."

In view of the commission's confirmation of the urgency felt by civil-rights supporters around the country, President Ford ought to follow through in the spirit of his meeting with black civil rights leaders last fall. He assured them of enforcement of federal desegregation law.

But Mr. Ford has not yet made that public "ringing affirmation" of the nation's commitment to racial justice which the black leaders asked for. Will he take a lead in both word and deed before the law is further thwarted?

The Detroit News
Detroit, Mich., March 13, 1975

Like the imperious Queen of Hearts, who cried "Off with their heads," the Commission on Civil Rights this week urged the government to give segregated school districts 90 days in which to desegregate and, if they fail, to cut off their funds.

Commissions far removed from the scene of an actual problem may voice such sweeping demands without worrying about details. In real life, equities are not always so easy to determine and to enforce.

As the commission itself admits, much of the segregation of schools results from residential segregation. In many communities residential segregation occurred primarily because whites moved away to neighborhoods with more pleasant surroundings and more benefits for their children. Less fortunate persons remained behind.

Nobody has yet offered a fair and reasonable solution to that problem. After all, you can't order people to live in certain places against their will, just as you shouldn't prevent them from living in places where they want to live and have the means to live.

Detroit schools provide a vivid example of school segregation stemming from residential segregation of the kind described above. Detroit's case also illustrates how hard it is to deal with that kind of school segregation. After working on the problem for four years, the community is back where it started.

The Supreme Court, dubious about driving buses across school district lines to join segregated neighborhoods, ruled out a massive cross-district concept that had emerged from lower courts. Detroit must now try to find a solution within its own borders.

Obviously, a school district that is 75 percent black will continue to have a substantial amount of segregation under such a solution. Such a district is not going to alter the laws of mathematics in 90 days. Meanwhile, to withdraw funds from that district will merely intensify the difficulty of providing quality education, which after all should be everybody's main objective.

The Civil Rights Commission wants a uniform national standard for school desegregation. We see the advantage of drawing up a list of basic principles, but any standard should leave room for dealing fairly and intelligently with peculiar local conditions.

Arthur S. Flemming, chairman of the commission, says the uniform standard is needed "to eliminate, once and for all, all forms of school segregation."

If it were only possible to do so. Unfortunately, a problem created over a period of more than a century will not be eliminated by a 90-day miracle.

Like New Detroit, Inc., which last week issued an eminently sensible statement on Detroit's school desegregation problems, we think it best to focus on "the achievement of the possible" instead of resorting to an idealistic theory "which, while persuasive in its appeal, is not practical in its approach."

The Morning Star
Rockford, Ill., March 13, 1975

For years, there was a smug assumption in the American North that desegregation was something for the South to do.

Now comes the U.S. Commission on Civil Rights with a 20-year overview of desegregation — and guess who's foot-dragging? The South? No, the North where many of the finger-pointers live.

Certainly, in our own city of Rockford, the fact that our Board of Education faces a desegregation suit — and possible loss of state and federal funds by the thousands of dollars — should convince somebody that there is blame to be shouldered in our midst.

Platitudes about "voluntary desegregation" won't carry the day. Wishful thinking won't either.

As the Civil Rights commission hastens to point out, more than 71 per cent of our Northern blacks attend predominately black schools.

In the South in the last 20 years, blacks attending predominantly white schools has gone from 19 to 46 per cent.

To carry integration forward, says the Civil Rights report, the voice of President Ford is needed to remind the country that "separate remains unequal" and that black separatists are as off-base as their white counterparts in seeking racially separated schools.

After all, we are supposed to be "one nation under God with liberty and justice for all."

We trust that President Ford will depart from the example of his predecessor and give the Commission on Civil Rights his sincere backing.

We also commend to our neighbors a careful reading — and acceptance — of the commission's conclusion that "integration must move forward for moral and legal reasons, irrespective of the difficulties along the way."

The Evening Bulletin
Philadelphia, Pa., March 22, 1975

In the two decades since the U.S. Supreme Court struck down the doctrine of "separate but equal," ruling that it "has no place" in public education, the school desegregation struggle has advanced slowly and unevenly.

The U.S. Commission on Civil Rights noted in a report issued last week that desegregation efforts over the last 20 years "present a conflicting picture of success and failure" which, viewed overall, "is much at odds with the expectations of many ... who looked upon the decision as a turning point in the racial life of the nation."

Significant progress has been achieved in desegregating public schools in the South. Nearly half of the black pupils in that region attended predominantly white schools as of 1972, where less than 19 percent did only four years earlier. However, the lack of progress in the North and West was equally significant. Over the same four-year period desegregation gains in those regions were minimal, and as of 1972 more than 70 percent of the black public school pupils attended predominantly minority schools.

As discouraging as the overall results of the last 20 years are, the future outlook is even less encouraging. The commission warned that unless positive action is taken, "segregation in urban areas, both North and South, appears likely to increase, and urban-suburban racial divisions will be intensified."

In spite of the difficulties involved in eliminating de facto segregation — segregation resulting from housing patterns — in large urban areas such as Philadelphia and the strong resistance to desegregation now being mounted in northern and western cities, the nation can't afford to retreat on the issue.

In the Brown decision the court contended that "separate" was inherently unequal. And the disparity that so often exists between the quality of predominantly white schools and predominantly minority schools within the same school system tends to substantiate the court's contention. In spite of the counter arguments put forth by opponents of desegregation — both white and black — the commission believes that the court's position is still valid.

Viewed solely from a political perspective, school desegregation is a no-win proposition for public officials. However, it is imperative that officials at all levels of government stop playing politics with what essentially is a legal and educational issue.

The leaders who continue to undermine the desegregation effort by their public statements or legislative attacks are in effect thumbing their noses at the law and the constitutional rights of a significant segment of the population.

As long as school desegregation is kicked around as a political issue, racial isolation in public schools — and racial hostility along with it — will continue to increase.

ARKANSAS DEMOCRAT
Little Rock, Ark., March 16, 1975

There's irony in the news that the civil rights commission is calling on anti-buser Gerald Ford to push for total school integration — particularly in the North and especially by busing. But we would like to see Ford do it.

We feel as he (and 80 per cent of Americans) feels about busing — we don't like it. But it can be stopped only by constitutional amendment. The quickest way to get congressional consensus on an amendment would be for Ford to do as the commission says: Apply to the North "the strongest possible federal enforcement" of Supreme Court decrees; impose "all available sanctions." If that doesn't fetch northern lawmakers, nothing will.

The rights commission furnishes the ammunition for the offensive: Though 54 per cent of Southern Negroes are still in predominantly black schools, 71 per cent of northern Negroes are still in black schools. Are we going to have a national busing policy or aren't we?

Granted — the North has never had anti-mixing laws on its state books. It hid behind that fact for years, while drawing school districts to keep the races separate as residential districts.

This used to be called "de facto" segregation. Northerners spread their palms wide in innocence — until the Supreme Court decided that implicit agreement among school boards and state and local governments to maintain racial school separation is as bad as passing laws to perpetuate it.

Judicially, that high court change-of-face put North and South in the same mixing pot. That was why Denver, Detroit, Boston, etc. began to feel the fire. But northern mixing has lacked one powerful push that was always applied in the South: Presidential leadership.

The court could rely on it when the Democratic predecessors to Nixon and Ford held office. Not only did the Justice Department suits fly thick and fast — the Department of Health, Education and Welfare used an even bigger club to force integration: The cutting off of school aid.

Nixon, who was no friend of busing, haltered HEW. Ford has continued that policy. Both the polls and events have supported their opposition to busing. When the court moved North, it also seemed probable that northern legislators would soon join with Southerners to produce a congressional consensus for an anti-busing amendment.

That hasn't happened, and one reason it hasn't happened is that when northern busing began neither Nixon nor Ford ordered HEW in to administer a financial flogging. HEW Secretary Caspar Weinberger, who served under both men, has always been anti-busing, like his bosses. Though he has commented on the curious Northern reluctance to do what it insisted that the South do, Weinberger has made it plain that he is against pushing integration anywhere. He hasn't cut off funds.

The Justice Department hasn't been nearly as active either, as its Democratic predecessors were, in filing suits. What the rights commission wants is for Ford to turn both Justice and HEW loose on the North.

Equity demands it, and we'd like to see it — not as a punishment but as a jab to northern legislators to get behind an anti-busing amendment. All through the busing years, Congress has been a laggard. Ten years ago and more, when busing was new, it did legislate against busing for racial balance, but the courts ignored the legislation. Congress has since limited itself to killing bills that would hamper busing while refusing to take any action on the fact that four-fifths of the people want it stopped.

Ford can put the lawmakers on the spot. The rights commission has given the pretext to impose an evenhanded national busing policy: Bus everybody. Busing everybody is the only way to produce the policy Americans really want: Bus nobody.

The Charlotte Observer
Charlotte, N.C., March 18, 1975

The U.S. Civil Rights Commission has called for creation of a uniform national standard for school desegregation and even offered to draw up one for Congress and the White House. That is certainly a worthwhile effort. But what is really needed is not a national standard but a national commitment to end school segregation. Until the Ford Administration and Congress make such a commitment, no standard will do much more than remind us how little has been done outside the South.

It has long been obvious that the problem of racial discrimination in America goes far beyond the existence of Jim Crow laws in the South. Throughout the country, longstanding practices — often enforced by government policies or customs as strong as law — have shunted most blacks and some other minorities into second-class citizenship.

The segregation laws have been knocked down. But what has happened now that the anti-discrimination effort has come up against the more subtle, engrained causes of school segregation, such as discrimination in housing, zoning and jobs? For the Nixon-Ford Administration, the answer has been "very little."

The Nixon-Ford Administration's attitude has been that school integration should be required in the North only if it can be done without disruption. Caspar Weinberger, secretary of health, education and welfare, said as much a few months ago in attempting to justify his do-little policy in the North. "The public has been much more willing to accept desegregation in the South," he said.

Mr. Weinberger, as we said then, was talking nonsense. The primary difference has been the federal government's willingness to enforce the law in the South as opposed to its lack of willingness to do so in the North. Few Southern school boards considered the disruption necessary to integrate the schools to be worthwhile until they were faced with the probability of a greater disruption if the schools remained segregated. The threat of a cutoff of federal funds or a citation for contempt of court for failing to carry out desegregation orders provided sufficient encouragement in most cases.

The same will be true in the North. Allowing Northern schools to continue to violate the law only encourages the belief that they need never obey it. The Civil Rights Commission also advocates use of federal funds to help Northern schools desegregate and denial of federal funds to schools that refuse to do so. The Nixon-Ford Administration has relied upon voluntary compliance with the law, but that method has failed in the North as it failed in the South. It is time for the Ford Administration to decide that the law and the Constitution apply to the North as well as the South.

DAYTON DAILY NEWS
Dayton, Ohio, March 12, 1975

It was just a day after the local U.S. District court ordered a desegregation plan that may not integrate Dayton schools (and won't integrate them much even if it works) that the U.S. Civil Rights commission issued its report commemorating 20 years of school desegregation and called for stepped-up political, legal and moral leadership against school segregation particularly in the North.

That means us. Or it should. As the civil rights commission reasserted, the mutual, black-white experience of integrated schooling is the best route yet found —indeed, about the only route — that eventually promises a racially agreeable society instead of the racially antagonistic, perhaps violent, one that could tear this country apart.

Not so ironically, the South is doing much better than the North. Nearly half of its black kids are now studying in thoroughly integrated situations, and many of the remainder are in schools that are pretty much integrated. But more than 70 per cent of the North's black kids remain in classrooms and schools as deeply segregated as the Jim Crow systems of the Old South ever achieved.

The problem is partly legalistic. The law against formal segregation is clear, the solution straightforward. The law against the North's fuzzier de facto segregation is uncertain, and it has been made additionally weak by the falsely named Equal Educational Opportunity act that Congress passed last year.

That new act hampered U.S. District Judge Carl Rubin in his order here. Or he let it hamper him. The appeal will decide which. The act asserts, without the justification of evidence, that "the neighborhood is the appropriate basis for determining public school assignment." It bars busing except where it is necessary to satisfy the law.

Congress, when it adopted the act, understood that its mishmash of conflicting language was mainly for political purposes. It let the lawmakers show off against busing, without actually slashing tires. If the courts take the act more seriously than Congress — and perhaps they must — its effects will be pernicious everywhere, as they have already been here.

But whatever the legal impediments and uncertainties, the problem is mainly political and moral. The voices that once dared Americans to the high moral purpose of racial justice have become silent — killed, as Martin Luther King's was, or fatigued and despairing. In their place, the white backlash has established itself, and hearing its crack, the politicians have catered or equivocated or run.

The racial challenge facing the nation—facing Dayton — is different in only one important way from what it was a decade ago. We have 10 years less time.

ST. LOUIS POST-DISPATCH
St. Louis, Mo., March 13, 1975

The U.S. Civil Rights Commission has surveyed 20 years of progress and lack of same since the Supreme Court ordered public school integration, but it is the future prospect that is alarming. Without positive action, the commission asserts, racial segregation is likely to increase in America's urban centers.

Who can dispute that? The nation has not had positive action since Richard Nixon became president. And the cities have constantly grown blacker, and the suburbs whiter. The schools have been affected, of course, but so has everything else. The old color line has been drawn in new places. Minorities generally can cross it only by paying a toll, which is to say, they can move from ghetto to suburb if they have money.

Because of economic conditions, the movement of minorities into majority situations is less likely now than it was a few years ago. White America's recession is black America's depression. Twice as many blacks as whites are jobless. The Government says 41 per cent of all young blacks lack jobs; others put the figure at 65 per cent.

That is part of the racial imbalance, and there are other illustrations. About 30 per cent of black families earned more than $10,000 a year in 1973 but one third lived in absolute poverty. In a decade 800,000 Negroes did move to the suburbs but 2,800,000 more were added to the overcrowded central cities. There are more than 2900 black elected officials in the nation but that is less than 2 per cent of the total.

Finally, it might be noted that while 65 per cent of all blacks in their twenties are high school graduates, 63 per cent of the black children still attend predominantly black schools. The Civil Rights Commission puts the figures at 71 per cent in Northern cities and about 50 per cent in the South which, by contrast, has made a greater accommodation to its minority.

The commission focuses on schools: it insists that school desegregation remains the most certain guarantee of equal opportunities in education and of constructive race relations. It urges the Government to set a uniform standard for measuring each school system's advance toward integration; it reminds the Government, ironically enough, that it should enforce existing laws. And it warns that more controversial busing may be required.

Yet, because busing seems so controversial, it should be apparent that more is wrong than segregated schools. When 43 per cent of the country's school children are bused, but only 4 per cent are bused to interracial schools, the constant controversy over the latter suggests that the nation has not really made up its mind to attack its historic problem of racism.

The Civil Rights Commission urges one further step: that the President issue an executive order to pool federal resources to bring about desegregation, and that he name one official to direct the use of these resources. So massive a problem as national disunity might, indeed, be thought to call for a massive effort. But the problem of leadership remains, and when presidents are less than enthusiastic, no subordinate official can do much.

The last President who understood the evil of racism and the need to unite the nation was Lyndon Johnson. His attempt at domestic leadership was tragically undone by his war policy. Yet if America is to return to the attack against its destructive racial division, it will need a leader, and it will need one in the White House.

THE ROANOKE TIMES
Roanoke, Va., March 20, 1975

Law and Sociology...

What has happened in 20 years of school desegregation illustrates a good rule: No argument is completely wrong. In the most contrary proposition there is an element of truth. The angry critics of the Supreme Court decision in *Brown v. Board of Education* (1954) are being proved right in their argument that the decision should not have turned on sociology and psychology.

The philosophical 1954 Supreme Court decision had footnotes on work by Dr. Kenneth Clark, New York psychologist, and by the Swedish sociologist Gunnar Myrdal. Their authority was used to work out the proposition that "Separate educational facilities are inherently unequal." Blacks themselves have been the first to question that proposition by insisting on something separate—black studies in public schools; whole departments, courses and degrees, complete with separate faculties and dormitories, in colleges.

The Clark and Myrdal findings, while containing some truth, might not have matured enough to deserve being cemented into the law. Certainly anyone old enough to remember the expectations of 1954 and 1955 realizes that the predicted harmonies and gains for education have not taken place. Instead, public school systems in many localities are simply being torn apart.

The trickest sentence in *Brown* was this: "Whatever may have been the extent of psychological knowledge at the time of Plessy v. Ferguson, this finding is supported by modern authority." Plessy v. Ferguson did not mention psychology at all. The dissenting opinion dealt with segregation as a matter of right. The late Justice Harlan, father of one of the justices in the *Brown* case, began by saying: *"In respect of civil rights, common to all citizens, the Constitution of the United States does not, I think, permit any public authority to know the race of those entitled to be protected in the enjoyment of such rights."*

How right Justice Harlan was! How much better the United States would be today if, starting in 1896, railroads, buses, industries, the police, government agencies—and the school boards—had ignored race as something they were not permitted to know. From 1896 to 1960's, school buses would not have taken black children past all-white (and usually superior) schools to distant (and usually inferior) schools. And from 1967 to this day, school children would not be bused back and forth to meet some mathematical ratios of races. Race would have been ignored in both situations.

In working itself out of the wrong 8 to 1 decision in *Plessy v. Ferguson*, the Supreme Court ignored wisdom of the ages already plainly written in the Constitution and relied on then-current belief that: "Separate educational facilities are inherently unequal." That might be true in some places and at some times. It has not been proved enough to warrant elevation to constitutional law. The doctrine has brought the Supreme Court back to its starting point: school assignments based on race.

... Proving the Point

Practical proof is at hand to reinforce the proposition of the above editorial: That it was wrong to base the Supreme Court desegregation decisions of 1954 and 1955 on then-current beliefs about sociology and psychology.

Where desegregation law has been based on a plain finding of Constitutional right and wrong, it has been successful: in restaurants, bus stations, airplanes, railroads, civic gatherings and in the voting booth. Successes have not been astounding in housing, but they have been scored, and blacks are working in places and at levels they were not found in before the 1960s.

Even in the areas where success has been relatively modest, such as house-purchases in suburban generally white areas, there is an attitude of apology for an attempt to disguise discrimination. There are a lot of problems and a debate about quotas in job allotments. But there is almost a universal agreement that it is wrong, a violation of the Constitution, to make choices in the economy on the basis of race.

Only in the area of schools is there still fierce and disheartening disagreement. There, choices are forcibly and specifically based on race!

The Supreme Court has come full circle in its attempt to prove that first proposition: "Separate educational facilities are inherently unequal." That may be true in some instances and at some times. It has not been proved long enough or universally enough to deserve a place in constitutional law.

The forthcoming retirement of U.S. Supreme Court Justice William O. Douglas (which is assumed because of his illness) may give the Supreme Court a new majority and a new will to get back on the right track. If it doesn't there will be new support for the worst remedy of all: an anti-busing amendment to the Constitution.

Democrat Chronicle
Rochester, N.Y., March 17, 1975

Twenty years after the U.S. Supreme Court struck down the separate but equal doctrine, public schools in the northern United States are more segregated than those in the south. Greater Rochester is no exception to the rule.

In the South today, more than 46 per cent of black students attend predominently white schools, as compared with less than 19 per cent 20 years ago.

But in the North, nearly three-fourths of all black children attend schools which are substantially segregated, and many white children have practically no contact with fellow students of another race.

Let's look at some statistics from the 1973-74 school year for schools in the Rochester metropolitan area:

Where, for instance, could there be a school more segregated than the City of Rochester's School 2, which last year was 99.6 per cent black? Or a school more segregated than Gates-Chili's Warren Harding School, which last year had 671 white children and no minority children of any kind?

The city's School 4 did not have a single white child in attendance in 1973-74. But it did have nine Spanish-surnamed children attending classes with its 611 blacks.

More than three thousand city elementary school children last year attended schools which were more than 95 per cent black.

THE U.S. COMMISSION on Civil Rights, in deploring deepening northern segregation, recommends that federal school construction aid be withheld from districts not complying with integration standards it is now devising.

But the trouble is that, with school populations declining, few schools are being built, so that leverage would not be very strong even were it approved. There is a better way.

Segregation can be ended best by voluntary local action to break down racial divisions in all aspects of community life. Before such progress can be made in Rochester however, people will have to talk about segregation again. Somehow they've stopped.

City School District is now considering moves which could have a great effect on racial balance . . . the closing down of buildings which have too few students. Yet the issue is getting practically no public discussion at all.

A proposal by school board member Brenda Fraser to create a task force to discuss the issue was voted down. And nobody, so far, is suggesting that the decisions be made in ways which would provide a little better racial mix.

So into the defending silence on the subject of racial integration, let us introduce some ringing phrases from the Civil Rights Commission's recent report:

"Separate remains unequal," the Commission said. "Integration must move forward for moral and legal reasons, irrespective of the difficulties along the way."

Who will be brave enough to help move integration forward here?

The Courier-Journal

Louisville, Ky., March 19, 1975

PRACTICALLY SPEAKING, the U.S. Civil Rights Commission's call for a coordinated federal initiative to fully enforce school desegregation is hardly likely to be implemented, given President Ford's willingness to embrace the Nixonian view that equal rights are good unless they might cost an election.

But the principle is sound. The federal government's abysmal failure to enforce a string of Supreme Court decisions dating back more than 20 years has compounded the enormously sensitive task of implementing desegregation plans in countless communities. The furor over busing has been fanned to the point that the real goal of ending second-class citizenship for blacks and other ethnic minorities has been obscured.

Can we, as a nation on the eve of our bicentennial, find our way back to the equalities our founders proclaimed? If we do, clearly the leadership won't come from Washington, where the civil-rights legacy of Presidents Truman, Kennedy, Johnson and even Eisenhower has been largely forgotten as the North suddenly realized that it wasn't immune.

So the leadership, if there is to be any, must come from people of goodwill and conscience elsewhere. Why not from such a place as Louisville?

At a crossroads

Obviously, school desegregation in metropolitan Louisville, as we move toward the elusive goal of becoming a color-blind society, will be shaped to a great extent by the national mood. But this poses all the more challenge, for a city that in 1956 became the focus of national attention for its voluntary and peaceful compliance with *Brown v. Board of Education,* to once more reaffirm a standard of conscience for an America still at odds with itself.

That the nation seems at a crossroads on school desegregation is evident. Last fall's violence in Boston has disappeared from headlines, but armed state and local police still give South Boston the look of an occupied military zone. President Ford has publicly disagreed with a federal judge's busing order; and another federal judge, for the third time in four years, is compelled to order the U.S. government to enforce school desegregation requirements in 16 states, including Kentucky.

A renewed effort is expected in Congress — this time supported by part of the House Democratic leadership — to pass an anti-busing amendment to the Constitution; and the odds that such an effort will succeed may be better than in the past. One-third of the

states have passed resolutions calling for a national constitutional convention to outlaw busing. Kentucky joined those ranks last year.

The public furor over busing unfortunately ignores, as the Civil Rights Commission pointed out last week, that the country, and the South particularly, have made enormous strides in school integration since the 1954 Supreme Court ruling. Much remains to be done, especially in Northern and Border states, where the number of minority students attending predominantly white schools has increased less than one per cent since 1968. But in the South, more than 46 per cent of black students attend predominantly white schools, compared with only 19 per cent in 1968. In addition, the number of black high school and college graduates has tripled, according to the rights commission.

The Louisville example

Southern school desegregation, however, was accomplished under the almost puritanical eye of the North and with a federal government commitment much stronger than it is now. The Civil Rights Commission's call for a federal initiative to enforce the law is precisely what's needed if school desegregation is to work at all. But the fact that the commission even had to issue such a plea (which is likely to fall upon deaf ears in Washington) also illustrates how far we have strayed in the seven years since the Nixon administration turned busing into a code word and made obedience to the law subservient to political expediency.

It was in a similar climate of opposition that Louisville drew national headlines nearly 20 years ago. That was when the late city school superintendent, Omer Carmichael, and the city government showed the rest of an uneasy nation how quiet desegregation of the schools could be accomplished. Now, the city system will shortly become part of the Jefferson County school district, but the same opportunity exists for the successor, merged district to set a national example once more.

The opportunity exists, that is, if the administrative and elected leadership of the newly merged district will resist the temptation of part-time integration, and if elected city and county leaders are responsible enough to avoid demagoguery and instead to make it known that the full weight of local government is behind enforcing the law.

It is one thing to stand up for the neighborhood school and to oppose the obvious inconveniences of busing children to schools in other neighborhoods. It's quite another to

say that these are obstacles that should stand in the way of ensuring that every child, regardless of his skin color, has the opportunity for equal education.

Opposition to court-ordered desegregation often seeks refuge in the mountain of academic studies that show busing to be beneficial or detrimental, as the case may be, to black and white children. A recent survey of desegregation research from the University of Massachusetts, for example, concluded that, while all the evidence isn't in, the impact of desegregation on the nation's children "must be judged neither a demonstrated success nor a demonstrated failure." Somewhat belatedly, the Civil Rights Commission has asked for funds for a Rand Corporation study of the desegregation impact on children in 1,600 school districts. That study will take six years.

The real goal

While such a study obviously will be useful, the rights commission itself notes that the outcome simply doesn't matter that much. That may sound closed-minded, but, as the commission says, "decisions affecting desegregation rest on legal and moral grounds, rather than on scientific research, regardless of its results."

The commission also reminds a nation that needs reminding that the underlying philosophy of the 1954 Supreme Court decision was not that blacks would somehow be better off by associating with whites, although true desegregation does presume that each race will benefit by association with the other. The commission quotes from a 1970 decision by the U.S. 4th Circuit Court of Appeals, in which the court said that "relegation of blacks to separate facilities represents a declaration by the state that they are inferior and not to be associated with." The court went on to call separate schools a "living insult to the black children."

Eradication of that dual educational standard is a goal that will be easy to lose sight of as this community comes to grips with U.S. Judge James Gordon's desegregation order. While a final desegregation plan is unlikely to be implemented until a year from this fall, the more critical time for developing the kind of community involvement that surely could avoid another Boston is now.

Louisville has a rich heritage as the nation's conscience on school integration. It would be tragic if that opportunity to once more lead the way were lost through a failure of local government and school leadership to show the difference between what's comfortable and what's right.

The Cleveland Press

Cleveland, Ohio, March 14, 1975

It is hard now to remember the emotionalism that swept Cleveland a decade ago over school integration — the marches, picketing, sit-ins, even the death of a minister in a demonstration at a school construction site.

The emotionalism is largely gone. But the issue remains.

The Greater Cleveland Interchurch Council and the Institute of Urban Studies of Cleveland State University have invited 150 community leaders to a conference Tuesday to discuss it.

These days many blacks have cooled on integration. They prefer to develop a separate black identity and to use available money for improving black schools rather than busing students to white neighborhoods.

Many whites remain violently opposed to integration, especially if it involves busing.

Boston's experience in the last few months is evidence of that.

The U.S. Supreme Court, by a 5-to-4 decision in a Detroit case, has apparently ruled out busing between central cities and suburbs, although the scope of its decision will not be clear until rulings are made in other cases.

In Cleveland, an integration suit filed by the NAACP is still awaiting trial in Federal Court, and it will be years before there is a final ruling. School officials are unfortunately using the pending suit as an excuse to avoid talking about the problem.

Finally, even many backers of integration are beginning to have doubts. Certainly the troubles at Collinwood High School and several suburban schools, most recently Maple Heights High, are evidence that bringing races together does not in itself bring understanding.

In the face of all these objections, certain facts remain:

BLACK STUDENTS who attend segregated schools do less well than those in integrated schools. On top of their other disadvantages, they get a second-class education.

WHITE STUDENTS who attend all-white schools miss the chance to learn about other people. Their segregated world is reinforced by a segregated education.

In calling the conference, the council and the institute did not suggest they had any easy solution. Frankly, neither do we.

But we applaud them for reminding us and the community of a problem that will not go away and yet, we firmly believe, is one that, black and white together, we shall overcome.

The State

Columbia, S.C., March 20, 1975

PREJUDICE is reputed to be a dirty word in federal circles these days, except when it is applied against the South.

That conclusion is inescapable when one considers recent developments which obviously aim at crucifying the South all over again on the false cross of "civil rights —" especially as they relate to school desegregation.

South Carolina and the South generally have made astounding progress in achieving a genuine if often grudging compliance with the federal government's judicial, legislative, and administrative requirements for race mixing in the public schools. Indeed, the progress toward true desegregation in the South not only has surpassed but has shamed the rest of the nation. One need look only at such strongholds of liberalism and tolerance as New York City and Boston to appreciate the difference between Southern performance and Northern resistance.

Yet despite the South's demonstrably better record, federal harassment of the region continues unabated; indeed it is becoming accentuated. A federal district judge in the District of Columbia ruled just last week that a number of school districts in the South (including South Carolina) have not achieved an acceptable racial balance in the distribution of students.

And, in something of a novel departure from the traditional American concept that a person is innocent until proved guilty, Judge John H. Pratt is requiring the school districts to justify the existence of racial ratios which Uncle Sam (that is, Judge Pratt) finds unacceptable. What the judge overlooks is the fact that most of the school districts already have been found in compliance with desegregation standards set by the Department of Health, Education, and Welfare.

But HEW apparently does not itself know what it is doing — unless its aim is the deliberate harassment of school officials in South Carolina and the South. In recent weeks, a number of South Carolina districts have been burdened (the term is inadequate) with the necessity of compiling voluminous data reflecting the racial composition of student bodies, classrooms, faculties, groups involved in extracurricular activities, special groupings by ability, and recipients of disciplinary action.

It becomes apparent that the South once more is under the gun, this time perhaps as a device to divert attention from real school problems in Northern and non-complying states. School officials report that non-Southern states are not being subjected to the same pressures as those being brought to bear against Dixie.

There is a mounting body of educational and lay opinion throughout the nation which questions whether compulsory race mixing in the schools actually serves the true needs of education. The point is debatable, but it cannot be denied that the cause of effective schooling is seriously impaired when federal bureaucrats continue to harass teachers and administrators with paperwork and pressure.

And since the avowed aim of desegregation is to remove discrimination, let it be noted that the South is undergoing considerable discrimination at the hands of HEW and the federal courts.

One is led to believe that if there were no such thing as the South, one would have to be invented to serve as a handy scapegoat for the federal autocrats and bureaucrats who thrive on petty tyranny.

The San Diego Union

San Diego, Calif., March 16, 1975

The U.S. Civil Rights Commission is urging that the federal government continue to use the full force of both the law and the federal purse to achieve greater racial and ethnic integration in American schools. Meanwhile, Congress is being asked to renew the Voting Rights Act of 1965 which forms the basis for federal intervention in state and local election procedures to encourage more participation by minorities.

This is a good time to take stock of the progress that has been made in treating racial problems in our society, and to project the best course to follow to achieve goals that still elude us.

The Civil Rights Commission concedes that the South has responded admirably in wiping out the school segregation which had been enforced for many years by local laws. The focus now is more on segregation which arises from the racial patterns of communities and neighborhoods—patterns determined by individual choice and economics than any deliberate policy of segregation.

The resistance to bussing and redistricting plans, often as vocal from negroes as from whites, has exhibited how much more difficult it is to overcome this kind of racial imbalance in public schools. Sociologists are not of a single mind on whether this kind of forced mixing of pupils is really enhancing educational opportunities or encouraging racial tolerance.

The door to the political process in our country is now so wide open to minorities that it is hard to justify an extension of the 1965 Voting Rights Act. Procedures have been established which hardly need the heavy hand of the federal government to see that they are continued. The spectacular increase in the number of Negroes elected to public office, especially in the South, refutes any argument that politics is dominated by the white majority.

In employment, a federal law passed in 1968 has established firmly the principle that job opportunities must be open without consideration of the race, ethnic background or sex of applicants who can otherwise meet the qualifications. The government's attempt to go beyond this with Affirmative Action programs—which the Civil Rights Commission is encouraging—has put many employers in the awkward position of practicing "reverse discrimination" in hiring and promoting members of minority groups. Along with school bussing plans, such policies can set back the spirit of tolerance rather than nourish it.

The American people can be proud of their collective achievements of the last 20 years in breaking down old patterns of segregation and discrimination. Many prejudices have received the burial they deserve. We have formed a foundation on which to achieve more. We must avoid the danger that too much pushing from Washington could interfere with progress that now has a momentum of its own.

Public Reactions: 1970-71

Colorado

Denver buses dynamited. Nearly one third of Denver's school buses were destroyed or damaged Feb. 6 when at least 12 dynamite bombs exploded under their gas tanks while they were parked overnight in a fenced school lot. There were no injuries.

Some school officials indicated they believed the explosions were the work of whites opposed to the city's arrangement of busing schoolchildren to achieve racial balance.

Denver's acting fire chief said the bombs had been tied together, and in his opinion "it was a strictly professional job." Damage was estimated at $200,000.

South Carolina

Carolina police rout mob. About 100 South Carolina state troopers used riot clubs and tear gas March 3 to rout a mob of angry whites, wielding ax handles and baseball bats, who stormed buses transporting Negro schoolchildren to a formerly all-white school in Lamar, S.C. About 200 white men and women rushed the buses, smashing windows, after they rolled up to deliver 39 students to Lamar High School.

The troopers drove the angry whites away from the buses by lobbing tear gas into the crowd long enough to get the children safely into the school. The mob then rushed the empty buses and overturned two of them. After a final fusillade of tear gas was fired in their midst, the mob dispersed.

Several Negro children received minor injuries from flying glass and the effects of the tear gas. Several troopers and members of the mob also suffered from the effects of the gas fumes. There were no arrests, the troopers said, because they were outnumbered.

A spokesman for Gov. Robert E. McNair said later the troopers would have opened fire with their pistols "if the tear gas had not worked as effectively as it did."

The U.S. attorney for the district, Joseph O. Rogers, said he would seek federal court orders for the arrest of the mob's leaders. A spokesman for the Justice Department said federal marshals were on their way to Lamar to join Federal Bureau of Investigation agents who were already there.

Polls and Studies

Gallup Poll finds 86% oppose busing. The Gallup Poll organization reported April 4 that by nearly an 8-1 margin, people questioned about the busing of schoolchildren said they would oppose the busing of black and white students to achieve racial balance in schools. The final statistics: Those who favored busing totaled 11%, 86% were opposed to it; and 3% said they had no opinion.

Busing role studied. The Southern Regional Council reported May 2 that one of its studies showed that private academies in the South bused more students farther than public schools in the region.

The council, a research and information agency based in Atlanta, Ga., reported its study in the May issue of South Today, a monthly digest of Southern affairs.

The council said it had studied 10 "segregation academies" and found that "public schools in the eight states are busing an average of 49.5% of their pupils and the academies are busing an average of 62%."

The study also reported that the academies were busing their children farther than the area public schools. The authors of the report wrote that "the figures indicated that bused students in public schools are traveling an average of 10.1 miles a day each way and bused students in segregated academies are traveling an average of 17.7 miles each way."

The South

Charlotte, N.C. elections. In Charlotte, the only Negro on the district school board was defeated in a runoff election May 31 that completed a sweep of the board's seats by antibusing candidates. Two other anti-busing candidates were elected to the board May 3. All three winners ran under the banner of the Concerned Parents Association, a local group that had opposed student busing for the Charlotte-Mecklenburg district and advocated a school boycott if the controversial desegregation plan was implemented.

Alabama Primary Runoff. Former Gov. George C. Wallace, 51, won the Alabama Democratic gubernatorial primary election runoff June 2. Wallace campaigned largely on one issue—that his opponent, Gov. Albert P. Brewer, 41, who won more votes than Wallace in the first balloting, was a favorite of the "bloc vote," a code word for the Negro vote. Wallace emerged with a narrow victory —51.5% of the vote to Brewer's 48.5%, or some 32,000 more votes out of more than a million cast.

Wallace, who won 13.6% of the national vote and 32.6% of the Southern vote in the 1968 presidential election as a third-party candidate, challenged President Nixon June 3 to deliver on his "two-year-old unfulfilled pledges to stop busings and school closings and to re-establish freedom of choice as the law of the land in public education." Indicating the possibility of another Wallace presidential bid "if Nixon don't give us back our schools," Wallace said "the Republican party knows it cannot win without the South in the next election and as governor I'll be able to convince them that they should implement their Southern strategy completely."

Georgia Primary. Jimmy Carter, 45, a peanut farmer and businessman polled a surprising 48% of the vote in the Democratic gubernatorial primary to lead former Gov. Carl Sanders, who had 38%. Sanders was backed by most of the state's larger newspapers, politicians and business leaders. A runoff was scheduled.

Another candidate in the field of nine was the state's first black gubernatorial candidate since Reconstruction, lawyer C. B. King, who ran a distant third.

Carter ran a campaign against "the establishment," with asides against school busing and for Alabama's George C. Wallace.

Arkansas Primary. Charleston lawyer Dale Bumpers, 45, won 59% of the vote Sept. 8 to gain the Democratic nomination for governor and halt the comeback bid of former Gov. Orval E. Faubus (1955-67), 60. It was the first try for statewide political office for Bumpers and the first statewide political defeat for Faubus, who sought to make busing in desegregated school districts the major issue. Bumpers contended that busing was not an issue since all candidates opposed it.

Schools in South integrate. More than 200 school districts across the South that had resisted integration since it was ordered by the Supreme Court in 1954 reopened quietly Aug. 31 with newly desegregated classrooms. Nearly 300,000 Negro schoolchildren from Virginia to Louisiana began classes with whites as threatened school boycotts organized by parents protesting desegregation plans failed to materialize.

Despite the compliance in the 200 districts, 175 others continued to be regarded by Nixon Administration officials as holdouts. Most of the 175 recalcitrant districts were involved in litigation on the controversial issue of student busing and other desegregation problems. Some of the others were involved in meetings with government officers in an attempt to dismantle the dual school systems.

(Chief Justice Warren E. Burger announced Aug. 31 that the Supreme Court would consider a broad test of school desegregation measures as its first order of business when the new court term began Oct. 12. He said the court would hear two days of oral arguments on six appeals covering a wide range of desegregation problems.)

School administrators in the 11 Southern states reported that the transition in the 200 districts was orderly and generally peaceful. In Richmond, Va., Gov. Linwood Holton accompanied his 13-year-old daughter to a newly desegregated high school. Holton said it was "hard for a child to change schools" but that his children "go where they are assigned."

In Atlanta and Columbia, S.C., there was peaceful compliance with court-ordered desegregation plans. In Poplarville, Miss., a rural district that in the past had experienced racial clashes over school integration, the schools were peacefully integrated.

Southern educators said that despite the successful integration in most of the schools in the 200 districts, the government still faced two significant problems: the busing issue and the rise of segregated private academies.

The most pressing problem was reported to be opposition to busing. White parents in Augusta, Ga. picketed a newly desegregated school the week of Aug. 24, insisting that their protest had nothing to do with desegregation of the school. They said that they were protesting the busing plans set for their children. The federal courts had handed down busing orders in cities and large towns where all-black schools were located in all-black neighborhoods to increase the incidence of desegregation.

The courts handed down the orders despite requests by officials in the Nixon Administration that busing be kept at a minimum. Parents had joined school administrators in some districts in filing suits and appeals to seek delays in opening their schools until the busing issue was resolved.

The Charlotte-Mecklenburg County, N.C., school board, which had been conducting a series of legal battles to delay implementation of a desegregation plan that called for extensive student busing, was denied a petition for a delay Aug. 25 by Chief Justice Burger. At the same time Burger refused to grant similar delays sought by Winston-Salem, N.C.; Forsyth County, N.C.; Broward County, Fla. and Dade County, Fla. All four districts had asked the chief justice to set aside the busing orders until the Supreme Court decided the busing issue.

Burger's refusal to grant the motions for stays of the orders meant that the busing plans ordered by lower courts for the districts would go into effect before the next regular Supreme Court session.

Officials for the two North Carolina districts said they would reopen their schools on schedule despite widespread opposition to the busing plans.

Burger rejected without comment Aug. 29 a similar appeal submitted by the Richmond, Va. school board. Officials on the Richmond board contended that the the busing plan, which would involve 13,000 students, would cause mass disruptions in the schools.

Charlotte-Mecklenburg schools open. There was little resistance Sept. 9 as the Charlotte-Mecklenburg, N. C. school system, one of the largest in the South, began to reopen its schools under a court-ordered desegregation plan. Although students in only four grades reported back to school, most of them were quietly brought in by a busing plan that had stirred up much community opposition in Charlotte.

Henderson riots. National Guardsmen remained bivouacked Nov. 9 in Henderson, N.C. following four days of sporadic sniper fire and burnings Nov. 5-8 that erupted in the aftermath of a dispute over the county's school desegregation policies. Henderson officials announced Nov. 9 that because of the return of order, a dusk-to-dawn curfew which had been imposed Nov. 6, was lifted.

Police reported that 101 persons had been jailed for curfew violations. Three more were arrested on charges of firearms violations. One fireman was killed Nov. 7 when a gun he was carrying fell to the pavement and discharged, fatally wounding him in the head. Two other persons sustained minor injuries.

Dissatisfaction among Henderson's black community over a school desegregation plan for Vance County was believed to have been the underlying cause of the outbreak. Black leaders had staged protests in Henderson for weeks over the decision by school officials to reopen an all-black school in the community. Black spokesmen charged that the board was trying to evade desegregation by reopening the school.

New Jersey

Busing sparks Trenton violence. Trenton, N.J., public schools were shut down for two days Oct. 29-30 due to racial disorders stemming from the city school board's decision to implement a student busing plan. The board voted Nov. 1 to reopen the schools, and a dusk-to-dawn curfew that had been imposed on Trenton Oct. 29 was ordered relaxed by Mayor Arthur J. Holland.

The violence erupted Oct. 29 when fighting broke out between 100 black and white youths at a school in the city's predominantly Italian section. The fighting spread into the downtown district when bands of black youths surged into the area, hurling bottles at policemen and breaking store windows. State troopers joined local police and county detectives in bringing the disorders to an end.

More than 200 persons were arrested during the three days of disorders. The police reported that most of those arrested were charged with violations of the curfew. More than 25 persons were reported injured, including two policemen.

The fighting was apparently triggered by the board's decision to implement a busing plan to achieve racial balance in the schools. Holland had opposed the plan, which called for the cross-town busing of 100 white and 55 black students.

Trenton's school busing plan voided. New Jersey's state commissioner of education Nov. 14 annulled Trenton's controversial school busing plan in the wake of a boycott by white parents who had kept their children at home rather than have them bused to schools outside their neighborhoods.

The action came a month after racial disorders stemming from dissatisfaction with the busing plan forced the Trenton school board to shut down many of its schools.

In a 26-page decision canceling the plan, Commissioner Carl Marburger said that "meaningful school integration cannot be achieved by the involuntary busing of children in urban areas where the majority of the public school youngsters consist of children of the nation's minority groups." His decision cited "serious procedural defects" in the busing plan as cause for its cancellation.

Under the proposed plan, 55 white children were to be bused to a school with a 95% black enrollment. As part of the plan, about 100 black and Puerto Rican students were to be bused to several predominantly white schools.

1971
South Carolina

3 whites guilty in Lamar rioting. An all-white jury in Darlington County, S.C. Feb. 17 convicted three white men of rioting in connection with an attack on school buses carrying Negro children to newly desegregated public schools in nearby Lamar in March 1970.

The jury of five men and seven women deliberated nearly 22 hours before convicting James D. Marsh, 43; Delmer Kirven, 46; and Jeryl Best, 42, of common law rioting. Kirven was also convicted of assault and battery on a police officer. He and Best were acquitted of charges that they maliciously destroyed property.

Presiding Judge Wade Weatherford Jr. praised the verdict. He said "there is not the slightest shadow of a doubt that there was a riot on March 3, 1970, in this county at Lamar," terming the violence "a day of tragedy."

Weatherford sentenced Kirven March 8 to a year in prison suspended to four months with three years' probation on the riot charge. On the assault and battery conviction he was sentenced to two years, suspended to eight months with three years' probation.

Best was sentenced to two years in prison and fined $1,000. Weatherford said he must serve six months with two years' probation.

Marsh was sentenced to 18 months, with all but four months suspended. He was fined $100 and placed on probation for two years.

South Carolina Gov. John C. West hailed Weatherford's sentencing of the three March 11, saying that "justice is now color blind" in the state.

Mrs. Mitchell

Mrs. Mitchell assails court. Martha Mitchell, wife of Attorney General John N. Mitchell, said April 21 that the Supreme Court "should be abolished" for its decision upholding the constitutionality of busing schoolchildren to achieve racially-balanced schools.

Mrs. Mitchell said "it's absolutely asinine for those nine old men to rule against the people. We should extinguish the Supreme Court. We have no youth on the court, no Southerners, no women—just nine old men."

In another outburst, Mrs. Mitchell called the Washington Evening Star, saying "I have never been so furious. Nine old men should not overturn the tradition of America."

The North and West

Busing resistance in North, West. For the first time since the Supreme Court ordered an end to racial segregation in public education in 1954, resistance to court-ordered integration centered in the North and West as schools reopened for the fall term Aug. 30-Sept. 8.

In the South, which for years had been the citadel of resistance to integrated schooling, newly desegregated schools reopened quietly and without major incident, even those with new busing plans.

Some federal and state officials had voiced fears over the possibility that there would be widespread and turbulent protests over the flood of new busing plans ordered for school districts across the nation. Except in a few communities, there were no extensive protests.

Southern school officials expressed satisfaction with the way in which the latest round of school integration was achieved with a minimum of friction and tension. Unofficial statistics indicated that about 500,000 of the South's school children would be involved in new integration during the 1971-72 academic year.

In San Francisco, Chinese-Americans indicated that they intended to resist a court-ordered busing plan that was to be implemented when the city's schools reopened Sept. 13. The decision to defy the busing plan was made after Associate Justice William O. Douglas of the Supreme Court rejected an appeal Aug. 29 to stop the busing order.

Leaders of San Francisco's Chinese-American community said the busing plan would undermine the cultural integrity of Chinatown's neighborhood education.

Under the plan, 6,500 Chinese-American students were to be among 48,000 youths bused to integrated schools.

More than 1,000 Chinese-American pupils were reported signed up to attend private schools in their neighborhood.

Parents of about 300 children assigned to a new racially-balanced elementary school in Boston refused Sept. 8 to enroll their children in the new school and instead took them to the neighborhood schools they attended the previous term. There was no violence.

In Evansville, Ind., students enrolled in the same schools they attended during the 1970-71 academic year in defiance of a federal order that the district submit a new "racial balance" plan.

Integration took place without incident in Indianapolis, Minneapolis and Kalamazoo, Mich.

Minimum of disruption in the South. Throughout the Southern and Border states most school districts reopened newly desegregated schools with a minimum of disruption. White attendance in formerly all-black schools was lower than expected in some areas of the South, while black registration at formerly all-white schools was near expected levels.

Even in most of the districts where children were riding buses out of their neighborhoods to distant integrated public schools, there was little protest activity.

There were scattered protests in Chattanooga, Tenn., Columbus, Ga., Kannapolis, N.C. and Pembroke, N. C. And in Norfolk, Va., controversy over a court-ordered plan increasing the number of pupils bused to achieve racial integration led the school board to delay for at least a week the reopening of Norfolk's schools.

In Chattanooga, public protests over new integration plans resulted in the absence of more than 3,000 students when the city's schools opened. A bomb damaged a high school Sept. 6, but city and police officials insisted that they had found no relationship between the explosion and the opening of the city's schools. The school hit by the blast was the scene of racial disorders during 1970.

A dynamite bomb damaged two classrooms in a vacant school Sept. 1 in Columbus. Schools in Columbus were set to reopen despite a jurisdictional dispute between a state judge and the federal courts over a desegregation plan.

In Kannapolis, an elementary school was damaged by eight firebombs. Schools remained open Sept. 4.

Indian parents armed with hatchets and machetes staged a demonstration Sept. 2 in Pembroke to protest the busing of their children.

School officials in Norfolk decided Sept. 6 not to reopen the city's schools for at least a week until they worked out a way to implement a new court-ordered busing plan. Under the original plan, 11,000 of Norfolk's 57,000 schoolchildren were bused out of their neighborhoods, but a federal court ordered a new plan under which 18,000 students were to be bused.

The decision to delay reopening the schools was made after Supreme Court Chief Justice Warren E. Burger refused Sept. 5 to grant an injunction to halt the new plan.

In Little Rock, Ark., schools reopened Aug. 30 with new busing and pairing plans which produced a consistent 2-1 white-black ratio throughout Little Rock's 24,000-pupil system. There was no public opposition in the city where federal troops once protected black schoolchildren from angry whites.

More than 110,000 children returned to integrated classrooms in Birmingham, Ala., and in adjacent Jefferson County Aug. 30 without incident. A school spokesman said of the schools' reopening: "We had a little confusion—not much more than on any first day."

Downstate in Mobile, more than 6,000 schoolchildren were bused out of their neighborhoods. Despite a suggestion by Gov. George C. Wallace that the city defy the court-ordered busing plan, the new busing arrangement worked smoothly and did not evoke appreciable opposition.

In Nashville, Tenn., elementary school children registered without incident Sept. 8. There was some opposition, however, to a federal court-ordered busing plan. Nashville school officials attributed some first-day low attendance levels to the antibusing sentiments, but said they were confident that attendance figures would reach expected levels on the first full day of classes.

A final effort to block implementation of the busing plan had failed Sept. 2 when Supreme Court Justice Potter Stewart refused to stay its implementation. Under the plan, about 47,000 of the city's 96,000 pupils were to be bused.

Michigan

Students injured in Pontiac protests. In Pontiac, Mich., eight white students and one black youth were injured Sept. 8 in fights during protests against a busing plan.

The protests in Pontiac over busing were among the most violent in the U.S. Protesters carrying American flags marched in front of the school bus depot Sept. 8 daring bus drivers to run them down. Police arrested nine persons at the depot, but busing opponents vowed to continue their protests. One group, the National Action Group, the center of white opposition to busing in Pontiac, demanded that the schools be closed but the Pontiac school board refused.

Pontiac School Superintendent Dana Whitmer said Sept. 8 that attendance on the second day of classes was about the same as opening day, with 60% of the children attending classes. But the figures showed that a high percentage of white parents were heeding a boycott. More than 75% of Pontiac's 8,000 black students were in classes. Total student enrollment was 24,000.

School buses burned in Pontiac. Arsonists slipped through a chain-link fence Aug. 30 and set firebombs that destroyed 10 school buses parked in a school lot in Pontiac, Mich.

The buses were part of the city's school bus fleet which was to be used to help carry out a court-ordered integration

plan that called for extensive busing. The plan, which would involve the crosstown busing of more than 8,000 schoolchildren, had evoked widespread community opposition.

Attorneys for the Pontiac school board had filed a petition with the Supreme Court Aug. 25 requesting a stay of the order. The board said, however, that it was preparing to meet the busing order if the court did not rule on its petition before classes began Sept. 7.

Klansmen charged in Pontiac bombing. Agents of the Federal Bureau of Investigation arrested six members of the Ku Klux Klan Sept. 9 in connection with the bombing of 10 school buses in Pontiac, Mich.

The six Klansmen were charged with plotting at a statewide meeting of the Klan in July to blow up the buses while they were parked in a Pontiac bus depot. Specifically, the six were charged with conspiracy to violate the public education section of the Federal Civil Rights Act, to violate federal bomb statutes and to obstruct federal court orders.

One of the six charged was Robert E. Miles, 40, who was described as the grand dragon of the Michigan Realm of the United Klans of America.

The five others arrested were Wallace E. Fruit, 29; Alexander J. Distel Jr., 28; Dennis C. Ramsey, 24; Raymond Quick Jr., 24 and Edmund Reimer.

Miles, Reimer and Distel were arrested by FBI agents in the Detroit area. The others were picked up in a car at the Mackinac Bridge.

An affidavit filed in U.S. court in Detroit Sept. 10 charged that the Klansmen also planned to "knock out" a power station in the Pontiac area as a diversion for a full-scale mortar attack on the city's 90-bus fleet.

The affidavit also disclosed that an unpaid undercover agent had been involved with the Pontiac group of the Klan and had reported to the FBI on its activities. The six Klansmen were released on $10,000 bail each.

5 indicted in Pontiac bombing. A federal grand jury in Detroit indicted the former grand dragon of the Michigan Ku Klux Klan and four of his associates Oct. 20 on conspiracy charges in the bombing of 10 school buses in Pontiac, Mich. Aug. 30.

Indicted were Robert E. Miles, Alexander J. Distel Jr., Wallace E. Fruit, Raymond Quick Jr. and Dennis C. Ramsey. Miles was identified as a past grand dragon of the Michigan Klan.

The five were charged with conspiring to intimidate black students in the exercise of their constitutional rights to attend public schools in Pontiac.

Baptist Convention

Nixon urged to back busing. The National Baptist Convention of America, which represented about 2½ million Negro Baptists, called on President Nixon Sept. 11 to declare himself in support of the "law of the land" on school busing.

The convention, meeting in San Francisco, endorsed school busing as a means of furthering racial integration. The convention's leaders sent a telegram to the President expressing the pro-busing views of the 10,000 persons who attended the group's meeting.

In an address to the convention Sept. 9, the Rev. Ralph David Abernathy, president of the Southern Christian Leadership Conference, accused the President of causing much of the turmoil over school integration.

Abernathy said Nixon "has created the climate for the opposition to busing. Those who follow his views have been given moral support to protest."

Gallup Polls

Opposition to busing drops. The Gallup Poll reported Sept. 11 that while an overwhelming majority of Americans continued to oppose the busing of pupils to achieve more racially-balanced schools, there had been some decline in antibusing sentiments since the last poll in March 1970.

In the new survey, involving interviews with 1,525 persons, 18 and older, 18% of those polled said they favored busing to further racial integration. Nearly 76% expressed opposition to busing.

In the March 1970 survey, 14% had said they supported busing, while 81% expressed opposition.

One of the sharpest increases in support of busing was found among college-educated persons, with the proportion nearly doubling since 1970—from 13% to 23%.

76% oppose busing. The Gallup Poll reported Oct. 31 that 76% of the public sample surveyed opposed the busing of pupils to achieve more racially balanced schools.

The polling organization maintained, however, that antibusing sentiments had eased somewhat from a survey in March 1970 when 81% expressed opposition to busing.

According to the latest poll, 18% of the public favored busing, the same as in the previous survey.

200 WHITE MEN AND WOMEN STORM BUSES CARRYING NEGRO CHILDREN

South Carolina state troopers had to use riot clubs and tear gas March 3 to rout a mob of angry whites who stormed buses transporting Negro schoolchildren to a formerly all-white school in Lamar, S.C. About 200 white men and women, wielding ax handles and baseball bats, rushed the buses as they rolled up to deliver 39 students to Lamar High School. Several Negro children were injured by flying glass from smashed bus windows and the effects of the tear gas, but they managed to get safely into the school. The mob then rushed the empty buses and overturned two of them.

South Carolina Governor Robert McNair called the mob's action "unspeakable." State police arrested 13 whites on charges of rioting and prepared warrants against 17 others on the same charges. The Justice Department is investigating the incident.

THE KNICKERBOCKER NEWS
*** UNION-STAR ***

Albany, N. Y., March 5, 1970

Several school buses full of Negro children make their way toward a once all-white school in Lamar, S.C. The children are being taken to the school under an integration order of a federal court.

Suddenly a shouting, cursing crowd of 200 white men and women surrounds the buses, forces them to stop, overturns them, smashes the windows with ax handles and terrifies the children with vile obscenities and shouts like "Let's kill the niggers." Several children are injured by flying glass.

Only the timely intervention of state police prevents much more serious harm to the children. At one point, the outnumbered police prepare to fire into the crowd with their pistols to prevent the mob from getting at the children, if the tear gas barrage fails.

The horrible aspect of this scene in an American city in 1970—16 years after the U.S. Supreme Court ordered integration of public schools "with all deliberate speed"—is that virtually all the 200 white adults who attacked the buses containing Negro children are the so-called "solid citizens" of the community: parents, home owners, working people—you know,

the kind of people who deplore riots and protests (when OTHER people are involved) and who demand "law and order" (enforced, of course, against OTHER people).

South Carolina Gov. Robert E. McNair rightfully described the violence as unspeakable and "defying all human reasoning," adding that he was "equally appalled at those who have helped to create the type of dangerous and inflammatory attitude which makes such an act possible."

That responsibility lies not only with those irrational whites who instigated the cowardly attack against innocent children, but with an attitude, fostered back in Washington, D.C., by an administration that has indicated by word and deed that it's really not very serious about civil rights—an attitude that has led two key administration civil rights aides to quit in disgust and 125 government civil rights lawyers to protest.

And there's a final irony in this depressing episode. The federal judge who ordered the Negro children sent to the former all-white school is Clement F. Haynsworth Jr. Remember him?

Arkansas Gazette.
Little Rock, Ark., March 8, 1970

As we had predicted, the country is being earnestly assured that the beating of Negro school children by a mob of white men *and* women at Lamar, Darlington County, S.C., did not in any way represent the thinking of the good white people of South Carolina. As might have been expected, the good white people of the South Carolina community concerned have gone on to do their best toward making their defenders' position untenable.

The dust had barely settled and the black children's blood been stanched when Robert Mardian — a former aide to Barry Goldwater who recently was named as staff director of Vice President Agnew's segregation-loaded committee to "ease" desegregation in the South — was issuing a statement saying that a United States attorney on the scene had just called him to report "feelings of remorse among the townspeople * * *: they are ashamed of their own conduct."

Next day the remorseful Lamar citizenry was out again in force to cheer the best known of the defendants in the case — the leader of a local "freedom of choice" committee — upon his release from jail, under modest bond.

Following, in the same vein, is a random sampling of statements made by the penitents of Darlington County the day after Mr. Mardian's "remorse" statement, as reported from the scene by news services and passed on here without editorial comment, "slanted" or otherwise:

"You nigger-loving highway troopers make me sick," one woman screamed at one of the state troopers escorting the prisoners.

One man in the crowd commented: "I wonder if they're [Darlington County sheriff's deputies] Communists. I've got more respect for a Communist than I have for those nigger-loving deputies.

Another white man interrupted her [Mrs. Jeryl Best, wife of the bailed out freedom-of-choice leader] to say, "God made man white and he made them black and he did not mean for them to mix."

"We have been betrayed by our city leaders" [Mrs. Best herself.]

The Greenville News

Greenville, S. C., March 8, 1970

Acrimonious political debate over who was to blame for the Lamar school outrage makes a bad situation worse and delays repairing the damage done to South Carolina.

In a sense the continuing attempts of Democrats and Republicans to saddle each other with the onus underscores the real gravity of the situation. All of them deplore the white mob's attack on peace officers and Negro school children. All of them realize it is a dangerous situation.

But the partisan controversy over blame-fixing actually obscures the real problem by diverting attention from rational assessment of the damage and a search for realistic ways to repair it.

Make no mistake about it. The Lamar mob action by 150 to 200 people has created a grave situation for South Carolina.

Lamar is the first serious breach of our people's strict adherence to law and order and to the fundamentals of human decency and bi-racial respect which hitherto had characterized this state's record in the nationwide racial crisis.

It reveals the existence of an ugly disregard for the processes of law and for human decency on the part of enough people to create chaos in certain localities.

The cause of law and order — the only defense of all South Carolinians, white and black, against crime and anarchy — has been hurt.

Externally the Lamar episode has blunted and may have reversed the effort to restore sanity to the handling of school affairs, including desegregation.

Much of the national goodwill for South Carolina created by the recent heroic actions of thousands of Greenvillians has been lost because of the cowardly attack by a mere handful of people in Lamar.

Instead of moving forward in the long, difficult struggle to restore common sense to school affairs, we are once again on the defensive in the national arena.

And that is a tragedy for all citizens of this state, black and white.

The damage must be repaired. It can be, if and when the political leaders of this state quit the silly business of finger-pointing and get down to tin tacks.

The politicians of all parties — and all South Carolinians — must realize that some things need to be done and done quickly.

The State of South Carolina has to realize that decent Negro citizens now have been given real reason to fear for their safety and the safety of their children. It's that simple and that terrible.

In order to remove the fear, the state has to make special efforts to show Negro citizens it can and will protect their persons and their homes and their right to attend the public schools of this state.

Responsible officials of both major parties should confer immediately with Negro leaders to see what special efforts might be helpful. A good faith offer to establish around-the-clock protective patrols in Negro communities of the affected area might be of some benefit, even if it would be costly.

In addition, there can be no let-up in the state's efforts to arrest and prosecute those who participated in the mob action. The open violations of state laws and the elemental codes of human decency must be redressed.

South Carolina also has an obligation to remove the publicly-expressed suspicion that the action of lawmen during the Lamar outbreak was not forceful enough because no on-the-spot arrests were made. The charge is that the peace officers would not arrest white people.

The state should take steps, even to the point of bringing in nationally-respected riot control authorities to explain in detail to the Negro citizens of this state why the officers acted as they did at Lamar.

The reason really is simple. Those officers could not disperse and make on-the-spot arrests without abandoning the Negro children and exposing them to grave danger. Their first responsibility was to protect the lives of those children.

They had to remain in a compact, defensive shield around them in the face of the mob's numerical superiority.

The lawmen on the scene followed nationally-accepted riot procedures by protecting the children first and taking pictures of the mob in order to make arrests later.

It is evident that many citizens do not understand the tactical situation and the state ought to make it clear to them in every possible way.

The central fact is that the Lamar incident challenges the state to show to all its citizens, regardless of race, that its protection extends to all alike and that its law and order is even-handed. That is a serious matter in these times of turmoil.

The overwhelming majority of law-abiding citizens of South Carolina cannot allow the current political controversy over Lamar to obscure the hard facts of the situation.

Soon, we hope, the politicians, all of them, will get around to taking a firm position against any repetition of the Lamar tragedy.

Frankly, Lamar has modified our view. Awhile back we commended our senior United States senator for what we then thought was a beautiful law-and-order statement to the effect that South Carolinians do not need to be reminded to obey the law. Now we know they do need to be reminded to follow the law.

All our political leaders need to reassess positions as a result of the Lamar incident. We believe they will when they have tired of the finger-pointing game.

State officials must stick courageously to South Carolina's long-standing policy of keeping its own peace and operating its own schools without trying to shift responsibility for enforcement of state law and maintenance of state institutions to the federal government. Any vacillation by state officials in this area is disturbing.

We still have the hope and the faith that South Carolinians will insist that "ax handle" politics and "ax handle" rhetoric will not be translated again into "ax handle" mob action.

THE CINCINNATI ENQUIRER
Cincinnati, Ohio, March 6, 1970

THE INEXCUSABLE mob action that imperiled the safety of 39 Negro youngsters being bused to Lamar (S. C.) High School this week recalled to mind the equally militant and lawless resistance at Little Rock (Ark.) High School.

On the earlier occasion, Gov. Orval Faubus winked at the resistance, and President Eisenhower responded by dispatching paratroopers to the scene. This week, Gov. Robert E. McNair recognized his responsibility and sent state troopers to Lamar to restore order.

It is easy to imagine that the 200 South Carolinians who made school children the target of their viciousness this week would be the first to characterize themselves as rock-ribbed defenders of law and order. That, at least, is the mask they wear in protesting the excesses of civil rights activists.

But they cannot have it both ways.

If they recoil from lawlessness on the part of Negroes seeking what they feel to be their rights, they must refrain from lawlessness themselves. And if they are opposed to governmental policies they should use the legal and political remedies available to them. By refraining from doing so, by choosing instead to make and execute the law, they have made a mockery of their self-righteousness and incensed the nation in the process.

The Birmingham News
Birmingham, Ala., March 5, 1970

The only good thing that anyone can say about the violence at Lamar, S. C., High School this week is that it is the exception, not the rule.

Regrettably, some people in other regions will sieze upon a white mob's attack on Negro school children as proof of their darkest suspicions about the South. But no one can fairly use this isolated incident to indict all of the people of South Carolina or the South as a whole.

The very fact that such a reprehensible thing can be called an isolated incident is evidence that the overwhelming majority of white Southerners, contrary to earlier warnings of widespread violence if schools were desegregated, have accepted desegregation and have sought to implement it peaceably.

There have been and still are, to be sure, protests against what many consider to be unreasonable conditions imposed by federal agencies and courts. But most of the leaders of those protests have insisted at the same time that the search for relief should follow legal, orderly channels and that violence and lawlessness cannot be condoned.

The people who attacked the school children at Lamar did themselves or their "cause" no service. They may instead have undone much of what's been accomplished in recent months toward winning a more sympathetic understanding of the South's position.

That, needless to say, is less important than the simple revulsion any citizen of any race must feel toward attacks on school children by adult mobs.

White Southerners especially, since many of those who participated in this outrage may have considered themselves acting in behalf of the white South, must join President Nixon and Gov. Robert McNair of South Carolina in condemning what happened at Lamar. Those responsible can't be too proud of themselves.

Let no one—*no* one—get the idea that violence is an acceptable form of protest, whatever the color or the cause of the protester.

The Morning Star
Rockford, Ill., March 7, 1970

What happened when a busload of black children arrived at their newly-integrated school in Lamar, South Carolina, this week may create lifelong hatred for all whites.

What the children saw was not just a strange new school. There also was a screaming mob of 200 white adults, including women, some bearing clubs and chains, awaiting their arrival.

The frenzied mob attacked the bus. Police used tear gas to fight off the attackers of the helpless children. The bus was upset and its windows smashed. No children were injured. But it was a disgraceful performance from beginning to end.

Regardless of individual feelings about school integration or other racial matters, there is no justification for intimidation of school children, black or white, by mobs, black or white.

Police in Lamar made no arrests on the spot — they didn't explain why — but 28 of 30 persons identified as participants in the attack on the bus were arrested the next day.

Violent dissent is becoming altogether too common in America. It must be ended. There is no place for violent dissent in a nation founded upon concepts of freedom, equality and justice. That tactic should and must be totally rejected.

Vice President Spiro Agnew described the South Carolina action as "reprehensible and entirely senseless."

A White House spokesman said the FBI is involved in the investigation and that the President "deplores and opposes" the action of the white adults who attacked the school bus.

The wounds of the Lamar, South Carolina, action are deep and are likely to be lasting. Long-range effects on the Negro children, the innocent victims of the Lamar incident, are the most tragic.

WINSTON-SALEM JOURNAL
Winston-Salem, N. C., March 8, 1970

THE argument over what federal marshals did or did not do when a white mob ran amok in Lamar, South Carolina, has descended into partisan outrage. Sen. Strom Thurmond claims Gov. Robert McNair should have called for federal assistance in dealing with the rioters. McNair points out that a federal marshal (a Republican appointee) and his deputy marshals sat in a car on the Lamar school grounds throughout the riot — while state troopers were busy defending a federal court order to integrate the school.

Moreover, said the governor, Attorney General Mitchell and the local U. S. attorney were warned in advance that there might be trouble at Lamar; but nothing was done to bring a larger number of federal marshals to the scene.

The Justice Department argues that its federal marshals were sent in merely as "observers" — but this won't wash. The department was forwarned about the possibility of disorder. The issue at stake was enforcement of a federal court order; and the department failed to provide federal law officers to enforce it. This failure culminated in the rare spectacle of southern state policemen protecting children affected by such a court order while officials of the federal government sat and watched.

President Nixon and Mr. Agnew and others in the administration deplore the violence at Lamar. This is commendable. We all deplore it. But the failure of the administration to send more than an ineffectual shadow force to Lamar High School could be construed, in itself, as part of the White House's attempt to be all things to all men.

Sooner or later, Mr. Nixon is going to have to break some eggs to make his omelette. He cannot escape responsibility for enforcing the laws of the land, nor can he escape the onus that will arise among those who oppose these laws. This is what being a President is all about — the buck stops with him, the responsibility is fixed in his executive authority, and all the rhetoric in the world won't change this.

The Courier-Journal

Louisville, Ky., March 6, 1970

THE RACIAL CONFLICT in Lamar, South Carolina, was like a montage of racial conflict of 10 years ago. White adults turned out to prevent the integration of local schools, overturned two school buses, and engaged in physical clashes with Negro pupils and police. The white adults were armed with ax handles, chains and bricks. Several Negro pupils suffered cuts and bruises and at least two police officers were injured slightly. The white demonstrators were finally dispersed with tear gas.

Governor McNair ordered the schools closed until order could be restored and called the incident "unspeakable."

It was dreadful enough, to be sure. That it occurred shouldn't be too surprising. The hard-core segregationists of the type that caused the violence have been there all along. They have been subdued, more or less, in recent years because they knew such behavior would not be tolerated, as a matter of national policy. The actions of the Nixon administration, however, have kindled new hope in the hearts of the segregationists; the words of spokesmen for the administration have fed this hope. Is it any wonder that the racists are becoming more aggressive?

The Nixon administration has embarked on a deliberate policy of slowing down school desegregation in the South. Spokesmen for the administration, including Vice President Spiro Agnew, have appeared before Dixie audiences and used all the code words of segregationist politics, have implied that they are in sympathy with those who want to preserve segregation awhile longer, have forced out people in Washington who tried to enforce the law of the land and the mandate of the Supreme Court on school desegregation, have, in short, tried to turn back the clock on racial justice, and have succeeded in doing just that in Lamar.

Having done all this the administration responds to its consequences by expressing shock and dismay. In the aftermath of Lamar, Mr. Agnew piously announces: "I want to make it clear that this administration does not condone and will not tolerate violence resulting from the lawful desegregation of schools anywhere."

Perhaps the administration means it. White suspects have been arrested in connection with the Lamar flare up, and state and federal law enforcement people are on the scene. Is it possible that top people in the Nixon administration see no connection between administration policies on school desegregation and the violence in Lamar?

It is quite possible, judging from statements emanating from the White House staff, and in a way this lack of comprehension is more disturbing than if the administration were following some grand design in racial politics.

Apparently, the two White House aides who have Mr. Nixon's ear on racial problems are Harry Dent and John D. Ehrlichman, and that is a bad combination. Harry Dent is Strom Thurmond's man in the White House; John D. Ehrlichman is the President's chief adviser on domestic affairs on the White House staff.

It is safe to assume that Mr. Dent at least knows what he is trying to do, and that is to throw every possible obstacle in the way of school integration in the South. Mr. Ehrlichman doesn't even seem to understand the problem. He is either naive or confused. Telling reporters that Mr. Nixon would soon issue a statement to clarify the administration's stand on school integration—and God knows it needs clarifying—Mr. Ehrlichman gave the gentlemen of the press a sample of *his* thinking on the issue.

Mr. Ehrlichman said he opposes the integration of Negro and white pupils in public schools if it only serves the social purpose of mixing the races and does not improve overall education standards. Now there's some food for thought. His elaboration didn't help. "I think," he said, "that when a change in the racial makeup of the schools is undertaken for a purely social end, that's a misuse of the schools."

Who is going to define when integration is serving a social rather than an educational purpose? If school desegregation is ordered because it is the law of the land, but if it doesn't improve educational standards (nor lower them), what then?

Is it busing that Mr. Ehrlichman has in mind? Southerners resisting school integration are making a lot of noise about busing. It is a phony issue. The truth is that as integration has increased in the South busing of students has *declined*. To put it another way, busing has been used on a large scale to preserve segregated school systems in many areas of Dixie.

Achieving genuine school integration is difficult in many parts of the country, North and South. We do not minimize the complexities and subleties of the problem. What is lacking, however, in too many places is a good faith effort to work out the problem. The Nixon administration has only added to the difficulties, and if Mr. Ehrlichman's thinking is representative of the President's then we are in for more trouble.

ARGUS-LEADER

Sioux Falls, S. D., March 6, 1970

The Nixon administration acted wisely to express promptly its sharp distaste of the riot in Lamar, S. C.

The riot was an expression of the attitude that was too prevalent in the Old South —an attitude of mob control without benefit of courts or justice in the treatment of the blacks. It is a form of action that is intolerable by all civilized standards of equality under the law. It revealed the worst of the South.

There was a day when many persons in the South—far too many—failed to recognize the blacks as human beings. They contended that the blacks must be made "to know their place" and resorted to intimidation, midnight raids, mutilation and actual murder to enforce their beliefs. When a crime was committed, they often proceeded to lynch one black or several of them "as a lesson."

That was a horrendous way of doing things and it was responsible in no small degree for the extreme criticism that developed throughout the nation.

The South Carolina episode revealed that a segment of that spirit still exists in benighted areas and most certainly it shouldn't be tolerated. It was good, therefore, that Vice President Agnew spoke out so vigorously in his own forceful way to emphasize the administration's position. It was more than talk, however. It will be supplemented by all the power that federal agencies can develop to make sure that the offenders are prosecuted and punished. It is to be hoped that the administration will have—as we like to believe it will—the full support of the law authorities in the South.

Oregon Journal

Portland, Ore., March 7, 1970

Evidence is all around us that men can behave like mad dogs.

But the vicious attacks by a white mob on Negro children in school buses in Lamar, S.C., boggles the imagination of people who like to believe they live in a civilized country.

The children were saved from serious injury only by the intervention of police. Two buses were overturned after the children had been evacuated.

Nevertheless, events in the wake of this barbarous act seem to prove that the South is not like it used to be in race relations.

Prompt law enforcement steps against the offending whites are being taken, with the issuance of warrants against 30 men on riot charges and the jailing of suspects. Gov. Robert E. McNair, who is quite a different person from Georgia's Gov. Lester Maddox, used the weight of his office to prod state and local authorities into action.

In Washington, Vice President Agnew, whose verbal firepower has been turned in different directions lately, described the mob attack as "reprehensible and entirely senseless." Agnew, who himself has been under fire for allegedly lacking interest in the aspirations of minority peoples, promised "this administration is going to make certain that all children, regardless of color, have equal access to quality education."

Headlines out of the South rarely give an accurate picture of what is happening there. Columnist Joseph Kraft made the surprising comment the other day that even in Georgia Gov. Maddox is losing his grip and that integration is moving steadily forward.

Racial understanding is hurt, of course, by events like that in Lamar, S.C., just as it is when militant blacks threaten or commit violence.

But the day is past when criminal acts by whites against blacks are condoned by white society in general and overlooked by authorities. A sense of shame over that day in Lamar is widely felt among whites in the South as well as in the nation at large.

The Charleston Gazette
Charleston, W. Va., March 9, 1970

Immediately after the shocking and puerile attack by a mob of white parents against a group of Negro school children in Lamar, S. C., both the President and the Vice President denounced what they called the "senseless" violence.

Did it occur to either of them how their own actions have encouraged such violence?

The federal government, which once presented a unified front on desegregation with the Supreme Court calling the turn, now presents instead a mixed bag of confused directives. While the President supports the principle of integration out of one side of his mouth, the other side is busy pandering to the very people who attacked a school bus full of children in South Carolina.

This President who claims to support the principles of racial equality is the same President who named that flaming racial liberal, Spiro T. Agnew, to be his running mate. And also the same President who was able to find no candidate for associate justice of the Supreme Court better qualified than Clement Haynsworth or Harrold Carswell.

God help us all

Des Moines Tribune

Des Moines, Iowa, March 6, 1970

The physical assault by 100 men in Lamar, S.C., on school buses with children in them is enough to make an observer despair of the human race. Gov. Robert McNair of South Carolina called the incident "unspeakable".

His attitude is the one hopeful element in the situation. He tried hard to prevent it, urging South Carolinians to submit to the federal court orders to end racial segregation.

School officials got the 32 black youngsters off the buses before the rioters overturned them — but not before several children suffered cuts and bruises and deeper pain within. Local police and state highway patrolmen ended the violence within a few minutes. FBI men and U.S. marshals were soon on the scene, and arrests by local and federal authorities followed.

Perhaps this incident will galvanize President Nixon, as the Little Rock situation did President Eisenhower, to a more unequivocal stand: enforcing the law of the land and protecting children from abuse.

San Francisco Examiner

San Francisco, Calif., March 9, 1970

IT WAS gratifying to see the authorities in South Carolina spring into action as if they meant it in the disgraceful attack by whites on school buses carrying Negro children.

We in the North have been guilty of derogating the South too much and too often on racial matters without paying due attention to our own shortcomings. Now a deep Southern state, both officially and privately to judge from press dispatches, has reacted with revulsion against an act of blind brutality committed by a band of ignoramuses.

It is a hopeful sign.

Meanwhile, Northerners must remind themselves to stand vigilant against the same breed of redneck, for such, alas, are in our midst.

TULSA DAILY WORLD
Tulsa, Okla., March 5, 1970

A MOB of white persons angered by school desegregation attacked three school buses filled with Negro children at Lamar, South Carolina, Tuesday. Some of the children were hurt—and so was the cause the mob represented.

To say this was a senseless and dangerous adventure is surely an understatement. It was insane—an act of mindless brutality. The persons responsible for it should be brought to justice as an example for others who may be so inclined.

Gov. ROBERT E. McNAIR made it clear that South Carolina does not countenance such violence. Although he has opposed the desegregation orders in his State, he found the attacks on the school children "unspeakable."

"We now see the consequences which result from an open defiance of the law," he said. "We now pay the penalty for the type of disrespect and disregard for authority which has been publicly advocated by many in recent days."

This statement covers the anti-law attitudes on both sides of the desegregation question—and it can be applied to other situations on campuses, around courthouses and wherever serious controversies have erupted. The growing tendency for mobs to lose all restraint goes back to lynch-law days that should be long forgotten.

The children on the bus at Lamar were not responsible for the inroads of integration. But even if they had been, the attack on them would have been indefensible. There are legitimate arguments to be made against busing students to achieve racial balance in schools, but even those who sympathize with that point of view cannot condone an attack on innocent children—or any other violence by an animalistic mob.

THE LINCOLN STAR
Lincoln, Neb., March 5, 1970

It would be too simple—and patently unfair—to suggest that the Nixon administration is to blame for the kind of racial disruption which occurred in Lamar, S.C., this week. But the President's always ambiguous, mostly negative position on school desegregation is certainly a contributing factor in encouraging resistance to the law of the land.

White adults overturned school buses in Lamar this week, injuring a number of black children during the melee which ensued. That kind of assault is only a step away from the ultimate horror of race warfare. If you believe that overstates the case, consider your reaction if they had been your children.

The President has been playing politics with the most dangerous dynamite in America. School desegregation is not an issue which the President should use to make political points. His obscure intransigence, combined with what might most fairly be described as apparent disregard for the special problems of black Americans, will only unleash the awful furies which lie not far below the surface in many American communities.

School desegregation is now the law of the land. The courts have so declared, and what remains is to determine the best and most orderly manner in which to implement the law. Busing is one way to accomplish desegregation — but it is not the only way and, in some cases, no doubt, it is not the best way.

The delicate task of determining the best way to accomplish desegregation is a matter for local school boards if they act in good faith, and for the courts if they do not.

Rather than standing in the way, the President would best serve his country if he provided on this issue, above all issues, that element of presidential authority which he has so often promised—moral leadership.

The Charlotte Observer
Charlotte, N. C., March 6, 1970

Clear-thinking people on both sides of the school desegregation issue in Lamar, S.C., and elsewhere can only condemn the unreasoned violence that occurred in that community on Tuesday.

This shocking attack on school buses containing young children serves no cause except that of the forces of fear and lawlessness. South Carolina Gov. Robert McNair, who termed the mob action "unspeakable," and all good citizens of his state were sickened by the conduct of a few irrational people.

No school problem, indeed no community problem of any kind, is going to be satisfactorily resolved with destruction of property and the terrorizing of children. Federal and state officials have moved swiftly to see that those interfering with court orders and violating laws of the state are brought to justice. Payment of the consequences of such a deplorable action must come for the guilty.

There has been widespread condemnation, and rightly so, of demonstrators on the national scene who have taken the law into their own hands. This has gone so far in recent days that an official as highly placed as the vice president of the United States has called for the newspapers to take the "kooks and demagogues" off the front pages.

But when "law and order" is so clearly threatened by so many elements of our society, including people who are referred to only as "parents" in the vice president's comments on Lamar, the news media cannot and should not bury the facts. The public can deal intelligently with such anarchy only if it is fully appraised of the facts.

Lamar's unhappy experience is not representative of the people of Darlington County or, for the most part, the people of the South. The stark horror of the event there should enable us to keep perspective elsewhere on the problems of school desegregation. Blind emotions and disobedience to law are a volatile combination that can harm even innocent children.

WALLACE WINS ALABAMA RUNOFF ON PLATFORM OF RACIAL BIAS

Former Alabama Gov. George Wallace won the Alabama Democratic gubernatorial primary election runoff June 2, on a platform appealing to racial bias. It was a narrow victory. Wallace received 51.5% of the vote to 48.5% for his opponent, Gov. Albert Brewer. Although considered a political moderate, Brewer had outpolled Wallace and five other candidates in the May primary. In the runoff, Wallace campaigned largely on one issue: that Brewer was a favorite of the "bloc vote," a code word for the black vote.

Amid speculation about his plans for the 1972 presidential election, Wallace said in his victory statement that he might run for president again "if Nixon don't give us back our schools." He challenged Nixon to deliver on his "two-year-old unfulfilled pledges to stop busings and school closings and to reestablish freedom of choice as the law of the land in public education." Said Wallace, "The Republican party knows it cannot win without the South in the next election and as governor I'll be able to convince them that they should implement their Southern strategy completely."

The Birmingham News
Birmingham, Ala., June 3, 1970

One of the most dramatic, emotion-packed—and historic—gubernatorial campaigns in Alabama's history is over. Now is the time for all Alabamians, regardless of which candidate they favored, to unite behind the man a majority has chosen to lead us.

This will be difficult for many, frankly, because of George Wallace's regrettable resort to the race issue in the run-off campaign to overcome the lead compiled by Gov. Albert Brewer in the first primary.

Gov. Wallace's reliance on the "bloc vote" issue reflected a disturbing willingness to divide Alabamians, to set race against race at a time when the state and the nation already are too much divided and when someone is needed to put salve on our wounds, not to rub salt in them.

Given that campaign strategy, it obviously was difficult for many people to take at face value Wallace's vow that he intended to be the governor of all the people—implying that no group would get favored treatment and that none would be discriminated against.

Nevertheless, the vow was made, and the people of the state now must come together behind the man chosen through democratic processes to lead them, and give him full opportunity to prove to those who had misgivings that he meant what he said.

Alabama doesn't need crisis and confrontation, trial and turmoil. It needs to be building for the future, with every citizen contributing to the work and every citizen having equal opportunity to share in the fruits of his labor.

That kind of job needs full-time leadership, and we are certain that Gov. Wallace doesn't need to be reminded that that is what he was elected to give—full-time service as governor of Alabama.

We trust that he will assume those responsibilities fully and that the duties (and prerogatives) of the most important office the pepole of Alabama can bestow will not be parceled out to persons not elected by the people to exercise them.

We trust, too, that—now that the votes are counted and the victory is won—he will review in a more critical light the array of promises he made during the campaign and bring them into more realistic perspective.

It simply isn't possible to give the voters all the things they were promised, and still lower their taxes. To attempt to do so would be no service to the voter who is also the tax-payer.

Many of the things the former governor promised are, of course, desirable and potentially beneficial, but we hope he arranges them in some sort of priority permitting the state to handle them on an orderly, as-possible basis.

Albert Brewer, meanwhile, is far from finished as a public figure in Alabama. The governor is still young and still full of immense promise for important service to this state. He ran an outstandingly decent, positive campaign, and in the two years he has held the state's highest office he has demonstrated much capacity for leadership.

Alabama needs such men, and will need them more than ever as the years go on. We are confident that Albert Brewer will have other opportunities to serve.

ST. LOUIS POST-DISPATCH
St. Louis, Mo., June 4, 1970

The victory of George Wallace in the Alabama runoff election Tuesday is a happening of more than a little importance for the country. Had Gov. Albert Brewer won he probably would have wiped Mr. Wallace from the national scene for good, a consummation devoutly to be wished. But having lost, he allowed Mr. Wallace to rise again to prominence and prepare to lead a third-party ticket in 1972 as he did in 1968.

In that year Mr. Wallace won five Southern states and 45 electoral votes, and it is these votes that President Nixon and Vice President Agnew have been pursuing assiduously for the last year.

Mr. Nixon has sought to bring Wallace votes into the Republican camp by such actions as the aborted Haynsworth and Carswell nominations to the Supreme Court. Mr. Agnew has moved through the South attacking the Eastern liberal press, dissident students and Negro militants, and appealing to the prejudices of the unsophisticated little people who think George Wallace's cheap slogans are answers to world problems.

Now it appears that the joint efforts of Messrs. Nixon and Agnew failed to cut the ground under George Wallace, and the big question is: What turn will the Nixon-Agnew strategy take now? On the eve of the election the Republican national chairman, Rogers Morton, said that if Mr. Wallace won, "Mr. Nixon will have to think this out and move very cautiously." Mr. Wallace's final campaign appeal was entirely on racial lines; will Mr. Nixon move further to the right, further toward denying justice to blacks? Or will he abandon the divisive racial issue and move in the opposite direction?

Part of the answer will depend on Administration evaluation of the Wallace victory. This suggests, but does not necessarily prove, that the GOP Southern strategy has failed throughout the South; analysis could show the failure is significant mainly in Alabama. But there is no doubt that the results in Alabama have dealt a blow to Mr. Nixon's carefully laid scheme to add the deep South to the border, midwestern and mountain states that gave him a narrow victory in 1968.

In 1968 Mr. Nixon got no support from the big cities, which constitutes one reason why he feels free to ignore the needs of the cities in favor of concentration on his Indochina war. But should he decide that Gov. Wallace denies him a Southern base, he may have to revise his strategy for 1972.

If Mr. Nixon would bring the Indochina involvement to an end and devote his energies to helping the cities and uniting the people, as he pledged in 1968, he could assuredly make inroads on Democratic strength in the next two years. Where else can he go, if the Wallace votes in the South are denied him, to find the support that would give him a comfortable chance for success in 1972?

We are sure of one thing, that, as Mr. Morton said, Mr. Nixon (and the architect of his Southern strategy, Attorney General Mitchell) is having to think this out. And the conclusion the President reaches can affect every American in the next two years.

CHICAGO Daily Defender

Chicago, Ill., June 12, 1970

The Wallace victory in the Democratic primary runoff for Alabama's Governorship nomination, throws the nation back into the sizzling kettle of the unresolved racial issue. Though it presents the Nixon Administration with alternatives that may strain its resourcefulness and political know-how, it provides a compelling opportunity for the American electorate to decide once and for all whether it wants to be saddled with segregation of the races or whether it wants to keep alive the dream of Freedom of which the late Dr. Martin Luther King spoke with such eloquence and earnestness.

So, the choice is not Mr. Nixon's alone. The fate of the Republican Party, of course, rests with the decision the Administration makes about how to counter the Wallace threat. It can outdo the Alabama segregationist, drop the Southern strategy or appeal to moderates in the North and West with much emphasis on the black vote.

In a larger sense, the voters must decide for themselves whether America should remain a permanent battlefield where the forces of racial oppression and the fighters for freedom are locked in a death struggle, or a land where the alluring promises of democracy may reach their fulfillment without blood and tears.

Wallace is undoubtedly the most dangerous demagogue of the twentieth century. He will divide the country as it has never been divided before. In fact, he has the inflammable tongue with which to drive the nation to the very brink of a civil war far more disastrous and fierce than what the United States experienced in 1860. A war which would decide not only the political image of this nation, but its very fate as an independent state.

All these calculations are predicated upon Wallace throwing his hat in the Presidential ring in 1972. There is scarcely any doubt that he will do so. That's the strategy behind his election to the Governorship of Alabama so as to provide the proper national platform on which to spit out his racist rhetoric on the American people.

The Sun Reporter

San Francisco, Calif., June 6, 1970

We expected that George Wallace would win the Democratic nomination for governor in the sovereign state of Alabama. The Wallace victory should be a sober reminder for those wishful thinkers in the nation who still believe white racism will roll over dead without a continuing struggle to eradicate this cancerous problem from the nation.

The defeat of Wallace would have indicated the success of Richard Milhous Nixon's Southern strategy to woo the racist South despite its blighting effect upon the hopes of millions of blacks-- those in the South who daily suffer under the yoke of overt Southern racism, and those in the North who endure covert racist duplicity.

George Wallace made an immeasurable contribution to the meagerness of Nixon's '68 victory over Humphrey. It is poetic justice that Nixon must now continue to bear the albatross of George Wallace around his neck for the next two years, so that Nixon and Wallace standing together in '72 might be judged by the American electorate for the evil, callous politicians they are.

Arkansas Gazette.

Little Rock, Ark., June 4, 1970

GEORGE WALLACE is alive and well in Alabama after surviving an extremely close election which, on the shift of two percentage points, could have eliminated him as a figure on the national political scene.

The election was close enough that it might have been decided on the weather election day, which was rainy and more discouraging to Albert Brewer's voters than to the Wallace fans, who are nothing if not dedicated. However, even a victory by some 30,000 votes out of more than a million is still decisive: George Wallace will be governor of Alabama for another four years and almost certainly will be a third party presidential candidate again in 1972, once again siphoning off votes from the regular party nominees.

Why did Wallace win?

If political analyses are sometimes complicated, this one is simple enough. Wallace won simply because a diminished but still decisive majority of Alabama white people still hate Negroes enough not to care very much on election day about anything else. In the showdown Wallace rode the "nigger" issue hard and the election was his. Governor Albert Brewer — who got the black vote by default — certainly is not a liberal by anyone's standards, nor even a moderate by any standards except those of Alabama and Mississippi.

It is a tragedy for Alabama that Brewer lost and that Wallace won, for Albert Brewer is a decent enough type and he had actually been trying to bring Alabama back into the Union. As it is, Alabama will be marching on back down the road of rebellion and disruption, more alienated than ever from the rest of the country even as the division between Alabama blacks and whites becomes deeper and deadlier than ever.

As for the country as a whole, we are not at all sure that the survival of George Wallace as a national political figure matters very much one way or the other. It is true that the victory or defeat of an important demagogue is always a matter of significance. Nevertheless, we are not at all sure that there is all that much difference between George Wallace and Spiro T. Agnew; we are sure that Wallace has not done nearly as much recently to unsettle the American society as Spiro T. Agnew, in his position as vice president.

* * *

IN NATIONAL politics, the outcome in Alabama is subject to all kinds of contradictory speculation. It is now entirely probable that Wallace will run again for president in 1972 (from Wallace's point of view, what does he have to lose?) and the question is whether he will cut more into the popular and electoral vote of President Nixon than into the vote of the Democratic nominee, whoever the nominee proves to be.

If this question does not lend itself to easy answers, there is one conclusion that rises clear in our mind: The Nixon "Southern strategy" has been dealt a serious, if not deadly, blow. One major objective of the strategy was to eliminate George Wallace one way or another and bring the "Wallace states" into he Republican fold, to give Nixon in 1972 a solid Republican South(!) to support his re-election campaign. Wallace may not carry five states again in 1972 — certainly we would hope that he would lose his plurality (42 per cent) in Arkansas — but he has every prospect of carrying three or four of them.

What President Nixon and the Republican high command have not quite understood is this: For the true habituated zealot in the George Wallace following, nothing will really satisfy except the hard stuff dispensed without mixer by Wallace and a few others like him. When Messrs. Nixon and Agnew dilute their own brand of demagoguery a little in concern for Northern reaction, they leave the true Wallaceite more convinced than ever that Wallace alone is fit to bear their standard.

THE DALLAS TIMES HERALD

Dallas, Tex., June 4, 1970

GEORGE CORLEY WALLACE, the banty, big-mouthed battler from 'Bama, is back. And that means trouble. Trouble for the hippies and the peaceniks. But trouble also for President Nixon—and, ultimately, for the two-party system and the nation.

By eking past incumbent Albert Brewer in the Alabama governor's race (it was only the Democratic primary, of course, but you know what that means), Wallace has recaptured the spotlight he had lost after his 1968 presidential race. It seems a foregone conclusion that he will make for another three-cornered presidential sweepstakes in 1972.

So what does this mean? Well, it means that Wallace will be driving a wedge, just as he did in '68, between two camps of sober, responsible, and concerned Americans. Between those—largely middle-class, fairly prosperous —who are content to work within the two-party system and those—largely working class—who (quite rightly) want an end to permissiveness and anarchic protest, and the two-party system be damned.

There may even be an additional wedge between South and North, for Wallace indicates that next time he will run a strictly regional—not a national—campaign.

Wallace dilutes the massive voting power of the silent majority. In 1968, Richard Nixon would have had a far more impressive mandate than he did if it had not been for Wallace. But Wallace lured away millions of voters who thought he talked tougher than Nixon. He thereby came within a whisper of throwing the election to Hubert Humphrey.

In the second place, Wallace's candidacy menaces the two-party system as we know it. The system has faults, but it has made for reasonable stability over the years. It has kept us free of the splinter parties that still make life unbearable for so many European government leaders.

Wallace thinks he can force the Nixon administration rightward. In the end, he may only destroy the administration. It needs Southern votes, but it cannot make Wallace-inspired deals and trades without compromising its integrity, and thereby alienating many moderates.

The South that Wallace says he speaks for indeed deserves a better break than it has received lately from the two major parties. But all signs indicate that Mr. Nixon is trying to give Southerners just such a break.

The thing now is for the South to keep cool and play the game it already is in. In the game that Wallace wants to play, nobody wins, and everybody loses.

THE ROANOKE TIMES

Roanoke, Va., June 4, 1970

George Wallace, like the Mississippi, just keeps rollin' along. And Alabama, and the Nixon "southern strategy," and the entire country, all are the worse for it.

For a time, last month, the inconceivable seemed conceivable. Gov. Albert Brewer—promising to be a *full-time* governor of *all* the people—actually edged out Wallace in the initial Democratic gubernatorial primary. Alabama, for a fleeting moment, seemed ready to take the first halting steps into a new era of political maturity.

Such, however, was not to be. Once, years back, George Wallace promised himself that he would never let another candidate "out-seg" him'; or, as Dixie's segregationist politicians used to say, he would thereafter shout "nigger, nigger, nigger" louder than anybody else. And, in the campaign leading up to Tuesday's runoff primary for the Alabama governorship, Wallace harked back to that evil tactic.

Unlike his 1968 race for the presidency, when code words and euphemisms were subtly employed to appeal to the fading bigot vote, Wallace's 1970 runoff campaign was openly keyed to the politics of racism. Brewer's "black bloc vote" became the only issue, and the old Wallace coalition of small-town voters, blue-collar workers and farmers was shrewdly resurrected. A vote for Gov. Brewer, Alabama was told, was a vote for a takeover of the statehouse by blacks; false though it was, that was all that white Alabamans needed to be told.

Brewer ran well, nonetheless. He was, after all, running against the Deep South's hero: the man who "forced" Richard Nixon into a southern strategy; the fiery "law'n order" man who stood at schoolhouse doors, brayed at the Supreme Court and promised to run over street demonstrators. Even so, the quiet-spoken, businesslike Brewer polled 48 per cent of the vote, nearly all of it apparently accounted for by upper income, better educated whites and by the 20 per cent of the electorate that is newly registered —and black.

While Brewer lost, his strong race hints that even the Deep South is seeing emergence of a formidable new coalition of moderate voters—such as Virginia and the Upper South already boast—that in time will put the Wallaces in the unemployment lines, where they belong.

For the present, however, Wallace once again has shown that the raw politics of race is not yet dead, and that the "bloc vote," "big boys" and "outsiders" (press, pointy-headed Potomac bureaucrats, the banks and the utilities) remain a latter-day Dixie populist's most effective targets.

The Wallace victory demonstrates, it seems to us, that the Nixon-Agnew administration can never expect fully to undercut George Wallace. It ought, therefore, to quit trying.

Wallace is a Deep Dixie phenomenon, probably the last of his breed. For a few more years he will boast a wide following in the Old Confederacy of Louisiana, Alabama, Mississippi and Georgia—but nowhere else.

Mr. Nixon won without the Wallace states in '68; if he gets out of Vietnam, the inflationary recession and the domestic antagonisms of the moment, his chances of winning re-election without the Wallace states will be at least fair, probably good. And if he doesn't come to grips with these problems, he's going to be another one-term President, irrespective of Wallace.

In recapturing the Alabama governorship, Wallace may have thought he was telling the President that only more Harrold Carswell nominations to the Supreme Court, more equivocal statements on school desegregation and more firings of HEW law-enforcers would allow him to retain the White House in '72.

Instead, the Wallace vote has dramatically shown Mr. Nixon the political futility of ever trying to build a Republican party on a Deep South foundation. In place of a Wallace-inspired southern strategy, the President ought therefore to be acting with dispatch in devising the kind of national strategy that he wrongly contends is already operative —one patterned after Lin Holton's black-white coalition in Virginia, one that will neither punish white South or black South, one that will close rather than widen the raw wounds found not just in Alabama but across the troubled land.

TWIN CITY SENTINEL

Winston-Salem, N.C., June 4, 1970

"All over Alabama the lamps are out."

—James Agee

THE George Wallace campaign for governor will go down as another dark episode in Alabama's history. In his effort to regain the governorship Wallace and his followers exploited racial feelings more openly than anybody since the days of Mississippi's Sen. Bilbo and Georgia's Gene Talmadge—more openly than he himself has done since his first successful campaign for high office.

Wallace's strategy—his only hope really—was to get out a massive white bloc vote to offset the black bloc vote which his opponent, Gov. Albert Brewer, had received in the first primary and would obviously receive again. Ads showing vote totals in Negro precincts (Brewer, 1,781; Wallace, 6) appeared in most of the state's newspapers, along with out-of-context quotes and pictures of the governor in company with Negro leaders. This was the old Wallace of the "segregation forever" days, so anxious to regain power that he had to abandon the shabby "I'm-no-racist" pretense built up during his two presidential campaigns.

Even so, he barely managed to pull it out. With most of the votes counted his total hovered somewhere around the 52 per cent mark. The race puts to rest whatever belief there was in Wallace's invincibility, and, incidentally, was close enough to keep Brewer alive as a plausible candidate for some other office, possibly for the Senate in 1972.

Wallace's performance is all the more unimpressive when compared to his late wife's landslide victory in 1966 and raises doubts about how effective he will be in governing the state and in organizing resistance to federal desegregation policy.

With his cry of "nigger" he has thoroughly disenchanted responsible leadership in the state. He has also alienated Democratic party leaders and legislators who believed Brewer deserved a second term and who dread the disrupting effect another Wallace-for-president campaign—who, quite simply, dislike the man's self-glorifying tactics even though they may agree with his politics.

Under Albert Brewer Alabama had been on the point of recovering from the Wallace years. There were no Selmas while Brewer was in office, no schoolhouse-door charades. Air and water pollution, educational financing, the quest for new industry—these and other matters had begun to push the race issue out of the headlines.

Wallace's return to power comes at a time when school districts are beginning to feel the full brunt of federal desegregation decrees, and at a time, furthermore, when the Nixon administration is making a play for southern support. Although Wallace may never regain the national or even the regional stature he once had, the administration cannot afford to take that risk. This means that during the next couple of years we are likely to hear the President and vice president promising the South more than they can deliver—more perhaps than they, deep down, really want to deliver.

THE WALL STREET JOURNAL.

New York, N.Y., June 5, 1970

It would have been healing for the body politic and convenient for President Nixon if George Wallace had been defeated in his latest race for Governor of Alabama. We're not sure that his victory, though, makes any real difference in what the Administration ought to do about the South, or indeed in what it will do.

Naturally Mr. Nixon and his lieutenants are interested in improving the fortunes of the Republican Party in the South, from which it has so long been excluded. The screaming about the inherent depravity of trying to win Southern support would be a lot more meaningful if it did not come from the liberal Democrats who have profited so long and so handsomely from their party alliance with Senator Stennis, Senator Eastland and the rest.

It is in fact altogether desirable that both parties try to win votes in the South. Such a competition will tend to keep both white and black factions there within the political mainstream, where disputes are most likely to be peacefully resolved. The question is not whether a Republican Administration should try to win votes in the South; it should. The question is how, and the considerations here far transcend anything George Wallace can do.

To begin with, moral considerations preclude any attempt to win Southern votes by giving the white South its head on racial policy, by completely stopping Federal pressure toward further desegregation. But we find it quite another matter to modify and qualify those pressures in ways that might placate the white South's sense of grievance at past enforcement policies. For Senator Stennis was right that courts have ordered things in the South that simply would not be put up with in the North. This double standard may be justified as a response to widespread Southern bad faith, but in the long run a vindictive approach is almost sure to be self-defeating.

In particular, until this year school integration policy had been rather rapidly evolving toward the position that absolutely no consideration could be thrown into the balance other than the numerical ratios of black and white children. Educational quality, the convenience of children, the practical possibility of resegregation into private schools or suburban enclaves—none of these could be considered.

We doubt that so stark a policy is in any sense morally justified; you cannot entirely dismiss moral considerations in reasonable treatment of first-grade children. Even more clearly on a practical level, this sort of evolution was bound to carry overtones that seem unreasonable to the majority of the American people, both South and North. Unless integration policy was cut back to more defensible ground, there was a long-run danger of its complete collapse.

It has become increasingly evident, we think, that the integration policies of the Nixon Administration have been directed not at eliminating Federal pressures toward integration, but in culling out the excesses that might lead to a total collapse later.

This distinction has at times been hard to pinpoint. Many people do believe integration policies should be enforced with literally no limit and have done their best to picture even the most reasonable limits as outright capitulation to the segregationists. For its part, the Administration took some time to get a grip on its policy, and in wavering it did do some things beyond the minimum needed to avoid excesses.

In recent weeks, the tone of Administration policy has become clearer. The President's pledge of financial aid to desegregating school districts, the substitution of the carrot for the stick, is being widely hailed in liberal circles among others. The reconsideration of the Charlotte school busing decision closely reflects the President's announced policy, and it plainly shows that it's possible to reject an unreasonable amount of busing without totally removing pressures toward further desegregation.

As a "Southern strategy" in the political sense, these efforts will not satisfy the most militant segregationists, regardless of whether Mr. Wallace had or had not won in Alabama. But to go further is not only morally indefensible, but politically senseless as well. A capitulation to segregation would write off Northern votes. Within the South itself, militant segregationism is obviously still potent enough to elect George Wallace in an Alabama primary, but that there was ever any question of his victory suggests its potency is declining, and rather rapidly at that.

The Administration, in short, has been settling into a policy of maintaining pressure toward further desegregation but in a more even-handed and less vindictive fashion. Take George Wallace or leave him, it's hard to see how the Administration could allow itself to be nudged off the course it has already set. The moral, practical and political considerations too manifestly indicate that course is the right one.

Los Angeles Times
Los Angeles, Calif., June 4, 1970

George C. Wallace's narrow victory in the Alabama gubernatorial election is a disastrous setback for those who have wanted, and worked for, racial progress and harmony in that state. It is also a misfortune for the country as a whole.

Ever since his election in 1968, President Nixon has been anxious—some would say overly anxious—to build Republican strength in the South and head off another Wallace bid for the presidency.

Republican strategists, accordingly, had been hoping that Wallace would go down to defeat in his campaign to recapture his old job as governor of Alabama.

In addition to crippling his chances of mounting another third-party effort in 1972, a Wallace defeat would have made it easier for the Nixon Administration to ease off on the so-called "southern strategy."

The latter, by its rhetoric more than by its substance, has contributed to the alienation from the Administration of black people and college youths.

Gov. Albert Brewer, a former Wallace protege, is hardly an integrationist. But on the thesis that Alabama has outgrown a politics based on racial fears and ob-sessions, he declined to campaign on that basis.

As a result, he had heavy support not only from Alabama Negroes, but also from whites who are embarrassed by the kind of image which Wallace has given Alabama nationally.

Unfortunately, it was not enough. In what Brewer called a hate campaign . . . the dirtiest campaign I've ever seen in Alabama," Wallace charged that a Brewer victory would turn the state over to black control, and he won.

Wallace proved to be a candidate with only regional appeal in 1968, when he failed to carry a single state outside the South, and lost several Southern and border states to Mr. Nixon.

Most political observers doubt that he will do even that well if—despite present disclaimers—he makes another run for the presidency in 1972.

Still, there is no question but that Wallace's inflammatory presence on Mr. Nixon's Southern flank makes it more difficult for the President to deal resolutely with the problems which are tearing this country apart. The difficulty is one, however, which Americans have a right to expect Mr. Nixon to overcome.

THE COMMERCIAL APPEAL
Memphis, Tenn., June 4, 1970

THE MONTGOMERY, Ala., address for George C. Wallace for the last year has been The Wallace Campaign, P.O. Box 1972. It took on new significance Tuesday when the voters of Alabama gave him the margin he needed to regain the governorship.

Wallace retired from the political scene after the 1968 presidential election in which he garnered 9,906,473 popular votes and 45 electoral votes. His wife, Lurleen, who had stood in for him in the governor's office after Wallace's first term, had died before the presidential race was well under way, and he had lost his platform temporarily. But few doubted during those days of 1969 that he would try to make a comeback in Alabama politics.

It was not easy. Gov. Albert Brewer, who came to office through the lieutenant governorship on the death of Mrs. Wallace, had grown in popularity during the last two years. In fact, his following was so large that he was able to force Wallace into the Tuesday runoff election. And even then Wallace had to resort to tactics that roused voter fears of Negro domination of Alabama politics for many future years in order to gain the needed margin over Brewer.

The question now is whether after this difficult victory he can succeed in using the governorship as the spring-board for another plunge into presidential politics.

While he was a third party candidate in 1968, his third party was in fact an amalgam of several state parties, held together only by the power of Wallace's own personality. When he subsided in late 1968, the third party movement fell into some disarray. Wallace did not even show up at the Louisville, Ky., meeting in early 1969 to organize a national conservative party. The state parties have fallen prey to differences and divisions.

Still, reports from Montgomery are that campaign contributions have continued to roll in to the P.O. Box 1972 address. And the tremendous task of getting official recognition on the ballots in all 50 states in 1968 will not have to be repeated in 1972 if he should run again.

BUT 1972 still is two years away. The Republican Party has sought to pick up strength in the South through what has been vaguely referred to as President Nixon's "Southern strategy." Awareness that Wallace again has a political base from which to operate surely will cause the Republicans to do all they can to offset this threat to their Southern building campaign. That reaction could have as much to do with Wallace's 1972 chances as the power of Wallace oratory.

The Charlotte Observer
Charlotte, N.C., June 4, 1970

By again making race the overriding issue, George Wallace has been renominated for governor in Alabama and preserved the base for his national platform.

The strategy Wallace used to overcome the primary lead of moderate Gov. Albert Brewer does not improve with age or repetition in the South. But the rejection of that strategy awaits a sophistication of the vote that comes slowly.

Wallace turned fears of what he called a "bloc vote" to his runoff advantage. Yet there is obvious peril, regionally and nationally, in urging and helping alienated and outnumbered people cast their lot with the system through the ballot box; then to have this use of the franchise turned as a weapon against them. This works against the creation of a stable, enduring, multi-racial society.

An equally important question rising from this election, however, is how it will affect the direction of the Nixon administration. There has been an effort nationwide to combine normal Republican support in the West, Midwest and Northeast, along with the growing conservatism of the suburbs, to the Wallace sentiment found in the South and other parts of the country among the "little people."

Wallace's latest success raises the question of how far any national administration must go to win the allegiance of true Wallaceites. Even now, he pledges that he will either move President Nixon more toward the Wallace position on race-related issues such as schools or prove that there's no difference between Nixon and the Democrats.

To date, the speeches of Vice President Spiro Agnew have probably been the chief attraction of this administration for many blue-collar workers and others who feel most menaced by racial and campus unrest and drastic social change. In Alabama, Brewer's margin over Wallace in the first election was cited by some observers as evidence that the Republicans had drained enough strength from Wallace to eliminate him as a threat in 1972.

The results Tuesday must make the politicians wonder. Anyone pursuing hard-core Wallace supporters will have to take a much harder turn to the right than any national administration can afford. It raises questions as to whether the real Wallace base is a part of the foundation the Republicans can or should rebuild on nationally.

The President is not amiss—either for the 1970 congressional elections or the 1972 presidential election — in trying to win all the "conservative" support he can get. But the Alabama election may be a sign that he should keep nearer the middle ground, where there is less risk in an already dangerously divided nation.

That way, Nixon will be in a better position in 1972 to damp down a presidential campaign that could have inflammatory racial and generational tones. All of us can help assure a decent campaign and moderation by putting in order the affairs of our own states and communities so that race is not an easily exploitable issue.

The Kansas City Times
Kansas City, Mo., June 4, 1970

Alabama duly informed Richard M. Nixon Tuesday that there is a George Wallace; that he is alive and well and plans to move to the governor's mansion soon, and that the President had better not forget that Southern strategy. We would guess that Mr. Nixon, who can read election results quite competently, will not forget it. Unfortunately for the nation, George Wallace is still a man to be reckoned with.

The fact is that Wallace still has his political base although, forced into a runoff which he won by a relatively small margin, he may stand on it a little less securely. He stands there, however—and this is perhaps the most disturbing aspect of

it all—as a victorious candidate who openly ran as a racist.

Two years ago, at the national level and seeking the presidency, Wallace at least went through the motions of denying that he was a racist. In Alabama, he had to do otherwise to win the statehouse. Here was a one-issue, openly segregationist politician, and Alabama bought his line.

In terms of national policy and politics, the uneasy prospect is that Mr. Nixon may feel compelled to buy it too. The South is a part of the Nixon geographical coalition that he expects to sustain him in 1972. George Wallace shakes the Southern pillars of the foundation, which carries (or, presumably, will carry) the weight of Nixon support along with the Mid-West and the West.

Thus—embarrassed as he may be by his inability to date to bring peace to Southeast Asia and shaken by the behavior of the economy—the President may very well find it necessary to counterattack in the South.

Which, of course, would mean more of the Southern strategy, and—measured in terms of Supreme court nominations, of attitudes toward school desegregation and civil rights, and in the administration's over-all relationship with minority groups—it has not been a healthy development. In the aftermath of George Wallace's hate campaign in one state, there may be national repercussions even before the campaign of 1972 rolls around. Tuesday, in Alabama, was not a very good day for Richard Nixon, or for the United States.

The Greenville News
Greenville, S.C., June 4, 1970

George Wallace's come-from-behind victory in the second Democratic primary race for governor of Alabama will have an important impact on Southern politics — and on the national political scene — from now through the 1972 presidential election. It's back to the political drawing boards for those who wrote the "Little Jedge" off after he placed second to Governor Brewer in the first primary last month.

As noted in our analysis of the first primary immediately after the results were known, the returns showed that Wallace had a good chance to win a big victory in the second race — and he did. He became the first man in Alabama history to pull it off after trailing in the first primary.

Wallace won largely because he lived up to the vow made many years ago after he lost a race because he was viewed as "too moderate" on the racial issue. Wallace said then that never again would anybody "out-seg" him in a political campaign. He played the racial issue for all it was worth in the second primary, topping it with a pre-election prediction that his defeat would lead to 50 years of black domination of Alabama politics.

That was enough to bring his supporters out in force all over the state and to turn the campaign completely around, overcoming Governor Brewer's lead which had been built on a record of good government, plus some resentment

against Wallace on grounds that he was trying to use the governor's office as a political stepping-stone.

Wallace obviously got much of the "blue collar" vote which went to Charles Woods in the first race on the basis of Woods' pledge to shift the tax load from the working man to big industry. He also managed to "energize" many rural voters who turned out in response to his plea against black political power.

The Wallace victory makes it clear that the possible shift of Southern political emphasis from the racial issue to economics, predicted by many political observers, has not yet taken place — at least in Alabama. A trend in that direction may be seen in

the fact that the Wallace victory margin was smaller than in some previous elections, but as of now racial considerations are decisive in Alabama, and probably several other Southern states.

This fact is bound to influence 1970 campaigns in Southern states and in some states outside the South. It will have impact on the gubernatorial race in South Carolina.

Obviously Wallace will plunge into the presidential race in 1972, perhaps running on a strictly regional basis instead of the national stance he took in 1968. One thing is certain: Southerners will be hearing — and seeing — George Wallace quite often in the immediate future.

Richmond Times-Dispatch
Richmond, Va., June 4, 1970

The former bantamweight Golden Gloves champion of Alabama will return to the statehouse in Montgomery, and it's not good news for the President of the United States.

George Wallace came in second in the state Democratic gubernatorial primary a month ago, but he came in first in the runoff Tuesday. The Republicans don't plan to field a candidate in the general election in November, so Wallace is assured of being the next governor of the Cotton State.

The fiery little Alabaman's return to the governor's office may or may not be good for the state, but it certainly will be no cause for rejoicing at the White House in Washington. For if Wallace runs for president in

1972 he will do exactly what he did in 1968, and that is to take votes away from Richard Nixon.

In 1968, running on the American Independent party ticket, George Wallace polled nearly 10 million votes, 320,272 of them in Virginia. If Wallace hadn't been in the race, Richard Nixon's victory would not have been as narrow as it was, since most of Wallace's supporters would have been in the Nixon camp if their prime hero hadn't been on the ballot.

Of course, even though Wallace is making noises now which indicate he is contemplating running for the top job in '72, he may find the political climate at that time not conducive to his making the effort. And it can be taken for granted that President

Nixon hopes to create that kind of climate between now and 1972.

But weather-making is not easy. In the face of Northern pressure, civil rights laws and court rulings, Mr. Nixon may not be able to comply with Wallace's post-victory demand that the President "give us back our schools" — at least not with the demand as Wallace means it.

If the South — and to some extent the nation as a whole — remains in turmoil over school desegregation, and if the administration fails to cope effectively with militant protesters on the campuses and elsewhere, then the stage may be set for George Wallace to appear in a starring role in the presidential drama. Not as the winner, of course, but

as the third party candidate with strength enough to keep victory out of Nixon's reach on election day, 1972.

Apart from all this, many Americans undoubtedly are saddened by the apparent fact that the race issue was a major factor in Tuesday's Alabama primary. There seems no doubt, on the one hand, that incumbent Gov. Albert P. Brewer received the black bloc vote, while Wallace benefited from encouraging fear among whites that a Brewer victory would give blacks and their ultraliberal white friends conarol of the state. In all elections there are people who vote on the basis of emotion rather than reason, but this kind of ballot-marking seemed especially widespread in Alabama Tuesday.

SCHOOLS REOPEN: SOUTH IS CALM; NORTH, WEST RESIST BUSING

For the first time since 1954 when the Supreme Court ordered an end to racial segregation in public education, defiance of court-ordered integration was centered in the North and West as schools reopened for the fall term. In the South, which for years had been the citadel of resistance to integrated schooling, newly desegregated schools—even those with new busing plans—opened quietly and without major incident.

The stiffest protest against busing came in Pontiac, Mich. On Aug. 30, arsonists firebombed and destroyed 10 school buses, part of Pontiac's fleet of 90 buses which were to be used to carry out a court-ordered integration plan calling for cross-town busing of more than 8,000 children. Ten days later the FBI arrested six members of the Ku Klux Klan and charged them with the bombing. Protest continued in Pontiac throughout the first two weeks of September, led by an anti-busing faction calling itself the National Action Group. NAG demanded that the schools be closed but the Pontiac school board refused. Protesters carrying American flags then marched in front of the school bus depot daring bus drivers to run them down. Police arrested nine persons. Later, hundreds of women and children carrying anti-busing picket signs forced the closing of two large General Motors plants in Pontiac as more than half the workers refused to cross the picket line.

The Charlotte Observer

Charlotte, N. C., September 9, 1971

Charlotte-Mecklenburg parents, students, teachers and school officials have every right to be proud this week. Schools opened with business-as-usual the first day. No mass rallies, no threats of boycott, no fist-shaking, sign-waving or voice-raising. Only a quiet resolve to get on with the important business of education.

The local mood contrasts sharply with the parental protests arising elsewhere in the nation, in communities getting their first taste of integration's uncomfortable demands. But empty threats and demonstrations in the face of court orders have proved in the past to be just that—empty.

As Charlotte-Mecklenburg has shown, school desegregation—and the additional transportation needed to achieve it—must be treated as a challenge instead of a threat, an opportunity instead of a death sentence.

Indeed, the most visible sign of "protest" in Charlotte-Mecklenburg has been staged by a ridiculous band of Nazi-uniformed die-hards. Riding through city streets in an orange school bus decorated with rebel flags, they have made a futile plea to "BOYCOTT BUSING."

The showbiz overtones of the hopeless crusade says only one thing: Charlotte Mecklenburg has ridden out the crisis. The passengers on the orange bus may not realize it, but they will have to travel on. These are no longer fertile pastures for self-defeating slogans.

There is still discontent, of course. Northwest parents, for example, feel they have been slighted by the Board of Education's "feeder plan." But they are taking their fight to the courtroom, where it belongs, instead of the street corner, where it does not. The plaintiffs are to be congratulated for the relatively calm and rational way in which they have conducted their own "protest." It reflects the sophisticated attitude the community is now taking toward the desegregation dilemma.

The burden remains on the community leadership and school-oriented organizations to see that whatever unhappiness parents and children still feel stays at a minimum during the coming year. Education must continue to receive emphasis over the mechanics and difficulties of busing. We can show the nation a thing or two, not about busing but about true education, which is what it has been all about.

BUFFALO EVENING NEWS

Buffalo, N. Y., September 2, 1971

The fact that millions of children in the South have returned quietly to desegregated schools reflects glowingly on the moderation and decency of people in that region of the country.

And the progress toward desegregated schools there stands in sharp contrast to the violence in Pontiac, Mich., where explosions ripped 10 empty school buses to be used under a court-ordered integration plan.

Trouble could easily have erupted in several cities, north and south, where strong opposition existed to bussing. But the general calm that prevailed as the first round of southern school openings began serves both as an example for school openings later on and as a welcome reproach to the noisy demagoging on the anti-bussing issue recently by Alabama Gov. George Wallace. Nor did the anti-bussing remarks a few weeks ago by President Nixon help arm moderates, north or south, against the verbal extremes of Wallace or the explosives in Pontiac.

Unquestionably, bussing is a searingly controversial issue around the country. But it is difficult to reject the contention that if bussing was used to perpetuate a dual school system in the past, then it can appropriately be used to establish a unitary system now. The Supreme Court, in ruling bussing constitutionally permissible as a means of breaking up segregated systems, noted last April that 18 million of the nation's public school children, or 39 per cent of the total, rode buses in the 1969-1970 school year. The Supreme Court properly conceded, however, that valid objections might be raised to a bussing plan where the distances traveled were "so great as to risk either the health of the children or significantly impinge on the educational process."

While Gov. Wallace was generating headlines with words and deeds to defy the courts last week, another southern governor, Reubin Askew of Florida, was getting less national attention but making more sense. He urged Floridians to encourage "reason and calm in your own communities in the days ahead." While nobody really wants bussing, "not even the courts," he said, the "law demands, and rightly so, that we put an end to segregation in our society." We could all benefit from that counsel. And perhaps, if the quiet and early openings of many southern schools are any indication, it is southern voices like that of Gov. Askew, rather than those of the Wallaces, that increasingly are being listened to.

Arkansas ✠ Gazette.

Little Rock, Ark., September 10, 1971

IT IS September, 1971, and the public schools of Little Rock and elsewhere in Arkansas are back in session much the same as in any year, except for one critical difference: This fall the integration of public education in the city and state, at long last, has been accomplished.

Such achievement could not have been claimed previously in all the years of "gradual" integration since the beginning 14 years ago. In the past there have always been obvious omissions, obvious delinquencies in the elimination of racially identifiable schools. This year, the full force of the United States courts has finally been brought to bear, and tokenism has been eliminated "root and branch." Some important details and questions are left to be ironed out before the next school term, especially at the elementary level, but the desegregation still to be effected in Arkansas will surely be anti-climactic.

In the second week of school there has been hardly anything that could be called an "incident" in the state. This is the experience even though the schools about Arkansas have been desegregated thoroughly, for the most part, and even though the city school district in Little Rock has employed "busing" to move substantial numbers of pupils across town, as necessary, in establishing a racial ratio of approximately 2-1 in "middle" schools and junior and senior high schools (serving altogether, the top seven grades.)

How far we have come since the memorable year 1957 and the token integration of Central High by the "Little Rock Nine"!

★ ★ ★

LET US claim certain credits at this juncture for the people of the city and the state, for what has been accomplished this fall.

We would not and do not suggest that the integration of schools has been done voluntarily, for, indeed, it has been done under the gun of federal court orders all the way. But once the last recourse was exhausted, the last loophole closed, the white majority has accepted the inevitable this September with surprisingly good grace and an eminently practical sense of resignation.

No trouble of any consequence has broken out in the school system. There has been remarkably little demagoging of the issue by Arkansas officialdom — Governor Bumpers having set the example of a scrupulous "hands off" policy. A few more scattered private "academies" have opened, including one lonesome (and expensive) academy in suburban Little Rock which had enrolled 200 pupils at last account ahead of its scheduled opening next week. In Arkansas there is no consequential threat to public education arising from private schools.

In Little Rock it is true that some thousands of pupils have been put to some inconvenience in attending schools that are not always the nearest at hand for a given student. The reopening of school has been smooth, nevertheless, and School Sup't. Floyd Parsons and his staff may take justifiable pride in the work they put into this climactic transition. As for the "busing," there is evidence showing that many students actually *enjoy* the outing, as many alumni of rural schools have anticipated all along in the memory of a time when riding a schoolbus was regarded as neither painful nor sinful.

The whole "busing" inconvenience has been magnified out of all reason. There is some artificiality to the use of buses for a better racial mix, but, even so, "busing" is an indispensable measure at this stage in breaking down the old racial school system. Everywhere students, black and white, will learn more about what the whole society they live in is really like, and for many of both races it will be a revelation. Whites have been "sheltered" and blacks placed apart, and both have been in a real sense deprived.

In addition there are bonuses that we have mentioned previously: The democratization of "snob" schools like Hall High; the stabilization of Central High, largest and oldest of the high schools, which now has a broad-based attendance zone reaching into the fashionable "Heights" neighborhoods; and finally the outlook for more stabilized property values as the "white flight" to the suburbs is slowed — there being no "white" schools left to flee to.

★ ★ ★

THE "BUSING" would not be necessary if we lived in a better world. Nevertheless, in the summing up, it is not more than an inconvenience, presumably a passing one, although none of us may know how long it will have to continue.

If there have been no "incidents" of importance, this is not to say that there have not been revelations. The Gazette's Tucker Steinmetz rode the schoolbuses in Little Rock for two days at the opening of schools. On one of these memorable rides he observed one schoolgirl on the soapbox, waving her finger and declaring that "the majority of the people don't want busing; it's just a little minority that wants it." Across the aisle, Steinmetz recounted, another girl rejoined: *"they say they don't want busing, but they really don't like integration — that's what it is."*

Whatever it is that they don't like, the people of Little Rock, and of Arkansas, have kept their cool and their common sense this fall. Parents and students alike have accepted the rule of law and of reason so well that four black leaders held a press conference in Little Rock early this week to compliment the community on its response to the school opening. Governor Bumpers later in the week added his own words of praise.

It has been a September to remember, with a sense of reassurance in looking to the years ahead.

THE MILWAUKEE JOURNAL

Milwaukee, Wis., September 12, 1971

The truly significant thing about this month's school reopening has been the calm with which tens of thousands of white and black children a c r o s s the land have been bussed to newly integrated classrooms.

There were senseless and unusual incidents, such as the brainless dynamiting of 10 empty busses in Pontiac, Mich., and the picketing there and elsewhere by angry parents. But school busses rolled without i n c i d e n t in hundreds of other communities.

Desegregation has not always been accomplished with parental enthusiasm, but it has been done for the most part with the parents' l a w f u l acquiescence. Sen. Muskie (D-Maine) probably reflects parental views more accurately than did President Nixon's antibussing statements, which rekindled passions of diehard racists. Muskie said that, "like everyone else, I don't like bussing," but added: "It is the law of the land and we m u s t a c c e p t it. . . . B u s s i n g is an inadequate answer, an answer we don't like. Yet it is an answer that is being used and it must be used to make a beginning on this problem."

Racial segregation — whatever the cause — is the real crux of this problem. Eliminating it is the ultimate goal. In some areas that may eventually h a v e to mean broadening school district boundaries, as proposed in a plan being discussed in Richmond, Va. And a federal judge in Indianapolis, recognizing that his desegregation order might drive more whites from the city, asked school officials to study the possibility of expanding the district to include nearby suburbs.

The lesson of the school bus this fall is that desegregation can and will take place, peacefully, in communities w h e r e it was believed to be unlikely or impossible, because of presumed parental a t t i t u d e s. It is a lesson that should embolden other communities that have too timidly hesitated to make this necessary step toward racial integration.

THE SAGINAW NEWS

Saginaw, Mich., September 1, 1971

THERE IS no law which prohibits any man from the right to believe that the only lunatics in the country are those wearing judicial robes and interpreting the nation's laws. But when that same man takes the law into his own hands and breaks established law he defeats the very thing he seeks to enjoin and ruins his own credibility.

Man or men, who at this hour remain nameless, have in fact joined the lunatic fringe in the city of Pontiac. It comes down to that when individuals in the dark of night plant explosives and shatter 10 costly school buses.

True, this radical demonstration against public property has not resulted in death or injury. Thus it is well understood that the criminal act is taken for symbolic protest against court-order busing of students to achieve racial balance in that city's schools. It is a sad day indeed, however, when the school bus has come to represent a symbol of racial antagonism and disdain for the law in the absolute.

We are fond of saying, of course, that this is not the American way. But sadly, in Pontiac, is another example for those to cite who claim that violence is the American way —"as American as apple pie." At the very least it is the last thing Pontiac needed. Pontiac is a troubled city at this hour caught in the swirl of controversy over a federal court order to proceed with busing to achieve a semblance of racial balance in its public schools.

This newspaper has consistently expressed its doubts over the value of busing children to strange schools out of home neighborhoods to achieve what at best is artificial balance in the school room. We have just as consistenly supported the law of the land that has directed communities to stop denying children access to certain schools strictly because of the color of their skin.

In all of the movement toward fulfillment of equal rights promises of the 14th Amendment for every American, the busing issue has been the greatest of growing dilemas. Our own position admittedly would seem to smack of inconsistency as we measure it against dejure and defacto segregation. Let us repeat another point we have earlier recognized. Dejure segregation is not difficult to identify, measure precisely or adjudicate. Defacto is less easy to deal with. But it is also a sham and a delusion to pretend that defacto segregation, the result of housing and ethnic patterns, in many instances deliberately contrived, doesn't produce the same end result —in effect, segregation of pupils by races, also in many instances virtually total.

The first has been the historic pattern in the South, the latter the pattern in the North. Only now as the effort to end segregration in the classroom moves northward do we begin to witness the human failing in places like Pontiac.

In all of this there is reminder of hypocrisy in two forms, one southern, the other northern. In the South it says to the minority, we don't mind you living near us or next to us—but don't try to take our jobs. In the North it runs, we don't mind factoring you into the working mainstream, but don't get too neighborly.

None of this moves the country nearer to solution of the basic human rights—equal rights problem. When vile mischief takes the form it has in Pontiac it is no more tolerable there than in South Carolina or Alabama or Mississippi. But be certain those who carry out such acts take their cue from men like George Wallace who openly defy federal law and advocate civil disobedience. Mr. Wallace certainly doesn't preach destruction of school buses. He doesn't have to. It is but a short step from standing in the door of one to block court-ordered transfers of students to moving to the next plateau of anger.

Those in Pontiac and other northern cities who now decry federal orders as the prelude to "absolute disaster in race relations" and the commencing of a tidal wave of white abandonment of the city for the suburb may unfortunately prove accurate prophets of doom. But what does an inicident like this one in Pontiac do for restoration of sensibility?

It has always seemed to us that the central question over equal education must be answered. Is the question in the classroom one of integrating colors or one of opening up minds? The world we live in today and the society of tomorrow which we rapidly move toward certainly suggests much for bringing children of different races together in reasonable balance for sharing the learning process when such balance can be reasonably attained without working undue hardship on student and parent alike.

Far more important, however, is the equalizing of educational quality within the classrooms of all schools wherever they are. Merely playing chess games with bodies does not do that. When busing to achieve racial balance means transporting children unreasonable distances and keeping them on buses from wee hours of the morning until dinner time the intent of the law of the land is clearly being carried over the brink to point of maximum antagonization. More and more parents of all races are sharing that view.

What is needed even more than busing on a mammoth and irrational scale is an additive of rationale. This must be supplied by the White House, the Congress and the courts —that and much greater investment on the school itself so that no child need be deprived of the best tools with which to learn.

Nobody in government — from South to North—has yet faced up to these simple truths. Until they do the busing issue will be fraught with confusion and absurd response.

"I hope this will wake up the people of Pontiac to the fact that they have unsolicited help — radicals— that they don't want," says Mayor Robert F. Jackson. That says it all from the mayor of a city whose school board seeks relief from the federal order on appeal now pending before the U.S. Supreme Court. This is where Pontiac must find its way —not in an unguarded city bus yard under the cover of night. That is a futile game played by losers. It is not the American way—but it hands those who say it is a very good case.

The Charleston Gazette
Charleston, W. Va., September 9, 1971

Despite discouragement or denunciation for political or other purposes by some leaders—such as George Wallace, Richard M. Nixon, and Robert C. Byrd —busing to achieve racial balance in the public schools moved smoothly this week in many parts of the country, particularly in the South.

Ironically, disturbances or resistance over desegregation plans were confined largely to so-called liberal cities of the North—Boston, Detroit, Pontiac, Seattle, San Francisco, Baltimore, Los Angeles, Phoenix and others—while the Deep South for the most part made unprecedented civil-rights progress by proceeding quietly and peacefully toward full scale desegregation.

►All of South Carolina's 92 school districts were operating under court-approved desegregation plans for the first time in history—and in Columbia only 13 per cent of the city's black students remained in all-black schools compared with 50 per cent last year.

►Notwithstanding Gov. George Wallace's pre-presidential campaign against school busing, desegregation spread without incident in Alabama to the extent that only four all-black schools remained in the state.

►In Jackson, Miss., where the business community once led the fight to make Jackson more or less the segregation capital of the country, this same business community has now joined the school board in an advertising campaign to boost the city's busing plan and "develop the nation's finest school system."

Indeed, except for a few minor incidents, massive desegregation was carried out peacefully in almost all of the 2,700 school districts in the South, a good portion of it through busing.

It remained for the North, which has been prodding the South about desegregation for years, to continue America's shame of segregation. It was hardly a source for pride in such trouble spots as Pontiac, Mich., where 10 school buses were destroyed by a dynamite blast a few days ago and where television viewers were treated to the degrading sight of shouting mothers urging their children to "hold your signs higher" and to join in the attempted blockade of school buses.

There was good reason to believe that desegregation by busing was acceptable to many of the children, but resisted by the parents. For example, there was the case of the little girl who said she liked the way she got to school because "I like to ride the bus." And the little boy who, asked why he was protesting, replied: "I don't know." And another little boy who gave a direct answer to a question as to why he was being bused: "So we all can be friends."

On the side of those protesting busing to achieve desegregation is the oversimplified argument that it makes no sense to bus a child across town when he lives near a neighborhood school. As Sen. Byrd put it, the busing rulings of the federal courts were "preposterous . . . authoritarian . . . nonsense . . . and pure folly."

But for anyone willing to think the matter through, full desegregation of the school—even through busing—is necessary if the blacks and whites of America are ever to learn to live peacefully together, and if we are to avoid a nation divided on racial grounds.

The truth is that the schools of many Northern cities are becoming increasingly resegregated as a result of white flight to the suburbs. The trend is to further segregation or resegregation, brought on by racial housing patterns and a strong tradition of neighborhood schools.

The blacks and other minorities of this country suffer most from what might be called economic segregation, and they are going to be locked ever deeper in their ghettos unless their children and the children of more affluent whites are permitted to learn that that they can live together. The best and perhaps the only way this can be achieved is by growing up together in the public schools, and in many cases this racial balance can be brought about only through busing.

The point was perhaps best made by a sensible mother in Pontiac. She lives across the street from a neighborhood school and she doesn't particularly relish the idea of her son being bused to a school in another part of town. But, she said with admirable philosophy, "We've got to get along together in this world, and he may as well start learning it now."

THE KNICKERBOCKER NEWS
*** UNION-STAR ***
Albany, N. Y., September 15, 1971

Disclosure by the FBI that a leader of the Ku Klux Klan and his associates had plotted to blow up school buses in Pontiac, Mich., should not be surprising.

Pontiac is one of a number of communities where emotions are running high as the result of the school busing issue. Whenever emotions and prejudice are involved, the extremist hate-mongers who lurk under sheets and rocks feel it is safe for them to come out and commit their evil deeds.

Had they been successful in Pontiac, many children—both black and white— would have been killed and injured.

This is an example of what happens when public officials shilly-shilly on enforcement of the law of the land. or blatantly defy it. Although the U.S. Supreme Court repeatedly has ruled that busing of students is proper to achieve desegregated education, President Nixon has weaseled around the subject so obviously that he has undercut and embarrassed his own Health, Education and

Welfare Department. And Alabama's Gov. George C. Wallace—ever ready to stir up trouble—has defied the law, contending, with his demagogic tongue in cheek, that since President Nixon says he's against busing, he—Wallace—is only trying to help the President.

While certainly no responsible public official, from President Nixon on down, would condone violence, is it any wonder that various nuts and fanatics occasionally get the idea that since some of their elected leaders wink at and evade the law, anything goes?

The Salt Lake Tribune
Salt Lake City, Utah, September 7, 1971

The essence of the Pontiac, Mich, bus bombing is the utter futility and mindlessness in it all. Assuming the act was meant to prevent integrating local schools by busing. it didn't work. Neither school nor court authorities backed down. Moreover, by such senseless destruction, opponents of busing further weaken whatever merit their position might have had.

Even more puzzling on the other hand, were comments from those few Pontiac residents who approved the bombings as an answer to the busing program they openly hate. Where, a less involved observer wonders, is the simple reasoning which would inform them that the buses being blown up were bought and must be restored by their tax money?

Further, how is it they mistake inanimate objects — the buses — as the cause of their distress?

When answers to such questions are fully understood, this country will be much closer to shedding its reputation for being a dangerously violent society. Certain violent crimes span the centuries, but does it follow that indiscriminate, brutal mayhem is inevitable.

The United States is a land of many handsome settings, where quiet and serenity can be searched out. But for extreme, inexplicable acts of malign fury, it is also a place with few equals. And the worry is that as the nation grows more urban, as its people live increasingly closer together, this tendency to homicidal outbreaks will not be controlled.

The country's history is punctuated by violence but usually of a limited kind. Revolutionary and civil wars, labor and agrarian movements, the settling of a frontier and defending the national existence — all have set force against reason. And yet the conflict was usually identifiable and the use of violence a last resort.

That doesn't appear so much the case today. Rather, there seems a blind lashing out in fear, in anger or in despair and without exhausting all avenues to a peaceful reconciliation. A few severe pains don't necessarily mean certain collapse, but a nation that continually ignores the abnormality in mounting, stupid violence is heading for disaster.

The Des Moines Register

Des Moines, Iowa, September 9, 1971

Busing to achieve racial integration of schools comes to a large northern city next week when San Francisco attempts to carry out a federal District Court desegregation order. About 25,000 of the city's 48,000 elementary school pupils are scheduled to be bused under the plan. Many parents have vowed to boycott the schools rather than comply.

The federal court found that only 29 per cent of San Francisco elementary school pupils are black but 80 per cent of them have been concentrated in 27 of the city's 102 elementary schools. The court found this wasn't wholly a result of housing patterns. The court said the school district had advanced segregation by zoning new schools and setting attendance boundaries to concentrate Negro youngsters in a few schools.

This form of discrimination can be as effective in creating segregated schools as the laws requiring segregation that were struck down by the Supreme Court in 1954. Busing to eliminate the dual schools created by Jim Crow laws has been upheld by the high court. Busing is just as justifiable in cases where school officials used their authority to create the equivalent of dual schools.

A complicating factor in the San Francisco situation is that blacks aren't the only minority group affected. About 6,500 Chinese-American youngsters attend predominantly oriental public schools. Though blacks object to their segregation and brought the desegregation suit, Chinese-American parents approve the predominantly oriental character of their schools and object to the busing program.

How much of this is due to opposition to mixing with blacks and how much to cultural factors isn't clear. Spokesmen claim the busing program would make it difficult for Chinese-American youngsters to be returned home in time to attend after-hours private schools for instruction in Chinese language and culture. But it is evident that many oriental parents also share the same objections as white parents to sending their children to school with blacks.

About 2,000 Chinese-American youngsters have been taking the private language and cultural instruction for two hours daily. It shouldn't be impossible to re-arrange the public and private school hours to enable the youngsters to continue to receive this training.

The public schools in Chinatown are among the oldest and most rundown in the city. No new school building has been constructed in the area in the last quarter-century. Busing the youngsters from their neighborhood school might be inconvenient, but it might also result in better education.

Los Angeles Times

Los Angeles, Calif., September 5, 1971

Nobody seems to like the bussing of school children. It wasn't always so. Rural school children for years have been bussed many miles to consolidated schools. The school bus is a familiar sight on city streets all over the country.

But the bussing that arouses opposition is bussing used as one means to integrate schools. President Nixon is not against all bussing, only bussing to desegregate schools. He accepts it only "to the minimum required by law." Some people in Pontiac, Mich., are against it regardless of the law. They dynamited 10 school buses the other night in a city where children have been bussed for years to segregated schools.

Residents of San Francisco's Chinatown oppose bussing. They want their children to remain in neighborhood schools. The fate of the Los Angeles judge who ordered full integration of city schools, which would require heavy bussing, is one indication of sentiment here.

Chief Justice Warren E. Burger is, by his own word, "disturbed." He said some federal judges may be "misreading" the Supreme Court's April decision and ordering more school desegregation in Southern cities than the law requires. That decision, he said, did not require "a fixed racial balance," which is true, and some Southern school districts, with increased bussing, are achieving a better racial balance than they would have been forced to accept by the law. Is that potentially harmful or disturbing?

Bussing now has become an easy code word for anti-integrationists, but opposition to it, especially for long distances, is not altogether that. The community school has a strong and valid appeal, particularly in the great metropolitan centers, where it is one of the truly unifying forces.

As an instrument of integration, bussing, as the Supreme Court said it could be, is being employed in the smaller communities, and to great advantage. And bussing —although to what extent has not been decided—will be one of the tools of integration in the big cities. It must be kept in mind when the difficulties of the present are considered, great as they may be, their roots in our history cannot be dismissed. We must pay our dues.

Integration of schools, the center of attention at this point in the struggle, is only one aspect of the broader goal. A Southern governor, talking recently at commencement exercises, said, "You have the ability and the opportunity to seek the broad community desegregation and cooperation which ultimately will make bussing unnecessary. Only in this way will we put the divisive and self-defeating issue of race behind us once and for all."

The governor of Florida was going beyond the cold letter of the law: He was attempting to appeal to something greater: the idealism and hope of the American people.

These qualities, too, have their roots in our history.

San Francisco Chronicle

San Francisco, Calif.

September 15, 1971

LIKE IT OR NOT, those San Franciscans who have elected to boycott busing by keeping their children out of school in protest against it are ill-advised.

The law requires integration. The Federal court directed the school authorities to implement their so-called Horseshoe Plan to achieve integration. The school authorities found that to achieve it a large degree of busing would be necessary. The schools have now opened and the thing to do is to send the children back to school.

Happily, the anticipated first-day crisis has passed peacefully. School attendance was appreciably better yesterday, the second day, than it was the first, and school authorities are predicting that organized support for the boycott will continue to dwindle.

JUDGE STANLEY A. WEIGEL'S order of July 9 to institute the Horseshoe Plan, with its massive busing requirement, was based on the premise that San Francisco's was a de jure (i.e., deliberately) segregated school system. There are many who have expressed strong doubts about this premise. Whether the premise was right or wrong, however, is at the moment beside the point.

Nevertheless, to say that children belong in school and that their parents are lawfully bound to send them does not dispose of the criticism that the San Francisco Board of Education's plan is an overplan. When its advisory citizens' committee was drawing up Horseshoe, its criteria did not include the one objective which is most obvious, that of achieving racial balance with the least transferring of children. Close observers of the Horseshoe Plan have concluded that Horseshoe is a hopelessly computerized scheme for overbusing, not minimum busing.

CLEARLY, IN A SENSITIVE area like race relations and race-balancing, one cannot safely or sensibly turn over to a computer all the decisions governing the school assignments and educational lives of 25,000 elementary school youngsters.

This becomes painfully obvious when we find that the computer has decreed that black children, already integrated in their school on Treasure Island, shall be bused into the city to be reintegrated in a different school.

Nor has the computer made sense in decreeing that black children, formerly in a well-integrated school in the central city, should be bused to schools in Hunters Point.

RATHER THAN WITHHOLDING children from school, the busing boycotters would be better advised to direct their attention to studying, devising and seeking support for revisions of the Horseshoe Plan that would require minimum busing.

Public Reactions: 1972-73

Primary Elections

Florida. Gov. George C. Wallace of Alabama began another quest for the Presidency Jan. 13, declaring that he would run in Florida's March 14 presidential primary as a Democrat.

Wallace, who ran against President Nixon and Hubert Humphrey in 1968 as a third party candidate, refused, however, to rule out the possibility that he would make the 1972 White House race as an independent.

Wallace, 52, formally announced his candidacy in Tallahassee. He said that he alone in a field of 14 Democrats gave Florida voters a chance to protest the busing of their children out of neighborhood schools and other intrusions of "big government" into their private lives.

"I make this prediction," Wallace said: "If the people of Florida vote for me, Mr. Nixon in 30 to 60 days after this campaign is over will end busing himself." Wallace said the President was "waiting to see if you're really as opposed to this trifling with children as he thinks you are."

Florida referendum. Florida Gov. Reubin Askew announced Feb. 14 he would not veto a bill passed the previous day placing the school busing issue on the March 14 primary ballot, although he would ask voters to reject the antibusing proposal. At his insistence, an additional referendum was to be placed before the voters on equal educational opportunity. A third proposal on school prayer had been attached during legislative debate.

The ballot questions would read:

"Do you favor an amendment to the U.S. Constitution that would prohibit forced busing and guarantee the right of each student to attend the appropriate public school nearest his home?

"Do you favor providing an equal opportunity for quality education for all children regardless of race, creed, color or place of residence and oppose a return to a dual system of public schools?

"Do you favor an amendment to the U.S. Constitution to allow prayer in the public schools?"

The governor, who had supported busing as a "necessary evil," said the two proposed amendments "may begin the destruction of what is one of the greatest documents ever conceived." Observers believed the referenda, by attracting a larger than usual turnout among former segregationists might help Gov. Wallace in the presidential preference poll.

Wallace wins primary. Gov. George C. Wallace won the Florida Democratic presidential primary March 14, collecting 42% of the vote against 10 other candidates. He picked up 75 of the state's 81 delegates to the Democratic National Convention.

Wallace dominated the campaign as well as the voting. He chided the other candidates on the necessity of focusing on his issues—school busing, taxing the rich and cracking down on crime. But busing, like Wallace, became the major issue.

Wallace flatly opposed any form of busing to desegregate schools. Humphrey opposed forced busing and busing children from good schools and neighborhoods to bad ones. He condoned busing if the education were improved thereby. Jackson proposed a constitutional amendment to prohibit mandatory busing. Muskie, busy in New Hampshire much of the Florida campaign, resisted the issue of busing, which he considered an undesirable but sometimes necessary tool to achieve desegregation. Lindsay, McGovern and Mrs. Chisholm also competing for the liberal vote, firmly supported busing as a way to desegregate until integrated neighborhoods, which would eliminate the need for busing, were attained.

Voters approve antibusing amendment. The Florida primary also featured two straw votes on the busing issue through questions on the ballot, without legal effect. The results: 74% of the voters favored a constitutional amendment to prohibit busing and to guarantee the right of a student to attend the public school nearest his home; 79% favored an equal opportunity for quality education for all children and opposed the return to a dual system of public schools.

The voters also were asked whether they favored an amendment to allow prayer in public schools. 79% did.

The school busing question was put on the ballot from a Republican initiative in the state legislature. Opponents tried to kill it by adding the school prayer question, which was accepted instead. Then Gov. Reubin Askew (D) tried to negate the busing question by insisting, prior to signing the bill authorizing it, on the equal education question.

Askew campaigned actively against an expression of support for the school busing amendment. After the outcome was evident March 14, Askew called upon President Nixon to exert leadership on the problem and "start talking about alternatives that will not carry us back to a dual [school] system."

Final Florida Results		
Democrats		
Wallace	515,916	(41.5%)
Humphrey	231,219	(18.6%)
Jackson	167,667	(13.5%)
Muskie	109,653	(8.8%)
Lindsay	81,322	(6.5%)
McGovern	74,880	(6.1%)
Mrs. Chisholm	44,786	(3.6%)
Republicans		
Nixon	357,356	(87.1%)
Ashbrook	35,983	(8.8%)
McCloskey	16,985	(4.1%)
Straw Votes		
To prohibit compulsory busing of schoolchildren:		
Yes 74%	No 26%	
To provide equal opportunity for quality education:		
Yes 79%	No 21%	
To allow prayer in public schools:		
Yes 79%	No 21%	

Tennessee. Wallace won 68% of the vote in Tennessee's first presidential preference primary May 4, but the primary was marked by the almost total absence of any campaign or organized opposition.

The primary featured a non-binding referendum, similar to the one in the Florida primary, on whether the voters favored a constitutional amendment to ban busing of schoolchildren for the purpose of racial integration. A nearly complete tally favored the busing ban, 420,500–105,571.

North Carolina. Alabama Gov. George Wallace took 50% of the vote to win the Democratic presidential primary in

North Carolina May 6 and rebuff a progressive Southerner, former Gov. Terry Sanford, who won 37% of the vote. Wallace captured 408,785 votes, Sanford collected 304,397.

Riding his opposition to the busing of schoolchildren as a top issue, Wallace won, as the proportion of his statewide popular vote, 37 of the state's 64 delegates to the national convention for a first-ballot vote. Sanford won the remaining 27 delegates. On the busing issue, Sanford supported integrated schools as a national goal with implementation left to local governments.

Wallace sweeps Michigan primary. Gov. Wallace won a sweeping victory in the Michigan Democratic presidential primary May 16 with 51% of the vote, his first plurality in a Northern state election since he entered such competition in 1964.

The busing of school children to attain racial balance in public schools, which Wallace adamantly opposed, was a dominant issue. Both McGovern and Humphrey, when they opened their last-minute campaigns May 11–12, were immediately confronted with the issue and both "wavered" from liberal support of busing as a tool of integration, if necessary, to express reservations about federal courts possibly having gone "too far" in demanding massive busing.

Resolutions, Polls and Demonstrations

AFL-CIO takes probusing position. The AFL-CIO Executive Council, at its meeting in Florida Feb. 15, approved a statement supporting busing "wholeheartedly," opposing any antibusing amendment and reaffirming support for "quality, integrated education." They criticized those who were stirring a "divisive political issue," which included the White House, according to President George Meany.

CORE takes antibusing position. Although most major black organizations opposed the antibusing moves, some 50 members of the Congress of Racial Equality (CORE) invaded the Washington offices of Rep. Augustus Hawkins (D, Calif.) Feb. 11 to demand that blacks opposing busing be given a voice in black national meetings. CORE stressed community control and "separate but really equal" schools, according to leader Victor A. Solomon.

Roy Wilkins, executive director of the National Association for the Advancement of Colored People, said Feb. 15 that President Nixon's proposed moves "would return segregation to this country, return 'Jim Crowism' to the schools," and "nullify the Civil Rights Act of 1964." He said "the President of all the people" had erred in inviting only busing opponents to his meeting, ignoring "22 million people who have millions of children in the schools."

Georgia boycott fails. A proposed Feb. 28 statewide boycott of Georgia public schools to protest a court-ordered integration plan in Augusta failed to develop outside that city, Savannah and Albany.

But in Augusta and surrounding Richmond County about 65% of the system's 36,000 pupils stayed home, in a repeat of a Feb. 14 boycott, when the first stage of a three-part integration plan was scheduled to begin.

U.S. Supreme Court Justice Lewis F. Powell had refused Feb. 11 to stay the desegregation order issued by U.S. District Court Judge Alexander A. Lawrence and upheld by the 5th Circuit Court of Appeals. The plan, which would involve the busing for integration of 5,681 students when fully implemented in September, was based on a cluster school system, in which several neighboring schools were combined into zones, and the pupils transferred to achieve racial balance.

Republican U.S. Rep. Fletcher Thompson called Feb. 16 for the statewide boycott, to pressure Congress into passing a constitutional amendment against busing for integration. Gov. Jimmy Carter (D.) had tentatively supported the statewide boycott, it was reported Feb. 16.

One half the students in Savannah participated in the Feb. 28 boycott, along with one quarter of those in Albany.

69% oppose busing. Newsweek magazine reported in its March 13 issue that a telephone Gallup Poll it commissioned found that busing children for desegregation continued to be opposed by large majorities cutting across geographic and even racial lines, while support for desegregation in general remained strong.

Although only 3% of the parents of school age children said their children had been affected, 68% of Northern whites, 74% of Southern whites, and "nearly half" the small sample of blacks opposed "compulsory busing" for desegregation. Of the sample of 548 adults, 46% supported an antibusing constitutional amendment, while 35% were opposed.

In answer to a question whether "schools in this country, both North and South, should be desegregated," 58% of Southern whites and 68% of Northern whites agreed.

Lawyers vs. Nixon bills. A letter signed by Harvard University President Derek C. Bok and 34 members of the law school faculty, sent to the chairmen of the House and Senate Judiciary Committees April 12, said President Nixon's proposals to limit court-ordered busing would "sacrifice the enforcement of constitutional rights," and "impair the functions of the judiciary under a rule of law." The signers recorded their "strong doubts" about the bills' constitutionality.

Antibusing march ends. Mrs. Irene McCabe and five supporters April 27 completed a six-week march from Pontiac, Mich. to Washington, D.C. to pub-

licize support for an antibusing constitutional amendment. Mrs. McCabe had helped organize opposition to a 1971 Pontiac school busing program.

Parent, teacher resolution on busing. The annual convention of the 8.5 million member National Congress of Parents and Teachers passed a resolution May 23 by a 303–296 vote asking government and educational authorities "to search for solutions that would by rational means reduce racial isolation through transportation." A resolution against busing across district lines was defeated by a 342–331 vote.

Polls show Nixon support. According to a Harris Survey reported July 17, Americans who were polled agreed with President Nixon rather than with Sen. McGovern on 15 of 16 key policy issues. Among them:

■ Ending U.S. involvement in Vietnam—Nixon 52%, McGovern 33%;

■ Checking rises in the cost of living—Nixon 47%, McGovern 24%;

■ Busing children to school to achieve racial balance—Nixon 49%, McGovern 23%.

Blacks

Blacks oppose Nixon move. Prominent black spokesmen, including the Congressional Black Caucus, the Council of Black Appointees of the Nixon Administration and leaders of black organizations spoke out against plans to limit busing March 15–28.

The 13 Black Caucus members issued a statement March 15 saying "we strongly reaffirm our support of busing as one of the many ways to implement the constitutional requirement of equal opportunities in education," although "massive busing" would usually not be required. They criticized "those who would exploit this issue for personal, political or monetary gain."

The same day, Gary, Ind. Mayor Richard G. Hatcher, who had helped chair the National Black Political Convention in that city March 10–12, reported that the convention, after passing a resolution against busing that was widely reported in the press, passed a supplementary resolution supporting the practice "in cases where it serves the end of providing quality education for black people."

The Council of Black Appointees of the Nixon Administration said in a March 20 statement it was studying ways to amend Nixon's legislative proposals "to safeguard the rights of black Americans," since the bills posed "grave constitutional questions" which "unintentionally, may adversely affect" blacks.

Black groups split on busing stands. Clarence Mitchell, Washington, D.C. office director of the National Association for the Advancement of Colored People, said March 28 his organization would challenge Nixon's proposals in the courts "before the ink is dry" if passed by Congress. He called the bills "the most blatant products of racism that I have seen in the federal government."

National Black Convention. Some 3,300 voting delegates and 5,000 observers met in Gary, Ind. March 10–12 as the first National Black Political Convention and voted to set up a permanent representative body to set the direction for black political and social actions. However, the convention failed to resolve strategy differences between those who favored working within the traditional two-party structure and those favoring separatist action. The convention also recorded itself against school busing to achieve integration, endorsed an agenda calling for radical social and economic changes, and refused to back any candidate for the Democratic presidential nomination.

The proposed National Black Assembly would have 427 delegates chosen from the District of Columbia and the 43 states represented at the Gary convention. The assembly would choose a council of 43 members, with guaranteed representation for all regions, viewpoints, organizations, youth and women. While the functions of the assembly, which was authorized by a 2,404–405 vote March 12, were left largely undefined, Imamu Amiri Baraka (formerly known as LeRoi Jones), one of the three convention co-chairmen, said it "could endorse candidates, support candidates, run national voter education and registration drives, lobby for black issues, assess black progress, make recommendations to the national convention" (which itself would be convened every four years) and "be a chief brokerage operation for dealing with the white power political institutions."

Black agenda ratified; NAACP quits. The National Black Political Convention released the 58-page "black agenda" May 19 that had been approved by the March founding meeting in Gary, Ind. Provisions on school busing and on Israel, although modified by the steering committee, continued to provoke controversy, and the National Association for the Advancement of Colored People (NAACP) withdrew from the group.

The agenda contained a broad range of political and economic proposals to be presented to the Republican and Democratic national conventions and to the presidential candidates. The group's co-chairmen, Gary Mayor Richard Hatcher, Rep. Charles C. Diggs Jr. (D, Mich.) and Newark, N.J. activist Imamu Amiri Baraka, pledged to campaign against candidates who opposed the proposals.

The school integration provision, originally calling busing "racist" and "suicidal," was modified into a criticism of the Nixon Administration for "making busing an issue," a commitment to finding "supreme quality education for all

our youngsters," and a demand that blacks retain control of any busing program.

The NAACP withdrawal was announced May 16. It attributed the break to "a difference in ideology," reflected in a "separatist and nationalist intent" in many of the agenda's provisions and in its preamble. The busing and Israel provisions were cited as "particularly outrageous" examples by Assistant Executive Director Dr. John A. Morsell. Executive Director Roy Wilkins had written the three co-chairmen May 3 that the agenda, by concentrating on seizing control of ghetto institutions rather than demanding "an equitable black share of control" in the white-dominated mainstream institutions, would "fetter black America" in poverty.

Armour Report

Integration gains denied. A study of school integration programs involving busing in six Northern cities, reported May 21, found no improvement in either academic achievement among black students or racial cooperation.

The study was conducted by Harvard University professor David J. Armor, and included programs in Boston, White Plains, N.Y., Ann Arbor, Mich., Riverside, Calif. and Hartford and New Haven, Conn. While no significant academic differences were found between black students bused and control groups which remained in ghetto schools, the first group tended to show declines in self-esteem and in educational and job aspirations. Armor recommended, however, that voluntary busing programs be continued since the bused students tended to get better opportunities for higher education.

Armor emphasized that his study involved only short-term effects, but wrote "it appears that integration increases racial identity and solidarity," and "at least in the case of black students, leads to increasing desires for separation."

Integration report challenged. A study by Harvard University professor David J. Armor questioning the benefits for black pupils of school busing for integration programs was criticized in a June 3 newspaper interview by fellow Harvard professor Thomas F. Pettigrew.

Speaking for a group of Harvard scholars challenging the report, Pettigrew said the report ignored some successful busing experiments, did not cover a long enough time span, and was based on too few individuals to be meaningful. In addition, the report allegedly averaged out widely differing results in different participating schools. Pettigrew said evidence of increased race consciousness among bussed black students could be explained by the assassination of Rev. Martin Luther King Jr. in 1968, when most of the data was recorded.

Mayors Conference

Mayors meet. The 40th annual U.S. Conference of Mayors met in New Orleans June 17–21. Resolutions favoring or opposing school busing for integration were tabled June 18 by a 9–5 vote of the resolutions committee.

Resolutions favoring or opposing school busing for integration were tabled June 18 by a 9–5 vote of the resolutions committee.

Party Platforms

Democratic platform drafted. The Democratic National Convention's Platform Committee completed work June 27 on a draft platform for presentation to the convention. Extreme proposals from the right and left were rejected and the majority of McGovern members took to the middle ground. The committee rejected, by a 78–16 vote June 26, a Wallace proposal opposing "forced busing" of school children and approved, by a 70–27 vote, another supporting busing as one tool for achieving desegration in areas where segregation was legally imposed.

Few changes in liberal document. In a marathon 11-hour session July 11–12 the convention adopted with only two minor changes the liberal draft platform prepared by the 150-member platform committee in Washington two weeks before.

Despite a dramatic wheelchair appearance by Gov. George Wallace to support the conservative minority reports, the convention rejected by large voice vote margins his stands on school busing, school prayer, gun control, defense and Vietnam.

The conservative report asked for a strong stand against school busing for desegregation, a constitutional amendment allowing school prayers, support for the right of citizens to bear arms, a strong military establishment and a pledge to remain in Vietnam until American prisoners were released. The Wallace forces did not demand roll call votes, and the planks were defeated by lopsided voice vote margins; former Humphrey and Muskie backers added to the majority on some issues.

A compromise busing plank offered near the end of the session by a Michigan delegate to oppose "massive or cross-district busing" or busing to "schools of lesser quality" was also defeated, after McGovern leaders reported the senator's opposition. Ted van Dyk, chief McGovern platform aide, explained that attempts to reach compromises with Wallace forces had failed in platform committee hearings.

The Supreme Court of the United States in Brown v Board of Education established the Constitutional principle that states may not discriminate between school children on the basis of their race and that separate but equal has no place in our public education system. Eighteen years later the provision of integration is not a reality.

We support the goal of desegregation as a means to achieve equal access to quality education for all our children. There are many ways to desegregate schools: School attendance lines may be redrawn; schools may be paired; larger physical facilities may be built to serve larger, more diverse enrollments; magnet schools or educational parks may be used. Transportation of students is another tool to accomplish desegregation. It must continue to be available according to Supreme Court decisions to eliminate legally imposed segregation and improve the quality of education for all children.

Republican platform approved. With perfunctory debate, the convention approved by voice vote Aug. 22 the 1972 Republican party platform, a document that was written largely under the guidance of the White House.

We are committed to guaranteeing equality of educational opportunity and to completing the process of ending *de jure* school segregation.

At the same time, we are irrevocably opposed to busing for racial balance. Such busing fails its stated objective—improved learning opportunities—while it achieves results no one wants—division within communities and hostility between classes and races. We regard it as unnecessary, counter-productive and wrong.

We favor better education for all children, not more transportation for some children. We favor the neighborhood school concept. We favor the decisive actions the President has proposed to support these ends. If it is necessary to accomplish these purposes, we would favor consideration of an appropriate amendment to the Constitution.

Presidential Campaign

Agnew's acceptance speech. In his acceptance speech Aug. 23, Agnew defined his role as vice president, lauded President Nixon's leadership, deplored dividing Americans into "quotas" and posed what he considered the major issues of the campaign.

Agnew framed the issues in a series of questions. Should the U.S.: Continue to be a world power or retreat into isolationism? Continue to seek mutual arms curbs or "disarm unilaterally?" Continue to return power to state and local governments or "revert to the discredited paternalism" of recent Democratic Administrations? Utilize the free enterprise system to provide jobs for everyone or "make the government a preferred employer?" Continue to try to upgrade education for all children by improving neighborhood schools or seek "arbitrary racial balance in each school by busing children back and forth over long distances?"

Nixon opens campaign. President Nixon opened his campaign Aug. 24. He flew to Utica, Mich. to dedicate a new high school and issue a statement reaffirming his opposition to school busing to achieve "an arbitrary racial balance."

Nixon assails 'welfare ethic.' President Nixon upheld the "work ethic" and denounced the "welfare ethic" in a Labor Day statement issued Sept. 3. "We are faced this year," he said, "with the choice between the 'work ethic' that built this nation's character and the new 'welfare ethic' that could cause

that American character to weaken." The former taught that "everything valuable in life requires some striving and some sacrifice," Nixon said, while the latter "says that the good life can be made available to everyone right now and that this can be done by the government."

In citing areas in which the 'welfare ethic' posed challenges to traditional values, Nixon attacked (1) "a policy of income redistribution," generally associated with Democratic presidential candidate George McGovern, and (2) the involuntary busing of schoolchildren away from their neighborhoods for the purpose of achieving racial balance."

Visit to Atlanta. President and Mrs. Nixon received an enthusiastic greeting from a huge crowd during a motorcade along Peachtree Street in Atlanta Oct. 12. Nixon told a group of southern Republican leaders later that what his critics called a "Southern strategy" was in fact an "American strategy," that issues, such as busing, that affected the South were also at issue in other areas of the country. Among the issues from which he hoped to gain his "new American majority" were respect for law and order and strengthening "the peace forces against the criminal forces" in the nation, Nixon said.

Nixon defines 'new majority.' President Nixon defined the tenets of "the new American majority" Oct. 21 and outlined "the principles which will guide me in making decisions over the next four years."

In his third paid radio address of the presidential campaign, Nixon upheld individualism, self-reliance and hard work as the personal characteristics he would seek to foster in the national character. And he cited taxation, school busing, job quotas, income redistribution and national defense as the issues which embodied these principles.

He did not think it was right to charge a man with selfishness, he said, because he objected to seeing "more and more of the money he earns taken away by government taxation." He did not think it right to charge a mother with bigotry when she objected to seeing "her child taken from a neighborhood school and transported miles away."

He did not think it was right to condemn young people "as insensitive or racist" when they objected because they were shut out from jobs "in politics or in industry" because "they don't fit into some numerical quota despite their ability."

There was no reason to feel guilty, Nixon said, "about wanting to enjoy what you get and get what you earn, about wanting your children in good schools close to home or about wanting to be judged fairly on your ability."

Conceding that "some people oppose income redistribution and busing for the wrong reasons," the President said "they are by no means the majority of

Americans, who oppose them for the right reasons."

Radio speech on education. In a 15-minute nationwide radio campaign speech, the fifth such broadcast, Nixon restated Oct. 25 his opposition to court-ordered busing plans to desegregate public schools. He also promised to continue seeking legislation to stop it.

Nixon defended his Administration's antibusing proposals by contending that "the answer to inequities in our educational system is to spend more money on learning and less money on busing."

McGovern winds up two-week swing. Democratic presidential candidate George McGovern ended his second two-week campaign tour Sept. 26 with a 24-hour non-stop effort in San Francisco and Los Angeles accompanied by Sen. Hubert H. Humphrey (D, Minn.).

During the week, McGovern focused his attacks on what he called President Nixon's "special interest" government. He also accused Nixon of exploiting the school busing issue.

Elections

McGovern discusses his defeat. Losing Democratic presidential candidate George McGovern, in an interview published Nov. 14, expressed determination to "keep the heat on" President Nixon to end the Vietnam war, cut military spending and reorder national priorities.

The day "the handwriting was probably on the wall," McGovern said, was the day Alabama Gov. George C. Wallace was shot, which prevented his third-party candidacy and bid for the independent vote. This left Wallace supporters "vulnerable to a strong Nixon bid," which the President had been preparing "for some time," McGovern said. "I suppose the busing issue was the code word, and the attacks on welfare recipients."

Tennessee. Sen. Howard H. Baker Jr. (R), with 714,398 votes, won expected re-election over Rep. Ray Blanton (D), who garnered 441,251 votes.

Blanton, a conservative whose House seat had been lost in reapportionment, had given the McGovern ticket only nominal backing. He emphasized local issues in the campaign and charged that Baker had nominated a federal judge in Nashville who later ordered school busing.

Illinois. Incumbent Republican Sen. Charles H. Percy won a second term by a large margin over seven-term Rep. Roman C. Pucinski of Chicago, piling up votes in all sections of the state to surpass Nixon's statewide total. Percy had managed to regain support from conservative Republicans despite his relatively dovish stand on Vietnam and his votes against Nixon's Supreme Court nominees, and despite Pucinski's emphatic antibusing position. Percy's vote total was 2,825,772; Pucinski's was 1,678,784.

Michigan. Senate Minority Whip Robert P. Griffin defeated Michigan Attorney General Frank J. Kelley in a Senate race dominated largely by the issue of school busing, which both candidates opposed. Kelley had at first signed a statement supporting busing as one integration tool, but later recanted and led Michigan's fight against a court order for Detroit city-suburb busing. Griffin had helped lead the unsuccessful Senate fight for strong antibusing legislation. Griffin, along with President Nixon, ran strongly in working class Detroit suburbs, while low voter turnout in Detroit held down Kelly's total.

Calif. bus ban challenged. The National Association for the Advancement of Colored People filed a class action suit in Superior Court in Sacramento, Calif. Nov. 29 seeking to invalidate an antibusing constitutional amendment approved by voters Nov. 7.

The amendment, passed 4,905,247–2,877,596, banned involuntary pupil transfers for integration. The American Civil Liberties Union reported Nov. 11 it had also filed suit against the measure, as part of a pending Santa Barbara integration case, saying the amendment "significantly encourages and involves the state in racial discrimination."

New York

N.Y. school boycott ends. About 6,000 white students returned to nine schools Nov. 9 in New York's mostly white working class Canarsie section after a two-week boycott called to protest the transfer of 31 black and Puerto Rican students to a junior high school in the district.

The students had been ordered bused to the school from a housing project in an overcrowded neighboring area, but the community school board tried to countermand the order. The city board overruled its opposition, and the students were escorted by police into the building for the first time Oct. 27 past a jeering mob of whites.

Michigan

Five shot in Pontiac. A 16-year-old youth was charged Nov. 28 with assault and attempt to commit murder, and two other 16-year-olds were charged with conspiracy to incite a riot, after five students were shot and wounded the previous day at a Pontiac, Mich. high

school. The incident marred the smooth implementation of a large-scale busing and rezoning integration plan, which had polarized the city along racial lines the previous school year.

1973
NAACP

NAACP in Atlanta split. The Atlanta chapter of the National Association for the Advancement of Colored People (NAACP) approved a desegregation plan for Atlanta schools that required a minimum of busing, and accepted continuation of predominantly black or white schools in return for assurances of increased black representation in administrative posts, it was reported Feb. 24.

But the NAACP national office in New York said March 8 it had suspended the Atlanta unit for disobeying a directive opposing the compromise, and the U.S. District Court in Atlanta deferred all rulings until March 29. In a separate action, the NAACP Legal Defense and Educational Fund filed a motion in the court March 8 opposing the plan.

Under the plan, which had to be approved by federal courts, fewer than 2,000 blacks and fewer than 1,000 whites would be bused. It would raise the proportion of blacks in all schools to at least 30% and leave enrollment virtually unchanged in 86 nearly all-black schools. An earlier NAACP plan would have bused 18,395 pupils.

Lonnie King, Atlanta NAACP president, noted that 78% of the city's school children were black, and said the compromise was an attempt "to halt the white flight." Some black parents had waged a campaign against the massive busing plan.

NAACP affirms integration goal. The National Association for the Advancement of Colored People (NAACP), at its 64th annual convention in Indianapolis July 2–6, reaffirmed—despite opposition of some delegates—its long-standing principle of school integration, approving a resolution calling for desegregation of state-supported college systems and voting to suspend the officials of the Atlanta chapter, which had accepted a local school plan de-emphasizing integration.

Michigan

5 guilty in Pontiac bus bombing. Detroit District Court Judge Lawrence Gubow May 21 found five former members of the Ku Klux Klan guilty of conspiracy in the plot to bomb school buses in Pontiac, Mich. during a busing controversy in

1971. The defendants had waived a jury trial.

Those convicted, all Klansmen at the time of the bombing, were: Robert E. Miles, Alexander J. Distel Jr., Wallace E. Fruit, Raymond Quick Jr. and Dennis C. Ramsey. Each faced jail terms of up to 10 years and/or a fine of up to $10,000.

Polls and Studies

Integration effects reported. A study by the U.S. Commission on Civil Rights found that school desegregation had contributed to the improvement of education, it was reported Aug. 1. The study, conducted during the 1972–73 school year, covered 10 communities in various stages of integration.

The study found that in nine of the 10 communities surveyed, people either accepted or were resigned to the fact of integration. Only in Charlotte-Mecklenburg County, N.C. was there an "apparent hardening of white racial attitudes" in response to integration efforts.

While most parents interviewed reported satisfaction with desegregation as it affected their own children, the commission noted, many of the same parents had voted against the busing of students on local and state referendums.

Poll finds busing in disfavor. The Gallup Poll reported Sept. 8 that while a large majority of the nation favored integration of public schools, only 5% (9% of the blacks and 4% of the whites) favored busing as a means of achieving integration.

Offered two alternative methods of integration, 27% of those polled favored changing school boundaries to allow persons from different economic and racial groups to attend the same schools, and 22% chose creation of more housing for low-income groups in middle-income neighborhoods. The poll found 18% (19% of the whites and 9% of the blacks) completely opposed to integration.

Other questions found that opposition to busing was based more on fears of infringement of personal liberties and higher school taxes than on racial animosities.

While only 27% of Northern white parents said they would object to sending their children to schools where as many as half the students were black, 63% said they would object if more than half the students were black. The latter figure was an increase from 51% in 1970. Corresponding figures for Southern white parents were 36% and 69%, the latter figure unchanged from 1970.

A

B

C

D

E

F

G

BLACK POLITICAL CAUCUS CONVENES; DIVIDED ON BUSING, ELECTIONS

The first National Black Political Convention, attended by a wide range of delegates from Black Panthers to representatives of the Nixon Administration, convened in Gary, Ind. March 10–12. The purpose of the meeting, according to co-chairman Imamu Amiri Baraka, formerly Leroi Jones, was to shape "a concrete and specific means of gaining political power for black people." The convention, attended by more than 3,000 delegates representing 43 states, voted to establish a permanent National Black Assembly empowered to "endorse candidates, support candidates, run national voter education and registration drives, lobby for black issues, assess black progress . . . [and] be a chief brokerage operation for dealing with the white power political institutions."

The convention was sharply divided over political cooperation with whites, school integration and the presidential candidacy of Rep. Shirley Chisholm (D, N.Y.). The agenda, adopted at the meeting's close, called for a "reparations payment" to the black community, a national black development agency, and a constitutional amendment to guarantee black Congressional representation in proportion to population. It opposed school busing for racial integration. The delegates refused to endorse any candidate in the presidential election.

THE POST-TRIBUNE

Gary, Ind., March 14, 1972

It would be easy to find fault with the now closed Black National Political Convention.

On balance, however, we believe it must be viewed as a success.

It should be noted that it has been easy to find fault in the past with Democratic and Republican conventions when they have had major differences—and they have been holding conventions for many years. This, it should also be noted, was the first time around for the black convention, at least within recent years.

It was a success because it gave focus to a voice not only demanding, but deserving to be heard. True, in one sense the voice was a cacophony of voices, but in its central lament that the American political system will lack validity until it recognizes the too long denied aspirations of one vast segment of society it sounded in attuned chorus.

Fault finders will cite a certain lack of organization which resulted in delayed meetings and in adoption of an agenda as a number of delegates walked off the floor. It was, however, over all, as orderly as most political conventions which face up to controversy. That, considering the lateness of the call—a mistake which could be corrected only by hindsight—was in itself an achievement.

Others will dissent from several specific portions of the adopted agenda. The demand for a national constitutional convention within a year seems unattainable. A call for 15 black senators and 66 black representatives in Congress is a goal which can be achieved only by state-by-state action. A $6,500 guaranteed annual income seems higher than most within the national establishment believe is attainable. Separate black unions would require long and vigorous organizing. The stand against

school busing was hotly disputed within the convention itself, though the stressing of more realistically adequate school financing as a more viable alternative is gaining ground.

But despite differences and goals which may in some cases be set too high, the agenda itself represents a refining of that voice into something which can be heard with more clarity than has been the case in the past. Even the adopted agenda itself is to be refined in later, smaller sessions, but it is vital as a starting point.

There were those who emphasized differences between Gary Mayor Richard Hatcher and the Rev. Jesse Jackson in their back-to-back keynote speeches, with the mayor calling for one more try within the established parties and the minister-organizer for a black party and a black nation. We believe, however, Post-Tribune reporter Guy Slaughter was more accurate in reporting that they played "variations of the same theme." Both speakers paraded the past sins of the white race in its dealings with blacks and both emphasized that the time had arrived for meaningful black political unity to force corrections of many of those sins. Both speeches may have been more in the tradition of religious revivalism than of deep political decision, but in the launching of a new movement that revivalist approach is vital.

A very definite plus for the convention was that those attending—representative of leadership in the black community from throughout the country—got to meet each other for the first time, and delegates, who have heard of varied black leaders, got a chance to meet them and hear them personally.

The convention's makeup ran the gamut from radical advocates of separatism and governmental overthrow to those who have made it on their own within the establishment and have much to gain from it. Out of such diverse backgrounds uniformity could not and should not develop.

But out of the shared background of denial which hopefully can be overcome by intra-racial cooperation, there came a clearer, more persistent voice. Giving rise to that voice was the Black National Convention's accomplishment.

THE WALL STREET JOURNAL.
New York, N.Y., March 11, 1972

The National Black Political Convention in Gary, Ind., over the week-end indicated that there is no uniform black position on most national issues, even in a group with a high level of political awareness.

The convention ended with only some one-third of the nearly 3,000 delegates still participating, the others having walked out over various disagreements. A final resolution called for a steering committee to try to reconcile the varying positions expressed by the delegates, who represented 43 states.

But if the results were confusing perhaps they will at least give pause to those people who profess to speak for the nation's blacks as if they represented a homogeneous bloc. That would seem to be particularly true on the issue of forced busing and other formulaic approaches to school integration. There appears to be as much disagreement among blacks on this issue as among whites.

The black convention at one point passed a resolution condemning busing, largely at the behest of delegates who also are members of the Congress of Racial Equality (CORE). Roy Innis, CORE's executive director, said that busing is counter to the interests of black people, who are "tired of being guinea pigs for social engineers and New York liberals."

Proponents of busing may well write off Mr. Innis's comments as black racism and the convention itself as not being representative of the views of blacks. Those are plausible criticisms, particularly in light of the differences that erupted within the convention.

But it would be well to pay some heed to what Mr. Innis said, nonetheless, because his attack on "social engineering" is of importance to citizens of whatever hue. Securing and protecting the rights that are promised to all Americans by the Constitution are one thing. Engineering a society in which everyone is expected to conform to the concepts of an intellectual elite is quite another.

The black convention demonstrated that blacks are not yet prepared to conform to the concepts of those who would mold them into a political bloc. Many prefer to find their own way, at a community and personal level, as well as in national political terms. That approach is in accordance with the American political and social tradition.

The black conventioneers can be thanked for reminding everyone that the busing issue is not easily divisible along racial lines, since there are blacks and whites alike who take contrary views on what best serves the interests of their children. And the convention is a further reminder that the heterogeneity of American society involves much more than racial differences. An understanding of that fact is a big step toward a better understanding of the American political process.

BUFFALO EVENING NEWS
Buffalo, N.Y., March 14, 1972

If one judged it only by concrete results, it would be hard to read much political significance, one way or the other, into the first-of-its-kind three-day national black political convention held in Gary, Ind., this week-end. For the convention endorsed no presidential ticket, launched no new party and brought forth no particularly ringing manifestos or platform proposals. In fact, some of the many resolutions it passed were as contradictory or as compromising in their thrust as are the typical platform straddles of the regular parties.

What the Gary convention did do, however, was plant some seeds of a black-identity or even a black-separatist movement that may grow a considerable harvest in future years. Whether this will be a harvest of bitterness and national disunity, or of a greater sense of black pride and identity within the dream of an America united, is something that only future events and future developments within this movement can determine.

The most specific accomplishment of the meeting was the creation of a proposed National Black Assembly, which will seek to cut across parties, philosophies and economic interest and to strengthen black effectiveness within the present political structure. The Assembly will hold its own black convention in advance of the regular party conventions each presidential year, which presumably would enable it to stay loose and either keep working within the existing system or form its own party whenever it so chose.

As with all major interest groups, the black political leadership covers a wide ideological spectrum from moderate all the way over to militant revolutionary. So long as the moderates can work within the system and get results which most blacks regard as fairly satisfactory, the call of the militants for separatism and revolution will presumably have little appeal. But this year's national campaign threatens to strain the faith of black moderates in the system in two ways.

One is the danger that both major parties will tend to take the heavily-Democratic black vote for granted — the Democrats treating them as if they have no place else to go, the Republicans as if they'll get few black votes anyway so why bother. The other is the danger that the major parties may get so emotionally hung-up on this year's issue of "forced bussing," or that they will handle it with such insensitivity to the feelings of most moderate blacks that they will contribute to a widening sense of black alienation from the system.

What the black convention in Gary seems to symbolize, then, is a wary readiness to stay with the two-party system for now, but a determination at the same time to keep all separatist options open in case this nation moves, as the 1967 National Riot Commission starkly warned, "toward two societies, one black, one white, separate and unequal." We hope the voices of black political moderation will continue to win enough victories within the system to keep the movement going in their direction.

The Boston Globe
Boston, Mass., March 15, 1972

There is obviously as much diversity among America's 25 million blacks as there is anywhere else in this melting pot nation. The miracle and the triumph of the three-day National Black Political Convention in Gary, Indiana, last weekend is that this fact was recognized and wrestled into a structure that clearly has the will to endure under the banner of "unity without uniformity."

Its purpose, in the words of 38-year old Newark nationalist Imamu Amiri Baraka, who formerly wrote poems and plays as LeRoi Jones, is to be "an issue-oriented focal point of black politics in the United States . . . a chief brokerage operation for dealing with the white power political institutions." And the fact that the 3331 voting delegates created a 51-member steering committee charged with naming a Black Assembly of 427 that will represent all regions and all ideologies — specifically women and the elderly, specifically integrationists and separatists — bodes well for the success of its mission.

And it bodes well for the American system that this was a true political convention, complete with Miss Indiana and Rev. Jesse Jackson's PUSH band, complete with time-consuming credentials checks and still more time-consuming speeches, wracked by frustrations and moulded in compromise.

The separatist black nationalists, who had drawn up a hard-line agenda and worked to stack delegations from the 42 states represented, failed to carry the day on such issues as the naming of a "black national assembly." It will be called the National Black Assembly. And it was in the rush to take up the question of endorsing Shirley Chisholm for President that CORE's Roy Innes was able to put through a motion to condemn busing and forced integration, in favor of local control.

The matter of endorsement, pushed by New York, failed as did the formation of a third party, at least for now. The question of a stand on busing and integration will be taken up again under a detailed reworking of the agenda by the steering committee, with Mayor Richard Hatcher of Gary, head of the 4000-member Black Elected Officials and one of the nation's most respected blacks, opposed on the grounds that it gives solace to white racists.

The resolutions contained in the agenda will all be reviewed by the steering committee. And many of the participants at Gary are scheduled to meet at Harvard on April 5 for a conference on national priorities.

The more important objectives of self recognition and an understanding of the nuts and bolts of obtaining a consensus within a political format were achieved. And the ongoing spirit was with the forces from the White House and the labor unions, the Panthers and the NAACP, the workers, the students and the housewives alike as they left for North and South at the convention's end.

The Dallas Morning News

Dallas, Tex., March 14, 1972

IN A BURST of enthusiasm, delegates to the National Black Political Convention have approved an agenda in which the organization takes a firm and uncompromising stand on both sides of the important issues.

With a delegate walkout beginning, the motion was made that the organization resolve conflicts by accepting everybody's preferred proposals, including those that directly contradicted each other. The motion was approved, as thousands cheered.

In doing so, they seem to have put their organization on record as being both for and against busing. The group is opposed to supporting any presidential candidate and, at the same time, dedicated to the support of candidate Rep. Shirley Chisholm.

Community control of schools is both an unmet need that must be filled and a cruel hoax that means a return to segregation—both views were offered, and apparently approved.

Sponsors of the caucus declared that the programs were advanced "with no real notion that white politics can endorse their direction."

That part of the agenda, certainly, is not debatable. It is extremely unlikely that "white politics" can figure out what the direction of this passel of programs is.

However, with millions of black votes at stake, there will undoubtedly be whole herds of white politicians who will try their hardest to determine what this new movement wants and will promise to deliver upon election.

Indeed, the most difficult thing to understand about this new politics experiment is what is new about it. The black convention seems to have operated under the same ground rules that govern most conventional caucuses and sessions these days. After bitter squabbles threatened to break up the meeting, the delegates decisively refused to let logic stand in their way. They remembered the three commandments of election year political meetings: Avoid offending. Promise all things to all voters. Head off dangerous internal conflicts at all cost.

Thus the new political body has united to speak to the waiting voters out of both sides of its mouth. That's political, all right. But that's nothing new.

WORCESTER TELEGRAM.

Worcester, Mass., March 14, 1972

The National Black Political Convention held in Gary, Ind., last week was right in line with a long American tradition.

Over the generations, many special interest groups have organized in this country to achieve specific goals. The Grangers, the Single Taxers, the Prohibitionists, the Anti-Masonic groups, the Suffragettes, the Irish, the Italians, the Jews, the Free Silverites, the America Firsters and countless others have used the tools of organization and political pressure to get a more favorable response from the American system.

The Gary convention was significant because it was the first time since perhaps the founding of the National Association for the Advancement of Colored People 60 years ago that U.S. black leaders have attempted to develop a national consensus on goals and procedures.

Not surprisingly, the attempt was not wholly successful. Like all other Americans, American blacks are widely diverse in their beliefs and attitudes. Some of the resolutions adopted contradicted each other. Thus, one resolution backed integrated schools while another condemned busing to achieve it.

The important thing was not the lack of agreement, but the determined effort to work within the system to bring about improvements. The political process of seeking common ground produced a different attitude in some quarters. Thus Imamu Amiri Baraka (LeRoi Jones) forsook his familiar fiery and mystical rhetoric for conciliation. Strong-willed people, confronted with others just as strong-willed, found that adjustments and compromises had to be made.

But this is the American system. This is democracy. Rhetoric, no matter how impassioned, counts for little if it does not lead to effective, constructive action.

The National Black Political Convention may have disappointed those who expected a more unified, more activist program. But it was a beginning — a notable beginning, it seems to us. It organized a setting in which black resentments and demands could be expressed and analyzed. It took the constructive, American approach, rather than the road to defeatism and despair.

CHICAGO DAILY NEWS

Chicago, Ill., March 14, 1972

The fact that there was a national convention of blacks in Gary over the weekend remains a major achievement and a tribute to the initiative of those who brought it into being. Its results were disappointing, but perhaps the negative lessons learned were an essential prelude to future progress.

The initial handicap was the fact that not all the delegates were elected — some just came and paid their fee and took part. That made for a minimum of genuine grass-roots representation and a maximum of individual ax-grinding.

Still, the convention that brought 3,546 delegates together from 43 states was a useful and significant event, and could presage an upswing in the degree of impact blacks will exert on the national political scene. It will certainly do this if a majority of the black leaders and their thoughtful followers will digest and apply the lessons to be drawn from the weekend in Gary.

One lesson is that if the black radicals and the black moderates are to be accommodated under the same political roof there will have to be a far greater spirit of give-and-take than was evident at Gary. The busing issue presents a fair example. The radicals succeeded in writing into the agenda — which was adopted — a resolution against busing that must have confused a legion of white observers as well as confounding the black moderates at the meeting. No one, of course, should accept this as a significant fusion of the philosophies of black and white radicals—or as any true distillation of black attitudes. The agenda was rammed through a hectic session with the thought that an unsatisfactory result was better than no result — a shaky premise at best.

A more promising development was the assurance that the demands approved in the agenda will be refined in a document to be produced with greater deliberation by a much smaller body consisting of state chairmen and representatives of black national organizations. Such demands, including a guaranteed annual income and proportionate representation in Congress, are legitimate and reachable through intelligent political action.

Such a document might become a useful political instrument. And such a body conceivably could become the nucleus of a "third political force."

Whether that force can ever develop into a full-fledged political party is quite another question. For the convention powerfully demonstrated that blacks are not as different from their fellow-Americans as some of their radical leaders have contended. Their viewpoints were as unreconciled as white Americans', and their concerns tend to be those of all citizens, not just blacks.

Whether black Americans choose to go ahead with plans for a black political party is their own business. But a more rewarding function for the organization that grows out of the convention would be to alert blacks to their own potential strength as a positive part of the national electorate, and not as a protest group.

WALLACE WINS; BUSING IS DEFEATED IN FLORIDA, MICHIGAN, TENNESSEE

Alabama Gov. George C. Wallace won the Florida Democratic presidential primary March 14, gaining 42% of the vote in a field of 11 candidates. Wallace's Florida victory was expected as he had dominated the contest from the beginning by making his total opposition to school busing for racial integration the central issue in the campaign. The other candidates had wavered between qualified opposition and full endorsement of the concept. On primary day Floridians also cast votes on the busing issue directly through two non-binding questions on the ballot. The results: 74% of the voters supported a constitutional amendment to prohibit busing and guarantee the right of a student to attend the public school nearest his home; 79% favored an equal opportunity for quality education for all children and opposed the return to a dual system of public schools. (The second question had been put on the ballot by Gov. Reubin Askew, who actively opposed the anti-busing effort.) Wallace also won the May primaries in Michigan and Tennessee. He captured respectively 51% and 68% of the vote. The statewide referendum in Tennessee resulted in a 4–1 vote against busing.

Portland Press Herald

Portland, Me., March 16, 1972

Ed Muskie's dismal showing in the Florida primary, following hard on the heels of his less-than-spectacular win in New Hampshire, takes much of the forward motion out of a campaign that has depended on momentum from the beginning.

Still, it would be foolish to count Sen. Muskie out at this point on the basis of these first two primary results. He remains the frontrunner, although Sens. McGovern and Humphrey are breathing hotly down his neck right now, and Sen. Jackson is getting up some momentum of his own.

A poll taken in the closing days of the Florida primary showed that the two dominant impressions voters there held of Muskie were that he was "too emotional" and that he waffled on the issues.

The first impression obviously sprang from his tearful outburst in the snows of New Hampshire. As for the second, in a state where everyone has very strong opinions on the subject of "forced busing," Muskie's temperate views may have sounded indecisive.

The busing issue, which dominated the Florida race, is one reason the primary results there may be misleading.

There are stronger, more important tests ahead for Muskie. If he wins the Illinois primary next week, as expected, it will go a long way toward getting him back on the momentum track heading into such crucial primaries as Wisconsin, Massachusetts and Pennsylvania.

Those are primaries in which Sen. Muskie must make a good showing. Any further stumbling could prove fatal to the Maine senator's presidential ambitions.

The Burlington Free Press

Burlington, Vt., March 16, 1972

THE RESULTS OF the Florida Presidential preference primary have really separated the men from the boys. Especially significant are the following:

(1) In a field of 11 Democratic candidates, George Wallace won a massive victory with 42 per cent of the vote. He also captured 75 of the 81 convention votes, giving him by far the largest number of votes accorded any Democratic candidate in this election year. Is it really so certain that Wallace won't be nominated by the Democrats?

(2) Hubert Humphrey came in second with a respectable showing of 18 per cent and the other six convention votes. A rerun of the 1968 Nixon-Humphrey battle seems a distinct possibility.

(3) Henry Jackson demonstrated unexpected strength with 13 per cent of the vote, but most observers doubt he has any chance for the nomination. He's a prime Vice Presidential possibility, however.

(4) Edmund Muskie suffered a drubbing, receiving only 9 per cent of the vote. He is probably finished as a candidate to be taken seriously.

(5) John Lindsay spent huge amounts of money, much of it on a lavish television saturation campaign, and he spent more time in the state than most other candidates, yet he suffered a crushing rejection — only 7 per cent of the vote. This was a fitting response to the shallow opportunist from New York.

(6) It was said that Lindsay and George McGovern would split the "liberal" vote. What "liberal" vote? Together the two of them received fewer votes than Henry Jackson!

(7) Some observers were suggesting yesterday that the Democrats may have to turn to Teddy Kennedy. If the Democrats do they will be committing political suicide. Kennedy's recent far-out statements (Northern Ireland, amnesty, etc.) and peculiar conduct (cheap allegations in the ITT flap) have angered large segments of the American public.

(8) On the Republican side, President Nixon won another smashing victory with an incredible 87 per cent of the vote and all 40 convention votes. John Ashbrook, the conservative challenger, won 9 per cent of the vote and Paul McCloskey, the liberal challenger who can't decide whether to stay in the race or not, received a dismal 4 per cent of the vote.

(9) On the important three straw vote questions, 74 per cent of Floridians want to prohibit forced busing of school children, 79 per cent want to provide equal opportunity for quality education for all children, and 79 per cent want to allow prayer in the public schools. The results only confirm the overwhelming public opposition, throughout the nation and among both blacks and whites, to forced busing.

(10) As of this writing, it appears there are only three "live" candidates for the Democratic nomination: Wallace, Humphrey and Kennedy. And Humphrey is obviously the only one of the three who would have a ghost of a chance of defeating President Nixon. — F.B.S.

The Miami Herald

Miami, Fla., March 16, 1972

GEORGE WALLACE won Florida by a landslide. He also won it by surprise — including his own. He carried every county. He carried every congressional district save one. He even carried Dade County, but only with 27 per cent of the vote compared to his statewide plurality of 42 per cent.

The analysts are busy at their charts and even at their microscopes. What happened in Florida?

For one thing, there were 11 Democratic candidates and the so-called "liberal" vote was splintered. Yet if we look at the spectrum, the "conservative" candidacies of Gov. Wallace And Sen. Henry Jackson piled up 682,000 votes to the "liberals'" 539,000.

What, however, is the true spectrum? Jackson is a populist domestically with a hard line abroad. Wallace is a populist and a racist with no known comprehension of foreign policy.

Then there was busing. The anti-busing amendment straw vote drew nearly as many votes as all those of the 11 Democratic candidates. The straw vote in favor of a continued program of integration drew even more. An anomaly.

Is Florida a microcosm of the national electorate? Politically, it certainly is variegated. In the Sunshine State there are many Floridas. In Presidential matters, however, most often Florida is conservative.

Many conservative Democrats and some re-registered Republicans voted openly for Wallace with no intention of voting for anyone but Richard Nixon in November. This switcherooing has happened more than once in Florida, most recently in the High-Burns contest for the Democratic gubernatorial nomination in 1966.

If Florida is a miniature model of the United States, does the Wallace sweep mean a hard rudder to the right? We'd like to see more returns, say from more politically oriented Wisconsin, before making a judgment.

So, what happened?

We think that George Wallace skillfully put together everything that rubs peoples' nerves raw, the frustrations, the things that make living painful, the issues in government no voter can get at directly. The Wallace campaign was a mobilization of discontent, orchestrated by a superb demagogue in simplistic phrases.

Whatever happened, George Wallace is right. He is now a national, not a regional, figure. The Democratic Party, which he shattered in Florida, must reckon with him.

So must sober Americans who know that discontent must have answers lest it become total disunity; that these answers are not simple or emotional, and that the kind of leadership contrived by Wallace in Florida is not along a path to glory but to the destruction of the human values which the power-hungry in every age and in every place seek first to corrupt.

Miami, Fla., March 15, 1972

"They" done sent "them" a message.

Florida's outsized vote for Alabama Gov. George Wallace, though it varied from district to district in intensity, reads about as clearly as Gov. Wallace's speeches:

Governments are run by big shots who forget the source of their power lies in people. Governments and other fatcats live it up, give money away to no-accounts for no decent reason and do not respond to the needs of the folks who carry crushing tax burdens.

Governments try to readjust people's natural social arrangements by carting kids unnecessarily on buses instead of just leaving people to work things out for themselves.

"Send them a message," read George Wallace's ads. The message has to be one of protest.

Sens. Henry Jackson and Hubert Humphrey subdued their New Dealism under attacks on busing. They pulled the second and third highest vote. They received the message clearly. Both are alive politically to test their slightly new image in some other state.

Sen. Ed Muskie, embittered by what he feels were erroneous press estimates of his status, plans to maintain his campaign. But more than any other candidate his chances have been seriously damaged in Florida.

Serious harm, also, was rendered to New York Mayor John Lindsay. He fought hard in Florida, spent much and barely edged out Sen. McGovern, who made an effort but hedged it enough so that he now appears neither helped nor hurt, just still in the fight.

President Nixon, of course, won the Republican primary solidly. He was not pitted against George Wallace and, besides, he proved his ability to defeat the Alabaman back in 1968.

With an almost solid Wallace delegation, except for six Dade Countians, headed for Miami Beach in July, Florida certainly seems in a mood now to lay a sort of vengeance on Democratic liberals, perhaps through a return to Mr. Nixon in November. We still do not believe the national party will nominate a five-state winner in 1968 to do battle with the incumbent.

Everyone expected George Wallace to win Florida. His victory exceeded the general assumption. It is an embarrassment to party leadership which now will have no opportunity to influence national party platform policy nor even play the participating host. Those duties will fall to Wallace delegates and none of the in-Democrats even know who they are.

Gov. Wallace deserves recognition of his victory. His outrage at the unresponsiveness and contrariness of government is no more than ours, but his method of stating it has prevailed this time.

We hope there is not an overreaction to his win. Smoldering outrage can carry elections but it doesn't really generate solutions of the problems that started it in the first place.

THE RICHMOND NEWS LEADER

Richmond, Va., March 15, 1972

George Wallace has achieved precisely what he set out to do. He plunged into the Democratic china shop and smashed everything in the place—even to the dentures on the heretofore hottest-selling Democratic figurine. Senator Edmund Muskie went all-out in Florida, and came home with a measly 9 per cent of the vote; the Senator was hateful about the Wallace performance, but more about that below. You may have forgotten about George Wallace: Most of the time during the past four years, Br'er Rabbit Wallace lay low in his briar patch. Yesterday was soon enough to make his presence known.

In Florida he made compulsory busing the essential issue. The national Democratic party has disintegrated into little more than a rallying point for perhaps the saddest collection of presidential would-bes and political has-beens that the American electorate ever has seen. With a good deal of accuracy, Mr. Wallace said that the national Democratic party has become "a party controlled by intellectual snobs who ignore the true expressions of rank-and-file citizens across America." He said: "There is more pluperfect hypocrisy in this election than ever before. (All the Democratic candidates) either supported or voted for busing. Every one." He was right in that, too. Mr. Wallace threatens to wreck the national political system as the nation has known it. And unless the Democrats and Richard Nixon face up to the busing issue, Mr. Wallace just might do it.

Last night, after most of the returns were in, George Wallace said something else that contained a good deal of truth. The returns, he said, indicate that he is not merely a regional candidate, but a national candidate. Florida is a peculiar State, in that its people run the gamut from the very rich to the very poor. As a haven for retirees, it contains people from across the country. If one State ever constituted a microcosm of the American electorate, Florida is that State. And in every part of Florida, from the tumble-down shacks in the panhandle to the Sodom called Miami Beach, George Wallace ran well. He walked off with 75 of Florida's 81 delegates to the Democratic national convention. George Wallace took on 10 other candidates, among whom 5 per cent of the United States Senate was represented, and he carried nearly a majority of the votes cast. It was a dazzling performance of the bantamweight at the Democratic punching bag.

And his performance was dazzling solely because Floridians, as most other Americans, are adamant in their opposition to compulsory busing. In two advisory referenda, 79 per cent of Florida's voters said they support integrated schools, but 74 per cent of the voters said that they cannot and will not abide compulsory busing. George Wallace was the only Democratic candidate in Florida who effectively articulated the profound antagonism to compulsory busing that three-quarters of the voters in Florida obviously feel. Senator Henry Jackson, who ran third, currently opposes compulsory busing, but he could not match the rhetorical capacities of the suzerain of Alabama. All the other Democrats either supported compulsory busing, or they waffled. Isn't it too bad that Virginia's General Assembly declined to put similar advisory referenda on the November ballot, so that Virginians might have had an equal opportunity to express themselves on the matter of compulsory busing?

In reacting to Mr. Wallace's electoral performance, big Ed Muskie hardly sat tall in the saddle. As his post-primary statement printed below adequately reveals, he was petulant and verbally small. Any candidate who just has had his eyeteeth shaken out is entitled to a portion of sour grapes. He is not entitled to be mean; he is not entitled to disparage the voters who cast their ballots for the other candidates. And that is exactly what Senator Muskie did. Trust Muskie? With his statement, Senator Muskie went a long way toward making himself the George Romney of 1972.

Consider. Senator Muskie said: "I hate what (Wallace) stands for." In the Florida primary, Mr. Wallace stood foremost for the reversal of compulsory busing edicts. Given the compulsory busing referendum, Mr. Wallace was standing up for roughly three-quarters of the Florida electorate. So Senator Muskie is saying, in effect, that he hates the sentiments of three-quarters of the voters throughout the South, and nearly three-quarters of the voters throughout the nation. In a portion of his statement not printed below, Senator Muskie said—ever so anti-democratically—that Mr. Wallace's showing indicates that "the worst instincts of which human beings are capable, have too strong an influence in elections." He said that he was appalled at the Wallace margin of victory, which he viewed as a "threat to humanism" and "decency."

It would be difficult to imagine a statement more suited to verify all the darkest suspicions of rational men—particularly rational men in the South—as to the philosophical and political malice nourished by the leading presidential contenders in the national Democratic party. Mr. Muskie is pre-eminent among those who have been pounding the South with compulsory busing edicts for the past decade. He disdains the emotions and intellects of non-racists. He castigates Mr. Wallace for speaking for those who have no other champion. Senator Muskie personifies all the reasons why George Wallace is riding a crest of popularity today: The oppressed will find their champions, whom the oppressors will deplore.

If there is a message for the Democrats in the Wallace victory, there is a message for President Nixon as well. Mr. Wallace is Mr. Nixon's darkest shadow. The Alabama governor is the ghost of Banquo to Nixon's Macbeth, threatening to be the death's head at Mr. Nixon's political feast. In 1968, Richard Nixon could not possibly have been nominated and elected without the support of rational conservatives, or without the South. But far more than in 1968, the votes that Mr. Wallace may take this year are likely to be Nixon votes. If Richard Nixon does not come forward with a program that halts compulsory busing—now—it is likely that this year Mr. Wallace will be able to draw off enough Nixon votes to prevent Mr. Nixon from winning re-election in the electoral college. In such an event, the presidency would go up for grabs, with George Wallace in the role of broker.

It is all very well to say that behind the Wallace facade, one senses some caesarism. But Mr. Wallace is a political poltergeist to Mr. Nixon and to the Democrats, and he is rattling the chains of compulsory busing. He has tapped a current of support that runs silent through the American electorate—and runs deep. One can philosophize all night on the question: Ultimately, will Mr. Wallace be a force for good or a force for evil? The Florida primary has shown that Mr. Wallace is the only national politician who thus far has aired the sentiments of the vast majority of the American people on the essential issue of the moment, and that is good. Whether Senator Muskie likes it or not, this still is a free republic grounded in democratic principle. Because of what the Muskies have done, Mr. Wallace is riding again to the private cheering of countless Americans who know that compulsory busing is wrong.

The Chattanooga Times

Chattanooga, Tenn., March 17, 1972

From the welter of conclusions drawn from the results of Florida's preferential primary Tuesday, only two seem sound enough to stand on bases for predictions of pre-convention trends in the Democratic party. And even they have to be subjected to the stresses suggested by a vote taken under unusual circumstances in an atypical state.

The first is obvious. George Wallace of Alabama is a stronger candidate within the ranks of the party he manipulates at home and has disavowed nationally than many thought. He had been expected to ride the school busing issue to a big lead. For him to take 42 per cent of the total, more than double runner-up Hubert Humphrey's 18 per cent, was surprising.

Nor does all his strength stem from the emotion-laden busing controversy. A special poll taken of 400 persons as they left the voting booth revealed that they were about equally divided in considering busing and economic issues as of first importance. Those who said they had voted for Mr. Wallace were not so strongly influenced by economic questions

of taxes and prices, but the governor had stressed this issue and is certain to have captured some votes on its appeal. The presumption follows that he could rely on his populist demands for more services to the poor and higher taxes for the rich in states where busing was not as hot an issue as in Florida.

The second conclusion is that Mr. Humphrey's somewhat tarnished image as a "has-been" has been significantly brightened. Freed from the burdens he carried four years ago as the vice president of a discredited Administration, Sen. Humphrey revealed much of his earlier ebullience and political savvy in picking the issues and appealing to the visceral responses of the voters without approaching the demagogic overtones of the Wallace race. Mr. Humphrey has re-established himself as a candidate in the running for the nomination.

We do not believe Sen. Edmund Muskie, who has been the unenviable target of concentrated attacks as the front-runner, was hurt as badly as some would claim. His was a lost cause in Florida—and perhaps much of

the South—from the start, because he is honest enough to say he does not think school busing is an issue of paramount importance in today's world. Sen. Muskie has had lapses in which he showed bitter anger or distress; they hurt him. These are not the things the voters long remember, however, and he is a man who tends to gain rather than lose from the way he answers questions. The road to Miami is still a long one, on which strengths can be developed or weaknesses can destroy.

The non-binding referendum on busing both showed the predictable opposition, three-to-one, and brought out the voters to swell the Wallace total. Those who make the most of this result say little or nothing of the still higher percentage, four-to-one, which favored quality education for all and no return to segregated schools.

George Wallace can be given no reasonable chance to win the Democratic nomination for president. There is no doubt, however, that he is the oil in the Democratic tank. As long as he is present, cohesiveness will be close to impossible.

The Virginian-Pilot

Norfolk, Va., March 16, 1972

Alabama's Governor George C. Wallace received more votes in the Florida primary Tuesday than Hubert Humphrey, "Scoop" Jackson, and Edmund Muskie put together.

Had Mr. Humphrey or Mr. Jackson or Mr. Muskie pulled Mr. Wallace's vote, or had any one of the leading "respectables" made a respectable race against Mr. Wallace, the candidate's camp-followers and the experts would be finding national significance in the showing.

But under the curious ground rules that apply to Governor Wallace, his votes don't really seem to count in the Democratic primary.

Even among the red, white, and true-blue believers in Mr. Wallace, there aren't many who seriously think he is ever going to be President of the United States. Their hero himself talks of influencing the Democratic Party platform and having a say in the choice of the nominee at the convention next summer.

Obviously Mr. Wallace is going to have some say about who'll be the Democratic nominee, and a greater say about who won't be the nominee. He is the apparent winner of 75 of Florida's 81 convention delegates and he probably will win additional delegates in other primaries. But Mr. Wallace is only going to do well in states where he is on the ballot and can exploit

popular resentments. (See Joseph Alsop's column on the opposite page today.) He cannot hope to overcome the opposition of almost all the established leaders and the power brokers within the Democratic Party. He might destroy the party, but he cannot capture it.

If Mr. Wallace isn't going to be nominated, then why did a half-million people vote for him?

Because a vote for Mr. Wallace is a "free" vote, and a protest vote. It is most obviously a vote against busing, reinforcing the nearly 3-1 rejection of busing in the Florida straw vote. It is also a protest against all the targets of Mr. Wallace's wrath, and against conventional politics and politicians. By voting for Wallace, the man in the street says that he doesn't like the way the country is going. That is always tempting.

Some statistics should be useful. In 1964 Governor Wallace ran very well against a series of stand-ins for President Johnson in Democratic primaries. In April he got 33.8 per cent of the Wisconsin vote, and in May he polled 29.8 per cent in Indiana and 42.8 per cent in Maryland. (That was when "white backlash" was coined to explain the Wallace vote as an expression of resentment against the civil rights movement.) After the early primaries Mr. Wallace withdrew

from Presidential politicking, and Barry Goldwater pursued a "Southern strategy" to the GOP nomination and disaster in November. There was little evidence of the "white backlash" in the November returns.

In 1968 Mr. Wallace stayed out of the Democratic primaries and campaigned as an independent for President. He carried five Deep South states and received 13.6 per cent of the total vote. (He got 28.9 per cent of Florida's votes in '68, running third.) Significantly, the Wallace vote, as measured by the polls, fell off sharply in the campaign's closing weeks.

But if the Wallace vote is a protest again against busing, taxes, and whatnot, it is also an evidence that the Democrats' "respectables" aren't exciting the people.

The big loser on Tuesday was Edmund Muskie, who finished fourth with just 9 per cent of the vote. The Democratic "front-runner" is now in serious trouble. His campaign was premised upon snowballing through the early primaries, stampeding the waverers, and cinching the nomination before the convention met. After Florida, Mr. Muskie is holding a melted snowball; if he can't produce a solid victory in a big state soon there will be a stampede away from him to the likeliest-looking winner.

That very well could be Hubert Humphrey, who ran second to Mr.

Wallace with 18 per cent of the Florida votes. Mr. Humphrey, the erstwhile joyful warrior, is rejuvenated and restyled this year. He is anxious for a rematch with Mr. Nixon, whom he came close to defeating in '68 against all odds. The Democrats were bitter, bloodied, and broke in '68. They aren't in '72, at least not yet, and Lyndon Johnson is off in Texas. The ever-eager Mr. Humphrey looks like the Democrats' fail-safe selection, the man the party can always turn to.

Of the others, Mr. Jackson (3rd, 13 per cent) and Mayor John Lindsay (5th, 7 per cent) stayed alive on Tuesday. Both campaigned extensively in Florida, escaped humiliation in the numbers game, and can't claim much of a positive showing. In the liberal sweepstakes, Senator George McGovern (6th, 6 per cent) and Representative Shirley Chisholm (7th, 4 per cent) had little to lose, and did.

President Nixon won 87 per cent of the Republican votes, and conservative challenger John Ashbrook did poorly (9 per cent) in a state where he had hoped for right-wing support. But while the GOP house is in order, Mr. Nixon may have to reckon, too, with Mr. Wallace. The Democrats are in disarray, as Florida shows, and that is tailor-made for Mr. Wallace. If he tastes another triumph or two, will he again run for President on his own ticket? And if so, will he help or hurt Mr. Nixon? It is too soon to say.

The New York Times

New York, N.Y., March 16, 1972

The score sheet of the Florida primary indicates that a majority of the voters were united on just one issue—opposition to school busing. This message is certain to affect those who plan their candidates' campaign strategies, Republican and Democrat alike.

Widespread fear of busing is an undeniable fact throughout the country. Irrational anxieties have been reinforced by occasional abuses of busing, without sufficient regard for educational and social realities.

It would nevertheless be a tragic error to let the Florida experience magnify the anti-busing issue out of all proportion to its actual importance. The anti-busing forces on the Florida campaign trail skilfully orchestrated a one-issue sales campaign in a territory friendly to their product. President Nixon provided some supportive mood music with his reminder that he was hard at work codifying his own busing views. The separatist anti-busing resolutions passed by the National Black Political Convention on the eve of the primaries also strengthened the segregationists' case.

The combination of these special factors should argue persuasively against a panicky retreat into a Democratic version of Mr. Nixon's unprincipled Southern strategy, with anti-busing rhetoric as the ideological soundtrack.

A more rational conclusion to be drawn from the Florida experience is the need to put the busing issue into perspective to prevent it from distorting the entire candidate-selection process. It is ludicrous to choose the next President on the basis of an issue which is peripheral even to the matter of school desegregation itself. And it is both cowardly and foolish not to challenge the segregationists' deliberate deceptions.

A responsible campaign should talk sense to the voters about these facts:

Excessive, long-distance busing, far from being required, has been held undesirable by the Supreme Court. Those Federal court rulings which specifically ordered busing generally did so in exasperation over local resistance to any school desegregation whatsoever. Busing, which is the way almost twenty million children daily go to school, has been used extensively as a means of keeping the schools segregated.

Finally, responsible candidates ought not overlook that other Florida referendum, overwhelmingly endorsed by the voters, which urged quality education for all children and rejected a return to a dual, segregated school system. The Nixon Administration has failed miserably to formulate strategies and provide leadership for effective school integration. It is on the capacity to fill that void, and not on the basis of rhetoric about the busing sideshow, that the candidates should be judged.

Arkansas Gazette.

Little Rock, Ark., March 16, 1972

The news from Florida was Wallace with the jockeying for place and show and the relative place in the running of candidates who have not even finished yet reduced to even more of an exercise in glum futility than the poor also rans had conceded in advance it would be. Wallace's 42 per cent showing exceeded all expectations—even, if we can believe the man, his own, which we know from experience are unlimited and illimitable.

So what we are expected to believe is the lesson for the country is that the Democrats in July will accept as their candidate for President a man who ran for the office as a third party candidate the last time out, just because he now has achieved a considerable popular triumph in a crowded preferential primary in a state that rejected both him *and* the Democratic nominee in that same 1968 general election. It does not follow.

However, the national campaign—which wasn't going to be any bargain to start with—inevitably has been further coarsened and cheapened by what has happened in Florida, predictable as it was in its broad outlines. For what we have seen there is a kind of object lesson in the Politics of the Lowest Common Denominator, dross driving out gold, with some political figures that hitherto had been thought to be as warrantable as the real stuff turning a little green in the process, and not wholly with envy of Wallace, who, though he may be made of fool's gold (i.e., the gold of fools) had been at the game of racial demagogy longer than anybody else in either of the Florida primaries.

To claim, as the Wallace supporters will, that what we had here was an issue —busing—in search of a man, rather than a man in search of an issue, is to ignore the whole principle of positive leadership, which principle was demonstrated again in this very Florida primary. The Wallace victory was of course inseparable from a non-binding vote on the same ballot overwhelmingly in favor of an amendment to the federal Constitution that would seek to bar "forced" busing of school children for purposes of furthering integration of the public schools.

But the complicating factor in the Florida primary results was a companion ballot measure in which, for the first time anywhere in the country, the people of Florida expressed themselves in favor of equal educational opportunities for children of all races, which in the context means, in favor of what used to be called "integration." And, lest it be forgotten, the opportunity for Floridians to express themselves thusly was the work of one man—the state's young liberal Democratic governor, Reubin Askew—exhibiting positive leadership for good.

The fact that Governor Askew failed in his larger effort to defeat the anti-busing amendment is attributable in considerable measure to a lack of any such positive leadership at the effective national level, meaning in the White House at Washington. Where, in the months immediately after May, 1954, there was a kind of dead-air hiatus on the issue of school integration in the absence of any positive leadership from the Eisenhower White House, with the effective racist damagogues moving in only belatedly, there no longer are any dead-air silences left unexploited even for an instant whenever the school integration process takes some new turn, such as, for once, two-way busing.

So, if Florida is not the world ("Tomorrow the world") or is not yet even the country, there will be fall-out aplenty from the Tuesday balloting there.

The task of the courts and of the local school a d m i n i s t r a t o r s and School Boards that have conscientiously tried to obey the law will have been further complicated.

The effort of Senate conferees to prevent a weakening of the Mansfield-Scott Amendment in conference will have been weakened vis-a-vis their hard-line opposite numbers from the House, some of whom still would not be content with an unconstitutional anti-busing law but must needs insist upon an unconstitutional *constitutional amendment.*

Richard Nixon, who is easily influenced by such things, will be influenced, having already done so much both by direction and indirection to create the situation in which he might be so influenced. (A not insignificant factor in the Wallace triumph was the cross-over of regular R e p u b l i c a n s hoping to weaken the national Democratic candidates.)

It is quite enough for now.

The Detroit News

Detroit, Mich., March 16, 1972

George Wallace's startling victory in the Florida primary illustrates above all the failure of the Democratic Party to develop strong moderate leadership as an effective alternative to Wallace demagoguery.

Senator Edmund Muskie, who had to settle for fourth place and 9 percent of the Democratic vote, warned in a bitter post-election speech that Wallace constitutes a threat to national unity. Very true.

But that threat exists in part because neither Muskie nor any of the other candidates has managed to capture the imagination of Democratic voters and unify the party's moderate sentiments. While Wallace was holding his bloc of voters together in Florida, his 10 weak opponents were dividing the remainder among them.

Some Democratic leaders shrug off Wallace's backing as "the bigot vote." Wallace certainly is a bigot and no doubt many people support him because they recognize in him a fellow bigot who expresses their point of view exactly.

But we suspect that many who vote for Wallace do so because he seems to be concerned about their legitimate complaints. With the finesse of a consummate demagog, Wallace has for the wrong reasons put himself on the right side of a host of issues not the least of which are taxes and bussing and big government.

If Wallace's foes start addressing themselves positively to the mundane frustrations which Wallace has been exploiting, they will stand a chance of blunting his disruptive influence. It is no mystery why Senator Jackson shot up from virtual obscurity to beat out Muskie for third place in Florida. Jackson conducted a strong anti-bussing campaign.

The thinking of Florida's voters on that issue was decisively expressed in a straw vote. They balloted 3-1 against the forced bussing of school children away from their neighborhood schools. They also voted overwhelmingly in favor of equal opportunity for quality education for all children.

In short, they favor integration but not at the heavy cost and inconvenience of illogical bussing programs. That is exactly the view of many moderates and liberals, so these straw votes cannot be dismissed as the hypocrisy of essential bigotry, as some bussing advocates suggest.

The big loser of the Florida primary was Senator Edmund Muskie. Stumbling out of New Hampshire where he got slightly more than 46 percent of the vote — not the 48 first reported — he hit the skids for the second time in a week. When you come in fourth, it's hard to maintain the claim that you are the "front-runner."

Meanwhile, aside from Wallace, Hubert Humphrey has become the man to watch. In his first outing against Muskie, he beat the senator from Maine and took second place in the field of 11 candidates. If Muskie continues to fall apart, Humphrey is poised to replace him as the most likely to succeed at the Democratic Convention next summer.

This assumes, of course, that anybody other than Ted Kennedy will be able to win the nomination after Wallace gets through splintering the party into a dozen pieces.

THE DALLAS TIMES HERALD

Dallas, Tex., March 16, 1972

EDMUND MUSKIE blew it — not just the Florida presidential primary, but his candidatorial cool, for good measure.

It wasn't just that Muskie, long regarded as the front-running Democratic presidential candidate, gathered in a measly nine per cent of the vote, barely ahead of John Lindsay's seven per cent and way behind George Wallace's 42 per cent.

No, Muskie then had to commit another of his increasingly frequent faux pas: He had to uncork a pettish attack on Wallace.

Now when a given opponent has won a landslide victory (as did Wallace) in a state sometimes regarded as the U.S. in microcosm, it would seemingly behoove the runners-up to behave graciously about it. Muskie didn't. Instead, he called Wallace "a demagogue of the worst kind" and "a threat to the unity of this nation." Whereby he gave Wallace a marvelous chance to respond with charitable forgiveness. Being a canny fellow, Wallace did just that—and assuredly made himself additional votes.

All of which casts increasing doubt on Muskie's potential as a candidate. Even more than the New Hampshire primary— where he won only a plurality in what was basically a two-man race with George McGovern— last Tuesday's contest in Florida shows Muskie to be an inadequate vote-getter. Somehow his image as the cool, collected man of reason doesn't come across. Well, certainly it doesn't come across when he indulges in personal vituperation, such as he hurled in New Hampshire at publisher William Loeb ("a gutless coward," said Muskie) and in Florida at George Wallace.

Worse, Muskie misreads the temper of the electorate. What bothers him most about Wallace, one gathers, is Wallace's opposition to racial-balance bussing. Yet in a straw vote referendum Florida voters by 3 to 1 endorsed a constitutional amendment to outlaw bussing. Muskie favors bussing. And he thinks anyone who doesn't is a rednecked bigot.

Not so. For in the same referendum, the voters endorsed by an even wider margin the principle of equalized education for all children. What's bigoted about that, senator?

At all events, the Florida primary shows that the voters in this microcosmic state don't care for leftish candidates. Muskie, McGovern, Lindsay, Chisholm— among them they garnered only 26 per cent of the vote. To George Wallace, to the anti-bussing, law-and-order-minded Scoop Jackson, and to Hubert Humphrey, with his now-moderate rhetoric went all the rest of the votes.

There's a very definite lesson here. And it's one Muskie ought to heed—if it isn't already too late. The farther left a candidate leans, the worse his prospects appear. If a Democrat's to have any chance at all against Richard Nixon, he's got to straddle the center. Muskie and McGovern can talk all they wish to "the poor, the black, and the young."

But George Wallace, Scoop Jackson, and Hubert Humphrey are talking to a lot of other folks, too. And so far, they're the ones who are getting the votes.

The Oregonian

Portland, Ore., March 16, 1972

The Florida Democratic primary election knocked Sen. Edmund Muskie out of the "front runner" role for the presidential nomination, established Gov. George Wallace of Alabama as a Democrat to be reckoned with, put Sen. Hubert Humphrey back in contention and gave Sen. Henry Jackson an encouraging boost.

It did nothing for Sen. George McGovern, who came out of New Hampshire looking pretty good, or for Mayor John Lindsay, his chief competitor for liberal left support.

All of which says that neither the New Hampshire nor Florida primaries added much except confusion to the Democratic race. In the meantime, with 79 per cent of the Republican vote in New Hampshire and 87 per cent in Florida against conservative Rep. John Ashbrook and liberal Rep. Paul McCloskey, President Richard M. Nixon rolls onward in a favored position for reelection.

The importance of Gov. Wallace's surprisingly large plurality, 42 per cent, in a race of 11 candidates, is not that it will bring him the nomination at the Democratic National Convention in July. The importance is in its impact on the political parties, other candidates, the Nixon Administration and the Congress.

Wallace may be a demagogue, as the embittered fourth-place candidate in Florida, Sen. Muskie, charged. But the size of his vote in mixed up, semi-South, semi-cosmopolitan Florida shows that there are a lot of voters who may not consider themselves demagogues but who will vote for one.

The reason is obvious: Gov. Wallace beat the drums on the issues that anger and frustrate millions of Americans, in the North and West as well as the South—compulsory busing, pornography, lawlessness and violence, oppressively high taxes, waste in welfare, inadequacy of Social Security, astronomic government expenditures, drug abuse, foreign aid.

Florida is not unique, although different from northern states. Republican Vice President Spiro T. Agnew has been called a demagogue, too. But he got a tremendous, write-in vote for re-election in New Hampshire, far outdistancing that for a respected Negro liberal Republican, Sen. Ed Brooke of Massachusetts. Agnew has found a lot of support among irritated Americans on some of the same issues Wallace emphasized.

What the vote for Wallace in Florida should do, aside from the presidential race, is to bring home to Congress—particularly to the Senate—that Americans are angry and frustrated by the pressures of the times and the apparent inability of government to move to relieve them.

The Democratic candidate in Florida who came closest to recognizing these frustrations and promising to do something about them, without abandoning his liberal record and without demagoguery, is Sen. Jackson of Washington. By polling more votes than Sen. Muskie, partly in response to much more active campaigning in that state, Sen. Jackson has moved into contention for the nomination.

All of these gains and losses in opening primaries, of course, can be and probably will be altered in succeeding primaries, which will come almost weekly until the course of 24 is run. Sen. Muskie could recoup in the Illinois primary Tuesday against McGovern and ex-Sen. Eugene McCarthy; or Humphrey could emerge on top in Wisconsin's 11-candidate race, or a lot of other things could happen. Unfortunately for the moderate and liberal candidates, however, George Wallace will be in there demagoguing in 10 more primaries to tarnish their claims and aspirations.

Gov. Wallace is certain to go to the Democratic National Convention with a hatful of delegates and what the convention does about it may make or break the party's presidential chances in November. After all, Wallace makes Nixon look like a flaming liberal.

The Courier-Journal

Louisville, Ky., March 16, 1972

If the people of Florida elect me in this campaign, in my judgment Mr. Nixon in 30 to 60 days after this election is going to end busing himself.
—Governor George Wallace

WELL, THE PEOPLE of Florida have anointed George Wallace, they've voiced their strong desire for a constitutional amendment to prohibit "forced busing" of school children, and they may have guaranteed us a sordid, emotionalistic election campaign in which the President of the United States will play "me, too" to the wily Alabama racist's "I was first."

Governor Wallace won't be the Democratic nominee on the November ballot, but his code word will be emblazoned on the campaign banners of the South this year, just as it has so many times in the past, and on many banners in the North as well.

There was a time when Governor Wallace didn't speak in code. His word was simply "nigger." But when it appeared that his constituents' public vocabulary was outgrowing his, he changed "nigger" to "states' rights," then to "crime in the streets." During his last campaign for governor, when it appeared that moderation might prevail at last in Alabama, it became "nigger" again. And now it's "forced busing." The words change, but the meaning remains the same, and it remains clear.

A 'national problem'

The Wallace code entered Republican national politics in 1964 with Barry Goldwater, and became nationally popular in 1968, during the "crime in the streets" era. The new President immediately set to work building a "Southern strategy" for 1972 which included the removal of the Department of Health, Education and Welfare (HEW) as an agent of school desegregation and the construction of a Justice Department that wouldn't prosecute for minority rights.

As the primary season opened, the White House called the busing of children to integrate schools—a remedy ordered reluctantly by the federal judiciary—a "national problem," and the President announced that he wouldn't reveal his position on that "problem" until after the Florida electorate—spurred by Governor Wallace—had expressed its will.

What will Mr. Nixon say now?

Will he say that Governor Wallace is exploiting racial prejudice and fear, that "forced busing" is code for "nigger," that the issue is unworthy of a presidential election campaign?

Will he remind us that children across the nation have been bused to school at public expense since 1919? That buses have been used for years, in both North and South, to perpetuate school segregation? That in 1969-70—before the Supreme Court ruled that busing was a valid means to eliminate state-imposed segregation—39 per cent of the entire public school population was bused to school?

Will he cite the several studies which indicate that children who are bused to better schools tend to improve in their school work; that white suburban children aren't harmed academically by the infusion of black ghetto children into their classrooms; that the children themselves readily adjust to busing—and sometimes acknowledge school desegregation as personally beneficial—when their parents allow them to do so?

Will he acknowledge that the *real* "national problems" are segregated housing and urban school systems starved by the flight of money to the suburbs, and that busing will be unnecessary when those more basic problems are solved? And will he commit himself to solving them?

To do so would push Governor Wallace into another third-party candidacy against the President, and might force Mr. Nixon to solicit the South's votes—and the votes of many Northern suburbanites—on the basis of principle rather than fear. It would encourage Southern moderates such as Florida Governor Reubin Askew—who has staked his political career on a plea for justice—in the battle of reason against fear.

Governor Askew's brand of courage—a courage which elevates the duties of responsible leadership higher than the natural desire for re-election—is rare in politics, and hasn't been typical of Mr. Nixon's career, nor of the three years since he promised to "bring us together."

If he now endorses Florida's cry for a constitutional amendment, or some other attempt to curtail the power of the federal government's judicial branch to protect the rights of minorities against fear-impassioned demands of the major" —and if the leading Democratic candidates continue to vacillate and equivocate on the busing issue—the pitch will be established for one of the most demeaning presidential campaigns in American history.

It's a pitch hummed first by George Wallace —the first note of a siren song, luring us back to the darkness of our racist past.

THE COMMERCIAL APPEAL

Memphis, Tenn., May 7, 1972

MORE THAN two-thirds of the registered voters of Tennessee thought the state's first presidential preferential primary election so unimportant they didn't bother to vote.

As for the results of the half-million votes which were cast, you needn't have tuned in on radio or television on election night to find out. As predicted, Alabama Gov. George Wallace swept up about 68 per cent of the ballots in the Democratic primary, leaving the other 10 in the field to chop the remaining votes into small segments. With the outcome so predestined, no wonder Tennessee saw little of the candidates, and that so few Tennesseans thought it worth a trip to the polls.

What probably got out those who did vote was the issue of public school busing. The statewide referendum on a constitutional amendment to prevent busing for the purpose of school desegregation undoubtedly brought in a goodly bundle of votes for Wallace, an outspoken foe of busing.

Wallace and the busing opponents would like to think that this election gives them momentum. Time will tell, but at the moment it is difficult to see the Tennessee primary as much more than an emotional escape valve for the anti-busing people.

On paper, George Wallace has won the 49 Democratic delegates Tennessee will send to the July convention at Miami Beach. Presumably they would be committed to him on the first two ballots. But these delegates, to be chosen under the party's new rules demanding representation for all kinds of minorities and factions, have yet to be selected. Some of them will be blacks, who are unlikely to feel any loyalty for Wallace.

By the latest count, George McGovern leads in Democratic delegates with 285½. Hubert Humphrey has 181. And Wallace is third with 169 — if you count all 49 from Tennessee, which would be pretty risky.

Governor Wallace may not know until the Tennessee delegation is polled on the first convention ballot just where he stands with the state he won so easily.

THE REFERENDUM on busing was no more meaningful than a Gallup Poll. The people who bothered to vote had a chance to express their feelings. Now they've done it. They've let their congressmen know they want a law to prevent federal judges from issuing school desegregation orders which require busing. The 4-1 outcome is now a matter of record, in case anyone ever wants to look it up.

And that's about all the great, first Tennessee presidential primary meant, except that it allowed the electorate to express some current frustrations — and it gave Knoxville a chance to vote in liquor by the drink.

THE NASHVILLE TENNESSEAN

Nashville, Tenn., May 6, 1972

FOR SUPPORTERS of Governor George C. Wallace the Tennessee preferential primary was an overwhelming success, but for the state it was little more than an expensive way to confirm facts that were already well known.

The primary, which cost at least $300,000 and did not bring money into the state as anticipated, proved that the people in this state do not like busing for racial balance in public schools. But, then, everybody knew that. As the proponent of that view Mr. Wallace's election was a foregone conclusion. Even though three-fourths of the eligible voters did not choose to participate, it is unlikely that the outcome would have been any different had the turnout been large.

In retrospect it seems clear that mistakes and events reduced the primary to virtual insignificance in terms of having a bearing on the national political picture. The timing was disastrous, for the primary was sandwiched in between other contests in which other candidates had better reason to spend their time and money. Also the primary was held so late that candidates who may have given Mr. Wallace competition had already been forced out of contention by other state tallies.

Mr. Wallace benefited from a heavy Republican cross-over vote, as evidence by the large number of traditional GOP precincts which voted in the Democratic column. Of course it is impossible to tell if GOP partisans were trying to spoil the Democratic contest, if Mr. Wallace's appeal drew support across party lines or if — as in Davidson County — Republicans were induced to cross over so that they could have a voice in local elections. In any case, Mr. Wallace did not need the Republican votes to win in Tennessee.

But Mr. Wallace will gain from his victory in Tennessee, even if he does not get the convention support of all the 49 delegates bound to him by state law — a real possibility because of national Democratic party rules. By rolling up a clear majority of 68% Mr. Wallace's momentum has been pushed along — perhaps enough to help him win in North Carolina today where he faces his only serious challenge in a Southern primary. A North Carolina win would give Mr. Wallace a clean sweep of all Southern primaries.

With each passing primary Governor Wallace presents more of a problem to the national Democratic party. There is no clear indication from Mr. Wallace that he will be in the party come November.

Despite the fact that Mr. Wallace is now talking to other issues — big government, tax loopholes, the plight of "the little man" in dealing with the political system, his followers in this state seem satisfied to have his victory in Tennessee a win against busing.

Nobody knows for sure where the Wallace candidacy is going. To Miami Beach and the Democratic convention, it seems certain. But he confirms that he will take only about 300 delegates with him — and that is some 1200 delegates shy of victory. Mr. Wallace has sent his message to Washington on busing. Now the Democratic party waits to hear his message on what his future political party plans will be. Will he stay in, or will he bolt? Until that is clear he will continue to serve as Democratic spoiler, a role he played to perfection in Tennessee Thursday.

DEMOCRATIC PLATFORM SUPPORTS BUSING; REPUBLICAN IS 'IRREVOCABLY' OPPOSED

The Democratic national convention July 11–12 adopted the liberal draft platform presented by the platform committee. Despite Gov. George Wallace's dramatic wheelchair appearance, his opposition to busing was not supported. A Michigan delegate's compromise busing plank against "massive or cross-district busing" was also rejected. The final platform stated that "Transportation of students is another tool to accomplish desegregation."

The Republican party platform was approved by a voice vote at the convention Aug. 22. The platform reflected the President's views on virtually every plank. The Republicans were "irrevocably opposed to busing for racial balance," while committed "to guaranteeing equality of educational opportunity and to completing the process of ending *de jure* school segregation."

THE INDIANAPOLIS STAR
Indianapolis, Ind., July 13, 1972

Radical delegates listened more or less politely to Governor George Wallace, but their response, like much else at the Democratic National Convention, was rigged.

On orders from the McGovern radical command, the delegates listened with closed minds. Wallace's attempt to influence the platform was — before he made it—doomed.

The delegates shouted down, one by one, Wallace's proposals to curb "senseless, asinine busing of school children," maintain a strong national defense, cut welfare s p e n d i n g and foreign aid, strengthen law enforcement, demand release of prisoners of war, allow prayers in schools, authorize states to impose capital punishment and affirm the right to bear arms.

Wallace had won the Democratic primaries in states with a total population of more than 32 million and placed second in primaries in states with a total population of over 26 million. That is some evidence of the extent to which his views on key issues are shared by other Americans.

The rejection of the Wallace proposal at the convention is one significant measure of how far the radical Democrats are out of touch with millions of Americans.

It is another instance of the dominant idea behind leftist thoughts and actions — that the leftists know better what is good for the people than the people do.

The radicals in control of the Democratic convention have shown they know how to cast a hex.

As spells sometimes do, this one may return to hex the sorcerers who cast it—in November.

WORCESTER TELEGRAM.
Worcester, Mass., July 13, 1972

Reflecting in general the views of the man whose nomination was assured even before yesterday's balloting, the 1972 Democratic Party platform provides Sen. George McGovern with the stage from which he hopes to make his way to the White House. It is a curious structure.

The platform, as adopted, indicates McGovern's eagerness to avoid major embarassments during the campaign and to bring about some sort of party unity. The delegates respectfully listened to Gov. George Wallace tell them that "75 to 80 per cent of the American people are against senseless, asinine busing of school children" — but then went on to shout down his entire eight-part package of dissenting planks. And an even clearer demonstration of McGovern power came when the convention defeated a number of amendments favoring liberal abortion policies, nondiscrimination against homosexuals and all the major goals of the National Welfare Rights Organization, including a $6,500 income guarantee for a family of four. Similarly torpedoed was the populist call for repealing the income tax code and substituting a system of lower tax rates and personal credits, but no deduction.

Still, the platform is enough to make every conservative or moderate hair stand on end: Immediate withdrawal from Vietnam — although McGovern has softened his own attitude, hinting that he would leave residual U.S. forces in Thailand until the American war prisoners are returned — replacing the welfare system with income grants, closing all tax "loop holes" and accepting busing as a means of achieving racial balance in schools.

The document is wholly doctrinaire with a strong populist flavor. It pays lip service to the free enterprise system, but the praise seems merely ornamental. It sees American industry in terms of "the power of corporate giants". It appears preoccupied with class distinctions — the "rich", as contrasted with the "working people" and the "poor". In places it sounds like a declaration of socialist principles: "We must restructure the social, political and economic relationships throughout the entire society in order to ensure the equitable distribution of wealth and power." And in the best egalitarian fashion, the platform also calls for "an equitable ratio of women and men" in federal appointments and proportional representation of the "poor" at all levels of the Democratic party

There are serious contradictions. The platform demands "an end to inflation". But then it endorses a long shopping list that would feed the fires of inflation, more federally subsidized housing, a $2.50 minimum wage, free maternity benefits, expensive health care and heavier tax burdens on industry.

The platform stresses the social, political and economic ills of the nation, concluding that the Republicans in general, and the Nixon administration in particular, are largely to blame. It neglects to mention that, except for four years, the Democrats have controlled both houses of Congress for 40 years.

It has been said that party platforms are important only during convention time, to be tucked out of sight soon after the confetti is swept up. It may be that the new Democratic document, too, will wind up on a dusty shelf.

It may also be that the McGovern platform does not truly represent the philosophy of most Democrats. If it does, the party has pulled up stakes and moved to new and shakier ground.

The Courier-Journal
Louisville, Ky., August 28, 1972

THE REPUBLICAN platform makes it perfectly clear that the party intends to play a cruel game with one of the most serious and most emotional issues bothering tne people during this presidential campaign.

First, the party declares a noble goal for itself: "We are committed to guaranteeing equality of education opportunity and to completing the process of ending *de jure* school segregation."

But how does it propose to achieve that goal? By opposing "busing for racial balance," on the ground that it creates "division within communities and hostility between classes and races" (the reason that Dixie's governors used to cite for opposing the very idea of desegregation and every civil rights bill passed during the 1960s). By favoring the "neighborhood school concept" (a "concept" devised to justify the continued segregation of black schoolchildren in ghetto neighborhoods). By proposing "$2.5 billion of federal aid to school districts to improve educational opportunities and build facilities for disadvantaged children. . . ."

It's a strange map the party has drawn, for it points the way to neither equality of opportunity nor the end of segregation. Busing —which everyone concedes is one of the least desirable ways of ending segregation—is opposed, yea, even unto a constitutional amendment prohibiting it. But the platform mentions not a single means by which the Republicans intend to redeem their pledge to end *de jure* segregation. Nor does it even say that President Nixon will come up with one later.

Of course, there *are* other ways. If President Nixon doesn't know them, he may find them listed in the Democratic Party platform: "School attendance lines may be redrawn; schools may be paired; larger physical facilities may be built to serve larger, more diverse enrollment; magnet schools or educational parks may be used." These methods have been used more widely than busing to bring about desegregation.

But, as the Supreme Court has noted, these methods aren't always viable, and when they aren't viable, busing may be called for. "Transportation of students is another tool to accomplish desegregation," the Democratic platform states. "It must continue to be available according to Supreme Court decisions to eliminate legally imposed segregation and improve the quality of education for all children."

That "quality of education for all children" is what both parties say is the real school issue in this campaign. The Democrats, paraphrasing the Supreme Court's 1954 decision in *Brown v. Board of Education*, contend that "equal access to quality education for all our children" is the very purpose of school desegregation. But President Nixon and the Republicans pretend that quality education and desegregation aren't related.

After the courts' efforts to achieve desegregation have been squelched, the Republican platform implies, the federal government will spend $2.5 billion to buy "high-quality education" for those kids who have been stranded in the ghettos.

Even if this were a good-faith promise, $2.5 billion in "new" federal money wouldn't begin to bridge the educational-opportunity gap between the ghettos and the suburbs of this country. But the $2.5 billion that President Nixon has proposed isn't even "new" money. It's money that has already been authorized by Congress—but not spent by the President—for other educational needs.

The criticism that several House Democrats leveled against President Nixon's compensatory education bill when it was introduced last March still holds: If Mr. Nixon *really* wants to improve education for needy youngsters, he doesn't need a new law to do it. Title I of the 1965 Elementary and Secondary Education Act authorizes full funding of more than $6 billion for this purpose. Yet current outlays under Title I total about $1.5 billion, and President Nixon hasn't asked that they be increased.

The Democrats, by calling for full funding of Title I, plus additional help for educationally deprived children, seem to have a more realistic idea of the magnitude and seriousness of the "quality education" problem. Their proposals, Mr. Nixon will point out, will cost more money. And so they may be more unpopular. But if the cry for "quality education" is anything more than a dodge around the segregation issue, surely the voters see that more money is the first essential step toward solution.

Mr. Nixon won't tight the battle along those lines. He'll continue to call only for no busing and more funds for the ghettos, which, being translated, means "separate but equal." And we all know how well that idea worked.

Oakland Tribune
Oakland, Calif., August 23, 1972

The party platform agreed to by the Democratic National Convention last month was, by and large, a product of the thinking and a reflection of the philosophies of the man delegates later selected as their candidate for the presidency.

In turn, the Platform Committee of the Republican National Convention listened attentively to White House suggestions in preparing the document made public Sunday and adopted last night.

Which is as it should be. Platforms should honestly and clearly reflect the consensus opinion of each party's membership and leadership.

So now, with the official adoption of the Republican platform, the differences between the two party's policies, which this year appear considerable, can be illuminated by and for the public.

Under the welfare heading, for instance, the Democrats emphasize the need for "income security" and flatly promise federal assistance for those who claim they need it.

The GOP welfare plank declares the "nation's welfare system is a mess" and offers a "decent level of payment to the genuine needy." But the big differences come in the Republican insistence that all adult welfare applicants register for work or job training and to accept such offers when made.

In net, the Democrats offer a government guaranteed income. The Republicans specifically reject that principle.

Another big difference is in defense policy, where the GOP platform warns against meat-ax slashes in spending that would substantially weaken this nation's deterrent capability.

The Democrats' defense plank calls for major reductions in virtually all defense spending categories and particularly in overseas forces.

On Vietnam, the Democrats would, if McGovern is elected, immediately withdraw all U.S. forces from Indochina and presumably abandon our allies in South Vietnam and other countries to whatever fates the Communists would have in store for them.

The GOP position endorses the continuing Administration effort to negotiate a settlement with Hanoi that would permit the people of Southeast Asia to "live in peace under political arrangements of their own choosing."

Perhaps the most glaring platform difference is on the touchy school busing question. Here, the Democratic policy statement describes busing as "another tool to accomplish desegregation." The Republican position rejects "busing for racial balance" and favors consideration of an "appropriate constitutional amendment to that effect."

On amnesty, tax reform and health care there are equally evident differences between the two party positions, with the Democrats consistently taking a more liberal position.

Thus, for all the voters a comparison of the two party platforms now offers a singular opportunity. Without particular regard to candidate personalities, it is now possible to confirm the thrust of one's political philosophy, or indeed, to find out a new, more comfortable political "home."

The Evening News

Newark, N.J., July 13, 1972

Because the platforms of political parties frequently bear little relevance to the campaign program a party's presidential nominee ultimately puts together, or to what he can reasonably be expected to accomplish, they tend to be catch-all documents, distinguished mostly by the multiplicity of the issues, frequently minor, that they cover and the vagueness of the language in which they are couched.

The platform adopted by the Democratic convention in Miami Beach fits into the accepted mold. In addition to obvious issues of major import that offer no surprises (get out of Vietnam posthaste, massive federal programs for the cities, mass transit, the environment, etc.) we are

exhorted to choose our own "life styles" without fear of discrimination or prosecution, to refuse to ingest non-union lettuce and to break up large conglomerates.

Enhancing the occasional aura of unreality one finds in the document is the lack of specificity. We are spared the vulgarity of price tags on an idealistic program of guaranteeing jobs for everyone, and on replacing the existing welfare system; we are not told how an "equitable" distribution of wealth would be accomplished or what constitutes an "appropriate" occasion for the taxing of environmental polluters.

The platform finally adopted unmistakably matches the liberal convictions of the day. That it was not

even more liberal can be attributed to the new moderation being practiced by the McGovern organization as it faces up to the reality of appealing to the American political center in the campaign that lies ahead.

To insure that the platform as fashioned in committee did not undergo any radical re-structuring on the floor of the convention, McGovern aides were on hand to head off minority-sponsored plans on abortion and guaranteed incomes ($6,500 for a family of four).

Similarly, the McGovern forces made sure that Gov. Wallace enjoyed no success in trying to turn the convention rightward. Down to defeat went the Wallace anti-busing proposal in favor of one that identified busing

as only "one tool" in the desegregation of schools. Other Wallace proposals on national defense, welfare, tax relief, foreign aid, and cutting back on the federal bureaucracy never got anywhere.

In short, the platform projects a generalized, occasionally profound, sometime silly, program that the liberal Sen. McGovern can live with and run on, with considerable room for maneuvering, as he seeks to tone down the radical image some of his public statements have fostered.

Adoption of the platform without any significant amendment also demonstrates that the Democratic party in this era of New Politics is now firmly in Mr. McGovern's control and ready to do his bidding.

Detroit Free Press

Detroit, Mich., July 13, 1972

MIAMI BEACH — When they needed it most, the McGovern supporters came up with the secret ingredient no one suspected they had — discipline.

They were known for being smart, dedicated and energetic. But the old pros are also smart, dedicated and energetic, and here this week the old pros had the extra incentive of fighting for their lives. So the smart money said that when it came to the push and shove of convention politics, the balloting, the maneuvering, the willingness to suppress causism for concert, the amateurs wouldn't have it.

The smart money was wrong. From the meetings of the rules, credentials and platform committees in Washington last month until the last shout of approval of the platform itself Wednesday morning, the McGovernites kept it all together.

The greatest danger to their success — as it will be from now on — came not from the anti-McGovern coalition but from their own enthusiasm. As hundreds of experts have written in millions of words, they represent an amalgam of separate causes which coalesced behind McGovern because his campaign embraced more of them than did anyone else's. But they were neither pros nor dedicated Democrats.

They made mistakes. The most grievous, of course, was their failure to dominate the Credentials Committee as they dominated the other committees. It was this failure which could have cost them the vital 151 extra votes in California.

They almost overkilled George Wallace and the Platform Committee. After the

Alabama governor, then in a suburban Washington hospital, rejected a moderate plank which referred to school busing as only one tool which might be used to promote quality education, the McGovernites threatened to push through a plank practically demanding busing. In the end, moderation prevailed and the final version said, "Transportation of students is another tool to accomplish desegregation. It must continue to be available according to Supreme Court decisions."

They threatened to shatter over such issues as women's lib, abortion reform, legalization of marijuana and the ending of criminal penalties for consensual homosexuality. Each of these had its advocates, and if anyone of them had stirred too much friction within their mutual camp, it could have provided the wedge the opposition needed.

But the dangers, though real, were also reckoned with. McGovern strategists had seen every possibility and had planned accordingly.

The tip-off, as everyone now recognizes, came on the first crucial vote Monday night on the South Carolina credentials challenge. The details are too complicated to repeat here but essentially it was a noble battle but on a disastrous battlefield. To win the battle would have been to lose the war.

Responding to more discipline than anyone knew they possessed, they deliberately lost the battle. They lived to fight another day — on the far more important California challenge.

From then on it was easy. Some of them must have been torn at times Tuesday night and Wednesday morning, as individ-

ual minority reports on the platform came before them. But the price of fervor was too high, and suddenly these amateurs, these causists, became pros.

This is not to say that the platform they adopted or the campaign that will be waged this fall will be just another campaign run on just another platform. It is not a radical document, but it is reformist. Much of it isn't going to be popular with large elements of the citizenry, whether they are beneficiaries of oil depletion allowances or scared householders who like to keep a .38 in the dresser drawer for self-protection. No accommodation was made to the real issues raised by George Wallace, which could be fatal in the finals.

But the fact is that an overwhelming proportion of the delegates here put it together, are willing to stand on it and are willing to defend it. And the man who put them all together, into one cohesive mold, is their candidate. He is, without any question, his own best strategist. What he did in one year of planning and four months of campaigning was to build a powerful structure on organization and education.

It may easily come apart in the strains of the campaign. Too much divisiveness remains, too much bitterness, too many dashed hopes. Too many power brokers may have been offended for a winning coalition to emerge.

But Republicans who tend to underrate McGovern's chances four months from now might do well to remember where and who he was four months ago.

The Virginian-Pilot

Norfolk, Va., July 13, 1972

With the voluminous Democratic Party platform to draw upon, Senator McGovern need not ever be at a loss for words in his quest of the Presidency. For that matter, President Nixon will find the document a help in attacking the Democrats at some points.

It differs from platforms of other years in being assembled not by a few closeted politicians, but by a 150-member committee that held 30 public hearings throughout the country. Political scientist Richard Neustadt was the committee's guide. If nothing else, the Democratic platform is a fascinating compendium of everything that all shades of the American people want, or think they want, in 1972.

Ironically, the delegates now pressing their demands on Congress excluded, for the most part, Congressmen from their midst. In fact, elected officials of any sort form the great minority of this convention. It is an enthusiastic assemblage of political newcomers.

But the old folks will have their day. One plank provides that the aged, like the young and other minorities, be represented hereafter at conventions in proportion to their numbers in the population.

What with birth-control programs and lengthening life spans, the nation's senior citizens soon will be in a position to inherit the Democratic Party, or what's left of it. They should live so long.

(The Arrangements Committee brought back former House Speaker John McCormack to introduce a platform section, and the faded old eagle, ticking off a few achievements of the Roosevelt-Truman era—Social Security and what-not —reminded the delegates gently that the old politics had not been entirely bereft of progress.)

Among the platform's less forthright planks is the one on busing. It is an embarrassment, shrinking from any mention of the dreaded word, saying only that "transportation" is another tool to accomplish desegregation. It reminds one of how the Democrats in the 1950s used to tiptoe through the tulips on fair employment practices. Governor Wallace appeared with stronger stuff, a resolution condemning busing, and he served as a sort of tar baby against which the liberals punched. They got their kicks in roaring down the Wallace antibusing proposals, along with other far-right sentiments from preservation of capital punishment to prayer in the public schools.

The rich get short shrift in the platform. Verily, it is easier for a camel to get through a needle's eye than for anyone with a sizeable income to get a favorable place in the Democratic platform. The convention's oratory has been marked by vows to abolish "tax-welfare aid for the wealthy, the privileged, and the corporations."

The platform is unusual in facing, here and there, the Democrats' own defaults. It notes, for instance, that the Democratic Party must share responsibility for Vietnam, but says the task now is to end the war, not decide who is to blame for it. It pledges "as the first order of business, an immediate and complete withdrawal of all U.S. forces from Indochina. All U.S. military action in Southeast Asia will cease."

Thanks to the public hearings' input (a much-used word here), the Democratic platform is strikingly different from the party's 1968 model. They could be separated by a decade instead of a mere four years. The current version shows a much greater sense of social justice. It seeks legal counsel for juveniles in trouble, better education for mentally retarded children, protection of the rights of prisoners.

It also would replace the sacrosanct Highway Trust Fund with a single Transportation Trust Fund to aid local transit systems as well as roads. Recognizing the core cities' burdens, it would encourage urban-suburban cooperation in education of children.

Many of the dozens of proposals are meritorious; all are worth pondering as reflecting the hopes and fears in these United States.

The Washington Post
Times Herald

Washington, D.C., July 11, 1972

At this writing, the outcome of the Democratic Convention's credentials fight is yet unknown, and the convention's platform deliberations—which will doubtless be influenced by the way the credentials fight is resolved, if it is—have yet to take place. They have been scheduled for this evening, to be sure, but everything is subject to change in a political convention, especially when the Democrats are involved. Even so, it seems to us that a few observations can be made at this moment on what is likely to be a principal element of conflict over the prospective party platform—namely, its so-called "busing plank." Should the convention be in shape to go forward with the platform this evening, then the odds are that this will be Governor Wallace's night —the first moment thus far at Miami Beach in which the Alabama governor and his supporters will have become a principal focus of attention.

Traditionally (and this convention is no exception), the specific language of party platforms is less important as a guide to future policies of an elected administration than it is as a guide to the political complexion of the party at a given moment. Its language and its compromises and fuzzinesses and inconsistencies in particular reflect something of both the prevailing public mood and the relative clout of the various elements within the party coalition. Thus, there are three variations on the "busing" plank in the Platform Committee's draft: a committee-backed, McGovern-favored plank, a Wallace plank and a plank that Senators Muskie and Humphrey had a hand in and which represents a kind of middle position between the other two planks.

Contemplating this focal point in the party's platform, conflict is necessarily to be struck by the strange context in which it occurs, a context which is worth noting because it says something not just of the meaning of the busing argument but also of the manner in which the party as a whole has changed. The plain fact is that black delegates are present at the Miami Beach convention in unprec-

edented numbers; and yet mention of the party's obligation to bring about racial justice specifically for black Americans is notably scant in the proposed platform. It is also a fact that the black delegates at Miami Beach, functioning as a caucus with sharply divided groups within, have concentrated their energies thus far on the more conventional assertions of power politics that go with a nominating convention, even as "busing"—a more or less conventional civil rights or desegregation issue for Democratic gatherings has been dominated by white delegates arguing with each other.

To some extent this unfamiliar condition represents a wholesome development within the party itself. For the presence of large numbers of black delegates, their comfort in conducting a classical political drive to gain and exert influence, and the fact that they have (along with various black lobbyists and protestors) bent their attention to issues other than the establishment of constitutional rights (jobs, income maintenance programs)—all this suggests that a certain number of the critical battles of the past have in fact been won, that the party like the country can at least begin to move on to issues other than the time and pace of granting what should have been granted long ago and what never should have been in question in the first place.

At the same time, there are disturbing aspects of the convention which also go a certain way to explain the framework in which the "busing" dispute takes place. Only four years ago and even in the wake of the turmoil in the cities and the dispute over the conclusions of the Kerner Commission, the Democratic platform made a point of recording the party in favor of strong execution of the provisions of the Civil Rights Act of 1964—possibly the last occasion on which the party would witness a fairly clearcut North-South argument over implementation of civil rights for blacks.

What is distinctive in this year's platform is the

dwelling upon the rights of practically every other group imaginable within the society, the downplaying of the issue as it has traditionally been applied to blacks and the fact that the single issue—"busing"—on which the orthodox struggle has come to turn now crosses regional lines: George Wallace is not representing a Southern resistance movement; rather he is exploiting the genuine confusions and legitimate controversies that surround the issue nationwide and he has plenty of Northern support in his cause. It is worth remembering that the Wallace minority plank on busing, calling for "immediate relief from busing" and for an exercise of congressional power to limit the courts contains very little that is at odds with the position taken by Michigan's liberal Democrats who have been fighting the Detroit and Pontiac decisions in Washington.

All this surely has something to do with the eerie silence of the platform as a whole on certain aspects of the fulfillment of black people's rights, and it does not bode particularly well for the convention's disposal of the issue. As it happens, the draft plank of the committee itself is far from radical or militant or even overly precise. The key sentence, embedded in a couple of paragraphs of unexceptional generalities merely accepts "transportation" as one of several "tools" to achieve desegregation and asserts that it should remain "available" as such in accord with certain "Supreme Court decisions." Perhaps because the black political community is itself divided on this question and certainly because the white political community is so frightened of it, there is a fairly strong chance that one of the alternative planks will have a good run on the convention floor. The party, however, should stick with the language as drafted by the committee. That language is hardly extreme or inflammatory. In a minimal way it acknowledges the authority of the federal judiciary to remedy violations of black people's constitutional rights. That strikes us as being the minimum that the reconstructed Democratic Party should do.

Public Reactions:
1974-75

Center for National Policy Review

Rights efforts in North, West assailed. A private civil rights study group charged Sept. 5 that the federal government had failed to desegregate schools in Northern and Western states despite legal requirements that it do so.

In its report, the Center for National Policy Review said government efforts had been characterized by "bureaucratic caution, needless delays, administrative inefficiency and sloppy investigation."

The report said the Department of Health, Education & Welfare (HEW) had not made sufficient use of a weapon that had proved effective in integrating schools in Southern and Border states—the cutoff of federal funds to segregated districts.

In preparing the report, the center reviewed HEW files on 84 cases involving Northern and Western schools undertaken since 1964. Of these, the report said, 52 were still "open" as of July 1, 1973, and no enforcement of any kind had been undertaken in 37 of the 52 cases. The report noted that the average case remained unresolved for more than three years before the district involved was informed that it was violating the law.

According to the report, only four of the 84 districts investigated had been forced to undergo formal enforcement proceedings in which a fund cutoff was threatened.

The report included statistics which, while not perfectly analogous, showed the differences among regions in the progress of integration. In 1964, the report said, 98% of black students in 11 Southern states were in all-black schools; the figure had fallen to 9% by 1972. The latest figures for the North and West, however, showed 1.6 million of 2.8 million black students (57%) were in schools that were at least 80% black.

Responding to the report Sept. 6, HEW Secretary Caspar W. Weinberger said the cutoff of federal school funds was an extreme weapon which in some cases should be supplanted by "persuasion and discussion." He said there were instances in which fund cutoffs had increased the degree of segregation.

Weinberger denied that HEW was lax in enforcing the law, contending that delays were caused by the "very fierce" public opposition in many Northern cities. He said the public in the South had been "much more willing to accept desegregation."

Massachusetts

Boston ballot vs busing. In a nonbinding referendum May 21, Boston voters rejected 30,789–2,282 the assignment of children to particular schools to achieve racial balance without parental consent. The 12% voter turnout was the lowest in the city's history.

An election official suggested that the low turnout might have been caused by Gov. Francis W. Sargent's proposal during the previous week that a freedom-of-choice plan encouraging voluntary desegregation be substituted for the current state law, which limited the number of black students in any school to 50%.

Boston busing protested. Scattered violence and successful boycotts of some schools marred the opening of Boston public schools Sept. 12 under a court-ordered integration plan involving busing of several thousand pupils.

Trouble was focused in the predominantly white South Boston area. At South Boston High, a boycott proclaimed by white parents and fear of violence kept attendance Sept. 12–13 at fewer than 100 pupils out of the 1,500 expected to be enrolled. Buses carrying black students were stoned as they left the school on both days, although Mayor Kevin White had ordered police escorts after the first incidents Sept. 12. In another neighborhood, a bus carrying white students was stoned as it passed through a black area.

The busing plan was carried out without serious incident in most other areas of the city, and system-wide attendance was about 65% of normal.

Protests continued in South Boston on the third day of busing Sept. 16, with crowds of mostly young whites staging antibusing marches. Police reported 19 arrests in the area.

The situation was generally calm by the next day as police lined the streets of South Boston to prevent demonstrations. But attendance at the boycotted high school remained low (about 210 pupils), while city-wide attendance had risen to about 73%. **C**

The busing plan had also been the target of protest before school opened. Attempting to speak at an antibusing rally at City Hall Sept. 9, Sen. Edward M. Kennedy (D, Mass.) had been chased from the speaker's stand by a jeering, rock-throwing crowd.

Boston calls out extra police. The office of Boston Mayor Kevin White announced **D** Oct. 9 that 300 Massachusetts state police, 100 Metropolitan District Commission police and their supervisory personnel had been placed under the control of the city's police commissioner, Robert J. diGrazia. The police were made available by Gov. Francis Sargent following a request by White, who had been ordered by U.S. District Court Judge W. Arthur Garrity to exhaust all potential help from local law enforcement **E** agencies to quell racial violence resulting from a four-week-old, court-ordered program of busing to desegregate the city's public schools.

In issuing his order for a "gradual escalation" of force up to the point necessary to insure public safety and implementation of the desegregation order, Garrity rejected a petition by White asking for at least 125 U.S. marshals to **F** augment Boston police, who the mayor said were stretched "razor thin" and whose presence in one ethnic enclave—predominantly Irish South Boston—was itself a contributing factor "to the incredible intensity of emotion." Use of federal marshals would be nothing more than a "symbol" that a federal court order was being enforced, Garrity said, adding that blacks being bused to South Boston were in "serious danger daily" and needed protection, not symbolism. (A **G** Justice Department representative indicated that his superiors in Washington also opposed use of marshals to protect the children.)

Meanwhile, outbreaks of violence continued to occur. At least 38 persons—

A 24 whites and 14 blacks—were reported injured in various incidents in the city Oct. 8. Police were summoned to the predominantly black Roxbury section, where hundreds of black students had poured out of a high school, pulling fire alarms and stoning passing cars as they dispersed. In South Boston, a white mob set upon and injured a lone black man caught in traffic.

B White demonstrators, numbering about 5,000, had marched through South Boston Oct. 4 protesting forced busing. A collateral one-day, citywide school boycott cut school attendance in half. Marching at the head of the demonstration were state legislators, members of the School Committee and all but one member of the Boston City Council.

C **President Ford opposes forced busing.** President Ford deplored the violence that had occurred in Boston at his press conference Oct. 9. "Respectfully" disagreeing with the court decision in the case, which he did not consider "the best solution to quality education in Boston," he stated his opposition to forced busing to achieve racial balance as a solution to quality education. He added that it was "of maximum importance that the citizens of Boston respect the law" and he **D** hoped that it was not necessary to call in federal personnel to help keep order.

Guard mobilized in Boston. Massachusetts Gov. Francis Sargent Oct. 15 ordered the mobilization of 450 National Guardsmen and called on President Ford to send federal troops to Boston, as racial violence in the city's schools continued to erupt. Sargent acted after a melee be-**E** tween black and white students at South Boston's Hyde Park High School resulted in the stabbing of a white student.

The call-up of the National Guard—two riot-trained, military police units—was criticized by Boston Mayor Kevin White, who asserted that the guard comprised "an inept, incompetent, ill-equipped, undisciplined or undertrained militia." The guardsmen, garrisoned on an alert status at two Boston armories, were issued riot control gear (face shields, armored vests and riot batons) but not **F** guns.

President Ford declined to act on Sargent's request. Use of federal troops to deal with violence in Boston schools, Ford said Oct. 15, should be only as a "last resort." A request for U.S. troops would not be in order until Sargent had exhausted the full resources of the state, a White House statement indicated. (A unit of Army paratroopers was placed on low-level alert at Ft. Bragg, N.C. Oct. 16, but **G** the alert was canceled two days later.)

The President had been accused by White Oct. 10 of fanning "the flames of resistance" to school integration. The mayor's criticism was in response to Ford's Oct. 9 press conference remark that he deplored forced busing to achieve

school integration. A Presidential spokesman subsequently denied that Ford had given "aid and comfort" to busing opponents.

By Oct. 22, a general calm, punctuated by minor racial flare-ups, had returned to the Boston schools. Searches with metal detectors at two high schools in the Roxbury-South Boston area, the focal point of the controversy, had apparently prevented students from bringing weapons into the schools. (As the violence subsided, school attendance at all grade levels rose to a city-wide average of 75% Oct. 18. However, attendance in the Roxbury-South Boston district hovered at 28% of a projected enrollment of 3,361.)

Civil Rights Commission Report. A staff report of the U.S. Civil Rights Commission Nov. 27 said President Ford had acted wisely in not sending federal troops to Boston to stem school violence, but it added that Ford would have been more effective if he had come to Boston and met with the officials involved.

The court-ordered desegregation plan, the report said, "is being imposed without any effective planning or preparation of students, teachers, administrators, parents or the community. . . ."

Boston school reform measure defeated. A referendum to abolish the independent Boston School Committee and replace it with a decentralized system of local advisory boards appointed by the city's mayor was defeated by Boston voters Nov. 5 by a recorded vote of 76,769 to 46,656. Mayor Kevin White had campaigned for passage of the measure, while a group of antibusing whites known by the acronym ROAR (Return Our Alienated Rights) had strongly opposed approval. The five-member School Committee, which was white and predominantly Irish-Catholic, had been the leader in the fight against forced busing and integration of Boston's schools.

Meanwhile, Mass. Gov. Francis Sargent ordered a two-third reduction Nov. 1 in the 450-man contingent of National Guardsmen placed on alert Oct. 15 because of violence resulting from the forced busing.

School system officials Dec. 17 decided to keep South Boston and Roxbury High Schools closed until Jan. 2, 1975. The schools had been closed Dec. 11 when a crowd of whites, angry over the stabbing of a white student by a black, trapped 135 black students in South Boston High School for four hours. Two days before at the school, four white girls had been injured in racial fighting.

In reaction to the violence, Judge W. Arthur Garrity Dec. 13 banned all gatherings of more than three persons within 100 yards of South Boston High School. He also prohibited use of racial epithets on school grounds.

As tension escalated, demonstrations by pro- and anti-busing forces became

more frequent and grew larger than during initial weeks of the busing plan. Supporters of the court-ordered program marched through downtown Boston Dec. 14, protesting the chaos that accompanied implementation of the plan. The crowd, estimated by police at 15,000-20,000 persons, contained contingents from Washington, Chicago, Newark and other areas of the nation. Opponents of forced busing mounted a counterdemonstration Dec. 15 in the Boston Common. The size of the crowd was estimated at 6,000 persons.

1975

Massachusetts

Busing foes attack masters' plan. The publication of the Phase Two, or masters' plan, for Boston evoked criticisms from opponents of busing March 22. At a press conference, State Rep. Raymond L. Flynn of South Boston said that the masters seemed to have realized that "forced busing is a bad trip." He regretted that they did not have "enough vision to see that the cancer of forced busing can not be treated piecemeal, but can only be cured by total elimination."

State Sen. William Bulger of South Boston agreed with Flynn. "The first plan was horrendous, and this is an attempt to retreat from it. Implicit in that attempt is an admission that the original approach is wrong. . . . At some point, Judge Garrity should stand up and admit that he has made a terrible mistake with other peoples' lives."

College heads view Phase Two. Presidents of the 17 colleges and universities in the Boston area called upon to help in the implementation of the Phase Two desegregation plan began to outline their possible contributions March 22.

Robert Wood, president of the University of Massachusetts (at Boston), called the masters' plan "a great promise" and "a great step forward" in an interview in the *Boston Globe.* He said that the universities could contribute to the desegregation process through curriculum planning, teacher training, and student counseling.

Boston University's president John Silber said he saw "no insurmountable difficulties" in the plan, and suggested that college faculty and graduate students might consult daily with Boston teachers and principals. He said that leaves of absence or more staff might be needed for the university-community cooperation.

Rev. Donald Monan, president of Boston College, mentioned the possibility of the School of Social Work's conducting workshops for the community in an effort to avoid racial tensions.

Dedham opens antibusing information center. An antibusing information center was opened March 31 in Dedham, a Boston suburb. It was the first center to open outside of Boston, where nine now exist in white neighborhoods. George D. Keller, chairman of Dedham Parents Against Forced Busing estimated that the group had 500–700 members, out of a town population of 28,000. Ten candidates for town election spoke at a meeting March 29, all of whom opposed forced busing.

NAACP says plan needs revisions. Thomas Atkins, president of the Boston branch of the NAACP said April 4 that the masters' plan would have the effect of ordering "permanent segregation in Boston." He cited the following racial percentages approved by the plan: 95% white schools in East Boston, 80% white schools in West Roxbury, 75% black schools in the Burke district, 70% white schools in South Boston, and 70% black schools in Madison Park (a proposed district). Atkins also attacked the plan as requiring black children to be bused outside of their areas, while most whites could walk to the nearest school.

NAACP files written complaint. The NAACP, representing black parents in Boston, filed a written complaint with Judge Garrity April 7. The group contended that the masters' plan was flawed by a "failure to provide the degree of actual student desegregation the constitution and the case law requires." The NAACP found that the proposed closing of some schools "would place a disproportionate busing burden on non-white children." A third objection raised by the NAACP was the alleged weakness of the planned community role in monitoring the scheme.

Boston march planned. Roy Wilkins, executive director of the NAACP, announced April 7 that a march would be held May 17 to commemorate the 21st anniversary of the *Brown v. Topeka* decision. Boston was chosen as the site of the march, Wilkins commented, since "Boston is the cradle of the revolution, but it appears to be fighting the Constitution because it wants to be the last holdout of segregation." Wilkins charged that more violence and threats had occurred in Boston than in any southern city.

NAACP march commemorates Brown decision. The March Against Racism, sponsored by the NAACP, was held in Boston May 17. Police estimated the marchers at 5,000, later reaching 12,000–15,000. At the Common, where the march terminated, the crowd was 30,000–50,000.

Nearly 200 busloads of demonstrators arrived in Boston. New York sent 77 busloads and Houston three planeloads.

NAACP Boston Branch President Thomas Atkins stressed the importance of the courts to the busing cause: "While we were helping to bring soul to the cradle of the confederacy, the cradle of liberty was being sacked here in Boston. We took the only course open to us. We went back to the federal courtroom...."

Kennedy jostled by white crowd. Sen. Edward M. Kennedy was jostled by an angry crowd of 300 antibusing white protesters in Quincy April 6. As he left a

school in the Boston suburb where he had addressed a Knights of Columbus breakfast, the crowd surrounded his car and prevented him from entering it. Policemen escorted him to a subway station as the crowd chanted, "Why don't you take a bus, Ted?"

After the incident, Kennedy repeated his support of busing. "I've taken a stand. I haven't changed it. We'll have to let the chips fall where they may. Part of the reason for these demonstrations is the press. I think that this particular group is more interested in getting publicity than resolving what is an extraordinary, complex and difficult issue."

ROAR vows to continue protests. Rita Graul, president of Restore Our Alienated Rights (ROAR) said April 7 that the group would continue harassing Sen. Kennedy whenever he appeared in the Boston area. The group claimed credit for the demonstration the day before, and explained that "The parents and children of Boston are just trying to get to him, to ask him to take a fair stand and help us out of the present forced-busing situation." Kennedy had refused to meet with ROAR members, asserting tnat they were "not anxious to talk, only to disrupt the meeting."

Dukakis rejects ROAR's platform. Gov. Michael Dukakis rejected most of the demands presented to him at a Jan. 22 meeting with ROAR representatives, the *Boston Globe* reported April 9. In a letter to ROAR dated March 25, Dukakis refused to petition President Ford and House Majority Leader Thomas P. O'Neill (D, Mass.) to press legislation against forced busing. He also refused to "initiate action" for a constitutional amendment to restrict forced busing. Dukakis said he believed that legislation against forced busing would not "further the cause of quality education" and probably would be "struck down by the courts as unconstitutional."

ROAR rally draws thousands. Coinciding with the NAACP's march in Boston, ROAR held a convention the weekend of May 17–18. Its purpose was to form a national antibusing organization. A rally ended the convention May 18, when an estimated 3,000–6,000 met in Commonwealth Pier.

Many wore pins with the word "never" superimposed on a school bus. The crowd waved American and antibusing flags, the latter combining the colors and symbols of the Irish and Italian flags.

Although the featured speaker, Gov. Meldrim Thomson of New Hampshire, did not arrive on schedule, his aide told newsmen that the governor later praised the antibusing group's efforts as in "the best tradition of Americanism."

A West Virginia minister active in the book protests was another speaker. Pastor Avis Hill said, "We're fighting with them [ROAR] as a coalition against the elements in government, the judiciary, that would take a parent's rights away."

School Committee argues against plan. The Boston School Committee filed a written complaint with Judge Garrity on April 7. It refuted the major points of the masters' plan: "This court cannot restructure the School Committee, cannot change the curriculum, cannot place others in positions of responsibility within the school system which heretofore had not existed, cannot permit any officials or colleges to assume roles in the school systems which are historically those of the School Committee's...." The School Board estimated that 24,320 students would have to be bused under the masters' plan, rather than the alleged maximum of 14,000.

Enrollment, attendance decline. Boston School Department statistics reported April 7 reflected the effect of the court-ordered, interim desegregation plan for the 1974-75 school year. Official enrollment declined 8% from the previous year from 93,647 students to 85,826. Of those enrolled, between 35% and 40% were absent on any given day. In the areas directly affected by busing, attendance was worse. At South Boston High School, into which blacks were being bused and where officials had originally expected an enrollment of 358 blacks and 1,094 whites, attendance was running about 130 blacks and 425 whites a day. At the formerly all-black Roxbury High School, into which whites were being bused, about 40 white and 240 black students were showing up each day instead of the 535 whites and 486 blacks initially expected.

Other official statistics showed that as of Jan. 30 that 5,184 suspensions had been meted out. Of that number, 3,099, or 60%, involved black students, although they made up but 38% of the system's total enrollment. (At least one observer, the head of the Massachusetts Advocacy Center, a Boston organization dealing with issues concerning children, suggested that large numbers of blacks were being suspended to discourage them from attending school. Larry Brown, the center's director, said this pattern was common in Southern schools during their first year of desegregation.)

State board of education criticizes plan. The Massachusetts state board of education filed its objection to the masters' plan April 8. It criticized the plan as not being "constitutionally valid" in its written argument to Judge Garrity. The proposed nine neighborhood districts were viewed as "incorrect" because of the racial percentages the masters scheduled for the schools. The board recommended that district lines be redrawn to attempt to "achieve racial ratios that are similar to citywide ratios."

Dukakis disagrees with board. Gov. Michael Dukakis, in rebuttal to the April 8 brief filed by the state board of education, cited several federal court decisions that approved racial variations ranging from 20% to 62%. "A fair reading of these decisions," Dukakis said, "will not support a categorical conclusion that the masters' plan proposes unconstitutional

A districts." Board Chairman John S. Sullivan said April 11 that with the addition of the proposed adjustments in the district lines, "we endorse the plan wholeheartedly."

Busing acceptance polled. The *Boston Globe* reported May 7 that 61% of Boston whites opposed elementary school busing, and 65% of blacks polled favored it. The *Globe's* poll was conducted between April 18 and 25, based on 1300 adults

B listed in the Boston telephone book.

Questioned on high school busing, 53% of the whites were opposed, and 77% of the blacks were in favor. A similar poll was held last year, but did not differentiate between elementary and high school busing. The overall percentages in 1974 were 68% of whites opposed and 57% of blacks in favor.

Asked if they were willing to have their own elementary school children bused,

C nearly two-thirds of the whites were opposed, while two-thirds of the blacks were willing.

Coleman

Expert pessimistic about integration. James S. Coleman, sociologist and the principal author of a 1966 study often cited to justify school desegregation, said that the flight of whites from desegregating city school systems threatened to defeat the purpose of integration, it was reported April 6.

Addressing the American Educational Research Association in Washington, Coleman offered a somber assessment of the impact of desegregation during the past few years. More attention should have been paid to how middle-class whites would react to rapid racial mixing of their schools, he suggested. Given the premise that culturally disadvantaged children tended to learn better when their classmates came from culturally advantaged homes, Coleman said, the flight of the middle class from the cities dimmed the prospect of black children being more successful in school through desegregation.

Careful analysis of whites' reactions and the other indirect effects of desegregation might yield results advocates and opponents of desegregation would find preferable to what was currently happening, Coleman contended. Federal, state and local officials were fearful of political consequences, Coleman said, and left desegregation almost entirely to the courts. As the courts were necessarily "blind" to such factors as white flight, they turned out to be "probably the worst instrument of social policy," he said. "Desegregation through the courts probably will have served in the long run to separate whites and blacks more severely than before," Coleman stated.

BOSTON CROWDS RIOT IN PROTEST OF COURT-ORDERED SCHOOL BUSING PLAN

Massachusetts Gov. Francis Sargent Oct. 15 ordered the mobilization of 450 National Guardsmen and called on President Ford to send federal troops to Boston, as racial violence in the city's schools continued to erupt. Sargent acted after a melee between black and white students at South Boston's Hyde Park High School resulted in the stabbing of a white student. The guardsmen, garrisoned on an alert status at two Boston armories, were issued riot control gear (face shields, armored vests and riot batons) but not guns. President Ford declined to act on Sargent's request. Use of federal troops to deal with violence in Boston schools, Ford said Oct. 15, should be only as a "last resort."

The office of Boston Mayor Kevin White announced Oct. 9 that 300 Massachusetts state police, 100 Metropolitan District Commission police and their supervisory personnel had been placed under the control of the city's police commissioner, Robert J. diGrazia. The police were made available by Gov. Francis Sargent following White's request. The mayor had been ordered by U.S. District Court Judge W. Arthur Garrity to exhaust all potential help from local law enforcement agencies.

At his press conference Oct. 9, President Ford deplored the violence that had occurred. "Respectfully" disagreeing with the court decision in the case, which he did not consider "the best solution to quality education in Boston," he stated his opposition to forced busing to achieve racial balance as a solution to quality education. He added that it was "of maximum importance that the citizens of Boston respect the law." At the request of Sen. Edward W. Brooke (R, Mass.), President Ford taped a message Oct. 12 to the people of Boston, asking them to "reject violence of any kind." The President said "I know that nothing is more important to you than the safety of the children in Boston and only your calm and thoughtful action now can guarantee that safety."

At least 38 persons—24 whites and 14 blacks—were reported injured in various incidents in the city Oct. 8. Police were summoned to the predominantly black Roxbury section, where hundreds of black students had poured out of a high school, pulling fire alarms and stoning passing cars as they dispersed. In South Boston, a white mob set upon and injured a lone black man caught in traffic.

Judge Garrity had ruled June 21 that Boston had deliberately maintained a segregated public school system, and ordered a state-devised racial balance plan. The state plan put into effect with the opening of the schools Sept. 12 reduced black-majority schools from 68 to 40. At least 6,000 black and white pupils (out of 94,000) were to be bused.

Attempting to speak at an anti-busing rally at City Hall Sept. 9, Sen. Edward M. Kennedy (D, Mass.) had been chased from the speaker's stand by a jeering, rock-throwing crowd. Further violence marked the opening of school Sept. 12 and continued for several more days. At South Boston High, a boycott proclaimed by white parents and fear of violence kept attendance Sept. 12–13 at fewer than 100 pupils out of the 1,500 expected to be enrolled. Buses carrying black students were stoned as they left the school on both days. In another neighborhood, a bus carrying white students was stoned as it passed through a black area.

Boston Herald American

Combining the best features of the Herald Traveler and Record American

Boston, Mass., September 12, 1974

Today can be a momentous day in Boston's history if only everyone will remember that it is not the bus ride which is important but the opportunity for quality education for all children which awaits at its end.

It is not merely a matter of obeying the law of the land, though that is important, too. More significant is that Boston is supposed to be the educational center of the country and its public school system has fallen far short of that reputation for a long time.

Dr. John R. Silber, president of Boston University, focused the goal most clearly in an Op-Ed page article in these papers yesterday.

He said: "There can be no equality of education in a segregated school system, and there can be no equality of opportunity without equality of education . . . Neither is the public interest served by denying (it)."

No one, certainly, should discount the admitted attraction of the familiar neighborhood school and it would be callous to disparage the natural anxiety felt by many parents for the well-being of their children attending classrooms distant from their homes.

But their fears should be calmed by the tremendous efforts exerted by a lot of people to do everything possible to assure their safety at all times. And they should be encouraged, too, by the fact that the same process has been carried out smoothly and without incident this month in many other communities across the land — in Denver and Pontiac and Detroit, where discord bowed to a spirit of harmony and cooperation.

Students and teachers, public and civic leaders, clergymen and parents have joined in a massive effort to prepare a smooth opening for the city's schools. What remains now is a show of unhesitating cooperation by the rest of the community to guarantee its success.

Whether or not, at this late hour, we are personally happy about busing, the time for further protest and other forms of negativism has passed. What Boston needs today — and in the days and weeks to come — is a calm and positive commitment to the improvement of the school system. Considering all that is at stake have we any right to do less?

THE DALLAS TIMES HERALD
Dallas, Texas, September 15, 1974

IT MUST BE one of the greatest ironies of our time when black children quietly and peacefully board buses to desegregated schools in Selma, Atlanta, Richmond and Dallas, but are stoned in Boston.

Boston, to many Southerners, symbolizes the accusing finger of Northern hypocrites who decried the sins of the South while overlooking problems in their own communities.

Today the situation is markedly clear to the nation. The South has made and is making tremendous strides in racial integration. There are, according to the U.S. Commission on Civil Rights, more desegregated classrooms in the South than in the North.

The South can be justifiably proud that an era of racial violence may be ending in the South, particularly violence directed against school children.

But because there has been progress in the South, Southerners should not gloat over the violence in Boston. It is sad. It is tragic. Southerners have learned from experience just how much so.

The South, we should hope, is now a mature region which has ended the caste system of legal segregation, is trying to work on improving human relations, but still faces difficult problems of school integration in its big cities and must come to gripes with many other urban problems.

These problems, like the problems in Boston, are problems of the nation. Every large American city is in a similiar situation where housing patterns tend to create de facto segregation.

Two of the top 10 largest U.S. cities—Texas' own Houston and Dallas—have urban problems not much different from Boston or Detroit or Philadelphia.

Solving some of these problems will require no more accusing fingers but real cooperation to share ideas and resources.

Arkansas Gazette.
Little Rock, Ark., September 15, 1974

It is 17 years since "Little Rock" and 20 years since the Supreme Court ruled against school segregation. In some ways much has changed in the two decades, but in other ways nothing has changed except that the racial battleground has moved North to centers of population like Detroit and Boston.

The Friday morning news report gave us in Little Rock an uncomfortable feeling of coming full circle back to 1957 and Central High, only the dateline this time was reading "Boston, Mass." Certain schools in Boston that had been segregated in fact, although not in law, were integrated under court order Thursday after a long legal battle. The integration was accompanied by disorderly scenes, all too familiar, as crowds of New England rednecks jeered children going to school, roughed up policemen and stoned school buses.

It is a sad business for Boston just as it was a sad business for Little Rock in 1957. This late in the day no one needs further reminder that bigotry, like pollution, recognizes no North or South, no artificial or regional boundaries of any kind. Indeed, there is some reason to think, on the record of the last six years, that the South is winning this battle of the Second Reconstruction just as it won the First, for on such critical issues as the "busing" of pupils the North has been joining US rather than vice versa.

It is the "busing" which the Boston segs are using as an excuse for the disorder and defiance of law. It is no more than an excuse. In Boston as in Little Rock an adequate desegregation of schools cannot be accomplished without transporting a portion of the pupil population to schools not in their immediate neighborhoods. "Busing" imposes some inconvenience and occasional hardship but the alternative, in the cities, is to accept de facto segregation and in effect give up the fight for a unitary school system.

In comparing the performance of the two cities, Little Rock comes off better on one point while Boston fares better on another, even if the racists throwing stones (or tomatoes at U. S. Senators) are the same in either venue.

In Little Rock the "busing" orders (a decade after the Central High riot) were carried out without violent street scenes or boycotts although the majority of people didn't like "busing" then or now.

In Boston the authorities have moved forcefully against the mobs and the mayor has made it plain he will not tolerate any further nonsense. Here in Little Rock, Ark., our governor at the time of our own trouble was inciting disorder rather than trying to suppress it. The response of officialdom *does* make a difference.

The Hartford Courant
Hartford, Conn., October 13, 1974

Non-involvement can be a copout. For some, it's the refuge of cowards; for others, the stance of the unconcerned. Whatever the reason and whether it be looking away from a street mugging, walking away from the screams of a ravished woman or, as in the case in point, merely looking askance at South Boston, playing it safe means, in time, everyone loses.

Sooner or later, the evils of society will be too close and too encompassing for anyone to escape or ignore. Inaction because it is someone else somewhere else being engulfed or destroyed is simply postponing the day when the same fate, or worse, will befall all who today cling to the spectator area, as vulnerable they may know it to be.

Leadership has failed, and in South Boston that failure has caught up with the fact. The seemingly insoluble situation there may well erupt in many other northern cities: wherever leaders have lacked the foresight or the courage to redraw school districts, or have ignored the pleas of blacks for new schools in areas that would naturally serve both black and white pupils.

Court orders are now being substituted for what could have been gradual and permanent integration, and the reaction to sudden insistence is violent resistance. Implicit also in the problem are class issues which cut across racial prejudices. South Boston's Irish certainly are not opposed to blacks solely because of color differences. Nor is their concern only with schools, they also fear competition with blacks over jobs, housing and social services. Nor are they unaware that the demand for sacrifice and cooperation has usually fallen upon poorer urban working people while little or nothing is asked of the middle class and the affluent in the suburbs.

Especially unfortunate, the breakdown in leadership extends also to Washington, where in recent years, specifically the Nixon years, racial integration has been less government policy and more political strategy. And all the while, most of the country, cowards and unconcerned alike, have looked and walked the other way.

Today, South Boston has no other way to look or to walk or to run. The same trap, it may be said, awaits every sister community where, for reasons of cowardice or copout, racial inequities and imbalances have been shamefully, dangerously, painfully, prolongedly ignored.

THE ATLANTA CONSTITUTION
Atlanta, Ga., October 11, 1974

Boston, where it may be said America was nurtured and born, has as proud a history as any city in The United States. Now Boston's fine name—a name that stood for freedom, high principle, and equality through most of the nation's life—has been shamed.

Like every other city everywhere, Boston has its share of individuals who know and care for nothing but the meanest human values. They are rampant now in the streets of Boston where the school system, under court orders, has been busing school children. The ugliest and most vicious scenes that took place in the South during the school desegregation struggle are now taking place in the city where much of the intellectual and moral impetus in that struggle originated.

It would be too easy for Southern cities like Atlanta to liken the events in Boston, where the mayor has called for the aid of federal marshals, to the ordeal in Southern cities like Little Rock, Birmingham and Selma. Race hatred is not confined to geographic regions. The good people of Boston are learning that lesson now. The South learned it over a decade ago.

The Boston Globe
Boston, Mass., October 9, 1974

What we prayed wouldn't happen has happened. The city of Boston has got out of control. There is a breakdown of law and order now that goes beyond the school busing issue to pit citizens and city police against each other. The law and the schoolchildren are in the middle.

Mayor White has done the right thing in calling for Federal aid. The city needs help and needs it immediately before things get further out of hand. And the symbolic presence of Federal marshals is not enough to do the job. Nor is the National Guard. Nor are the State Police. What is needed is a highly visible, highly disciplined outside presence. And that means US troops.

This is a very serious and very sad thing. Federal troops are a last resort in this country. And it is a serious blow to the pride of a city and state that have always stood for decency and compassion. But it would be worse to ignore the reality that people's lives are now in danger on the streets of this city as frustrations escalate.

The Boston police have done a brave and tireless job here in the past three weeks in circumstances that offered only anguish. But if some charged them with underreacting earlier, there is growing evidence that the Tactical Patrol Force overreacted at the least in their raid on the Rabbit Inn on Saturday night.

Perhaps this was inevitable in a situation that put local men on the firing line, working overtime in their own community under incredible tensions in a situation where their own feelings were often mixed. The price of that strain was Saturday's episode in South Boston. That hurt police credibility in a taut neighborhood.

Calling in Federal troops is strong medicine. But the costs of delay and prolonged unrest are far higher.

Those costs are already seen in terms of children getting no education or a delayed one, with the resulting harmful effect on careers and on jobs and on the health and harmony of the city itself. What is really so damaging for Boston, which has led a charmed life for so long, is that even the most realistic observers are surprised by the degree of ugliness that is surfacing here.

Boston was supposed to be an enlightened city, the Athens of America. Now our collective conscience is stunned by brutal attacks on children in school buses and on innocent citizens going about their business on our streets.

We had a fierce pride in our way of doing things and always thought we could handle our own affairs. Now, for the time being, that is largely gone.

The past three weeks will cost the city, its economy, and its residents very heavily. And, with the rest of the country comparing Boston to Little Rock and watching to see what happens here, it would be false pride indeed to deny that we need outside help.

But nothing is forever. The 101st Airborne Division was sent to Little Rock in 1957 and integrated classes have been functioning there for years. Civil disruptions worse than what we have seen here so far have come and gone. Kent State is open and operating normally. Campuses from Harvard to San Francisco State are quiet. Black and white students are in classes together peacefully today in Pontiac and at the University of Mississippi.

This, too, will pass. But it will pass with less pain in the long run if we act decisively now.

The escalating violence we are seeing now is something every person in the city must dread. And it is what makes Federal troops imperative to break the cycle.

The Afro American
Baltimore, Md., October 8-12, 1974

Many white parents, notably in Boston and Baltimore this fall, but as a general rule throughout the United States, keep stirring up racial tensions in schools then leaving their kids and black ones in the trenches to dig out as best they can.

Because it seems fairly certain that school desegregation will continue to be enforced by the courts, no matter how lax the Department of Health, Education and Welfare may be, this is a rather cruel and unjustified burden white parents are imposing on their children and communities.

Any way they slice it, the basic argument of the white parents has to boil down to "you are better than they are."

But their children are going to find out from day in and day out experience that those black students from economic backgrounds similar to their own, as a general rule, will match their efforts and achievements.

And among the questions they will come to ask is why their parents think a public school system should be run so that a race which historically has enjoyed advantages would be assured of still additional preferential treatment?

If there are good and bad schools, topnotch and inferior teachers, peaceful and rowdy schools or new and old buildings, should not all students be required to share alike?

If in the long-run the overall quality of education will be enhanced nationally through desegregated education, is it not time the 1954 Supreme Court mandate be accepted?

Is it not time that the goal of quality education for all children be worked at rather than talked about?

When will "quality education" in the United States include proper attention to learning to live together as a nation of people with equal opportunity and citizenship rights?

Until we can drastically curb the kind of racial poisons being imbedded into the hearts and minds of Americans by situations such as witnessed in Boston and Baltimore, the country is going to be handicapped in efforts to solve other national and international problems.

The Seattle Times
Seattle, Wash., October 9, 1974

AFTER more than a month of almost constant disorders and racial unrest triggered by a federal court's school-desegregation order, Boston Mayor Kevin White has sent out a call for help.

Citing the mounting number of acts of violence, physical injuries and arrests, particularly in South Boston, White asked that federal marshals be sent in to help protect school children and carry out the court's order on mandatory bussing.

Despite the daily assignment of as many as 900 police officers to trouble spots—nearly half the city's police strength at a given time — White warned that in South Boston, at least, "this city is unable to continue to maintain both public safety and implementation of the court order."

The situation in Boston is, of course, deplorable and has spread beyond the jeering and rock-throwing episodes at the affected schools. In one incident Sunday, for example, a mob of whites chased and beat a black motorist whose car was tied up in traffic. Bands of youths, both black and white, have been roaming the South Boston area and precipitating numerous clashes.

While Boston is the focal point of the present difficulties (of the Northern cities that have resisted court-ordered desegregation plans of the past 20 years, none has held out longer than Boston), the events there call into fresh question the advisability of forced bussing as such in any community.

Other responses to the need to improve educational equality — curricula changes, voluntary transfers, special training for teachers, etc.—have met the test of public acceptance. The same obviously cannot be said of compulsory bussing, however.

Feelings on the issue of forced bussing can run so high, in fact, that its divisive effects may well outweigh the presumed academic and social benefits attributed to it. And that, in turn, raises doubts as to whether it should remain a mechanism in the array of techniques being applied to problems involving racial deprivation.

At the moment, the United States Supreme Court's views on the bussing issue give signs of change and experts in both black and white communities are rethinking the larger question of whether the schools alone are capable of correcting social and economic problems rooted in highly complex causes.

Meantime, the shocking events in Boston—which evoke mournful recollections of the racial disruptions of the 1950's and 1960's—demonstrate that a court order by itself cannot compel either the spirit or reality of peaceful school desegregation.

HOUSTON CHRONICLE
Houston, Texas, October 11, 1974

H o w unfortunate that American should be pitted against American in such a situation as we find in Boston with public schools there trying their best to implement court-ordered busing to desegregate South Boston and Roxbury schools.

This is but another example of what happens when the federal courts force something upon the public that large blocs of people oppose, many of them for justifiable reasons.

Regardless of how bitter the parents are over the busing of their children out of their neighborhoods, they are wrong to make the streets and school campuses battlegrounds. What a fine example for the school children of Boston. The adults who are so upset about the busing should take their grievances to the school board, their elected representatives, the courts. Involving the children so directly is completely unjustified. The cross fire is unhealthy for many reasons.

President Ford capsuled our sentiments at his press conference when he said: "The court decision was not the best solution to quality education in Boston. I respectfully disagree with the court. But it is of maximum importance that the citizens of Boston respect the law."

Perhaps all of us shall learn something from the sad situation in Boston, above a l l those individuals w h o thought such problems somehow were restricted to the South.

The Charlotte Observer
Charlotte, N.C., October 9, 1974

The people of Boston are doing for the cities of the North what Oxford, Miss., Birmingham, Ala., and Lamar, S.C., did for the South. They are proving the need for federal enforcement of civil rights laws.

The rocking of school buses and beating of black parents in Boston reminds us again of the ugly street scenes that brought national opprobrium to the South in the 1950s and 1960s. The marshals at Ole Miss, the cattle prods at Birmingham and the overturned buses at Lamar only hastened the change that some Southerners sought to resist.

Now, from afar, Southerners themselves can see the repugnance and brutality of racist mobs and join with people elsewhere in condemning it. A Charlottean, reading a newspaper story while riding a bus to work, commented to his seat mate: "You know, the people of Boston are about to give us Southerners a good name."

The country did not really need the events in Boston to remind us that racial injustice transcends the Mason-Dixon line. Brutalities against blacks in the North, East and West are too old and too well known. Even during the Civil War, when Union soldiers from New York were' fighting in the South to free black slaves, black refugees sometimes had to defend themselves against white mobs in New York City.

During World Wars I and II, when blacks left the South to take jobs in the big industrial centers of the Midwest, they discovered that segregation accompanied them. There were race riots in Chicago and Detroit.

Among the many ironies in the Supreme Court's school desegregation decision of 1954 was that the defendant in the Brown case was not a Southern school board but one in Topeka, Kan., in the heartland of the country. In choosing Brown as the case of record among the five suits that made up that decision, the Supreme Court seemed to recognize that race was a national rather than a regional issue.

Because it has largely come to terms with desegregation, the South has something to teach the people of Boston, Detroit and other cities undergoing racial turmoil. The South has learned to beware of political leaders who promise to roll back the social forces or hold them at bay. For too long, Southerners believed the rhetoric of such false hopes. Southerners also learned, all too often the hard way, that threats, brutality and lawless resistance bring harsher judgments and swifter justice. The people of Boston should profit from that bitter experience. And perhaps the trouble there will force the Ford Administration to reexamine its policy of regional bias in the enforcement of the law.

The State
Columbia, S.C., October 9, 1974

A WHILE AGO, some wags claimed there was a distinction between busing, a means of transporting children to school, and busin', the hauling of kids out of their neighborhoods to improve the racial balance of schools. Busin' was often spit out, George Wallace fashion, and it had a bad connotation in Southern circles.

The distinction has been lost as this connotation spread northward. Busing now means student shuffling for racial balance almost everywhere.

It has also meant big trouble in Detroit and Boston, once the national capital of bleeding-heart liberalism. But it is also viewed with distaste elsewhere in the North, if a survey taken by The Ohio Poll is any indication.

Citizens of that great Midwestern state were asked two questions: do you favor public school integration, assuming that busing is not required? Do you favor it, assuming busing is required?

The wording of the final phrases made a big difference in the response. Of the entire sample, 74 per cent favored integration, with 17 per cent opposed. The black segment was 78 per cent for, and 14 per cent against, and the Jewish sample was 100 per cent for the concept of school mixing.

But with busing added, the results were almost reversed. Of the total sample, 71 per cent nixed busing, with only 22 per cent favorable. Only 18 per cent of the whites said "yes" and a surprising 36 per cent of the blacks disapproved, as opposed to 62 per cent for busing."

And that Jewish group that was all for integration was 80 per cent against busing.

Why these flip-flops? The best we can figure, integration is viewed in the abstract. It connotes equality of educational opportunity and equal treatment under the law. It is an educational and social good.

But integration tumbles off these lofty pillars of principle when busing is added. It brings it home and makes it real and personal. "Our little Johnny" is threatened, and attitudes change.

Hypocrisy? Maybe. Human nature? Surely.

The Virginian-Pilot

Norfolk, Va., October 10, 1974

Twenty years and five months after the Supreme Court's school desegregation ruling, Boston is reviving the spirit of John Kasper. This week a white mob attacked a black man stuck in a South Boston traffic jam and stoned a bus carrying black students to South Boston High School. The next day blacks stoned cars in which whites were riding. South Boston High has been nearly empty throughout the month of the new school term, symbolizing white resistance to a Federal court's integration decree.

Mayor Kevin White has said the Boston police force is unequal to the worsening emergency and petitioned the judge who handed down the busing order to back it up with U.S. marshals. That the Mayor was forced to plead for assistance is remarkable. When integration was blocked in Little Rock, President Eisenhower sent in Federal troops. When it was challenged at the University of Mississippi, President Kennedy directed U.S. marshals to take over the campus and authorized the Secretary of Defense to call the 11,000 men of the Mississippi National Guard into "the active military service of the United States."

In the Little Rock and Oxford instances, state governors defied the law. In Boston, mobs are defying it—but as ugly and more effectively than Orval Forbus and Ross Barnett managed. Washington is mistaken to view the Boston shame, as it appears to be doing, as a local affair.

The law of the land is concerned. Boston racists are not immune from it.

DAILY NEWS

New York, N.Y., October 12, 1974

The ugly rioting and vicious attacks on blacks by South Boston busing opponents can only be stopped by cool heads and firm hands.

President Ford was right when he said at his recent press conference that Boston citizens should "obey the law." But he needlessly and carelessly added that he disagreed with court-ordered busing decisions and always had.

That gratuitous remark was untimely and uncalled for. It quite possibly fanned the flames of resentment in Boston still higher, as Boston's Mayor Kevin White has charged.

White needs all the help and support he can get in quelling the disturbances and ending the strife. With added police and public support, he may be able to persuade the people to adhere to the law.

The most important thing now is to restore order in Boston, cool passions and bring the violence, venom and hatred under control.

WORCESTER TELEGRAM.

Worcester, Mass., October 9, 1974

Ever since the court-enforced integration of Boston's public schools went into effect last month, it has been hoped that opponents of the plan would temper their protest and stay within the law.

Unfortunately, that has not always happened. Encouraged by a small group of political leaders, anti-busing demonstrators have grown more and more violent. It is no longer safe for black and white children to cross certain neighborhood boundaries on their way to school. And the unprovoked mob attack on a black man in South Boston the other day was one of the ugliest incidents we have seen in a long time.

Forced school integration is a bitter pill to swallow for many persons, and neighborhood pride is strong throughout Boston. But the court-ordered school plan — which affects about 94,000 children in the Hub — is the law, and no mob action can change that.

Boston city and school officials have shown wisdom and flexibility in trying to cope with the situation.

If present measures to protect the children and keep the schools open are not enough, perhaps stronger action is in order. That may include assistance by federal marshals.

The anti-busing leaders have a special responsibility. It is up to them to calm their followers before serious tragedy occurs. They ought to make it clear that stopping school integration by force is a no-win proposition.

While much attention is being focused on a couple of schools in South Boston and Roxbury, it ought to be noted that calm has prevailed in most of Boston's 200 other public schools, and attendance has been over 70 per cent. It is only a small minority that gives Boston a bad name.

Boston — the "Athens of America" — has the oldest school system in the country. With patience, tolerance and understanding, there is no reason why it should not also have one of the best for all its children. But first mob violence must be stopped. Thoughtfulness and civility do not have a chance while fists and stones are flying.

Des Moines Tribune

Des Moines, Iowa, October 2, 1974

Despite the recent outbreaks of violence in Boston, busing to end racial segregation in schools is not the political issue it was in 1972. The Supreme Court let much of the steam escape when it overturned a federal district judge's plan for cross-busing between city and suburbs in the Detroit area.

By that decision the court removed for suburban parents the fear that their children would be taken to inferior inner-city schools. It also made desegregation a practical impossibility in cities with a majority of black school children.

But within the city of Boston, and most cities, busing could bring black and white children into almost every school in proportion to their numbers in the population without submerging the whites in a black majority. Experience has shown this to be the fastest way to desegregate schools.

Yet even in cities such as Boston where the white-black ratio would be three to one busing is unpopular. Roy Wilkins, executive director of the National Association for the Advancement of Colored People, offers this telling quote from a white mother in South Boston: "The coloreds aren't getting an equal education, right? Now (the authorities) want to put our children into those schools. Then our children won't get an equal education, either."

Right — and wrong. In many cities better facilities and better faculties are provided when white children are in the classroom. So busing, in effect, makes white children hostages until the school board has provided equal educational opportunity throughout the district, as it should have done all along.

But white parents don't like having their children held hostage in poor schools — any more than black parents have liked having their children held in those schools. Where white families for economic or other reasons are unable to escape, as in South Boston, they throw rocks at buses.

Where they have the means, and where crossing a street into another district provides "safety" — thanks to the Supreme Court — then busing will not work well, because unfair housing practices often close that escape route to blacks.

The Chattanooga Times

Chattanooga, Tenn., October 11, 1974

In Boston, Mayor Kevin White has been refused federal marshals to combat the strife that erupted following implementation of a court-ordered busing program and which has nearly exhausted the resources of Boston police. But additional area law enforcement officers have been obtained, said the mayor, to prevent someone from being killed in the controversy. It is, of course, ironic that such widespread racial violence is going on in Boston, where so many events associated with American independence occurred. But it is even more ironic when one considers that American independence is predicated on the rule of law, not of mobs, whose actions in the agony of Boston has been nothing short of degrading.

CHICAGO Daily Defender

Chicago, Ill., October 15, 1974

Muffled during the stormy days of Watergate, school busing has flared up again in all of its ugly companionate features of resistance and racism in Boston, the cradle of liberty. The resurgence is painfully reminiscent of Little Rock, Ark., and Oxford, Miss., where two Presidents, one after the other, saw clearly that the law had to be obeyed, and they did not back away from their constitutional responsibility.

Eisenhower dispatched federal troops to Little Rock and later Pres. Kennedy sent federal marshals on the campus of the University of Mississippi to enforce the order of the courts. President Ford has chosen a different course. He has elected to throw the weight of his personal opinion and emotion on the side of the misguided Bostonians who are in defiance of the courts.

His tape-recorded statement urging the people of Boston to "reject violence of any kind," was a feeble pronouncement made at the urging of Mass. Senator Edward W. Brooke. The half-hearted exhortation came too late to have any redeeming psychological or moral effect on those hard-core segregationists who look upon Mr Ford's earlier criticism of the busing order as an approbation of their resistance to the law.

By his blind, indefensible criticism of the judges for discharging their judicial responsibility in ordering Boston public schools integrated in confirmity with the course prescribed by law, Mr. Ford was not fulfilling his presidential obligation. He has in fact, fanned the flames of resistance, as Boston Mayor Kevin H. White correctly puts it.

The lives of black children are endangered. They have already sustained injuries when the buses carrying them to school were stoned by angry white mobs. Ford's lukewarm, adulterated admonition does not alter his profile as a Nixon disciple.

The Washington Post

Washington, D.C., October 10, 1974

THE FIRST THING to be said about the violence in Boston, which was occasioned by efforts to enforce a court-ordered school desegregation plan and which has disrupted the schools and caused a great deal of bloodshed. is that local and federal authorities have a clear obligation to restore and maintain public order. By that we mean they have an obligation to protect the school children and adult citizens involved and also to ensure that the schools stay open and that the law is upheld. Whether this dual imperative can be fulfilled without the help of federal troops—now that the city's request for U.S. marshals has been turned down—we do not know. But Mayor Kevin White shoud not hesitate to request and Washington should not hesitate to provide whatever assistance is necessary to guarantee the citizens' well-being and the school system's compliance with the federal court order.

Given the volatility of the situation in Boston and the rising curve of violence and resistance of the past several days, we are hard put to think of a more untimely, unfortunate and unhelpful statement than that offered by President Ford at his press conference yesterday. The by-now pat formulation he followed—a pro forma statement deploring violence leading to the inevitable "however" and a subsequent expression of distaste for the court's order—is only likely to give further hope and encouragement to those who have taken the law into their own hands. The city of Boston, as we understand it, has no shortage of local politicians at the moment who are plying this line and whose principal effect has been to incite the violent to further action. What the people of Boston need to know is that street violence is not and cannot be permitted to become a substitute for orderly legal and/or political efforts to change laws they consider unfair.

In this connection we would add only that one grimly ironic aspect of the violence in Boston is the light it sheds on the inadequacy and perils of the so-called "antibusing" legislation that has become so popular in Washington in recent years. One of these provisions would limit busing for desegregation to older children —precisely those who are most caught up in the violence in Boston, as distinct from the younger children whose integration appears to be going much more smoothly. Another—the so-called "next nearest school" provision, which would keep busing within close geographical confines—would generally entail bringing black ghetto children into poor white neighborhoods where racial tensions are highest and violent resistance most likely, places very much like South Boston.

But there will be plenty of time for reflection on these things. What is needed now is an end to the disorder in Boston. It is a great pity that President Ford, who had an opportunity to help in his remarks yesterday, failed to take it.

VIOLENCE CONTINUES IN BOSTON; KENNEDY IS JOSTLED BY CROWD

Violence resumed in Boston in antibusing protests during January and April. More than 100 policemen patrolled the corridors of Hyde Park High School Jan. 14, after racial clashes the day before had resulted in three injuries and 13 arrests. Racial fighting had also resulted in arrests of 15 Hyde Park students Jan. 9 on charges of disorderly conduct. South Boston High School, closed since a Dec. 11, 1974 stabbing incident, reopened Jan. 8. The approximately 400 students—31 of them black—who returned to classes were guarded by an estimated 500 state, metropolitan and city policemen.

Sen. Edward Kennedy (D, Mass.), a supporter of busing to achieve integration, was heckled and jostled by a crowd of antibusing demonstrators April 6 when he tried to make his way to a car after emerging from a suburban Boston junior high school, at which he had spoken. When police and the senator's aides were unable to clear a path to a waiting automobile, Kennedy made his way to a nearby subway station, where he caught a Boston-bound train. Kennedy was not injured, although one woman repeatedly jabbed at him with the point of a small U.S. flag.

Amsterdam News

New York, N.Y., January 18, 1975

The time clock of racial violence is ticking away in Boston while President Gerald Ford, like Nero of old, fiddles as the racial fires burn.

The NAACP and others standing for decency in this country have appealed to President Ford, to take urgently needed action in enforcing law and order in Boston.

But in spite of the fact that a Black man was beaten and almost lynched on October 7th by white mobs, and despite the fact that Boston's racist violence has become a regular weekend occurrence nevertheless, there is no new word from the White House on Boston.

The last word we had from the White House on Boston was that the President did not agree with the judge who told the Boston bigots to desegrate their schools.

What do we have to do in order to get the President to take responsible action in Boston? Must we wait until someone is killed in the violence?

There was a time when this nation deplored Dwight Eisenhower's reluctance to act. That was the time when Orvil Faubus thumbed his nose at federal laws and used the National Guard to take away the rights of Black children in Little Rock.

But even Dwight Eisenhower had his breaking point, and he finally did what he should have done earlier. He sent federal troops into Little Rock to restore law and order and uphold the Constitution.

What does it take to get Gerald Ford to act?

WORCESTER TELEGRAM.

Worcester, Mass., January 10, 1975

Not enough voices of reason have been heard throughout the long Boston school busing controversy. Politicians have been jockeying for position or keeping carefully away from the controversial issue. Opponents and advocates struck repeated blows for inflexibility. Courts, lawyers, police and demonstrators carried the day more often than not while education received short shrift.

The voice of Mrs. Peggy Coughlin is refreshing in this din of discontent. A South Boston mother of nine, she is opposed to "forced busing" but dislikes violence and the closing of the high schools even more. She has just about had it with trouble-makers and noisy activists and wants to see the mothers of the deprived children stand up and be counted. Mrs. Coughlin informed the Boston School Committee that she had persuaded more than 100 mothers to help her keep the peace.

Hers may have been the most constructive voice in the South Boston school integration issue for a long time. No one knows how much the restraint of Mrs. Coughlin and others had to do with the relatively trouble-free reopening of the schools — hundreds of police stood by just in case. But if more and more people begin to think and act like Mrs. Coughlin and her volunteers, there may be new hope for that troubled neighborhood.

Los Angeles Times

Los Angeles, Calif., January 5, 1975

The leaders of the public schools in Boston are teaching a dangerous and destructive lesson.

It was their neglect of the problem of racial segregation that left no alternative but a court-ordered integration plan.

Now they are defying the authority of the court to take the next appropriate step, enlarging and extending the integration.

This is not a question of resisting what a community may regard as an unwise plan, of appealing through appropriate legal channels orders that are thought to be contrary to the public interest. Not at all. This is a case of deliberate defiance of the federal courts, and with that defiance a debasement of the rule of law. It is a response that can only inflame prejudice, enhance fears, encourage disorder.

In fact, the situation has deteriorated to a point at which police have proposed the permanent closing of one high school complex in South Boston. The opening of those schools has been postponed until Monday. The police are concerned that they will not be able to give adequate protection to the students.

That is a terrible indictment. The federal judge controlling the integration plan has wisely postponed a decision on permanent closing, asserting that such action should be applied only as a last resort and when alternative school facilities became available.

Protection of students is imperative. But to separate this imperative from the imperative of constitutional rights would be to expose all law to the depredations of the lawless.

There can be no turning back in Boston. The law will and must be observed. The task will be easier, the transition smoother, if the school board members begin teaching by example the paramount requirement of respect for the law, for due process.

The News and Courier

Charleston, N.C., April 14, 1975

Despite the fact that his position is opposed by constituents in large numbers, Sen. Ted Kennedy has been stubborn as a mule in adhering to ideas on busing. His inflexible position suggests that the senator is out of touch with the feelings of voters on crucial subjects, a not uncommon phenomenon in Washington where Congress is gradually building walls around itself, away from the people.

How Mr. Kennedy's attitude will be affected by his recent visit to South Boston where he was jeered by a mob of not-so-proper Bostonians, we can only speculate. It is often a revelation to people in high places when they get down to earth with the rest of us and find out what's going on. Surely some message was conveyed by the lady who poked Mr. Kennedy about the ribs with what the Associated Press described as the point of a small American flag.

Roughing up senators is not an approved method of getting one's views before Congress. But we are reminded of a formula for handling mules: the way to get the mule's attention is to slap him around a bit.

Herald ☙ News
Fall River, Mass., April 10, 1975

The mistreatment of Senator Kennedy by three hundred anti-busing demonstrators in Quincy was a disgrace. Anti-busing opponents have a perfect right to express their opinion; even further, they have a right to make that opinion known in the presence of elected officials like Senator Kennedy.

But their abuse was so violent in this case that the senator was unable to get into his car and retreated to a subway under police protection. Later on he cancelled a speech he was scheduled to make in Sharon when he learned that anti-busing demonstrators had gone there to confront him.

This kind of mistreatment, which included the slashing of tires on his car, fortunately stopped short of physical injury, but that is all that can be said for it. The demonstrators were flagrantly interfering with the senator's right to express his own views and, presumably, trying to frighten him into switching his pro-busing stand.

Whatever one thinks of the busing issue itself, there is simply no way of justifying the behavior of these demonstrators. They acted like an unruly mob, not a group of responsible citizens. They forgot entirely the respect that should be displayed toward a man holding high public office. The treatment accorded Senator Kennedy fell far short of the respect he has a right to receive.

The anti-busing advocates have done their cause no good whatever by their performance in Quincy, and, as they might have expected, Senator Kennedy has pointed out that their behavior will have no effect on his own stand regarding the busing issue.

FORT WORTH STAR-TELEGRAM
Fort Worth, Tex., April 10, 1975

The spectacle of a U.S. senator being jostled and poked by a heckling crowd in his own state has once again pointed up a disgusting, even disturbing, strand in the fiber of modern America.

We're talking about the roughing up Sen. Edward Kennedy received as he walked to his car from a Quincy, Mass., junior high school where he had delivered a speech.

The crowd of about 300 angry, shouting adults — brandishing pickets ripped from a nearby fence — were protesting Mr. Kennedy's stand on court-ordered busing for racial balance in Boston schools.

In the past we've disagreed vehemently with many positions espoused by Ted Kennedy. We still do.

We've opposed the principle of busing school children of various races away from their own neighborhoods and across long distances as a means of solving the problem of providing equal educational opportunity for all children, regardless of race. We still do.

So, in protesting Mr. Kennedy's views and in protesting the idea of court-mandated busing, we have something in common with the distraught citizens of Quincy.

And we can understand and sympathize with their frustration.

But the method the Quincy crowd chose for its protest appalls us. Such violence has no place in the American system of solving problems.

It involved pushing the senator jabbing at him with the fence pickets and, in one case, grabbing him by the leg.

The irony of this exhibition of un-American conduct was blatantly illustrated by the action of a woman in the crowd. As she bombarded Mr. Kennedy with abusive language, she kept jabbing at him with the point of a small American flag standard.

When the busing furor descended on Fort Worth, we deplored the busing principle. We believe the majority of Fort Worth parents agreed with us.

But we also said that, for this to be a law-and-order country, the orders of our federal courts, including the busing order, had to be obeyed.

It's a tremendous credit to the people of this community that they too recognized this; and violence was avoided.

Many developments, both in education and human relations, indicate that busing is as far from a solution to equality in education as we all expected it to be.

But that shouldn't stir any of us to violent behavior. It should only prompt us to attack the problem of inequality the more vigorously through the facets of reason and goodwill that constitute the spirit of the American way.

Every child is entitled to be exposed to educational opportunities that will provide him the chance to enter society as a productive, contributing citizen with worth and dignity.

A United States senator, however repugnant his views may be to some, is entitled to walk the streets of this country unmolested.

If that's not so, then America, as we've always understood the term, doesn't really mean anything.

The snarling mob in Quincy said, in effect, they don't care what it means.

Here in Fort Worth, thankfully, the people said they care.

Whatever others may do, let's keep on caring.

The Afro ☙ American
Baltimore, Md., April 22, 1975

Ominous rumblings and actions from the anti-busing Restore Our Alienated Rights group in Boston are significant warnings of what is happening in democratic America.

After about 200 antibusing protesters poked, grabbed and jostled Senator Edward M. Kennedy because of his position that busing is a tool to be used in desegregating schools (the Supreme Court's edict), ROAR executive board member Elvira Palladino declared:

"We'd like to destroy him politically, and we will.

"He's voting his conscience instead of the will of the people.

"If you read that, then it's no longer a representative government.

"He said, let the chips fall where they may, and the chips are coming down like a snowstorm.

"We don't wish the man any harm, basically—we only wish he'd get out of politics."

What these people are saying with their unAmerican actions and declarations is Kennedy has to go, or at least be hounded by them every time he appears in his home state, simply because Kennedy agrees with the law of the land and they do not.

They're so confused they claim representative government is not working because Sen. Kennedy votes his conscience rather than kowtow to them when they clearly are out of step with the law.

Senator Kennedy should have broad national support of his position.

The Boston Globe
Boston, Mass., April 8, 1975

Antibusing protestors on Sunday again availed themselves of public appearances by Sen. Edward M. Kennedy to cause disturbances, forcing him to detour by subway from Quincy and later to cancel a speech in Sharon. In two other such incidents in Boston, demonstrators prevented the senator from addressing a rally in Government Center on Sept. 9 and interrupted a subcommittee hearing on airline fares on Feb. 15.

In Quincy the crowd escalated its tactics beyond the jeers and taunts of the earlier episodes. Protestors slashed the tires of Kennedy's car and barred him from reaching it. Some of them jabbed at him with American flags. Others threw rocks at the subway train, as Sen. Kennedy departed.

Such harassment and intimidation discredit the cause the demonstrators espouse. They cast doubt, for instance, on their avowed concern for the safety of their children when they place them under the wheels of an automobile, as they did yesterday in Quincy.

In encroaching on rights of free speech, they antagonize law-abiding persons across the political spectrum. Their actions on Sunday deprived an audience in Sharon, for example, of hearing Sen. Kennedy's views on national health insurance.

The assault on the senator's rights is all the more indefensible since he has shown a continuing willingness to listen to viewpoints on school desegregation different from his own. He has met with opponents to school busing on numerous occasions, including Sunday morning, when he conferred with a group of parents from the South Shore.

Rather than access to Sen. Kennedy for exposition of their views, these abusive protestors apparently want to exploit the media attention that surrounds him for their own publicity. This strategy can lead only to further confrontations ultimately at the expense of the protestors' own credibility and of the democratic process.

The Standard-Times
New Bedford, Mass., April 10, 1975

A Boston group called ROAR is opposed to busing as a means of integrating schools and to Sen. Edward M. Kennedy, D-Mass., because of his refusal to condemn busing as a means of achieving racial integration.

As a result, ROAR (Restore Our Alienated Rights) members have shown up at Kennedy speaking engagements in the state seeking to prevent his talking and to force him to change his mind on busing. In other words, intimidation.

The most ugly incident occurred in Quincy when a crowd of 200 attempted to mob the senator, slashed the tires on his car, placed their children under the wheels of a backup car and forced him to flee under police protection to a nearby subway station.

There are conflicting reports about whether Kennedy suffered minor injuries. He has sought to make light of the situation even after the same group forced him to cancel another speaking engagement in Sharon later in the day.

The next day, a ROAR official, one Elvira "Pixie" Palladino, confided to reporters the group will continue to harass the senator and, if possible, "destroy him politically unless he switches to an anti-busing position."

We have differed sharply with the senator in the past—and fully expect to in the future—but this strong-arm approach is not the way to win support to any cause.

In fact, we suspect this assault on the right of free speech will alienate many persons who feel at least some degree of opposition to forced busing. ROAR's tactics smack too much of the Nazi storm troopers and Communist goon squads.

These tactics seem particularly unjustified since Kennedy has demonstrated time and again his willingness to sit down with anti-busing elements. In fact, he spoke for 20 minutes with another anti-busing group before his talk in Quincy.

ROAR is entitled to its point of view, but so is Sen. Kennedy. In pursuing its rights, the group has violated the right of those persons in Sharon to hear their U.S. senator. And the Sharon gathering is not the first that they caused to be canceled.

Violence breeds more violence, as we all saw during the demonstrations in South Boston and elsewhere last fall. And violence is not going to change the law of the land.

If ROAR's methods trigger a resumption of the rock-throwing, the knife-wielding, the thuggery and racial strife in Boston schools, the ultimate losers will be the children.

The Detroit News
Detroit, Mich., April 14, 1975

Can Detroit avoid the bitterness and violence which have accompanied forced bussing of schoolchildren in Boston?

Not that massive bussing is a foregone conclusion for Detroit. Federal Judge Robert E. DeMascio may well approve a plan requiring limited use of school buses. However, if the court does order extensive bussing, this community will face a stern test of tolerance and maturity.

Let's hope Detroit possesses a fuller measure of those qualities than Boston has displayed.

Emotion has blinded the better judgment of many Boston citizens. Last week, for example, angry anti-bussing protesters dogged the footsteps of Sen. Edward Kennedy. They grabbed and clawed him, prevented him from entering his own automobile and hurled stones at the subway car in which he finally made his escape.

We neither approve massive bussing nor feel a high regard for Sen. Kennedy. However, a U.S. senator or anybody else should be able to express his views on bussing or any other topic without having his freedom of speech and movement restricted by a mob.

The harassment of Sen. Kennedy offers but one example of Boston's hysterical reaction to bussing. Since last September, when a federal judge ordered the bussing of students, violence has occurred with clockwork regularity.

Mobs stone buses; officials close some schools temporarily to avoid bloodshed; police must patrol the halls of some schools; many students stay home because they're afraid to enter the school yard; Boston enrollments have dropped 8 percent; on a given day, absenteeism in a school may reach as high as 35 percent.

This newspaper opposes massive forced bussing and defends the right of citizens to protest official acts with which they disagree. And we can see how blacks and whites, alike, would be disturbed by a bussing program and would want to display their feelings.

Still, any citizen genuinely concerned about the welfare of the community and its children should keep in mind that violent protest could only make a bad situation worse. Action for change should be directed at all times through legal channels.

The Constitution allows for the picket line and the public rally. Anti-bussing forces can always appeal to higher courts or seek relief through congressional action. When the protester starts throwing rocks, his conduct is no longer legal or acceptable and he loses our support.

In turn, the public has a right to expect responsible restraint on the part of the court and all those involved in the desegregation case. Detroit will more readily accept a desegregation plan if convinced that those who devised the plan did their utmost to produce a reasonable formula for desegregating and educating Detroit schoolchildren.

A reasonable formula will respect certain principles:

Quality education is more important than bussing for bussing's sake; it's better to invest in children than in buses.

Local control is an important factor in public support of schools. The concept of local control must not get lost in plans to haul children in wholesale quantities away from neighborhood schools.

If the schools are to be integrated, they must contain the ingredients for integration. They won't contain those ingredients if an immoderate plan causes still more whites to flee to the suburbs.

Finally, any remedy that creates graver ills than it cures cannot be seriously regarded as social progress.

If those responsible for producing a desegregation plan keep their eyes on such principles, they can reasonably expect a peaceable reaction to their handiwork.

Boston Herald American
Combining the best features of the Herald Traveler and Record American
Boston, Mass., April 8, 1975

Senator Edward M. Kennedy has attempted to make light of the rowdy incident in Quincy Sunday in which he was vocally harassed and — technically, at least — physically assaulted by anti-busing demonstrators.

It would be a mistake, however, to minimize the seriousness of the demonstration, in which agitated dissidents resorted to something very close to mob violence to deny the right of conscience and free speech to a member of the United States Senate.

The ugliness of the scene raises doubt, too, that the small band of hecklers, who have been following Senator Kennedy from one public appearance to another for the purpose of embarrassing and silencing him, according to his aides, are representative of the majority of law abiding citizens who obviously differ with his stand on the busing issue.

What occurred in Quincy — after similar outbursts elsewhere — is a warning to all that radical extremism is not the exclusive weakness of young campus rebels but can be just as threatening to human freedom and dignity when resorted to by adults.

Forced busing and school desegregation are worrisome issues for many of us. But they will not be resolved by shouting epithets and throwing punches at public officials, slashing the tires of their cars or rock throwing, which only encourages other more despicable forms of violence. The answers will be found only through respect for each other's right to disagree.

The Dallas Morning News

Dallas, Texas, June 6, 1975

WHEN THE federal courts began ordering the school buses gassed up, in order that the integrated society might at last be achieved, the name of Prof. James S. Coleman was very often invoked.

Coleman, of Johns Hopkins University, was author of a massive study for the federal government which declared that "for those children whose family and neighborhood are educationally disadvantaged, it is important to replace this family environment as much as possible with an educational environment"—by busing, in other words, and by busing as early as possible. Black children had to be gotten away from their families and taken to white school districts, else they could not learn.

How interesting and enlightening to learn, therefore, that Dr. Coleman himself believes busing to have become—in the jargon of our times—counterproductive. It is driving white families out of the large cities, Coleman has been saying in newspaper interviews, and has led to resegregation; it is "accelerating the very racial isolation we are trying to overcome."

Not that Coleman is any the less committed to integration; he emphasizes that he still thinks black children learn best in economically and racially mixed classrooms. He believes, though, that the courts have gone much too far.

"When the will for integration does not exist," Coleman now acknowledges, "the imposition of it by the courts doesn't make it successful."

"The courts," he maintains, "have tried to take on the function of educators. And for the advocates of busing, who worked through the courts, the integration fight became a matter of realizing a principle regardless of the consequences."

Coleman's reading of the pro-busers' mindset is accurate enough. Busing though the heavens fall! they have cried. The heavens remain in place, but not the white families whose children were expected to be the pawns in the courts' social experiment. Numerous of those families have gone to the suburbs, thus reducing the tax base of the school districts where once they resided.

Yet there are still righteous busers to demand that the horse not only be led to water but have the water forced down his throat.

Naturally, the busers will not in the end succeed. That does not make their activities any the less harmful. Where will it all end? In the destruction of American public education? Not Coleman, nor any one else, knows. But toward that destruction the busing fervor—a fervor worthy of Cromwell's Roundheads or similar hot-eyed zealots—already is leading us.

THE RICHMOND NEWS LEADER

Richmond, Va., May 1, 1975

The American Educational Research Association threw a bash in Washington a few days ago, and a couple of sociologists turned up to review the progress of school integration since the Brown decision 21 years ago. Their appraisals were melancholy.

The first was James S. Coleman, now a professor at the University of Chicago. Coleman was the author of the Coleman Report, issued in 1966, in which he proclaimed that the "hostage theory" would improve the educational advantages of black children when they attended predominantly white schools. White children would act as hostages, because their parents would continue to demand high levels of educational quality in the schools — a quality from which the minority black students would benefit.

Coleman has a different view now. Taking into account the white flight to the suburbs generated by compulsory busing, he said, the momentum toward true integration in the schools has wavered. In the push to integrate the schools, courts and governmental officials failed to consider the reaction of whites whose co-operation they tried to coerce. That reaction came when middle- and upper-income white families fled to the suburbs. They left behind lower-income and working-class white families who resented and fought all attempts to use their children as pawns in racial balance games.

Coleman singled out the courts as "probably the worst instrument of social policy" in effecting school integration. "Desegregation through the courts," he said, "probably will have served in the long run to separate whites and blacks more severely than before. As white flight accelerates, the cities are left with large black populations and fewer whites to be used for racial mixing." But Coleman was long on realities and short on suggested remedies.

The second speaker was Robert G. Wegmann, a University of Houston professor who addressed himself to the subject of "tipping." He told his audience that courts and other agencies ignored the fact that whites flee when black percentages in schools reach a level between 30 per cent and 50 per cent. Tipping already has caused Richmond's school system to become 76 per cent black. In Detroit, the schools are 72 per cent black; in Chicago, 71 per cent black; in New York City and in Philadelphia, 66 per cent black; in Baltimore, 70 per cent black.

When a school system's enrollment reaches 30 per cent, Wegmann said, "Integration may then put each of the schools in the city beyond the tipping point, leading to an agonizing process of resegregation which will, over time, significantly alter the character of a city's population." He held out little hope that true integration could occur in any school system with a black enrollment of 30 per cent or more.

The courts will hear no pleas from local school officials about human reactions to judicial coercion, nor will they consider such evidence as white flight and tipping. In the numbers game they play, they consider only the presumed necessity for providing a satisfactory racial mix in every school throughout a system. Those who resist compulsory busing have been talking and writing about white flight and tipping for years, and it is unlikely that either Coleman's or Wegmann's appraisal of the real world will have much effect on public policy.

And so we have violence in Boston, as we had violence in Pontiac and in Canarsie. The battlefront now moves north, across the Mason-Dixon Line, and Northerners who thought it commendable to coerce Southerners find themselves resisting the same coercion. In time, though, as Coleman and Wegmann point out, the courts will put themselves out of the school integration business. When a school system becomes so predominantly black that only a small minority of whites remains to be spread around, judicial pronouncements don't count for much. Judges need only look at Washington — the showcase of the nation — which now has a black school enrollment of . . . 96 per cent.

Boston Herald American

Combining the best features of the Herald Traveler and Record American

Boston, Mass., May 25, 1975

Court-ordered desegregation of schools — especially when it has involved the forced busing of a large number of students — has been stoutly opposed and angrily denounced for many years. The resistance and criticism, too, have been just as strong in the North as in the South — in some cases even stronger.

Recently, however, a number of new and rather surprising voices have been added to the anti-busing chorus. They include several people who have played key roles in the long legal and political battle to end racial segregation. Today they are not only having second thoughts about forced busing and other forms of compulsory integration which they have advocated in the past; they now admit that they were wrong.

Although their arguments may be different from the traditional case against busing, their conclusions are the same: it doesn't work and usually is counter-productive.

Last week pro-busing forces were jolted by the news that one of their heroes had abandoned the cause. Professor James S. Coleman, whose scholarly report on school segregation in the U.S. in 1966 served as the basis for numerous lawsuits in subsequent years and earned him the title of "architect" of court-ordered desegregation, announced that the experience of the past nine years has forced him to alter his views.

The author of the Coleman Report still believes in integration. But he says that the main goals of busing — which were to improve the quality of education and to end racial isolation — have not been achieved.

In fact, he adds, the result in most cases has been the disruption and deterioration of schooling, and more racial segregation, not less.

Several days earlier, a superior court judge in California who had ordered forced busing in Inglewood five years ago to achieve racial balance in that city's schools, threw in the towel, conceding that his order had been a failure.

The judge noted that before busing began the city's schools had a student population that was 60 percent white and 40 percent black; now it's 80 percent black, 20 percent white.

Thanks to five years of busing — and white flight to escape it — Inglewood is segregated.

"As a practical matter," said the judge, "we are now busing black children from predominantly black schools to other predominantly black schools."

The same thing has occurred in Detroit, Denver, Richmond, Atlanta and many other cities. In fact, from all indications we've seen, forced-busing hasn't worked anywhere, except perhaps in Prince Georges County, Maryland, and a few small towns.

In the big cities and large school districts, North and South, the tragic result in almost every case has been white flight, resegregation, all too much violence and increased racial antagonism.

And the costs of court-ordered desegregation — measured in terms of the exodus of taxpayers to the suburbs, the closing of schools, the expense of police protection as well as the funds required to keep buses shuttling back and forth across town — have been a heavy burden.

Most people would willingly bear those costs and other burdens if they were convinced that the end result would be an improvement in the quality of education for their children and the elimination of racial isolation and intolerance.

But they are not convinced. And can you blame them? When such erstwhile advocates of busing as Professor Coleman conclude that the experiment has not only been a failure, but has actually done more harm than good, making the illness it was designed to cure even worse, it should surprise no one that resistance to court-ordered desegregation has become stronger than ever.

As long as that resistance is peaceful and non-violent, as long as it is in compliance with the law and within the proper channels of legal and judicial change, it cannot be ignored.

Des Moines Tribune

Des Moines, Iowa, May 16, 1975

Two sociologists recently reported on the phenomenon of "white flight" from racially integrated schools.

James S. Coleman, who directed the landmark "Equality of Educational Opportunity" report in 1966, and Robert W. Wegmann, a former Milwaukee school board member who is now at the University of Houston, gave their reports at the April meeting of the American Educational Research Association.

Neither presented his findings as an argument against efforts to integrate schools, although Coleman's statement has been used that way by others. Rather, both stressed that without parental support, beneficial school integration may not occur.

Coleman is studying "white flight" from large desegregating school systems for the Urban Institute. He cited one instance where rapid and massive integration had resulted in a 30 per cent drop in the white population of a district within five years. It is the affluent middle class which moves while the low-income workers stay behind.

Findings of the 1966 Coleman study give that shift an ominous cast. The 1966 study found that "black" schools were as good as "white" schools in outward measurement of quality: per pupil spending, facilities, teacher experience, etc. It found such differences as existed had no relation to pupil achievement. It found that racial makeup had no relation to pupil achievement.

What affected achievement, the report found, was a pupil's classmates. Those in classes with children from affluent homes did better than those with classmates from lower socio-economic levels. The integration of poor whites and poor blacks seemed to accomplish nothing. And that is the kind of integration which occurs when affluent families move out.

Wegmann pointed out that this moving out can result from the school board's doing nothing as well as from integration efforts. He found that schools in Milwaukee "tipped" — soon became almost all black — once the proportion of blacks reached 33 per cent. The board could have prevented "tipping", he suggested, by acting to keep the black ratio below that level.

He also found junior high racial balances the most volatile and subject to change, with whites leaving "black" junior highs more precipitately than either elementary or high schools.

Coleman used his findings to argue for integration efforts which acknowledge parental feelings, not as an argument for no effort at all. He said that metropolitan school districts might hold an answer to the problem — but only if they were developed with parental support. Otherwise they could only broaden the range of "white flight."

Though there are some similarities in Des Moines to the findings reported by the sociologists, there are some important differences. Those elementary schools not in a predominantly black junior high attendance zone have maintained black proportions at the 50 per cent level for seven years without "tipping".

White Des Moines parents have shown no aversion to the kind of black ratio (10 to 15 per cent) which thorough integration programs could accomplish within the city.

But as in other cities, the black percentage in Des Moines public schools runs well ahead of the percentage for the total population. It was 40 per cent greater in 1970 than the census figure for that year. It is now 60 per cent above the 1970 census figure. (School enrollment is 9.9 per cent black; 1970 city population was 5.7 per cent black.)

Coleman acknowledged that courts, in ordering integration, had to be blind to the consequences of "white flight." But he viewed his findings as an argument for more sensitive voluntary plans, not as a reason to do nothing.

Index

This index includes references to information in the news digest and in the editorials. Index entries referring to the news digest can be identified by a marginal letter identification, e.g. 11G3, page 11, section G, column 3. Editorial references have no identification other than the page number, e.g. 18, page 18. In both cases the date of the event is given when possible, e.g. 2-25-70, February 25, 1970.